DISSENT

Dissent

THE HISTORY OF AN AMERICAN IDEA

Ralph Young

NEW YORK UNIVERSITY PRESS

New York and London

NEW YORK UNIVERSITY PRESS
New York and London
www.nyupress.org

References to Internet websites (URLs) were accurate at the time of writing. Neither the author nor New York University Press is responsible for URLs that may have expired or changed since the manuscript was prepared.

ISBN: 978-1-4798-0665-2

For Library of Congress Cataloging-in-Publication data, please contact the Library of Congress.

New York University Press books are printed on acid-free paper, and their binding materials are chosen for strength and durability. We strive to use environmentally responsible suppliers and materials to the greatest extent possible in publishing our books.

Manufactured in the United States of America

10 9 8 7 6 5 4 3 2 1

Also available as an ebook

To the memory of Pete Seeger and Allen Ginsberg,
who taught us how to march to the beat
of a different drummer

CONTENTS

ACKNOWLEDGMENTS

Dissent: The History of an American Idea is my personal take on how dissenters shaped American history. Although the interpretation is mine, many people have contributed to broadening my insights and sharpening my thinking during the research and writing.

My colleagues at Temple University David Farber, Bryant Simon, and Heather Ann Thompson, as well as Kryštof Kozák of Charles University in Prague, generously offered their time to read several chapters and offer valuable suggestions that have improved this book. Drew Isenberg, Elizabeth Varon, David Waldstreicher, David Wrobel, and Gregory Urwin read portions of the early chapters when I first set out to write the history of American dissent and made many recommendations that helped guide my way. This book is better because of their insights and criticism. Any errors are solely mine.

My thinking about dissent also benefited from conversations with Richard Immerman, Bob Wintermute, Istvan Varkonyi, and Jim Hilty at Temple; Leopoldo Nuti, Leila Tavi, Azzurra Meringolo, and Renato Moro at the University of Rome (Roma Tre); and Gyorgy Toth and Barbara Capinska at Charles University.

Teaching "Dissent in America" and leading the weekly teach-ins at Temple University since 2002 has been the most amazing experience of my professional career. *Dissent: The History of an American Idea* is the product of the course, the teach-ins, and the extraordinary discussions I participated in with my students. I especially want to thank former students Brianne Murphy, Sierra Gladfelter, Sarah Khan, Evan Hoffman, Wafai Dias, Lauren Spahr, Armond James, and Julia Foley, as well as my colleagues Richard Immerman, Vlad Zubok, Beth Bailey, Arthur Schmidt, Lila Corwin Berman, Ken Kusmer, Phil Evanson, Howard Spodek, Mohammad Kiani, Rebecca Alpert, Laura Levitt, Ruth Ost, Terry Halbert, and Teresa Scott Soufas, who have supported and participated in the teach-ins despite efforts to silence us by two political organizations that objected to the teach-ins' dissenting point of view.

Discussing and analyzing controversial subjects, even in the United States, even in the twenty-first century, evidently has its detractors.

I wish also to thank the Fulbright Specialist Program for the grant to teach my "Dissent in America" seminar in 2009 at Università Degli Studi Roma Tre, Scuola Dottorale in Scienze Politiche, in Rome, and the American embassy in Prague for supporting the seminar in 2012 at Univerzita Karlova. Thanks also to Alison Young, Margaret Cronan, and Kerry Sautner at the National Constitution Center for bringing me in for talks and workshops on dissent and the Constitution.

Ashley Dodge and Priscilla McGeehon were the driving forces behind pushing me to write about American dissent when I first began collecting and editing hundreds of documents of American dissenters. I am forever indebted to them for their suggestions and their inspiration. At New York University Press Clara Platter instantly saw the value of this book the first time we spoke about it. I am very grateful to her as well as Constance Grady for their indispensable role in bringing *Dissent: The History of an American Idea* to fruition.

Many other people had a more personal impact. I want to thank Daniel Wood for teaching me to fall in love with words, Leif Skoogfors for showing me how to look at the world through an artist's eyes, Ellen Gibson and Cyndy Jahn for their always-lively opinions that seemed to touch on every subject under the sun, the "Friday Night Gang" for taking us under their collective wing, Peter Hiler for his unbounded generosity, Millie for being my sister, Cara and Sean for letting me be a part of their lives, my late parents, Ralph Eric Young and Emily Mildred Young, for making sure I did not become part of the military-industrial complex, and my wife, Pat, for her constant energy, compassion, and love.

I first met Pete Seeger in 1969 and over the years between then and 2012 spoke with him on several occasions at the Philadelphia Folk Festival and the Clearwater Hudson River Revival. He was always accessible, always willing to talk about his latest cause (and there were many). He graciously read my *Dissent in America* reader of dissenting documents and offered suggestions as well as a blurb for the book's cover. In February 1980 I spent a day and evening in lively conversation with Allen Ginsberg and continued a correspondence with him for the next eight years. These two men had, before we met and then for a long time thereafter, a profound influence on me and the way I perceive the joys and the sorrows and the complexities of this planet we all share. *Dissent: The History of an American Idea* is dedicated to their memory and to all the other courageous dissenters who have inspired us to live up to the better angels of our nature.

Introduction

If a man does not keep pace with his companions, perhaps it is because he hears a different drummer. Let him step to the music which he hears, however measured or far away.
　　　　—Henry David Thoreau, Walden Pond, 1854

All we say to America is to be true to what you said on paper. . . . Somewhere I read [*pause*] of the freedom of speech. Somewhere I read [*pause*] of the freedom of press. Somewhere I read [*pause*] that the greatness of America is the right to protest for right.
　　　　—Martin Luther King, Jr., Memphis, April 3, 1968

There are many ways to tell the story of the United States, many possible perspectives. This is the story of the U.S. told through a somewhat unlikely assortment of voices. It is the story of religious dissenters seeking refuge in a New World; Native Americans defying the onslaught of European settlement; political revolutionaries launching a government "of the people, by the people, for the people"; enslaved Africans resisting their oppressors while creating a new culture; immigrants fighting to assimilate into American society; women persevering to gain equality; and minorities demanding their share of the American Dream. It is also the story of a countless number of Americans who prodded, provoked, and pushed the United States to actually be the nation it imagined itself to be. Throughout these stories runs the thread of dissent, protest, conflict, and change.

Dissent: The History of an American Idea is the personal reflection of a historian on the centrality of dissent in American history. Of course dissent in not sui generis an *American* idea, but Americans have instinctively understood, even if mostly unconsciously, the interrelatedness of dissent and what it means to be an American. Dissent created this nation, and it played, indeed still plays, a fundamental role in fomenting change and pushing the nation in sometimes-unexpected directions. My goal has been to write a narrative history of the United States from the standpoint of those who did not see eye to eye with the powers that be, from the standpoint of those who marched to the beat of a different drummer constantly challenging the government to fulfill the promise laid down in the nation's founding documents. There has not been a time in American history when dissenters have not spoken out against the powerful and entrenched interests. At the same time, there were many occasions when dissenters against the dissenters fought ever harder to maintain, or restore, a social order that they feared would vanish if dissenters had their way. And so dissent did not propel the United States on a steady path toward the progress that dissenters sought. It was a rocky road.

Naturally it is impossible to include all those who dissented during the four-hundred-year history of the United States in a single volume. Although I have included a large number of dissenters in these pages, the reader should keep in mind that those discussed here are only a fraction of those who had an impact on the development of the United States. There are literally hundreds of others I would have liked to include, from the Merrymount Settlement to the Catholic Worker Movement, from Aaron Burr to Angela Davis, from Henry Demarest Lloyd to Paul Krassner, but that would have resulted in an impossibly unwieldy book. My goal has been to cover a representative selection of the most important dissenters and dissent movements that have influenced the course of American history, while at the same time touching on some of the less significant, less successful dissenters. Even those who did not achieve their goals had an impact because they created an atmosphere of debate. Impassioned debates over conflicting issues compelled Americans to look more deeply not only into the issues but also into their own attitudes and behavior, and as a result they either reaffirmed or revised their beliefs. This has been the case in the past. It will continue to be the case in the future.

* * *

Dissent is one of this nation's defining characteristics. Every decade since the earliest days of colonization Americans have protested for just about every cause imaginable, and every time they did, defenders of the status quo denounced the protestors as unpatriotic and in more recent times as un-American. But protest is one of the consummate expressions of "Americanness." It *is* patriotic in the deepest sense.

Even before the United States was conceived, there was dissent. During the seventeenth century religious dissent played a significant role in the planting and development of the English colonies. In the eighteenth century political dissent led to the open rebellion that resulted in the birth of the United States. In the nineteenth century dissenters demanded the abolition of slavery, suffrage for women, fair treatment of Native Americans, and the banning of immigrants. And they protested against the War of 1812, the Mexican War, the Civil War (on both sides), and the Spanish-American War. In the twentieth century dissenters organized to prohibit alcohol but also demanded workers' rights, women's rights, African American rights, Chicano rights, reproductive rights, and gay rights. They also protested against every war (declared and undeclared) fought by the United States. In the twenty-first century dissenters protest against abortion, NAFTA, globalization, the Iraq War, the PATRIOT Act, the National Security Agency, bank bailouts, and out-of-control deficits. On the right the Tea Party movement has arisen, perceiving itself as the true heirs of the patriots of the American Revolution standing firm opposing despotic government; and on the left the Occupy Wall Street movement denounces the control of government by corporate interests and the finance industry. Clearly, dissent has many faces.

On the broadest level, dissent is going against the grain. It is speaking out and protesting against what *is* (whatever that *is* is), most often by a minority group unhappy with majority opinion and rule. However, history has shown that dissent is far more complex, that it comes from all political perspectives and in a variety of categories: mostly religious, political, economic, and cultural/social. Religious dissent is the insistence that everyone be allowed to worship according to the dictates of conscience and not according to the rules of an established religion. Although most religious dissent occurred during the colonial period, when individuals insisted on religious liberty, and during the early national period, when the new nation endorsed the principle of separation of church and state, the demand for religious autonomy persists to this day. Religious dissent was expressed when new sects such as the

Shakers, the Mormons, or the Branch Davidians were formed, and it is still being expressed on a different level in the debates over school prayer, intelligent design versus evolution, abortion rights, capital punishment, and the right to die.

Political dissent is a critique of governance. As the United States grew from a fledgling nation into a world power, political dissenters expressed dissatisfaction about the way those who were in charge governed, and usually (but not always) they provided a plan or recipe for redressing what they perceived as wrong. Most often they used the nation's founding documents as the authority to legitimize their protest. Antebellum abolitionists demanded the end of slavery, declaring that holding persons in bondage was contrary to the principle that "all men are created equal." In recent years hundreds of thousands of Americans protested the decision to launch a preemptive invasion of Iraq, proclaiming that doing so transforms the United States into an aggressive imperial power and that by embracing imperialism the United States is renouncing its democratic birthright.

When the economy crashes, economic dissent comes to the fore. People take to the streets protesting economic injustice and inequality. And as distress and suffering expands from the lower classes to the middle class, so too does protest. One thinks of the Richmond bread riots and the food riots in Georgia and North Carolina during the Civil War, the violent labor disputes of the nineteenth century, Coxey's Army marching on Washington in 1894, the Bonus Army's encampment at the Capitol in 1932, the militant labor activism during Franklin Delano Roosevelt's liberal presidency, the tax revolts of the 1970s, the occupation of Zuccotti Park in 2011.

Cultural and social dissent is a rejection of the predominant attitudes, beliefs, and behavior of mainstream society. Utopian groups in the nineteenth century, such as the Oneida Community, defied the conventional values of their time and established a community where all men and women would be treated equally. "Beatniks" and "hippies" in the mid-twentieth century rejected the conventional middle-class morality of their time, urged their fellow Americans to "do their own thing," and influenced millions to reevaluate their views of race, gender, and sexuality.

But this is only part of the story. There is significant and frequent overlapping of religious, political, and cultural/social dissent. For example, many dissenters, such as temperance activists in the early twentieth century and the Christian right today, can be labeled as political, religious, *and* social dissenters. The 1960s counterculture's challenge to American values was also intricately tied up in the political protests against the Vietnam War and the struggle for racial equality. Furthermore, there are economic and psychological factors that often play a role in all dissent movements.

There are some decades that are relatively quiet dissentwise and others when significant problems intensify so rapidly that tens of millions of people get involved in the discussion to find solutions. During these periods we see a sharp rise in dissent, and that dissent can take many forms as different groups propose different solutions. Some dissenters are *reformers* who wish to fix the problems through a process of reform. Some are *reactionaries* who seek to address the problems by returning to the policies that existed before the problems arose. Some are *radicals* or even *revolutionaries* who propose to solve the problems by smashing the system and starting over. The debate over slavery and the events leading to the Civil War, the Progressive era, and the 1960s were periods when dissent, in all its diverse forms, exploded.

There are several levels or stages of dissent. At the beginning individuals might simply disagree with a policy or a law or an issue. Perhaps they are willing to tolerate a wrong or an injustice for a while, but when it becomes less tolerable, the next step is to become active. Individuals might write a letter or an article, give a speech, lead a protest march, or conduct a demonstration. Dissent and protest carried to a higher level entails resistance, civil disobedience, breaking laws, or even participating in a riot or insurrection. At the last extreme, as in the American Revolution or in John Brown's raid, outright conflict breaks out. At this point dissent has metamorphosed into something much larger and is either crushed or brings about a radical transformation.

The methods and forms of dissent are wide-ranging. Many protestors express dissent through petitions and protest marches. Some use music or art or theater or comedy to articulate their message. Some engage in acts of civil disobedience, willfully breaking laws to put pressure on the system to force those who have political and economic power to acknowledge and address the issues. They are often marginalized individuals and groups that lack power but have a legitimate grievance against the way things are. Most times these types of dissenters have criticized the United States from the left. They have sought more equality, more moral rectitude, more freedom. They have demanded that America live up to what it had committed itself to on paper at the Constitutional Convention. Many of these dissenters have viewed the Constitution and the Declaration of Independence as binding contracts between the people and the government and protested when they believed the government was not fulfilling its part of the contract.

Dissenters often have a keen sense of history and build on the experiences and methods of earlier dissenters. It is not unusual to see dissenters quote those who have gone before as well as draw on the successful tactics and strategies of earlier dissent movements. The civil rights movement of the 1950s and 1960s employed many of the tactics of the labor movement of the 1930s, while antiwar activists adopted the tactics of the civil rights movement in their protests against the war in Vietnam and later the Iraq War. Dissenters with a vision for the future look to the past for inspiration.

Individuals and groups that protest against the protestors are also expressing dissent. Reactionaries have frequently resisted change and fought to maintain the special privileges and supremacy of their class or race or gender. Some have wanted to maintain the status quo and prevent change, while others have sought to turn back the clock to a simpler, more "trouble-free" time. When abolitionists denounced slavery, antiabolitionists argued just as passionately to preserve the institution. When women demanded equality, millions of Americans reacted with hostility and formed antisuffrage associations.

Although most dissent springs from those who lack political power, there are instances when a dissent movement is part of the power structure—the temperance movement and the Know-Nothings of the nineteenth century; the antitax ideologues of the twentieth and twenty-first centuries. There are also notable individuals who fought entrenched interests from a position of political power—Representative Clement L. Vallandigham and Senators Theodore Frelinghuysen, Robert M. La Follette, and Margaret Chase Smith, for example, all spoke out against what they believed was a usurpation or misuse of power on the part of the federal government. Founding fathers Thomas Jefferson and James Madison dissented forcefully against the Alien and Sedition Acts.

Over the years dissenters achieved varying levels of success. Some got in trouble. Some were arrested. Many were beaten. Some were killed. But they kept hammering away at the powers that be until those powers began to listen. As a result, public opinion was swayed, laws were enacted or repealed; slavery was abolished, unions were organized, women got the right to vote, the Jim Crow laws were invalidated. In fact many dissenters who were maligned, vilified, and even demonized as unpatriotic and anti-American by their contemporaries are now considered heroes. Some dissenters never achieved the change they were seeking, but though their goals were dismissed, they raised new questions and had an influence on the political discussion.

For the most part dissenters have embraced lofty ideals and have a moral purpose. And most of them believe they are acting to ensure that the United States lives up to its promise to secure Americans' natural rights. But there are dissenters whose goals are not well intended or virtuous and who use questionable means to attain their goals—they are not in it to grant equal rights to a downtrodden minority but to restrict rights or to promote their own narrow interests at the expense of others.

During times of heightened passions—the 1850s, the Progressive period, the Great Depression, the Vietnam War—dissenters have protested from liberal, conservative, *and* radical standpoints. In the debates about the war in Vietnam, for example, there were those who believed that America was acting as an imperial power and that the capitalist system should be toppled. There were those who opposed the war primarily on ethical grounds because the United States was acting immorally. And there were those who opposed the war simply because the United States was losing it and thus argued that if the government was not going to go all out in its effort to destroy communism in Vietnam, then there was no point in being there. For completely different reasons radicals, doves, and hawks, in the end, all came to protest the war in Vietnam.

Obviously not all dissenters are created equal. Nor are the consequences of their efforts necessarily positive or socially useful. There is a difference between dissenters whose goal is to create a more just society by expanding the rights of the disempowered, and those who are self-aggrandizing troublemakers interested only in disrupting society or denying rights to others. Historian Eric Foner, in *The Story of American Freedom*, points out that "freedom" is a "contested concept."[1] So too is "dissent."

Seventeenth-Century Dissent

Early seventeenth-century religious dissenters, refusing to conform to the practices of the Church of England, crossed the Atlantic and founded the colonies of Plymouth and Massachusetts Bay. Most of these early settlers were committed to setting up churches according to the only polity sanctioned, in their view, by scripture. In 1620 Puritan Separatists settled in Plymouth, so they could worship according to the principle that each church was wholly separate from the Church of England. A decade later Puritan Congregationalists, seeking to reform the church from within, founded Massachusetts Bay Colony, where they organized churches in which ministers were chosen by the members, not appointed by the bishop of London; and membership was restricted to those who could provide evidence of "saving faith" to the congregation.

The Puritans, however, were not promoting the principle of religious freedom. They were only seeking to practice religion the way they saw fit. Those who did not see eye to eye with them were not to be tolerated. It was Roger Williams who pushed for religious freedom. Williams, one of the first dissenters in the English colonies, took exception to several tenets of the Puritan oligarchy. He called for the complete separation of church and state and for a broader religious toleration. Williams argued that to compel people to conform to a specific, authorized religious belief was counterproductive because it simply convinced people that the imposed beliefs are false. In the end, Williams's dissension eventually led to banishment. He established a new colony that became a haven for those who held unpopular views. Over the next century and a half, as the colonial settlements grew increasingly diverse and multicultural, Williams's advocacy of toleration and the separation of church and state became a fundamental part of eighteenth-century political discourse. Shortly after the ratification of the Constitution these principles, regarded by then as natural rights, were enshrined in the First Amendment.

Incidents of political dissent also cropped up in the early years of colonial America. By the 1670s fertile land in Virginia was becoming increasingly scarce. Indentured servants were forced to work as tenant farmers for wealthy landlords or move to less desirable acreage on the frontier. But much of this land was off-limits because it was reserved for Indians. Seething with disdain for the wealthy landholders and filled with racial hatred of the Indians, a band of indentured servants and some slaves, led by Nathaniel Bacon, marched on Jamestown in the summer of 1676, torched the town, and plundered the landed gentry's estates. In the aftermath of the rebellion the Virginia governing authorities, in a decision that had profound historical consequences, decided no longer to rely on unruly, disgruntled indentured servants to fill the colony's labor needs but on African slaves whose lifelong subjugation would prevent them from becoming a potential threat to the colony's stability. From this point on slavery became entrenched in colonial America.

Not only does Bacon's Rebellion show how dissent shaped the Chesapeake colonies, but to a large extent the rebellion also reveals the ambiguities in dissent. On one hand it appears as a straightforward class struggle—an uprising by the lower classes against the Virginia aristocracy—but on the other hand it was a venting of deep-seated racism against the Indians that demonstrates how racism can conceal deeper economic issues. The rebels were attempting to *expand* their rights, while simultaneously *diminishing* the rights of the Indians. Further obfuscating the issue is the fact that it was also a power struggle because not all of the rebels, indeed not Bacon himself, were truly lower class, but they wanted to wrest political and economic power from Governor Berkeley.

Eighteenth-Century Dissent

In the eighteenth century Indians clashed with whites invading their territory, slaves rebelled in South Carolina and New York City, Quaker abolitionists condemned the institution of slavery, women spoke out against male authority. In the 1730s John Peter Zenger fought for freedom of the press, and thirty years later dissenters fought for the unalienable rights of life, liberty, and the pursuit of happiness.

Of course, the most momentous dissent movement of the eighteenth century was the protest against British taxation policies that led to the American Revolution. When Parliament passed the Stamp Act, colonists took to the streets in protest: effigies of tax collectors were burned, royal officials were tarred and feathered, and in Boston mobs destroyed government offices and even demolished and plundered the lieutenant governor's residence. Parliament, stunned at the severity of the protests, repealed the act in 1766, but each subsequent attempt to raise revenue only provoked more protest, until shots were eventually exchanged at Lexington and Concord. This time political and economic dissent led to revolution.

Despite the enthusiasm for independence a large percentage of the population remained loyal to England and protested against the war and against the rebels. Loyalists, such as the royal governor of Massachusetts Thomas Hutchinson, clashed uncompromisingly with those who advocated rebellion against Britain. In 1776 he found himself in the unusual position of defending the status quo against a rising new status quo. When the Second Continental Congress issued the Declaration of Independence and in the face of a tide of proindependence thinking, arch-loyalist Hutchinson dissented against the dissenters. He published a pamphlet vehemently criticizing every one of the points Jefferson made in the Declaration. Hutchinson argued that because some of the signers demanded freedom for themselves while denying it to others, the Declaration of Independence was a hypocritical document, a piece of propaganda that confirmed his belief that the rebellion was dishonest and criminal and the idealistic principles it espoused based on false logic. Although Hutchinson's protestations went against the increasingly popular view that independence from Great Britain was a noble cause, his example anticipates those who in the nineteenth and twentieth centuries protested against the unwanted political and social change that was taking place around them, such as the Ku Klux Klan's efforts to subjugate newly freed slaves and antiabortion activists who fought to overturn the *Roe v. Wade* Supreme Court decision legalizing abortion.

Dissent was so important to the revolutionary generation that they enshrined the right to dissent in the First Amendment of the Constitution. And Americans, ever since, have taken that right seriously.

Nineteenth-Century Dissent

Once the United States was established dissent intensified rather than diminished. In the nineteenth century hundreds of thousands of Americans, troubled by the discrepancy between the nation's democratic/republican principles and reality, spoke out against the injustices that still persisted. Social reformers urged radical changes in education, rehabilitation of criminals and the mentally ill, and the elimination of alcohol. After 1831 abolitionism grew so widespread that it inflamed passions to such an extreme that the issue was only resolved through civil war. During the Civil War thousands of Americans on both sides protested against the war, against conscription, and against violations of the Bill of Rights. When the war ended, many southerners formed terrorist organizations such as the Ku Klux Klan and the Knights of the White Camellia to protest the new social order, while in the North and West farmers, Indians, Chinese immigrants, laborers, and women organized alliances, protest groups, and unions to demand the rights that were denied them. After America's victory in the Spanish-American War in 1898 many citizens condemned the United States as an imperialist power and warned that democracy at home was in danger if the nation abandoned its ideals.

Arguably the most significant example of political dissent in all of American history was the antebellum abolitionist movement. Abolitionists were dissenters who opposed, mostly peacefully, sometimes violently, the institution of slavery. However, federal and state law protected slaveholders, while slavery itself had the sanction of the highest law of the land—the Constitution. To oppose a practice that was embedded in the economic, political, and social structure was a formidable task, but hundreds of thousands of Americans joined the abolitionist crusade. In 1831, William Lloyd Garrison began publication of a weekly antislavery newspaper, the *Liberator*, in which he unconditionally condemned slavery and demanded immediate emancipation and the granting of full citizenship and voting rights to all slaves. Garrison eventually went so far as to propose that the United States abrogate the Constitution because of its complicity with slavery and expel the southern states from the Union. Like flag burners in the twentieth century, Garrison incurred the wrath of his fellow citizens after he publicly burned a copy of the Constitution in Boston Common, thus alienating many of those who might have been sympathetic to his cause.

Some abolitionists expressed their dissent more moderately than Garrison. The former slave Frederick Douglass, after he escaped from bondage, traveled from town to town speaking out against slavery. Listeners were so amazed by his intelligence and eloquence that it caused them to rethink all the racial stereotypes they had been brought up to believe. The arguments of abolitionists like Garrison and Douglass, as well as those of hundreds of others, educated Americans about the horrors of slavery and compelled them to examine their conscience and decide on which side of the issue they stood. This process has occurred over and over again in all dissent movements. Protestors go on marches, write books, deliver speeches, and hold demonstrations to inform the public, raise consciousness, and win converts to their cause.

The issue of slavery brought about still another type of dissent once the Civil War ended and slavery was abolished. The Ku Klux Klan was founded in 1865 for the explicit purpose of preventing former slaves from gaining political and economic power. In a campaign of terror and violence Klansmen rode through the South intimidating and murdering freedmen and creating a climate of subjugation and suppression that lasted for more than a century. The Klan was not interested in extending constitutionally guaranteed rights. Rather its goal was to make sure that African Americans were denied those rights. The KKK illustrates one of the paradoxes of dissent. If dissent is defined merely as opposing the status quo, challenging the way things are without regard to moral considerations, then the Klan is a dissent organization. Certainly the Klan is an example of reactionary dissent. The post–Civil War status quo was that former slaves were legally free and equal. The Klan opposed African Americans' new status and sought to restore white supremacy. But since white supremacy was always at the heart of social relations in the South, the Klan, despite the fact that it was opposing the (new) status quo, was not expressing what I would view as a legitimate form of dissent. The Klan's dissent was simply a continuation of the effort to maintain the old status quo.

Twentieth-Century Dissent

In the twentieth century dissent proliferated at an exponential pace. Political dissent was expressed in both world wars and dozens of undeclared military conflicts. Writer Randolph Bourne, Senator Robert M. La Follette, and Socialist Party leader Eugene V. Debs were among the hundreds of thousands who opposed U.S. entry into the Great War. The Second World War also had its share of protestors, despite the fact that a vast majority of Americans believed it was necessary and honorable to fight against fascism. Isolationists such as Charles Lindbergh, conscientious objectors such as David Dellinger, and writers such as Henry Miller all condemned American involvement in the war.

The most divisive war in our nation's history was the Vietnam War. The antiwar protests of the 1960s and 1970s were distinctive in that they were part of a wider protest movement that began with the African American struggle for civil rights. By the 1960s activists were taking to the streets for a host of reasons—African American rights, women's rights, gay rights, Chicano rights, and opposition to the war in Vietnam. The dissent of the 1960s was unique in that it brought political, cultural, and social dissent together. Everything, from politics to militarism to racism to sexism to "American values," was questioned.

Many of the protests followed the nonviolent civil disobedience format that Martin Luther King, Jr., espoused. Echoing Henry David Thoreau and Mahatma Gandhi, King argued that if an individual believes in justice, then he or she *must* oppose injustice: "Injustice anywhere is a threat to justice everywhere."[2] If a law is unjust, King wrote in his "Letter from Birmingham Jail," that is, if it does not universally apply to all people and if it is not in harmony with moral law, then it is the duty of anyone who believes in justice to break that law. King never advocated breaking a just law, but he did advocate breaking unjust laws, such as those that sanctioned segregation. But when one breaks an unjust law, one must be willing to pay the penalty. King also argued that protest marches intended to call attention to injustice must be peaceful. If demonstrators destroyed property or responded violently to attacks they would be breaking just laws that were meant to protect people.

Some demonstrations, however, did get violent when protestors got impatient with delay and inaction. The government, it seemed to many frustrated activists, was moving too slowly to eradicate racial discrimination and to end the Vietnam War. Protests at the 1968 Democratic Convention in Chicago became violent when police and demonstrators clashed in full view of television cameras. Millions of Americans watched in dismay as they viewed images of bloodied demonstrators being arrested and carted away by the police. In May 1970 a demonstration at Kent State University took the lives of four students when the Ohio National Guard opened fire on the crowd. The scope and intensity of antiwar dissent wound up having a fundamental impact on shaping American policy for the remainder of the century. For more than twenty-five years after the end of the war in Vietnam, American foreign policy focused on avoiding, as far as possible, any commitment of U.S. forces in other conflicts around the globe.

Simultaneous with this retrenchment and rethinking of America's role in the world, a conservative backlash also set in during the last quarter of the century, when millions of Americans sought to return to the conformity, complacency, and "family values" of an earlier time. Still, dissent was alive and well, as a multitude of dissenting groups, with a wide variety of agendas, proliferated.

The power of dissent in shaping history became further apparent over the issue of abortion when, after decades of women pushing for reproductive rights, the Supreme Court legalized abortion in the 1973 *Roe v. Wade* decision. Dissent had changed the law. However, after the decision, a new dissent movement came into being: the prolife movement. Thousands of Americans protested at abortion clinics and on university campuses around the country in an all-out effort to make abortion illegal once again. By the 1980s antiabortion dissent turned violent when some protestors bombed Planned Parenthood clinics and murdered clinic employees and abortion-providing physicians. The perpetrators argued that doctors performing abortions were committing acts of murder and therefore that killing them was a moral duty. As in previous occasions when dissenters brought about change, those who had previously dissented against the restrictions on abortion found themselves defending the new reality, and those who had once favored the status quo found themselves as the dissenters. What is particularly complicated about the abortion issue is that it is not as simple as one group wanting a right and the opposition wanting to deny that right, because antiabortion protestors argue that they are not trying to restrict rights but rather are seeking to expand them to unborn children.

In the 1980s and 1990s Theodore Kaczynski, convinced that technology was leading to the inevitable destruction of civilization, conducted an eighteen-year campaign of mailing letter bombs to scientists, researchers, and industrialists. The Unabomber's method of protest resulted in the deaths of three researchers and the maiming of twenty-three. In 1995 Gulf War veteran Timothy McVeigh, believing that the federal government had become a malevolent force that endangered the U.S. Constitution, set off a bomb at a federal office building in Oklahoma City that killed 168 people. Such methods of dissent went far beyond the philosophy of civil disobedience and even the boundaries of dissent. In these dissenters' fight for what they perceived as a threat to their rights, they broke the most fundamental just law—the law prohibiting murder.

A New Century

September 11, 2001, opened a new chapter of dissent. In the first weeks after the terrorist attacks most Americans united behind the president, the War on Terror, and the PATRIOT Act (designed to root out would-be terrorists). But as time went by, many Americans began criticizing the policies that they believed provoked Al-Qaeda terrorists to attack the United States. By 2002 thousands of Americans, from both ends of the political spectrum, fearing the erosion of civil liberties, signed petitions and protested against the PATRIOT Act. And in February 2003, a month *before* the American invasion of Iraq, hundreds of thousands of demonstrators took to the streets protesting a war that had not yet begun, believing that it was a terrible decision that would only strengthen terrorism, not defeat it. Among the most resolute protestors were veterans of previous wars, such as West Point graduate David Wiggins, who published an open letter to the troops embarking for Iraq, telling them that invading Iraq will lead to "a more dangerous world."[3] A multitude of political groups, grassroots peace organizations, soldiers returning from Iraq, and Gold Star Mothers like Cindy Sheehan spoke out by holding vigils and marching in demonstrations, hoping to convince the administration to end the war in Iraq.

In addition to the political protests focusing on American foreign policy, the first years of the twenty-first century also saw an escalation of social and cultural dissent in the ongoing protests for and against same-sex marriage, health care reform, immigration reform, abortion, and the government's violation of privacy rights. In a century that is only in its second decade, we cannot foresee the scope and extent of future protest movements, but if the history of the past four hundred years has taught us anything, it has taught us that dissent and protest in all its numerous manifestations is not going away and will continue to shape the United States.

CHAPTER I

The "Free Aire of a New World"

Now if you do condemn me for speaking what in my conscience I know to be truth I must commit myself unto the Lord.
—Anne Hutchinson, 1636

After more than a century of conflict with and exploitation of the First
Nations of the New World, Spain had successfully established scores
of missions and permanent colonies from Florida to California, while
French explorers and missionaries were setting up outposts along the
St. Lawrence River. Into this volatile mix of cultures thousands of English colonists began in the early seventeenth century to establish permanent settlements along the east coast of North America. Most were
seeking economic opportunity, but many, especially those arriving in
New England, were religious dissenters who believed the only possibility for them to worship according to the dictates of their conscience was
to abandon England and seek refuge in the New World. Almost as soon
as these religious dissenters arrived in New England, dissidents such as
Roger Williams and Anne Hutchinson rose up among them to challenge
the authorities. Dissent also erupted in Virginia, when Nathaniel Bacon
and hundreds of indentured servants revolted against the colonial elite
and the forces that limited their economic prospects. Native Americans
too, such as Powhatan in Virginia and Metacom in Massachusetts, took
up arms to protest English encroachment on their lands.

Something changes when people break from their day-to-day existence and take action to build something new. Forces are let loose that
create a climate conducive to independent thinking and a sense that the
individual has to take a stand at some point for what she or he believes
is right. And if that goes against the majority feeling in the body politic, then so be it. So it was in the "free aire of a new world"[1] that dissent, already widespread in the old country as a result of the forces
unleashed by the Protestant Reformation, took root at once in receptive
and fertile soil.

∗ ∗ ∗

The Puritans who settled in Plymouth and Massachusetts Bay had a profound influence on the development of American history, yet most Americans have a distorted image of them. The most common misconception about the Puritans is that they were uptight spoilsports. In fact we still use the word *Puritan* as an adjective to describe an entire set of strict, rather self-righteous values; this is a false representation. They were not, as the common stereotype holds, uptight spoilsports. Contrary to H. L. Mencken's acerbic twentieth-century observation that Puritanism is "the haunting fear that someone, somewhere, may be happy,"[2] the truth is that the Puritans of seventeenth-century Massachusetts were much more down-to-earth, sensible, and intellectual than our image of them. They valued education, they enjoyed life, they wore colorful clothing, they were not against alcohol, nor did they believe that sex was evil. True, they were very religious—they took God, the Bible, and morality seriously—but they believed that God is good. Therefore it followed that everything God created is good and is there for humans to enjoy. Increase Mather, one of the most famous Puritan ministers, once delivered a sermon titled "Wine Is from God, the Drunkard from the Devil," meaning that God made wine for us to drink and enjoy. Drinking to the point of drunkenness, however, is an abuse, and that is a sin. Examination of the church records of the 1630s and 1640s reveals that the principal expenses churches incurred were the costs for the wine and ale that was consumed at ordination ceremonies for new ministers. God also created sex, and he made it enjoyable for our pleasure. Sex was not just for procreation; it was a joyous sign of our love and devotion. There are cases in colonial court records of women divorcing their husbands for refusing to have conjugal relations, and vice versa. Increase Mather's son, Cotton Mather, the most influential Puritan clergyman by the 1690s, censured a couple that wished to practice sexual abstinence thinking that it would heighten their spirituality. Mather believed that such a practice was a denunciation of the purity of sexual love within matrimony and was therefore a denunciation of God. To be sure, Puritans did not tolerate pre- or extramarital sex or promiscuity (although from the birth records and court transcripts of seventeenth-century Massachusetts we learn that many Puritans did engage in premarital sex), but within marriage sex was a blessed thing.

In essence the Puritans ultimately believed that life and the pleasures of life were all gifts of God to be relished. Denying this was a sin, just as becoming obsessive or fixated on pleasure was a sin. The key was moderation in all things.

The covenant theology that the Puritans devised touched political and social relationships as well as spiritual ones. God, they believed, made an original covenant with Adam. If Adam would obey God's laws, God would bless Adam with eternal life. However, Adam broke the covenant when he ate the forbidden fruit. Later, when God sent his only son into the world, he instituted the covenant of grace whereby those who would have faith in him would receive forgiveness and redemption from Adam's sin. God also made covenants with nations. Puritans believed that when Henry VIII turned his back on Rome, God covenanted with England that as long as England would continue to reform God's church, he would bestow his blessings. After all, was not the "Protestant wind" that destroyed the Spanish Armada a clear example of God's approval of England? Covenants did not only exist between God and mankind on a spiritual or national level; they also existed throughout the whole chain of relationships. For example, there were covenants between magistrates and the people on all levels of national and local government: the people agree to obey the laws; the magistrates and governors will protect the people's rights. On the personal level there was the covenant between a man and a woman in which they agree to love and honor each other; a covenant between parents and children; a covenant between masters and servants. Just as the nation was subordinate to God, the people were subordinate to magistrates, wives to husbands, children to parents, servants to masters. The clearly defined logic of the covenant approach shaped all political, social, and personal relationships and established a set of mores and assumptions that were dutifully followed for generations. However, within this subordinate/dominant structure, on the spiritual level, salvation was equally available. Class and gender did not separate people; only faith did. And perhaps it was this element of spiritual equality that wound up fueling dissent and inciting challenges to authority.

* * *

The Puritans were religious dissenters, but they did not come to the New World for the noble cause of "religious freedom." What the

Congregational Puritans of Massachusetts Bay were seeking was to practice what *they* regarded as the one true faith, not freedom for all religions. They did not favor religious toleration, as anyone entering the colony wishing to worship according to a "false" belief system quickly discovered. Those who did not see eye to eye with the Bay Colony's authorities found themselves ostracized and banished. These men and women were the first dissenters within the colonies, and although they had no way of knowing it at the time, they were the vanguard of what was to become a defining American character trait.

One of the most noteworthy dissenters was Roger Williams. Williams arrived in 1631 and became the teacher of the Salem church (larger churches had two ministers: the pastor and the teacher). Almost immediately he began calling for the complete separation of the Congregational churches of New England from the Church of England, warning that God would punish the people of Massachusetts if they did not do so. But the Puritans had no wish to separate. They wanted to reform the church, and how could that be done from *outside* the church? Williams irritated them even further when he disputed the king's authority to grant the charter to Massachusetts Bay because Charles had no right to the land. The land belonged to the Indians, and no one had consulted them! This, of course, was a challenge to the validity of all land claims and deeds obtained by individual settlers. And finally Williams called for toleration of all religious beliefs and the separation of church and state. Civil authorities, he maintained, should have no power to monitor people's beliefs, nor was it their prerogative to enforce the Ten Commandments or punish breaches thereof. Such practices endangered religious freedom. At first the magistrates tried to convince Williams to tone down his dissent; but he did not, and they banished him in 1636. Williams spent that winter with the Narragansett Indians, purchased land from them, and founded the settlement of Providence. In 1644 he traveled to London to obtain a charter for the colony (to be called Rhode Island) that gave him the legal authorization to govern the colony.

Before returning to Rhode Island, Williams published *The Bloudy Tenent of Persecution* to defend his views—that all religious faiths should be tolerated and that there should be a total separation of church and state—against the attacks of the Boston clergy, as well as to promulgate them in England. If governing officials seek to enforce one religion in a society, then they obviously have to punish those who refuse to accept the authorized religion. "A *civill sword*," meaning the punishment that civil authorities must use to enforce conformity of religion, Williams argued with impeccable logic, "is so far from bringing or helping forward an *opposite* in *Religion* to *repentance* that *Magistrates* sin grievously against the *worke* of God and *blood* of Soules by such proceedings. . . . *Violence* and a *sword* of *steele* begets such an *impression* in the sufferers that certainly they conclude . . . [that] that *Religion* cannot be true which needs such *instruments* of *violence* to uphold it so." Regarding separation of church and state, Williams maintained that it is imperative to keep a well-defined distinction between the two to protect freedom of religion. If there were too much blurring of the lines between church and state, both institutions would be endangered, but worst of all it would mean religion would have to be sanctioned by the state. And as far as Williams was concerned, he did not want the colony to have, like the nations of Europe, an established religion. Religious belief should not be dependent on the whim of a monarch. "Magistrates," he insisted, "have no power of setting up the Forme of Church Government, electing church officers, [or] punishing with church censures." Likewise

the Churches as Churches, have no power . . . of erecting or altering forms of Civill Government, electing of Civill officers, inflicting Civill punishments . . . as by deposing Magistrates from their Civill Authoritie, or withdrawing the hearts of the people against them, to their Lawes, no more than to discharge wives, or children, or servants, from due obedience to their husbands, parents, or masters; or by taking up arms against their Magistrates, though he persecute them for Conscience: for though members of Churches who are publique officers also of the Civill State may suppress by force the violence of Usurpers . . . yet this they doe not as members of the Church but as officers of the Civill State.[3]

The most influential of the Puritan ministers in the colony was John Cotton. He had a large following in England, and when he migrated to Massachusetts, many members of his congregation followed him to Boston, including Anne Hutchinson, who had greatly admired his sermons. Shortly after her arrival Hutchinson began holding Wednesday-evening meetings in her home in which she summarized and analyzed

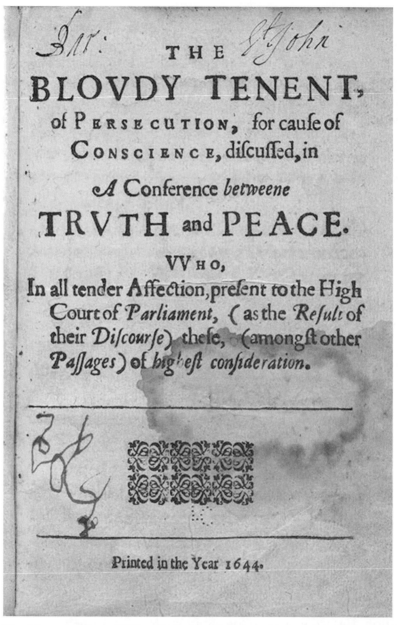

The title page of Roger Williams's *The Bloudy Tenent of Persecution, for Cause of Conscience, Discussed in a Conference between Truth and Peace* (1644), in which Williams presents his argument for religious freedom, tolerance, and separation of church and state. (Public domain; courtesy Library of Congress)

the previous Sunday's sermon for women who had been unable to attend church that week. Hutchinson, who was a highly intelligent woman who studied the finer points of theology and was unafraid to step out of the usual role of submissive housewife in articulating her views, provided an incisive commentary that so energized the sessions that they soon became the most popular event in Boston. So many women (and men) began filling her home that she had to schedule a second weekly meeting. A problem arose, however, when Hutchinson began criticizing John Cotton's colleague at the Boston church. She made the accusation that the pastor, John Wilson, was preaching that salvation could be achieved through good works, whereas John Cotton's sermons were in line with the Calvinist view that faith alone led to salvation and that no amount of effort would ease the way.

Over the next several months, as Hutchinson intensified her critique of Wilson, she also attended worship services at other churches and began accusing other ministers of preaching the covenant of works. In fact by the summer of 1636 she was claiming that only John Cotton and her brother-in-law John Wheelwright, of all the Bay Colony's ministers, were preaching the covenant of grace. She argued that good behavior could never lead to salvation and that it was only through a mystical experience that a sinner could be saved. This was one of the paradoxes with which Puritans wrestled: if salvation came only through faith, if it did not matter how sinful or pious a person was who was predestined for eternal life in heaven, how does a society get people to live according to good conduct and moral law? The Puritan answer was that good conduct was a sign of piety, but Hutchinson's contention that only mystical experience mattered, thus rendering a person's behavior insignificant, was getting perilously close to the heresy of Antinomianism: denying the need for law and paving the way to anarchy.

In a society that expected women to be subservient, Hutchinson's assertiveness exacerbated her problems. But her gender was not what got her banished. She was banished by the Bay Colony authorities because of her belief that God guided each individual's morality. To the powers that be, this was anarchy. Nor was she banished because she advocated religious freedom; she was just as intolerant of her adversaries as they were with her. At her trial in 1637 Governor John Winthrop and several magistrates and ministers debated with her for two days over theological matters. She insisted that they prove to her where she was in error, while they insisted that she present scriptural evidence that would support her accusation that Wilson was preaching the covenant of works. After they kept pressing her, she finally announced that it was not through a passage of scripture but that God had spoken to her "by an immediate revelation": "By the voice of his own spirit to my soul."[4] This was sufficient for the court to condemn her. If direct revelation took precedence over the Bible or law, what then was to prevent any person from breaking the law because he or she had an immediate revelation from the Holy Spirit? This would lead to the breakdown of law and the breakdown of society. Hutchinson was banished, and in early 1638 she and a number of her followers went to Narragansett Bay and established the colonies of Warwick and Newport. (Later, wishing to remove herself farther from the reach of the authorities in Boston, she moved to the Dutch colony of New Netherlands, where, in 1643, Indians massacred her and her family. When word of the massacre arrived in Boston, the Puritans there saw this as God's divine judgment on her heretical views.)

* * *

Although Charles I's efforts to force Puritans to conform to the Church of England drove thousands of them to resettle in Massachusetts, most Puritans remained in the mother country. By the end of the 1630s they dominated Parliament, and in 1642, led by Oliver Cromwell, they took up arms against Charles. After six years of bitter fighting the English civil war came to an end with the king's defeat and execution. This was perhaps the single most extraordinary event in the development of English constitutionalism. With one stroke of the axe Parliament had established its authority over the monarchy. For the next ten years Cromwell exercised executive power; but after his death Parliament restored the late king's son, Charles II, to the throne, and the eleven-year Puritan interregnum came to an end.

During the chaos of the civil war religious dissent continued to grow. One of the dissenting sects that emerged at that time was the Quakers. Believing that each individual should interpret scripture according to his or her own light, George Fox preached that this "Inner Light" would lead to salvation and that clerics were not necessary to interpret God's word. Although Fox's followers called themselves the Society of Friends, the English irreverently labeled them Quakers, for their penchant of "trembling before the Lord." Believing it was sinful how both Protestants and Catholics eagerly found ways to justify war, Quakers became outspoken pacifists. They practiced civil disobedience and passive resistance. They believed that the Sermon on the Mount was a code by which to live. They also refused to swear oaths in court, wore plain clothes, and valued humility. However, their humility did not prevent them from going about the realm doggedly proclaiming the truth of their vision to such a degree that most people regarded them as extremely annoying. (Later, in New England, Quakers sometimes proselytized by marching nude up the aisle during Puritan church services.) Christians were also horrified that Quakers had no clergy, denied the concepts of original sin and predestination, and did not discipline their children by trying to break their will but instead treated them as innocents who were not born sinful and who only needed love and nurturing to bring out their inner spark. Quaker views, it appeared to other Christians, were leading straight to anarchy.

When Charles II was restored to the throne, he sought to repay a loan of £16,000 he had received from one of his supporters, Admiral William Penn. But Penn had died, and so Charles offered the money to Penn's Quaker son, also named William. The younger Penn asked instead for a charter so that he could establish a colony in the New World as a refuge for the Society of Friends. Charles granted the charter with the stipulation that all laws Penn enacted must be submitted for approval and that Anglicans would be guaranteed religious freedom.

Penn put a lot of thought into his "Holy Experiment." His intention was to provide a place where Quakers could worship freely without fear of harassment, and unlike the Puritans who attempted to erect a socially and religiously homogeneous society, Penn wanted Pennsylvania to be open and welcoming to people of all beliefs. He composed a "Frame of Government" that guaranteed due process of law, trial by jury, liberty of conscience, and moderate punishments.

One of the most unusual features that set Pennsylvania apart from the other English colonies was that the settlers arrived there without weapons. Penn sincerely wanted to maintain friendly relations with the Indians and treat them with respect. And for a time, at least until Pennsylvania established its first militia in 1740, peaceful coexistence was successful. The Quakers dealt fairly with the Indians, treated them as human beings, and made sure to pay for lands they sought.

In Pennsylvania Quakers were able to worship freely. But they faced enormous hostility in other colonies. In Boston in 1657 one Quaker, Mary Dyer, was arrested for proselytizing her religious views. The Puritans banished Dyer from the colony, but when she returned in 1659, they arrested her again. This time when they banished her, they warned her that if she returned to Boston, she would be hanged. In October of that year she did return and was arrested, tried, and convicted. She stood on the gallows while two fellow Quakers, Marmaduke Stephenson and William Robinson, were hanged at her side. At the last minute, after watching the two men die, she was reprieved and told that if she ever came back to Massachusetts, she would be executed. She was not intimidated. She returned in May 1660, and this time, on June 1, the Puritan authorities followed through with their threat and hanged her.

* * *

Throughout the seventeenth century, while colonial settlements were digging in deeper roots and formally establishing English institutions of law and government, there was considerable social upheaval, conflict, and even political revolt. Relationships with the Indians frequently turned hostile, despite some of the best, and sometimes misguided, efforts of settlers to deal honorably with the Native Americans. And even among the colonists themselves serious social discontent and grievances led to open rebellion, notably in Virginia in 1676 and in New York, Massachusetts, and Maryland in the aftermath of the Glorious Revolution in 1689.

The expansion of New England meant increased competition for land, and this led to a drastic deterioration of relations between the colonists and the Indians. In 1637, in an effort to resist English encroachment into the Connecticut and Mystic valleys, the Pequot sought to form an alliance with other Indians. But before the alliance could fully form, the English launched a predawn surprise attack on a Pequot village. Men from Massachusetts and Connecticut, together with their Narragansett allies, surrounded the village, while one contingent broke through the palisade, killed women, children, and elderly men as they slept, and set fire to the village. Terrorized people, fleeing the flames, ran into a withering barrage of bullets that claimed the lives of hundreds. Within a year the English rounded up the remnants of the Pequot that had survived the attack and either executed them or sold them into slavery. The Pequot's efforts to resist English encroachment proved, in the end, suicidal. The Pequot were never again an obstruction to English expansion.

Physical extermination was not the only approach the English took with respect to the Indians. They also sought to destroy the Indians' traditions and religious beliefs by converting them to Christianity and pressuring them to abandon their rituals and customs. In the 1640s the Reverend John Eliot began to minister to the Indians, translated the Bible into the Wampanoag language, and set up what he called "praying towns" where Indians would live adjacent to whites and learn Christianity and farming. At the same time, Thomas Mayhew and his son preached to the Indians on Nantucket and Martha's Vineyard, although they did not try to do away with their cultural identity the way Eliot did. By the mid-1670s, of the ten thousand Indians left in New England, about twenty-three hundred had converted to Christianity. It was clear that it would take all the skill the Indian nations of New England could muster to avoid annihilation not only from the disease and warfare that decimated them but also from the missionaries who undermined the survivors' culture and beliefs. The interaction between whites (despite the different approaches of the Spanish, the French, and the English) and the First Nations always wound up with destructive results, even when the Europeans believed they were doing God's work in converting people they viewed as "heathens."

The year 1675 was the breaking point for Indian-white relations in New England when the Wampanoag chieftain Metacom led his people in the most momentous and terrifying uprising against the settlers in colonial New England's history. Unlike the Pequot War, which was a brief clash against a single Indian nation, King Philip's War (the English called Metacom King Philip) was a far more extensive conflict between the English and a united force of Wampanoag and Narragansett that took on the character of a racial war. When the brutal killing finally came to an end, English attitudes toward Native Americans had hardened, and racial hatred was profoundly intensified. The war began when an Indian, John Sassamon, warned the colonists that the Wampanoag were preparing for an attack. When Sassamon was murdered, presumably by the Wampanoag for his betrayal, whites executed three Indians. Shortly thereafter Metacom led his coalition of Wampanoag and Narragansett in a broad attack against more than fifty English settlements throughout the region. The colonists were shocked at how successful the Indians were. Metacom's alliance was organized, they had acquired firearms, and they employed superior tactics by ambushing colonial forces from the cover of trees and rocks. However, the English prevailed with the help of the Mohawk Indians. The Mohawk, the easternmost of the Iroquois nations of New York, wanted to prevent the New England Indians from encroaching into their territory, and so they did not hesitate to ally themselves with the colonists. It was the Mohawk who finally captured Metacom and several of the Wampanoag and Narragansett leaders. When they executed Metacom and brought his head to Plymouth, the war was over. But the devastation in the yearlong struggle was appalling. Thousands of Indians and colonists were killed, twelve New England towns were destroyed, and hundreds of Indian survivors, even those who had not taken part in the war, were sold into slavery.

* * *

Farther south, with over forty thousand colonists living in Virginia, competition for land also greatly intensified. As more and more settlers served out their indentures, they were disappointed that the land they received was not suitable for growing Virginia's main cash crop: tobacco. Since most of the good-quality land was in the hands of the planter elite, former indentured servants were shunted westward to the piedmont region, where they were in constant conflict with the Indians. The settlers believed that an agreement made in 1646 between colonial authorities and the Powhatan, granting exclusive land rights to the Indians in areas beyond white settlement, had been much too favorable to the Indians and should be amended so that more arable land would be opened for settlement. They also harbored deep-seated resentment against the wealthy planters who had kept so much of the most fertile land for themselves. When hostilities broke out with the Indians in 1675, this resentment and anger boiled over. It began when a party of Doeg Indians, trying to collect a debt from a settler, clashed with several whites. When settlers seeking revenge went after the Doeg, they also attacked a band of Susquehannock Indians, whose land they coveted, and hostilities escalated sharply. During the winter the Susquehannock struck back, killing thirty-six Virginians. In the spring Nathaniel Bacon led a ragtag army of frontiersmen, runaway indentured servants, and slaves against the Indians. Governor William Berkeley wanted nothing more than to maintain peace and prevent the economic dislocation a war would cause. When Bacon would not desist from his attacks, the governor, calling Bacon a rebel, sent three hundred militiamen to apprehend him and bring him back to Jamestown to stand trial. Throughout the summer of 1676 Berkeley's troops tried to outmaneuver Bacon and his men, but Bacon continued killing Indians (mostly friendly Indians). Then Bacon's force marched on Jamestown, confiscated Berkeley's estate and those of his supporters, and terrorized the surrounding countryside by raising havoc and plundering the property of other colonists. What began as a conflict with Indians became a civil war. Berkeley escaped to the eastern shore, where he raised a force and retook Jamestown in August. Bacon's foraging men returned, laid siege to the capital, and forced Berkeley to retreat again to the eastern shore. In September Bacon burned Jamestown to the ground and boldly declared that he would unite Virginia and Maryland with Carolina, make an alliance with the Dutch, and set up an independent republic of the Chesapeake. Within a month, however, before he could turn his boasts into reality, he died of dysentery, Berkeley regained control, and twenty-three of the rebels were summarily hanged.

This episode, which became known as Bacon's Rebellion, was the most violent social upheaval in the colonies prior to the American Revolution. The uprising exposed a deep-seated distrust of authority and an intense antipathy toward the planter elites that had been building for some time. Bacon and his men felt that their opportunities for economic advancement and political power were severely limited, and so they took up arms. But that is only half the story. Even though some slaves and free blacks participated in the rebellion, it also demonstrates how racism, in this case aimed at the Indians, can mask deeper economic issues. Both the backcountry settlers and the Indians were competing for an area of land that was fast diminishing because the elite class had taken possession of nearly all the desirable acreage, and this competition fanned the flames of white racism. Although Bacon and his men were dissenters who fought for radical changes to the system, they were not attempting a revolution to attain idealistic goals such as natural rights and individual liberties; they were embroiled in a struggle for economic and political power.

The most important impact of Bacon's Rebellion is that it wound up changing the way the Chesapeake colonies approached the need for a sizeable cheap labor force in a labor-intensive economy. Bacon's army consisted of indentured servants—men who came from the lower classes of English society, who had no resources and could not afford to pay their own passage to Virginia. The planters who controlled the colony saw this underclass, this rabble, especially after Bacon's Rebellion, as potential troublemakers, rebels, and revolutionaries. And so in the aftermath of the rebellion colonial officials in Virginia and Maryland determined that labor needs would no longer be met by low-class, landless whites but by African slaves. Unlike indentured servants, slaves were entirely under the control of their masters, they would never be freed, they would never be armed, they would never be able to act on aspirations to possess their own land, and if they escaped from bondage, they could not blend in with other settlers and remain undetected.

* * *

When James II succeeded his brother as king in 1685, he announced that he was a Catholic. Needless to say, this did not sit well with Parliament. Parliament's concern deepened when James issued the Declaration of Indulgence guaranteeing freedom of worship to Catholics and intensified further when James began appointing Catholics to positions of power. Still, the king was old, his wife was thought to be beyond child-bearing years, and his two adult daughters (by a previous marriage), who were next in the line of succession, were Protestants. However, in 1688, to everyone's dismay, the queen gave birth to a son. The boy was to be brought up as a Catholic. The prospect of a long reign of a Catholic king who would presumably restore Roman Catholicism as the established church was unacceptable, and so Parliament formally invited James's daughter Mary and her Dutch husband, William of Orange, to London to become joint monarchs. James, mindful of what happened to his father when he had opposed Parliament, fled to France at the end of December. In January 1689 William III and Mary II were proclaimed king and queen, while Parliament passed a Declaration of Rights limiting the monarch's power and establishing a Protestant succession, as well as a Toleration Act granting freedom of religion to all Protestant dissenters. This bloodless Glorious Revolution was the final phase (after the civil war and Restoration) in England's progress from an absolute to a constitutional monarchy. Clearly, Parliament, not the king, was supreme. Kings did not rule by "divine right" because God had willed it so. They ruled by the authorization of Parliament.

The Glorious Revolution reverberated in the colonies. Charles II, during the last year of his reign, had revoked the Massachusetts charter in order to coordinate London's control over the colonies more efficiently. This was the Puritan colony's worst nightmare come true— losing the charter and thus undermining the entire basis for their holy commonwealth. Church membership had already been steadily declining in Massachusetts; losing the charter only exacerbated Puritan worries that their society was in decline. And then their anxiety deepened when James II tightened London's control by dissolving the colonial governments and combining the New England colonies with New York and New Jersey into a centrally controlled Dominion of New England. James appointed Sir Edmund Andros as governor general and sent him to Boston. The Puritans were infuriated when Andros levied taxes by executive order, issued a decree requiring religious toleration, commandeered a Puritan church in Boston for Anglican worship services, abolished the General Court, and set up restrictions on town meetings. Many colonists protested, but they were quickly thrown in jail. When news of the Glorious Revolution arrived in April 1689, hundreds of jubilant Puritan insurgents took to the streets in an uprising against the reviled Andros. They imprisoned the governor general and seized the fort in Boston Harbor. Andros escaped, but Massachusetts was back under Puritan control and remained so for the next three years while they waited patiently for the Crown to reissue their charter. Unfortunately for the Puritans the new charter was a profound disappointment. Although Rhode Island and Connecticut resumed the right to elect their own governors, this was not the case for Massachusetts, which now became a royal colony with a governor appointed by the Crown, not elected by the freemen. The charter also removed church membership as a requirement to vote and incorporated Plymouth into Massachusetts Bay.

The Dominion of New England's lieutenant governor, Francis Nicholson, as second in command to Andros, was the Crown's appointee in charge in New York. When Nicholson refused to acknowledge the accession of William and Mary in 1689, he too faced an insurrection. Because the lieutenant governor remained loyal to James II, New

Yorkers viewed him as part of a papist conspiracy to restore Catholicism. At this point Jacob Leisler, a merchant who had migrated to New
Amsterdam from Germany before the English had taken the colony
(and who very much resented English discrimination against Dutch and
German residents), stepped forward to lead a revolt against Nicholson.
The rebels ousted Nicholson and replaced the king's governing council
with a Committee of Safety. Renouncing James II and declaring loyalty
to William and Mary, Leisler seized Fort James at the southern tip of
Manhattan and renamed it Fort William. For the next thirteen months,
with his son-in-law Jacob Milborne serving as deputy, Leisler ran the
government, encouraged the lower classes to attack the property of the
wealthy English elite, and freed debtors from prison. Despite the fact
that Leisler proclaimed his allegiance to the new monarchs, he did not
immediately hand over power when English soldiers and the new royal
governor, Henry Sloughter, arrived in 1691. This hesitation prompted
Sloughter to have Leisler and Milborne arrested and tried for treason.
Many of the English in the colony, even those who opposed James II
and the Dominion of New England, never warmed to Leisler and con-
temptuously considered him a German upstart. Consequently very few
defended him. Leisler and Milborne were found guilty and sentenced to
be strung up "by the Neck and being Alive their bodyes be Cutt downe
to Earth and Their Bowells to be taken out and they being Alive, burnt
before their faces."[5]

When Protestants in Maryland got word of the Glorious Revolution, they too took to the streets. Vowing to annihilate the papists in
the colony, John Coode and a group of militants calling themselves the
Protestant Association deposed Lord Baltimore's Catholic regime and
seized control of the government. They petitioned William and Mary
to establish a Protestant government and the Anglican Church in the
colony. The request was granted, and the Calvert family lost their pro-
prietary rights to govern the colony until 1715, when they converted
to Protestantism.

* * *

The seventeenth century was a critical period in the prehistory of the
United States because the English colonies that were established helped
mold the institutions, philosophy, and character of a nation that had
not yet been born. In addition, many complex problems that the United

States was eventually to face, as well as the responses to those problems, had their roots in the seventeenth century. By 1700 misunderstanding, condescension, competition, and conflict had become the accepted manner of dealing with the Indians. By 1700 Puritan theology and attitudes in New England had taken such deep root that they still permeate American philosophical, religious, social, cultural, and political thought. By 1700 slavery and the plantation system had become so entrenched in the South that a century and a half later it was to lead to the most devastating and bloody war in the nation's history, and a century and a half after that racism still persisted as one of the country's most vexing and enduring problems. And by 1700 the middle colonies of Pennsylvania, New York, and New Jersey were already emerging as centers of diversity, multiculturalism, commerce, and toleration that would also be a force helping to shape the American character.

Puritans in New England sought a refuge where they could worship according to the dictates of their conscience, yet among them dissenters arose challenging their doctrines and beliefs. As a result, a number of individuals and groups broke off from the mainstream and sought their own refuge. Planters and indentured servants in the Chesapeake colonies expected to improve their lives through economic opportunity in the new settlements, but a widening gap between the planter elite ruling the colony and the lower classes led to frustration, resentment, protest, and eventually armed conflict. Political upheaval in the mother country, from the execution of Charles I in 1649 to the deposing of James II in 1688, had extensive ramifications in the colonial settlements. The aftermath of the Glorious Revolution led to popular uprisings in Massachusetts, New York, and Maryland that troubled the authorities both in the colonies and in London. From the beginning of settlement, dissent, protest, and resistance were central features of the English colonies. As the Age of Faith gave way to the Age of Reason, political dissent supplanted religious dissent. And dissent, in the end, gave way to revolution.

CHAPTER 2

Dissent in an Age of Reason

Wee your humbell and poore partishinners doo begg Sir
your aid and assistance in this one thing. . . . Releese us out of
this Cruell Bondegg.

—anonymous slave, 1723

As the English colonies grew from fledgling outposts of empire into
burgeoning provinces, a number of significant forces came together
that had the combined effect of intensifying dissent. During the first
decades of the eighteenth century the Enlightenment arrived in the New
World; a religious revival swept through the colonies; slavery became
entrenched as the preferred system for filling the need for cheap labor,
especially in the South; and the colonies participated in a series of wars
between England and France. All the while dissenting opinion became
more and more visible. Enlightenment ideas raised the consciousness of
influential educated people and initiated a meaningful discourse about
the nature of government and the concepts of natural rights, freedom of
speech, and freedom of the press. Colonists protested against Britain's
policy of pressing men involuntarily into military service. Native Americans embraced a variety of methods to resist white encroachment.
Quakers and others spoke out against slavery. And on several occasions
slaves rose up in rebellion. By the 1760s the colonists were acquiring
a distinct awareness of themselves as set apart from their brethren in
Great Britain. And many of them were struck by the conviction that if
they spoke their minds, they could produce change.

* * *

By midcentury intellectual trends from Europe became the vanguard
of a new rational age—the Age of Reason, or the Enlightenment—
that sought to explain the phenomena of life scientifically, logically,
and rationally rather than as manifestations of God's will. Although
the Enlightenment also gave rise to such spurious notions as scientific

racism and sexism, it encouraged critical thinking and challenged time-honored beliefs and principles. Coterminous with Enlightenment thinking, a decades-long religious revival swept the colonies, the Great Awakening, when scores of clergymen decried the mounting rational secularism that seemed to be turning religion into a cold, emotionless ritual. These ministers sought to reverse this process and to restore emotion and enthusiasm to religious conviction by initiating a serious of spiritual revivals. Ironically these conflicting trends—the impulse to understand the material world rationally and the desire to experience spiritual awakening and salvation—both, in their own way, stimulated discontent with the existing realities and helped stir up dissent. Both impulses encouraged ordinary people, as well as the intellectual elite, to question authority and to think for themselves. Moreover, these impulses motivated individuals to examine the meaning of natural rights and personal salvation and whether these principles universally applied to all people.

As early as the sixteenth century the Scientific Revolution had been altering ways of thinking. Astronomical discoveries by Nicolaus Copernicus, Tycho Brahe, Johannes Kepler, and Galileo Galilei, as well as the advent of Newtonian physics, established that the Earth was not the center of the universe as had been previously assumed; therefore it only stood to reason that humankind was not the center of God's attention. The educated classes that had been following the discoveries reasoned that *individuals*, not kings and popes, were responsible for their own fate. The growing emphasis on science and rational thinking raised significant doubts about, and was a potent challenge to, traditional assumptions about politics, religion, social relations, and culture.

Over time, these ideas filtered down to the general public and promoted the growth of rational thinking in everyday life. Many historians consider the Enlightenment to have begun when the English philosopher John Locke published his *Second Treatise of Government* in 1690, justifying Parliament's action to replace King James II with William and Mary. In his treatise, Locke applied the scientific method (in which scientists conduct objective experiments in order to discover the laws of nature) to political thought. The *Second Treatise* states that all men are born equal in a state of nature and possess the natural rights of life, liberty, and property. Locke argues that government becomes necessary in order to preserve and safeguard those rights; and so people enter into a social contract in which they give up a portion of their rights (for example, the right to punish a transgressor) to the government, and in return they gain a higher portion of security. If the government, however, does not protect life, liberty, and property or if it in fact infringes on those rights, then the people have the right to rebel—they have the right to overthrow that government because it is violating its part of the social contract—and set up another government that will protect those rights.

Locke's views on government spread throughout Europe and the American colonies. With his *Second Treatise* a new age dawned that repudiated the long-standing belief in the "divine right of kings"—the view that rulers were ordained by God—and replaced it with the principle that rulers got their authority from the people. As Enlightenment ideas filtered through the social order, more and more people began to accept the belief that they had the ability to determine their own fate.

The Enlightenment's emphasis on rational thought stimulated the growth of scientific study and research. Throughout the century intellectuals, from professors to theologians, from political philosophers to dilettantes, dove into mathematics and what was then called "natural philosophy"—physics, chemistry, and astronomy. Not only that but scientific methodology was also employed in philosophical and social inquiry and consequently was instrumental in giving rise to a modern education system. Locke had postulated that the human mind was a *tabula rasa* (blank slate) at birth and that all knowledge, all insight, is externally imposed knowledge—knowledge that is written on the blank slate by the teacher or by experience. Thus, since it is so important to be mindful of what is written on the slate, education is crucial to human progress. This thinking took hold, especially in New England, where education-minded Puritans had already established schools and Harvard College in the early seventeenth century. By the mid-eighteenth century public and private schools and colleges were founded throughout the colonies. Colleges, such as William and Mary, Yale, Princeton, and the University of Pennsylvania featured a multitude of courses in the sciences, modern languages, and law, and their graduates entered business, politics, and science as well as the ministry and education. Provincial society was becoming more secularized. Additionally students studied the works of Locke and other Enlightenment political philosophers such as Montesquieu, Voltaire, Berkeley, and Hume, and as the eighteenth century wore on and more young men were exposed to modern ways of thinking that went well beyond the scope of a classical education, these colleges became breeding grounds for the development of many key dissenting political ideas and attitudes that were to shape the second half of the century.

Historians still debate the significance of religion in eighteenth-century America, but recent studies have shown that, as the colonies expanded, church attendance began to decline. In fact, by the last decades of the seventeenth century there were signs that piety had fallen off in direct proportion to the growth of the colonies.[1] Once settlements spread into the interior, it became increasingly difficult for people to attend worship services, and consequently church membership plummeted. Moreover, as a nascent consumer society was beginning to take root, many colonists devoted more time and energy to improving their economic position instead of attending to their spiritual state. As a result, clergymen, influenced by the Enlightenment emphasis on reason, tempered their theology by embracing and advocating Christian rationalism, the view that individuals possess free will and can achieve salvation by living rationally and morally. Christian rationalism in a sense was a form of dissent against the traditional Protestantism of Luther and Calvin.

By the 1720s many conservative ministers in the colonies, especially those rooted in the Calvinist tradition, were appalled at this revisionist theology. To them God was still the omniscient, omnipotent, angry God whose hand was evident in the everyday affairs of individuals, and no amount of striving for salvation would be of any use for escaping his wrath on the day of judgment. An attempt to bring rationalism to religion, they argued (quite rationally), was anathema, and these preachers fervently implored individuals to examine their hearts for God's grace and to seek a personal conversion experience. This line of reasoning fostered a religious revival that had a massive impact on the colonies.

The Great Awakening, as it was called, was not a cohesive phenomenon but a series of local revivals that took place in rural backwoods areas and urban centers from New England to Georgia and every colony in between. Solomon Stoddard in New England and Theodore Jacob Frelinghuysen in New Brunswick, New Jersey, were among the ministers that initiated the Great Awakening. Soon Gilbert Tennent in New Brunswick and his brother John in nearby Freehold, New Jersey, also began holding revivals. Then, in 1734 in Northampton,

Massachusetts, Stoddard's grandson Jonathan Edwards followed suit by preaching "hellfire and damnation" sermons insisting that the only path to salvation was to experience an immediate, personal, emotional conversion experience.

The Great Awakening spread even wider when the charismatic English preachers George Whitefield and John Wesley, who had been converting thousands of Britons with their riveting sermons, arrived in the colonies in the late 1730s. Both men preached extensively to large audiences up and down the Atlantic seaboard. Whitefield's sermons were especially effective in enthralling the thousands who came to hear him. From Georgia to Philadelphia, New England to South Carolina, Whitefield preached the message of redemption through faith and converted thousands of sinners with sermons that were so emotional that listeners wept and fell to the ground overwhelmed with the prospect of eternal damnation. Even Benjamin Franklin attended one of Whitefield's rallies in Philadelphia and was genuinely impressed with this mesmerizing speaker (although not moved enough to fall to the ground weeping).

To some extent the Great Awakening was a reaction to the cold rationalism of the Enlightenment and brought comfort to those who did not have their needs met by a purely intellectual approach to salvation. For them spiritual needs could only be assuaged by a personal and mystical relationship with God. Ironically Whitefield, Wesley, and Edwards, who exhorted worshipers to seek such a relationship, argued in their sermons and writings according to the same methodology and logic of the Enlightenment thinkers. They were intellectuals who believed that spirituality was also a deeply emotional experience. In this paradoxical sense the Great Awakening was both a reaction to the intellectualism of the Enlightenment and a product of Enlightenment thinking. Taken together, the Great Awakening and the Enlightenment were powerful forces pushing individuals to be skeptical of all types of authority and to rely instead on their own capacity for critical thinking.

The Great Awakening also revealed the underlying social and economic tensions that existed in the colonies. Many of those who were caught up in the revivals were from the lower classes and began more openly to voice their displeasure with the economic elite. Itinerant preachers in the rural South condemned wealthy planters for making their fortunes on the backs of slaves while they wiled away their time indulging in sinful pleasures, and evangelists in Massachusetts denounced the greed of merchants and money lenders. Even some blacks and women began going about preaching the gospel and criticizing those who were more interested in worldly goods and pursuits than in spiritual values.

The Great Awakening was the first colonial-wide experience that showed colonists that there was a common bond linking them together greater than their Englishness or their self-perception as Virginians or New Yorkers or New Englanders. It boosted an emerging "American" identity while inducing people to examine their basic assumptions and to rethink their view of themselves as individuals, as souls seeking redemption. Although the revivals focused on faith, not politics, the Great Awakening had the unforeseen impact of encouraging the sort of open and critical questioning of authority that within a few decades inspired and encouraged a new, revolutionary, generation to challenge king and Parliament.

* * *

One and a half million Africans, three times the number of European immigrants, were abducted and taken to the British colonies as slaves. Because of the exceptional profitability of sugar most of these slaves were imported into the West Indies. During the eighteenth century, as demand for workers increased on the mainland, tens of thousands of Caribbean slaves were sold to brokers in South Carolina, Georgia, and the Chesapeake. About half of the slaves imported into the southern colonies were women, and this meant there was a much more equitable gender balance among the slave population there than in the Caribbean, where the majority of slaves were men. The gender balance meant that there was a steady natural increase in the slave population through procreation. The slave population also grew because the mainland environment, especially in the Chesapeake region, was significantly healthier than in the Caribbean, where fatal tropical diseases ran rampant. By the time of the Revolution there were over half a million slaves in the thirteen colonies, most of them living in the South.

Slaves were an indispensable part of colonial life. They plowed, they hoed, they constructed houses, they built roads, and they cultivated lush rice paddies that increased South Carolina's prosperity enormously. They also gave their white owners the opportunity to engage in such leisure pursuits as travel, reading, hunting, horse racing, and engaging in political and philosophical discussions and debates about natural rights, liberty, and the future of the colonies.

But slaves resisted.

The most common forms of resistance were the sabotaging of crops, barn burnings, and the intentional loss or destruction of tools. Also slaves frequently tried to escape by fleeing to Spanish Florida or to the frontier, where they would be beyond the reach of authority. Rebellions, however, were rare occurrences. Although there were dozens of slave insurrections in the West Indies during the colonial period, the first one in the mainland British colonies occurred in 1712 in New York. Twenty slaves, armed with hatchets, swords, and a few guns, torched a building and then ambushed the whites who came to put out the fire. Nine people were killed and six wounded. The New York militia rounded up twenty-seven slaves; thirteen were summarily hanged, three were burnt alive, one was tortured to death, and another six committed suicide before such retribution could be enacted on them.

As a result of this uprising, the New York Assembly enacted laws that prohibited slaves from owning weapons, forbade more than three slaves from assembling, and in an unsuccessful effort to discourage manumission, required masters to post a £200 bond if they should free a slave. Despite such setbacks, slaves continued to rebel. The 1739 Stono Rebellion in South Carolina—the largest slave revolt of the colonial period— started when twenty slaves, led by a literate Angolan named Jemmy (some historians have called him Arnold, others Cato), seized weapons in a store in Stono, about twenty miles from Charleston, killed several whites, and then headed south for St. Augustine. It was rumored that, because England and Spain were involved in the War of Jenkins' Ear—a conflict that later expanded into King George's War—the Spanish would protect the slaves if they could make it to the Spanish colony. The slaves raised a flag proclaiming "Liberty" and recruited other bondsmen as they marched south. By late afternoon they had traveled about ten miles when, by chance, the lieutenant governor, William Bull, and several companions encountered them. Bull called for reinforcements, and when one hundred militiamen eventually arrived, a firefight ensued that claimed the lives of about forty rebels and twenty whites. Fifty slaves, many of whom had not actually joined the rebellion, were rounded up, tortured, and hanged. As a warning to others who might contemplate such an uprising, the executed slaves' heads were impaled on posts and strategically and publicly placed around Charleston. In 1740 South Carolina passed the Negro Act, which established stricter penalties for owners who taught their slaves to read, outlawed manumission, and prohibited slaves from earning money, cultivating their own gardens, or assembling. The act also made it mandatory for whites to serve in the South Carolina militia.

The Stono Rebellion took place in a decade of considerable slave unrest in Britain's colonies—uprisings in St. John (1733), the Bahamas (1734), Antigua (1735), and Savannah, Georgia (1738). These events put whites on edge. In fact they were so nervous that even a rumor of rebellion could result in swift, precipitate action. White fears came to a head in a disturbing incident in New York City in 1741. Between March and April 1741 seven arson fires broke out in Manhattan, including one that destroyed Fort George. Suspicions that there was a plot by slaves to instigate an insurrection prompted the city government to offer a reward for any information on the culprits. A teenage indentured servant, Mary Burton, stepped forward and claimed that her boss, the tavern keeper John Hughson and his wife, along with several whites and slaves had formulated a plan to burn down the city. The accused, when summoned before the court, denied any knowledge of the plot. Nevertheless, all of them were hanged. Mary Burton continued to name names, and when the hysteria had run its course, thirty-one slaves had been executed (thirteen of them by burning at the stake) along with the four whites whom the servant had accused. It is impossible to determine whether there was an actual conspiracy or whether the incident was the result of white paranoia at the prospect of a slave rebellion.[2]

Armed slave resistance was a compelling and violent manifestation of dissent against slavery. Many compassionate whites, especially Quakers and others with strong religious convictions, believed that slavery was morally abhorrent. Increasingly they spoke out against the institution. Quakers recognized that slavery was a form of institutionalized violence—after all, violence was necessary to maintain slavery and to quell slave uprisings—and therefore slavery went directly against their pacifist principles. As early as 1688 Pennsylvania Quakers and Mennonites in Germantown signed a petition against slavery on the basis of the biblical argument that no person would consent to being "sold or made a slave for all the time of his life."[3]

Other Quakers protested against the institution and publicly censured all those who would own slaves or profit in any way from the slave trade. In 1718 William Burling published the first of a series of antislavery tracts calling attention to the glaring contradiction between the practice of slavery and Quaker beliefs. Ralph Sandiford, a merchant who refused loans from businessmen who made money on the backs of slaves, spent much of his life campaigning publicly against slavery. In 1729 he expressed his antislavery views in a pamphlet, *A Brief Examination of the Practice of the Times*, by quoting from the Bible to discredit slaveholders who maintained that slavery was God's curse on Africans because they are the descendants of Cain or of Ham. He also drew on Enlightenment principles to reinforce his argument. "What greater injustice," Sandiford asked, "can be acted, than to rob a man of his liberty, which is more valuable than life[?]"[4]

Benjamin Lay was notorious for using unconventional ways to protest against slavery. Once, in a Burlington, New Jersey, Quaker meeting, Lay denounced Quakers who owned slaves by theatrically thrusting a sword into a Bible in which he had concealed a bladder full of pokeberry juice. As the red juice splattered all over him (and several of his fellow worshipers), he cried out, "Thus shall God shed the blood of those who enslave their fellow-creatures."[5] Another time he abducted the child of a neighbor who owned slaves and then asked the frantic man if he thought perhaps the parents of his slaves might feel the same distress that he was feeling. Lay went so far in his opposition to slavery as to practice what he preached by living in a cave in Abington, Pennsylvania, and refusing to wear any clothing that had been produced by slave labor. Despite such eccentricity Lay's 1737 antislavery book, *All Slave-Keepers That Keep the Innocent in Bondage, Apostates*, was printed by community stalwart Benjamin Franklin.

In Nantucket, Elihu Coleman also used scripture in his *A Testimony against the Antichristian Practice of Making Slaves of Men* (1733) to convince Quakers that the concept of owning a human being was antithetical to Christianity. "This practice of making slaves of men," he wrote, is "so great an evil . . . that for all the riches and glory of this world, I would not be guilty of so great a sin as this seems to be."[6]

The most influential antislavery activists of the time were the Quakers John Woolman and Anthony Benezet. Woolman, from Burlington County, New Jersey, believed in the interconnectedness of all beings, that there was a spark of divinity in all of God's creatures. As a young man Woolman worked as a bookkeeper. When his employer instructed him to write up a bill of sale for a female slave, he was suddenly struck with the epiphany that "slavekeeping" was a "practice inconsistent with the Christian religion" and that the institution was evil because it denied the divine spark that existed in Africans.[7]

Along with preaching against slavery Woolman wrote two pamphlets, *Some Considerations on Keeping Negroes* (1754) and *Considerations on Keeping Negroes, Part Second* (1762), in which he insisted that "Negroes are our fellow creatures" and that to keep them in bondage is nothing but a crime. How "can an honest man," Woolman asked, "withhold from them that Liberty, which is the free Gift of the Most High to His rational creatures?"[8] Not only is slavery devastating to an entire race of people; it is an unchristian practice that also harms the slaveholder. Woolman argued that those who own slaves would be unwittingly teaching their children lessons in moral depravity. His antislavery stance is unique in that he anticipates future antislavery arguments by combining Christian morality with the secular Enlightenment principle that all men innately possess the natural rights of life and liberty.

Woolman's views led him to collaborate with Anthony Benezet and Benjamin Lay in order to convince the Philadelphia Society of Friends to adopt resolutions in 1755 and 1758 condemning slavery and denying membership to anyone who owned slaves. Eventually Woolman's ardent campaign against slavery convinced many of his fellow Quakers and others that they must be true to a deeper morality and refrain from participating in either owning slaves or being involved in the slave trade.

In addition to working with Woolman and the Philadelphia Society of Friends, Anthony Benezet contributed a great deal to the antislavery position. Benezet, a teacher at a Quaker school in Germantown, set up evening classes there for slave children. Later, in 1770, he established the Negro School of Philadelphia. In 1762 he wrote *A Short Account of That Part of Africa Inhabited by Negroes, with General Observations on the Slave Trade and Slavery* "to invalidate the false arguments which are frequently advanced for the palliation of this trade."[9] Benezet never accepted the prevailing notion that Africans were inferior to Europeans, and all his subsequent works were attempts to counteract such views. His most widely read pamphlet, *Some Historical Account of Guinea* (1771), influenced many individuals in Britain and the colonies, including such notables as John Wesley, Thomas Clarkson (who became the leading antislavery activist in England), and to a lesser extent, Benjamin Franklin. In this pamphlet Benezet describes in vivid detail the horrors of slavery and the slave trade, and even more than Woolman, he combines Enlightenment ideals with Christian values by copiously quoting such Enlightenment thinkers as Montesquieu as authorities to substantiate his attack on slavery. Benezet argues that it is hypocritical for slaveholders to stand up for the right to own slaves. Moreover, such an argument is contrary to Enlightenment principles and the doctrine that all humans have natural rights. If the colonists have natural rights, how can they deny these rights to Africans?

Despite such enlightened sentiments Benezet himself was not a radical abolitionist like those who came to prominence several decades later. He was a gradualist; that is, he espoused the gradual elimination of slavery, and he advocated the colonization of freed slaves to lands west of the Allegheny Mountains. Benezet's focus was not on immediate emancipation but chiefly on outlawing the slave trade. Still, his influential antislavery stance was not confined to mere theorizing. In 1775 he was instrumental in founding an abolitionist organization, the Society for the Relief of Free Negroes Unlawfully Held in Bondage, and he lived his life according to the principle of equality. (He also took up the causes of Acadians who had been forced into exile during the French and Indian War, pacifism during the American Revolution, and the plight of Native Americans, publishing *Some Observations on the Situation, Disposition, and Character of the Indian Natives of the Continent* in 1784, calling for the compassionate treatment of Indians.) Anthony Benezet affected so many people that at his death over a thousand mourners, including more than four hundred African Americans, attended his funeral.

Some slaves embraced the Quaker model of nonviolent dissent by adopting such forms of peaceful protest as publishing critical accounts condemning the institution as well as taking advantage of the English legal system to petition for freedom. Two eighteenth-century slaves, Quobna Ottobah Cugoano and Olaudah Equiano, hoping to gain converts for the antislavery cause, published critical accounts of life under slavery.

Quobna Ottobah Cugoano was abducted from the west coast of Africa around 1770 and enslaved in the Caribbean for two years. In

1772 his master took him to England, where a year later he was freed. He formed a fraternal organization, the Sons of Africa, and published *Thoughts and Sentiments on the Evil and Wicked Traffic of the Slavery and Commerce of the Human Species* (1787), in which he described his ordeal as a slave in Grenada, analyzed the economics of slavery, and concluded that Great Britain, as a Christian nation, must commit itself to ending the institution. "To put an end to the wickedness of slavery and merchandizing of men," he wrote, "and to prevent murder, extirpation and dissolution, is what every righteous nation ought to seek after; and to endeavour to diffuse knowledge and instruction to all the heathen nations wherever they can, is the grand duty of all Christian men."[10]

Olaudah Equiano also published an autobiographical antislavery narrative. In *The Interesting Narrative of Olaudah Equiano, or Gustavus Vassa the African* (1789)[11] Equiano vividly described his experience as a slave and demanded an end to racism and slavery. Like Cugoano, Equiano used both moral and economic arguments against slavery. Free wageworkers, he argued, would be far more efficient and cost-effective than slaves. If whites would treat the "slaves as men, every cause of fear would be banished. They would be faithful, honest, intelligent, and vigorous; and peace, prosperity, and happiness would attend [whites]."[12]

Both Cugoano's and Equiano's autobiographies were extensively read at the time and convinced many people that slavery was a brutal, repugnant institution. At the same time, the moving narratives demonstrated that Africans, contrary to the prevalent racial stereotypes of the eighteenth century, were just as urbane and sophisticated as any European. In the nineteenth century their example encouraged escaped slaves to publish accounts of their own personal experience under slavery as a means of raising antislavery sentiment among whites.

Starting around 1770, many unheralded slaves in Massachusetts began to draw on the British legal system to sue for their freedom and make claims to receive all the wages they earned after the age of twenty-one. Every one of these cases resulted in victory for the slaves. One such Massachusetts case was that involving Prince Boston, a Nantucket whaler. When the ship's captain paid Prince Boston his wages, the slave's master, William Swain, sued the captain for the money on the grounds that whatever a slave earned rightfully belonged to the master. The Court of Common Pleas ruled against Swain, and so he appealed to the state supreme court. When John Adams was named as counsel for the defense, Swain dropped the case, and as a result Prince Boston was recognized as a free man. Equally as important the case reinforced the principle that slaves, in Massachusetts at least, possessed the right of litigation.

Within a few years Nantucket freed its slaves, and many towns in Massachusetts began to pass ordinances doing away with slavery. In 1773 and 1777 slaves petitioned the legislature for emancipation, which induced lawmakers to adopt resolutions that eliminated slavery in stages. These peaceful methods of dissent—submitting petitions and using the legal process to eradicate slavery—did not go unnoticed by whites and certainly had an impact on what people were thinking about the great natural-rights issues of the day.

* * *

Dissent continued to mount. Indians never stopped protesting the efforts of colonial officials to deceive and trick them out of their land, and they increasingly used violence against the white settlers who were moving into their territory. Women began to resist the subservient role they were duty bound to play. Laborers and poor farmers increasingly protested against colonial elites who set prices and levied taxes that they believed were exploitative and unfair. It is clear that a significant number of eighteenth-century Americans were drawing on the new Enlightenment principles that were circulating through the colonies to provide them with some ammunition for making their cases. And each of these occurrences was a harbinger of things to come. After the establishment of the United States, Native Americans, African Americans, women, poor workers, and farmers, inspired by their predecessors' protests, continued to agitate for more liberty, more equality, and more opportunity. The forces of dissent determining the direction of the colonies were setting the precedent for, and evolving into, the forces that would continue to shape the nation after independence.

The word *dissent* does not adequately describe the intensity of Indian resistance against white encroachment. Much of their resistance went far beyond the parameters of protest and took the form of outright warfare. There were many instances, however, when Indians employed the tactics of white settlers and even slaves by using such methods of dissent as negotiations, petitions, and letters. Often, like white settlers and some slaves, they tried to reason with colonial authorities by using the arguments derived from Locke's views of natural rights, which they knew resonated with white authorities. For example, in 1727, when English negotiators attempted to convince the Penobscot envoy Loron Sauguaarum that his people must acknowledge the king of England as their rightful sovereign, Loron Sauguaarum refused to do so. While shrewdly agreeing that George I was sovereign in England, he warned the colonial officials, "[Do not] infer that I acknowledge thy King as my King, and King of my lands. Here lies my distinction—my Indian distinction. God hath willed that I have no King, and that I be master of my lands in common."[13] In other words (Locke's words) Loron Sauguaarum and the Penobscot Indians refused to consent to the king's authority. This is a revealing example that at least some Indians were familiar with Enlightenment concepts and grasped that the best way to stand up for their rights was to make their case from the white man's point of view.

Most often Indian dissent was unsuccessful. For example, in 1740 the Lenni Lenape petitioned Pennsylvania authorities, protesting the so-called walking purchase. Thomas Penn (William Penn's son) claimed that the Lenni Lenape chiefs had granted his father the rights to all the land "as far as a man can go in a day and a half" from the Delaware River. To carry out this "walking purchase," Thomas Penn had a trail cleared and sent three men instead of one walker to run in stages as far as they could. The third runner got to a point sixty-five miles from the river. When the lines were drawn, the colony encompassed all of the land up to the Lehigh Valley. Penn then sold tracts in this area to white settlers, and the outraged Lenni Lenape protested. "We Desire Thomas Penn," they wrote, "Would take these People off from their Land in Peace that we May not be at the trouble to drive them off for the Land WE Will hold fast With both Our hands not in privately but in Open View of all the Countrey & all Our Friends & Relations That is the Eastern Indians & Our Uncles the five Nations & the Mohikkons."[14] Unfortunately for the Indians their petition was ignored, and the result was that Indian-white relations in Pennsylvania deteriorated rapidly.

Other Native Americans put forward their views just as dramatically. In 1752, during negotiations with Massachusetts officials, Atiwaneto, an Abenaki Indian, asserted that although his people did not want to go to war with the English, they would do so if the English continued taking their land. "We ask nothing better than to be quiet," he said, and ultimately "it depends, Brothers, only on you English, to have peace with us." He made it clear that the Abenaki would not submit to the settlers' demands. Indeed the Indians had demands of their own with which the English must comply. "You have the sea for your share from the place where you reside; you can trade there; but we expressly forbid you to kill a single beaver, or to take a single stick of timber on the lands we inhabit; if you want timber we'll sell you some, but you shall not take it without our permission."[15] Another example of Indian protest also occurred in 1752 when the Mashpee of Massachusetts petitioned the General Court for protection from further white encroachment. "We truly are much troubled," they wrote, "by these English neighbors of ours being on this land of ours. . . . Against our will these Englishmen take away from us what was our land. . . . And as for our streams, they do not allow us peacefully to be when we peacefully go fishing. They beat us greatly, and they have houses on our land against our will."[16]

Despite such pleas and defiance whites continued to outrage Native Americans even after Parliament issued a proclamation in 1763 prohibiting any further westward expansion into Indian lands. Whites simply ignored the edict and swarmed into the Ohio Valley. As a result, in 1771 Indian representatives, fully appreciating English legal principles and the reverence the English claimed to have for the rule of law, met with the governors of Pennsylvania, Virginia, and Maryland demanding that they enforce the law. At the meeting Lenni Lenape chieftain John Killbuck warned the authorities that if they did not enforce the proclamation line, warfare would almost certainly break out. "You have always told us you have laws to govern your people by (but we do not see that you have). Therefore, brethren, unless you can fall upon some method of governing your people . . . who are now very numerous, it will be out of the Indians' power to govern their young men, for we assure you the black clouds begin to gather fast in this country."[17]

There are many such examples of Indians showing determination to be heard and accommodated. Usually they first attempted to reason with the English in a manner consistent with English political thinking. But experience taught most Native Americans that no matter how doggedly they protested, even when they adopted natural-rights philosophy and logic, their entreaties were disregarded. When formal appeals were denied, they resorted to more drastic, oftentimes violent, means of resistance. Rarely did they submit without defiance.

During the century subtle changes in gender relationships challenged previously accepted assumptions about women's place. Although throughout Europe and the colonies women were regarded as the "weaker" sex, colonial women began to experience a shift in their customary role. Because of the labor shortage it was necessary in many frontier environments for women to work side by side with men, oftentimes in roles usually reserved for men, such as the planting and harvesting of crops. Frequently these women were referred to as "yoke mates" or "deputy husbands," terms that reflected society's view that they were engaging in work that was usually regarded as the male's domain. But despite the fact that married women forfeited the right to enter contracts or own property in their own name (whatever property women possessed going into a marriage became the husband's), small changes were occurring. For example, many colonial assemblies passed laws giving women some rights over their property, and in some families women were taking on a more dominant position (albeit subordinate to the husband's). As women's roles in some spheres were gradually shifting, these modest changes were preparing the way for dissenting voices that increasingly demanded more fairness, more rights, and more equality.

One of the most common assumptions prevalent in the eighteenth-century world was that women were inferior to men. Although women had little opportunity to experience the level of independence that men enjoyed, there were occasions when women, employing the natural-rights philosophy of the Enlightenment, spoke out against male-dominated society.

One example of women standing up for themselves in prerevolutionary America is the advertisements that "runaway women" placed in newspapers. Under English law women were considered *femes covert*. In other words their legal identity was "covered" by their husbands. Legally they did not exist. A woman's duty was to serve and obey her husband. The husband had the legal right to beat his wife (as long as he observed the "rule of thumb" that specified he could not use a stick wider than his thumb to strike her). Furthermore, women were not allowed to make contracts. In the rare case of a divorce husbands always got custody of the children. If a woman was injured and her husband sued for damages, he got the settlement, not her. This also meant that if a woman incurred debts, the husband was responsible for them. A woman's property, even her clothing, belonged to her husband. It was illegal for a woman to run away, but even so there were frequent cases during the century when women fled from an abusive or loveless marriage. When this happened, the husband, as a matter of course, put a legal notice in the newspaper informing the public that his wife had run away and that he was no longer responsible for her debts. In most cases the husband was probably hoping to shame his wife into returning to him.

But some wives responded by publishing their own advertisements to justify their actions. For example, when James Dunlap of New Jersey published a notice in the *Pennsylvania Gazette* that his wife, Elizabeth, had eloped (run away), Elizabeth responded with her own advertisement informing the public that she had done so because she "was obliged in safety of her life to leave her said Husband because of his threats and cruel abuse for several years past repeatedly offered and done to her." Furthermore, in the event that her husband attempted to put his estate up for sale, she "thought [it] proper to give this notice to any Person or Persons that may offer to buy, that she will not join in the sale of any part of said lands, but that she intends to claim her thirds (or right of dower) of and in all the lands" that had been acquired since their marriage. Similarly in 1746 Mary Fenby responded to her husband's notice by claiming that they had "parted by Consent" but that he had not yet relinquished her share of their material possessions. She concluded her advertisement with the wry comment that "as she neither has, nor desires to run him in Debt, believing her own Credit to be full as good as his; so she desires no one would trust him on her Account, for neither will she pay any Debts of his contracting."[18]

Women's dissent, however, was not limited to protesting against patriarchal society and the laws that underpinned it. As tensions between the colonies and London worsened after 1763, women increasingly stood shoulder to shoulder with the men resisting the policies of king and Parliament. Women organized protests and boycotts; established groups such as the Daughters of Liberty; wrote broadsides, poems, articles, letters, and petitions; and spoke out for liberty and equality. For example, in 1768 Hannah Griffiths published a poem addressed to the Daughters of Liberty:

If the Sons (so degenerate) the Blessing despise,
Let the Daughters of Liberty, nobly arise,
And tho' we've no Voice, but a negative here.
The use of the Taxables, let us forebear, . . .
Stand firmly resolved & bid Grenville to see
That rather than Freedom, we'll part with our Tea
And well as we love the dear Draught when a dry,
As American Patriots,—our Taste we deny.[19]

Despite widely held beliefs in female inferiority and helplessness women were neither diffident nor silent in the eighteenth century. By expressing such dissent against the tyranny of the king, as well as against the despotism of their husbands, they had no small impact on the course of events and also inspired women in later ages to speak out for their rights.

Ordinary middle- and lower-class whites also protested against policies that limited their liberty and hampered opportunities for improving their lives. Throughout much of the colonial period the working classes as well as tenant farmers, fully aware that women, slaves, and Indians were also questioning authority, dissented periodically against the economic and political dominance of the wealthy classes. In towns this usually took the form of demonstrating, protesting, and on occasion rioting against the high price of food and manufactured goods. In agrarian areas protest was primarily over land distribution and ownership, since most of the arable land was owned by the landed gentry, while the poorer classes had to settle for what was left over.

In Boston soaring food prices and the scarcity of grain led to an uprising in 1719. At the time it was common for merchants to export grain to the West Indies market, where it fetched a higher price because of the demand to feed the thousands of slaves there. Sometimes this led to a grain shortage in New England, which in turn made bread prohibitively expensive. In May 1719 over two hundred of the working poor protested in Boston Common against the exportation of corn and wheat. The protest turned violent when scores of people broke into a wealthy merchant's warehouse looking for grain to loot. When the lieutenant governor tried to convince the mob to disperse, he was shot. Despite the violence, or perhaps because of it, the bread riot ended favorably for the poor. The General Court stepped in and eased tensions by passing legislation prohibiting the export of grain during times of shortage and putting a cap on grain and bread prices. Bread became affordable again.

A protest over land occurred in New Jersey in 1745 when wealthy landowners demanded increased rents from tenant farmers who believed they had just as much right to the land (on the basis of deeds they had signed with the Indians) that they worked and lived on as did the proprietors. After three tenant farmers, Nehemiah Baldwin, Robert Young, and Thomas Serjeant, were arrested for nonpayment, a mob of over two hundred attacked the officials who were transferring Baldwin to the courthouse in Newark. Baldwin was set free, and then the protestors proceeded to the jail to liberate the other two men. When the sheriff and his men appealed to the citizenry to defend the prison against the rabble, no one came forward. The mob quickly "broke the ranks of the soldiers, and pressed on the prison door, where the Sheriff stood with a sword, and kept them off, till they gave him several blows, and forced him out from thence. They then, with axes and other instruments, broke open the prison door, and took out the two prisoners."[20]

Other riots broke out sporadically over such issues as prices, election fraud, boundaries, land distribution, taxes, and impressment for several years, before culminating in the anti-king, anti-Parliament revolutionary fervor of the 1760s and 1770s. It is clear that the participation of colonists in such acts of protest helped to popularize a culture of resistance and to strengthen, at just the right historical moment, the conviction that dissent works.

Perhaps the most significant act of dissent during the period was newspaper publisher John Peter Zenger's protest against political corruption in New York. In November 1733 Zenger's paper, the *Journal*, in a deliberately partisan attack began running a series of articles scathingly denouncing Governor William Cosby for his corrupt administration of the colony. It was public knowledge that Cosby was bribing legislators and judges, embezzling funds from the colony's treasury, and falsifying election results. The *Journal* argued that freedom of the press was necessary because the press was the only institution that could serve as a watchdog against political corruption and the misuse of power. Zenger maintained that if the magistrates and rulers were not held accountable to the law and for their actions, then Britain and its colonies had not progressed at all from the absolutism of the Tudors. "If men in power were always men of integrity," the *Journal* argued, "we might venture to trust them with the direction of the press, and there would be no occasion to plead against the restraint of it."[21] But men are corruptible, and therefore a free press is essential to keep them in check. If freedom of the press and freedom of speech were restricted, liberty itself would be snuffed out.

Governor Cosby ordered the publisher's arrest on charges of seditious libel and had the newspaper shut down. According to eighteenth-century British law, it was only necessary to prove that Zenger had published the articles in order to obtain a conviction. The question of whether Zenger's allegations against Cosby's administration were true or false was irrelevant, because "truth" was not deemed a valid defense against libel. The Philadelphia lawyer Andrew Hamilton, however, argued that truth *was* a defense: "If Libel is understood in the unlimited Sense urged by [the attorney general], there is scarce a Writing I know that may not be called a Libel or scarce a Person safe from being called to Account as a Libeller: For *Moses*, meek as he was, Libelled *Cain*— and who is it that has not libeled the Devil?"[22] When the court acquitted Zenger, it was a momentous victory for the principle of freedom of press. The acquittal also was pivotal in establishing the precedent that no political official was exempt from public censure. The Zenger case also had a significant impact in the coming of the Revolution, for in the ensuing decades it made it easier for those who were protesting against king and Parliament to publish and distribute newspapers, pamphlets, tracts, and broadsides condemning the Crown's policies and drumming up support for civil disobedience and, eventually, revolution.

* * *

During much of the century European nations competed with each other and with the Indians for control of North America. These military conflicts sowed the seeds for even more dissent. Resentments began in the 1690s during King William's War. The war ended in a draw, but after a brief peace a second war flared up again in 1701 in what became known in the colonies as Queen Anne's War. For New Englanders Queen Anne's War and King William's War were excessively costly in both lives and treasure. The taxes needed to support the military and defray the exorbitant debt incurred caused great financial hardship in Massachusetts, as did the burden of taking care of numerous widows in the aftermath of the two conflicts. Resentment against England for leading the colonists into these wars was especially strong among the classes that had supplied the bulk of the military force and suffered the heaviest casualties—farmers, apprentices, newly arrived immigrants, and indentured servants.

During King George's War in the 1740s battles were fought along the Canadian border, where France and its Indian allies repeatedly attacked New England settlements. New England troops launched a massive assault on the French fort at Louisbourg, the "Gibraltar of North America," located on Cape Breton Island, which guarded the entrance to the St. Lawrence River. News of the capture of Fort Louisbourg by New Englanders swept through the colonies and was heralded as the greatest military victory ever in the colonies. However, despite this exhilarating triumph that puffed New Englanders' chests with pride, there was significant antiwar dissent. The colonists deeply resented Parliament's decision to involve them in yet another war fought primarily over complex geopolitical disputes in Europe, which seemed to have no bearing on the colonists and which cost too many lives and too much money.

On top of having to fight the French and Indians the colonists also had to deal with the Royal Navy. The navy routinely filled its ranks by deploying press-gangs to round up able-bodied young men and essentially kidnap them into involuntary service. Parliament had ruled that press-gangs could operate in the colonies without the approval of colonial legislative assemblies. This led to a series of protests and riots on the part of enraged colonists, the most significant of which occurred in 1747 when Admiral Charles Knowles sent a press-gang into Boston to recruit sailors. However, before the press-gang could transport the captives to the fleet, thousands of angry Bostonians took to the streets. They captured several British officers, burned a barge, surrounded the governor's house, and demanded that the pressed men be released. The governor called out the militia to subdue the mob, but the militia, sympathizing with the protestors, refused the order. Admiral Knowles threatened to shell the city, but after a standoff, more demonstrations, and negotiations he finally agreed to release the men. It was an early example of colonists mustering together to protest an infringement on their natural right to liberty. And the memory of the anti-impressment riots (and their triumphant outcome) was still vivid thirty years later when men took to the streets protesting Parliament's attempt to tax the colonies without their consent.

Even the treaty ending the war added enormously to mounting tensions between the colonists and the mother country. By the terms of the Treaty of Aix-la-Chapelle all territory captured during the war was returned to its original holder. New Englanders were infuriated that Louisbourg, after their tremendous sacrifice to capture it, was simply handed back to the French. The status quo ante bellum had been restored. The war had settled nothing. The colonists were feeling constantly imposed on without receiving any benefit from being part of the British Empire. For some it was proof that politicians in London were out of touch and had no interest in acting for the well-being of the colonies.

The fourth major war between England and France, the French and Indian War, broke out in the colonies but quickly spread to Europe and colonial possessions around the world. By the time the war ended in 1763, American colonists were ambivalent about their place in the British Empire. On one hand they were proud of being a part of the most powerful empire in the world, but at the same time they deeply resented the press-gangs as well as the arrogant condescension of the British toward colonial troops. And then when London insisted that the colonists should pay for the war that was fought for their benefit, it seemed that a powder keg of resentment and anger awaited only the spark of protest to ignite an explosion.

* * *

At the beginning of the eighteenth century there was little doubt in the colonists' minds that they were first and foremost British subjects. Their allegiance was to the Crown, and their enemies were the French, the Indians, and the Spanish. However, as the colonies expanded, a sense of Americanness was awakening. Much of this change had to do with the spreading of Enlightenment thinking. The theories of Locke and Montesquieu, Voltaire and Hume, infiltrated into the colonies and were discussed and debated by politicians, ministers, the intelligentsia, and even, to a surprisingly large extent, the masses. The Great Awakening impressed on many the idea that the individual was responsible for his or her own salvation, and this belief had a momentous impact on encouraging independent thinking. By the 1760s colonists became increasingly alarmed that Parliament, in collaboration with King George III, was becoming more and more arbitrary, more and more despotic, and was endangering the fundamental liberties and rights of British subjects.

Considerable social changes were also taking place. The middle decades of the century saw an influx of African slaves as the system of chattel slavery took firm hold in the southern colonies and became the bedrock of the economy. However, slaves resisted—in South Carolina, in New York. Quakers, like John Woolman and Anthony Benezet, took up the issue of slavery and became effective voices for abolition. Dissent in the colonies was also expressed when John Peter Zenger exposed corrupt politicians in New York and championed the principle of freedom of the press—and again when women, Indians, and the poor fought against the powerful and demanded better, more equal treatment. Most of their demands fell on deaf ears, but they did help to raise awareness of their plight. Furthermore, dissenters were aware of each other. When one group spoke out against injustice, it set an example for others to speak out. In many respects the eighteenth-century protests had the effect of setting precedents and laying the foundations for future forms of dissent and dissent movements.

CHAPTER 3

Revolution

Our cause is just. Our union is perfect. . . . With hearts for-
tified with these animating reflections, we most solemnly,
before God and the world, declare that, . . . the arms we have
been compelled by our enemies to assume we will, in defiance of every hazard, with unabating firmness and perseverance, employ for the preservation of our liberties; being with
our mind resolved to die free men rather than live [as] slaves.
—Second Continental Congress, 1775

For a century the English and French had fought for control in North
America, but at the end of the French and Indian War Great Britain
emerged triumphant. France ceded all of its mainland North American
possessions to the English, and England was at the height of its glory.
However, the long-term impact of the war had consequences that were
as momentous as they were unanticipated. Every step London took to
pay for the war and assert its authority over the colonies deepened the
colonists' resentment toward king and Parliament. Resentment led to
organized protest, and Parliament's attempts to curb the protests worsened the situation. By 1775 what started as opposition to the Crown's
policies had become a full-fledged revolt.

The experience of the French and Indian War had the paradoxical
effect on the colonists of both creating pride in being part of the British
Empire and stirring up antipathy over the condescending way the English treated them. General James Wolfe was not alone among British
officers who viewed Americans as "the dirtiest, the most contemptible,
cowardly dogs that you can conceive. There is no depending upon them
in action. They fall down in their own dirt and desert in battalions, officers and all."[1] The British felt they had some justification for their view
of the colonists since it was not uncommon for colonial troops to refuse
to follow the orders of officers whom they had not elected. Further
complicating the issue was the tendency of many colonial merchants

to continue to trade with the French during the war, and the failure of colonial assemblies to pass legislation providing adequate revenue to supply troops. Moreover, as in all the previous wars fought in North America, the colonists seethed over the forced recruitment of men into the Royal Navy and the standing army. Britain relied on press-gangs to fill the ranks, but the colonists were so outraged by being forced to serve unwillingly that Britain finally abandoned the practice in 1758 to avoid causing more problems with the colonists. For the British this only reinforced their view that Americans were at best unreliable and at worst disloyal.

The war had other consequences as well. It marked the first time the colonists experienced an awareness of common interests and solidarity with one another. War had created a sense of identity as *Americans*. To be sure, colonists still thought of themselves, above all, as British and then secondly as New Yorkers, Virginians, Pennsylvanians, but there was now a subtle shift as they became more cognizant of their shared interests. Gradually they began noticing their "Americanness," no doubt stimulated by British soldiers' tendency to refer to them as "Americans." (To the British *American* was a pejorative term, code for "insufficiently British.") Also, with the French no longer a threat in the Ohio Valley or Canada, the colonists began to feel more secure and less dependent on Britain for protection. Their wish to expand into the Ohio Valley would mean, of course, conflict with the Indians, but this was something they believed they could handle.

* * *

Though the war was a great success, it had nearly bankrupted the treasury. So one of the first tasks Parliament faced was the need to raise revenue. Moreover, London was concerned that land-hungry colonists pushing into the Ohio Valley would provoke a war with the Indians. This must also be dealt with.

In order to prevent another costly war Parliament acted to station British troops permanently in the colonies and issued a proclamation prohibiting expansion west of the Appalachians. This Proclamation Line of 1763 only stirred up resentment and did little to dissuade land speculators and settlers from penetrating beyond the crest of the Appalachians. Many flocked into the area, and the British found that it was impossible to enforce the proclamation. Once the colonists began moving west of the line, the Indians reacted immediately. The Ottawa chieftain Pontiac formed an alliance of Seneca, Delaware, Huron, Chippewa, and other Indian nations and led them on a series of attacks against encroaching whites.

While British soldiers were busy dealing with Pontiac's Rebellion, a contingent of Scots-Irish settlers in Lancaster County, known as the "Paxton Boys," convinced that the Quaker-dominated provincial government in Philadelphia was doing nothing to protect whites, decided to take matters into their own hands. They murdered a band of Christian Indians in Lancaster and then marched on Philadelphia. Before they arrived, however, the Pennsylvania legislature averted a showdown by agreeing to send one thousand troops to western Pennsylvania to protect the settlers against the Indians. This mollified the Paxton Boys, but their attempt to take the law into their hands was an ominous sign that the times were changing. An attitude of defiance was clearly emerging, a feeling that if government was not going to protect and preserve the natural rights of life, liberty, and property that Locke wrote about, then it would be necessary for citizens to take action.

* * *

To begin tackling the £145 million national debt, Parliament passed the Sugar Act in 1764. "It is just and necessary that a revenue be raised . . . in America for defraying the expenses of defending, protecting, and securing the same."[2] On the heels of the Sugar Act, Parliament passed the Currency Act, which forbade the thirteen colonies from issuing their own paper money. Many merchants and colonial legislatures now began grumbling that these acts were hurting economic recovery and hampering trade. However, it was the Stamp Act in 1765 that provoked the most feverish protests.

The Stamp Act (already in force in England) levied a tax on all printed documents—newspapers, wills, marriage licenses, death certificates, deeds, pamphlets, and even packs of playing cards. The reaction to the Stamp Act in the colonies was swift and hostile and took Parliament completely by surprise. The Virginia colonial assembly (the House of Burgesses) met in May and, led by the young Patrick Henry, passed the Virginia Resolves proclaiming that Virginia was not going to be coerced into paying externally imposed taxes and that it was the colony's inherent right not to pay any tax that was not approved by the House of Burgesses. In Boston a radical group consisting of merchants, artisans, craftsmen, and farmers, identifying themselves as the Sons of Liberty, called for a boycott to protest the act. Tensions escalated in August when an unruly mob hanged a stamp-duty official in effigy and held a mock funeral; they then destroyed the office building where it was thought the stamps were stored. Two weeks later violence broke out again when they plundered and demolished Lieutenant Governor Thomas Hutchinson's mansion. There were other violent protests in Newport and New York, along with dozens of effigy burnings throughout the colonies, which prompted tax collectors to resign their posts.

The acts of destruction not only alarmed British authorities but also even worried the Boston merchants who were opposed to the stamp tax. The merchants and the Sons of Liberty tried to reestablish control of the demonstrations by reining in the more extreme protesters, but this outbreak of violence revealed the depth of antipathy toward the elite classes and drew attention to the class struggle that was seething below the surface.

Eventually London merchants, apprehensive that trade with the colonies would be impaired, pressured Parliament to repeal the Stamp Act in 1766. However, Parliament did not want to give the colonists the impression that their protests had prompted the repeal, so it issued the Declaratory Act affirming Parliament's power to levy taxes on the colonies and approved the so-called Townshend Duties—new taxes on tea, lead, paper, and paint.

The colonial reaction was immediate. The Massachusetts legislature sent out a circular letter to the other twelve colonies urging noncompliance. London responded by sending four regiments to Boston to protect customs officials and to force compliance with the Townshend Duties. From this point on activists implemented a general boycott of British goods. Boston, New York, Philadelphia, and several of the southern colonies all passed nonimportation and nonconsumption agreements. This resulted in significant financial hardship for American merchants, and when some attempted to carry on business as usual, bands of young radicals made the rounds in every port, enforcing the boycott by "liberating" (i.e., destroying) merchandise before the merchants could do business. With the boycotts and petitions dissenters were beginning to shape the direction of events.

The Townshend Duties only netted £21,000, while the boycott cost the British economy £700,000. London businessmen and merchants were so angry over the economic impact that they lobbied Parliament to repeal the duties. In March 1770, under a new ministry led by Frederick Lord North, all the duties, except that on tea, were repealed. Before news of the repeal arrived in the colonies, however, an incident occurred in Boston that stunned everyone.

For more than a year the presence of the four British regiments stationed in Boston to protect customs officials was an increasing irritant to the populace. Not only that, but working-class Bostonians were also seething with anger that many of the underpaid British soldiers took jobs working on the docks and were thus directly competing with them for jobs. This volatile mixture exploded on a cold night in March 1770, when an unruly, somewhat inebriated mob began taunting British soldiers on sentry duty at the Customs House. Many of the civilians were street toughs and dockworkers, and along with their insults and verbal abuse, they began throwing snowballs and chunks of ice. When it seemed that the crowd was going to attack the sentries, a British squad appeared on the scene, and shots were fired. When the smoke cleared, five people lay dead.

News of the "Boston Massacre" spread rapidly throughout the colonies, aided by skillful propaganda pamphlets claiming that belligerent British regulars had maliciously opened fire on a peaceful crowd. Colonists from New England to Georgia were shocked and indignant when they read the inflammatory pamphlets and viewed Paul Revere's famous engraving that, instead of showing the unruly dockworkers who provoked the confrontation, depicted unarmed, middle-class civilians being gunned down by sneering British soldiers. Thousands were convinced that London was bent on subjugating the colonists and trampling fundamental liberties.

In the aftermath of the Massacre Boston formed a Committee of Correspondence to proclaim "the Rights of the Colonists and of this Province in particular, as Men, as Christians, and as Subjects; to communicate and publish the same to the several Towns in this Province and to the world."[3] Other Massachusetts towns followed suit, and by 1773 ten of the thirteen colonies had established such Committees of Correspondence. This was another important step linking the colonies together in their growing opposition to the Crown's policies.

A number of those who organized the protests and formed the core of the Committees of Correspondence and the Sons of Liberty were wealthy merchants (such as John Hancock). But other agitators had working-class connections, such as Samuel Adams, a founder of the Sons of Liberty. Adams was the foremost radical polemicist of the era. He found his true calling in politics after his business failed in the mid-1760s, and by the time of the Boston Massacre, he had emerged as the leading propagandist in the colonies. He insisted that colonists should only be required to obey laws that they had a hand in framing and that they must resist all attempts on the part of king and Parliament to stifle liberty. Through pamphlets and speeches he protested against England's rule, kept the Boston Massacre uppermost in people's minds, and continually reminded his fellow colonists that they were being arbitrarily taxed by an autocratic Parliament. In Adams's 1772 report, "The Rights of the Colonists," he emphasized that, "among the natural rights of the Colonists are these First, a Right to *Life*; Secondly, to *Liberty*; thirdly, to *Property*; together with the Right to support and defend them in the best manner they can." Adams maintained that when Parliament imposes taxes on those who do not have representation, it is in essence taking away property. "The supreme power cannot justly take from any man any part of his property, without his consent in person or by his Representative."[4] It was essential that the colonists take a stand against this abuse of power.

While dissent against London's taxation policies rapidly accelerated, a different form of dissent arose internally, pitting colonists against each other. In western South Carolina, for example, prosperous farmers grew increasingly resentful that the colonial government in far-away Charleston was doing nothing about protecting them from bands of outlaws that were freely going about the countryside plundering and robbing and making life miserable for them. They decided to impose law and order themselves by regulating and punishing outlaws and those who aided and abetted them. But more than five hundred people targeted by the "regulators" organized themselves into a makeshift army to confront them. It appeared that a civil war was about to break out, but in 1769 the governor finally agreed to create a circuit court and to send officials to the western part of the colony to establish the rule of law.

A separate regulator movement emerged at the same time in North Carolina. The North Carolina regulators' grievance was not that there was too little government but that there were too many corrupt governmental officials and bureaucrats who were extorting money from the backcountry settlers. In 1768, after failing to convince the governor to recall the corrupt officials, the regulators banded together and vowed not to pay any of the fees and taxes that were being levied on them. Within a few years the regulator protests had escalated to the point where they were kidnapping local officials and committing acts of violence against property and persons, even capturing and whipping Edmund Fanning, the corrupt clerk of the Orange County Superior Court who was notorious for extorting fees from the populace. Finally, in May 1771, the governor sent a force of one thousand militiamen to engage a much larger, although ill-equipped, regulator army. The regulators were routed, several of their leaders were executed, and the movement fell apart. Tensions, however, between backcountry farmers and the eastern elite still seethed.

* * *

In 1773 Parliament sought to mitigate the colonists' grievances by passing the Tea Act. The act granted the nearly bankrupt East India Company the right to ship tea directly to the colonies rather than, as it had always done, through London, where the tea passed through the hands of English customs agents and English middlemen. By allowing the East India Company to sell tea directly in the colonies, even with the modest tax imposed on the tea, it meant that tea from India would be cheaper than the tea that colonial merchants were smuggling into the colonies. London expected the colonists to be delighted.

The colonial reaction, however, stunned Lord North's government. Colonial merchants, furious that their tea-smuggling business was threatened, denounced the act as giving the East India Company a monopoly on the tea trade. If the colonists allowed this to happen, the merchants ominously predicted, other monopolies would soon follow. Radicals raised the issue that if colonists drank the taxed, albeit cheap, tea, they would be tacitly abnegating their right to tax themselves. In several colonies merchants and the Sons of Liberty held meetings and protest marches denouncing the tax and the East India Company. In

"Americans Throwing the Cargoes of the Tea Ships into the River, at Boston." Engraving in W. D. Cooper, *The History of North America* (London: E. Newberry, 1789). (Public domain)

New York and Philadelphia tea ships were prevented from landing, but in Boston protest went a step further.

On December 16 members of the Sons of Liberty and the Boston Committee of Correspondence boarded the East India Company's ships, chopped open 342 tea chests and heaved £10,000 worth of tea into the harbor. The Sons of Liberty had crossed the line separating dissent from criminal activity. News of the "Boston Tea Party" sent shockwaves through England. Both the king and Lord North recognized that the controversy now no longer revolved around taxes but around the more basic issue of Parliament's right to rule the colonies. In response to this act of property destruction Parliament closed the port of Boston, restricted town meetings, gave the army the authority to quarter troops in private dwellings, and appointed the authoritarian commander in chief of the army, General Thomas Gage, to be the new royal governor.

Outraged colonists denounced these "Intolerable Acts" as designed to take away their rights and liberties as British subjects. Samuel Adams declared that the acts were nothing less than an attempt to enslave the colonists. Thousands of people from New England to the Carolinas vowed support for Massachusetts and vigorously protested against the despotism of a repressive government. In Edenton, North Carolina, for example, fifty-one women initiated a boycott against English imports. In October 1774 they issued a statement saying, "We, the Ladys of Edenton, do hereby solemnly engage not to conform to the Pernicious Custom of Drinking Tea," and furthermore, "We, the aforesaid Ladys will not promote ye wear of any manufacturer from England until such time that all acts which tend to enslave our Native country shall be repealed."[5]

In May 1774 colonists called for a meeting of delegates from each colony to formulate a united response to these acts. In September representatives from twelve of the colonies (Georgia did not attend) met in Philadelphia, where they issued a statement of grievances and demanded that all the repressive legislation passed since 1763 be repealed. They called for a comprehensive boycott of trade with the mother country, formed a "Continental Association" to enforce the boycott, and endorsed a resolution that the colonies begin arming and training local militias to be ready at a minute's notice in case Britain launched a military campaign. And finally they agreed to meet again the following spring for a Second Continental Congress. Before the Congress met again in the spring of 1775, however, incidents at Lexington and Concord, Massachusetts, changed everything.

* * *

In the winter of 1775 reports arrived in London that colonists, preparing for an armed insurrection, had assembled a cache of weapons in Concord, Massachusetts. Lord North ordered General Gage to confiscate and destroy the weapons and to arrest two of the leading agitators, John Hancock and Samuel Adams. In mid-April Gage sent a force of seven hundred troops to Concord. However, the Sons of Liberty had a network of informants who tipped them off that the British soldiers would be making their move during the night of April 18. And so when the redcoats arrived in Lexington at dawn, several dozen militiamen confronted them. As the greatly outnumbered militia prepared to withdraw, a shot rang out. Both sides claimed the other fired first. Regardless of which side fired the "shot heard round the world," that musket ball instigated a fusillade of shots that left eight of the militia dead and nine wounded. Although no one realized it at the moment, revolution had begun.

As the redcoats proceeded toward Concord, the entire countryside began swarming with minutemen rushing to engage the soldiers. When the troops arrived at Concord, they only found a few barrels of gunpowder (which they set on fire) and a contingent of militiamen on Concord's Old North Bridge (which they engaged). However, all along their march back to Boston hundreds of minutemen fired at them from behind trees and stone fences, killing and wounding more than 270 redcoats. The Americans suffered ninety-five casualties.

Through newspapers and broadsides news of the bloodshed swept through the colonies. In the following weeks, twenty thousand men volunteered to fight the British as each colony began raising troops. Not only did thousands of men volunteer for the militia, but quite a few women also got involved. In one instance a contingent of thirty-five women (some disguised as men) took up arms to guard a bridge on one of the main roads leading to Boston in order to block British reinforcements that might be sent down from Canada. John Adams's wife, Abigail, who was never hesitant about voicing her opinion, wrote that American women were more than up to meeting the challenges of armed conflict: "If our men are all drawn off and we should be attacked, you would find a race of Amazons in America."[6]

On June 17 the British attacked the colonial position on Breed's Hill in Charlestown. This "Battle of Bunker Hill" (named after the neighboring hill) was a costly victory for the British. The Americans suffered 441 casualties; the British, however, lost 40 percent of their men in securing the hill, 1,054 out of 2,400. The Americans, despite their defeat, still occupied positions around Boston and continued the siege, while 250 miles to the south delegates meeting in Philadelphia grappled with the thorny issue of what to do next.

Opinions among the delegates at the Second Continental Congress were deeply divided. John Adams of Massachusetts and Richard Henry Lee of Virginia argued that British aggression and atrocities had gone too far and that there was no recourse but to form a confederation, declare independence, and take up arms against a despotic government. However, many, if not most, of the delegates hoped for a diplomatic solution. They were unwilling to sever ties with Great Britain and pursue a course that could only be labeled as treasonous. Instead, they sought to find a middle way, a compromise to heal relations before it was too late. Moderates such as John Dickinson convinced Congress to approve an "Olive Branch Petition" affirming their loyalty to the Crown while at the same time imploring the king to work with them in seeking a compromise. However, they also resolved that in order to achieve military success it was necessary to convert the various colonial militias into a more disciplined and organized "Continental army" that would undergo training and be financed by Congress. And on John Adams's recommendation the delegates appointed George Washington as commander in chief of this new army.

Even though the Continental Congress was taking on the responsibilities of a government, the members continued to agonize over the proper course of action. If there was any chance for reconciliation with Britain, most of the delegates wanted to pursue it. However, they did feel it was necessary to issue a declaration coinciding with the appointment of Washington as commander in chief of the Continental army that would justify the colonists' resort to arms and bolster their opposition to the Crown's policies. The delegates declared that Parliament, in its thirst for "unlimited domination" and its "inordinate passion for power," had gone well beyond its legitimate authority. For a decade Parliament levied taxes on the colonists without granting them representation, and it stationed troops in Boston in order to enforce these revenue measures. The delegates denounced Lord North's decision to send troops to Concord as an act of unprovoked aggression (even though the delegates were well aware that militiamen had stored munitions there), and opening fire was the final straw. The colonists had no choice but to take up arms in self-defense. "We most solemnly, before God and the world, declare that . . . the arms we have been compelled by our enemies to assume we will . . . employ for the preservation of our liberties; being with our [one] mind resolved to die free men rather than live as slaves."[7]

For the remainder of 1775 the Continental Congress busied itself with the particulars of financing the rebellion while continuing to debate whether to seek accommodation with Britain or outright independence. By the end of the year, however, as battle casualties mounted, news arrived that George III had spurned the Olive Branch Petition with his proclamation that the colonies were in "open and avowed rebellion."[8] This, along with reports that Britain was sending another twenty thousand troops along with German mercenaries to the colonies, pushed many of the moderates into the radical camp. If the colonists were in open rebellion, as the king had declared, then they had already crossed the line and become traitors in London's eyes. There was no turning back.

Finally, the last hesitant southern delegates abandoned their efforts at accommodation when they learned that the royal governor of Virginia, the Earl of Dunmore, had issued a proclamation offering freedom to all slaves who helped put down the rebellion. Slaveholding delegates were infuriated at this outrageous attempt to destroy the sanctity of private property, and without any sense of irony they announced they had no choice but to take up arms to fight for independence, freedom, and liberty.

Britain considered the colonists rebels, terrorists, and traitors whose acts of rebellion would not be tolerated. As far as the colonists were concerned, though, Parliament was turning its back on the Glorious Revolution of 1688 and the Lockean principle that each individual has inherent natural rights—rights that no government has the right to violate. Parliament, in some respects, incurred more of the colonists' wrath than the king did because Parliament was supposed to represent the interests of *all* British subjects, and somehow it too had become a tyrannical body. If Parliament could not be trusted to protect the rights of the people, the only recourse was to set up a new, independent government. Had not Locke written that when a legislative assembly no longer defends and protects life, liberty, and property, it has broken its part of the social contract with the citizenry? Therefore, does not the citizenry have the right to revolt against such a government?

While the Continental Congress pondered the purpose of the rebellion, Thomas Paine, a recent immigrant to the colonies, published a pamphlet in Philadelphia in which he put forward the case for independence. In *Common Sense*, Paine urged Congress to stop wasting time debating and simply declare American independence. It was absurd, he argued, that the thirteen North American colonies should allow themselves to be ruled by a government situated on a small island three thousand miles away that was out of touch with their interests and concerns. "'TIS TIME TO PART," Paine exclaimed, not only because of the king's attempt to coerce, exploit, and tyrannize the colonies but also because "even the distance at which the Almighty hath placed England and America, is a strong and natural proof, that the authority of the one, over the other, was never the design of Heaven." To Paine, it was "common sense" that a continent should not be ruled by a distant island, for "there is something very absurd, in supposing a continent to be perpetually governed by an island." To those who contended that the colonists should remain loyal because Britain was the mother country, Paine responded that England was a tyrant that should be ashamed of its conduct. "Even brutes do not devour their young; nor savages make war upon their families." Elevating dissent to a higher level, Paine issued a clarion call to Americans to stand firm against an oppressive despotism. "O ye that love mankind! Ye that dare oppose, not only the tyranny, but the tyrant, stand forth!"[9]

Within a week the first printing of one thousand copies of *Common Sense* sold out. Between January and April thousands more were reprinted, and eventually it went through twenty-five editions before the year was out. From Philadelphia it was disseminated to New York and eventually to Boston. Although *Common Sense* was printed primarily in the northern colonies and had its greatest impact there, one edition was printed in Charleston, South Carolina. It was the most important publication of the colonial era and appealed to both the educated elite and the common folk with its easy-to-understand rationale for a break with England. Clearly, *Common Sense* had an impact on the delegates meeting in Philadelphia. Just a few months after the pamphlet's publication, Virginia's Richard Henry Lee submitted a resolution to the Continental Congress calling for independence. Accordingly, Congress appointed a committee of Thomas Jefferson, John Adams, Benjamin Franklin, and others to draft a statement for the delegates' consideration.

Although the Declaration of Independence is revered today for its soaring pronouncement that "all men are created equal" and that all men have the unalienable rights of "life, liberty, and the pursuit of happiness," it was not the first document to express these sentiments. For decades before the rebellion dozens of pamphleteers and politicians had been quoting or paraphrasing Locke's natural-rights philosophy that the duty of government was to protect "life, liberty, and property." Jefferson simply consolidated much of this thinking into a succinct statement of purpose. After the philosophical basis was expounded, the bulk of the declaration went on to list the specific grievances the colonists had against George III. In one sense the Declaration was a propaganda instrument meant to persuade other governments that the colonists were not a radical mob mindlessly fomenting chaos and anarchy but were serious, responsible men who had good cause to separate from England. In this justification for the rebellion the delegates hoped that the Declaration would serve to sway England's archenemy,

France, to recognize the new nation and perhaps even to form an alliance with it.

On July 4 Congress voted to adopt the Declaration. Several days later the Declaration of Independence was read publicly for the first time to the throngs assembled before the statehouse in Philadelphia. Church bells rang, jubilant cheers filled the air, and in a gesture symbolizing the irrevocable transference of allegiance from the king to the new United States, the crowd tore down and burned the king's coat of arms that had been mounted above the statehouse doors.

As the Declaration circulated through the colonies in July 1776, the Continental Congress framed another document, the Articles of Confederation, which formally created the United States of America. Even though the Articles were not fully ratified and adopted until 1781, it was the instrument by which Congress conducted the war. Under this document the thirteen colonies became thirteen independent sovereign powers delegating certain federal powers to the Confederation in order to facilitate governance. Congress alone ruled the Confederation. Those who had been protesting for so long about the abuse of executive and judicial power by the few made sure that neither an executive nor a judiciary would play a role in the new government, and they decided to strictly limit the power of the legislature. While Congress was empowered to create a postal system, to coin money, to conduct foreign affairs, to make war, and to deal with the Indians, it had no power to raise an army or impose taxes. These restrictions, however, severely limited Congress's ability to conduct the war and continually threatened to undermine the entire war effort.

* * *

The American Revolution was not only a struggle to gain independence from Great Britain but also a civil war. Many of the class issues that had occasionally manifested themselves, such as the regulator movement in the Carolinas, emerged more forcefully during the disorder and confusion of the Revolution. But on an even larger scale within all thirteen colonies there was a second equally significant conflict between Patriots who protested London's policies and desired independence and Loyalists who remained faithful to the Crown. This second conflict had the bizarre twist of turning those who remained loyal into dissenters. As the war progressed and Patriot sentiment increased, Loyalists found themselves increasingly on the outside dissenting against those who would wrest power from London.

After the war John Adams estimated that about one-third of the people favored independence, one-third opposed it, and another third were either neutral during the Revolution or, like the Quakers, had moral objections to war. Those who opposed independence valued nothing more highly than British citizenship. Great Britain, Loyalists wholeheartedly believed, was the most enlightened, most advanced nation in the history of the world. Who, in their right mind, would ever want to turn their back on Britain? The Loyalists thought those who sought independence were traitors who should be rounded up and imprisoned, or worse.

Thomas Hutchinson, a descendant of Anne Hutchinson, was a preeminent Loyalist. At the time of the Boston Tea Party he was the royal governor of Massachusetts, and as the representative of the Crown, he often found himself the target of Sons of Liberty demonstrations and hostility. His role as one of the earliest conservative (or reactionary) dissenters in American history who sought to resist sweeping forces of change that were threatening his privileged position is evident in his response to the Declaration of Independence. In October 1776 Hutchinson published a pamphlet, *Strictures upon the Declaration of the Congress at Philadelphia*, in which he analyzes and discredits every one of Jefferson's assertions in the Declaration. According to Hutchinson, most colonists were "easy and quiet. They felt no burdens. They were attached, indeed, in every Colony to their own particular Constitutions, but the Supremacy of Parliament over the whole gave them no concern. They had been happy under it for an hundred years past: They feared no imaginary evils for an hundred years to come."[10] The unrepresented colonists, Hutchinson points out, were perfectly willing to accept laws that protected or benefited them, and they had no objection when Parliament replaced James II with William and Mary. He argues that it is therefore unfair and hypocritical for them to reject laws that would raise the revenue necessary to protect them.

After emphatically discrediting each of Jefferson's statements, Hutchinson concludes that the Declaration of Independence is nothing more than a litany of distorted facts attempting to sway the majority to favor independence, and although these so-called Patriots demand freedom of speech and thought, they are denying those very rights to

anyone (like him) who points out Jefferson's distortions and misrep-
resentations. He claims that discerning, intelligent men are forced to
keep silent, "because under the present *free* government in America,
no man may, by writing or speaking, contradict any part of this Declaration, without being deemed an enemy to his country, and exposed
to the rage and fury of the populace."[11] Most tellingly, he attacks the
Declaration's core assertion ("We hold these truths to be self evident
that all men are created equal") when he sarcastically comments that he
no doubt would be considered "impertinent" if he should ask "in what
sense all men are created equal; or how far life, liberty and the *pursuit of
happiness* may be said to be unalienable": "only I could wish to ask the
Delegates of Maryland, Virginia, and the Carolinas, how their Constituents justify the depriving more than an hundred thousand Africans of
their rights to liberty, and *the pursuit of happiness*, and in some degree
to their lives, if these rights are so absolutely unalienable."[12] Of course,
Hutchinson was not advocating the abolition of slavery and the granting of liberty and equality to slaves; rather, he was merely attacking the
shaky logic of the Declaration's assertion that rights were unalienable.

Loyalists in all of the colonies, especially in the commercial centers
of New York, New Jersey, and Pennsylvania, found themselves at odds
with the direction the colonies were taking. Some Loyalists (about fifty
thousand of them) formed regiments and fought alongside British regulars in an effort to bring down the rebellion and defend the British
Empire. But tens of thousands of Loyalists also left the country, fleeing to Britain, Canada, or the British West Indies. Those who remained
were subjected to hostility and violence from neighbors who supported
the war. Loyalist sentiment was not confined to the elites; it reached
into all classes of colonial society. Many merchants and public officials
were Loyalists, but so too were numerous tenant farmers in New York,
poor farmers in Maryland, and backcountry settlers in South Carolina,
who all viewed the Patriots (not the Loyalists) as an oppressive eastern/
coastal elite.

Patriots also consisted of a diverse assortment of people from all
classes who had little in common except the bond of protesting London's policies. Men, women, free blacks, slaves, aristocrats, and paupers
all contributed to the Patriot cause. The Continental army was made up
primarily of members of the lower classes. The lure of financial reward
and owning land influenced many indentured servants, vagrants, free

blacks, debtors, and the unemployed to join the army in 1777 when Congress offered a bounty of twenty dollars and a postwar land grant of one hundred acres to encourage men to enlist (by 1779 the bounty was raised to two hundred dollars).

Women played a big part in the Patriot cause. Thousands assumed the male role when their husbands, fathers, and sons went off to war, and they had to take over supervision of farms and small businesses. Many of these women worked at supplying the troops with clothing and provisions and also defended their homes from marauding British and Hessian troops. Several hundred women even fought in the army. Deborah Sampson disguised herself as a man and enlisted in the Continental army as "Robert Shurtleff." She fought in several battles and was only found out when she was wounded. Pennsylvania's Margaret Corbin lost an arm defending Fort Washington. Other women served as spies, while more than twenty thousand "Women of the Army," as George Washington called them, traveled with the troops, performing such important functions as cooks, nurses, laundresses, and water carriers (the fabled "Molly Pitcher" was probably a composite of several of these women of the army).

African Americans and Indians also joined in the fight for independence. In the North many free blacks, as well as some slaves, volunteered for the Continental army. It is estimated that over five thousand African Americans, free and enslaved, enlisted in the Continental army or one of the state militias or served at sea as privateers. Slaves could not help overhear their masters' heated discussions before and during the Revolution, and many of them felt the stirrings of hope in their hearts that they too might one day be free. For some this hope was fulfilled, and they did gain their freedom at the end of the war; but for most this was not the case.

Northern slaves who were caught up in the revolutionary rhetoric filed petitions for emancipation with state legislatures. For example, eight Massachusetts slaves signed a "Petition for Gradual Emancipation" in January 1777, humbly beseeching "your honours to give this petition its due weight & consideration & cause an act of the legislature to be passed whereby they may be restored to the enjoyments of that which is the natural right of all men."[13] In the South slaves who were inspired by the slogans and chants of liberty showed their defiance against authority by running away. In Georgia, Virginia, and the

Carolinas tens of thousands of slaves ran off, some of them even forming insurrectionary cadres ready to fight for their own freedom. As many as four hundred thousand slaves in the South sought refuge behind British lines after Lord Dunmore's declaration that any slave fighting for the Crown would receive freedom as a reward for his services, and over one hundred thousand of them fought on the British side. Thomas Peters, for example, a North Carolina slave, ran away from his master (who was a member of the Sons of Liberty) and fought with the British army. Slaves were enamored by the rhetoric of freedom and equality, but they fully realized that most Patriots excluded blacks when they proclaimed that all men are created equal. "One of the less-well-known facts about the Revolutionary War," historian David Waldstreicher has written, "is that African Americans fought on both sides, primarily with their own freedom in mind."[14] They were committed only to the goal of their own freedom, not to the goals of either the colonists or the British. African Americans, throughout the war, deeply distrusted a society that reserved such lofty ideals only for whites.

Native Americans were also divided. Many, like the Androscoggin Indians in New England, aligned with the British hoping to reclaim their lost land. The Abenaki of northern Maine and southern Quebec deeply resented the American thirst for their land but at the same time hated the British for allowing the Americans to take it from them. As a result, some Abenaki fought on the British side hoping to keep future American incursions at bay, while others fought on the American side hoping that a British defeat would mean the return of the more Indian-friendly French. In addition, Penobscot Indians were scouts for the Continental army, while a number of St. François Indians accompanied Benedict Arnold and Richard Montgomery on their invasion of Quebec in the winter of 1775–1776 and aided in the siege of Boston in the spring of 1776. There is also evidence that some Pigwacket, Maliseet, and Passamaquoddy Indians fought with the Americans against the British. Many Seneca, Cayuga, Mohawk, and Onondaga allied themselves with the British, while some Oneida and Tuscarora fought for the Patriots. In the South large numbers of Cherokee, Chickasaw, and Choctaw fought on the British side, while some Catawba fought on the American.

The divided nature of the war resulted in cases when Patriots and Loyalists themselves changed sides. For example, in New Jersey, Loyalist sentiment ran high at the outset of the rebellion, but the British and Hessian soldiers who occupied the colony committed so many atrocities (murders, rapes, confiscation of property) that it spawned an insurgency that drove New Jersey into the Patriot camp. But there were also times when Patriots shifted to the British side. The most infamous case was when Benedict Arnold, chafing at not being sufficiently appreciated as an officer of the Continental army and claiming that Congress betrayed America's Protestant heritage with the French alliance, switched sides. And New Jersey's Richard Stockton, a signer of the Declaration of Independence, recanted and swore an oath of loyalty to the Crown when he was captured and imprisoned.

* * *

The Revolution resulted in independence for the United States, but the war, as is the case with all wars, had many unanticipated political, economic, and social consequences. Not surprisingly the Revolution had a devastating effect on Native Americans, because without the constraining pressure of Parliament there was no authority to hinder the westward expansion of a growing population hungry for land. Moreover, the ideological rhetoric and the notions of freedom and equality that had been formulated to justify the Revolution had an inspiring effect on two groups that had not even been considered during the struggle: women and African Americans.

The roles women took on during the Revolution gave them a taste for what it was like to expand beyond the confines of the male-dominated social order, and many found that their attitudes toward this social order were rapidly changing. Some women believed they too had a right to the new liberties and opportunities at the center of the American promise, and they became actively engaged in the political discussions raised during the Revolution. Many of them dissented against the policies, laws, and customs that elevated men while keeping women subjugated, and they openly demanded changes in the new society that was evolving. Mercy Otis Warren published essays and plays maintaining that the republican principles of the Revolution should apply to all people. Esther DeBerdt Reed, breaking with feminine stereotypes, organized Philadelphia women to renounce "vain ornaments" and to contribute the money they would have spent on clothing and hairstyles to the Continental army. After the British invasion of South Carolina in 1780 Eliza Wilkerson declared, "None were greater politicians than the several knots of ladies, who met together. All trifling discourses of fashions, and such low chat were thrown by, and we commenced perfect statesmen."[15]

The most famous woman of the period who spoke out for women's rights was Abigail Adams. In March 1776 she urged her husband, John Adams, not to leave women out of the new system of government that the delegates to the Second Continental Congress were establishing. "By the way," she wrote,

> in the new Code of Laws which I suppose it will be necessary for you to make, I desire you would Remember the Ladies, and be more generous and favorable to them than your ancestors. Do not put such unlimited power into the hands of the Husbands. Remember, all Men would be tyrants if they could. If particular care and attention is not paid to the Ladies we are determined to foment a Rebellion, and will not hold ourselves bound by any Laws in which we have no voice, or Representation.[16]

As the new nation took shape, Abigail Adams's entreaty went unheeded. It was more than 140 years of continued protest and activism on the part of women before they gained the right to vote or hold political office in the United States. Clearly, though, her views reveal that the ideology of equality was widespread and was being taken seriously even by those for whom it was not intended. And the fact that she and other women raised these issues inspired generations to come.

Many of the slaveholding founding fathers, notably George Washington and Thomas Jefferson, were acutely aware of the paradox of slaves participating in a revolution for freedom while they were denied their own freedom. Though some of these men were disturbed by the inherent contradiction, most of them saw no alternative to the institution. They wondered, if slaves were freed, what would become of them? No one seemed to have an adequate answer, and no one thought freed slaves could ever be integrated into white society. Jefferson, who believed that if there was a just God, the white race would surely pay for the sin of slavery, commented forty years later that slavery was like holding a wolf by the ears. You didn't like it, but you didn't dare let it go.

The irony of the highly touted revolutionary ideals of freedom and equality is nowhere more apparent than in one of the first orders issued by George Washington within days of Cornwallis's surrender at York-town. Washington ordered his troops to hunt down and capture all slaves—some of whom were still within British ranks, while others had represented themselves as free and were working as servants for French or American officers—and return them to their masters. "It having been represented," Washington wrote,

> that many Negroes and Mulattoes the property of Citizens of these States have concealed themselves on board the Ships in the harbor; that some still continue to attach themselves to British Officers and that others have attempted to impose themselves upon the officers of the French and American Armies as Freemen and to make their escapes in that manner, In order to prevent their succeeding in such practices All Officers of the Allied Army and other persons of every denomination concerned are directed not to suffer any such negroes or mulattoes to be retained in their Service but on the contrary to cause them to be delivered to the Guards which will be establish'd for their reception at one of the Redoubts in York and another in Gloucester.[17]

While Cornwallis's surrender at Yorktown meant independence and liberty for white Americans, it resulted in far different consequences for African Americans. The thirty thousand fugitive slaves who had accompanied Cornwallis found themselves in a desperate situation. Many were killed, most were reenslaved. But the fact that George Washington had to issue this order clearly demonstrates that innumerable African Americans were emboldened to attempt to flee a society that persistently, and hypocritically, denied them freedom.

* * *

What began as a protest in the 1760s against taxation rapidly mushroomed into a full-scale condemnation of a government that was perceived as out of touch with the people's concerns. When king and Parliament responded with a show of military force, colonial dissent escalated into outright rebellion. At first the colonists were unsure of their goals. Did they want to be treated fairly and equally as British subjects? Did they want the Crown to recognize the validity of their grievances and restore their rights as Englishmen? Or did they want independence? With each passing day of bloodshed the Continental Congress analyzed, debated, and weighed the consequences before deciding, after more than a year, that the goal of the Revolution was independence.

Dissent, militant activism, and rebellion gave birth to the United States. It was only the beginning.

CHAPTER 4

Discord in the New Republic

This government will set out a moderate aristocracy: it is at present impossible to foresee whether it will, in its operation, produce a monarchy, or a corrupt, tyrannical aristocracy; it will probably vibrate some years between the two, and then terminate in the one or the other.

—George Mason, 1787

We are overwhelmed! Our hearts are sickened, our utterance is paralized, when we reflect on the condition in which we are placed, by the audacious practices of unprincipled men, who have managed their stratagems with so much dexterity as to impose on the Government of the United States, in the face of our earnest, solemn, and reiterated protestations.

—Cherokee Chief John Ross, 1836

The Articles of Confederation were the perfect expression of American republicanism—the view that government should be small and representative and close to the people in order to guard against corruption and despotism. Fearful that too much authority in the hands of an executive would lead to tyranny, the creators of the Confederation made no provision at all for a chief executive. Power was not centralized; it was dispersed locally. A representative congress was the only branch of government in this "firm league of friendship" known as the United States of America.[1] "Each State," in this league, was to retain "its sovereignty, freedom and independence, and every power, jurisdiction, and right, which is not by this confederation expressly delegated to the United States."[2] This meant that while Congress had the authority to regulate Indian affairs, negotiate treaties, and establish diplomatic relations, it had little real power. Responsibilities such as lawmaking, taxation, and the regulation of commerce remained in the hands of the states. Congress could request revenue from the states but had no authority to require it.

The weaknesses on the national level of this loose form of government were clearly evident throughout the Revolution as the states squabbled incessantly with each other and regularly disregarded Congress's appeals for taxes to finance the war. After independence the inability of Congress to raise the necessary revenue to retire the national debt further underscored the inherent weakness of the Articles. Within a few years many of the men who had been the force behind the Revolution and the Articles began to call for revision.

A violent protest in Massachusetts, however, was the spark that brought about change. The Revolution had saddled each of the states with heavy debt, and as a consequence the states were forced to raise taxes. Most of the tax burden fell on property owners. This was especially difficult for small farmers, who owned substantial parcels of land but had little capital. When farmers failed to pay taxes, the state confiscated their land and sold it at public auction. In the summer of 1786 farmers in western Massachusetts petitioned the state legislature to ease their financial woes by lowering taxes and putting a moratorium on farm foreclosures. Their petition was ignored. In response a band of farmers, led by the former Revolutionary War captain Daniel Shays and believing they were acting in the same spirit of dissent and revolutionary fervor as the Patriots of the 1760s and 1770s, took up arms, marched into Springfield, and temporarily occupied the courthouse. When the legislature in Boston continued to disregard their pleas, Shays led an attack on the federal arsenal in Springfield. The Massachusetts state militia repulsed the Shaysites, and after several days of pursuing the rebels finally arrested Shays and the other leaders of the rebellion. At the subsequent trial Shays and fourteen others were convicted and sentenced to death, but they were later pardoned by Governor John Hancock.

While Thomas Jefferson was enthusiastic about Shays's Rebellion ("I hold it," he famously opined, "that a little rebellion now and then is a good thing, and as necessary in the political world as storms in the physical," and that rebellions should not be discouraged, for they are "a medicine necessary for the sound health of the government"),[3] most politicians were deeply troubled. The fact that so many common folk would take up arms against their government alarmed the privileged classes. Mob rule, they reasoned, would lead to tyranny just as surely as despotic government. Alexander Hamilton and others had already been arguing for a revision of the Articles of Confederation; now, in the aftermath of Shays's Rebellion, men of property agreed that this task should be undertaken as soon as possible. In this way "a little rebellion" was the final prod prompting political leaders to call for a convention in Philadelphia to establish a more efficient system of government.

By the end of the summer of 1787, after much wrangling and compromise, the Constitutional Convention produced a document that was ready to be submitted to the state legislatures for ratification. However, it was not at all certain that the states would ratify the Constitution. In a new nation wary of centralized authority that had just fought a revolution against tyranny, there was deep-seated skepticism about forming a government that might one day become as authoritarian and repressive as Britain's. After all, despite the Glorious Revolution of 1688, less than a hundred years later king and Parliament had become so tyrannical that natural rights were in jeopardy. Supporters of the Constitution, "Federalists" such as James Madison, John Jay, Alexander Hamilton, and George Washington, urged their state conventions to ratify it. But George Mason, Timothy Bloodworth, and numerous other "Anti-Federalists" denounced it because they feared it would establish a government so strong that it would endanger natural rights. For this reason they campaigned energetically against ratification, urging the states not to approve it as long as it lacked a Bill of Rights. Anti-Federalists also were very protective of states' rights and prerogatives. Good government, they believed, could only be accomplished on a local level.

In an effort to counter these objections Hamilton, Jay, and Madison published a series of pamphlets intended to convince the people of the merits of ratification. They claimed that the Constitution could not lead to tyranny because of the checks and balances written into it and even more importantly because ultimate authority rested not in either the federal government or the state governments but in "we the people." If factions arose (one of the Anti-Federalist objections), this would not be a bad thing. As Madison argued in *Federalist No. 10*, factions and parties helped promote an atmosphere of healthy debate that would ensure the survival of liberty. But Anti-Federalist hostility persisted until finally the Federalists agreed to add a Bill of Rights guaranteeing basic natural rights, especially freedom of religion, speech, assembly, and protest. "Congress shall make no law respecting an establishment of religion, or prohibiting the free exercise thereof; or abridging the freedom of speech, or of the press; or the right of the people peaceably to assemble, and to petition the Government for a redress of grievances." In this way the right to dissent was ensconced in the First Amendment and has become a cornerstone of American polity.

When George Washington was inaugurated as the nation's first president in 1789, Americans rejoiced. The world had changed. A new nation with a *written* constitution was about to step onto the world stage. Optimism and great hopes ran high. "Nothing but harmony," George Washington declared, "honesty, industry and frugality are necessary to make us a great and happy people."[4]

* * *

Almost as soon as the new government became operational, Washington's vision of harmony quickly evaporated as divisions within the administration surfaced. Secretary of the Treasury Alexander Hamilton and Secretary of State Thomas Jefferson were dedicated to the new republic, but their views about republicanism differed widely. Both men believed in the *virtues* of republicanism, that is, representative government, but Hamilton, who distrusted the judgment of the masses, felt the only way a republic could survive was through a strong central government that had the power to keep the democratic excesses of the people in check. Moreover, he believed that industry, commerce, and banking should be the focus of American development and therefore that government should cater to the wealthy, because tying the interests of the country with their interests would promote prosperity and bring economic benefits to all classes. Hamilton wanted to see a federal government so strong that state governments would be little more than agencies for administering federal directives.

Jefferson, in contrast, believed that the people should have the ultimate say in shaping policy. He feared that catering to the upper classes would create a government that could potentially restrict liberty, and so he insisted that all powers not specifically granted to the federal government should be reserved for the states. Central to this debate was the clash between the Jeffersonian "strict constructionist" view that the Constitution must be interpreted literally and the Hamiltonian "loose constructionist" position that the government had the power to do anything that the Constitution did not expressly forbid.

By Washington's second term in office the battle lines had been drawn between Hamiltonian Federalists and Jeffersonian Republicans, and despite the president's loathing of factionalism, a nascent political party system was emerging. The disputes between the two factions were instrumental in shaping national identity, and while many of the debates were hammered out among politicians and lawmakers and while ordinary citizens had little say in influencing the political discussion, this partisanship stimulated dissent and encouraged later generations to be less hesitant about speaking their minds. During the first decades of the new republic's existence it was customary for ordinary citizens to protest, in articles, speeches, and broadsides, policies they deemed undemocratic. The Revolution was over, but dissenting opinions were digging even deeper roots.

The liberal natural-rights ideals on which the United States was founded generated a plethora of alternative views. Dissent and conflict challenged Washington's ideal of consensus and harmony. Those who felt their needs and concerns were not being addressed sought empowerment by protesting against policies they found repressive. They took seriously the First Amendment right to seek "redress of grievances." However, especially in the case of farmers and Indians, the new government did not tolerate dissent gladly but confronted it with force.

The most significant protest during Washington's presidency was the violent response to a new excise tax on whiskey. Backcountry farmers who relied on exporting surplus grain to eastern markets found that the most efficient and economical way of transporting bulk grain was by distilling it into whiskey. The excise tax, however, soaked up all their meager profits. The farmers' frustration was exacerbated by the knowledge that the backcountry was economically lagging far behind the more profitable East Coast centers of commerce and that eastern elites as well as the Federalist politicians who had authorized the whiskey tax tended to look down their aristocratic noses at the "lesser folk."

In the summer of 1792 citizens in western Pennsylvania held protest meetings in which they condemned the tax in words reminiscent of the objections to the Stamp Tax and the Townshend Duties. President Washington issued a warning that such "unlawful" gatherings would not be tolerated. Still the farmers protested frequently, even going so far as to tar and feather federal tax officials. Tensions escalated in 1794

"Famous Whiskey Insurrection in Pennsylvania." Protestors tarring and feathering a tax official. (Public domain)

when one of the excise officials attempted to serve eviction papers on farmers near Pittsburgh who had not paid the tax. An angry mob of about five hundred men surrounded the excise official's house. Shots were fired, and a shootout ensued that lasted for several hours. The official escaped; but several people were killed, and the mob burned the house to the ground. In the aftermath more disgruntled farmers gathered to debate whether to take up arms against the government, while others erected liberty poles around the state.

The protests alarmed President Washington. He feared that acts of rebellion could spread to other areas of the country, and with stories arriving from France of the horrors of the Reign of Terror, he knew that he had to act forcefully and demonstratively. In August 1794 the president, with Hamilton riding at his side, personally led an army of thirteen thousand federalized militiamen into western Pennsylvania to confront the mob. Washington's aides, fearful for the safety of the president, convinced him to return to Philadelphia, but the secretary of the treasury remained at the head of the force; however, the anticipated battle did not occur. The farmers dispersed as word spread that an army larger than any the Americans had put on the battlefield during the Revolutionary War was on the way. Several ringleaders were arrested, two were condemned to death for treason (Washington later pardoned them), the Whiskey Rebellion was quashed, and the government had made its point that resistance to federal law would not be tolerated.

Farmers in western Pennsylvania were not alone in rebelling. Indians, vexed that the American triumph over the British had removed the

last impediment to American expansion, increasingly defended themselves against settlers and land speculators moving into their territory.
As whites poured into eastern Tennessee and Kentucky, the Cherokee,
Shawnee, and Creek Indians took up arms against them. In a series of
bloody battles, both sides fought with brutal ferocity, killing and scalp-
ing men, women, and children.

When Indians north of the Ohio River formed a confederacy "for a
general defense," as they put it, "against all Invaders of Indian rights,"[5]
Washington ordered an army of fourteen hundred soldiers into the
Northwest Territory to smash the confederacy. But a coalition of Shawnee, Chippewa, Delaware, Cherokee, and Miami under the leadership of
Little Turtle and Blue Jacket engaged the American force and inflicted
over nine hundred casualties. Washington then dispatched envoys to
meet with the Indians to negotiate a treaty, but the Indians murdered
the envoys and sent a proposal to Philadelphia: "Our only demand is the
peaceable possession of a small part of our once great Country. Look
back and view the lands from whence we have been driven to this spot,
we can retreat no further, because the country behind hardly affords
food for its present inhabitants. And we have there fore resolved, to
leave our bones in this small space, to which we are now confined. . . .
We shall be persuaded that you mean to do us justice if you agree, that
the Ohio shall remain the boundary line between us, if you will not consent thereto, our meeting will be altogether unnecessary."[6]

The United States did not consent, and the following year Washington sent an army under the command of Major General Anthony
Wayne to subdue the Indians. At the Battle of Fallen Timbers, in August
1794, the Indians were decisively defeated and within another year were
compelled to sign the Treaty of Greenville, in which they ceded the land
that later became the state of Ohio. Their resistance was heroic, but it
only delayed their ultimate defeat.

* * *

The government regarded backwoods farmers and Indians who resisted
federal authority as troublesome minorities, but it was a different story
when a far larger group began to chafe at the restrictions limiting their
liberty. Women were becoming more and more frustrated by the contradiction of living a life of enforced subservience in a revolutionary
republic that championed liberty and equality for all. Even though John

Adams and the other founding fathers paid no attention to Abigail Adams's entreaties to include women in the new system of government, growing numbers of women were unwilling to remain submissive in a society that continuously espoused liberty and equality while denying them the rights they reserved for themselves.

The most famous of these early feminists was Judith Sargent Murray. Because of her gender Murray did not have a formal education. Nevertheless, with the aid of her brother, who tutored her in literature and the classics, she educated herself and soon became an eloquent advocate for women's rights. In her 1790 essay "On the Equality of the Sexes" she demanded that women be granted the same educational opportunities as men. Only through education would women be able to gain equal rights. "Ye lordly, ye haughty sex," she wrote,

> our souls are by nature *equal* to yours; the same breath of God animates, enlivens, and invigorates us. . . . I dare confidently believe, that from the commencement of time to the present day, there hath been as many females, as males, who, by the *mere force of natural powers*, have merited the crown of applause; who, *thus assisted*, have seized the wreath of fame. I know there are [those] who assert, that as the animal powers of the one sex are superiour, of course their mental faculties also must be stronger; thus attributing strength of mind to the transient organization of this earth born tenement. But if this reasoning is just, man must be content to yield the palm to many of the brute creation, since by not a few of his brethren of the field, he is far surpassed in bodily strength. Moreover, was this argument admitted, it would prove too much, for occular demonstration evinceth, that there are many robust masculine ladies, and effeminate gentlemen. . . . Besides, were we to grant that animal strength proved any thing, taking into consideration the accustomed impartiality of nature, we should be induced to imagine, that she had invested the female mind with superiour strength as an equivalent for the bodily powers of man.

But, she went on to assure her male readers, her battle was not for superiority over men, as men feared, but "for equality only."[7]

Soon after the publication of Murray's essay British feminist Mary Wollstonecraft's *A Vindication of the Rights of Women* appeared in the United States. This seminal work further provoked discussion and debate about women's rights, as did Hannah Webster Foster's novel *The Coquette . . . Founded on Fact*, which was a critical commentary on the inequality of women in the new republic. Another early American feminist was writer and actress Susanna Rowson, who performed a number of plays aimed at raising public awareness that the subjugation of women was a problem that needed to be addressed.[8] Although most men (but not all) tended to ridicule women's discontent, Murray's essays, Wollstonecraft's book, and the writings of other feminists were widely read and taken seriously by many people and had a significant influence on subsequent generations of women. By 1800 women had higher expectations than their mothers had.

It was obvious that there was a major contradiction between the liberal ideals of the Revolution and the reality of denying liberty to African Americans. Even in the Upper South, people were keenly aware of the hypocrisy inherent in fighting for liberty while holding slaves. Also many religious groups, most notably the Society of Friends, found slavery sinful and morally repugnant. Whether for political or moral reasons large numbers of Americans began actively calling for the elimination of slavery, in both the North and the South. However, economic factors, coupled with the influx of European immigrants filling the labor ranks, were just as important in the withering away of bondage in the North. Slavery simply was no longer a profitable institution in the North, where farms were smaller and the chief crops were not cash crops such as tobacco and cotton. Between 1789 and the 1820s the northern states gradually did away with slavery, but after the invention of the cotton gin in 1793, the slave-based economy in the South prospered and thrived at a level that was scarcely imaginable a decade earlier.

* * *

Despite Washington's hope to leave behind a truly united nation when he retired, the election of John Adams in 1796 intensified the division between the rival political factions. Shortly after his inauguration Adams was faced with a serious international crisis—the "XYZ Affair"—that further inflamed protest. Ever since the French Alliance of 1778 France had somewhat condescendingly regarded the United States as an inferior power that it had the right to manipulate in whatever way benefited France. When Washington refused to join France in its war with England in 1793, the French were affronted. By the time Adams became president, tensions between France and the United States were running high, and the French began routinely seizing American merchant ships at sea. In order to avert war Adams sent commissioners to Paris to negotiate a settlement, but three French diplomats, identified only as "X, Y, and Z," agreed to receive the Americans only if they first paid a bribe of $250,000. Adams refused, and when he released the details of the "XYZ Affair," Congress and the American public were outraged. Some Americans clamored for war, while others were equally outspoken against a resort to arms. The French, Adams believed, must be taught a lesson and learn to treat the United States with respect. But unwilling to risk all-out war, Adams conducted a "Quasi," or undeclared, war that lasted until 1800. Throughout the uproar Republicans such as Jefferson publicly condemned the French diplomatic insult but were unwilling to support the Federalists. Moreover, they were apprehensive that the Federalists would find a way to manipulate the anti-French fervor against them.

They did not have to wait long.

In the summer of 1798 Federalists pushed the Alien and Sedition Acts through Congress. The Alien Acts gave the president the authority to deport any alien "he shall judge dangerous to the peace and safety of the United States."[9] This was primarily aimed at recent Irish and French immigrants who supported the Jeffersonians. The Sedition Act, in effect, made it illegal for anyone to criticize the administration's policies. The act prohibited "any persons unlawfully [to] combine or conspire together, with intent to oppose any measure or measures of the government of the United States." Furthermore, it was forbidden to "write, print, utter or publish . . . any false, scandalous and malicious writing or writings against the government of the United States, or either house of the Congress . . . or the President."[10]

By equating legitimate dissent and political criticism with sedition, these laws not only were aimed at weakening the Republican opposition but were also an infringement on two of the most prized liberties guaranteed by the Bill of Rights—freedom of press and freedom of speech. The acts limited the power of the people and their right to dissent, and once they took effect, dozens of men were arrested and tried under the Sedition Act. Ten were convicted and sent to prison. Some of those arrested included newspaper editors, as well as Vermont congressman Matthew Lyon, who had criticized Adams for mishandling the Quasi-War, and even a drunk, Luther Baldwin, who, while watching an artillery salute in honor of President Adams, had puckishly commented that he wished the cannonball had "fired through his ass."[11] Baldwin was arrested, tried, convicted, and jailed for sedition.

Jefferson and the Republican opposition wasted no time going on the offensive and attacking the Federalists for subverting the Constitution. Jefferson penned the Kentucky Resolutions, and James Madison the Virginia Resolutions, expounding the principle that states had the right to nullify a federal law if it went against the Constitution, especially if the law threatened civil liberties. Although no other state adopted this nullification policy, the strategy was successful in identifying the Federalists as enemies of basic American liberties. The Republicans were in effect accusing the Federalist Party of turning against the principles of the Revolution. Much of the public sided with the Republicans on this issue, and it was clear that the Federalists, in their imprudent attempt to stifle political opposition in order to strengthen their control of the government, had badly miscalculated. The protests over these acts had a determining influence on the election of 1800 and a significant impact on the future of the country. By enshrining the right to protest in the First Amendment, the United States had committed itself to the belief that dissent can bring change. The Federalists' attempt to take away that right doomed their prospects for maintaining power.

At the same time as the Alien and Sedition protests, Adams also faced a small-scale rebellion—a miniature version of the 1794 Whiskey Rebellion. During the Quasi-War with France, Congress authorized a $2 million tax on real estate and slaves in order to expand the army and navy. When tax assessors made the rounds in southeastern Pennsylvania assessing householders' tax liability, angry residents rose up in revolt. They refused to pay the tax, claiming it was unconstitutional. Tax resisters, led by John Fries, harassed, captured, and threatened the tax assessors. The "rebellion" was finally put down and the leaders captured by the local militia. Fries and two others were tried for treason and sentenced to death, but President Adams pardoned them. The so-called Fries Rebellion was not the first instance, nor the last, in the history of the United States in which citizens passionately protested about the always-controversial issue of taxation.

* * *

At the beginning of Thomas Jefferson's first term as president, he was confronted with the nation's first hostage crisis. Throughout the 1790s American merchant ships that traded in the Mediterranean fell victim to pirates operating out of the Barbary shore of North Africa—routinely American ships would be seized; the crew was subjected to imprisonment, torture, and enslavement. And adding insult to injury, the United States was forced to pay an annual tribute to the Barbary States to keep the pirates from seizing other American ships.

Jefferson took steps to put an end to this humiliating extortion by sending the U.S. Navy and Marines to "the shores of Tripoli" in an attempt to oust the pirates' patron, the pasha of Tripoli. The invasion failed, but it did compel the pasha to negotiate a settlement with the United States that ultimately secured the release of the Americans held captive there. This affair triggered an outbreak of anti-Muslim feeling in the United States in which newspapers condemned the Muslims of North Africa as uncivilized, and as a result, seeds of misunderstanding and distrust between the United States and Islamic nations began to take root in the first decade of the nineteenth century. (It is ironic that as enraged Americans protested against North African Muslims enslaving a few hundred white American seamen, few people seemed to make the connection that there might perhaps also be something criminal about the American institution of black slavery.)

During Jefferson's second term the United States again got caught up in an international crisis. The Napoleonic Wars in Europe were a constant threat to American security. The United States with its minuscule military was in no position to get involved in the interminable warfare between the British and the French, and consequently Jefferson pursued a policy of neutrality. But problems arose in 1806 when Britain issued the Orders in Council, which prohibited neutrals from trading with its European enemies. Napoleon responded by closing all Continental ports to British goods, even goods that were carried on neutral ships.

American merchants found themselves in an impossible situation. If an American vessel attempted to sail into a Continental port, the Royal Navy would seize it, but if it sailed to England, it risked capture by the French. A further complicating factor was that Britain continued to impress Americans into the Royal Navy. In 1807 the British intercepted the American ship the *Chesapeake*, looking for able-bodied men. When the *Chesapeake* refused to allow the Royal Navy to board, the British opened fire. Several Americans were killed and wounded; the *Chesapeake* was forced to surrender, and the British pressed four of its sailors into service. The uproar in the United States was loud and instantaneous. Jefferson, however, hoping to avoid war, responded by persuading Congress to pass the Embargo Act in December 1807. He reasoned that if neither England nor France had access to American goods, it would force them to reopen trade. Angry American merchants protested the act by flagrantly flouting the embargo. This forced Jefferson, for the remainder of his last year as president, to issue a series of increasingly harsher measures to enforce the embargo, which, in turn, only worsened the situation and further inflamed the protesting merchants.

In 1809, just days before James Madison was sworn in as president, Congress repealed the Embargo Act and replaced it with the Non-Intercourse Act, which reopened trade with all countries except England and France, with the proviso that the United States would renew trade with those nations if they pledged to respect neutral rights; however, it seemed that neither Britain nor France had any intention of allowing American merchants to trade with its enemy. Further, the Royal Navy continued its practice of impressment. Thus, in the early years of Madison's presidency, he was faced with a persistent conflict that threatened at any moment to drag the United States into a war that it was neither willing nor prepared to fight.

By 1812 a faction of "War Hawks" was having more sway in Congress. Chafing at the humiliation that the United States was forced to endure at the hands of the Royal Navy and blaming the British for encouraging and supporting violent Indian resistance to American settlement in the Northwest Territory, these War Hawks began to push for war with England. Chief among them were two young congressmen—South Carolina's John C. Calhoun and Kentucky's Henry Clay—who took the lead in drumming up support for a declaration of war. Both men argued passionately that a war with Britain would restore international respect for the United States and give the nation the unique opportunity to expand into Canada (perhaps even to wrest Canada from the British), as well as Spanish Florida. On June 1, 1812, President Madison succumbed to the pressure and asked Congress for a declaration of war.

There was, however, considerable antiwar opinion. Federalists especially opposed the war not only because of their pro-British and anti-French predisposition but also because they saw the war as purely a

Republican venture. New England Federalists regarded the war as a ruse to expand U.S. territory, expand slavery, create new states, and diminish New England's influence in Washington. Massachusetts congressman Josiah Quincy denounced the war from the floor of the House of Representatives and submitted a statement, signed by a number of Federalist congressmen, protesting the war.

> The undersigned can not refrain from asking, what are the United States to gain by this war? . . . Let us not be deceived. A war of invasion may invite a retort of invasion. When we visit the peaceable, and as to us innocent, colonies of Great Britain with the horrors of war, can we be assured that our own coast will not be visited with like horrors? At a crisis of the world such as the present, and under impressions such as these, the undersigned could not consider the war, in which the United States have in secret been precipitated, as necessary, or required by any moral duty, or any political expediency.[12]

So-called Blue Light Federalists in New England were even more radically opposed to the war. They protested against recruitment drives, supported those who refused to enlist, urged all citizens to withhold taxes, and openly traded with the enemy by ignoring trade restrictions with Britain and Canada. They were even suspected of signaling the Royal Navy (with blue lights) every time American vessels left port. The governor of Massachusetts, reflecting the antiwar position of his constituents, secretly attempted to negotiate a separate peace with Britain, offering territory in Maine in exchange for peace. Such radical antiwar activity clearly crossed the line into treason.

Antiwar fervor in New England remained strong throughout the conflict. In December 1814 New England Federalists held a convention in Hartford in which they openly discussed secession from the United States if the war continued. Moderate delegates at the convention, however, toned down the final resolutions so that they only called for several new constitutional amendments and not secession. But the War of 1812 came to an end on Christmas Eve when American commissioners in Paris signed the Treaty of Ghent. However, since news of the signing of the treaty did not arrive in America until February 1815—several weeks after the Battle of New Orleans—most Americans viewed the outcome as the result of Andrew Jackson's spectacular victory at New

Orleans. Americans felt proud that the United States had successfully defeated, or at least held off, the most powerful military force in the world. In this atmosphere Americans denounced the Hartford Convention and the Federalist Party as disloyal, a charge from which the Federalists were never able to recover. Antiwar dissent, in this case, resulted in the collapse of a major political party.

* * *

Throughout these years Indians in the old Northwest Territory (the area north and west of the Ohio River) continued to resist the onslaught of land-hungry Americans flooding into their lands. Between 1800 and 1809 two Shawnee brothers, Tecumseh and Tenskwatawa, put together a powerful confederacy of Miami, Shawnee, and Potawatomi Indians, with its headquarters at Tippecanoe in northern Indiana. For three years Tecumseh, hoping to strengthen the alliance further, went on diplomatic missions to the southern Indians—the Cherokee, Chickasaw, Choctaw, and Creek—urging them to join the confederacy. Tecumseh warned the southern Indians that they must not remain passive, for if they did, they would suffer the same fate as the Pequot, the Mohawk, and the Narragansett. "Your people, too," he predicted in a speech to the southern tribes in 1811, "will soon be as falling leaves and scattering clouds before [the whites'] blighting breath. You, too, will be driven away from your native land and ancient domains as leaves are driven before the wintry storms." The only hope to preserve Indian lands was to unite. "Sleep not longer, O Choctaws and Chickasaws, in false security and delusive hopes. Our broad domains are fast escaping from our grasp. Every year our white intruders become more greedy, exacting, oppressive and overbearing. . . . Before the palefaces came among us, we enjoyed the happiness of unbounded freedom, and were acquainted with neither riches, wants nor oppression." Indians, Tecumseh argued, had lost their land and their liberty. Whites had oppressed and subjugated them, treating them just as terribly as they treated their African slaves. "How long will it be before they will tie us to a post and whip us, and make us work for them in their cornfields as they do them? Shall we wait for that moment or shall we die fighting before submitting to such ignominy?" Indians have no choice, Tecumseh declared, but to join forces in a great confederation and rise up against the whites and either "destroy them all, which we now can do, or drive them back whence they came."[13]

The Shawnee Indian chief Tecumseh. Wood
engraving, c. late nineteenth century. "The
white people have no right to take the land from
the Indians." (Public domain; courtesy Library
of Congress)

Despite Tecumseh's appeal the Choctaw and Chickasaw refused to
join the confederacy. Confrontation with the whites continued to escalate, and while Tecumseh was on another mission to promote his Indian
confederacy, the governor of the Indiana territory, William Henry Harrison, negotiated with a band of Ohio Indians to purchase three million
acres of land in southern Indiana. When Tecumseh found out, he wrote
an angry letter of protest to Harrison claiming that the sale was invalid.
"The white people," Tecumseh argued, "have no right to take the land
from the Indians. . . . Any sale not made by all is not valid. . . . [For] all
red men have equal rights to the unoccupied land."[14] Harrison ignored

Tecumseh's protest and in 1811 led a force of one thousand men against the Indians at Tippecanoe. Although the battle was inconclusive, the Indians retreated the following day, and Harrison burned the village to the ground. The following year, when the United States went to war with England, Tecumseh and the remaining Indians in his confederacy joined with the British to fight the Americans in a final attempt to hold on to their remaining lands. For a time he led successful raids against American troops at Fort Nelson, Fort Wayne, and Detroit, but in 1813, at the Battle of the Thames in Canada, Tecumseh was killed by troops led by Harrison. Tecumseh's death marked the end for the northern Indian confederacy.

Although the southern Indians refused to join Tecumseh's confederacy, they did put up a fight to protect their lands. In central Alabama a series of increasingly bloody encounters occurred between Americans and the Creek Indians. In the summer of 1813, after Creek raids killed five hundred whites, including women and children, the Tennessee legislature sent Andrew Jackson and five thousand militiamen to destroy the Indians. In March 1814, at the Battle of Horseshoe Bend, Jackson and a force of two thousand defeated one thousand Creek warriors, killing eight hundred of them. The southern Indian resistance continued sporadically for more than a decade afterward, but at Horseshoe Bend it was dealt an irreversible blow from which it never recovered.

* * *

Beginning in the first decade of the nineteenth century and continuing after the War of 1812, the United States experienced a second evangelical revival. Thousands of Americans underwent religious conversion experiences. Itinerant preachers without any denominational affiliation traveled the nation spreading the message of the gospel mingled with a heavy dose of Jeffersonian ideals and egalitarianism. It was repeated over and over again that each person was responsible for his or her own salvation and that all people, men or women, blacks or whites, slave or free, were equal in the eyes of God.

Along with personal salvation the revivals also brought people together from all classes and religions, including slaves. This Second Great Awakening encouraged and reinforced the belief that individuals had something to say and that they could and should say it. Like the First Great Awakening of the eighteenth century the evangelical impulse was a leveling, socializing experience that created a milieu that later in the century helped underpin such reform movements as abolitionism, temperance, and women's rights.

The sense that individuals had agency in improving their lives, along with the return of peace, raised hopes that the nation would expand, that the economy would boom, and that all Americans would experience the benefits of prosperity, liberty, and equality. But the festering issue of slavery continued to plague Americans by challenging their most basic idealistic assumptions. Enlightenment philosophy had convinced many Americans, especially in the North, that slavery had no place in a society that was grounded on the idea that all men are created equal. Still, most white Americans considered blacks inferior. This was not so much because of skin color but because slaves were treated as property, kept illiterate, and forced to live in such humiliating and degrading conditions that it seemed they could never rise up to be the whites' equal. Thus northerners, despite the fact that they abhorred slavery, were just as firmly opposed to racial mingling as southerners were.

One of the first antislavery organizations, the American Colonization Society (founded in 1816), reflected this assumption of black inferiority. The society sought to end slavery not by freeing the enslaved and granting them citizenship and equal rights but by sending them back to Africa. In fact, the society was as much concerned with ridding the country of free blacks as it was concerned with freeing slaves. Despite the promise of freedom from slavery many slaves and black abolitionists opposed this form of racism and organized to protest colonization. They were, after all, more American than African. Why should they have to leave the United States when it was their blood, sweat, and tears on which the nation's prosperity had been built? In 1817 a group of free blacks in Philadelphia sent a petition to their congressman attacking the colonization project. "Whereas our ancestors," they wrote,

> (not of choice) were the first successful cultivators of the wilds of America, we their descendants feel ourselves entitled to participate in the blessings of her luxuriant soil, which their blood and sweat manured; and that any measure or system of measures, having a tendency to banish us from her bosom, would not only be cruel, but in direct violation of those principles, which have been the boast of this republic. . . .

> Resolved, That we never will separate ourselves voluntarily from the slave population in this country; they are our brethren by the ties of consanguinity, of suffering, and of wrong; and we feel that there is more virtue in suffering privations with them, than fancied advantages for a season.[15]

In the end, only about twenty thousand slaves were transported to West Africa through the efforts of the American Colonization Society, which hardly affected the natural increase that expanded slavery over the next four decades. But what is important is that African American opposition to colonization shows that there was an organized core of antiracist, as well as antislavery, activism. In the ensuing decades this burgeoning militancy helped fuel a more radical abolitionist movement.

Along with the stirrings of abolitionism there was another ominous sign that the nationalism that had united Americans so tightly ever since the Revolution was eroding. When Missouri applied for admission to the Union as a slave state in 1819 (which would upset the eleven-to-eleven balance of slave and free states and thus give slaveholding interests dominance in the Senate), northerners balked. Eventually a potential crisis was avoided when York County was separated from Massachusetts and admitted to the Union as the free state of Maine, while Missouri was admitted as a slave state. The settlement also prohibited slavery in any future states carved out of the Louisiana Purchase north of the 36° 30′ parallel (the southern border of Missouri). The Missouri Compromise simply postponed the vexing question of what, ultimately, ought to be done about the institution of slavery. And it was a warning, as Thomas Jefferson observed at the time, like "a fire bell in the night," that a conflagration awaited the nation.[16]

At the time of the Missouri Compromise Jeffersonian Republicans were for all practical purposes the only political party. President James Monroe had authorized America's first protective tariff, established the Second National Bank of the United States to regulate and stimulate the economy, and initiated a program whereby the federal government would finance the building of interstate roads and canals. Some Republicans, such as John Quincy Adams and Henry Clay, were enthusiastic about these measures; others, such as John C. Calhoun and Andrew Jackson, however, were alarmed that the party was forsaking its Jeffersonian states'-rights roots. By the time Jackson won the presidential election of 1828, the party had irrevocably split into National Republicans (those favoring federally sponsored programs) and Democratic Republicans (those favoring states' rights and smaller government).

Jackson's two terms in office were a turbulent time. Even within his party—the Democratic Party, as it came to be known—there was division. A series of clashes with Vice President John C. Calhoun over everything from the "Tariff of Abominations" to the Peggy Eaton Affair—a veritable soap opera in which Secretary of War John Eaton married his mistress, Peggy O'Neal, immediately after her husband died under suspicious circumstances—led Calhoun to resign. Calhoun became a bitter enemy of Jackson's and the leading proponent of nullification—the doctrine, originally proposed by Jefferson and Madison, that the states have the sovereign right to nullify federal laws they deem unconstitutional. Although Jackson himself was a strong supporter of states' rights, he rejected nullification out of hand. To Jackson individual states did not have the right to go against federal law because this would risk breaking up the Union. Calhoun's argument was that the United States "are not a nation, but a Union, a confederacy of equal and sovereign states."[17] Note the use of the plural "*are.*" Calhoun, and indeed most Americans, certainly most southerners, commonly referred to the United States as a plural entity, not singular. The implication, of course, was clear: the individual states were more important than the united whole.

It was also an era of impressive economic growth and expansion. The nation was spreading westward, industry was booming, and canals and national roads were creating a transportation revolution, which in turn further stimulated the burgeoning economy. A new mood enveloped the country, and although banking and industrial interests continued to dominate politics and the economy, the so-called age of the common man was on the rise. Universal manhood suffrage, in which property qualifications for voting were rescinded, became a reality, and white men began to believe they had an important say in how the government was run. But how much power was truly in the hands of the common man? What special interests dominated the governing of the nation? These questions resulted in an accelerating debate between states'-rights adherents and those who wished to see a stronger central government in Washington. Native Americans, of course, found themselves at odds with all this "progress." Some tried to accommodate themselves and adjust to the inevitable, while others resisted; but no matter how well they accommodated themselves or how strongly they resisted, the results were tragic and disastrous for them. Workers too found that the age of the common man did not provide quite as much opportunity for them to advance as it did for bankers, industrialists, and planters.

* * *

As president, Jackson's attitude toward Indians changed little from what it had been when he won fame as an Indian fighter. The Cherokee, Creek, Seminole, Chickasaw, and Choctaw were, in Jackson's eyes, a barrier to progress. Even though the Cherokee had assimilated to a large degree into white society—accepting Christianity, translating the Bible and Protestant hymns such as "Amazing Grace" into Cherokee, abandoning Cherokee traditions, wearing white man's clothing, learning to farm, even purchasing slaves (by 1830 the Cherokee owned approximately one thousand slaves), which further enhanced their credentials as Americans—they were still regarded by Jackson and whites living in the southeastern states as uncivilized savages. Naturally, underlying this racist attitude was the basic economic issue of white lust for Indian land. If whites could convince themselves that Indians were inferior and uncivilized, it would ease whatever pangs of conscience that might otherwise have reminded them that the insatiable desire for Indian land in and of itself was dishonorable.

In 1830 Jackson sent a bill to Congress calling for the removal of these five Indian nations to an area west of the Mississippi. However, many humanitarians, largely evangelical Christians and Quakers, protested. They believed that the Indians, especially the Cherokee because of their acceptance of white civilization and Christianity, had the right to remain on their ancestral lands. Partly for religious/humanitarian reasons and partly for partisan advantage, Senator Theodore Frelinghuysen of New Jersey led the congressional opposition to the Indian Removal Bill. Frelinghuysen argued that the Indians, living on the continent for thousands of years, had title to the land, not Americans. "Our ancestors," he reminded senators, "found these people, far removed from the commotions of Europe, exercising all the rights, and enjoying the privileges, of free and independent sovereigns of this new world. They were not a wild and lawless horde of banditti, but lived under the restraints of government." The whites, when they first arrived, "approached them as friends" but soon began to take over their lands and destroy their way of life. The Indian has been wronged. "Do the obligations of justice," Frelinghuysen asked rhetorically, "change with the color of the skin? Is it one of the prerogatives of the white man, that he may disregard the dictates of moral principles, when an Indian shall be concerned? No, sir. . . . If the contending parties were to exchange positions, place the white man where the Indian stands, load him with all these wrongs, and what path would his outraged feelings strike out for . . . ?" Frelinghuysen scoffed at Jackson's claim that removing the Indians would benefit them by ensuring their moral and political improvement as well as their physical comfort. "The end, however, is to justify the means. 'The removal of the Indian tribes to the west of the Mississippi is demanded by the dictates of humanity.' . . . Who urges this plea? They who covet the Indian lands—who wish to rid themselves of a neighbor that they despise, and whose State pride is enlisted in rounding off their territories."[18] Despite Frelinghuysen's determined efforts as well as the opposition of those who did not wish to see the Indians suffer further injury, the Indian Removal Bill passed. The Indians' fate was sealed.

But the Indians pushed back. The Cherokee refused to comply with the Removal Bill and even took their case to the Supreme Court. In *Cherokee Nation v. Georgia* (1831) Chief Justice John Marshall ruled that the Cherokee "have an unquestionable right, and, heretofore, unquestioned right to the lands they occupy until that right shall be extinguished by a voluntary cession to our government." And in *Worcester v. Georgia* (1832) Marshall declared that "the Indian nations had always been considered as distinct, independent, political communities," and hence the Cherokee people were indeed a sovereign nation that had a lawful right to its own territory. Efforts to remove them were therefore unconstitutional. It was reported that when Jackson learned of the court ruling, he responded defiantly, "John Marshall has made his decision. Now let him enforce it."[19]

In the face of Jackson's unconstitutional refusal to implement the Court's rulings the Creek, the Choctaw, the Chickasaw, and some Seminole agreed to relocate; however, the Cherokee and a contingent of the Seminole refused to do so. In 1836 the Seminole chieftain Osceola led a faction of his people in what was called the Second Seminole War, a bloody, protracted battle that cost the United States $20 million and fifteen hundred soldiers before Osceola was captured and the Seminole vanquished. (Although many Seminole were removed to the west, most

Cherokee chief John Ross, c. 1843. Lithograph published by Daniel
Rice and James G. Clark, Philadelphia. "Our hearts are sickened
. . . in the face of our earnest, solemn, and reiterated protestations."
(Public domain)

of them avoided capture by disappearing into the swampy Everglades,
where their descendants still live today.)

The Cherokee response to Indian removal was more complicated. A
minority faction negotiated a treaty at New Echota in which they agreed
to give up their lands. This incensed the majority of the Cherokee. They
declared that the Cherokee who signed the New Echota Treaty had no
right to speak for the Cherokee Nation. Chief John Ross denounced the
treaty in no uncertain terms. "By the stipulations of this instrument," he
protested to Congress,

> we are despoiled of our private possessions, the indefeasible property of
> individuals. We are stripped of every attribute of freedom and eligibility

for legal self-defence. Our property may be plundered before our eyes; violence may be committed on our persons; even our lives may be taken away, and there is none to regard our complaints. We are denationalized; we are disfranchised. We are deprived of membership in the human family! We have neither land nor home, nor resting place that can be called our own. And this is effected by the provisions of a compact which assumes the venerated, the sacred appellation of treaty.[20]

Ross's appeal was to no avail, and in 1838 seven thousand American soldiers forced seventeen thousand Cherokee at bayonet point on the one-thousand-mile trek along the infamous "Trail of Tears." Historians have estimated that fully one-fourth of the Cherokee died on the trail before they reached the bleak reservation set aside for them in the Oklahoma territory. It is quite clear that what the Cherokee and the other southeastern nations endured in the 1830s can only be viewed as a near-genocidal experience. Although the Indian nations were not exactly wiped out, they were decimated and their ways of life forever altered.

Every Indian nation that stood in the way of American expansion suffered, in its own way, a similar fate—the Powhatan Confederacy, the Pequot, the Iroquois, the Shawnee, the Sac and Fox, the Natchez, the list goes on and on. Still, many Indians continued to resist, not only on the battlefield but also in speeches and writings in which they protested the hypocrisy of whites who used grandiose natural-rights philosophy to validate and justify ignoble and sordid purposes.

One nineteenth-century Indian who scornfully drew attention to the discrepancy between what the white man said and what the white man did was William Apess. Apess, a Pequot Indian who studied theology and was ordained a Methodist minister, published an essay in 1833 titled "An Indian's Looking Glass for the White Man." In this piece he cleverly uses scripture and the principles of Christianity so often invoked by whites to condemn Americans' treatment of the Indians. "Is it right," Apess writes, "to hold and promote prejudices? If not, why not put them all away? I mean here, among those who are civilized." He describes the abject poverty and disgraceful conditions on the reservations and says that if any Christian man or woman would visit one of them they would be horrified at the unchristian conditions that the Indians are forced to endure. The Indians are exploited and demoralized, and some are forced into prostitution; while whites enter the reservations brazenly

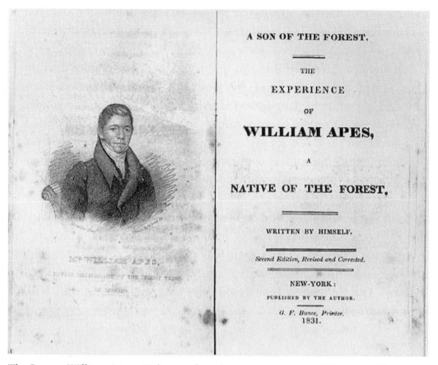

A SON OF THE FOREST.

THE

EXPERIENCE

OF

WILLIAM APES,

A

NATIVE OF THE FOREST,

WRITTEN BY HIMSELF.

Second Edition, Revised and Corrected.

NEW-YORK:

PUBLISHED BY THE AUTHOR.

G. F. Bunce, Printer.
1831.

The Pequot William Apess. Title page from his memoir, *A Son of the Forest: The Experience of William Apes, a Native of the Forest* (New York, 1831). "Is it right to hold and promote prejudices? If not, why not put them all away? I mean here, among those who are civilized." (Public domain)

and take what they want, even cutting down the "most valuable timber," because they view it as no crime to commit an offense against an Indian. "Why are not we protected in our persons and property throughout the Union?" he asks. "I would ask you if you would like to be disfranchised from all your rights, merely because your skin is white, and for no other crime." He then points out that for every white person in the world there are at least fifteen nonwhites. Do whites *really* believe, Apess asks sardonically, they "are the only beloved images of God"?

Assemble all nations together in your imagination, and then let the whites be seated among them, and then let us look for the whites, and I doubt not it would be hard finding them; for to the rest of the nations, they are still but a handful. Now suppose these skins were put together, and each skin has its national crimes written upon it—which skin do you think would have the greatest? I will ask one question more. Can you charge the Indians with robbing a nation almost of their whole continent, and murdering their women and children, and then depriving the remainder of their lawful rights, that nature and God require them to have? And to cap the climax, rob another nation to till their grounds and welter out their days under the lash with hunger and fatigue under the scorching rays of a burning sun? I should look at all the skins, and I know that when I cast my eye upon that white skin, and if I saw those crimes written upon it, I should enter my protest against it immediately and cleave to that which is more honorable.[21]

As in the seventeenth and eighteenth centuries, Native Americans in the 1830s, such as William Apess, had no illusions about the aims of the interlopers. They knew that their way of life, their very existence, was under attack and that the whites' aim was the total destruction of the Indians. And they knew that despite the impossible odds, they had no choice but to fight back.

* * *

The defining issue of Jackson's second term was his refusal to recharter the Second National Bank of the United States. Jackson's successful war on the bank was perceived at the time as a triumph for democracy. The president was considered the champion of the common man, fighting for the rights of the less privileged against the advantages of a privileged aristocracy. However, ironically, for nearly a century after the destruction of the bank the United States went through a series of financial panics, recessions, and depressions that caused significant economic hardship and suffering for the common man and helped to foment further dissent, protest, and activism.

In some areas of the country, most notably New England, a factory system was developing, and by the 1820s several textile mills were operating in Waltham, Lowell, and Chicopee, Massachusetts. The mill in Lowell was notable because most of the workers were young farmwomen. The New England agricultural economy had been shrinking, and so the modest income these women earned helped their families survive. They worked as much as eighty hours a week, but the mill provided housing and food. At a time when it was considered scandalous for young unmarried women to live away from home, the Lowell mill gave women a unique opportunity. Despite the long hours, they could live and work at the mills in a safe, secure environment and develop friendships, camaraderie, and a feeling of female solidarity, while experiencing a wider world.

But labor unrest was brewing. The expansion of industry and the exploitation of workers by factory and mill owners propelled some workers to organize and form unions. Printers, masons, carpenters, and others formed the first trade union in Philadelphia in 1827, and within seven years the first nationwide union—the National Trades Union—was founded. By the mid-1830s enough trade unions had organized that they initiated nearly two hundred strikes around the country demanding better wages, shorter hours, and safer working conditions. Even the "Lowell Mill Girls," who labored under somewhat better conditions than most workers, went on strike (unsuccessfully) in 1834. Carpenters, stonecutters, and masons in Boston struck to reduce the working day from thirteen hours to ten. After three strikes that did not lead to reduced hours, the workers issued a manifesto justifying their cause and calling for all workers to unite with them in demanding a ten-hour day. The workers were fighting, they proclaimed, "for the recognition of the Natural Right to dispose of our own time in such quantities as we deem and believe to be most conducive to our own happiness, and the welfare of all those engaged in Manual Labor." It was not right that the owners should subject hardworking people to give up so much of their lives in the cause of profits. Working thirteen hours a day was so exhausting that they were unable to enjoy life.

> We have been too long subjected to the odious, cruel, unjust, and tyrannical system which compels the operative Mechanic to exhaust his physical and mental powers by excessive toil, until he has no desire but to eat and sleep, and in many cases he has no power to do either from extreme debility. . . .
>
> No man or body of men who require such excessive labor can be friends to the country or the Rights of Man. We also say, that we have rights, and we have duties to perform as American Citizens and members of society, which forbid us to dispose of more than Ten Hours for a day's work.
>
> We cannot, we will not, longer be mere slaves to inhuman, insatiable and unpitying avarice. We have taken a firm and decided stand, to obtain

the acknowledgment of those rights to enable us to perform those duties
to God, our Country and ourselves. . . .
It is for the rights of humanity we contend.[22]

Despite such pleas, it was nearly impossible to put up an effective front
against the bosses and the companies. Small, incremental steps were
made, but opposition was so strong that it was decades before the labor
movement was powerful enough, or even recognized as legitimate, to
be able to exert sufficient pressure to achieve its modest goals. Although
workers did not win the ten-hour day in the 1830s, they set the foundation for future workers to carry on the struggle, and twenty years later
the ten-hour day *did* become a reality.[23]

In 1837, just weeks after the inauguration of Martin Van Buren as
president, the plight of workers worsened when the price of America's
major export, cotton, dropped by 50 percent. A panic set in. British
banks called in American loans. Prices of coal, wheat, and other necessities doubled, and unemployment hit 30 percent. Mobs took to the
streets protesting against unemployment, rising prices, and the government's inability to alleviate the crisis. The situation threatened to get
out of hand. Unemployed workers broke into warehouses and stores to
steal provisions. In cities around the country the police had to be called
in to stop the looting and to arrest the perpetrators. There were even
Luddite-style riots in which jobless workers broke factory machines
and destroyed manufactured products. In Philadelphia protesters vandalized the flats of Irish immigrants, who were reviled (and feared) as
unwelcome competitors for whatever jobs were available.

∗ ∗ ∗

Throughout the first half century of the nation's existence clouds of
discontent gathered. Indians pleaded, petitioned, formed alliances,
appealed to the Supreme Court, and took up arms in a desperate and bitter fight to defend their land and their lives. When some Indians as well
as whites pointed out that whites' treatment of Indians was contrary to
the liberal natural-rights philosophy on which the nation was founded,
they were told that the Indians were uncivilized savages and that those
principles did not apply to them. Backcountry farmers showed their
discontent with the government's taxation policies by echoing the pre-
revolutionary protests of the 1760s and 1770s. American women, basing

their arguments on the tenets of the Declaration of Independence and the Constitution, called for equal rights. When war was declared against England in 1812, thousands of Americans protested. African Americans fought as hard against racism as they did against slavery and resisted whites' efforts to return them to Africa. Workers took part in protest marches demanding the rights and privileges and opportunities they believed they were entitled to as American citizens; realizing that the only way to get better wages and safer working conditions was to make use of the power of their numbers, they began to form unions and initiate strikes. Of course, women were unable to gain equal rights, African Americans were unable to do away with slavery or racism, antiwar dissenters were unable to end the War of 1812, and workers were unable to get the ten-hour day. But the brave individuals who protested did make a difference by building the foundation for future feminist, antiwar, antislavery, and prolabor activists. And they all learned important lessons for the future.

CHAPTER 5

Slavery and Its Discontents

I have nothing more to offer than what General Washington
would have had to offer, had he been taken by the British and
put to trial by them. I have adventured my life in endeavour-
ing to obtain the liberty of my countrymen, and am a willing sacrifice in their cause: and I beg, as a favour, that I may
be immediately led to execution. I know that you have pre-
determined to shed my blood, why then all this mockery of
a trial?

—anonymous slave shortly before he was executed for
taking part in Gabriel Prosser's conspiracy, 1800

During the antebellum period cotton and slavery were central to the
nation's economic life, but the cotton kingdom was not a uniform,
homogeneous society. Most southern whites did not own slaves. Most
who did owned fewer than ten. The wealthy planters who owned the
large plantations and the large gangs of slaves of fifty or more represented less than 1 percent of the population. They were of course on
the top rung of southern society and enjoyed controlling the economic
and political life of the South and, to a lesser extent, the social and cultural life. Below the planter elite were the proprietors of small farms and
business entrepreneurs who owned fewer than ten slaves and usually
no more than five. Also the southern middle class consisted of nonslaveholding yeoman farmers who owned small farms, primarily in the
backcountry, who did all the work themselves. This middle class, both
slaveholding and nonslaveholding, accounted for the majority of southern whites. Below this group, living on the margins of southern society
on land that no one else wanted, were poor whites who owned virtually
nothing and who were, in some respects, hardly much better off than
the slaves.

Despite enduring the harshest of all possible conditions, living lives
of unending drudgery, and being overwhelmed with an incessant yearn-

108

ing to be free, slaves did not succumb to despair and passively submit to their fate. They developed a vibrant African American culture that has over the years influenced the United States as powerfully as has the dominant European culture that subjugated the continent. In a sense the slaves' creation of this distinct culture was a form of resistance, a form of dissent, against their circumstances. They were not giving up on life.

Masters, in order to secure more control and also to placate their own consciences, taught their slaves Christianity. When slaves were in attendance at the master's church (in a separate section at the back), sermons indoctrinated them in the virtues of work, and they were reminded over and over again of the biblical injunction that servants were to obey their masters and that Africans were descended from Noah's son Ham, who was cursed by God. But the Christianity the slaves absorbed was different from that of their masters. When slaves held religious services, they were far more emotional, more exuberant, and emphasized the biblical story of the ancient Israelites for the obvious reason that slaves could identify with the plight of the enslaved children of Israel. Usually the enslaved children of Africa adopted the denomination of their masters, most commonly Baptist and Methodist, but they also threw in a dose of African religion and belief. Elements of polytheism and voodoo seeped into slave Christianity. Frequent outbursts and joyful exclamations from the congregation accompanied sermons. There was hand clapping during the singing of hymns. There were spontaneous conversion experiences. Slave preachers continually retold the story of Moses taking his people to the Promised Land or the Lord calling his people home to dwell with him. The slaves used these images not only in their hopes for the afterlife but also for freedom now, or at least in the not-so-distant future. Masters who attended their slaves' services congratulated themselves on what a civilizing, Christianizing benefit slavery was, for how else could these children of Africa have come to know the Lord? Of course, most masters never caught on that what their slaves were preaching and singing about was deliverance from bondage in this life and not the hoped-for rewards of the next.

There were two main musical forms that were created by the slave experience: Negro spirituals and field hollers. The spirituals included such songs as "Swing Low, Sweet Chariot," "We Are Climbing Jacob's Ladder," "Go Down Moses," "Twelve Gates to the City," and hundreds

of others that were exuberant visions of freedom, expressions of longing for slaves' most desired goal. Songs expressed sorrow about being
"stolen from Africa," as well as joyful anticipation of a happy future.
Unlike the Negro spiritual, which has antecedents in European bal-
ladry and folk song, forms that tell stories, the field holler has deeper
African roots. Similar to the "call-and-response" form that abounded
in Africa, in which singers would call out a line of verse that would be
repeated by others, the field holler evolved during work hours. Field
hands found that singing helped get them through the long day. (It also
helped in synchronizing work that had to be coordinated.) Usually the
head field hand would take the lead and belt out a line, "Long John, he
done gone," and then the other field hands would repeat the line in a
rhythmic response. The type and pace of work the slaves were doing at
the time (hoeing, sowing, picking) determined the tempo of the song.

Musicologists and music historians have traced the roots of modern-
day blues to the field holler and of gospel music to the Negro spiritual.
After the abolition of slavery the themes of the songs had less to do
with the plight of African Americans as a group and more to do with
the individual's pain and misery, imposed by bosses or the composer's
romantic partner.

Naturally field hollers were sung a cappella, but slaves had plenty
of opportunity to become fine instrumentalists. They brought with
them from Africa the skill to make drums and banjos (originally called
banjar or *bangoc*). Drums were animal skins stretched over a frame;
the banjo was simply a gourd with a stick added, to which three (later
four) strings were attached. Eventually slaves began building a circular
frame with an animal skin stretched over it, much like a drum head.
The model of the original gourd banjo seems to have come from Gam-
bia in West Africa. During the antebellum period banjos were fretless.
Frets and a fifth string were not added until after the Civil War. (Today
most banjos have metal frames with synthetic, rather than animal-skin,
heads.) Some slaves also learned to play the violin and the guitar, and
most Saturday nights in the quarters were festive occasions of music,
singing, and dancing. They were determined to make the best of an
impossible situation.

Because most slaves were intentionally kept illiterate (masters certainly did not want their slaves to be able to read abolitionist literature or, heaven forbid, such pernicious doctrines as "all men are created

equal"), there was a very strong oral tradition within the slave community. Stories and fables of Africa were told and retold from one generation to the next (a custom that kept alive much of the African tradition). Slaves also invented new folk tales that they frequently used to entertain each other. These stories, which reveal a sophisticated intuitive wisdom, were an outlet for slaves to lampoon masters and overseers as well as implicitly to express a deep-seated rebelliousness toward the peculiar institution. Probably the best known of these tales are the Br'er Rabbit stories about the downtrodden con artist rabbit that, in the end, always seems to wind up one step ahead of his tormenters. The rabbit, of course, was the slave, the fox or tiger the master or overseer.

* * *

Although the United States prohibited the direct importation of slaves from Africa after January 1, 1808, the law was laxly enforced, and it was easy for traders to continue bringing slaves into the country. The historian John Hope Franklin estimates that 250,000 slaves were imported into the American South by smugglers along the unpatrolled coast. Moreover, there was a flourishing interstate slave trade that lasted all through the antebellum period right up to the Civil War. Much of this interstate trade was the movement of slaves from the Upper South to the Lower South. As the soil in the Tidewater areas of Virginia and Maryland as well as North Carolina lost its fertility, slavery became less profitable, and thousands of slaves were sold south, where the demand for slaves to work the cotton plantations was soaring. Conditions in Alabama, Mississippi, Louisiana, and East Texas were much harsher, and slaves were frequently treated with more brutality there. Masters in the Upper South made use of this knowledge, often exaggerating the rough treatment, as a tool to extract the maximum work out of their slaves. They would threaten slaves that if they did not work harder, they would be sold south. Indeed, this was often the case when masters finally gave up on slaves who persisted in defiance and rebelliousness and who were impervious to being whipped into submission. By the 1830s the internal slave trade was a multimillion-dollar enterprise. Slaves from the Upper South were usually transported to Alexandria, Virginia. From there they were shipped to the main depot in the Deep South, Natchez, Mississippi. Sometimes they were transported by ship to New Orleans and then upriver to Natchez, sometimes by railroad; sometimes they would be marched over land, chained together in coffles. As in any profit-making venture the traders attempted to maximize proceeds as much as possible. Before putting slaves up on the auction block they would take the older men and put black shoe polish in their gray hair and oil their wrinkled, withered skin so as to fool the potential buyer into thinking the slave was younger than he really was. By the 1840s the going price for a healthy field hand was anywhere from $500 to $1,700, depending on age. Young, sexually attractive women commanded higher prices. Slaves whose backs were scarred from numerous whippings (thus tipping off potential buyers that they were troublesome) went for less.

Masters were always cognizant that their slaves represented a significant financial investment, and this was the primary consideration in providing and caring for the slaves as well as punishing them. It was important to provide them with sufficient nutritional sustenance and medical care so that they would remain productive and healthy. Of course, in order to cut costs rations and medical care were kept at the bare minimum. If a dangerous job needed to be done on the plantation, such as building a dam over a snake-infested stream, masters were extremely reluctant to risk a field hand who might have cost $1,000 or more. For such jobs Irish immigrants were sometimes hired (for a dollar a day), and if an Irishman was bitten by a copperhead or water moccasin, the master would not have lost a valuable field hand.

Discipline was meted out with varying degrees of severity and cruelty. Punishments that left slaves incapacitated, mutilated, or handicapped meant that the master would have lost a great deal, or all, of a slave's productivity and value; nevertheless, severe infractions incurred severe penalties. The abolitionists Theodore Dwight Weld and Angelina and Sarah Grimké observed, in their polemical antislavery book *American Slavery as It Is* (1839), that masters treated slaves worse than animals because slaves were property with the discomfiting ability to be defiant, and defiance invariably incurred the master's rage no matter what the economic cost. Naturally, if a slave committed murder or rape, masters had no compunction about executing the person, but normally slaves would be whipped according to the seriousness of the offense. Slaves frequently suffered dozens of lashes for not working hard enough, stealing, lying, disobedience, and insubordination. Masters, on the whole, would rather punish for a slight infraction right away so as to set an example for other slaves and to make sure that a minor problem, if left unchecked, did not escalate into a major one. Whipping was the most common physical punishment; but also the stocks were used or branding, and sometimes masters set dogs on slaves to maul them.

Many slaves fought back when they were struck. Sylvia Dubois, for example, who worked as a slave in a Pennsylvania bar in the early nineteenth century, told her life story to a biographer after the Civil War. Her mistress, she recounted, "was the very devil himself": "Why, she'd level me with anything she could get hold of—club, stick of wood, tongs, fire-shovel, knife, axe, hatchet, anything that was handiest—and then she was so damned quick about it too. . . . Once she knocked me till I was so stiff that she thought I was dead. Once after that, because I was a little saucy, she leveled me with the fire-shovel and broke my pate. She thought I was dead then, but I wasn't." Sylvia vowed then and there that she would not take any more abuse. One day in 1808 her mistress ordered her to scrub the barroom, but Sylvia went about it half-heartedly; when her mistress scolded her for it, she talked back. For this her mistress slapped her. "Thinks I, it's a good time now to dress you out, and damned if I won't do it. I set down my tools and squared for a fight. The first whack, I struck her a hell of a blow with my fist. I didn't knock her entirely through the panels of the door, but her landing against the door made a terrible smash, and I hurt her so badly that all were frightened out of their wits, and I didn't know myself but that I'd killed the old devil." There were many people in the bar: "some of them were Jersey folks who were going from the Lake Countries home to visit their friends. Some were drovers on their way to the west. And some were hunters and boatmen staying a while to rest." They started toward Sylvia to restrain her. "They were going to take her [mistress's] part. . . . But I just sat down the slop bucket and straightened up, and smacked my fists at 'em, and told 'em to wade in if they dared and I'd thrash every devil of 'em, and there wasn't a damned a one that dared to come." Sylvia's master was so impressed with her audacity and courage that he actually freed her after this episode. As a free woman she moved to Hunterdon County, New Jersey, where she operated a tavern and lived for another eighty years dying at the age of 116 in 1889.[1]

Fighting back was one form of resistance. Running away was one of the most common. During the 1850s alone it is estimated that over one thousand slaves a year ran away. Most often slaves fled to a nearby plantation where their husband or wife or child had been sold in order to be reunited with their loved one. Masters would then send out a search party with dogs, and the fugitive would be caught within a day or two, brought back to the plantation, and punished as an example to the rest of the slaves. But numerous runaways did make it to freedom. Most of these were "passengers" on the Underground Railroad.

The Underground Railroad was a complex, sophisticated undertaking. Hundreds of people—free blacks, abolitionists, Quakers—participated in this effort to free the enslaved. Harriet Tubman, the most famous of all Underground Railroad conductors, escaped from a plantation in Maryland and managed to get to Philadelphia. Vowing to dedicate her life to the freeing of others, she returned to the South dozens of times, at great risk to herself, to escort slaves out of bondage. Usually she would arrive on a plantation at night, station herself outside the window of a slave hut, and whistle or hum a song such as "Swing Low, Sweet Chariot." This would be a signal to the slaves that someone was there to conduct them north. Not all slaves were willing to take the risk of running away, knowing as they did that being caught would mean severe punishment. Those who decided to make a break for it would travel with Tubman through the night. At daybreak they would find security in the "stations" along the way. Usually these were farmhouses of Quakers. Runaways recognized these stations by a light left burning in the window. During the day the "passengers" would rest in a suitable hiding place, such as the potato cellar, while the slave catchers were out and about hunting for the fugitives. At night again they would travel north, and this would be repeated for however long it took for them to get to a free state. Some even traveled to Canada, where the U.S. Fugitive Slave Law could not reach them. Crossing the Mason-Dixon line between Delaware and Pennsylvania or the Ohio River between Kentucky and Ohio was often a tense, scary experience. Quaker farmers would transport the runaways in the false bottoms of hay wagons. At the border intimidating guards would question travelers and search wagons, jabbing pitchforks into the hay to find concealed runaways. It is said that Tubman packed a pistol and told her passengers that if any of them got cold feet along the way, she would shoot them. She would not tolerate a slave turning back who would, when taken by the slave patrol, be coerced into revealing the identity of the conductors and the location of the safe houses along the way. A returning slave could jeopardize

Harriet Tubman with family and neighbors at her home in Auburn, New York. Photograph c. 1887 by William H. Cheney. (Public domain)

an entire network of the Underground Railroad. Evidently her passengers believed her because she never did shoot one of them.

Another way the enslaved rebelled was through shirking and sabotage, both effective methods of decreasing the profitability of slavery. Slaves would pretend not to understand the overseer's instructions, which meant that the overseer would have to spend an excessive amount of time showing, for example, how a field was to be hoed. If slaves were left alone for any amount of time, they frequently slowed their pace to a crawl, even at times stopping work. Rarely did they perform the tasks assigned to them with any diligence or perseverance. And everything they did to slow down production decreased the planter's profits. Slaves also resorted to sabotage by breaking equipment or machinery, burning down barns and sheds, or losing tools by dropping them into a pond or river. Household servants would sometimes serve their masters spoiled food hoping to get them sick. Some cooks even tried to poison their masters or put ground glass into the gravy. Of course, when an entire white family was sickened or died because of poison, the suspect was usually and quickly narrowed down to the cook. The most extreme form of sabotage was self-mutilation. After all, the slave was the master's most valuable property; if slaves mutilated themselves, they would decrease their value. One slave was told that he was going to be sold to Louisiana, and rather than suffering the emotional distress of separation from his family, the night before he was to be sold he made himself unsalable by chopping off his hand. This is also a rather gruesome indication of how terrified slaves were of being "sold down the river."

Fighting back, shirking, sabotage, stealing from the master, and even developing phony obsequious personalities, all these strategies were forms of dissent employed by people who were in an unbearable situation but who steadfastly refused to give up all hope. Some slaves went even further. Their resistance turned into outright rebellion.

* * *

Apologists for slavery right up to the mid-twentieth century maintained that slavery was not a cruel, immoral system but a benign institution with happy slaves living in comfort on plantations owned by kindly masters. If slavery was evil, they argued, then why were there so few rebellions? The historical record, however, reveals a different picture. True, there were not many large-scale rebellions and none that were successful, but there was constant, daily resistance in many forms by slaves all over the South, even by those with "kindly" masters. The fact that few rebellions took place and that they were put down quickly simply underscores the fact that slaves were well aware that open rebellion was suicidal. No matter how many weapons they could commandeer, a band of slaves would be no match for a well-armed, well-prepared militia.

While hundreds of individual slaves in the antebellum period courageously resisted their owners and while impromptu acts of rebellion sporadically flared up, there were several occasions when individual slaves designed plans for an uprising with the goal of destroying the peculiar institution. Two of these revolts were crushed before they could get off the ground. The last terrified southern whites so badly that they were never able to look at their slaves the same way again.

In 1800, as Toussaint Louverture's slave revolt in Haiti was nearing its successful conclusion, a twenty-five-year-old slave named Gabriel, who belonged to Thomas Prosser in Henrico County, Virginia, decided the time had come for Virginia's slaves to rise up and win their freedom. Gabriel was politically astute—co-coordinating his uprising with Louverture's—and evidently very charismatic. Many slaves in Henrico County looked to him as a leader. Along with two other slaves, George

Smith and Jack Bowler, Gabriel developed a strategy whereby they would lead slaves in a two-pronged attack. One group would destroy several buildings in Richmond, while the other would storm the state government houses and gain control of the armory. There they would arm themselves and recruit more slaves to join a statewide revolt. Their aim was to kill all the whites, except for Quakers, Methodists, and Frenchmen. Evidently they believed the Quakers and Methodists would be sympathetic to their cause, and they were aware that the United States was still involved in the undeclared Quasi-War with France. Some historians believe they had hopes that the French would come to the aid of their revolt. By the time of the designated day for the uprising, August 30, 1800, over one thousand slaves (some estimates run as high as seven thousand) were ready to move. Unfortunately a drenching rainstorm hit the Richmond area on the morning of the planned attack; and even worse for the plotters, a few slaves informed their masters of the impending uprising, and the state militia was put on alert. Gabriel decided to postpone the attack until the following day, but by the time one thousand slaves assembled on the thirty-first, armed with swords, knives, scythes, pitchforks, and a few guns, the state militia was ready for them. Dozens were arrested, while Gabriel escaped to Norfolk, where he was betrayed by another slave and brought back to Richmond to stand trial. At the trial he remained silent and refused to testify against any of his coplotters. Gabriel and fifteen others were hanged on October 7. By the time the executions ended, thirty-five slaves were hanged for the conspiracy.

Eleven years after Gabriel Prosser's abortive uprising an unplanned, spontaneous revolt broke out on a Louisiana plantation owned by Major Andry. As word rapidly spread from plantation to plantation, five hundred slaves gathered together and joined the insurgents. They had no guns, but with axes, hatchets, clubs, and knives made out of sugarcane stalks they attacked whites. Major Andry was wounded, and his son killed; then the slaves set out to attack other plantations. There is no telling how far they would have gone, but the state militia, bolstered by the U.S. Army arrived, killed scores of the rebels, and ended the uprising. At a subsequent trial sixteen slaves were condemned and executed.

Another eleven years went by before Denmark Vesey of Charleston, South Carolina, decided it was time for him to act. Vesey had purchased his freedom in 1800 with $600 of the $1,500 he had won in a lottery.

With the rest of the money he set himself up in the carpentry business. Vesey became a respected member of the Charleston community, and it is quite clear that he could have lived out his days as a free man and a successful carpenter; but he despised the institution of slavery and personally hated the master who refused to let Vesey buy his wife's freedom. Over the years he began urging the slaves of Charleston to rise up in rebellion. He took to denigrating and ridiculing them that they were too submissive, that they were spineless, and that they must fight for their freedom. By 1822 he recruited a core group to organize a revolt. Historians have estimated that as many as nine thousand slaves joined the plot to seize weapons at the armory, take possession of Charleston, burn the city to the ground, free the slaves, and set sail for Haiti. But, like Gabriel's Rebellion, too many people were in on the plot, and Vesey was betrayed by some of the conspirators. The insurrection was scheduled for July 14, 1822, but Vesey and his lieutenants were rounded up before it could unfold. On June 23 Vesey and forty-six others were hanged, and during the ensuing weeks scores of slaves, many of whom were not even involved in the plot, were summarily executed by nervous whites.

From the earliest days that slavery was introduced into the American colonies, there was always the fear lurking in the back of every slaveholder's mind of a slave rebellion. After all, by the 1830s in some states slaves outnumbered whites, and even in those states where they did not, they made up a substantial proportion of the population. The thought of slaves ever uniting and finding a way to arm themselves never ceased to send a jolt of fear pulsating through slaveholders' veins. In the immediate aftermath of the foiling of both Gabriel Prosser's and Denmark Vesey's Rebellions southern anxiety grew, and efforts were made by southern states to create and enforce more vigorous slave codes to regulate slaves' behavior and to put additional restrictions on the manumission of slaves. In 1831, however, a slave rebellion took place in Southampton County, Virginia, that actually did get off the ground, creating so much terror in the hearts of white southerners that the state legislatures studied and reevaluated all the laws that were intended to keep slaves submissive.

Nat Turner was born in 1800, the year of Jefferson's election and Gabriel's Rebellion. He was first owned by Samuel Turner; but no matter what master he served under he seemed like a model slave, and his masters gave him a smidgen of independence. Turner was a religious man, studied the Bible, and often preached to other slaves. He experienced, during his short life, three visions that God was preparing him for some special mission. He described one of them this way: "While labouring in the field, I discovered drops of blood on the corn, as though it were dew from heaven—and I communicated it to many, both white and black, in the neighbourhood—and then I found on the leaves in the woods hieroglyphic characters and numbers, with the forms of men in different attitudes, portrayed in blood, and representing the figures I had seen before in the heavens." Later, when he was twenty-eight, a third vision convinced him that he was put on earth to carry out God's plan:

> I heard a loud noise in the heavens, and the Spirit instantly appeared to me and said the Serpent was loosened, and Christ had laid down the yoke he had borne for the sins of men, and that I should take it on and fight against the Serpent, for the time was fast approaching when the first should be last and the last should be first. . . . And by signs in the heavens that it would make known to me when I should commence the great work, and until the first sign appeared I should conceal it from the knowledge of men—And on the appearance of the sign . . . I should arise and prepare myself and slay my enemies with their own weapons.[2]

In February 1831 there was a solar eclipse, and Turner interpreted this as the sign that the time had come. He now brought in several other slaves and revealed his intention to lead a slave revolt. After agreeing to support him, they decided that July 4 would be the day for the insurrection. But in early July Turner fell ill, and they postponed it to August. This time, however, unlike 1800 and 1822, when thousands of slaves were part of the conspiracy, none of Turner's few trusted lieutenants betrayed the plot. On the hot, humid night of August 21 they acted. At two a.m. Turner and six of his men sneaked into the house of his master, Joseph Travis, and as Turner related in his confession (dictated to Thomas Gray, who most likely embellished Turner's account),

> It was then observed that I must spill the first blood. On which, armed with a hatchet, and accompanied by Will, I entered my master's chamber;

it being dark, I could not give a death blow, the hatchet glanced from his head, he sprang from the bed and called his wife, it was his last word. Will laid him dead, with a blow of his axe, and Mrs. Travis shared the same fate, as she lay in bed. . . . There was a little infant sleeping in a cradle, that was forgotten, until we had left the house and gone some distance, when Henry and Will returned and killed it.

Then the killing spree began. For the next twenty-four hours they traveled from plantation to plantation, killing whites, arming themselves with the planters' weapons, and recruiting about forty additional slaves to join the uprising. "We started . . . for Mrs. Reese's, maintaining the most perfect silence on our march, where finding the door unlocked, we entered, and murdered Mrs. Reese in her bed, while sleeping; her son awoke, but it was only to sleep the sleep of death, he had only time to say who is that, and he was no more." After this, Turner and his band of men went to another plantation a mile away.

Henry, Austin, and Sam, went to the still, where, finding Mr. Peeples, Austin shot him, and the rest of us went to the house; as we approached, the family discovered us, and shut the door. Vain hope! Will, with one stroke of his axe, opened it, and we entered and found Mrs. Turner and Mrs. Newsome in the middle of a room, almost frightened to death. Will immediately killed Mrs. Turner, with one blow of his axe. I took Mrs. Newsome by the hand, and . . . struck her several blows over the head.

By this time Turner had collected about twenty slaves, who joined with him on his march to the Whitehead farm.

As we approached the house we discovered Mr. Richard Whitehead standing in the cotton patch, near the lane fence; we called him over into the lane, and Will, the executioner, was near at hand, with his fatal axe, to send him to an untimely grave. . . . As I came round to the door I saw Will pulling Mrs. Whitehead out of the house, and at the step he nearly severed her head from her body, with his broad axe. Miss Margaret, when I discovered her, had concealed herself in the corner, formed by the projection of cellar cap from the house; on my approach she fled, but was soon overtaken, and after repeated blows with a sword, I killed her by a blow on the head, with a fence rail.[3]

Turner's Rebellion, 1831. "Horrid Massacre in Virginia." Woodcut. (Public domain; courtesy Library of Congress)

By the time the rebels neared the town of Jerusalem, word had spread throughout the county, and they found themselves confronted by a substantial militia force. Shots were fired, and Turner's men scattered to the woods. The next morning they attacked another house but again were confronted by the militia, and in the ensuing fight several slaves were captured. By this time state and federal forces arrived, and a firefight broke out. One rebel was killed and many captured, while Turner and a number of others fled. Whites were horrified that when the death toll was counted, it was discovered that fifty-five whites, including women and children, had been shot, stabbed, and hacked to death, and no one knew where Nat Turner had gone. For the next two months, while masters all over the South spent sleepless, anxious nights with pistols under their pillow (one slaveholder even died of a heart attack, which his neighbors attributed to his fear that Turner would creep into his bedroom and cut his throat), a massive manhunt to find Turner was set in motion. Finally, on October 30, he was discovered hiding out in a cave not far from his master's house.

When Turner was asked at his trial how he pled, he replied, "Not guilty," not because he did not commit the murders of which he was accused but because he did not *feel* guilty about having committed them. He felt justified for he had carried out God's will. He was condemned to death and on November 11 hanged and skinned. More than fifty other slaves were also executed for taking part in the rebellion, and in the aftermath white gangs murdered about two hundred other slaves who had nothing to do with the insurrection.

Nat Turner's Rebellion shook southerners to the core. Throughout the South state legislatures put more teeth into the slave codes, ordered masters to exercise much more stringent control over their slaves, and strengthened their state militias (in Virginia alone 10 percent of the entire state's population was formally registered in the militia). What was particularly unnerving for whites was that Nat Turner acknowledged during his confession (perhaps under coercion) that his master was a kind man who allowed him a degree of liberty on the plantation that most slaves did not experience. Southerners, believing in their benevolent paternalism, convinced that slavery was a positive good for African Americans, who would otherwise be unable to care for themselves, were distressed to grasp that no matter how kind they thought they were, no matter how well they believed they treated their slaves, and no matter how obedient and seemingly happy their slaves appeared to be, the slaves were inwardly seething with hatred and, given half a chance, would gladly rise up and murder their masters. What most slaveholders failed to realize was that there was nothing redeeming about slavery, nothing redeeming about denying freedom to a human being. The words *kindness* and *slavery* cannot coexist in the same sentence.

In the wake of the Vesey and Turner revolts proslavery southerners blamed blacks' discontent on antislavery northern agitators, for Vesey and Turner's rebellions were not the only cause for southerners' sleepless nights. Earlier in 1831 a balding, unimposing young man began publishing a newspaper in faraway Boston with a message demanding the immediate and unconditional abolition of slavery. His message, and the way he presented it, compounded southerners' worst fears.

The South would never be the same again.

* * *

The antislavery crusade of the nineteenth century was perhaps the largest, certainly the most important, mass dissent movement in this nation's history. As we have seen, there were many activists—primarily Quakers, humanitarians, and free blacks—who called for the abolition of slavery before the Revolution and during the early years of the new republic. In the 1820s the American Colonization Society advocated the gradual abolition of slavery and the transportation of freed slaves back to Africa. By the end of that decade, however, those who opposed slavery adopted a new line of attack. Disdaining the idea of gradualism, they began calling for the immediate and complete elimination of slavery. Thousands of Americans, moved by the passionate arguments of hundreds of white and black abolitionists, examined their consciences and threw themselves into the antislavery cause. In a variety of ways, from moderate opposition to radical activists consciously breaking the law, and for a variety of reasons, moral, religious, political, and economic, hundreds of thousands of Americans called on the United States to repeal all laws sustaining slavery. Not enough lawmakers listened, and a dissent movement that began as a nonviolent protest to abolish the peculiar institution ended in the bloodiest war in the nation's history.

David Walker, a free black living in Boston, was one of the first to have an impact on the radicalization of the abolitionist movement. In the 1820s he moved from North Carolina to Boston, where he became the proprietor of a clothing shop, became a leader in the African American community, and cofounded the Massachusetts General Colored Association. He also distributed *Freedom's Journal*, the first African American national newspaper. In 1829 he published an incendiary pamphlet titled *Appeal to the Coloured Citizens of the World*, in which he attacked both slavery and racism. Walker's *Appeal* sent shockwaves through the nation. "America is more our country than it is the whites'—we have enriched it with our *blood and tears*," he wrote. "The whites want slaves, and want us for their slaves, but some of them will curse the day they ever saw us." If whites did not abolish slavery, then slaves should rise up and cut their masters' throats. "Kill, or be killed." Appealing to heaven, Walker declared,

> We, (colored people of these United States of America) are the *most wretched, degraded* and abject set of beings that ever *lived* since the world began, and that the white Americans having reduced us to the

wretched state of *slavery*, treat us in that condition *more cruel* (they being an enlightened and christian people,) than any heathen nation did any people whom it had reduced to our condition.[4]

How is it possible that a nation that prides itself on its Christian heritage would be so sinful as to commit the crime of slavery?

I have been for years troubling the pages of historians, to find out what our fathers have done to the *white Christians of America*, to merit such condign punishment as they have inflicted on them, and do continue to inflict on us their children. But I must aver, that my researches have hitherto been to no effect. I have therefore, come to the immovable conclusion, that they (Americans) have, and do continue to punish us for nothing else, but for enriching them and their country.[5]

The time has come for blacks to cast off the shackles that enslave them, both literally and metaphorically. Slavery cannot exist if slaves refused to submit to the institution.

Are we MEN!!—I ask you, O my brethren! are we MEN? Did our creator make us to be slaves to dust and ashes like ourselves? Are they not dying worms as well as we? Have they not to make their appearance before the tribunal of heaven, to answer for the deeds done in the body, as well as we? Have we any other master but Jesus Christ alone? Is he not their master as well as ours? What right then, have we to obey and call any other master, but Himself? How we could be so *submissive* to a gang of men, whom we cannot tell whether they are as *good* as ourselves or not, I never could conceive. However, this is shut up with the Lord, and we cannot precisely tell—but I declare, we judge men by their works.

The whites have always been an unjust, jealous, unmerciful, avaricious and blood-thirsty set of beings, always seeking after power and authority.[6]

Southerners were so outraged when they discovered that abolitionists were smuggling the pamphlet into the South that they put a price on Walker's head. Although Walker's pamphlet was inflammatory, his goal was reform, not an insurrection. His hope and emphasis was to combine a northern black culture of reform with a southern culture of resistance that would ultimately lead to slavery's demise. Walker's

Appeal marks the transition from moderate antislavery protests to the far more inflammatory, and sometimes fanatical, antislavery protests of William Lloyd Garrison, the Grimké sisters, Elijah Lovejoy, Frederick Douglass, John Brown, and numerous others. Southerners were convinced that Nat Turner had been inspired by Walker's *Appeal*, and now, added to their fears of a slave revolt, was the specter of radical northerners inducing slaves to commit murder.

The year Nat Turner's Rebellion sent a shudder of terror through the South, William Lloyd Garrison began publication of his antislavery newspaper, the *Liberator*. Garrison is an intriguing figure in American history. Early on he wrote for an antislavery newspaper in Baltimore that advocated gradual emancipation and the colonization of blacks in Africa, but he became so disillusioned with the idea of eliminating slavery only gradually that he moved to Boston and started his own newspaper. In the very first issue of the *Liberator*, January 1, 1831, Garrison trumpeted his new stance for all to hear. Condemning gradualism and colonization, he called for immediate abolition as well as the "immediate enfranchisement of our slave population."

> I am aware, that many object to the severity of my language; but is there not cause for severity? I *will be* as harsh as truth, and as uncompromising as justice. On this subject, I do not wish to think, or speak, or write, with moderation. No! No! Tell a man whose house is on fire, to give a moderate alarm; tell him to moderately rescue his wife from the hands of the ravisher; tell the mother to gradually extricate her babe from the fire into which it has fallen;—but urge me not to use moderation in a cause like the present. I am in earnest—I will not equivocate—I will not excuse—I will not retreat a single inch—AND I WILL BE HEARD.[7]

The newspaper had a wide distribution in the North, and within a year Garrison founded the New England Antislavery Society in Boston and in 1833 the American Antislavery Society. Within a few years nearly fifty antislavery societies were organized in New York, Philadelphia, Michigan, Ohio, Indiana, and other northern states. By 1840 the total membership of these local groups numbered more than one hundred thousand.

It was not only the intensity of Garrison's views that so alarmed southern slaveholders but also the uncompromising nature of his language. There was no give to the man, and his adversaries were frightened. Southern states also offered rewards for Garrison's capture, trial, and conviction. In 1835 a proslavery mob snatched him, put a rope around his neck, and dragged him through the streets of Boston with the intention of lynching him. The mayor saved his life by having him arrested and thrown into jail for safekeeping. Garrison, undaunted, wrote on the wall of his cell, "Wm. Lloyd Garrison was put into this cell Wednesday afternoon, October 21, 1835, to save him from the violence of a 'respectable and influential' mob, who sought to destroy him for preaching the abominable and dangerous doctrine that 'all men are created equal.'"[8] By the 1850s Garrison was one of the most radical and controversial men in America. On the fourth of July 1854 he went so far that he publicly burned a copy of the U.S. Constitution in Boston Common. It was, he proclaimed, "an agreement with death and a covenant with hell."[9]

Sarah and Angelina Grimké were born into a prosperous South Carolina slaveholding family. Seeing slavery firsthand as they grew up soon taught them the evils of the institution, and their trips to the North further fostered their antislavery sentiments. In the 1820s they moved to Philadelphia, converted to Quakerism, and joined the abolitionist movement. The sisters came to national attention after Garrison published one of Angelina's letters in the *Liberator*. Soon they were traveling about the country speaking at antislavery meetings and writing antislavery pamphlets. In 1836 Angelina wrote an appeal to southern women to join the abolition crusade, not just because slavery was evil in and of itself but because so many slave owners were sexually abusing female slaves and fathering so many children that it was destroying the sanctity of marriage and family life in the South. Slavery, she argued, was not only destroying African Americans; it was also another form of male domination over women. This pamphlet created an uproar, not only because of its linking slavery with the oppression of women but also because a woman wrote it. Women in the 1830s were not expected to be so outspoken, especially about such an explosive issue, and both Angelina and Sarah, the more outspoken they became, the more they found themselves criticized, even by other abolitionists. The Grimkés were the only white southern women who embraced the immediate abolition of slavery, exiled themselves, and wound up becoming feminist pioneers.

Calling slavery a violent institution, "a national sin" that would inevitably lead to bloodshed, Angelina urged southern women to rise up and join the abolitionist crusade before it was too late.

> If Southern women sit down in listless indifference and criminal idleness, public opinion cannot be rectified and purified at the South. It is manifest to every reflecting mind, that slavery must be abolished; the era in which we live, and the light which is overspreading the whole world on this subject, clearly show that the time cannot be distant when it will be done. Now there are only two ways in which it can be effected, by moral power or physical force, and it is for *you* to choose which you prefer. Slavery always has, and always will produce insurrections, wherever it exists, because it is a violation of the natural order of things, and no human power can much longer perpetuate it. The opposers of abolitionists fully believe this; one of them remarked to me not long since, there is no doubt there will be a most terrible overturning at the South in a few years, such cruelty and wrong, must be visited with divine vengeance soon. Abolitionists believe, too, that this must inevitably be the case if you do not repent, and they are not willing to leave you to perish without entreating you, to save yourselves from destruction.

"There is nothing to fear," she concluded, "from immediate Emancipation, but *every thing* from the consequences of slavery."[10]

During the religious revivals of the 1820s Theodore Dwight Weld fell under the spell of the evangelist Charles G. Finney. After much soul searching Weld had a conversion experience and dedicated his life to preaching the gospel. In the 1830s, as he led revivals in Ohio and western New York, he was swept up in the spirit of reform that was arising. And the biggest issue that captured his attention was slavery. At revival meetings Weld would deliver emotional sermons about the evils of slavery and about the immoral, sinful treatment of slaves and then exhort members of the audience to "come forward" and commit themselves to abolitionism. In 1834 the trustees of Lane Theological Seminary in Cincinnati, Ohio, banned him from preaching his antislavery message at the seminary. This attempt to censor him led Weld to lead a mass walkout of students. These "Lane Rebels" became a significant core group of abolitionists that later founded Oberlin College as a center for the antislavery movement.

Arthur and Lewis Tappan were wealthy New York merchants who financed the publication and distribution of abolitionist literature. Elijah P. Lovejoy operated an abolitionist press in Alton, Illinois, until one night a proslavery mob descended on his office and murdered him. Sojourner Truth was a former slave who traveled the country giving speeches denouncing slavery and supporting feminism. Wendell Phillips was an exceptionally eloquent orator who delivered hundreds of lectures calling for the end of slavery and denouncing the violence of the proslavery forces that intimidated, attacked, beat, and even, as in Lovejoy's case, murdered abolitionists. In an 1851 speech transcendentalist philosopher Ralph Waldo Emerson condemned the controversial Fugitive Slave Law that made it compulsory for state governments, even in states where slavery was abolished, to capture and return to their owners fugitive slaves seeking asylum in a free state. According to Emerson, such a law is immoral, and "an immoral law makes it a man's duty to break it, at every hazard. For Virtue is the very self of every man. It is, therefore, a principle of law, that an immoral contract is void, and that an immoral statute is void, for, as laws do not make right, but are simply declaratory of a right which already existed, it is not to be presumed that they can so stultify themselves, as to command injustice." The crux of the Fugitive Slave Law is that it "is a statute which enacts the crime of kidnapping,—a crime on one footing with arson and murder." Therefore it is clear that such a law is wrong and even goes against the most basic principle on which the United States was founded: "A man's right to liberty," Emerson declared, "is as inalienable as his right to life. . . . If our resistance to this law, is not right, there is no right."[11]

Frederick Douglass escaped from slavery on the Underground Railroad in 1838, and shortly after his arrival in New England he met William Lloyd Garrison. Almost immediately the two men became friends, and Douglass started accompanying Garrison to antislavery gatherings. Extremely intelligent and articulate, Douglass mesmerized audiences with his speeches. He would introduce himself as a "thief" who had "stolen this head, these limbs" from his master when he ran away. Plagued by fears that he might be apprehended in the North and sent back into slavery, he saved some of the money he made from his speaking engagements, and when he had enough, he sent the money to his master to purchase his freedom. Later he wrote his agitprop

Frederick Douglass, 1856. "There is not a nation
on the earth guilty of practices more shocking and
bloody than are the people of the United States,
at this very hour." Ambrotype, photographer
unknown. (Public domain; courtesy National Portrait Gallery, Smithsonian Institution)

Autobiography, published the abolitionist newspaper the *North Star*,
became influential in organizing black regiments during the Civil War,
and championed voting and civil rights for African Americans after the
war. In 1852, when Douglass was invited to speak at a Fourth of July celebration in Rochester, New York, he used the occasion to present one of
his most acerbic commentaries on the hypocrisy of the United States.
Douglass held back nothing. "What, to the American slave, is your 4th
of July?" he asked rhetorically.

I answer; a day that reveals to him, more than all other days in the year, the gross injustice and cruelty to which he is the constant victim. To him, your celebration is a sham; your boasted liberty, an unholy license; your national greatness, swelling vanity; your sounds of rejoicing are empty and heartless; your denunciation of tyrants, brass fronted impudence; your shouts of liberty and equality, hollow mockery; your prayers and hymns, your sermons and thanksgivings, with all your religious parade and solemnity, are, to Him, mere bombast, fraud, deception, impiety, and hypocrisy—a thin veil to cover up crimes which would disgrace a nation of savages. There is not a nation on the earth guilty of practices more shocking and bloody than are the people of the United States, at this very hour.

Go where you may, search where you will, roam through all the monarchies and despotisms of the Old World, travel through South America, search out every abuse, and when you have found the last, lay your facts by the side of the everyday practices of this nation, and you will say with me, that, for revolting barbarity and shameless hypocrisy, America reigns without a rival.[12]

Many abolitionists were keenly aware that slavery was not the only cruelty African Americans had to suffer. Racism and racial violence was just as prevalent in the North as it was in the South, and the plight of free blacks was nearly as bad as that of slaves. As Martin Delany, a free black living in Pennsylvania, toured the North delivering antislavery speeches in the 1840s, he frequently encountered the ugly face of racism. People called him "nigger," he was nearly tarred and feathered in an Ohio town, and when he was accepted to Harvard Medical School in 1850, he was told that he could only study at Harvard on condition that he practice medicine in Africa when he got his degree. On top of all that white students refused to attend classes if blacks were admitted. These experiences expanded Delany's activism from antislavery to protesting racism and motivated him to write a book advocating black nationalism. In *The Condition, Elevation, Emigration and Destiny of the Colored People of the United States* Delany called on blacks to relocate to Africa and establish a society in which they would have complete power over their own lives and destinies. It was not just slavery that kept African Americans down, Delany wrote, but the entire racist system that existed in the United States. "Were we content to remain as we are, sparsely interspersed among our white fellow-countrymen, we might never be expected to equal them in any honorable or respectable competition for a livelihood." The only option for blacks was to empower themselves. "No people can be free who themselves do not constitute an essential part of the *ruling element* of the country in which they live." Only by controlling their own fate would blacks win the respect of whites. "The claims of no people, according to established policy and usage, are respected by any nation, until they are presented in a national capacity."[13]

* * *

Chafing at the attacks on the peculiar institution, southerners launched a campaign to prove to the world, and perhaps to themselves, that slavery was not an evil, immoral institution but a positive good. William Harper, Thomas R. Dew, and other apologists published proslavery pamphlets and books that were widely read and discussed. Africans, they argued, were like children who lacked the tools to survive in America unless they were supervised by kindly, paternalistic masters who, like good fathers, would instruct them how to get by in this world. Slaves needed slavery because they were unfit for the competitive marketplace. The Bible was also used as an elaborate apology for slavery. Southern preachers and theologians scoured the Bible for passages in which slaves appeared or that could be construed as a divine sanction for slavery. The curses that God put on Cain and Ham were often interpreted as his curse on the entire black race, and the word "servants" in the injunction that they must obey their masters was taken to mean "slaves"; and because it was in the Bible, it meant that God approved of slavery. Biblical arguments, however, can be used both ways, and abolitionists found numerous verses that they threw back at the proslavery forces, verses that they interpreted as divine condemnation of slavery.

Southerners also used economic arguments, mixed with a dose of Jeffersonianism, to support slavery. Slavery was good, they argued, because it enabled a large area of the United States to remain agrarian in the face of the assault of the industrial revolution. Slavery would help preserve all that is good in the American character, whereas the industrialization of the North has already shown the evils attending manufacturing. Southerners saw themselves as the preservers of a great tradition. Perhaps the most potent proslavery argument was the

comparison with northern wageworkers. It was no secret that northern industrialists exploited and oppressed their workers as much as
they could get away with. The factory system, southerners argued, was
worse than slavery. People were worked to death for a bare subsistence
wage, which barely gave them enough money for food and rent. And if
a worker fell sick, got injured, or grew too old, he was out of a job and
invariably fell into abject poverty. Slaves, on the other hand, were not
thrown to the wolves when they lost their productivity. There is some
truth to southerners' criticism of working conditions for free laborers in
the North. However, their critique does not take into consideration the
obvious fact that northern workers were free. At least they had basic
civil rights and had legal protection for themselves and their families.

*   *   *

As cotton became king, the American economy flourished. But the
prosperity the nation enjoyed was made possible only partly by American ingenuity and industriousness. The economy benefited significantly
from the labor of an unfree workforce. White Americans, North and
South, prospered, while African Americans suffered under unendurable
conditions. Yet they endured—not only endured but developed a vibrant
culture and never gave up the hope that freedom would one day come.
Some slaves adapted, some resisted, some rose up in open rebellion.

As slavery expanded, so too did an aggressive antislavery crusade.
Whites and free blacks protested that slavery undermined American
democracy and that it was the duty of the nation to abolish the peculiar institution. Abolitionism grew to be the most important reform
movement of the antebellum years, but other reform movements also
emerged at this time. More and more Americans, with an unshakable
faith in the vision of a democratic America, took up the challenge to
eradicate the inequalities and ills that plagued American society.

CHAPTER 6

Reformers and Dissidents

The mass of men serve the state thus, not as men mainly, but as machines, with their bodies. They are the standing army, and the militia, jailers, constables, posse comitatus, etc. In most cases there is no free exercise whatever of the judgement or of the moral sense; but they put themselves on a level with wood and earth and stones; and wooden men can perhaps be manufactured that will serve the purpose as well. Such command no more respect than men of straw or a lump of dirt. . . . Yet such as these even are commonly esteemed good citizens. Others—as most legislators, politicians, lawyers, ministers, and office-holders—serve the state chiefly with their heads; and, as they rarely make any moral distinctions, they are as likely to serve the devil, without intending it, as God. A very few—as heroes, patriots, martyrs, reformers in the great sense, and men—serve the state with their consciences also, and so necessarily resist it for the most part; and they are commonly treated as enemies by it.
—Henry David Thoreau,
"Resistance to Civil Government," 1847

As the industrial revolution was ushering an era of great change, and while Andrew Jackson was immersed in the political dramas of nullification, Indian removal, and the war on the Second National Bank of the United States, a tidal wave of reform began to sweep over the country. Partially stimulated by the Second Great Awakening and the enthusiasm generated by the surge of American nationalism, a new spirit was abroad in the land. The optimistic belief that the American experiment in democracy elevated the common man to heights hitherto unattainable by ordinary people convinced many Americans that human suffering could be alleviated through human ingenuity. It was painfully obvious, however, that not everyone was enjoying the fruits of liberty.

The experiences of the Cherokee on the Trail of Tears and African Americans in bondage were nagging examples that "equality" was no more than a platitude. As we have seen, ever larger numbers of Americans were protesting against slavery, and this burgeoning abolitionist movement profoundly affected how Americans thought of themselves. Concurrent with the antislavery movement Americans began championing other causes: laborers sought better wages and working conditions; educators called for universal education; humanitarians lobbied to reform prisons and asylums; women demanded the right to vote and laws restricting the use of alcohol. The winds of change blowing over the land stirred up a new spirit of dissent.

Some reformers were inspired by religious revivalism and the belief that every man, woman, and child was equal in the eyes of God, regardless of race or class. Some were inspired by the secular philosophy of the Romantic movement and its distinctive American spin-off: transcendentalism. Others, hoping to expand democracy and make America more inclusive, applied the ideas of French socialism in establishing alternative utopian communities to experiment with new ways of living.

* * *

The Second Great Awakening, which began at the turn of the century, flared up again in the mid-1820s. Once again thousands of Americans flocked to churches in towns and tents at camp meetings to hear itinerant preachers exhorting them to dedicate (or rededicate) their lives to Christ. Untold thousands were overwhelmed by the enormity of their sins and accepted Jesus Christ as their personal savior. Once again the revivals were a leveling experience that brought men and women of all races and classes together and reinforced the popular notion that the United States was truly a democracy. From the late 1820s into the 1840s evangelists such as Charles Grandison Finney touched thousands of hearts. Finney's evangelical message was that individuals were capable of making a conscious effort to open themselves to Christ's mercy. And if only they did so, he would listen and grant them eternal salvation. Finney was a mesmerizing preacher who brought audiences to tears with his emotional fervor while simultaneously appealing to their reason with the rational arguments of an attorney.

Finney and other evangelists not only preached the message of salvation but also condemned such social evils as greed, alcohol, political corruption, and the maltreatment of fellow human beings. Faith, moral virtue, and dedicated work, they claimed, could, with God's help, reform America. Such messages promising a better life in the hereafter attracted thousands of men and women from all classes and races. The belief that the individual's soul could be saved not only gave hope for one's spiritual salvation but also underscored the conviction that the individual had some control over making life better in the here and now. If a person could achieve salvation in the future through the act of accepting Jesus Christ as personal savior, then each individual could also act to effect changes in the present. This conviction was strengthened with the importation of two new ideas arriving from Europe: French utopian socialism and Romanticism. These philosophies addressed the human condition and the grave injustices that kept the United States from living up to its democratic ideals. Together the ideas of socialism, Romanticism, and personal salvation came together to ignite and give strength to a wide variety of dissent movements.

* * *

As the industrial revolution transformed Europe and the United States, many intellectuals expressed alarm at the widespread abuses that seemed the handmaiden of industrial capitalism. Led by the French philosophers Joseph Proudhon and Charles Fourier, European socialists called for a new political/economic approach to government in which the people, through the government, controlled the means of production and the distribution of wealth. Proudhon's famous dictum "*Property is theft*" confronted the fact that industrialists accumulated their wealth and their property by paying their workers no more than subsistence wages.[1] Labor is the most significant cost in production, and thus it is essential for capitalists to keep wages as low as possible in order to maximize profit. In effect Proudhon argued that profit is money stolen from workers' pockets and that the government could alleviate poverty and suffering by controlling industry and redistributing profits more equitably. Another socialist was Fourier, who advocated *phalanxes* (communes) in an effort to solve the inequalities inherent in capitalism. A socialist commune, in which property is held in common and in which the participants, both men and women, share all work equally, would be the basis for a truly egalitarian society. Fourier claimed that capitalism penetrated so deeply into every aspect of society, even into

personal relationships, that marriage was nothing but legalized prostitution. By this he meant that there were so few educational and
employment opportunities for women in the early nineteenth century
that it was impossible for a woman to survive unless she married a wage
earner. In effect she made a bargain with a man to provide sex and bear
children in exchange for room and board.

French utopian socialist ideas and communal experiments had a significant impact in Europe, most notably at midcentury when Karl Marx
and Friedrich Engels wrote *The Communist Manifesto* and later when
Marx wrote *Das Kapital.* (Marx considered socialists too naïve in their
expectation that they could achieve their goals through reform. Such
change, Marx believed, could only come through the complete overthrow of the capitalist system.)

An artistic and more idealistic response to industrialism was another
European movement that began in the late eighteenth century. The
Romantic movement was a reaction to the rationality of the Enlightenment. The Enlightenment emphasized reason, science, materialism,
and logic, whereas Romanticism argued that such an emphasis ignored
the very real and important role of the emotions, creativity, and spirituality in human experience. To the Romantics it was futile to try to
understand life by dissecting, destroying, and analyzing. The scientific
method, Romantics claimed, meant that in order to understand a bird
you dissect it and examine how its organs work to create life, and in so
doing you wind up with a dead bird. To the Romantics the best way to
understand a bird is to watch it fly, listen to its song, observe it building its nest. "Sweet is the lore which nature brings," the English poet
William Wordsworth wrote. "Our meddling intellect / Mis-shapes the
beauteous forms of things:— / We murder to dissect."[2] Life, ultimately,
is unknowable, and those who seek to know everything are misguided.
There is perfection in what is unknown. Not knowing preserves the
mystery of life. And this is as it should be. This is good.

Enlightenment philosophy led to the industrial revolution, the triumph of technology, and the attempt to conquer nature. Romantic
artists, musicians, poets, and philosophers sought to restore spirituality, emotion, and the mystery of life; they sought to know themselves
through nature and through tapping into their creative instincts; they
sought self-realization. By the 1830s these ideas were gaining ground
in the United States, where many American writers and poets took to

this more intuitive worldview. From James Fennimore Cooper idolizing the woodsman to Edgar Allan Poe writing about the darker impulses of human nature, writers put their own, American, imprint on Romanticism. The poet Walt Whitman focused on the positive achievements of democracy and the way America elevated the common man, while the novelist Herman Melville wrote about the negative side of the quest for self-knowledge when it becomes obsessive and leads to self-destruction. And in Concord, Massachusetts, the Romantic movement evolved into a compelling individualistic philosophy that became the wellspring of American dissent then and well into the future: transcendentalism.

Ralph Waldo Emerson, Margaret Fuller, and Henry David Thoreau formed the core of a new way of looking at the individual's place in the world. Emerson claimed that there are two forms of knowledge: understanding and reason. Understanding is externally imposed knowledge — the knowledge we get through formal education and books — whereas reason is the innate, intuitive capacity that each individual has for recognizing truth and beauty. To Emerson reason is the highest human faculty. It is in intuitive awareness where our wisdom lies. He argued that in order to live a meaningful life each individual must strive to transcend the narrow confines of externally imposed knowledge and cultivate this intuitive wisdom. Learning a discipline, such as biology or mathematics, is important, but such knowledge is limited. Deeper insight, higher wisdom comes through an intimate and direct relationship with the universe. No one needs to read a book to know what truth is. No one needs to be told what beauty is. We recognize truth and beauty the moment we see it, because, in essence, at that moment we are connecting to the creative force of the universe. Emerson called this creative force the "oversoul," and our individual souls are all part of the oversoul. We are all part of the godhead. We all have a spark of divinity within us. When we see this, we achieve self-realization, we recognize our interconnectedness with nature, with the universe, with all living creatures. In this way we see that there is no difference between humans, there is no difference on the soul level between races or the genders. Therefore self-realization leads us to a deeper engagement with the world.

"To believe your own thought," Emerson writes in his essay *Self-Reliance*, "to believe that what is true for you in your private heart is true for all men, — that is genius." In order to live an authentic life each individual must resist the impulse to conform. Each individual must become self-reliant, must think for him- or herself and not be concerned about what everyone else thinks or expects. Have the courage to think broadly; have the courage to expand the mind, even when you have to change your mind. "Trust thyself," Emerson counsels: "every heart vibrates to that iron string. Accept the place the divine Providence has found for you; the society of your contemporaries, the connexion of events." But even though you are part of a society, a time, and a place, and even though it is your duty to respond to the events and issues surrounding you, you must be cognizant of the pressures that society constantly exerts to destroy individuality. "Society everywhere is in conspiracy against the manhood of every one of its members. Society is a joint-stock company, in which the members agree, for the better securing of his bread to each shareholder, to surrender the liberty and culture of the eater. The virtue in most request is conformity. Self-reliance is its aversion. It loves not realities and creators, but names and customs."[3]

The only way to live life authentically is to resist societal pressures and become a nonconformist. Do not assume, Emerson insists, that those in authority (parents, lawmakers, clergymen) know what is best for you. "What must I do is all that concerns me, not what the people think. . . . You will always find those who think they know what is your duty better than you know it. It is easy in the world to live after the world's opinion; it is easy in solitude to live after our own; but the great man is he who in the midst of the crowd keeps with perfect sweetness the independence of solitude."[4]

Conformity, according to Emerson, is for those who are not interested in the "truth" and are too timid to probe below the surface. Most people accept what others tell them and endeavor to impose that view on anyone who might question it.

A man must consider what a blind-man's-buff is this game of conformity. If I know your sect, I anticipate your argument. I hear a preacher announce for his text and topic the expediency of one of the institutions of his church. Do I not know beforehand that not possibly can he say a new and spontaneous word? . . . Do I not know that he is pledged to himself not to look but at one side,—the permitted side, not as a man, but as a parish minister? He is a retained attorney, and these airs of the bench are the emptiest affectation. Well, most men have bound their eyes with one or another handkerchief, and attached themselves to some one of these communities of opinion. This conformity makes them not false in a few particulars, authors of a few lies, but false in all particulars. Their every truth is not quite true.

The individual should strive always for honesty and integrity and not be stubbornly wedded to a particular viewpoint. A person should be ready to abandon a dearly held belief and acknowledge the truth of a contrary position even if it means appearing inconsistent.

A foolish consistency is the hobgoblin of little minds, adored by little statesmen and philosophers and divines. With consistency a great soul has simply nothing to do. He may as well concern himself with his shadow on the wall. . . . Speak what you think to-day in words as hard as cannon-balls, and to-morrow speak what to-morrow thinks in hard words again, though it contradict every thing you said to-day. Ah, then, exclaim the aged ladies, you shall be sure to be misunderstood. . . . Is it so bad then to be misunderstood? Pythagoras was misunderstood, and Socrates, and Jesus, and Luther, and Copernicus, and Galileo, and Newton, and every pure and wise spirit that ever took flesh. To be great is to be misunderstood.[5]

Emerson's friend Henry David Thoreau went even further in his advocacy of nonconformity. The individual, according to Thoreau, *must* resist the pressures to conform, *must* resist the pressures to do what society expects and instead follow his or her own instincts, dreams. Most people fail to see this and as a result are living "lives of quiet desperation." Thoreau conducted his two-year experiment at Walden Pond so that, as he put it, when it came time for him to die, he would know that he had lived. Rejecting the party politics and materialism of a nation whose prosperity was based on slavery, he wanted to simplify his life and experience the basics. He wanted to know what it felt like to be warmed by the fire that he himself built; he wanted to know what water tasted like that he himself carried from Walden Pond to his cabin. He chided those who were so busy chasing after material goods that they failed to see what is essential. We need to simplify our lives and recognize that most of what we own we do not need. We spend our whole lives striving to accumulate things without ever noticing what is meaningful. If we learned to see what really *is*, if we examined our hearts and followed in the direction of our own dreams, we would no longer be content with the false values of society.

> I learned this, at least, by my experiment: that if one advances confidently in the direction of his dreams, and endeavors to live the life which he has imagined, he will meet with a success unexpected in common hours. He will put some things behind, will pass an invisible boundary; new, universal, and more liberal laws will begin to establish themselves around and within him; or the old laws be expanded, and interpreted in his favor in a more liberal sense, and he will live with the license of a higher order of beings. In proportion as he simplifies his life, the laws of the universe will appear less complex, and solitude will not be solitude, nor poverty poverty, nor weakness weakness. If you have built castles in the air, your work need not be lost; that is where they should be. Now put the foundations under them. . . .
>
> Why should we be in such desperate haste to succeed and in such desperate enterprises? If a man does not keep pace with his companions, perhaps it is because he hears a different drummer. Let him step to the music which he hears, however measured or far away.[6]

True nonconformist that he was, Thoreau cautioned his readers *not* to follow in his footsteps. The experiment at Walden Pond was Thoreau's path to self-realization. Each man and woman must find his or her own path, must find his or her own direction and not simply copy or imitate him.

Like Emerson and Thoreau, Margaret Fuller believed that inwardly, on the soul level, all human beings are equal. There is no fundamental difference between races; there is no fundamental difference between man and woman. "Male and female represent the two sides of the great radical dualism. But, in fact, they are perpetually passing into one another. Fluid hardens to solid, solid rushes to fluid. There is no wholly masculine man, no purely feminine woman." Each man, according to Fuller, possesses the feminine principle just as each woman the masculine. It is through the union of the feminine and the masculine that human beings find fulfillment. Because the sexes *are* equal, women should no longer submit to being shunted aside as somehow less than

Henry David Thoreau, 1856. "Unjust laws exist: shall we be content to obey them, or shall we endeavor to amend them, and obey them until we have succeeded, or shall we transgress them at once?" Daguerreotype by Benjamin D. Maxham. (Public domain; courtesy National Portrait Gallery, Smithsonian Institution)

a man; they should have faith in their own innate abilities and intellect and strive for self-realization. "It is therefore that I would have Woman lay aside all thought, such as she habitually cherishes, of being taught and led by men. I would have her, like the Indian girl, dedicate herself to the Sun, the Sun of Truth, and go nowhere if his beams did not make clear the path. I would have her free from compromise, from complaisance, from helplessness, because I would have her good enough and strong enough to love one and all beings, from the fulness, not the poverty of being."[7]

If the central premise of transcendentalism is true—that the human soul is part of the oversoul, that all humans are part of the godhead— then the only reasonable conclusion that can be drawn is that all people are truly equal. So, to the transcendentalist, slavery is not only wrong, not only immoral; it is also illogical. After all, how can one individual own another when they are both divine? How can God own God? In this way transcendentalism, along with the egalitarianism of the evangelical revivals and the notions of fairness advocated by socialists, helped shape the philosophical foundation and gave more credibility to the two most powerful and far-reaching critiques of American society during the antebellum period: abolitionism and feminism.

* * *

At a time when there were few diversions and amusements, alcohol played a central role in the nineteenth-century social order. In cities and towns men congregated at taverns and saloons to discuss politics over pints of ale and drams of whiskey; in rural areas, where farmers stored most of their surplus grain by distilling it, jugs of whiskey were omnipresent at every social gathering, from dances to weddings to funerals to barn raisings. Drinking whiskey was more common than drinking water, especially in an era when people often succumbed to water-borne illnesses. Alcoholism cost men their families and their jobs; unemployment led to poverty; poverty led to crime, despair, suicide. One nineteenth-century antialcohol poster showed the nine steps of descending into an alcoholic hell, starting with the casual social drink to "a glass too much" to drinking with jolly companions to "poverty and disease," "desperation and crime," and eventually "death by suicide."[8] As a result, a temperance movement began in the 1830s that lasted well into the next century.

The movement was spurred by both evangelicals and the women's movement. Theodore Dwight Weld, who had brought evangelical fervor to the abolitionist cause, also brought the same fervor to temperance. In 1831 Weld preached a fiery four-hour sermon in Rochester, New York, about the evils of alcohol that motivated most of his listeners to join the antialcohol crusade. For years many people tried to keep alcoholism in check by advocating moderation and temperance, calling for the banning of strong spirits but permitting wine and beer. But after the founding of the American Temperance Society in the 1820s the word *temperance* essentially came to mean abstinence. Weld and other activists emphasized Christian ethics and morality to denounce drink. Many of those who joined the crusade and signed antialcohol pledges were middle-class Protestants who feared the rising number of poor people and who also sought some control over what they considered one of the major threats to the United States—the influx of numerous immigrants from Catholic Ireland. They hoped that a prohibition on alcohol would dissuade Catholics from migrating to America.

Another factor driving the movement was that many women viewed alcohol as the principal destroyer of the home. Drunken men neglected their families, abused them, beat their wives and children, and frequently abandoned them. Men who could not free themselves from "demon rum" lost their jobs and could not provide for their families. As families fell into poverty, the crime rate rose. Eliminating alcohol, therefore, would create a more wholesome, more moral society and preserve the sanctity of the family. The campaign led by evangelists, women, and reformers became so extensive that by the 1840s more than one million Americans had joined various temperance organizations. Men promised to set a good example to their sons by abstaining from drink and cursing, vowed to treat their wives with more respect, and pledged that they would spend more time with their families. The result was that alcohol consumption in the United States dropped by 50 percent.

* * *

In the late 1820s there were some attempts on the part of workers to organize, and as we have seen, in the 1830s Boston workers campaigned unsuccessfully for a ten-hour day. There were other efforts by workers to secure better wages and working conditions, and despite the fact that women made up a small minority of the workforce, one of the first major efforts to organize a strike was carried out by women. The Lowell Mill Girls initially had a rather good situation—along with their wages they were provided with room and board and also had the opportunity to experience a degree of independence that was rare for nineteenth-century women—however, in 1834, with competition on the rise, the mills cut wages by 15 percent. The Lowell Mill Girls, already a tightly knit group, decided there was strength in numbers, and they could fight the wage cut by going on strike. A poem in their petition to the mill owners equated their cause with that of the patriots of 1776:

> Let oppression shrug her shoulders,
> And a haughty tyrant frown,
> And little upstart Ignorance,
> In mockery look down.
> Yet I value not the feeble threats
> Of Tories in disguise,
> While the flag of Independence
> O'er our noble nation flies.[9]

And at a second strike in 1836 they marched through the streets of Lowell singing,

> Oh! isn't it a pity, such a pretty girl as I
> Should be sent to the factory to pine away and die?
> Oh! I cannot be a slave, I will not be a slave,
> For I'm so fond of liberty,
> That I cannot be a slave.[10]

Both strikes failed, but the experience was an invaluable lesson in organizing and in heightening political awareness. In 1844 Sarah Bagley, one of the workers, founded the Lowell Female Labor Association, and two years later, demanding the restoration of the pay cuts and a reduction of the working hours from twelve to ten, the workers struck again. "I am sick at heart," Sarah Bagley wrote after the strike ended without success,

> when I look into the social world and see woman so willingly made a dupe to the beastly selfishness of man. A mere donkey for his use and no right, even to her own person. I most fervently thank Heaven that I have never introduced into existence a being to suffer the privations that I have endured. . . . The man who tended this office before me had four hundred dollars per year. I [receive] three and still the business has been on the increase all the time. But I am a woman and it is not worth so much to a company for me to write a letter as it would be for a man.[11]

Still, despite the fact that the women did not achieve their goals, they emerged from the experience highly sophisticated in useful tactics to take on the bosses, and they inspired and informed future labor organizers.

There were other strikes and attempts to organize during the era. In Paterson, New Jersey, for example, children walked off the job at a mill, protesting that the lunch break was shifted from noon to one o'clock. The work stoppage lasted ten days before they were forced back to work. The mill later, quietly restored the lunch hour to noon. In Lynn, Massachusetts, workers in a shoe factory organized in the 1830s, and in 1860 they held the largest strike in the nation's history up to that time. Three thousand workers went on strike for higher wages and demanded that the company recognize their union. Within days shoemakers all over New England pledged their solidarity and walked off their jobs too. The work stoppage lasted for two months, with a total of about six thousand workers taking part. It ended in a partial victory. Wages were raised, but the union was not recognized.

* * *

The transcendental emphasis on the inherent equality of all human beings, combined with the socialism of Proudhon and Fourier, prompted several ambitious experiments in communal living in the United States. A number of enthusiastic reformers set up models of what they believed a perfect society would look like.

In Scotland the mill owner Robert Owen experimented with utopian socialism at his cotton mill in New Lanark by providing good wages, reasonable hours, and a good living environment for his workers, even to the point of providing education for their children and recreational facilities for the families. In 1825 Owen visited the United States and founded a utopian community in New Harmony, Indiana. In this community all property was held in common, and the residents shared all work equally. Many people went to live in the commune, but evidently there was too much disharmony in New Harmony. Within three years the community disbanded.

Frances Wright, also from Scotland and acquainted with Robert Owen, came to the United States and established a utopian socialist community for slaves at Nashoba, Tennessee. The idea was that slaves would live and work there, and their earnings would pay for their freedom. Wright believed that slaves working for their freedom would prove to be diligent workers and that the success of the experiment would show Americans that free labor was more profitable than slave labor. The United States would thus see the way clear to ending slavery. However, Wright caught malaria, and when she returned to Britain to recuperate, the people she left behind to manage the community mistreated the slaves, even to the point of whipping them and producing conditions that were hardly different from what slaves on southern plantations were experiencing. By 1828 the experiment collapsed.

In the aftermath of the failed New Harmony and Nashoba experiments a number of other activists, influenced by Fourier, set up about thirty phalanxes throughout the United States. All residents of these utopian communities shared the work, both manual labor and administrative duties, and all property was held in common. Although about one hundred thousand people lived in these communities during the ten-year period after 1842, all thirty of them lasted only about two years each. Socialists blamed the American emphasis on individualism for short-circuiting the whole idea of cooperative living. Americans, it seemed, were too individualistic to work together for a common goal.

George Riley, Bronson Alcott, and other transcendentalists conducted a utopian experiment at Brook Farm in Roxbury, Massachusetts. Their idea was that all residents would spend part of each day doing some manual labor, such as shoveling manure or hoeing fields, and then exercise the mind later in the day by studying literature and poetry. Time was set aside for meditation and contemplation as well as artistic endeavors. There were guest lectures by transcendentalists Ralph Waldo Emerson and Margaret Fuller. Many of the residents wrote articles for the *Dial*, a literary journal edited by Fuller. But by the end of the 1840s Brook Farm too could not sustain itself economically and disbanded. As Emerson later said, the problem with the idealistic utopian communities is that they "met every test but life itself."[12]

The Shakers also took up communal living. Founded in England by Mother Ann Lee, the Shakers were a religious sect that believed that God had both masculine and feminine traits and that therefore the sexes were completely equal. They believed in living a simple life separated from the outside world, in complete sexual equality, communal ownership of all property, and total celibacy. Their name derived from the practice of ecstatic dancing in such a way as to shake out sin through their fingertips. Since Shakers could not add to their numbers through reproduction, the only way to stave off the demise of the group was through conversion. All in all about twenty Shaker communities with a total of six thousand adherents were established in New England, the mid-Atlantic states, and Ohio and Indiana.

Perhaps the most successful utopian venture (certainly the most long-lived) was the Oneida Community, founded in 1848 by John Humphrey Noyes. Noyes was a Christian perfectionist who believed that once a soul was saved, it was perfect and the usual rules and moral constraints no longer applied. At Oneida all property was held in common, all people belonged to each other, all children were raised by all the residents. All men and women were equal and were therefore "married" to everyone else. The community looked at this as a way to free women from the demands of male lust. Women were free and were not considered anyone's property; therefore they were not forced to provide sexual favors to a husband every time he demanded sex. Sexual intercourse was permitted between any two consenting adults, but they were not permitted to get attached to each other. People in neighboring towns, however, looked with horror on this practice of "free love," and so the Oneida perfectionists were invariably faced with hostility whenever they traveled outside the community. Unlike the other utopian cooperatives, which usually survived through agricultural work, the Oneida Community did so through manufacturing. At first they produced steel animal traps, but they later branched out into making silverware, which was a very successful enterprise. Although the utopian experiment ended in 1881, Oneida still exists as a major tableware-manufacturing company.

In the end, all the utopian communities failed. No matter how hard visionaries tried to use human reason to create the perfect society, no matter how hard they tried to rectify the problems that were endemic to life in the real world, it seemed that perfection could not be achieved. Perhaps it was partly due to the hostility of neighbors who did not take kindly to such practices as open or plural marriages. In fact it seems that the sexual practices of most of the communes were just too scandalous and outrageous for nineteenth-century Americans. But the failure was also due to American antipathy toward perfectionist and socialist ideas in general and communal ownership in particular, especially at a time when the sanctity of private property was taken for granted and the desire to own land was each American's deepest desire. Still, these utopian visionaries raised profound questions that forced people to think about democracy and capitalism and, in some cases, to ponder their own personal values.

* * *

The reform spirit touched almost all areas of American life, not just the glaring issues of slavery, the exploitation of workers, and the subjugation of women. Some reformers dedicated themselves to transforming the way criminals were treated in the prison system as well as inmates in mental asylums. Others called attention to the way Americans looked at health and exercise and made proposals to overcome detrimental habits. Some people had concerns about the way children were treated and sought to create an educational system that would benefit both society and the individual.

For centuries lawbreakers and the insane were viewed as sinners. God was punishing them, and it was beyond our understanding to know why. The insane were allowed to wander about, unless they were dangerous, and in that case they would be confined. Criminals were whipped, placed in stocks or the pillory, or if they had committed a capital crime, hanged. But reformers now advocated a reevaluation of such treatment and punishment. The Enlightenment emphasis that humans can solve problems by using their intellect as well as the Romantic movement's elevation of the individual fostered the view that human defects could, with the right care and treatment, be corrected. If the insane were cared for with sensitivity and understanding and not cruelty, they could be cured. If criminals were given the time and space to reflect on their crimes and repent of them, they would see the error of their ways and turn their lives around.

Of all the outspoken critics of the barbaric treatment of the insane and prisoners Dorothea Dix was the most influential. She devoted herself throughout the 1840s and 1850s to investigating asylums and prisons and lobbying the states to reform the entire system of incarceration. She reported to the Massachusetts legislature that the insane in the state's hospitals were kept "in cages, closets, stalls, pens! Chained, naked, beaten with rods, and lashed into obedience!"[13] She urged lawmakers to do something about this deplorable treatment by creating new asylums with proper psychological care and a more humane attitude toward their inmates. Her efforts paid off. Not only did Massachusetts build a new asylum; fourteen other states established new hospitals for the insane.

A number of states constructed and staffed penitentiaries, whose purpose was to reform prisoners, not punish them. One of the most famous of these institutions was Eastern State Penitentiary in Philadelphia. The reformers believed that mixing criminals in a communal environment was a bad idea because it would only corrupt and harden them. Solitary confinement was preferable because convicts would have the opportunity to meditate and pray and become penitent (hence the term *penitentiary*) for their crime. They would be allowed to exercise each day in a small courtyard opening off their cells, and the wardens would act as educators aiding in their moral rehabilitation.

Unfortunately the theory seldom worked in practice. Many of the new institutions were underfunded and overcrowded, and the staffs were undertrained. Of course, psychotherapy was at such a rudimentary stage that even the trained caretakers in the asylums and the custodians in the penitentiaries did not know what they were doing. They frequently resorted to brutal methods to keep prisoners in line or to subdue unmanageable inmates. Many convicts spending years in solitary confinement did not reflect on their crimes or read the Bible or seek penitence; some of them went mad, some committed suicide.

Other reformers addressed the specific issues of physically handicapped individuals; for example, Thomas Hopkins Gallaudet founded the American School for the Deaf in Connecticut, and Samuel Gridley Howe founded the Perkins School for the Blind in Boston. Some reformers urged Americans to be more cognizant of their health and to be careful about what they ingested. Many became motivational speakers offering cures and panaceas for every possible ailment. Resorts opened all over the country promising to cure patients from whatever ailed them. Hot springs, mud baths, body purges, and hypnotism were methods employed for the healing process. Sylvester Graham took on a multitude of health and dietary subjects. Americans' eating habits, he declared, were unhealthy. There were too many additives in commercially baked bread so as to give it its white color. (White bread had become the rage because it was considered a status symbol by the upwardly mobile middle class, who disparaged the dark bread of the lower classes.) The additives, Graham claimed, were detrimental to the health. He espoused vegetarianism and invented a new cracker made of coarse, unsifted whole wheat flour without any additives that would have restorative effects on the digestive system: the Graham cracker. He also urged people to sleep with the window open and on a very firm mattress, and if they suddenly found themselves caught in the grip of uncontrollable sexual desire, the one sure remedy was a cold bath.

There were other significant trends prompting people to use science to discover unknown facets of the human personality, psychology, and even spirituality. Some of these became pseudosciences, such as phrenology, which purported to be able to determine an individual's intelligence and personality from the bumps on the head as well as its size and shape. By the 1850s spiritualism had become an extraordinary psychological phenomenon. Hundreds of thousands of Americans were convinced that by going to a medium and participating in séances they could communicate with the dead. For some people a séance was a form of psychological treatment, therapy, and perhaps even a cure for grief. There was, after all, solace and comfort in communing with a relative who had gone on to the great beyond. For other people spiritualism was a vehicle whereby the dead, possessing the wisdom of the spiritual world, could instruct the living how to create a better life and overcome the sufferings of existence. Spiritualism was thus another instrument for the reforming and perfecting of society.

While American children were nurtured, disciplined, and taught morality at home, it became increasingly obvious, especially among the reformers of the antebellum period, that formal education was a necessity and that some sort of system of universal free education should be implemented. The most influential and successful advocate of educational reform was the secretary of the Massachusetts State Board of Education, Horace Mann. The Bay State was more advanced than most other states as far as providing education for its children, but even here, as Mann began his campaign to get the state to fund universal free schools for all children, it was difficult convincing wealthy people and those without children that their tax dollars should support education. Most people could not see beyond their own private concerns and needs and wondered why they should support educating other people's children. But Mann cleverly argued that society as a whole benefits when all citizens are educated. Education provides opportunities for people and has an impact on cutting crime; the more people who are educated, the more society benefits from the inventions and discoveries they may provide; education creates stability, protects democracy, and prevents class conflict; it enables the swifter assimilation of new immigrant groups; and (in a line of reasoning that resonated especially well with industrialists and businessmen) education teaches common people to respect private property and the values of industrialism, making them fit in as productive workers, and productive workers can earn higher incomes, which in turn would be spent on consumer products.

In Mann's system schools were free and open to all, teachers were better trained and paid twice what they had been previously, and the school year was increased from a few weeks to six months. Mann established institutes for training teachers and librarians, and he also introduced new pedagogical methods into the classroom whereby children would be taught to think for themselves and learn to use their intellect. The Common Schools would also teach children proper middle-class values and morality, and thus those who were potential dissenters and troublemakers would be properly socialized. Teaching middle-class values would also enable the children of workers and immigrants to rise up the social and economic ladder. Mann also promoted the "whole word" approach to reading rather than the older method of teaching the letters and putting them together into words. The die-hard schoolmasters of Boston, however, first resisted Mann's innovative ideas, preferring the old techniques of memorization, repetition, and drill, and they also did not like Mann's prohibition on corporal punishment.

Mann had a huge impact on the movement toward free education to all, and by the 1850s his tireless efforts persuaded all states to establish tax-supported schools and in a few cases to pass laws making primary and secondary education compulsory. He also introduced Friedrich Fröbel's kindergarten model to American educators. According to Fröbel, children are like sensitive budding flowers, and they should be nurtured with all the love and care a gardener waters and tends a garden. Mann also incorporated the pedagogical theories of the Swiss educator Johann Heinrich Pestalozzi into the Common Schools. Pestalozzi argued that children learn through activities, not through being "talked at," and that the effective teacher, while guiding pupils through an activity, allows them to think for themselves and to draw their own conclusions. He called this approach "object teaching." For example, a teacher should use a tangible object to gain the child's attention, such as an owl pellet, and then construct the lesson around it by having the child dissect the pellet and deduce what the owl had eaten. Furthermore, the teacher should help train the "whole child," not just the intellect; the goal is to balance the hands, heart, and head. Because of Mann's advocacy for such pedagogical techniques and because he was the force behind the Common School movement, many educators today consider him to be the central figure in the evolution of the modern American education system. "Education," Mann had claimed, "is the great equalizer,"[14] and it is the natural right of every child. It was this view that by the end of the century opened up education in America for all people and influenced the way children today are taught.

It is ironic that Mann, who saw education as opening the door for social and economic advancement and who wanted to extend its benefits even to those who could not pay for it, was also an enthusiastic promoter of the interests of the business class. Of course, in order to get the moneyed elite to agree to a tax-supported educational system Mann employed every argument he could to convince them that their self-interest lay with the Common School system. But his arguments that education would mold immigrants and the poor into trustworthy citizens, who would dutifully become the workers in factories, mills, and industrial plants, have earned him a great deal of criticism from some historians. They see him as trying to thwart radical change through educational reforms and see Mann's Common School as really an instrument of social control whereby the wealthy could manipulate and indoctrinate the lower classes. Children were taught that they could advance socially if they cultivated the ideals of thrift, discipline, punctuality, and respect for authority, while in reality they were being trained to become useful as a source of cheap and cooperative labor. Still, many people today regard the Common School as an honest attempt to elevate the lower classes and see Mann's probusiness rationale as simply a ploy to get the upper class's support for the democratization of education. However one looks at the Common Schools, they did help regulate the growing gap between ordinary citizens and the wealthy in the nineteenth century—the gap continued to grow but at a slower pace.

Transcendentalists Margaret Fuller, Bronson Alcott, and Elizabeth Peabody also proposed new ways to educate children. They maintained that education should encourage, not interfere with, a child's natural connection with the universe. Children were basically good, and educators should concentrate on facilitating that goodness, that inner wisdom, and allow it to develop. Education should come out of the child, not be imposed on him or her. William Maclure, in charge of education at the New Harmony, Indiana, commune, was even more radical in advocating that schools should teach children how to avoid the dehumanizing impact of capitalism and to reject materialism and consumerism.

An especially significant outcome of the education reforms of the 1830s and 1840s was the feminization of the teaching profession. According to conventional wisdom, women were more nurturing than men. Therefore Mann and other educators, in order to ease the transition for young children as they entered school and found themselves for the first time spending hours each day away from their mothers, advocated a policy of encouraging women to enter the teaching profession. Female teachers in kindergarten or primary school would lessen the trauma a child might otherwise experience by being separated from his or her mother. Over the next several years more and more women entered college and teacher training schools in order to become teachers. Later in the century, as this trend accelerated when universal education became compulsory in all states, this had an enormous, unexpected effect on the women's movement. Although female teachers soon became customary in primary school, the upper grades and secondary schools were still dominated by men, and women regularly received lower wages than men. Administration, of course, remained a male domain.

* * *

Thomas Jefferson famously commented that a little rebellion now and then was good for a democracy. It kept the ideals of the revolution fresh and alive. In 1842, in Rhode Island—which was still governed under its seventeenth-century charter and which still did not recognize the right of propertyless adult males to vote—a group of men led by Thomas Wilson Dorr initiated a "little rebellion." Unhappy that they were denied voting rights, the Dorrites first called on the state government to frame a new constitution guaranteeing universal manhood suffrage. The conservative government refused to do so, whereupon Dorr called for a constitutional convention. Over the next several months both sides held conventions and framed new constitutions. A referendum was held, and both sides claimed victory and elected a full slate of officials. Invoking the clause in the Declaration of Independence that people have the right of revolution if the government infringes on their rights, Dorr led an armed attack against the state armory. When the assault failed, many of the insurgents were arrested, while Dorr escaped. In the aftermath violence continued, with demonstrations, riots, and a few armed skirmishes, until the state government agreed, in order to restore the peace, to address the Dorrite grievances. A new state constitutional convention was called, and the resulting constitution greatly reduced the property requirement for voting. With the Dorrites appeased, in 1843 Dorr returned to Rhode Island, where he was tried, convicted, and sentenced to life imprisonment for treason. He was, however, released in 1845, and later his record was wiped clean.

* * *

Involvement in the various reforms of the era was a political apprenticeship for thousands of women. Abolitionism in particular had an enormous impact on the emergence of the women's movement. By forcing a national dialogue on the issue of slavery, abolitionism raised the consciousness (and hackles) of ordinary Americans to such a level that by the 1850s few people could remain neutral about the subject. Even in the remotest regions of the United States Americans were compelled to take sides on the one issue that overshadowed all others: slavery. The more antislavery people used moral arguments against the institution, the more the apologists for slavery dug in their heels and defended it. And ultimately the issue proved unsolvable through compromise or the political process. As the nature of equality and freedom was hotly debated, the second-largest reform movement was spawned: women's rights.

Many women were involved in the antislavery crusade. Women such as the Grimké sisters, Sojourner Truth, Harriet Tubman, Elizabeth Cady Stanton, Lucretia Mott, and countless others emerged in the 1830s and 1840s to speak out vehemently against slavery. They soon discovered that the very act of speaking out was itself controversial. For nineteenth-century women to assert themselves in this way was considered a kind of immoral exposure, and so in their struggle to pressure the United States to act against the injustice of slavery, they became painfully aware that injustice was not confined to African Americans.

In 1840 the abolitionist Elizabeth Cady Stanton sailed with her husband to London to speak at the World Antislavery Convention. After making the exhausting voyage across the Atlantic and finally arriving in London, she was exasperated and infuriated to find that women were not permitted to speak at the convention. It was a startling realization that women needed to fight for their own emancipation, not just for the slaves'. Stanton met Lucretia Mott at the convention, and together they decided circumstances required them to become advocates for women's rights. In 1848 they organized a convention at Seneca Falls, New York, to "discuss the social, civil, and religious condition and rights of women."[15] Hundreds of women (and men) attended the convention and listened to speeches and reports and framed a manifesto calling for equal rights for women.

In a nation that prides itself that the people are sovereign, it is wrong that half the population has no say in formulating the laws that they are obliged to obey. "We are assembled," Stanton said during her opening remarks,

> to protest against a form of government existing without the consent of the governed—to declare our right to be free as man is free, to be represented in the government which we are taxed to support, to have such disgraceful laws as give man the power to chastise and imprison his wife, to take the wages which she earns, the property which she inherits, and, in case of separation, the children of her love; laws which make her the mere dependent on his bounty. It is to protest against such unjust laws as these that we are assembled today, and to have them, if possible, forever erased from our statute books. . . .
>
> The world has never yet seen a truly great and virtuous nation, because in the degradation of woman the very fountains of life are poisoned at their source. . . . So long as your women are slaves you may throw your colleges and churches to the winds. You can't have scholars and saints so long as your mothers are ground to powder between the upper and nether millstone of tyranny and lust.[16]

The Seneca Falls manifesto for women's rights, the Declaration of Sentiments, was modeled on the Declaration of Independence. It began with a reiteration of natural-rights philosophy but this time with the specific inclusion of women: "We hold these truths to be self-evident:

that all men and women are created equal." It went on to demand a complete restructuring of society and gender relationships, full social and economic equality for women, and the right to vote. Just as the Declaration of Independence catalogued the specific grievances that the colonists had against George III, the Declaration of Sentiments went on to list the specific grievances that women had against men: "He has never permitted her to exercise her inalienable right to the elective franchise. He has compelled her to submit to laws, in the formation of which she had no voice. . . . She is compelled to promise obedience to her husband, he becoming, to all intents and purposes, her master"— and a dozen more accusations.[17]

Although the majority of Americans were not receptive to the convention's proposals, a significant number were. The abolitionist Frederick Douglass proclaimed his solidarity when he reported on the Seneca Falls Convention in his newspaper, the *North Star*. Addressing the bigotry and hypocrisy of white men in the United States, Douglass sardonically conjectured that he suspected American men would look more favorably on a convention that met to discuss animal rights than women's rights. He then went on to endorse the women's movement and link it with the fight for African American freedom.

> In respect to political rights, we hold woman to be justly entitled to all we claim for man. We go farther, and express our conviction that all political rights which it is expedient for man to exercise, it is equally for woman. All that distinguishes man as an intelligent and accountable being, is equally true of woman, and if that government only is just which governs by the free consent of the governed, there can be no reason in the world for denying to woman the exercise of the elective franchise, or a hand in making and administering the laws of the land. Our doctrine is that "right is of no sex."[18]

The Declaration of Sentiments resonated with women, and with each passing year larger numbers began to challenge male-dominated society. The religious revivals had certainly prepared the way by assuring American women that they were equal to men, as did the demise of the practice of arranged marriages. But most important was women's centrality to antebellum reform and the lessons they learned about challenging accepted values. The experience of working for reform radicalized some women. Thousands of the women reading the Declaration of Sentiments, already feeling more independent than their mothers and grandmothers, were ready to take on the male power structure. Responding to rising concerns about women's rights, some states passed Married Women's Property Acts that overturned the prevailing laws that a married woman's property did not belong to her but to her husband. For example, in 1852 New York enacted a law specifying "that the real and personal property, and the rents, issues, and profits thereof, of any female now married, shall not be subject to the disposal of her husband, but shall be her sole and separate property, as if she were a single female."[19] These were modest gains at the beginning of the modern women's movement. It took seventy-two years of struggle after the 1848 Seneca Falls Convention before women finally achieved the right to vote.

* * *

Whether it was emancipating an entire race of people from lifelong servitude or freeing women from a lifelong role of submissiveness or curing the ills of a society stumbling around in an alcoholic haze or alleviating the injustices of poverty or attacking the evils of inequality or working for the humane treatment of the insane and criminals or striving to save souls, most reformers were seeking to create a perfect society in an imperfect world. Faith in the perfectibility of humankind was common to all these reformers, whether conservative Christians or radical utopian socialists. They also had faith in democracy and the American experiment in republican government, and even those who were not transcendentalists had faith in the capacity of the individual to achieve great things. Perhaps these notions seem naïve to us today (undoubtedly many reformers were wise enough to be realistic about their goals), but those who became activists, those who worked hard for change, felt that some problems were so appalling that they simply *had* to do something about them.

There was undeniable success in improving life for some people and rectifying some injustices, but even so, many reformers failed because ultimately none of them could fully deliver what they promised. No matter how ardent the campaign, prison reform would not end crime, temperance would not end the abuse of alcohol, educational reform would not create a nation of wise intellectuals, the ending of private property would not end aggression, disputes, and violence. Still, just because human beings are not perfectible, it does not mean sitting back and sinking into complacency. Even when antebellum reformers fell far short of their idealistic goals, they believed (as is the case with dissenters in every age) that apathy is not an acceptable alternative, that doing something was better than doing nothing. And they did awaken the consciousness *and* consciences of millions of Americans and showed that just trying to make a difference did, in its own small way, make a difference.

CHAPTER 7

Expansion and Conflict

[The cost of the war] is a question which the President seems
to never have thought of. As to the mode of terminating the
war, and securing peace, the President is equally wandering
and indefinite. . . . All this shows that the President is, in no
wise, satisfied with his own positions. . . . His mind, tasked
beyond its power, is running hither and thither, like some
tortured creature, on a burning surface, finding no position,
on which it can settle down, and be at ease. . . . He knows not
where he is. He is a bewildered, confounded, and miserably
perplexed man.

> —Congressman Abraham Lincoln, speech to
> the House of Representatives, January 1848

All men recognize the right of revolution; that is, the right to
refuse allegiance to, and to resist, the government, when its
tyranny or its inefficiency are great and unendurable.

> —Henry David Thoreau,
> "Resistance to Civil Government," 1847

In the thirty-year period after the Missouri Compromise Americans
were on the move. Thousands crossed the Mississippi River and settled
in farmland in a band running from Minnesota to Louisiana. Missionaries, mountain men, prospectors, and small farmers moved even farther
westward, following the path of Lewis and Clark into Oregon or pressing into sparsely settled northern Mexico. Some hoped to convert the
Indians to Christianity, some craved financial gain, and some merely
sought the relative freedom of the frontier; at bottom, though, all of
them desired to improve their lives. Advances in technology, machinery,
weaponry, canals, steamships, railroads, and the telegraph accelerated
the westward movement so rapidly that it seemed to most Americans
that, as the newspaper editor John L. O'Sullivan put it in 1845, it was

"our manifest destiny to overspread the continent allotted by Providence for the free development of our yearly multiplying millions."[1]

By the 1830s expansion fever was running rampant. Texas, as well as the vast Oregon territory spanning an area along the Pacific coast from California to Alaska, seemed ripe for the taking. And by the 1840s Americans were looking with covetous eyes at the Mexican provinces of New Mexico and California. When James Knox Polk was elected president in 1844, "Manifest Destiny" was the catchphrase. But not everyone was enthusiastic about expansion. For northerners, especially abolitionists, the quest for more land appeared to be a plot by southern slaveholders to expand the peculiar institution. Many northerners were already wary of southern dominance in the American government; after all, seven of the first ten presidents were slaveholders. And when southerners began migrating to the Mexican province of Tejas seeking more land for growing cotton, it seemed further proof that a southern plot was afoot to dominate national politics. If Texas entered the Union, potentially five or six slave states could be carved out of the vast territory, thus giving southerners a considerable advantage in the Senate. At first, after Texas gained its independence from Mexico in 1836, northern congressmen successfully blocked the admission of the "Lone Star Republic," but by 1845 the prevailing winds shifted, Americans seemed seduced by Manifest Destiny, and Texas was admitted to the Union as the fourteenth slave state. Later that year the United States negotiated its conflicting claims with Russia and Great Britain and got title to the Oregon territory south of the forty-ninth parallel. But the hunger for more land was not quite satisfied, and so within a year of taking office President James Knox Polk took the United States into war with Mexico.

*   *   *

Shortly after Texas entered the Union, Mexico broke off diplomatic relations with the United States. What made matters worse and increased tensions was that President Polk insisted that the southern boundary of Texas was the Rio Grande River, whereas the border of Tejas when it was a Mexican province was the Nueces River, 150 miles north of the Rio Grande. Mexico was still infuriated that American settlers had instigated a revolution in 1836 that resulted in Texas independence and that throughout the nine-year history of the Lone Star Republic the United

States had aided Texas in thwarting Mexican attempts to retake its province. The United States, Mexico believed, had clearly "stolen" Texas. Now that Americans were claiming that Texas extended 150 miles into Mexico, it seemed obvious that Washington was hatching an imperialist plot to appropriate more Mexican territory. Polk aggravated Mexican suspicions when he sent John Slidell to Mexico City to persuade Mexico to accept the Rio Grande boundary and to offer to purchase California and New Mexico. When the Mexican government refused to give Slidell an audience, Polk ordered the U.S. Army, under the command of General Zachary Taylor, into the disputed territory between the Nueces and the Rio Grande. As far as Mexico City was concerned, this was a blatant act of aggression.

When Taylor marched his thirty-five hundred troops to the Rio Grande and set up an encampment near Matamoros, one of the general's aides, Colonel Ethan Allen Hitchcock, confided the true purpose of the maneuver in his diary: "I have said from the first that the United States are the aggressors. . . . We have not one particle of right to be here. . . . It looks as if the government sent a small force on purpose to bring on a war, so as to have a pretext for taking California and as much of this country as it chooses, for, whatever becomes of this army, there is no doubt of a war between the United States and Mexico."[2]

On April 24, 1846, Mexican forces crossed to the north side of the river and engaged an outpost of American dragoons. Taylor wired Polk that "hostilities may now be considered as commenced."[3] The president, delighted that he had provoked the Mexicans into initiating a skirmish, informed Congress that Mexico had "invaded our territory and shed American blood on American soil."[4] Congress overwhelmingly voted to declare war. Within days thousands of young men volunteered for military service, and dozens of prowar rallies took place around the country. Americans were enthralled with the prospect of the riches that expansion would bring to the United States. The *New York Herald* enthused that "the universal Yankee nation can regenerate and disenthrall the people of Mexico in a few years; and we believe it is a part of our destiny to civilize that beautiful country."[5]

Although enthusiasm was high at the outset of the conflict, there was considerable antiwar opposition. The newspaper publisher Horace Greeley opposed the war on the grounds that it was contrary to the basic notions of American democracy, that a war for expansion was turning the nation into an imperial power. "Who believes," he wrote in the *New York Tribune*, "that a score of victories over Mexico, the 'annexation' of half her provinces, will give us more Liberty, a purer Morality, a more prosperous Industry, than we now have? . . . Is not Life miserable enough, comes not Death soon enough, without resort to the hideous enginery of War?" But it was within the ranks of the poorly supplied and underpaid soldiers that antiwar sentiment first took hold in a big way. Soldiers turned against the war not for moral or political reasons but because of the terrible conditions they had to endure and the denigrating and brutal way they were treated. "We are under very strict discipline here," one soldier wrote in Matamoros. "Some of our officers are very good men but the balance of them are very tyrannical and brutal toward the men. . . . Tonight on drill an officer laid a soldier's skull open with his sword. . . . A soldier's life is very disgusting."[6]

Thousands of soldiers expressed dissent with their feet. Historians estimate that approximately one-third of the 105,000 recruits who served deserted. In addition, some soldiers went so far as to mutiny against their officers and in some cases join the enemy. Because the United States was fighting against Catholic Mexico, anti-Catholic feeling ran high among the rank and file. The anti-Catholic bigotry, mixed with a dose of racism and xenophobia, was so intense that Irish Catholic immigrants serving in the U.S. Army faced widespread discrimination on a daily basis. Consequently more than two hundred Irish American soldiers deserted and went over to fight on the Mexican side, where they formed the Batallón San Patricio—the Saint Patrick's Battalion. When members of this battalion were captured later in the war, they were court-martialed, and seventy-two of them were executed.

As word filtered back to the public about the realities of army life and the brutality of the war, a modest antiwar movement began to take shape. Workers in New England issued a statement declaring their opposition to taking "up arms to sustain the Southern slaveholder in robbing one-fifth of our countrymen of their labor," and recently landed Irish immigrants in New York City called for the withdrawal of American forces from Mexico. Other civilians wrote letters to newspapers expressing opposition to the war. "Neither have I the least idea of 'joining' you," one young man wrote anonymously to a New England newspaper, or in any way assisting the unjust war waging against Mexico. I have no wish to participate in such "glorious" butcheries of women and children as were displayed in the capture of Monterey, etc. Neither have I any desire to place myself under the dictation of a petty military tyrant, to every caprice of whose will I must yield implicit obedience. No sir-ee! As long as I can work, beg, or go to the poor house, I won't go to Mexico, to be lodged on the damp ground, half starved, half roasted, bitten by mosquitoes and centipedes, stung by scorpions and tarantulas—marched, drilled, and flogged, and then stuck up to be shot at, for eight dollars a month and putrid rations. Well, I won't. . . . Human butchery has had its day. . . . And the time is rapidly approaching when the professional soldier will be placed on the same level as a bandit, the Bedouin, and the Thug.[7]

Northern Whigs opposed the war because they perceived it as "Mr. Polk's War," a Democratic Party scheme to strengthen its political power. A freshman Whig congressman from Illinois introduced a resolution that would have required (if it had passed) the president to travel to Texas to identify the exact spot on American soil where American blood was shed. Knowing full well that his "Spot Resolution" would not muster enough support to pass, Abraham Lincoln nevertheless submitted it as a protest against the war and a denunciation of President Polk. Another congressman, David Wilmot of Pennsylvania, introduced a proviso forbidding the introduction of slavery into any territories that might be annexed to the United States as a result of the war. The Wilmot Proviso did pass the House of Representatives but failed in the Senate. Other Whig politicians condemned the war as immoral and un-Christian, while still others argued that Polk was trying to extend the power of the presidency at the expense of Congress. In this case, they believed, the war was unconstitutional because it would destroy the balance of power and the checks and balances that were so essential for the preservation of American democracy.

Abolitionists almost unanimously opposed the war because it was clear that the war was being waged in order to seize more territory into which slavery could be extended. The most celebrated antiwar dissenter was transcendentalist Henry David Thoreau. When war was declared, Thoreau in a small gesture of protest famously refused to pay his poll tax because he could not in good conscience support a government that was initiating an unjust war to spread the unjust institution of slavery. In July 1846 he was arrested and jailed. Though his aunt paid his poll tax (against his wishes), and he was released after spending only one night in jail, the incident inspired him to write "Resistance to Civil Government."

In the essay Thoreau wrote that when an injustice exists, it is the individual's duty to oppose it. He argued that laws supporting the institution of slavery are unjust; therefore anyone who values justice must do all he or she can to overturn such laws. If this means breaking the law, then so be it. What is necessary is to put enough pressure on the government so that lawmakers would have no recourse but to change the law. When the United States is pursuing a war against a neighbor solely to expand slavery and increase the nation's wealth, it compels the individual to examine his or her conscience.

> How does it become a man to behave toward this American government to-day? I answer, that he cannot without disgrace be associated with it. I cannot for an instant recognize that political organization as *my* government which is the *slave's* government also. . . .
>
> . . . When a sixth of the population of a nation which has undertaken to be the refuge of liberty are slaves, and a whole country is unjustly overrun and conquered by a foreign army, and subjected to military law, I think that it is not too soon for honest men to rebel and revolutionize. What makes this duty the more urgent is the fact that the country so overrun is not our own, but ours is the invading army.[8]

To those who argue that we must obey the law, Thoreau drew a distinction between just and unjust laws. Unjust laws attempt to withdraw natural rights from individuals; just laws protect those natural rights. "Unjust laws exist: shall we be content to obey them, or shall we endeavor to amend them, and obey them until we have succeeded, or shall we transgress them at once?" But we must pick our fights carefully. "If the injustice is part of the necessary friction of the machine of government, let it go, let it go"; we should not engage in civil disobedience frivolously. But if the injustice "is of such a nature that it requires you to be the agent of injustice to another, then I say, break the law. Let your life be a counter-friction to stop the machine. What I have to do is to see, at any rate, that I do not lend myself to the wrong which I condemn."[9]

But civil disobedience means that when you break an unjust law, when you refuse to be part of the injustice, you must be ready to pay the consequences. And by paying the consequences, by going to prison, you force the system to change.

> Under a government which imprisons unjustly, the true place for a just man is also a prison. . . . If any think that their influence would be lost there, and their voices no longer afflict the ear of the State, that they would not be as an enemy within its walls, they do not know by how much truth is stronger than error, nor how much more eloquently and effectively he can combat injustice who has experienced a little in his own person. . . . A minority is powerless while it conforms to the majority; it is not even a minority then; but it is irresistible when it clogs by its whole weight. If the alternative is to keep all just men in prison, or give up war and slavery, the State will not hesitate which to choose. If a thousand men were not to pay their tax-bills this year, that would not be a violent and bloody measure, as it would be to pay them, and enable the State to commit violence and shed innocent blood. This is, in fact, the definition of a peaceable revolution.[10]

Not content to voice opposition to the war solely in philosophical terms, Thoreau reflected on his own decision to practice what he preached:

> I have paid no poll-tax for six years. I was put into a jail once on this account, for one night; and, as I stood considering the walls of solid stone, two or three feet thick, the door of wood and iron, a foot thick, and the iron grating which strained the light, I could not help being struck with the foolishness of that institution which treated me as if I were mere flesh and blood and bones, to be locked up. I wondered that it should have concluded at length that this was the best use it could put me to, and had never thought to avail itself of my services in some way. I saw that, if there was a wall of stone between me and my townsmen, there was a still more difficult one to climb or break through before they could get to be as free as I was. I did not for a moment feel confined, and the walls seemed a great waste of stone and mortar. . . . I saw that the

State was half-witted, that it was timid as a lone woman with her silver spoons, and that it did not know its friends from its foes, and I lost all my remaining respect for it, and pitied it.[11]

Although Thoreau's essay had no impact on the outcome of the Mexican War, "Civil Disobedience" became one of the foundation stones of American dissent. In subsequent decades the essay inspired millions of dissenters, not only in the United States but also around the world. In the 1880s a young Brahmin studying law in London, Mohandas K. Gandhi, read it and spent the rest of his life fighting injustice in South Africa and his native India, where he spearheaded the civil disobedience campaign for Indian independence. In the 1940s a young theology student in the United States also read "Resistance to Civil Government" and subsequently implemented Thoreau's philosophy when he led the Montgomery, Alabama, bus boycott in 1955. And then in 1963, when he wrote "Letter from Birmingham Jail," the Reverend Martin Luther King, Jr., too, like Thoreau, advocated the breaking of unjust laws.

* * *

By the terms of the Treaty of Guadalupe Hidalgo ending the Mexican War the Rio Grande was formally recognized as the border between Texas and Mexico, the United States received California and New Mexico (a vast territory out of which the states of California, New Mexico, Arizona, Nevada, and Utah were carved), and Mexico received $15 million as compensation. After gold was discovered in California in 1848, thousands of eager, hopeful individuals from back east as well as Canada, Europe, Latin America, and China poured into the territory acquired from Mexico. By the end of 1849 more than one hundred thousand Americans had arrived in California, and by 1852 the "forty-niners" had increased California's population to nearly a quarter million people. Most hoped to strike it rich and then move on. Few intended to settle in California. At first there was enough gold to be found that prospectors accumulated an average daily take of about twenty dollars—an exorbitant sum in 1849—but as more and more new arrivals flooded in and as the more easily accessible surface gold was taken, the average daily take fell to about six dollars. Within a few years prospecting for gold required the financial resources of large mining companies that had the capital to invest in the heavy equipment needed to bore tunnels and shafts into the hills. Most miners were men hired by the mining companies at subsistence wages, and they labored under conditions that were, if anything, worse than the conditions of their eastern counterparts working in factories in Philadelphia or Cleveland. The only people who got rich on mining were those who owned the mining companies, most of whom never picked up a shovel or pick axe in their lives.

Although the gold rush was a huge boon to the American economy, there was also a considerable negative impact, especially for ethnic minorities. Mexicans, African Americans, and Chinese found suffering, hardship, and racial discrimination rather than riches. Indeed, for many of the Spanish-speaking inhabitants of California, some of whom owned vast estates that had been in their families for generations, the arrival of fortune hunters spelled doom—Americans confiscated their estates, and the *rancheros* found there was no legal recourse for them to get their land back. Laws were passed requiring nonwhites to pay an exorbitant tax just for the privilege of prospecting for gold in California. Most Chinese moved to San Francisco, where they could make a better living running small laundries or restaurants than they could in the gold fields. Mexicans and African Americans barely scraped by and found themselves little better off than they had been before making the trek to California.

* * *

At first the Indians and Hispanics who had been living in the West for centuries welcomed the Americans, but this quickly changed when they encountered white aggression. In 1846 the Sioux presented to President Polk a petition in which they demanded compensation for the damage that white settlers were inflicting on them. Despite the fact that the Sioux treated the Americans cordially, "the Emigrants going over the Mountains from the United States," their petition read, "have been the cause that Buffalo have in great measure left our hunting grounds, thereby causing us to go into the Country of Our Enemies to hunt, exposing our lives daily for the necessary subsistence of our wives and Children and getting killed on several occasions."[12] When Polk ignored the Sioux petition, they took matters into their own hands and attempted to collect tolls from whites entering their territory. This, in turn, angered whites, who now demanded federal protection and even a federal response to punish the Indians for their audacity. The government in Washington, however, did nothing.

With the onset of the gold rush, friction between whites and Indians increased rapidly, forcing the federal government to formulate a policy that was designed to ease tensions. A series of forts were constructed to provide security, and Washington scheduled a conference to meet with the Indians to convince them to make peace with white settlers and each other and remain within specified geographical areas. In 1851 thousands of Indians from all over the plains met with federal officials at Fort Laramie. But the meeting did not go as peacefully as anticipated. Some Indian nations refused to send representatives because their enemies were attending, and there were even skirmishes between some of the Indians as they arrived at Fort Laramie. Nevertheless, American officials urged the Indians to accept the fact that the times had changed and that they must expect to live differently in the future. The Americans promised that the Indian nations would be compensated for the loss of their hunting and grazing grounds, and they drew up boundaries for land that would be reserved for each Indian nation. Many of the chiefs agreed to the Fort Laramie Treaty, but there were some who turned it down. The Sioux, for example, vigorously protested the agreement and refused to be a part of it. One of the Sioux told the officials that they would not give up their claim to the lands south of the Platte River that they had conquered from their enemies. "These lands once belonged to the Kiowas and the Crows," he said, "but we whipped those nations out of them and in this we did what the white men do when they want the lands of the Indians."[13]

The Treaty of Guadalupe Hidalgo had specified that all Mexicans living in the territories ceded to the United States would be granted American citizenship and accorded all the rights guaranteed by the Constitution. Unfortunately Hispanic Americans soon discovered that their rights as citizens were rarely protected. When hundreds of *Californios* (Hispanic Americans who had lived their entire lives in California) prospected for gold, they were met with discrimination, intimidation, hostility, and even lynching. In southern California and New Mexico, where they remained a majority of the population, they did not incur as much prejudicial treatment, but in all areas of the southwest, as more and more whites moved in, the rights and privileges of Hispanic Americans were increasingly eroded. Even wealthy *Californios* who owned vast estates found their centuries-old land titles that had been granted under Mexican law declared null and void in American courts. To their dismay many of these men suddenly found themselves impoverished as their large estates were confiscated and parceled out to the newcomers.

The same state of affairs prevailed in Texas, where by 1850 Anglo settlers outnumbered *Tejanos* twenty to one. Despite the fact that so many *Tejanos* had fought just as fervently for Texas independence as the Anglos, they found themselves second-class citizens. In one Texas county in 1856 all inhabitants of Mexican descent were expelled and their land confiscated. "To strangers this may seem wrong," a journalist admitted, "but we hold it to be perfectly right and highly necessary."[14] Whether Hispanics lived in Texas, California, or New Mexico, they (like blacks and Indians) learned the hard lesson that democracy in the United States was reserved for white men.

But many contested this treatment. In the 1850s Juan Cortina, a wealthy landowner and political boss in south Texas, led a protest campaign against Anglo bigotry, racism, and intimidation. When Anglos expropriated much of his family's property, Cortina sought legal redress but without success. He began stepping outside the law, raiding white settlements, and stealing cattle. When judges and lawyers in Brownsville, Texas, succeeded in running a number of poor *Tejanos* off their land by manipulating the legal system, Cortina's protests took a violent turn. The violence was triggered in July 1859 when Cortina witnessed the brutalization of a Mexican American by the Brownsville marshal. Cortina rescued the arrested man and shot the marshal. Two months later Cortina led a paramilitary band of more than fifty men into Brownsville shouting "Death to Americans!" and seized the town. On September 30 he issued a "Proclamation . . . to the inhabitants of the State of Texas," in which he denounced the "multitude of lawyers," whose "sole purpose" is the "despoiling the Mexicans of the lands and usurp them," detailed the history of abuse and exploitation that Mexican Americans suffered at the hands of whites, and demanded that Mexican Americans be accorded the full rights and protection of American citizenship. By the end of the year, however, Cortina evacuated Brownsville and was defeated by a band of Texas Rangers at the Battle of Rio Grande City. He retreated into Mexico, where he remained until the outbreak of

The Mexican rancher and militant outlaw Juan Cortina took up
arms to fight against the repression of *Tejanos* just before the
Civil War. Photograph c. 1860s. (Public domain)

the Civil War, when he launched a series of raids into Texas. Though he
remained in Mexico for most of the remainder of his life, Juan Cortina
became an inspiring symbol to Mexican Americans of open defiance
and fierce resistance to bigotry and racism.[15]

* * *

When the Mexican War ended, the nation was gearing up for a presidential election. The most significant issue during the campaign was the
future of slavery in the new territories. Mexico had already outlawed
slavery, but now as the United States took possession of California and

New Mexico, the question arose whether to reintroduce slavery. Northerners wanted to prohibit slavery in the new territories, but southerners, led by John C. Calhoun, introduced resolutions in Congress affirming slaveholders' rights to take their property with them into the territories. President Polk, although he had decided not to run for reelection, proposed that the Missouri Compromise line, 36° 30´, be extended to the Pacific Ocean. Both major parties, however, when they convened to nominate their candidates and devise their platforms, hoped to sidestep the volatile issue entirely.

The Democrats campaigned on the idea of "squatter sovereignty" (later called popular sovereignty), which called for the people living in each territory to decide for themselves whether to permit slavery. This fit in nicely with the American ideal that sovereignty rested in the people. The Whigs tried to ignore the issue entirely. But when they nominated war hero and slaveholder General Zachary Taylor for president, a significant number of antislavery Whigs broke with the party.

In August these "Conscience Whigs" joined with disgruntled antislavery "Barnburner Democrats" and the antislavery Liberty Party to form the Free-Soil Party. At their convention in Buffalo, New York, speakers condemned slavery and the southern plot to extend the institution into the new territories. Slavery, free-soilers proclaimed, was contrary to Christian principles and had no place in a free, democratic nation. Slavery was "a great moral, social, and political evil" that must be destroyed.[16] They nominated former president Martin Van Buren and drafted a platform with the slogans "no more Slave States and no more Slave Territories" and "free soil, free speech, free labor, and free men."[17] Although the free-soilers were opposed to the extension of slavery into the territories, their motivation was not an abhorrence of the peculiar institution. What they meant by "free soil" and "free labor" and "free men" was that the territories should be an area where free white men could settle and find employment and economic success without having to compete with slave labor. The Free-Soil Party wanted to keep slaves (as well as free blacks) out of the territories so that they would not be in competition with whites.

In the end, the Free-Soil Party won 14 percent of the popular vote, but the Whigs won the election. In March 1849 Zachary Taylor was sworn in as the nation's twelfth president, and it seemed that nothing much was going to change.

* * *

Back in the early seventeenth century John Winthrop referred to Massachusetts Bay Colony as a "citty upon a hill"[18] on which the eyes of the entire world would be fastened. In the eighteenth century American revolutionaries believed that the new republican form of government that they had created would encourage other nations to develop democracy. Now the nation had expanded to a distant ocean, and American democracy was on a stage three thousand miles wide. Would this experiment in democracy be an inspiration to the whole world, or would it be a disappointment? Whites were fiercely proud of American democracy. But not all Americans were experiencing the democratic dream—certainly not Indians, slaves, free blacks, Hispanics, and Chinese. The promise was there, but when would it be extended to them? Some members of these minorities resisted the forces of subjugation, some of them acquiesced in their lot, and others fought hard to attain the same rights and privileges that were considered the birthright of white Americans.

The nation was growing, but so too was the explosive quarrel about slavery. Disharmony, dissent, and disunion were in the air. At the dawn of the 1850s it was clear that the dispute was not going to go away and that it was imperative for Americans to find the wisdom and the courage to resolve it.

CHAPTER 8

Dissent Imperils the Union

I have only a short time to live—only one death to die, and I
will die fighting for this cause. There will be no more peace in
this land until slavery is done for.
　　　—John Brown, Osawatomie, Kansas, 1856

The U.S. victory over Mexico was a two-edged sword. It boosted nationalism and Americans' confidence in the future of the nation, while at the
same time the outcome of the war stirred up a veritable hornet's nest
of uncontrolled sectional conflict. The acquisition of a vast territory
containing a wealth of raw materials and natural resources portended
an era of unprecedented prosperity and growth, but would slavery be
permitted or forbidden in that territory? The perpetual impasse on the
subject of slavery continued to threaten the core democratic ideals on
which the republic was founded. By the 1850s antislavery dissenters
had hardened their position, while proslavery southerners stood firm
against the attacks on their way of life. For every law enacted to curb
slavery, dissident southerners sought ways to bypass, break, or overturn the law. Likewise for every law and judicial decision strengthening
the peculiar institution, antislavery activists pushed for laws that would
abolish or at the very least cripple slavery. Moderate reformers were
becoming irrelevant as radicals on both sides grew stronger and drew
increasing numbers of adherents into their camps.

Lawmakers hoped that the Compromise of 1850 would reduce passions. But they were wrong. The Compromise, as it was finally worked
out, admitted California as a free state but stipulated that the inhabitants of any future states carved out of the Mexican Cession would
decide for themselves on the basis of popular sovereignty whether
to permit slavery. Thus a sop was thrown to both northern as well as
southern interests. The final two points consisted of one concession
to the North and one to the South, by outlawing the slave trade (but
not slavery) in the District of Columbia and enacting a stricter Fugitive

Slave Law. This last point was the most controversial of all—it was the one point that southerners insisted on but the one that northerners most objected to.

The Constitution originally specified that an escaped bondsman be taken into custody and returned to the owner. With the rise of the abolitionist movement, however, northern state and municipal governments showed little inclination to cooperate with southern slave catchers. In order to make it easier for southerners to reclaim their slaves, the new Fugitive Slave Law contained several provisions that favored slaveholders. For example, captured slaves would no longer be granted a jury trial, nor would they have the right to testify in their own defense. This meant that even free blacks could be captured and returned into slavery without any legal recourse to prove they were free. Federal marshals and police officers were authorized to deputize bystanders to help restrain the fugitive. If the bystander refused, he was subject to arrest, fine, and imprisonment. These provisions angered northerners, even those not opposed to slavery. For many Americans, including those who believed blacks were an inferior race, it raised the question of whether human rights were subordinate to property rights. Was the natural right to own property superior to the natural right to be free?

During the first months after the law was enacted eighty-four "fugitives" were captured and, with no opportunity to mount a defense, were returned to slavery. But there was resistance—intense resistance. Several states enacted "personal liberty laws" that made it illegal for state officials to enforce the Fugitive Slave Law. Frederick Douglass defied the law by hiding runaways and assisting their escape to Canada, while the Underground Railroad stepped up its operations. In 1851 in Christiana, Pennsylvania, a slave owner who attempted to capture his runaway slave was killed. An antislavery mob broke into a Syracuse, New York, jail, rescued a fugitive, and helped him escape to Canada. The most notorious incident of northern resistance against the Fugitive Slave Law was the case of Anthony Burns, who was captured in Boston in 1854. During the extradition hearing an armed crowd stormed the courthouse and tried unsuccessfully to free him. When the federal government dispatched a ship to Boston to take Burns back to Virginia, the U.S. Army was needed to escort Burns to the vessel through a mob of twenty thousand enraged Bostonians. The impact of this event won many new converts to the antislavery cause—not so much because they

were morally opposed to slavery but because the sight of slave catchers forcing a man back into slavery (with the help of the U.S. Army)
was just too inhumane for many Americans. Amos Lawrence claimed
that he was radicalized when he witnessed the Burns episode. "We
went to bed one night old-fashioned, conservative Compromise Union
Whigs," he wrote, "& waked up stark mad abolitionists."[1] Antislavery
sentiment in Boston amplified throughout the decade, and antislavery
protestors took to the streets whenever a slave was caught and returned
to bondage.

* * *

In 1854 Senator Stephen A. Douglas of Illinois, eager to promote the
construction of a transcontinental railroad that would link Chicago with
San Francisco, introduced a bill in Congress that would facilitate building the railroad through Kansas. Douglas was aware that southerners
would resist organizing a territory in an area where slavery was prohibited (because it was north of the Missouri Compromise line), and so he
put together the act in a way that he believed would satisfy both slaveholding and free-labor interests. He proposed repealing the Missouri
Compromise line and forming the territories of Kansas and Nebraska
on the principle of popular sovereignty: the inhabitants would vote
whether the territory should permit or prohibit slavery. Presumably, he
reasoned, Kansas would come in as a slave state, Nebraska free.

Douglas unleashed a firestorm. Northerners of both major parties protested bitterly against what they saw as yet another plot to
strengthen the slave interest. Senators Charles Sumner and Salmon P.
Chase, Congressman Joshua Giddings, and other antislavery men published *Appeal of the Independent Democrats*, denouncing the act as a
plot to turn Kansas and Nebraska into a "dreary region of despotism,
inhabited by masters and slaves."[2] While senators and congressmen
debated the bill, protest rallies broke out all over the North. Abolitionists condemned the bill. Frederick Douglass claimed it was the "audacious villainy of the slave power" that was responsible for foisting the
act on the American people.[3] The bill aroused Abraham Lincoln "as
he had never been before" and persuaded him to reenter politics with
the express purpose of opposing the extension of slavery into the territories.[4] "The monstrous injustice of slavery," Lincoln said, "deprives
our republican example of its just influence in the world—enables the

Banner of the Know-Nothing Party, c. 1850. Members of this nativist political party were the most virulent anti-immigrant protestors of the nineteenth century. (Public domain)

enemies of free institutions, with plausibility to taunt us as hypocrites."[5] Instead of allowing slavery to spread into the territories, Lincoln called for a readoption of the principles embraced by the Declaration of Independence.

Anti-Nebraska Societies sprang up around the country, while political parties split along sectional lines. In the end, the Democratic Party managed to survive the Kansas-Nebraska Act; what was left of the Whig Party, however, wholly disintegrated. In its wake two new parties emerged, both products of discontent with the federal government's response to two of the most important issues of the time: the Know-Nothings and the Republican Party.

The xenophobia that had been growing since the 1840s was just as explosive an issue as the extension of slavery into the territories. Old-stock Protestants viewed the influx of Irish Catholic immigrants as a significant threat to the United States. Some even viewed the Irish immigrants as part of the advance guard of some sort of "popish plot" to undermine the nation's Protestant heritage. In 1849 the Supreme Order of the Star-Spangled Banner was founded in New York to prevent further immigration into the country and to increase the time

requirement necessary for immigrants already here to apply for citizenship. By 1854 they had established the American Party (popularly called
the Know-Nothings because members replied "I know nothing" whenever outsiders inquired about the party) and attracted tens of thousands
of disgruntled, anti-immigrant, anti-Catholic Whigs and Democrats.

The Republican Party also was formed in 1854. Its central principle
was opposition to the extension of slavery into the territories. Republicans, like the Free-Soil Party, believed in the principle of free labor—
the belief that all *white* men must have the economic independence and
opportunity to better themselves. There should be no obstacle in the
way of a common laborer rising up to the status of a landowning farmer
or business proprietor or skilled craftsman. American democracy was
dependent on this freedom, and if slavery expanded into the territories,
it would compete with free labor. And this would mean the death knell
of democracy. The Republicans were not abolitionists (although some
abolitionists were Republicans); they were not opposed to slavery on
moral grounds, but they did want slavery to die out for economic and
political reasons.

* * *

Concurrent with the restructuring of the political party system, a series
of events further inflamed tensions and led to escalating protests on
both sides of the Mason-Dixon line.

Several books published during the 1850s pushed many of those who
had been straddling the fence into taking sides over the slavery debate.
The most famous and influential of all was Harriet Beecher Stowe's 1852
novel *Uncle Tom's Cabin*, which relates the heartbreaking story of fugitive slaves. Only two years after politicians predicted that the Compromise of 1850 would settle the slavery issue, millions of Americans were
stunned by the story of slaves frantically trying to escape from bondage.
Readers wept when they read about the slave Eliza fleeing across the
ice-choked Ohio River in a desperate attempt to save her baby from
slavery, or when they read of the Christ-like Tom being sold away from
his wife and family, or when they read of the utter brutality of the slave
master Simon Legree. Within months of publication the book was the
best-selling novel of the nineteenth century. Northerners were horrified over the devastating impact of slavery on God-fearing Christian

families in the United States, while southerners were outraged and offended over what they considered an exaggerated, patently dishonest depiction of their way of life.

The book's impact is not to be underestimated. It was reported that as far away as England Queen Victoria wept when she read *Uncle Tom's Cabin*. Lord Palmerston was so moved when he read the novel that later, in 1862 when he was prime minister, he persuaded Parliament *not* to tender formal recognition of the Confederacy—a decision that may very well have affected the outcome of the Civil War. In America most readers were aware that *Uncle Tom's Cabin* was hardening lines and pushing the nation toward civil war. And the story is often told that when Abraham Lincoln met Harriet Beecher Stowe at a White House reception in 1863, he remarked, "So you're the little woman who wrote the book that made this great war!"[6]

In a less emotional vein Hinton Rowan Helper of North Carolina published a scholarly critique of slavery in 1857 that also intensified emotions both North and South. In *The Impending Crisis of the South* he denounced the oligarchical despotism that controlled the South and condemned slavery as the basic cause of the lack of southern economic growth. The southern elite, Helper maintained, had too much wealth and power, while most southerners languished behind in an economic and cultural backwater. The only way for the South to flourish was for whites who did not own slaves to unite and vote the slaveholding aristocracy out of office. "Slavery lies at the root of all the shame," Helper wrote, "poverty, ignorance, tyranny, and imbecility of the South."[7] *The Impending Crisis* was read throughout the North, and the Republican Party financed an abridged edition of it for distribution; but in the South it was effectively banned.

Still, many southerners did read the book and responded angrily. One was Virginian George Fitzhugh, who wrote *Cannibals All*, a passionate defense of the peculiar institution that became a best-seller throughout the South. In it Fitzhugh praised slavery as a much more humane system of labor than the northern wage-slave system. In the North, he wrote, when workers lost their jobs or could no longer work because of infirmity or sickness, they were quickly rendered destitute, whereas slaves in the South were taken care of. "Capital exercises a more perfect compulsion over free laborers," Fitzhugh wrote, "than human masters over slaves, for free laborers must at all times work or starve, and slaves are supported whether they work or not. . . . What a glorious thing to man is slavery, when want, misfortune, old age, debility, and sickness overtake him."[8] Unlike free workers, slaves need not fear old age or sickness. They would always be taken care of.

Publishing was one way agitators on both sides of the issue fanned the flames of discord. Stowe and Helper were two of many that used their writing skills to protest slavery; Fitzhugh was one of a multitude that railed against the abolitionists. Others decided that words and the most carefully constructed arguments were simply not powerful enough to defeat their adversaries. Some decided that the time had come to rely on the sword; others, the gun; and one, the cane.

The ink was hardly dry on the Kansas-Nebraska Act when both antislavery and proslavery forces mobilized to gain the upper hand in the new territory. In New England men were recruited and given financial support by the Massachusetts Emigrant Aid Society to establish free-soil communities in Kansas. But thousands of Missourians and inhabitants of other slave states also rushed into Kansas. The Democratic senator from Missouri, David Atchison, was especially vocal in organizing and pushing proslavery settlers to swarm over the border into neighboring Kansas. The senator encouraged the formation of secret societies and urged slaveholders to do whatever was necessary to prevent free-soilers from settling in Kansas, even if they had "to kill every God-damned abolitionist in the district."[9] In 1854, when proslavery settlers framed a state constitution at Lecompton that permitted slavery, thousands of Missouri "border ruffians" crossed into Kansas to vote in favor of it. In fact there were three thousand more ballots cast than registered voters in the territory! The following year angry antislavery settlers framed their own constitution at Lawrence, Kansas, and set up a free-soil government in Topeka. When President Franklin Pierce recognized the Lecompton government as the legitimate one, sympathizers around the country began supplying both sides with money, arms, and reinforcements to intimidate their opponents. An Alabama slaveholder raised an army of three hundred men to go to Kansas, while the abolitionist minister Henry Ward Beecher in New Haven, Connecticut, handed out Bibles and Sharp's rifles (dubbed "Beecher's Bibles") to men willing to go to Kansas to fight against slavery. There were fears that a civil war was about to break out in Kansas. And in May 1856 it did.

Firing guns and cannon, a proslavery mob raided Lawrence, Kansas. They sacked the offices of an antislavery newspaper, threw the printing presses into the river, and destroyed the Free State Hotel. A few days later antislavery forces retaliated. A band of seven abolitionists led by John Brown went to Pottawatomie Creek, where they hauled five proslavery settlers from their houses and, despite their frantic pleas, brutally hacked them to death with broad swords. For the next several months Bleeding Kansas erupted into an undeclared civil war, with more than two hundred people killed on both sides.

With Kansas descending into violence antislavery Republican Senator Charles Sumner of Massachusetts delivered a blistering speech in the Senate. He condemned Senator Atchison for instigating the crisis and Senator Andrew Butler of South Carolina for having taken the "Harlot slavery" as his mistress and denounced the "incredible atrocities of the Assassins and of the Thugs" that were taking slaves into Kansas.[10] Two days later Congressman Preston Brooks of South Carolina (Butler's nephew), outraged at Sumner's scathing attack (with its sexual innuendo) on his uncle and the South, strode into the Senate chamber and savagely beat the Massachusetts senator with a cane. Sumner suffered so much brain and spinal-cord damage that it was three years before he sufficiently recovered to resume his senatorial duties. Throughout the North people were shocked that such violence had reached the Senate floor, and Sumner instantly became a symbolic hero for the North fighting to preserve freedom against the interests of the slave power. Likewise, throughout the South, Brooks was hailed as the valiant defender of southern virtue. Although he was expelled from the House of Representatives, Brooks was overwhelmingly reelected. For months after his caning of Sumner hundreds of canes and walking sticks arrived in the post at Brooks's Washington office from southern supporters, with instructions that they might be useful if he came across another abolitionist in need of a good thrashing.

Tensions mounted even further just days after the inauguration of James Buchanan when the Supreme Court issued the *Dred Scott* decision. Dred Scott was a slave whose master had taken him for a time to Illinois and then to Minnesota, where slavery was prohibited by the Missouri Compromise. In 1846 Scott sued for his freedom on the grounds that his residency in a free state and a free territory meant that he and his wife were therefore free. The case dragged on for over a decade as it worked its way to the Supreme Court. Finally, in March 1857, Chief Justice Roger B. Taney delivered the Court's decision in *Dred Scott v. Sandford.* Taney ruled that because Dred Scott was a slave, he was not a citizen and therefore had no right to bring a lawsuit to the Supreme Court. Taney could have stopped there, but he went on to declare that a black man "had no rights which the white man was bound to respect." Africans, were not part of "the family of nations, and [thus are] doomed to slavery."[11] Furthermore, Taney declared, Congress had overstepped its authority when it had approved the Missouri Compromise prohibiting slavery north of the 36° 30′ line because the Constitution expressly forbids Congress from making any law infringing on private property. Therefore the Missouri Compromise (which had recently been voided by the Kansas-Nebraska Act) was unconstitutional in the first place. Therefore the Republican Party's central principle of preventing the extension of slavery into the territories was itself unconstitutional.

North and South the response was instantaneous and in some cases fanatical. President Buchanan, though a northerner, hailed the decision as the law of the land and declared that slavery was clearly permissible in all American territories. He moved quickly to admit Kansas as a slave state, even though the proslavery state constitution that was framed at Lecompton had not yet been submitted to popular vote. Southerners rejoiced that the Supreme Court had endorsed slavery and their constitutional right to take their property with them even if they moved into a "free" territory. Newspapers throughout the South exulted that the Supreme Court had once and for all settled the question of slavery in their favor. The South, they firmly believed, was vindicated in resisting northern pressure to limit or prohibit the God-given right to own slaves.

Northerners and specifically Republicans were horrified that the Missouri Compromise, which to them was nearly in the same pantheon of documents as the Declaration of Independence and the Constitution, was ruled unconstitutional. Republicans were convinced that the "Slave Power Conspiracy" had hijacked the Supreme Court of the United States. Their only hope was to elect a Republican in 1860 who would have the authority to reconstruct the Supreme Court by appointing antislavery men to the bench when vacancies occurred.

Abolitionists and moderate Republicans were also shocked that the Supreme Court ruled that property rights were superior to human rights and individual freedom. Frederick Douglass condemned the decision as "a most scandalous and devilish perversion of the Constitution" and said that no matter how hard Chief Justice Taney tried, he "cannot . . . change the essential nature of things—making evil good, and good, evil."[12] William Lloyd Garrison registered an "indignant protest against the Dred Scott decision, . . . against the alarming aggressions of the Slave Power upon the rights of the people of the North—and especially against the existence of the slave system at the South, from which all these have naturally sprung, as streams of lava from a burning volcano." Garrison vowed "to 'crush out' slavery wherever it exists in the land."[13] Abraham Lincoln, less emotionally, attacked the logic of the decision. Taney's argument that the Declaration of Independence and the Constitution did not apply to blacks, Lincoln reasoned, is false because free blacks were part of the electorate in five of the states that ratified the Constitution, and the phrase "We the People" applied to them as well.

In the midst of the explosive debate after the *Dred Scott* decision there was a financial panic. Scores of insurance companies and banks failed, speculators began dumping their stock, European demand for American grain declined, hundreds of thousands of workers lost their jobs. As the panic worsened, unemployed workers took to the streets in New York and other large cities protesting the government's incompetent response to the depression and demanding aid and relief. Buchanan was finally forced to deploy marines and soldiers to control the thousands of protestors.

Even the economic downturn exacerbated sectional tensions. Northerners blamed southern politicians for voting against higher tariffs. Southerners blamed the depression on the greed of northern industrialists and financiers and gloatingly declared that the panic was further proof that the slave system was superior to the wage-slave system; northern workers lost their jobs, became destitute, and went hungry, while southern slaves were not affected by the depression. In Congress northern Republicans fought with southern Democrats over how to stimulate a recovery. In the out-of-control acrimonious atmosphere on the heels of the *Dred Scott* decision every piece of legislation introduced by the Republicans, such as the Homestead Act, which would provide cheap land for midwestern farmers and hopefully mitigate economic hardship, was defeated by southern Democrats or vetoed by President

Buchanan. Within a year the economy began to recover, but the Panic of 1857 was a further reminder that there was little desire for cooperation between North and South.

* * *

Although Abraham Lincoln abhorred slavery and believed that each man should have the opportunity to rise as far as his potential would take him, he was not an abolitionist. He was a moderate antislavery man. He opposed interfering with slavery where it already existed but believed it was essential not to allow it to spread. Like most nineteenth-century men Lincoln shared the prevailing racial notions of the day that blacks were inferior to whites for historical and cultural reasons, but he earnestly believed that "all men are created equal." This did not mean that "all men [are] equal *in all* respects," for the founding fathers "did not mean to say all were equal in color, size, intellect, moral developments, or social capacity," Lincoln said in 1857, but that they were "equal in 'certain inalienable rights, among which are life, liberty, and the pursuit of happiness.'"[14] This meant that all human beings are born equally to these natural rights. "I want every man to have the chance," he said, "and I believe a black man is entitled to it, in which he *can* better his condition."[15] To Lincoln it was also clear that the founding fathers' intention, with the Ordinance of 1787 prohibiting slavery in the Northwest Territory was to confine slavery to the South, where it would eventually die a natural death. Lincoln's reputation grew as he spoke out ever more frequently on the slavery issue. "If slavery is not wrong," he declared, "nothing is wrong."[16]

Lincoln also had as much of an aversion to the anti-Catholic bigotry and ethnic prejudice of the Know-Nothings as he had for slavery. "Our progress in degeneracy appears to me to be pretty rapid," he commented.

As a nation, we began by declaring that *"all men are created equal."* We now practically read it "all men are created equal, *except negroes."* When the Know-Nothings get control, it will read "all men are created equal, except negroes, and *foreigners, and catholics."* When it comes to this I should prefer emigrating to some country where they make no pretence of loving liberty—to Russia, for instance, where despotism can be taken pure, and without the base alloy of hypocrisy.[17]

In 1858 Lincoln sought to unseat the architect of the hated Kansas-Nebraska Act, Senator Stephen A. Douglas. He challenged Douglas to a series of debates that became the highlight of the campaign and proved to be momentous. Lincoln repeatedly attacked Douglas on the concept of popular sovereignty. "A House divided against itself cannot stand," he famously said, meaning that the nation had to choose one way or the other between slavery or freedom. If the United States wished to be an example unto the world that democracy can work, then it must choose freedom over slavery. Douglas defended popular sovereignty as the perfect expression of freedom and democracy because the people have the right to choose how they would govern themselves. Douglas contended that Congress had no right "to force a good thing upon a people who are unwilling to receive it." Although Lincoln acknowledged that "self government is right," it was morally wrong when slavery entered the picture. "When the white man governs himself," Lincoln argued, "that is self-government; but when he governs himself, and also governs *another* man, that is *more* than self-government—that is despotism. If the negro is a *man*, why then my ancient faith teaches me that 'all men are created equal'; and that there can be no moral right in connection with one man's making a slave of another."[18]

Douglas attacked Lincoln's patriotism by calling him a radical who had "distinguished himself by his opposition to the Mexican war, taking the side of the common enemy against his own country." He also played to voters' racist attitudes by accusing Lincoln of being an extreme abolitionist who would subjugate the white race to the black. Despite Lincoln's liberal stance that blacks too were included in the "all men are created equal" doctrine, he made it clear that he believed blacks inferior to whites. When Douglas declared, "I am opposed to negro citizenship in any and every form. . . . I believe this government was made on the white basis . . . . I believe it was made by white men, for the benefit of white men and their posterity for ever," Lincoln replied that he was not interested in introducing "political and social equality between the white and the black races." Nevertheless, he pointed out,

There is no reason in the world why the negro is not entitled to all the natural rights enumerated in the Declaration of Independence. . . . I agree with Judge Douglas he is not my equal in many respects—certainly not in color, perhaps not in moral and intellectual endowment. But in the right to eat the bread, without leave of anybody else, which his own hand earns, *he is my equal and the equal of Judge Douglas, and the equal of every living man.*[19]

Lincoln's somewhat paradoxical stance underscores how much he was a man of his age. In the nineteenth century racial assumptions went unchallenged. But as Lincoln biographer Doris Kearns Goodwin has pointed out in analyzing his racial statements, Lincoln in many respects was ahead of his time in rejecting most (but obviously not all) racial stereotypes. Even though he asserted during the debates that he believed the black man inferior, it is worth noting that the former slave Frederick Douglass, who never flinched from criticizing Lincoln's delay in abolishing slavery, commented on first meeting Lincoln in the White House, "[He is] the first great man that I talked with in the United States freely, who in no single instance reminded me of the difference between himself and myself, of the difference of color."[20] Lincoln, Douglass concluded, was entirely free from racial prejudice.

* * *

As we have seen, throughout the 1850s antislavery activists from a variety of backgrounds and opinions protested against the institution, protested against the extension of slavery into the territories, protested against the Fugitive Slave Law. At the same time, thousands of others protested against those who would infringe on their sacred right to own property even if that property was human. Most often the protestations took the form of speeches, books, and pamphlets, sometimes as public protest demonstrations and acts of civil disobedience, and sometimes, as in Kansas and in the Senate chamber, violence erupted and blood was shed.

To this day John Brown remains a controversial character. Some historians have maintained that he was insane, a wide-eyed fanatic, a terrorist. Others claim that there was a method to his madness and that to consider him mentally imbalanced is to denigrate his commitment to ending slavery. Certainly he is one of the most significant radical dissenters in American history. Unlike some radicals he did not seek to overthrow the government and smash the system; he did seek, however, to overthrow the slave power, to overthrow a system that validated slavery. His radicalism is that he demanded that the United States live up to

John Brown, 1846. Brown was perhaps the most notorious of the
radical abolitionists. "I will die fighting for this cause. There will be no
more peace in this land until slavery is done for." This daguerreotype
of Brown was taken circa 1846–1847 by the African American photographer Augustus Washington. (Public domain; courtesy National
Portrait Gallery, Smithsonian Institution)

its principle that all men are created equal. Most Americans were unable
to fathom Brown's total devotion to the destruction of slavery and his
utter lack of racism. Most white abolitionists believed in the superiority
of whites and were just as racist as slaveholders. They opposed slavery
for moral or economic reasons, not because they thought blacks should
have an equal place in American society. Brown, however, believed in
the complete equality of the races. Throughout his life and throughout
all his antislavery operations all the African Americans who knew him
declared that Brown was the only white man in America they had ever
met who embraced them as equals. The portrayal of Brown as insane

began immediately after Harpers Ferry when Republicans, with an eye on the upcoming presidential election of 1860, distanced themselves from Brown's attack. Fearing that any connection with Brown would ruin their political prospects, they argued that although Brown was right in his opposition to slavery, he was insane to lead a terrorist strike against the South. Proslavery southerners also added to the legend of Brown's madness by proclaiming that only an insane man would think he could convince slaves to join him in an uprising against their masters. Slavery, southerners continued to insist, was a positive good for both slaves and masters, and to be so violently antislavery and to believe that blacks were equal to whites was an obvious sign of mental illness.

After Pottawatomie, Brown continued his operations in Bleeding Kansas while at the same time preparing another, more spectacular blow against slavery. His plan was to seize the federal arsenal in Harpers Ferry, Virginia, arm the local slaves, and repair to the Appalachians to launch a guerrilla war into the heart of the Deep South. In retrospect the plan seems foolhardy and bound to fail. But Brown did believe that slaves would rally to him and that he would be able to establish a base in the mountains. Even if he was killed during the operation or captured and executed, Brown was certain that his martyrdom would hasten the destruction of slavery.

By the autumn of 1859 Brown and his band of twenty-two men (five of them free blacks) were ready to move. On October 16 they crossed the Potomac River and attacked the arsenal at Harpers Ferry. At first they were successful, but as they waited for the slaves to join the rebellion, it was soon obvious that they would wait in vain. None of the slaves rose up, but the townspeople and the local militia did. After a shootout they forced Brown and his men to retreat to a nearby firehouse, where they were besieged for the next twenty-four hours. At first light on the morning of October 18, Colonel Robert E. Lee, commanding a company of U. S. Marines, stormed the building and captured the severely wounded Brown and the five surviving members of his band.

During Brown's trial for treason against the state of Virginia testimony revealed that northern abolitionists funded him. This infuriated southerners even more than Brown's attack had infuriated them. It confirmed their suspicion that *all* northerners were ready to finance acts of terrorism to destroy the southern way of life. Brown's majestic deportment during the trial, however, earned the admiration of northerners, many of whom saw Brown as a martyr ready to lay down his life for his fellow man. At his sentencing Brown faced the court and declared that although he was guilty of trying to free the slaves, he was not guilty of a crime. "Had I so interfered [invading Virginia] in behalf of the rich," he claimed, "and suffered and sacrificed what I have . . . , it would have been all right; and every man in this court would have deemed it an act worthy of reward rather than punishment." But in his heart he was content with what he had done and with the court's verdict. "Now if it is deemed necessary that I should forfeit my life for the furtherance of the ends of justice," he said, "and mingle my blood further with the blood . . . of millions in this slave country whose rights are disregarded by wicked, cruel, and unjust enactments. I submit; so let it be done!"[21]

On December 2, 1859, Brown went to the gallows. As he left his cell, he handed a note to a nearby soldier. "I, John Brown am now quite certain that the crimes of this guilty land will never be purged away, but with Blood. I had, as I now think vainly, flattered myself that without very much bloodshed, it might be done."[22] Even the governor of Virginia, the jailors, and the jury that had condemned him were impressed with his commitment to the destruction of slavery, his eloquence during the trial, and the courage he displayed as he faced his execution.

The reaction around the country was swift and disquieting. Although most Republican politicians, including Lincoln, deplored Brown's deed, thousands of northerners compared Brown to Christ. Church bells tolled, cannon were fired, and memorial services were held throughout the North. Ministers preached that Brown's mission was "holy" and extolled him as a martyr for a noble cause. Ralph Waldo Emerson claimed that Brown had made "the gallows as glorious as the crucifixion." Herman Melville later hailed him as the "meteor" of the Civil War, and Frederick Douglass confessed, "I could only live for the slave. John Brown could die for the slave!"[23] Southerners were appalled. They were absolutely convinced that Brown represented all abolitionists, who in turn represented all Republicans, who in turn represented all northerners. Southern newspapers decried Brown as a terrorist and murderer. A hostile North, they raged, was out to destroy the southern way of life. Immediately there was a redoubling of southern dissent against the federal government. Increasingly isolated and defensive, the South grew increasingly radical. And as southern radical "fire-eaters" protested in apocalyptic fury, they persuaded more and more southerners that there was no future for the South in the United States of America.

Brown's ultimate act of defiance, of uncompromising protest against the slave power, persuaded all southern states to expand their militias as rapidly as possible and prepare for the worst.

* * *

The nation was so divided in 1860 that four candidates ran for president. Republicans nominated Lincoln. Northern Democrats nominated Stephen A. Douglas; southern Democrats bolted the party and nominated John Breckinridge of Kentucky. A fourth party, the Constitutional Union Party, believing the only hope to save the Union was to ignore slavery and *not* take any political stance at all, nominated John Bell of Tennessee.

Breckinridge won the Deep South, while Bell took three border states (Kentucky, Tennessee, and Virginia); Douglas won Missouri and three of New Jersey's seven electoral votes; and Lincoln won the rest. Within hours of Lincoln's election newspapers throughout the South called for secession. In Charleston, South Carolina, one editor declared that "the tea has been thrown overboard; the revolution of 1860 has been initiated."[24]

From the founding of the republic the South had dominated American politics. Now a man who did not even appear on southern ballots was elected president. To southerners it seemed that their influence over American political life had suffered an irreversible setback. They would never again be able to dominate American political discourse, and their influence would diminish drastically as new territories would enter the Union as free states. Furthermore, southerners were infuriated at what they viewed as the hypocrisy at the core of northerners' antislavery stance. Southerners were feeling an economic pinch because the price of field hands had been rising steeply and could not be checked because the ban on the international slave trade removed the possibility of lowering prices by importing more slaves from Africa. But even as southern profits declined, northern merchants and manufacturers were profiting enormously from slave-based cotton.

One by one southern states began to secede. South Carolina was the first, on December 20, 1860. Six other states quickly followed suit,

Mississippi on January 9, Florida the following day, Alabama on the eleventh, Georgia on the nineteenth, Louisiana on the twenty-sixth, and Texas on February 1. In mid-February delegations from each of these states met in Montgomery, Alabama; proclaimed a new nation, the Confederate States of America; chose Jefferson Davis of Mississippi as president; and drew up a constitution that validated and protected slavery. As Alexander H. Stephens of Georgia put it, the Confederacy was founded on "the great truth that the negro is not equal to the white man, that slavery, subordination to the superior race, is his natural and normal condition."[25]

* * *

In the years before the Civil War the sheer number and diversity of anti-slavery critics and proslavery apologists created an enormous body of dissenting literature, speeches, and polemics, while protestors and militants committed acts of defiance, resistance, and even terrorism. With each passing year it seemed the nation was racing at a dizzying pace toward disaster: the Compromise of 1850 and the northern reaction to the implementation of the more stringent Fugitive Slave Law; the furor over the Kansas-Nebraska Act, popular sovereignty, and the dismantling of the Missouri Compromise; the outbreak of guerrilla warfare in Kansas; violence erupting in the Senate; and the intense joy and horror (depending on which section of the country one came from) that exploded after the *Dred Scott* decision all widened the chasm between North and South.

The formation of a new party dedicated to preventing the spread of slavery and the emergence of strong and opinionated political leaders such as Seward, Sumner, Lincoln, Douglas, and Davis also heated up the dispute that was driving a sectional wedge deep into the nation's psyche. But it was John Brown's attack on Harpers Ferry and the outcome of the election of 1860 that took the nation over the edge. As 1861 dawned, it seemed that compromise and cooperation, long-established strengths at the core of American politics, were hopelessly defunct. North and South radicals and fire-eaters, dissenters and protestors had brought the country to the brink of civil war.

CHAPTER 9

A Nation Divides

I have spoken freely and fearlessly to-day, as became an
American Representative and an American citizen; one
firmly resolved, come what may, not to lose his own Constitutional liberties, nor to surrender his own Constitutional
rights in the vain effort to impose these rights and liberties
upon ten millions of unwilling people.
—Congressman Clement L. Vallandigham's response to
President Abraham Lincoln's war policies, July 1861

After decades of heated antislavery debate and abolitionist activism,
southerners, even those who did not own slaves, were convinced that
emancipation would destroy the southern way of life. The threat was so
real, so frightening, that they believed they were left with no alternative
other than to take up arms against the United States. Like the revolutionary generation of 1776 that declared independence from Britain,
southerners in 1861 had come to view the government in Washington as
tyrannical. It was time to separate.

But not all southerners wished to secede from the Union or to go to
war against the Stars and Stripes. And not all northerners wanted to
fight a war to preserve the Union. North and South tens of thousands
went against the majority view of their sections, and both Presidents
Abraham Lincoln and Jefferson Davis were faced with the dual crisis
of fighting a war while concomitantly dealing with dissent on the home
front. It was not just the blood shed on the battlefield but the passionate arguments within both sections about civil liberties and waging war
that irrevocably transformed the American nation and ultimately set it
on a new course.

Lincoln spoke in his inaugural address directly to the seven seceded
states. He assured them that he had no intention of disturbing slavery
where it still existed, but he also reaffirmed his pledge to prevent the
extension of slavery into the territories. "In *your* hands," he declared,

shrewdly putting the responsibility for potential hostilities on the South's shoulders, "my dissatisfied fellow countrymen, and not in *mine*, is the momentous issue of civil war. The government will not assail *you*. You can have no conflict, without being yourselves the aggressors." Appealing to the common revolutionary heritage of all the states and to the inherent goodness in Americans' patriotic hearts, he hoped that "the mystic chords of memory . . . will yet swell the chorus of the Union, when again touched, as surely they will be, by the better angels of our nature."[1]

But Lincoln's eloquent appeal failed to convince the seceded states— which already viewed the United States as a hostile, foreign power—to return to the Union. Confederates felt a closer kinship to the patriots of 1776 than they felt for the Republicans, abolitionists, immigrants, factory workers, industrialists, and bankers of the North. The South, they argued, had not left the Union. The Union had left *them*. It was the North that had abandoned the principles of democracy and self-determination on which the nation was founded by trying to force the South to remain in the Union against its will. It was the United States that no longer carried the torch of liberty and freedom. The Confederacy, by going its own way, was the true heir of the American Revolution.

✳   ✳   ✳

The bombardment of Fort Sumter and Lincoln's subsequent call for troops ignited a wave of patriotism in the North. From Maine to Minnesota, Americans took to the streets in spontaneous demonstrations of support for the Union. Thousands of men enlisted in the army. Even the Democrat Senator Stephen A. Douglas rallied to Lincoln's side to endorse the president's measures for putting down the rebellion. But the Democrats remaining loyal to the Union split into two factions. War Democrats opposed secession and were willing to go to war to preserve the Union, but they were unwilling to fight for the abolition of slavery. Peace Democrats, however, would rather see the South go its own way than resort to military action. The Union, they believed, was not worth the sacrifice that war would entail. Even many Republicans and abolitionists were not convinced that war was the answer. In fact some, such as William Lloyd Garrison, claimed that the Union would be better off without the South. The South and its institution of slavery, they reasoned, was like a cancer that should be amputated before it infected the rest of the body. Let the southern states depart in peace, many northerners urged. It was going to be a significant challenge for Lincoln to unite the North behind the effort to preserve the Union.

The response in the South mirrored that of the North. A surge of southern patriotism swept over the Confederacy as young men rushed off to enlist—so many in fact that hundreds were turned away. "We are fighting for our liberty," one Confederate soldier declared proudly, "against tyrants of the North . . . who are determined to destroy slavery."[2] But, as in the North, not everyone was enthusiastic about going to war. Some southerners, especially in the backcountry, where there were few slaves, were reluctant to fight a war to preserve slavery and the interests of the planter class. But most of these men and women were torn between loyalty to their state and loyalty to the United States. In the northernmost slave states that remained in the Union in the aftermath of Fort Sumter, differences of opinion between Unionists and secessionists were more sharply drawn and led to fierce debate, arbitrary arrests, and in some cases, a civil war within the Civil War.

While both sides mobilized for war, Lincoln concentrated his political skills on preventing the secession of the four border slave states that were still, however tenuously, loyal to the Union. Although slavery existed in Delaware, Maryland, Kentucky, and Missouri, Union sentiment ran high in each of these states. Delaware's loyalty was never significantly in doubt. Kentucky at first attempted to remain neutral, and Lincoln was careful not to infringe on that neutrality. Lincoln's prudence paid off. Later, when the Confederates disregarded the proclamation of neutrality and invaded the state, Kentucky declared its loyalty to the Union. In Missouri both Union and secessionist feeling ran high, and though the deeply divided passions led to brutal partisan fighting that raged within the state for the duration of the greater conflict, Missouri did not secede. In both cases Lincoln's restraint and faith that Unionist sentiment was strong enough to keep Kentucky and Missouri from seceding bore fruit.

Maryland, however, was more problematic, and Lincoln resorted to harsh, unconstitutional means to prevent the state from seceding. Secessionist sentiment was so strong in Maryland that when the Sixth Massachusetts Regiment passed through Baltimore on its way to Washington shortly after the fall of Fort Sumter, it was attacked by a mob of over ten thousand secessionists. Five soldiers and nine civilians were killed, dozens were injured, the bridges leading out of Baltimore were burned, and Washington was cut off from the North. When the governor of Maryland and the mayor of Baltimore met with Lincoln in the White House a few days later, they demanded that federal troops be barred from traveling through Maryland. Lincoln emphatically refused to comply with their demand, although he did agree to route federal troops around Baltimore so as to forestall further acts of violence.

Lincoln hoped to lessen tensions in Maryland because if the state seceded, it would mean the isolation of the nation's capital inside the Confederacy. In that case the national government could be held hostage by secessionists, and the administration and Congress could conceivably become prisoners of war. Obviously such a scenario was unacceptable. When the state legislature opened debate on an ordinance to secede, Lincoln's response was to contravene civil rights by issuing orders to arrest the secessionist legislators. It was "necessary," Lincoln explained, "to suspend the writ of Habeas Corpus for the public safety."[3] (The writ requires that charges *must* be filed in order to hold a person in jail.) Hundreds of Confederate sympathizers, including the mayor of Baltimore and sixteen state legislators, were arrested, according to Lincoln's directive, "without resort to the ordinary processes and forms of law," and were left languishing in prison for months without being charged.[4] Supreme Court Chief Justice Roger B. Taney furiously denounced Lincoln's arbitrary usurpation of power in *Ex parte Merryman* (John Merryman was one of the men Lincoln had imprisoned), ruling that only Congress had the constitutional authority to suspend the writ of habeas corpus. Lincoln paid no heed to Taney's decision. Later in the year, after the secession crisis in Maryland had passed, Lincoln quietly freed the imprisoned secessionists.

Lincoln's violation of civil liberties, in flagrant disregard of the Constitution, caused a furor in the North. Alarmed citizens denounced the president as a despot, a tyrant, a dictator, who would destroy liberty and constitutional law. But Lincoln defended his actions by arguing that it was necessary to subvert one part of the Constitution in order to preserve the whole Constitution. In Lincoln's eyes if Maryland seceded, there was a good chance that Kentucky and Missouri would secede too and the game would be lost. The Union, Lincoln believed, could not be saved if the border states joined the Confederacy. In the end, Lincoln's controversial measures kept the four states in the Union.

The uproar over Lincoln's suspension of habeas corpus was not the only protest Lincoln had to deal with. There was also significant antiwar dissent. Thousands of northerners opposed the war for a variety of reasons. Peace Democrats opposed it for political reasons. Pacifists protested on moral or religious grounds. Draft dodgers did everything possible to avoid serving in the military. And there were hundreds of Confederate sympathizers who worked for the Confederacy as informants, spies, and saboteurs.

The most radical faction of the Peace Democrats went so far as to condemn Lincoln and the Republicans for foisting the war on the nation. Republicans viewed them as traitors and equated them with the venomous copperhead snake. But while it is true that the Copperheads denounced the war and criticized the constitutional abuses of the executive branch, they were not, despite Republican castigations, disloyal to the United States. In Congress the leading Copperhead was Representative Clement L. Vallandigham of Ohio. The Democratic congressman denounced Lincoln for the Maryland arrests and for raising an army by executive order while Congress was not in session. Vallandigham was convinced that even though blood had already been shed, compromise could still save the Union. He delivered several impassioned antiwar speeches condemning Lincoln, the administration, and the Republican Party for stifling civil liberties, overstepping constitutional authority, and rushing the nation into war. If Lincoln was not checked, Vallandigham insisted, Americans' cherished civil liberties would be a thing of the past. When Congress finally convened in July, Vallandigham gave a speech from the House floor in which he censured the president as a tyrant. He began by reminding his listeners that the Constitution stipulates that only Congress has the right to declare war and raise an army and navy, "yet, the President," he complained, "of his own mere will and authority, and without the shadow of right, has proceeded to increase, and has increased . . . a grand army, or military force, raised by executive proclamation alone, without the sanction of Congress, without warrant of law, and in direct violation of the Constitution, and of his oath of office." This alone, to Vallandigham, was an unforgivable "breach of the Constitution" that should not be tolerated by Congress or the American people. Not only that but Lincoln invaded "public liberty" by ordering officials to seize private citizens' telegraph dispatches without a search warrant, "in plain violation of the right of the people to be secure in their houses, persons, papers, and effects, against unreasonable searches and seizures." After citing specific examples of violations against the private property and personal liberty of citizens of Maryland, Vallandigham concluded that any cause "which demands the sacrifice of the Constitution and of the dearest securities of property, liberty, and life, can not be just; at least, it is not worth the sacrifice."[5]

Vallandigham continued to protest throughout the war. When he delivered a blistering speech in 1863 condemning the president for scheming to free the slaves and enslave the whites, Lincoln finally had had enough. He had Vallandigham arrested and, on rather dubious authority, deported to the Confederacy. Eventually the congressman made his way to Canada, where he campaigned in absentia for the Ohio gubernatorial race. He lost the election but subsequently slipped back into the U.S. Lincoln, realizing that arresting Vallandigham again would only boost his popularity among Democrats, wisely chose to ignore Vallandigham's return.

Vallandigham was the most notorious antiwar dissenter in the North, but there were thousands of other public figures as well as ordinary citizens who denounced the war. The mayor of New York City, Fernando Wood, for example, pushed for the secession of the city so that the cotton trade with the Confederacy would remain uninterrupted. Thousands were arrested for refusing to serve in the army. And there were hundreds who expressed their opposition to the Union by joining partisan gangs, especially in states that bordered the Confederacy. All through the war partisans attacked U.S. military patrols, sabotaged railroad lines, and destroyed supply depots. Historians estimate that over thirteen thousand protestors, militant activists, and partisans were arrested between 1861 and 1865. Many of the antiwar critics languished in prison without ever being tried, but those whose dissent was expressed through sabotage or other terroristic acts were tried and, not infrequently, executed.

In the Confederacy, although the majority of southerners supported the war and rushed to enlist, there was also widespread dissent. Thousands of southerners loyal to the Union protested when their states joined the Confederacy; many of them protested secession by joining the U.S. Army. But even among those who were in favor of secession, there was considerable dissent. Thousands denounced President Davis's leadership, his conduct of the war, and his violation of civil liberties.

Like the Loyalists during the American Revolution, Unionists in the South found themselves in the odd position of dissenting against the dissenters. In Tennessee, for example, newspaper publisher William Brownlow campaigned against the state's decision to secede. Brownlow, like most of his fellow eastern Tennesseans, loved his state and supported slavery, but he was deeply loyal to the United States and opposed secession. After Tennessee seceded in April 1861, Brownlow continued to fly the American flag and wrote editorials in his newspaper adamantly defending the right to fly the Stars and Stripes even if the state had joined the Confederacy. He was arrested, his printing press destroyed, and his newspaper, the *Knoxville Whig*, suppressed. Eventually he was tried for treason and banished from the Confederacy. Like Vallandigham in the North, Brownlow discovered that the price of dissent often meant the forfeiture of the right to free speech.

Unionist sentiment in the South was especially strong in those areas, such as eastern Tennessee, where there were few slaves. Such was the case in the hills of western North Carolina and Virginia. Unionist sentiment was so high in western Virginia, in fact, that the fifty western counties sent delegates to Wheeling in June 1861 to reject the secession ordinance and proclaim loyalty to the United States. These counties eventually seceded from Virginia, framed a new state constitution, and applied for admission to the Union in 1863 as the state of West Virginia. (Ironically, it was politicians who rejected the legitimacy of the doctrine of secession that admitted West Virginia, a state formed by counties seceding from Virginia, to the Union.)

In Arkansas more than a thousand Unionist war resisters banded together and formed a secret peace society. When the Confederate government in Richmond got wind of the Arkansas Peace Society, it sent agents to the state to destroy the organization. Members were arrested and tried for treason. Some were given the opportunity to avoid trial and possible execution if they consented to conscription into the Confederate army. Most of those who did, however, deserted across enemy lines as soon as they were sent into battle.[6]

In many counties throughout the South bands of Unionists, infuriated at the Confederate government's effort to raise revenue and conscript men, took up arms and engaged in partisan warfare. In eastern Tennessee and northern Georgia, for example, Unionists sabotaged bridges, railroads, and telegraph lines and ambushed Confederate patrols much the same way as prosouthern partisans did in the North.

There were numerous examples of other forms of dissent in the South. Many who were unquestionably committed to southern independence became increasingly unhappy with Jefferson Davis and the Confederate government's conduct of the war. Davis, like Lincoln, also stepped over the line protecting individual liberties. At the beginning of the war Davis liked to call attention to the Confederacy's undying commitment to the preservation of the civil liberties that the despotic Abraham Lincoln was determined to destroy. Davis's actions, however, belied his lofty words. On several occasions he suspended the writ of habeas corpus and routinely ordered the arrest, without charges, of civilians whose loyalty to the Confederacy was suspect. Most of these arrests, as in the North, took place in the border regions, such as Tennessee, Kentucky, Virginia, and Arkansas. For example, in January 1863 Davis suspended habeas corpus in Arkansas when he learned that there were thousands of traitors and deserters in that state. Clearly, both governments demanded the loyalty of their citizens even if it meant suspending some civil liberties.

One political leader who opposed Davis's policies was Governor Joseph E. Brown of Georgia. Brown objected to the suspension of habeas corpus and Richmond's frequent imposition of martial law. Brown viewed these policies, as well as the Confederate Conscription Act of 1862, as violations of the South's core principle of states' rights. The South, in Brown's view, had seceded because southerners were opposed to a strong central government. Ironically, in order to build an efficient war machine, finance the war, draft soldiers into the army, and appropriate property that could be used to fight the war, the Confederate government had to expand its powers at the expense of the individual states—the South, paradoxically, was turning into what it most despised. Brown, in 1862, wrote to Confederate Vice President Alexander H. Stephens deploring the fact that "military men are assuming the whole powers of government to themselves and setting at defiance constitution, laws, state rights, state sovereignty, and every other principle of civil liberty": "I fear we have much more to apprehend from military despotism than from subjugation by the enemy."[7] Later, in 1864, he sent a message to the Georgia state legislature condemning conscription and the suspension of habeas corpus as "the essence of military despotism," which, if not checked, would place "all civil rights in a state of subordination to military power, and [put] the personal freedom of each individual, in civil life, at the will of the chief of the military power. . . . When such bold strides towards military despotism and absolute authority, are taken, by those in whom we have confided, and who have been placed in high official position to guard and protect constitutional and personal liberty, it is the duty of every patriotic citizen to sound the alarm."[8]

* * *

Although Lincoln was opposed to the extension of slavery and believed it was an evil institution, he had no intention at the beginning of the war to put an end to it. Lincoln always held that if the institution was confined to the South, it would wither and die. But from the moment Lincoln took office, Frederick Douglass, William Lloyd Garrison, Senator Charles Sumner, Congressman Thaddeus Stevens, and other radical abolitionists rebuked Lincoln for his inaction. Even members of his Cabinet, most notably Treasury Secretary Salmon P. Chase, publicly criticized Lincoln for not making any move against slavery during his first year in office. But Lincoln was determined, above all, to move cautiously. Any precipitous move, he feared, would jeopardize his effort to hold the Union together. When General John C. Frémont, leading troops in Missouri, issued a proclamation in August 1861 emancipating Missouri slaves, Lincoln, alarmed that the proclamation would prompt the border states to secede, countermanded it and cashiered Frémont. Lincoln did, however, sanction General Benjamin Butler's policy of treating slaves as "contraband of war" as official Union policy. Slaves who escaped behind Union lines or came under federal authority in places where the army had advanced—notably in Louisiana and parts of Virginia and Tennessee—would be considered contraband. That is, since they could be used in the Confederate war effort to build railroad lines or transport supplies to the Confederate army, it was legitimate to confiscate and use them for the Union cause.

By July 1862, however, Lincoln decided to codify an official policy. At a Cabinet meeting on July 22 he read a draft for an emancipation proclamation that set January 1, 1863, as the day all slaves in states still in rebellion would be set free. After some debate the majority of the Cabinet approved. Secretary of State William Henry Seward suggested, however, that Lincoln hold off issuing the proclamation until a Union victory on the battlefield had been achieved; otherwise European nations would view the proclamation as a last-ditch, desperate attempt to gain international support because there was little progress on the battlefield. Seward, as secretary of state, was particularly sensitive to international reaction, as he was making every effort possible to prevent England and France from formally recognizing the Confederacy. Lincoln put the draft of the proclamation in his desk drawer and waited.

In August newspaper editor Horace Greeley published an open letter to the president in the *New York Tribune*, in which he blasted Lincoln for doing nothing about slavery. Lincoln's famous reply to Greeley is illuminating about the way his thinking was evolving as well as about his political sophistication. In a sense he was preparing the American public for the Emancipation Proclamation. "My paramount objective in this struggle," Lincoln wrote, even though he had already decided to issue the proclamation in the wake of a military victory, "*is* to save the Union, and is *not* either to save or to destroy slavery. If I could save the Union," he continued, "without freeing *any* slave I would do it, and if I could save it by freeing *all* the slaves I would do it; and if I could save it by freeing some and leaving others alone I would also do that."[9]

In September the moment arrived when Robert E. Lee's Army of Northern Virginia engaged Union forces at Sharpsburg. The Battle of Antietam, as it was called in the North, was essentially a draw; but the day after the battle Lee's army retreated south of the Potomac, and so Lincoln could portray it as a Union victory. On September 22, 1862, Lincoln announced the Preliminary Emancipation Proclamation, which decreed that on January 1, 1863, "all persons held as slaves within any state or designated part of a state, the people whereof shall then be in rebellion against the United States, shall be then, thenceforward, and forever free."[10]

The Emancipation Proclamation did not abolish slavery. Slavery was still permitted in slave states that had not seceded and in those areas of the Confederacy occupied by Union forces. By freeing the slaves in states that were still in rebellion, Lincoln was in effect offering an inducement to any Confederate state that if it rescinded its secession ordinance, it could keep its slaves. Lincoln did not expect any of the rebellious states to do so, but by framing the proclamation this way he was hoping not to alienate conservative northerners or slaveholders in the border states. The Emancipation Proclamation did, however, transform the conflict into a war for freedom. As the Union army advanced, all slaves coming under its jurisdiction were freed. The Union army became an army of liberation. And European nations that had already outlawed slavery were put into the position that recognizing the Confederacy would be seen as an endorsement of slavery.

* * *

Radical abolitionists who would not compromise on slavery and southern fire-eaters who defended the institution and the principle of states' rights with every fiber of their being were clearly responsible for setting in motion forces that led to the outbreak of the Civil War. Just as forces of dissent led to the war, the war itself created new circumstances that led to and inspired dissent movements in the aftermath of the war.

From the beginning of hostilities African Americans experienced a significant social transformation. Even before the Emancipation Proclamation affirmed the ending of slavery as one of the war's goals, African Americans demanded that they be allowed to participate in a war that would lead to freedom. In 1861 and 1862, as Union forces advanced into the Confederacy, thousands of slaves defied their owners by refusing to work unless they were paid; some destroyed plantations; others fled to the Union army, often bringing useful military intelligence with them. Even if Lincoln had not issued the Emancipation Proclamation, it seemed clear that slavery was on the way to extinction. In the North thousands of free blacks tried (unsuccessfully) to enlist in the army. By the beginning of 1862 the army was employing free blacks and escaped slaves as cooks and laborers, and in the months leading up to the Preliminary Emancipation Proclamation the army began to recruit former slaves in Missouri as well as in occupied sections of South Carolina and Louisiana. Influential abolitionists lobbied the president and Congress to sanction the formation of black combat regiments. African Americans, they argued, should contribute to the cause of their own freedom, but just as importantly, as Frederick Douglass put it, if they served as soldiers, it would facilitate their path to citizenship. "Once let the black man get upon his person the brass letters U.S.," Douglass said, "let him get an eagle on his button, and a musket on his shoulder and bullets in his pocket; and there is no power on earth which can deny that he has earned the right to citizenship in the United States."[11]

Lincoln yielded to the pressure and authorized the formation of the first black regiments in the fall of 1862. In early 1863, after the Emancipation Proclamation went into effect, the training of African American regiments began in earnest. The governor of Massachusetts invited Frederick Douglass to assist in recruiting blacks for a regiment, and Douglass enthusiastically toured a number of northern cities, organizing meetings calling for African Americans to enlist. By May the free blacks who had responded to Douglass's entreaties were being trained by white officers and formed the core of the Massachusetts Fifty-Fourth Regiment. In September 1863 the Massachusetts Fifty-Fourth, under the command of Captain Robert Gould Shaw (the son of a prominent Massachusetts abolitionist), led the attack on Fort Wagner in South Carolina. Although the regiment lost nearly half its men (including Shaw) and failed to capture the fort, the soldiers' heroism and courage made headlines around the country and did much to convince skeptical whites that the sons of Africa were indeed as brave and courageous as any white soldiers.

Over two hundred thousand African Americans served in the military during the war, 30 percent of whom became casualties. They suffered a heavier casualty rate primarily because enraged Confederates treated captured blacks as traitors, summarily killing most of them on the spot or forcing them back into slavery. But the overall experience of fighting for, and winning, emancipation was an empowering experience for the African Americans who served.

The Civil War also brought about a significant social transformation for women. On both sides of the Mason-Dixon line rural women from all classes had to do the plowing and sowing and harvesting and the day-to-day running of the farms and plantations; in the towns women worked in textile mills and factories or took over the management of the business or shop their husband owned. There was also demand for women to work in industries such as uniform and shoe manufacturing and as clerks and secretaries in civil service jobs. But the most striking way that the Civil War impacted women was in nursing. At the outset women volunteered to work as nurses, but since nursing was primarily a male profession, there was much reluctance to allow women to work in the hospitals. Part of the reluctance was because of the Victorian Age's prim sensibilities. It was not considered proper for women to attend to soldiers who had "stomach" (that is, groin) wounds. Furthermore, there was a prejudice that women who spent time with the army were women of ill repute or that the presence of women with the army would lead to a sharp rise in prostitution. Still, the bloody reality of the Civil War and the dire need for nurses to attend the huge numbers of wounded and dying soldiers finally overcame the reluctance, both North and South, to employ female nurses.

Nursing was not the only traditional male profession that women gained access to during the war. There were also instances of women acting as spies and enlisting in the army disguised as men. One of the most famous Confederate spies was Rose O'Neal Greenhow. At the beginning of the war she passed on military intelligence from her home in Washington to Confederate agents; the intelligence proved very useful during the First Battle of Bull Run. She was arrested soon after this but continued to provide the Confederacy with military intelligence even while in prison. In 1862 she was deported to Richmond and later served as a Confederate agent in Europe collecting diplomatic intelligence. Elizabeth Van Lew was one of the most successful northern spies. Known as "Crazy Bet," she convinced Confederate officials to allow her to visit Union prisoners of war in Richmond. While they thought she was doing humanitarian work, she was actually garnering information from prisoners (as well as unsuspecting Confederate guards) about Confederate troop deployments and then passing this information on to Union officials. She also contrived to get one of her servants a job in President Davis's household; the servant provided her with more valuable information that she forwarded to the Union army.

Hundreds of women disguised themselves as men and served in both armies. Mary Owens (John Evans) fought for eighteen months in the Union army before a wound revealed that she was a woman. Mary Stevens Jenkins spent two years in a Pennsylvania regiment, and even though she was wounded several times, it was never discovered that she was a woman. Among the hundreds who served on the Confederate side were Mrs. S. M. Blaylock, who enlisted with her husband in the Twenty-Sixth North Carolina Infantry, and Loreta Vasquez (Harry Buford), who served as a Confederate lieutenant.

By the end of the war thousands of women turned their backs on convention and experienced more independence and self-reliance than they had ever known before. Although those who served as nurses, spies, and soldiers were only a small fraction of the female population, their collective experience, along with that of the vast majority of women who daily dealt with the struggles and sorrows of the home front, underscores the transformational impact of the Civil War on women's roles in American society. Women were feeling the empowering potential of their own lives, which in turn drew attention to their political inequality. This, many women vowed, would have to change. After the Civil War gender relations would never again be the same.

* * *

The war was good for northern business. To be sure, the North was already rapidly industrializing before the war, but the Civil War significantly accelerated that development. Bankers, investors, and industrialists made huge profits by helping finance the war and supplying the military, which served in turn to enhance their political influence over the affairs of state. Despite the economic growth, however, there was much discontent. Inflation and shortages of products were sources of disgruntlement among workers and sparked several strikes during the war. Americans were angry over reports that speculators were making fortunes selling shoddy and defective supplies to the government. In such an atmosphere of greed and exploitation many northerners grew critical of the expanding governmental bureaucracy and unscrupulous opportunists. For some, patriotism metamorphosed into cynicism, and support for the war began to wane.

But what most troubled Americans and increased antiwar sentiment was the ever-increasing day-to-day brutality of the war. With casualties mounting at a frightening rate, civilians grew weary of the war and just wanted it to end. Young men of draft age and women who were trying to provide for their families on the home front became so distressed at the personal impact of the war that they began taking to the streets to protest their governments' policies. Some of these protests were violent. Draft riots in New York and food riots in Richmond shocked politicians and public figures on both sides of the Mason-Dixon line. In addition, conscientious objectors protested against conscription and refused to serve in the army on moral grounds; in the North hundreds of black soldiers protested their unequal pay; and in the South hundreds of civilians condemned the Confederate government for jeopardizing the core southern principle of states' rights. The disruption of war emboldened thousands of ordinary Americans, who had been privately skeptical or critical, to dissent more openly and more forcefully.

Needing more manpower, the Confederate Congress, in April 1862, passed a conscription act decreeing that all white men between the ages of eighteen and thirty-five were eligible for the draft. In October the age limit was extended to forty-five. In March 1863 the Union enacted a similar conscription act that all men between twenty and forty-five must register for the draft. Especially galling to both northerners and southerners was the loophole allowing draftees to hire a substitute to take their place or to pay an exemption fee of $300. Only the wealthy could afford such a fee. In the South resentment was further exacerbated by the so-called overseer exemption that one white man must remain on a plantation for every twenty slaves, thus providing exemptions for wealthy planters. The conscription acts led to draft resistance. Conscripts bitterly protested that it was a "rich man's war and a poor man's fight."[12] Some men dodged the draft by running away. Others deserted from boot camp. Still others made a living by becoming a substitute, absconding with the money, and then hiring themselves out again at a different recruitment office. Both North and South antiwar activists encouraged and aided hundreds of conscripts to desert. In some southern counties, such as Lumpkin County, Georgia, there was so much draft evasion and desertion in 1863 that the army was deployed to take the men into custody. Hundreds were rounded up and forced to serve, but scores escaped to the hills and formed guerrilla bands to attack officials trying to enforce the draft.

The most alarming manifestation of antidraft feeling was the draft riots and demonstrations that took place in multiple cities throughout the country. And the most violent and shocking of these riots took place in July in New York City when a mob exploded in an outpouring of class- and race-driven rage. Just a few weeks before the Conscription Act of 1863 went into effect, Irish immigrant dockworkers in New York went on strike. The shipping companies broke the strike by bringing in free blacks to replace the striking workers. On July 11 thousands of workers, believing that the U.S. government was compelling them to fight in a war to free slaves who would then compete with them for jobs, carried "No Draft" signs (mostly the Irish immigrants who had lost their jobs just a few weeks earlier) and marched on the provost marshal's office in Manhattan, where the draft lottery was being held. The demonstration quickly turned into a riot that lasted for five days. The mob torched the buildings housing the draft offices and then set out—with cries of "Down with the rich!" and "There goes a $300 man!"—to assault wealthy New Yorkers and Republicans whom they considered responsible for the war and the draft. They attacked Horace Greeley's *Tribune* offices as well as Brooks Brothers and other symbols of the upper class. Soon the riot spread into black neighborhoods, where it was no longer an antidraft uprising but a full-blown race riot. A Pennsylvania newspaper reported that one protestor shouted that he would fight for Uncle Sam "but not for Uncle Sambo,"[13] as the mob demolished the Colored Orphan Asylum, destroyed the homes of African Americans, attacked whites who tried to protect blacks, and brutally lynched scores of African Americans. Several men, such as William Jones, were beaten, hanged, and burned alive. Many blacks escaped to New Jersey, but many were caught while fleeing the city and killed.

After five days of rioting, looting, and murder, order was only restored when ten thousand exhausted troops rushed to the city from Gettysburg. All in all, approximately fifty thousand people participated in the violence; sixty-seven rioters were tried, convicted, and imprisoned; more than $1.5 million of property was destroyed; and an estimated 119 people, mostly African Americans, lost their lives. (There are no accurate statistics for the casualty count; some historians argue that as many as one thousand people were killed, both rioters and victims.) When the draft was resumed a month later, however, New York City's quota was reduced from twenty-six thousand to twelve thousand, so the rioters apparently did have some level of success in fighting against the Conscription Act.

In the aftermath, however, there was considerable backlash against the rioters. Many Americans were horrified at the racial violence and became more sympathetic to the idea that African Americans should be granted citizenship and the right to vote. For instance, the *Atlantic Monthly* argued (perhaps in a fit of anti-Irish pique) that if the Irish were granted suffrage, then so too should African Americans. "It is impossible to name any standard," the editor observed, "that will give a vote to the Celt and exclude the negro."[14] The antidraft protestors made their point that the draft was unfair, but in doing so they also unintentionally called attention to the inherent racism that festered in

New York Draft Riots, July 1863. Antidraft protests turned into a violent five-day riot during which more than a hundred people were killed. It took one thousand exhausted federal troops rushed from Gettysburg to restore order. (Public domain)

American society and to the fact that the discrimination that African Americans faced was equally unfair.

Although the New York City draft riot was a particularly violent example of dissent, there were also numerous examples of nonviolent dissent against the war. Pacifists and Quakers resisted the war and the draft by simply refusing to serve. Cyrus Pringle, a Vermont Quaker, was drafted into the Union army the same July 1863 day that the New York riot erupted. Pringle confided to his diary that he could not in all good conscience serve in the army because he was morally opposed to the concept of war. He would never wish for or accept the military protection of the U.S. government, and therefore he could not agree to engage in warfare for the government's sake. War, Pringle believed, was morally wrong, even when it is "waged in opposition to an evil and oppressive power and ostensibly in defence of liberty, virtue, and free institutions." When Pringle was offered the option of paying for a substitute, he declined because supplying such money would make him the agent "in bringing others into evil." Against his will he was forced into the army and spent his time like "a caged lion" in the training camps. Taken from Brattleboro, Vermont, to Boston, Pringle appealed his case, while officers threatened him with a court-martial that would result in capital punishment. Still Pringle refused to follow military orders. He refused to clean his gun and was punished by being staked to the ground for two hours. He refused hospital duty, because that would free up someone else to do military duty, and he was punished again. When he refused to clean his gun a second time, he was again staked to the ground—this time for four hours in the blistering sun. "I was very quiet in my mind as I lay there on the ground with the rain of the previous day, exposed to the heat of the sun, and suffering keenly from the cords binding my wrists and straining my muscles. . . . I wept, not so much from my own suffering as from sorrow that such things should be in our own country, where Justice and Freedom and Liberty of Conscience have been the annual boast of Fourth-of-July orators so many years."[15]

Eventually, after going through many such punishments, Pringle was taken to Washington, where his case was reviewed by the adjutant general and eventually referred to Secretary of War Stanton. Pringle was informed that both Stanton and Lincoln "sympathized with Friends [Quakers] in their present suffering, and would grant them full release," but that they were obliged to enforce the Conscription Act. Pringle then was offered the option to work as a nurse in a military hospital, and if he did so, he was promised that no one would be sent into military service in his place. This satisfied Pringle's conscience enough so that he consented. Still he resisted military protocol and refused to salute officers. Eventually President Lincoln interceded on behalf of Pringle and the other Quakers who resisted military service. "It is my urgent wish," Lincoln ordered, that "all those young men be sent home at once."[16] Pringle's personal protests worked. He was released from hospital duty and discharged.

By the summer of 1863 African American regiments, such as the Massachusetts Fifty-Fourth, had amply demonstrated their courage and fighting ability. But racism still plagued them on a daily basis. White troops received more and better supplies than black troops. From guns to shoes, whites were better treated. When African American soldiers learned that the War Department paid white troops thirteen dollars a month while they received only seven dollars, they were so angered that they began shirking their duties and refusing to carry out orders. They would obey orders again, they announced, when they received thirteen dollars a month. Some of the protesting soldiers were court-martialed and executed by firing squad. This, of course, was a potent deterrent. But then the soldiers came up with an innovative, rather ingenious tactic. They carried out all their military duties and obeyed their officers' orders but refused to accept any pay at all until the War Department would agree to give them equal pay.

Refusing pay was passive resistance, but the soldiers also actively campaigned for equal pay by writing letters to African American newspapers, articulating their stance. For example, an anonymous soldier identifying himself only as H.I.W. from the Fifty-Fourth Massachusetts wrote a letter to the editor of the *Christian Recorder* in June 1864 complaining that although he and his comrades rallied patriotically to the defense of the Union, the government was treating them shamefully. "I enlisted on the same terms as other soldiers," he wrote, but the regiment has not received any pay. At Fort Wagner "the men of the 54th suffered terribly, and still they [the U.S. government] have the cheek to wrest these brave men of color out of their rights. . . . If we are good enough to fill up white men's places and fight, we should be treated then, in all respects, the same as the white man. We have families as well as the white man." Another soldier of the Fifty-Fourth, J. H. Hall wrote to the same newspaper two months later arguing that African Americans are the equals of any white man. "If we are to be recognized as citizens, we want the rights of citizens!" Hall insisted. Blacks have benefited, he went on, from living in an enlightened country, and it is time for whites to recognize that fact. "I am gratified to know that the descendants of Africa, and the so-called adopted sons of America have more than kept pace with the Anglo-Saxon. We do not claim that we are more intelligent than our so-called superior race, but we are nearly equal in intelligence, and have acquired a knowledge of science and literature that would surprise the world, if they only knew of the difficulties we have had to encounter to acquire it for ourselves and for our children."[17]

African American soldiers' civil disobedience baffled the military brass, but the protests eventually succeeded. In August 1864 free blacks were granted equal pay, and in March 1865 all African American soldiers, regardless of their status before enlisting, were awarded equal pay, backdated to their enlistment.

As the war wore on, sizeable protests and riots also wracked the Confederacy. By 1863 there was a severe food shortage in the South. Those who suffered most from the scarcity were the women-led households of the working poor. But after nearly two years of the continual disruption of war, the hunger and misery extended to the lower middle class as well. The food shortage was caused by the Confederate government's inability to control runaway inflation as well as the Union blockade and the persistence of many large planters to continue growing cotton (because of the enormous profits they could potentially reap if they successfully ran the blockade) rather than food. By March 1863 the scarcity and high price of food (butter had soared from twenty-three cents a pound to three dollars, coffee from twelve cents to five dollars) propelled thousands of people to rebel. Bands of women in Salisbury, North Carolina, and Atlanta, Georgia—believing that the Confederate government had failed them after they had sacrificed so much for the war effort, including their husbands and sons—went on a rampage and sacked and looted government food warehouses.

On April 1 Minerva Meredith and Mary Jackson organized a meeting of working-class women in Richmond to discuss what to do after the government ignored their demand to make more food available. The following day hundreds of women, armed with axes and knives and pistols, stormed through the city streets vowing to have "bread or blood!" On their way to the city's commercial center they recruited hundreds more women, men, and children, until they numbered more than a thousand. They ransacked dozens of bakeries, food stores, and warehouses, carrying off whatever bread, meat, clothing, and shoes they could find. The police finally restored order and arrested more than sixty people. But there was little the Confederate government could do about hunger. Even the provisions that were reserved for the military—which frequently was forced to live off the land—were so scarce that there was no surplus that could be released for public consumption. Women continued to petition for relief for the remainder of the war, and when the government did not act (which was usually the case), they took to the streets. Bread riots erupted all over North Carolina as well as in Mobile, Petersburg, Atlanta, Savannah, and Macon. In each instance women banded together, put together a plan to storm a food storage facility, and then carried out the raid.

The wealthy and the upper middle class in the Confederacy were horrified at these riots. Unwilling to accept that so many people were in such bad straits that they resorted to violence and unwilling to see that the intensity of the violence revealed widespread class resentment, mainstream southerners viewed the rioters as criminals, not as desperate, hungry people. The *Richmond Examiner*, in its coverage of the bread riot, characterized the women as "a handful of prostitutes, professional thieves, Irish and Yankee hags, gallows-birds from all lands but our own,"[18] when in fact they were women (many of whom were widows of Confederate soldiers who died in battle or were the sole breadwinner while their husbands were serving in the army) whose only objective was to feed their families. When a society feels under attack and insecure, it is more comfortable to imagine that the problems are perpetrated by ne'er-do-wells or a criminal element or "outside agitators" than to acknowledge that the society has failed to take care of those who are most in need.

Increasing numbers of southerners grew so appalled at the terrible cost of the war in lives and money that they gave up on their vision of an independent Confederate States of America and urged the government in Richmond to make a peace settlement at any cost, even if it meant reunion. One peace activist was William Woods Holden in North Carolina. Holden published a newspaper, the *Standard*, in which he doggedly called for an immediate end to the war. His views were much too revolutionary for the government in Richmond. What concerned Confederate authorities more than Holden's antiwar stance was his radical proposal to overthrow the plantation aristocracy in the South and establish a more industrial and more progressive society based on the rule of the many and not the few. In September 1863 Confederate soldiers ransacked his office and destroyed his printing press. He continued to publish, however, until the Confederate government suspended (once again) the writ of habeas corpus and imprisoned him.

* * *

From 1861 to 1865 the United States went through a second revolution. Or perhaps more accurately put, the United States completed the eighteenth-century revolution that, although it was based on the principles of liberty and equality, had left slavery intact. Most Americans were mindful that the Constitution guaranteed the right to dissent, and the protests and debates leading up to the Civil War clearly show that both northerners and southerners did believe, passionately, that they were exercising their constitutional rights. Thousands of Americans spoke out against slavery, while thousands protested that those who would abolish slavery were the enemies of private property and personal liberty. The Civil War—the ultimate manifestation of dissent—brought about such massive social and political upheaval, especially for African Americans and women, that it created the conditions that generated more dissent in the decades ahead.

CHAPTER 10

Liberation and Suppression

The story of our inferiority is an old dodge . . . ; for wherever men oppress their fellows, wherever they enslave them, they will endeavor to find the needed apology for such enslavement and oppression in the character of the people oppressed and enslaved. . . . It is said that we are ignorant; I admit it. But if we know enough to be hung, we know enough to vote. If the Negro knows enough to pay taxes to support the government, he knows enough to vote. . . . If he knows enough to shoulder a musket and fight for the flag, fight for the government, he knows enough to vote.

—Frederick Douglass, 1865

At the end of the Civil War the South was in ruins, its economy shattered; dislocation reigned, hundreds of northern carpetbaggers—humanitarians as well as opportunists—flocked into the region, and everywhere there was the fear of the unknown. The only certainty was that slavery was dead, but what this meant for the freedmen and for southern whites was not at all clear.

After the war many African Americans hired themselves out to whites for a year at a time as contractors working for fixed wages. Most, however, were sharecroppers who lived and worked on a piece of land, receiving a share of the crop—usually divided fifty-fifty with the white landlord—for their labors. Unfortunately this was not much better than a new form of slavery, for sharecroppers frequently had to borrow money, especially during bad crop years, in order to survive. Creditors took a portion of the crop as payment, and when the harvest came in, there was virtually nothing left for the sharecropper. In fact in most cases they sank further into debt. There was little opportunity for people living in such a system ever to break out of poverty.

Still, there was significant progress for African Americans. The Freedmen's Bureau (Bureau of Freedmen, Refugees, and Abandoned

Lands) channeled federal funds to aid the freedmen between 1865 and 1870 primarily through providing food, shelter, and tools; finding jobs for former slaves; helping them find lost relatives; and promoting education for black children. Thousands of blacks joined Union Leagues that were formed for the purpose of raising political awareness, educating them about business practices and the latest agricultural developments, and advising them on education and legal rights. Perhaps the most important agency for change was the establishment of black institutions, businesses, schools, and churches. Under slavery blacks had attended their masters' churches; now they were able for the first time to establish churches of their own. The African Methodist Episcopal Church, the Negro Baptist Church, the Colored Presbyterian Church, the Zion Union Apostolic Church, the Colored Methodist Episcopal Church, and others were instituted and began attracting large congregations. These first African American churches served (then and now) not only the religious needs of their members but also as community centers and gathering places where social, economic, and political issues would be raised and discussed. In some respects the separation and eventual legal segregation of the races in the aftermath of the Civil War strengthened, rather than weakened, African American solidarity. In addition to the expansion of a sense of African American community, there were other important achievements for blacks during the era. Perhaps the most significant was in the field of education. Literacy increased dramatically throughout the period so that toward the end of the century the African American literacy rate was approximately 40 percent (for whites the figure was 50 percent). This was a remarkable accomplishment considering all the challenges African Americans faced emerging from slavery and struggling to make a living in a hostile atmosphere.

Freedmen also made some political progress by electing over six hundred blacks to local and state legislatures, as well as to the U.S. House of Representatives and the two senators from Mississippi. Many of these African American politicians, such as South Carolina congressman Robert B. Elliott, were instrumental in guiding important civil rights legislation through Congress. Elliott served in the House of Representatives from 1871 to 1874 and was an ardent supporter of the Civil Rights Bill that was eventually passed in 1875. During the debate on the bill Elliott denounced those politicians who considered states' rights superior to individual rights. He reminded his colleagues of Alexander Hamilton's view that "there can be no truer principle than this, that every individual of the community at large has an equal right to the protection of Government. Can this be a free Government if partial distinctions are tolerated or maintained?" The bill was essential because if the nation denied civil rights to blacks, it would jeopardize the civil rights of *all* Americans. "The passage of this bill," Elliott concluded, "will determine the civil status, not only of the negro, but of any other class of citizens who may feel themselves discriminated against. It will form the cap-stone of that temple of liberty."[1]

Other prominent African Americans continued to insist that freedom alone was not enough and that freedmen should be granted the full rights and privileges of citizenship. The guns had hardly fallen silent in April 1865 when Frederick Douglass delivered an impassioned address in Boston demanding the immediate, universal, and unconditional enfranchisement of the freedman. "Without this," he declared, "his liberty is a mockery; without this, you might as well almost retain the old name of slavery for his condition; for in fact, if he is not the slave of the individual master, he is the slave of society, and holds his liberty as a privilege, not as a right. He is at the mercy of the mob, and has no means of protecting himself." Douglass ridiculed the attitude so prevalent in white America that people were at a loss as to what to do with the former slaves. "Do nothing with us!" he exclaimed.

> Your doing with us has already played the mischief with us. Do nothing with us! . . . And if the Negro cannot stand on his own legs, let him fall. . . . All I ask is, give him a chance to stand on his own legs! Let him alone! If you see him on his way to school, let him alone, don't disturb him! If you see him going to the dinner-table at a hotel, let him go! If you see him going to the ballot-box, let him alone, don't disturb him! If you see him going into a work-shop, just let him alone,—your interference is doing him a positive injury. . . . Let him fall if he cannot stand alone![2]

But despite the widespread attempt to raise the nation's consciousness about the vital issues of enfranchisement and civil rights, many of the modest gains that African Americans achieved during Reconstruction quickly evaporated when whites regained political power and enacted laws and policies to reestablish, as far as possible, the antebellum world.

* * *

On Christmas Eve 1865, in Pulaski, Tennessee, General Nathan Bedford Forrest and other former Confederate soldiers founded the Ku Klux Klan. The name derived from the Greek word for "circle," *kuklos*, and they concocted an assortment of bizarre titles for the group's officers—Grand Wizards, Genii, Titans, Furies, Hydras, and Grand Dragons—in order to accentuate the mysteriousness and secrecy of the association. Some historians have argued that the original founders were only interested in creating mischief and frightening people, but as membership mushroomed during the first year, mischief making quickly turned violent. In the sense that the Klan was fighting against the (new) status quo, it was a dissenting organization. But if we define dissent more narrowly as a force for positive change, a force for the expansion of rights, pushing the United States to live up to its democratic promise, than it was not a dissenting organization. The Klan, and other racist groups such as the Knights of the White Camellia, the Red Shirts, and the White Leagues, was in actuality a paramilitary arm of the Democratic Party whose sole purpose was to preserve white supremacy in the South. White supremacy had always been the rule since the establishment of slavery in the American colonies, so the Klan was resisting change, not initiating it. As African Americans fought for civil and political rights, the Klan did whatever it could to intimidate, to terrorize, and to destroy the threat posed by the new realities. If an African American appeared to be advancing economically, if he had opened a small general store and was enjoying some moderate success, if he did not step off the sidewalk and act deferentially to a passing white, if he simply seemed too "uppity," Klansmen wearing white sheets would visit him in the middle of the night. The man might be whipped, a cross might be burned in his yard, his cabin might be vandalized or burned to the ground, or he might actually be taken out and lynched. The Klan also sought to undermine Reconstruction and to destroy the Republican Party by terrorizing, mutilating, and killing Union League members, as well as carpetbaggers (northerners who had come south) and scalawags (southerners who had joined the Republican Party). Between 1867 and 1872 hundreds of Republican leaders, as well as ordinary voters attempting to go to the polls, were murdered. Most of these victims of the Klan were black, but scores of whites were also killed. Klan violence was responsible for preventing most blacks from voting in Georgia and Louisiana so that those two states went Democratic in the 1868 election. By 1870 Republicans were so intimidated in North Carolina, Georgia, and Tennessee that Democrats had resumed control.

There were so many instances of Klan violence, both recorded and unrecorded, that it is impossible to know for certain how many people suffered at the Klan's hands. In Memphis, Tennessee, a white mob started a two-day riot that culminated in the death of forty-six African Americans. In Mississippi Klansmen dragged the president of the Republican Club, Jack Dupree, out of his house and, forcing his wife to watch, slit his throat and eviscerated him. In Meridian, Mississippi, town violence erupted during a hearing for three black leaders who had been arrested for giving "incendiary" speeches; the violence resulted in the murder of the Republican judge and more than thirty blacks. In Alabama, after the former slave George Moore had voted for the Republicans, the Klan appeared at his house, whipped him, shot one of his neighbors, and raped a young woman who was visiting his wife. Also in Alabama a young white teacher, William Luke, who was teaching in a black school was systematically harassed and threatened by the Klan for many months before they finally dragged him out one night and lynched him. In Georgia the Klan murdered three Republican members of the state legislature and drove ten others out of town. In Kentucky a mob hanged Sam Davis, George Roger, and William Pierce in separate incidents. In South Carolina white gangs participated in a "negro chase," killing thirteen blacks and driving 150 out of their homes. During the 1868 election campaign three members of the South Carolina legislature as well as Arkansas congressman James M. Hinds were assassinated; in St. Landry Parish, Louisiana, more than two hundred freedmen were murdered. By 1871 nearly all white men in York County, South Carolina, belonged to the Klan, and there were so many nightly raids that thousands of terrified blacks routinely sought sanctuary in the woods every night.

Southerners maintained (and many still do) that only poor whites joined the Klan and other terrorist groups. But there is extensive evidence that all classes of southern whites participated. Workingmen and farmers, middle-class shopkeepers and professionals, including the most reputable and respected citizens—physicians, lawyers, newspaper editors, ministers, politicians—all participated in Klan activities. While most of the midnight riders were the younger middle- and lower-class men, the leaders who planned the raids and chose the targets were the esteemed pillars of southern society.

Even though most southern whites vehemently opposed the Reconstruction regimes, not all supported the Klan. Some southern whites courageously sought to rein in the organization. In Arkansas, Governor Powell Clayton sent state militia units into ten counties to confront the Klan. Dozens were arrested and brought to trial, three were executed, and countless Klansmen fled the state. William G. Brownlow, the governor of Tennessee, who had been an antisecessionist before and during the war, attempted to control the Klan by having agents infiltrate the organization. But his spies were discovered and lynched. In 1869 he declared martial law and sent militiamen into nine Tennessee counties to suppress Klan violence. Texas governor Edmund J. Davis was more successful in the early 1870s when he arrested over six thousand suspected Klansmen and shut down Klan activities in the state. Despite the best efforts on the part of some southern political leaders, however, the Klan was in virtual control of political power in most areas of the former Confederacy, and it was clear to both federal and state authorities that the Reconstruction governments in the South were in effect facing an insurrection led by KKK terrorists. As one former Confederate put it, the Klan's purpose was "to defy the reconstructed State Governments, to treat them with contempt, and show that they have no real existence."[3] The Klan was unmistakably successful at achieving this goal.

In 1870 and 1871 Congress passed the Enforcement Acts and the Ku Klux Klan Act, empowering the president to send election supervisors into the South to prevent voting fraud, bribery, and intimidation and to ensure that no citizen was deprived of the right to vote, serve on juries, or hold office because of his race. Also the authority to prosecute certain individual crimes such as robbery, murder, and assault was taken away from local governments and made federal offenses if the intention was to deprive people of their right to vote. In addition, the wearing of masks and hoods and midnight rides were prohibited, and provision was made that if prosecutions were lackadaisically pursued, then the federal government could suspend habeas corpus and send in the military. The Department of Justice set to work implementing the laws, and in many southern counties hundreds of people were indicted for these

"The Louisiana Murders: Gathering the Dead and Wounded," *Harper's Weekly*, May 10, 1873, 397. The noted historian Eric Foner calls the Colfax Massacre of April 13, 1873, "the bloodiest single instance of racial carnage in the Reconstruction era" (*Reconstruction*, 437). However, the state of Louisiana views the murder of nearly 150 African Americans differently. The historical marker in Colfax refers to the event as a riot that "marked the end of Carpetbag misrule in the South." (Public domain)

offenses. Because most witnesses were afraid to testify and many defendants had access to expert lawyers, many of the cases resulted in acquittal. Still, a number of Klansmen were convicted and sent to prison. President Ulysses S. Grant, in October 1871, sent the military into western South Carolina, where hundreds of Klansmen were arrested and brought to trial. Even though most escaped punishment for their crimes, the rigorous federal crackdown served to break up the Klan and reduce violence throughout the region. What eventually terminated it, however, was not the crackdown but the final restoration of the former Confederate states to the Union. With the end of Reconstruction, Democrats regained complete political control, and the Klan was no longer needed to preserve white supremacy. State and local officials were able to accomplish this legally without the Klan's help.

Although African Americans did not themselves go on midnight rides committing acts of terror against their enemies, they took measures to protect themselves against Klan violence. They were at an enormous disadvantage, of course, since most of them had not received military training as had the Klansmen who had served in the Confederate army, nor were they familiar with firearms since they had been forbidden to possess or use firearms other than shotguns for small game hunting. Nevertheless, freedmen did fight back. The most notorious incident took place in Colfax, Louisiana, the county seat of Grant Parish. Both Democrats and Republicans had claimed victory in the recent gubernatorial election, and in the spring of 1873 a number of anxious freedmen, worried that Democrats would grab power and instigate a terror campaign against them, took up arms and seized the town. A few of them had served in the Union army and used their experience to supervise the digging of trenches and erecting defenses. For three weeks they held the town, until whites, armed with Winchesters and a cannon, attacked in force. In the ensuing battle about fifty freedmen were killed and another fifty were massacred after they surrendered. With more than one hundred African Americans dead the Colfax Massacre was the most brutal event of the Reconstruction era.

The first Klan did not survive Reconstruction, but its campaign of terror and intimidation achieved the desired effect. Keeping African Americans away from the polls swayed a number of elections and ensured the restoration of Democratic rule. Murdering and terrorizing freedmen as they attempted to improve their economic and social standing was a major impediment to their progress and ensured, once whites regained power, that African Americans would remain the underclass in the South for the rest of the century.

* * *

The abolition of slavery and the significant changes in gender roles that had taken place during the Civil War propelled the reemergence of the women's movement. When Congress began hammering out a voting rights amendment, women were optimistic that the right to vote would be granted to *all* citizens regardless of race *or* sex. But when the wording of the Fifteenth Amendment was finalized, it only extended the suffrage to black males: "The right of citizens of the United States to vote shall not be denied or abridged by the United States or any State on account of race, color, or previous condition of servitude." As a result, women launched an antiratification campaign demanding that the amendment be defeated unless Congress added the word "sex" to it. In 1866 Susan B. Anthony, Elizabeth Cady Stanton, and hundreds of other women and men founded the American Equal Rights Association. In a statement released in May 1867 they protested the disfranchisement of women. It is contrary to republican principles to deny women the right to vote, the statement declared,

> for male and female are but different conditions. Neither color nor sex is ever discharged from obedience to law, natural or moral; written or unwritten. The commands, thou shalt not steal, nor kill, nor commit adultery, know nothing of sex in their demands; nothing in their penalty. And hence we believe that all human legislation which is at variance with the divine code, is essentially unrighteous and unjust. . . . Woman has been fined, whipped, branded with red-hot irons, imprisoned and hung; but when was woman ever tried by a jury of her peers? . . .
>
> Woman and the colored man are loyal, patriotic, property-holding, tax-paying, liberty-loving citizens; and we can not believe that sex or complexion should be any ground for civil or political degradation. In our government, one-half the citizens are disfranchised by their sex, and about one-eighth by the color of their skin; and thus a large majority have no voice in enacting or executing the laws they are taxed to support and compelled to obey.[4]

Unfortunately schisms developed within the American Equal Rights Association, and the subsequent campaign to persuade Congress to extend suffrage to women introduced disturbing racist lines of reasoning and rancorous infighting that ultimately destroyed the decades-long alliance between suffragists and abolitionists and broke up the association. Elizabeth Cady Stanton, bitterly disappointed that so many former abolitionists refused to support women's suffrage, openly opposed the Fifteenth Amendment. How could educated upper-class women be denied the right to vote, she wanted to know, when ignorant immigrant and uneducated African American males were granted that right? "Think of Patrick and Sambo and Hans and Ung Tung who do not know the difference between a Monarchy and a Republic, who never read the Declaration of Independence . . . making laws for Lydia

Maria Child, Lucretia Mott, or Fanny Kemble."[5] Such racist statements turned increasingly vitriolic, and by 1869 the American Equal Rights Association disintegrated. Stanton and Susan B. Anthony founded the National Woman Suffrage Association (NWSA), while Lucy Stone and Alice Stone Blackwell founded the more moderate American Woman Suffrage Association (AWSA), which continued to back the ratification of the Fifteenth Amendment even though women were left out. Once the amendment was ratified, the NWSA began a campaign for a separate women's suffrage amendment, while the AWSA engaged in a strategy of getting each state to grant women's suffrage. It was twenty years before women reunited behind the effort to gain voting rights and another thirty years after that before the Nineteenth Amendment achieved that goal.

The women's movement was splintered, but protest against the disfranchisement of women continued. "There is no escaping the fact," Victoria Claflin Woodhull proclaimed in an 1871 speech, "that the principle by which the *male* citizens of these United States assume to rule the *female* citizens is *not* that of self-government, but that of despotism." She argued that women already had the right to vote and defiantly announced her candidacy for the office of president of the United States. In 1872 she ran as the candidate of the Equal Rights Party (although her name was not printed on any official ballots). During this time she also took on the conventional morality of the day in her newspaper, *Woodhull & Claflin's Weekly*, which, in addition to advocating women's suffrage, pushed for free love, sex education, and the legalization of prostitution and printed the first English translation of *The Communist Manifesto*. "I am a Free Lover," she boldly acknowledged. "I have an *inalienable, constitutional* and *natural* right to love whom I may, to love *as long* or as *short* a period as I can; to *change* that love *every day* if I please, and with *that* right neither *you* nor any *law* you can frame have *any* right to interfere."[6]

Other women spoke out just as defiantly as Woodhull, although few ventured into such controversial territory. For decades Susan B. Anthony had been an ardent participant in the abolition movement as well as a major force behind the struggle for women's rights, educational and labor reform, and the temperance movement. After the ratification of the Fifteenth Amendment she became even more militant. During the 1872 presidential election she went to the polls in Rochester,

New York, and cast a vote. She was arrested and brought to trial in June 1873. The judge found her guilty and imposed a fine of $100. When she stood up to challenge the guilty verdict, the judge told her she could not argue the question for she had been tried "under the forms of law." "Yes," she replied, "but laws made by men, under a government of men, interpreted by men and for the benefit of men. The only chance women have for justice in this country is to violate the law, as I have done, and as I shall *continue* to do. . . . I do not ask the clemency of the court. I came into it to get justice, having failed in this, I demand the full rigors of the law."[7] She refused to pay the $100 fine and insisted that she be sentenced to prison. The judge, however, well aware of the additional publicity and sympathy she would gain if he sentenced her to jail, ignored her demand and simply released her. Newspaper articles, however, as well as a speech she delivered around the nation titled "Is It a Crime for a U.S. Citizen to Vote?," brought a great deal of attention to her act of civil disobedience. "It was *we the people*," she insisted—"not we, *white male citizens*—nor yet we male citizens—but we the *whole people*, who formed this Union; and we formed it, not to *give* the blessings or liberty, but to *secure* them—not to the *half* of ourselves and the half of our posterity, but to the whole people, *women* as well as men. And it is downright *mockery* to talk to women of their enjoyment of the *blessings* of liberty while they are *denied the use of the only means of securing them* provided by this democratic-republican government [the ballot]."[8]

In 1878 Senator A. A. Sargent of California introduced to Congress what became known as the Susan B. Anthony amendment. In 1882 Senate and House Select Committees on Woman's Suffrage submitted favorable reports recommending passage of the amendment, but it took more than five years before the Senate voted on the issue. (It was defeated thirty-four to sixteen, with twenty-five senators not voting.) Subsequently, every time the matter was brought up, Anthony personally implored the legislators to pass the amendment. However, at each session it was repeatedly debated, tabled, defeated, reintroduced, and defeated again. She kept up her dynamic energy, campaigning for women's suffrage well into her eighties, but she never saw the passage of the amendment she had fought so ardently for before her death at age eighty-six in 1906.

* * *

When the last federal troops were pulled out of the South in 1877, political power quickly reverted back to the proslavery secessionists who had held power before the war. These "Redeemers," as whites called them (some pejoratively called them "Bourbons"—named after the ultimate aristocrats, the royal family of France's ancien régime), wished to return, as far as possible, to the old, established ways of the antebellum South. Despite the class distinctions that existed in the South, the overriding tenet that enabled the Bourbons to maintain power was white supremacy. They could easily defeat political opponents who tried to take them on simply by accusing them of attempting to divide whites and pave the way for a return to "Negro rule." Racism was central to the Bourbons' strategy of keeping poor whites ignorant of their shared economic and class interests with poor blacks. As long as racism kept them divided, the two poorest classes in southern society would never be a threat to Bourbon hegemony. Playing the "race card" kept power in the hands of the elites even when their policies did nothing to alleviate the economic hardships suffered by white farmers. By the 1880s and 1890s so many small farms went under that more and more whites were forced into sharecropping, and it seemed, briefly, that racial and class barriers might be eroded. But in the end, racism was too deeply ensconced. The Bourbons remained unchallenged.

Between 1877 and 1900 white regimes systematically restricted African Americans' civil and political rights. State governments concocted ingenious ways to circumvent the Fifteenth Amendment while simultaneously devising laws prohibiting racial mixing. One method they used to get around the suffrage amendment was the poll tax, which deterred not only impoverished African Americans from voting but poor whites as well. An even more effective technique for disfranchisement was the literacy test. This was not a problem for uneducated whites because they were merely asked to sign their name, or they were exempted from the test if their grandfathers had voted in 1865. For African Americans, however, the process worked differently. Often the registrant would be required to read a section from the U.S. Constitution and interpret it. No matter how well educated a black man might be, if the clerk did not want him to pass the test, the questions would simply become more and more difficult until the person failed.

For southern lawmakers, disfranchising blacks was not enough. In order to make sure that African Americans would forever be a race apart, they enacted a series of Jim Crow laws to isolate them from white society.[9] Blacks were forbidden to ride in the same railroad cars as whites; they could not attend the same schools, visit the same parks or beaches, or use the same waiting rooms at train stations. They were not allowed to use the same toilets and water fountains. If they went to the theater, they had a separate entrance and were compelled to sit in the balcony (sometimes referred to as the "Jim Crow Gallery," sometimes as "nigger heaven"). They were not admitted to the same hospitals or buried in the same cemeteries. These rules became so vigorously enforced and deeply entrenched in the southern way of life that it took nearly a century of protest, petitions, civil disobedience, and political activism before they were rescinded.

In 1892 Homer Plessy was traveling first class on a train in Louisiana when the conductor told him that because he was one-eighth black, he had to ride in the "colored car." When Plessy refused to move, he was arrested. At his trial he argued that the rule requiring blacks to ride in a separate car was in violation of the Thirteenth and Fourteenth Amendments. Plessy lost the case and subsequently appealed the decision to the Louisiana Supreme Court. Once again he lost, and once again he appealed, this time to the U.S. Supreme Court. In 1896 the case was finally decided when the high court ruled in *Plessy v. Ferguson* that the Louisiana Railroad had in no way infringed on Plessy's civil rights. It had not violated the Thirteenth Amendment by trying to enslave him, nor had it violated the Fourteenth Amendment, which guaranteed equal protection before the law. Plessy, the Court ruled, although dealt with separately, was also treated equally, and as long as the railroad offered "separate but equal" accommodation, it was acting constitutionally. With this landmark decision the United States validated the Jim Crow laws. Any state or local government could henceforth enact legislation that separated people as long as equal facilities were provided. Of course, for the next seventy years, although separate facilities were made available for African Americans, the "equal" part of the ruling was conveniently ignored.

In *Williams v. Mississippi*, in 1898, the Supreme Court upheld the literacy tests, and the following year the Court took the *Plessy* decision a step further in *Cummings v. Richmond County Board of Education* by ruling that the "separate but equal" doctrine also applied to public schools. By the time the new century dawned, the American system of apartheid was firmly (and legally) in place that was in due course to spawn the most powerful social movement in twentieth-century America.

The literacy tests, poll taxes, and Jim Crow laws were more than enough to keep African Americans from exercising political power. But southern whites, perhaps seeking to accentuate the imperative that white supremacy should never be challenged, made sure that no one ever misunderstood their intentions. African Americans were reminded daily that they were not fit for white society, through systematic and constant denigration, humiliation, and condescension. They were expected to be obsequious and deferential to whites, to step off the sidewalk if they encountered a white person, to show respect by lowering their heads, and never to make eye contact with a white woman. They were never called "mister" or "missus"; black men were called "boy" or "uncle." They were barred from industry and the skilled trades. The only option open to those who were not chained to a life of sharecropping was the low-paying, low-status jobs no one else wanted. Those who ran afoul of the law were subject to chain gangs and the convict lease system that put black prisoners to work (most of whom had been convicted for petty crimes or simply vagrancy) in hazardous, grueling, and often brutal jobs such as mining, clearing land, and constructing roads. These jobs were so hazardous that the mortality rate reached 25 percent.[10] And then there was the prevalence of lynchings. Even though the Klan had disbanded before the Reconstruction era ended, during the 1890s alone there was an average of 187 lynchings per year. Lynchings were so common, so widespread, that they became public spectacles conducted in a festive atmosphere. It was not uncommon for a lynching to become a social event, with scores of jubilant whites eagerly and cheerfully crowding around the victim's corpse to pose for the camera.

Black men who had been suspected or arrested for murder or rape or merely for petty theft or even a display of insolence would often be dragged out of jail and lynched. Lynching was not necessarily confined to hanging or shooting, nor was it only resorted to as a sort of vigilante justice perpetrated on someone actually charged with a serious crime. Frequently an African American whose only "crime" might have been that he had opened a business that was beginning to achieve some financial success was abducted and murdered. And all too frequently there were cases in which the victim was tortured and burned alive.

In 1891 a black man, Ed Coy, who had been arrested for raping a white woman, was seized by a mob and tied to a stake. While his tormentors poured oil over his body and the woman he was accused of raping set fire to him, the terrified man continued to cry out that he was innocent. In March 1899 nine blacks in Palmetto, Georgia, had been arrested on suspicion of arson. While awaiting trial a mob of over one hundred white men dragged them out of jail. The men were taken to a warehouse and tied together. While they begged and pleaded for mercy, the mob coolly and carefully took aim with their pistols and Winchesters and fired volley after volley until the moans and sobs of the victims ceased.

While such atrocities were spreading throughout the South, a courageous young editor of a Memphis newspaper, enraged by the injustices perpetrated on African Americans, initiated an antilynching campaign. Ida B. Wells-Barnett earned a degree at Fisk University in Memphis and during the 1880s worked as a teacher. In 1889 she became an editor of the *Memphis Free Speech*, writing articles on education and self-help for African Americans. In 1892 three of her friends who were partners in a small grocery store were lynched. She was so shocked by this event that she embarked on a campaign of writing articles, pamphlets, and books and eventually traveling around the United States and Europe giving lectures against lynching and demanding that the federal government enact strong, enforceable laws against the practice. She wrote that whites used racial stereotypes to justify murder. It was a boldfaced lie, she insisted, that black men were sexually obsessed with white women and were chomping at the bit to rape them. White reliance on this myth was merely a ploy to justify murdering African Americans whose real crime was that they were economic competitors for whites. Her newspaper editorials were so provocative that whites destroyed her office and drove her out of town. By the end of the year she had relocated to New York, wrote articles for papers there, and published a pamphlet, *Southern Horrors*.

In 1899 Wells-Barnett wrote *Lynch Law in Georgia*, in which she exposed the details of many of the lynchings she had researched. One of the cases that Wells-Barnett reported in this book was the lynching of Samuel Hose "by the Christian white people of Georgia." Hose had murdered a white man, Alfred Cranford, and while he was still at large, the *Atlanta Constitution* published several editorials inciting citizens to take the law into their own hands. On April 23 Hose was caught by

Ida B. Wells-Barnett, c. 1893. The outspoken journalist and civil rights activist led the fight for federal antilynching legislation. Photograph by Mary Garrity. (Public domain)

a mob of about two thousand people. They stripped him of his clothing and then tied him to a sapling. Wood was piled up around him, but before it was ignited, his ears, toes, fingers, and genitals were cut off. Though he remained conscious while being mutilated, he never groaned or begged for mercy.

The stake bent under the strains of the Negro in his agony and his sufferings cannot be described, although he uttered not a sound. After his ears had been cut off he was asked about the crime, and then it was he made a full confession. . . .

He writhed in agony and his sufferings can be imagined when it is said that several blood vessels burst during the contortions of his body. When he fell from the stake he was kicked back and the flames renewed. Then it was that the flames consumed his body and in a few minutes only a few bones and a small part of the body was all that was left of Sam Hose.

One of the most sickening sights of the day was the eagerness with which the people grabbed after souvenirs, and they almost fought over the ashes of the dead criminal. Large pieces of his flesh were carried away, and persons were seen walking through the streets carrying bones in their hands.[11]

Body parts and bones were auctioned off for twenty-five cents each. His "crisply cooked" liver sold for ten cents.[12] Even the remnants of the sapling were sold as a souvenir.

* * *

The two most influential African American civil rights proponents at the time were Booker T. Washington and W. E. B. Du Bois. Although Washington and Du Bois were rivals who relentlessly criticized each other's strategy for achieving equality, both men were highly regarded by the African Americans community and had an enormous impact on the emerging civil rights movement.

Booker T. Washington was only nine years old when the Thirteenth Amendment abolished slavery. Growing up and going to school during the Reconstruction era, Washington became a firm believer in the redemptive power of education. It was through education, he believed, that blacks would be able to rise and become productive U.S. citizens. Washington devoted his life to teaching African Americans how to advance, and in 1881 he became the principal of the Normal School for Negroes in Tuskegee, Alabama. Over the next decades he transformed the school into the Tuskegee Institute, creating an institution that catered to the educational needs of blacks.

Washington argued that blacks should not seek education purely for education's sake. It was impractical to study esoteric specialties such as Latin or Greek, philosophy or literature. Instead, African Americans should concentrate on scientific and technical fields of study that would enable them to find practical occupations that would be beneficial for their financial well-being. Useful subjects such as animal husbandry, agricultural economics, and mechanical engineering thus became the meat and potatoes of the Tuskegee Institute. If blacks became important contributors to the nation's economic growth, Washington assured them, this would be the surest path to acceptance and advancement. In an 1895 speech in Atlanta, Washington advised African Americans not to defy the Jim Crow laws but to focus instead on self-improvement. At the same time, he called on whites to encourage and promote black economic opportunity. By concentrating on bettering their lot, the sons and daughters of slaves would contribute so much to economic growth that whites would gladly grant them their civil and political rights. "No race that has anything to contribute to the markets of the world is long in any degree ostracized." At one point during the speech he held his hand aloft with fingers spread apart: "in all things that are purely social," he declared, "we can be as separate as the fingers, yet one" (and here he formed a fist) "as the hand in all things essential to mutual progress."[13] So if blacks worked hard for economic success, whites would treat them as valuable members of the community, even if they did not accept them socially. The pragmatic, submissive philosophy of Washington's "Atlanta Compromise" speech was music to the white South's ears but not to such prominent African Americans as Ida B. Wells-Barnett and W. E. B. Du Bois, who worried that such accommodationism would only add fuel to the fire of racism and lead to more lynchings. After all, if Booker T. Washington was right that whites would accept blacks who advanced economically, then why were lynchings, as Ida B. Wells-Barnett had already documented, of African Americans who were achieving some success on the rise?

Of course, one of the problems African Americans faced was the deep-seated racism of a society that had thrived and grown rich on the profits from slavery. And the Enlightenment's veneration of science and the unquestionable validity of empirical evidence led to a plethora of scholarly research and "scientific studies" purporting to prove the inferiority of blacks. By the late nineteenth century the assumption by most whites, including those who had opposed slavery and the subjugation of blacks, was that blacks were undeniably inferior, that they were inherently childish, emotional, docile, submissive, and dim-witted. Charles Darwin's theory of evolution was manipulated by pseudoscientists to prove the inherent inferiority of the nonwhite races. At the turn of the century numerous books were in print in both the United States and

Europe purporting to prove a multitude of racist theories. In practice this meant that blacks were denied educational opportunities because they were perceived as ill equipped for intellectual activity. This lack of opportunity mired them in ignorance and reinforced all the racial stereotypes that whites accepted as true. It was the ultimate vicious circle from which there was seemingly no escape.

While Booker T. Washington's response to scientific racism was to concentrate on economics, self-improvement, and submission, W. E. B. Du Bois proposed an alternative solution. Unlike Washington, Du Bois never knew slavery. He was born in Massachusetts in 1868 and, at the age of twenty-seven, was the first African American to earn a Ph.D. from Harvard. He became an influential figure in the struggle for civil rights and a harsh critic of Booker T. Washington's accommodationism, insisting that blacks fight for full and immediate political, social, economic, and civil rights. In *The Souls of Black Folk* Du Bois damns Washington's philosophy as detrimental and degrading and calls on the "talented tenth" of African Americans to settle for nothing less than a comprehensive and rigorous academic education and to seek all the benefits that had been traditionally reserved for whites. It is absurd, Du Bois insisted, to think African Americans would achieve equal rights by giving up rights. Concentrating on industrial education and the accumulation of wealth while giving up political power, civil rights, and the opportunity for higher education, as Washington urges, is madness. Whites will give blacks nothing, Du Bois maintained; therefore they must fight for their rights. "Is it possible, and probable, that nine millions of men can make effective progress in economic lines if they are deprived of political rights, made a servile caste, and allowed only the most meagre chance for developing their exceptional men?" Du Bois answers his rhetorical question with an emphatic "no." Even if blacks achieved economic success by following Washington's strategy, "it is utterly impossible," Du Bois writes, "under modern competitive methods, for workingmen and property-owners to defend their rights and exist without the right of suffrage." And how can a man have self-respect if he keeps silent about the humiliations he must face every day living in the Jim Crow South? Booker T. Washington "advocates common-school and industrial training, and depreciates institutions of higher learning; but neither the Negro common-schools, nor Tuskegee itself, could remain open a day were it not for teachers trained in Negro colleges, or trained by their graduates." Du Bois concludes by dismissing Washington's views because in his estimation the only "way for a people to gain their reasonable rights is not by voluntarily throwing them away" but to "insist continually, in season and out of season, that voting is necessary to modern manhood, that color discrimination is barbarism, and that black boys need education as well as white boys."[14]

Despite the vitriol that laced the quarrel between Washington and Du Bois, African Americans esteemed both men and believed both had valid points to make. In our present day, with the experience of the twentieth-century struggle for civil rights fresh in our memories, it is hard to disagree with Du Bois's argument that each person must be allowed to exercise full and equal rights. If we are the free society that we like to think we are, then it is imperative that no individual's rights be violated or restricted. But to give Booker T. Washington his due, there was a certain sense of realism and pragmatism in his argument that a race of people subjected for centuries to enslavement must start with the basics in order to get ahead, even if it is incremental and slow. He was not trying to convince African Americans to accept their inferiority but urging them to rise above the racial epithets and ignominy and prove to whites that their stereotypes were wrong. In the end, Du Bois and Washington together had the impact of elevating dissent to a rhetorical art. They raised questions that energized a debate on the tactics and strategies that would be required to achieve African American aspirations.

* * *

The euphoria and optimism that freedom and suffrage would elevate freedmen to the same status as whites was quickly replaced by the awful realization that the Jim Crow laws and literacy tests perpetuated a system that kept equality as unattainable as ever. And if one dissented against these restrictions, if one dared to go against the grain or demand equal treatment, there lurked the lynch mob. True, they were free. But that seemed to be the only positive change.

The last quarter of the twentieth century, which was so devastating for African Americans, was just as catastrophic for Native Americans desperately fighting to preserve their way of life and for the thousands of Chinese immigrants seeking a better life in the United States. Discontent, however, was not limited to African American, Indian, and

Chinese minorities. As the West was settled and exploited, industry flourished, and the nation grew enormously prosperous. But the lion's share of that prosperity was controlled by the fortunate few. In addition to the struggle for racial equality, income inequality was a rising source of societal unrest.

CHAPTER 11

Protest and Conflict in the West

If the white man wants to live in peace with the Indian he
can live in peace. There need be no trouble. Treat all men
alike. Give them the same laws. Give them all an even chance
to live and grow. All men were made by the same Great Spirit
Chief. They are all brothers. The earth is the mother of all
people, and all people should have equal rights upon it.
—Chief Joseph's appeal to
President Rutherford B. Hayes, 1879

As the United States was busy reconstructing itself, tens of thousands
of Americans pulled up their roots and headed into the trans-Missouri
west. Most of them sought to improve themselves economically. Some
sought new challenges and hoped-for riches, while others sought more
freedom or simply desired to escape problems back home. There were
recent immigrants from Europe and Asia, Civil War veterans, freedmen,
families, pioneers, speculators, and opportunists.

The region they entered, though vast, was not unpopulated. Millions of people from a variety of cultures already inhabited the West:
Spanish-speaking residents in the Mexican Cession; white prospectors
and mountain men; Chinese laying tracks over the Sierra Nevadas for
the Central Pacific Railroad; and more numerous than all the rest, the
Pueblo, Apache, Navajo, Comanche, Lakota, Pawnee, Nez Perce, Cheyenne, and scores of other Indian nations. As development accelerated,
the unquenchable thirst for land and economic betterment produced
a host of problems. And as these problems magnified, thousands of
Native Americans protested passionately and violently against the invasion of the newcomers that threatened to destroy their culture. Some
of the Indian nations on the Great Plains experienced a sense of déjà
vu, for they had already been driven west when whites took over their
homelands east of the Mississippi. Now in desperation they took up
arms in a final effort to preserve their vanishing way of life. Others

protested too. Chinese workers fought against racial discrimination, while white workers did all they could to make sure the Chinese would not compete with them for jobs. Mexican Americans unsuccessfully demanded that the U.S. government protect their property rights. With so many divergent interests colliding in the West, even white settlers soon began to fight against each other and against regulations that they believed curbed their opportunities. Homesteaders fought ranchers, miners and railroad workers struck against their bosses, and farmers protested angrily against the railroads and banks that were fleecing them and destroying their dreams. All of these groups appealed to the government in Washington to safeguard *their* interests.

* * *

Indians—notably the Sioux, the Cheyenne, the Nez Perce, the Navajo, the Pueblo, and the Apache—put up a strong resistance to the encroachment on their lands, but in the end, all of the Indian nations were conquered and forced onto reservations. Many were killed, and those who survived were treated despicably by corrupt Department of Interior agents. Even when Congress passed the Dawes Act, ostensibly to alleviate Indian suffering and reverse decades of ruthless policies, Native Americans' hopelessness and despair sank to new lows.

The Sioux in the Dakota Territory, the Cheyenne in Colorado and Wyoming, and the Comanche of the southern plains all engaged in a nomadic way of life based on hunting the enormous herds of bison that roamed the Great Plains. By the nineteenth century contact with Americans and modern technology had brought significant changes to the Indian lifestyle. By midcentury Indian use of firearms had reduced the size of the herds, and friction between tribes competing with each other for the buffalo led to escalating tribal warfare; and the availability of rifles in these conflicts led to much higher casualty rates. But it was the arrival of the whites that finally decimated the buffalo herds and ultimately destroyed the Indian way of life.

It is estimated that in 1860 there was close to fifteen million bison grazing on the Great Plains. But the completion of the Transcontinental Railroad in 1869, bringing vast numbers of settlers to the plains and transporting thousands of others to points farther west, had a devastating impact on the herds. The popularity of buffalo-hide coats back east and in Europe enticed hundreds of professional buffalo hunters to slaughter the beasts wholesale, leaving rotting skinned carcasses covering the plains. (The destruction of the bison was not entirely unconscious. Americans understood that the Plains Indians' livelihood depended on the buffalo.) To Indians who could not conceive of killing a buffalo without using the entire carcass for sustenance, to Indians who respected the land and the creatures living on it, this wanton slaughter was an appalling display of the white man's disrespect for life. By the end of the 1870s the buffalo was nearly extinct. Only a few thousand were left.

Further complicating the relationship between Indians and the settlers were continual American incursions into the Dakota Territory. Under the terms of the Fort Laramie Treaty of 1868 the U.S. government guaranteed that the Black Hills would forever be reserved for the Lakota Sioux. But American settlers and prospectors repeatedly violated the treaty by entering the Black Hills—considered by the Lakota to be sacred ground. In 1873 the U.S. Cavalry, under the command of George Armstrong Custer, entered Dakota Territory to guard railroad survey crews, and then in 1874 Custer led his men into the Black Hills. This time Custer announced that they had discovered gold. It was not a bonanza, but reports of the discovery led to the Black Hills Gold Rush. Within months thousands of whites poured into the Black Hills, and the Lakota, already troubled by the earlier forays into their territory and acutely aware that their protests to federal officials were ignored, resolved to go to war. To increase their numbers they united with other tribes—notably the Arapaho and the Northern Cheyenne—in a large confederacy to fight the Americans. Thousands of Indians, led by Sitting Bull, Crazy Horse, and Rain-in-the-Face, amassed in eastern Montana, while the U.S. Cavalry set out to round them up and force them onto reservations. On June 25, 1876, three columns of soldiers encountered the Sioux encampment on the Little Big Horn River in eastern Montana. Custer, leading a small contingent of 264 men from the Seventh Cavalry and apparently underestimating Indian strength, rashly attacked. The ensuing "Custer's Last Stand," when Custer and his entire command were wiped out, was the greatest single victory for the Indians in the Plains Wars, but in reality it was the "Indians' Last Stand," for within a year most of the Sioux were either captured and forced onto reservations or had escaped to Canada. Sitting Bull was one of those who sought refuge in the "Land of the Grandmother [Queen Victoria]," where he remained for several years. Crazy Horse surrendered in 1877, but later in the year he left the reservation and was killed by soldiers when they arrested him. Most of the Indians were eventually dispatched to Standing Rock, Rosebud, Pine Ridge, and other reservations.

Farther west, in eastern Oregon, the Nez Perce still lived on their ancestral lands in the Wallowa Valley. In 1877, however, General Oliver O. Howard informed the Nez Perce leader, Chief Joseph, that if he did not move his people onto Lapwai Reservation in Idaho, the U.S. Cavalry would remove them forcibly. Before Chief Joseph could comply, a band of young Nez Perce warriors impulsively attacked a nearby settlement, killing several whites. When Howard ordered his men to round up the Indians, Joseph decided that he must lead his people out of Oregon and find sanctuary in Canada. For several weeks the Nez Perce eluded the soldiers as they took a circuitous fourteen-hundred-mile journey through Idaho, Wyoming, and Montana. Although greatly outnumbered, the Nez Perce skillfully used guerrilla tactics to ambush and harass the soldiers tracking them, but forty miles short of the Canadian border they were finally surrounded by the Americans. Brigadier General Nelson A. Miles promised Chief Joseph that his people would be permitted to return to Oregon if he surrendered, but when they laid down their arms, they were taken to a disease-ridden reservation in Indian Territory (present-day Oklahoma).

In 1879 Chief Joseph was allowed off the reservation to press the Nez Perce case to President Rutherford B. Hayes in Washington. Like many Indians before him, Joseph protested the treatment his people had suffered by employing arguments and logic that came from the Enlightenment—logic that he knew Americans would understand. He implored the president to permit the Nez Perce to return to their homeland in Oregon. "Good words," Chief Joseph said, referring to the broken treaties, "do not last long unless they amount to something. Words do not pay for my dead people. They do not pay for my country now overrun by white men. . . . Good words do not give me back my children. . . . Good words will not give my people a home where they can live in peace and take care of themselves. . . . I am tired of talk that comes to nothing. It makes my heart sick when I remember all the good words and all the broken promises."[1] But the president turned a deaf ear to Chief Joseph's appeal. The Nez Perce were not allowed to return to the Pacific Northwest for another six years, and even then the tribe was

Chief Joseph (Hin-mah-too-yah-lat-kekt, or Thunder Rolling
Down the Mountain) of the Nez Perce, 1902. "I am tired of talk
that comes to nothing. It makes my heart sick when I remember
all the good words and all the broken promises." Photoprint by
Rudolph B. Scott, Spokane, Washington. (Public domain; courtesy Library of Congress)

divided between a reservation in Idaho and one in Washington State.
Chief Joseph never returned to his beloved Wallowa Valley.

The essential problem in the clash of the two cultures was that for
Americans nothing was more desirable than land. The Lockean/Jeffer-
sonian emphasis on the importance and inviolability of private property was sacred to Americans, and their thirst for land could not be
held in check. By the last quarter of the nineteenth century, however,
growing numbers of influential Americans were disturbed enough by

the Indians' plight that they resolved to do something to ease their suffering and prevent any further carnage.

In 1887 Congress passed the Dawes Severalty Act, designed to assimilate the Indians into American society. If "savage" Indians could be induced to live on the land like whites, lawmakers believed they could then become "civilized" members of the American community. The act divided land on the reservations into small tracts that would be deeded to individual Indian families. Also, Indian children were taken to Carlisle, Pennsylvania, where they were educated and indoctrinated with American principles, mores, and customs. Their hair was cut short, tribal attire was discarded, they were issued American clothes, and they were not allowed to speak their native languages.

The attempt at assimilation was a failure. Indians were not so easily integrated into American life. Most of them had no interest in farming when they desired, most of all, to hunt the buffalo that had all but disappeared from the Great Plains. Moreover, the Indians did not have a tradition of individual land ownership. In their view the land belonged to all people, and it was not easy to break the system of tribal ownership and adopt the notion of individual ownership. Many sold their allotments to land-hungry whites, and when their money ran out, they had no resources. Furthermore, after allotments had been dispersed, there were millions of acres on the reservations that had not been allocated. The federal government then auctioned these tracts to the public. In effect the Dawes Act became a land grab for white settlers and speculators. But most disheartening of all for the Indians was the education feature of the act. Although their children were "Americanized" at the Carlisle School, they were never fully accepted by whites, and when they went back to their families, they no longer fit in with Indian life. For many Native Americans the reaction to the Dawes Act was in essence, "first you stole our land, and then you stole our children." The Dawes Act did little to accomplish its goal of assimilating the Indians and only hastened the annihilation of Indian tradition and culture.

Indians' despair reached such a nadir by the end of the 1880s that they began clutching at a new religion that promised deliverance from their suffering and held out hopes for a bright new day when the buffalo would return to the plains and the white man would disappear. Combining elements of Indian religious thought and Christianity, a Paiute Indian, Wovoka, prophesized that the messiah was about to return to earth. This messiah had previously come to the white man, but the white man had killed him. Now he would return; but this time he would come to the red man, and he would bring back the buffalo along with new soil, new trees, and new streams to the Great Plains. The soldiers would be gone, and the earth and its bounty would once again belong to the Indian. By dancing the Ghost Dance to invoke the spirits of the ancestors, Indians would hasten the day when the prophecy would be fulfilled. "My brothers," Kicking Bear (one of the Indians who helped spread the Ghost Dance religion) declared, "I bring to you the promise of a day in which there will be no white man to lay his hand on the bridle of the Indian horse; when the red men of the prairie will rule the world. . . . I bring you word from your fathers the ghosts, that they are now marching to join you, led by the Messiah who came once to live on earth with the white man, but was cast out and killed by them."[2]

And so they danced the Ghost Dance clutching at the hope that it might actually work. Some were skeptical, but they danced as an expression of protest against their removal to reservations and the destruction of their lives and traditions. As the Ghost Dance spread through the reservations and the few remaining Indian communities, panicky whites feared that an Indian uprising was imminent. In December 1890 a band of Miniconjou Sioux, one of the few bands not yet confined to a reservation, were rounded up by the Seventh Cavalry and force marched to the Pine Ridge reservation. In the morning, after spending the last night of the journey encamped along the banks of Wounded Knee Creek, the soldiers ordered the Indians to surrender their weapons. One of the Indians, Black Coyote, refused to give up his rifle. Soldiers tried to wrest the rifle away, and during the scuffle Black Coyote fired a shot into the air. As if on signal, the troops surrounding the encampment immediately opened fire. For the next twenty minutes a barrage of gunfire, including shrapnel-filled artillery shells, rained down on the Indians. When it ended, more than 150 of the 340 Indians (mostly women and children) were dead, including their chief, Big Foot. Many of the survivors were wounded and crawled off to die, leaving bloody tracks in the snow. About twenty-five soldiers also had been killed, most by "friendly fire." For several hours soldiers continued hunting down Indians who tried to escape and killed them. "A mother was shot down with her infant," American Horse recalled later. "The child not knowing that its mother was dead was still nursing. . . . The women as they were fleeing with their babies were killed together, shot right through, and the women who were very heavy with child were also killed. All the Indians fled in these three directions, and after most all of them had been killed a cry was made that all those who were not killed or wounded should come forth and they would be safe. Little boys who were not wounded came out of their places of refuge, and as soon as they came in sight a number of soldiers surrounded them and butchered them there."[3]

Night was falling, and a blizzard was setting in. As the dead bodies were already beginning to freeze where they had fallen, soldiers left them and hastily loaded fifty-one wounded (forty-seven of them women and children) into wagons and took them to Pine Ridge. There they commandeered the chapel, covered the floor with hay, and arranged dozens of critically wounded Indians near the altar. It was December 29, and Christmas decorations still adorned the chapel. A banner above the altar proclaimed the message of Christ: "Peace on Earth, Good Will to Men."[4]

* * *

Even before the final subjugation of the Indians, white settlers had transformed the face of the West. Miners, homesteaders, ranchers, and large corporations all made their imprint on the West. Whether eking out a subsistence on the Great Plains or growing rich exploiting the seemingly unlimited natural resources of the region, Americans changed the West permanently. The expansion and development of the railroad made all this possible by bringing ever larger numbers of settlers, speculators, and businessmen into the region and providing the means by which the products of their labor were sent to markets in St. Louis, Chicago, and the East Coast. The railroad companies prospered enormously, but their ruthless business tactics eventually led to fierce resentment on the part of farmers, who found ever-increasing freight charges eating up all their profits. By the 1890s farmers' fear that railroads were threatening to destroy their livelihoods prompted thousands of them to ban together in one of the most significant protest movements of the nineteenth century—the Populist Revolt.

Prospectors, unable to resist the allure of gold and silver, continued to pour into the West after the Civil War, even though they were aware that most of those who flocked to the California Gold Rush in

1849 had *not* struck it rich. Like the "forty-niners," prospectors found that after the initial strikes the only way to extract the valuable ores was with heavy equipment for deep-shaft mining. No individual could afford such equipment. So mining soon came to be dominated by large companies such as the Anaconda Mining Company in Montana and the Homestake Mining Company in South Dakota. There was a tremendous fortune in the mines—more than $306 million in Nevada's Comstock Lode alone—for the mining corporations. The bulk of the wealth from gold and silver mining thus found its way into the pockets of stockholders back east, not into the pockets of the colorful, grizzled old prospectors of Hollywood myth.

When President Lincoln signed the Homestead Act into law back in 1862, his vision was that the West would be settled by thousands of family farmers living the respectable Jeffersonian dream on their 160 acres of land. But unfortunately expectations fell short. Even though the price for the land was minimal, most would-be homesteaders could not afford the cost of moving west and buying the tools, implements, supplies, and horses and mules necessary to start a farm. Moreover, most of the factory workers of the East who might have been tempted by the economic opportunities of the West did not have sufficient farming experience to be successful. Although it is true that many thousands of Americans did lay claim to land under the Homestead Act, life as a homesteader was so arduous that many of them gave up and sold their land titles, and so most of the acreage wound up in the hands of speculators and investors. The farmland of the Dakotas, Nebraska, and Kansas eventually proved productive when agricultural corporations began cultivating it. Agribusinesses that had the capital to invest in expensive mechanical equipment such as reapers, harvesters, and combines bought up homesteads, consolidated them into large farms, and employed farm workers (often the very homesteaders they had bought out) at subsistence wages.

Big business also found enormous profits in the heavily timbered areas of the Rockies and the coastal mountain ranges. Millions of acres of forest in California, Oregon, and Washington fell to the saw. The decimation of the forests, especially the destruction of so many California redwoods, gave rise to a dissent movement that continues to this day—environmentalism. At a time when most Americans assumed that the resources of the West were limitless, John Muir warned that the despoliation wrought by the lumber, railroad, and mining industries would lead to long-range environmental problems. Throughout the 1880s and 1890s Muir wrote articles calling for the preservation of America's wildernesses and forests. In 1890, along with Robert Underwood Johnson and other environmentalists, Muir began a successful campaign to convince Congress to preserve the Hetch Hetchy Valley in central California by establishing Yosemite National Park. In 1892 Muir founded the Sierra Club, and in subsequent years he lobbied for the creation of the Grand Canyon and Sequoia National Parks. It was essential, Muir believed, to treasure and preserve these beautiful valleys and forests and canyons, not only because of their natural beauty but because the ecosystem would be irreparably damaged if they were not preserved. Muir's position later influenced President Theodore Roosevelt to push for policies that would balance the nation's need for coal and iron and lumber with the desire to preserve America's scenic beauty. The modern environmental movement owes much to John Muir.

Like mining, agriculture, and lumber, ranching also required a large capital outlay, thus favoring individuals and corporations with considerable financial resources at their disposal. With the railroad opening the West, investors and entrepreneurs from the East Coast and Europe jumped at the opportunity to buy herds of cattle and water rights. Ranchers hired cowboys to do the grueling, tedious work of rounding up the steers and driving them to railroad towns in Kansas, Nebraska, and Colorado, where the cattle were shipped to Chicago's slaughterhouses. The cowboys' job was rough and monotonous; they worked in the blazing sun and frigid blizzards, breathed in unhealthy levels of dust along the trails, constantly faced the dangers of stampeding cattle and venomous snakes, and were paid no more than forty dollars a month. They were no better off than the factory workers back east. They were exploited labor.

Thousands of Americans raised crops or sheep on small family farms, and thousands worked for wages as miners or cowboys in the West. But it was the large mining, lumber, cattle, and agricultural corporations that dominated the region. Corporations dominated economic life in the East. Corporations dominated economic life in the West. Increasingly wage earners in both sections of the country felt they were missing out on the promises of American society. Increasingly they were feeling the injustice, in a land that promised so much, of their limited opportunities.

* * *

The experience of ethnic minorities and women in the West became a Petri dish for dissent. Mexicans living in the Southwest protested against discrimination and their status as second-class citizens and as a result preserved a powerful Mexican American culture that has indelibly stamped the American Southwest. African Americans, in small acts of protest against racial discrimination, aided the rapid development of the West by leaving the South and serving as soldiers, working as cowboys, or planting farms on the Great Plains. Chinese immigrants, who helped create a multicultural California, fought against statutes that deprived them of citizenship and civil rights even as they played an indispensable role in the construction of the transcontinental railroad. And women were so central to the development of the West that their contributions accelerated the women's movement and hastened the day that women throughout the nation finally won the right to vote.

The thousands of Mexicans living in the territory that the United States acquired from Mexico in 1848 originally retained title to their land on the basis of the age-old land grants they had received from Spain. But unscrupulous lawyers representing the Americans settling in the Southwest successfully challenged the Spanish titles, so that by 1880 almost all of these titles had been invalidated in American courts. Thus Mexican Americans in California and New Mexico (where they were actually in a majority) were forced off their land. But they did not give up without a struggle. In the early 1880s Mexican Americans formed Las Gorras Blancas (The White Caps), a secret militant organization that put up a fight against the invading Anglos. For over a decade they intimidated whites by burning barns, tearing down fences, scattering livestock, and burning crops, as well as vandalizing railroad yards and white businesses. Well into the twentieth century Las Gorras Blancas remained an inspiring model for Mexican American protest and resistance against discrimination and oppression. Despite facing unremitting bigotry and intolerance, Mexican Americans protested, adapted, and successfully maintained their cultural traditions.

Thousands of African Americans, like their white counterparts, also took the trek west hoping to improve their opportunities for economic success. Many young black men enlisted in the U.S. Army and were deployed to the frontier as "Buffalo Soldiers" (a name given them by the Indians) to protect settlers and railroad property from the Indians. Some became cowboys, while others took up homesteading. In the 1870s a former slave, Benjamin Singleton, set up a company and purchased land in Kansas as a haven for blacks. Hundreds of black families, fed up with prejudice and discrimination, left the South and went with Singleton to establish towns on the Kansas prairie. Over the next decade thousands of African Americans became "Exodusters" in Kansas. But unfortunately for them, as was the case with all small farmers on the Great Plains, the difficulties of making a living, the devastating droughts and blizzards of the 1880s, and competition from agribusinesses later forced many to abandon their farms and take jobs in the factories of Kansas City and St. Louis.

By the 1870s there were more than sixty thousand Chinese immigrants living in the United States. Although originally lured by the dream of striking it rich in the mountains of California, most of them were lucky to find employment as laborers laying track for the Central Pacific Railroad, as agricultural workers, or toiling in San Francisco or Sacramento in factory jobs. Those who were fortunate enough to save some money established small businesses—general stores, restaurants, laundries. Although the Chinese constituted a minuscule proportion of the total American population (only a fraction of 1 percent), they found themselves the target of rabid racial discrimination. White railroad workers, especially Irish and German immigrants, bitterly resented the Chinese, who were always willing to work harder and longer for less wages. (Railroad magnates, such as the president of the Central Pacific Railroad, Leland Stanford, observed that Chinese workers were "peaceable, industrious, economical," and "much more reliable" than white men.)[5] White resentment led to a mushrooming "anticoolie" movement. Workers took to the streets in violent anti-Chinese protests. They denounced these Asian competitors for jobs, smashed windows of Chinese stores, and demanded that California levy exorbitant taxes on Chinese businesses, pass laws prohibiting the education of Chinese children, and ban any further Chinese immigration into the state.

Increasingly whites terrorized the Chinese by vandalizing and destroying their businesses and houses, attacking them on the street, pelting them with rotten vegetables and eggs, beating them, humiliating them by cutting off their queues (pigtails), and on several occasions lynching them. President Hayes, in 1879, matter-of-factly revealed how far anti-Chinese bigotry had penetrated when he proclaimed, "The present Chinese labor invasion . . . is pernicious and should be discouraged. Our experience in dealing with the weaker races—the negroes and Indians, for example—is not encouraging. . . . I therefore would consider with favor any suitable measures to discourage the Chinese from coming to our shores."[6] In 1882 a suitable measure was indeed found when Congress enacted the Chinese Exclusion Act. The act forbade Chinese immigration into the country for ten years (when the ban expired, it was renewed and eventually extended indefinitely) and excluded those already living in the United States from citizenship. Anti-Chinese protestors were exuberant.

The Chinese, however, resisted. In San Francisco the Chinese Consolidated Benevolent Association protested against the Exclusion Act and the state ordinances, promoted Chinese American rights, and established schools for Chinese American children. Chinese workers in various industries, from railroad construction to cigar making, attempted to organize unions. Chinatowns on both coasts coordinated boycotts of American goods. Activists Ng Poon Chew in San Francisco and Wong Chin Foo in New York launched anti–Exclusion Act newspapers. Wong Chin Foo also founded the Chinese Equal Rights League of America in 1892 as an organization to coordinate the struggle for Chinese American civil rights. Unfortunately for him, however, his activism eventually resulted in his deportation to China.

Chinese also protested by challenging anti-Chinese laws in court. When San Francisco passed a law denying business licenses for Chinese laundries, Yick Wo took the city to court and persisted with his suit all the way to the U.S. Supreme Court. In 1886 the Court ruled in *Yick Wo v. Hopkins* that it was unlawful for a local government to issue statutes that would deny the right of an individual to make a living. In another case, in 1889, the Court ruled against Chae Chan Ping when it reaffirmed the government's right to exclude immigrants from China. But in the *United States v. Wong Kim Ark* (1898) the Court ruled for the plaintiff and upheld the Fourteenth Amendment when it concurred that any person born in the United States of Chinese parents was an American citizen. All in all, Chinese immigrants won most of the more than seven thousand lawsuits they filed in the 1880s and 1890s.

When France presented the United States with an iconic, inspiring gift for New York Harbor as a token of its admiration for American democracy, the Chinese American writer Saum Song Bo summed up the anti-Chinese furor best by wryly punning about America's legacy to the world. "Whether this statute against the Chinese [the Chinese Exclusion Act] or the statue of Liberty will be the most lasting monument to tell future ages of the liberty and greatness of this country," he wrote, "will be known only to future generations."[7]

Despite the protests, Chinese Americans did not accomplish much. In 1882, the year of the Exclusion Act, the number of Chinese living in the United States was 104,000. By 1920 that number had fallen to 62,000. In 1943, only because of the U.S. alliance with China in the war against Japan, the Exclusion Act was finally repealed. The quota for Chinese immigrants, however, was set extremely low, and their numbers grew at a slow pace. In 1965 the restrictions were eased, and the number of Chinese living in the United States rose abruptly. Still, today they make up only a little over 1 percent of the American population (about three million).

Women in the West contributed greatly to the grueling work of eking out a living, tending to flocks of sheep, plowing fields, all the while performing the child-rearing and domestic duties expected of their gender. Women's role in the growth and development of the West was so indispensable that several of the western territories, notably Wyoming, Utah, and Colorado, granted women the right to vote even before they applied for statehood.

The situation in Utah, where the Church of Jesus Christ of Latter-Day Saints (Mormons) presided over every aspect of the inhabitants' lives, played out somewhat differently because the federal government stepped in to prohibit the practice of polygamy. (It was Mormon defiance of bourgeois sexual morality and the severe persecution that they had faced that compelled them to migrate to northern Mexico back in 1847. Unfortunately their escape from the jurisdiction of the United States was short-lived when Mexico ceded Utah to the United States a year later.) In 1882 Congress passed the Edmonds Law abolishing plural marriage, and then, in 1887, Congress repealed women's suffrage in

Utah. Many devout Mormon women who had been enjoying the right to vote were outraged that Washington struck down an article of their faith and then rescinded their right to vote. Denouncing what appeared to them as a federal attack on Mormonism, women banded together and founded the Woman Suffrage Association of Utah. Emmeline Wells, the editor of the Mormon magazine the *Woman's Exponent*, defended plural marriage and demanded the restoration of the right to vote. Wells repudiated the popular perception that plural marriage was the equivalent of sexual bondage and instead argued that polygamy actually freed women from the conventional idea that female identity derived from a husband. Plural marriage was a boon for women because it gave them more freedom and allowed them to play a significant role in public life.[8] For nearly ten years the female activists of Utah carried on the campaign. Although they eventually gave up on their fight to reinstate plural marriage, they were successful in their fight for suffrage. In 1896 Utah was admitted to the Union with women's suffrage enshrined in the state constitution.

The experience of women in the West was a catalyst in bolstering the women's movement across the nation and raised the hopes of many women that suffrage would soon become a national reality. The West, it seemed, was paving the way to a future in which women would finally secure equal rights.

* * *

It did not take long before homesteaders ran up against powerful forces arrayed against them. By 1887, the year the Dawes Act confined Indians to ever-smaller parcels of land, farmers in the West realized that pursuing independence and economic self-sufficiency on the Great Plains was far more difficult than they had ever imagined. During the 1870s and 1880s small midwestern farms were hit with blizzards, hailstorms, scorching droughts, and plagues of grasshoppers. Although individual farmers suffered greatly from these natural catastrophes, crop production continued to rise. So much wheat was produced that there was a glut in the domestic market, and so, in order to survive, farmers became increasingly dependent on selling their wheat abroad. Disaster struck when crop yields in Europe increased to the point that demand for American grain fell drastically. By the late 1880s the price of wheat had dropped by more than 50 percent, and small farmers were forced to borrow money at exorbitant interest rates to pay for equipment, fertilizer, and seed. As their income dwindled, many defaulted on their loans and were evicted. In the South sharecroppers as well as middle-class farmers faced an economic catastrophe when the price of cotton halved during the 1880s (from approximately eleven cents a pound to five cents). They had no alternative but to borrow money at excessive rates of interest just to survive. Farmers' resentment toward the money-lenders began to bubble over.

In addition to the usurious interest rates demanded by financial institutions, the price-gouging tactics of the railroad companies equally angered farmers. Railroads routinely offered discounted rates to large agribusinesses and cattle companies (because of the volume of their business) while charging small farmers much higher rates. For American farmers it was clear: big business was out to destroy them.

Washington's monetary policy further convinced farmers that there was a conspiracy against them. Federal law required that paper currency should never exceed the amount of gold bullion in the treasury. Because the population was growing at a much faster rate than the gold supply, there was a shortage of currency in circulation, and this further deflated the price farmers received for their crops. A shortage of money also meant it was a lenders' market; thus interest rates soared even higher.

Farmers' recognition that the American banking and financial system was not working for their best interests radicalized them. Earlier cooperative organizations such as the Patrons of Husbandry (the Grangers) and the Farmers' Alliance (which farmers had formed to pool their resources so they could, for example, purchase expensive mechanized farm equipment to share) now metamorphosed into political action associations. The Farmers' Alliance, especially, became a major political force.

The first Farmers' Alliance was formed in Texas and expanded to hundreds of communities in most states of the Union. Eventually more than one million farmers joined the Alliance. The Alliance's objective was to push Washington to enact legislation that would regulate the railroads and the other businesses that were gouging farmers. (In 1887 Congress passed the Interstate Commerce Act, which specified that interstate railroad rates be "reasonable and just," and it created the Interstate Commerce Commission to implement the act. But the commission lacked sufficient teeth to enforce the law.) In the South, despite the Jim Crow laws and rampant racism, there was some cooperation between whites and blacks who recognized that they shared the same grievances against the "money power." Although most white Alliance chapters in the South did not accept black farmers, they did recognize, and to some extent work with, the Colored Farmer's Alliance.[9]

As the protest movement grew, farmers began exerting a more influential voice in state and national politics. In 1889 a number of representatives from various chapters of the Alliance met in St. Louis, Missouri. They formed the National Farmers' Alliance and Industrial Union as a large umbrella organization and deployed speakers to make their grievances a focal point of the 1890 election. Perhaps the most eloquent of the Alliance's speakers was Mary Elizabeth Lease, who traveled the circuit from her Kansas home protesting against the corporate greed that was wiping out the small farmer. Lease demanded that the government do something about regulating the banks and the railroads and urged farmers to recognize that if they banded together and channeled their dissent, they could force the government to respond to their needs and protect their rights. We are good, virtuous men and women, she reasoned, who have worked hard just to enjoy a modest standard of living. "Yet, after all our years of toil and privation, dangers and hardships upon the Western frontier, monopoly is taking our homes from us by an infamous system of mortgage foreclosure. . . . It takes from us at the rate of five hundred a month the homes that represent the best years of our life, our toil, our hopes, our happiness. How did it happen? The government, at the bid of Wall Street, repudiated its contracts with the people." The way to bring about change, the way to save the small, ordinary man from extinction, would be accomplished when farmers decided to "raise less corn and more hell!"

> Crowns will fall, thrones will tremble, kingdoms will disappear, the divine right of kings and the divine right of capital will fade away like the mists of the morning when the Angel of Liberty shall kindle the fires of justice in the hearts of men. . . . No more millionaires, and no more paupers; no more gold kings, silver kings and oil kings, and no more little waifs of humanity starving for a crust of bread. No more gaunt-faced, hollow-eyed girls in the factories, and no more little boys reared in poverty and crime for the penitentiaries and the gallows.[10]

Political activist and populist spokesperson Mary Elizabeth
Lease, c. 1890s. She enjoined farmers to "raise less corn
and more hell!" (Public domain; courtesy Kansas State
Historical Society)

When the results of the 1890 elections came in, the Alliance was
jubilant. Candidates committed to the Alliance's program won the
majority of the legislative seats in ten states. In addition, they won the
gubernatorial races in Texas, Georgia, South Carolina, and Tennessee
and sent three senators to the U.S. Senate and forty-four congressmen
to the U.S. House of Representatives. In December the Alliance held
a convention in Ocala, Florida, to explore the possibility of forming
an alternative political party, to frame an official platform, and to give
notice to the Republicans and the Democrats that if they were unwilling to be responsive to the needs of the people, then the Alliance would
replace them. They urged a reduction of the tariff to lower consumer
prices; they called for the direct election of senators by the people (the
Constitution stipulates that state legislatures select U.S. senators); they

demanded a national banking system controlled by the government; they insisted on the free and unlimited coinage of silver so that more money would be in circulation; they called for nationalizing the railroads; and they demanded a graduated income tax.

By 1892 Alliance members had given up on the two major political parties. As far as they were concerned, there was no difference between Republicans and Democrats. Both parties were in cahoots with Big Business. And so the Alliance launched the People's Party (dubbed the Populist Party by the press). In July hundreds of delegates met in Omaha, Nebraska, fine-tuned a visionary, progressive platform, and nominated James B. Weaver for president. Protesting that "corruption dominates the ballot-box" and all branches of government, that newspapers are "muzzled, public opinion silenced, business prostrated, homes covered with mortgages, labor impoverished, and the land concentrating in the hands of capitalists," the delegates announced they had no alternative but to organize a new party that would fight for the rights of farmers, miners, and industrial workers. "The fruits of the toil of millions are boldly stolen to build up colossal fortunes for a few, unprecedented in the history of mankind; and the possessors of these, in turn, despise the Republic and endanger liberty." On top of that, the two major parties are merely the handmaidens of the moneyed classes and pay absolutely no attention to the protests of poor farmers and workers. Republicans and Democrats alike "drown the outcries of a plundered people with the uproar of a sham battle over the tariff, so that capitalists, corporations, national banks, rings, trusts, watered stock, the demonetization of silver and the oppressions of the usurers may all be lost sight of. They propose to sacrifice our homes, lives, and children on the altar of mammon; to destroy the multitude in order to secure corruption funds from the millionaires."[11]

In order to restore government to the American people, the Populists endorsed the Ocala Platform of 1890 by calling for essential political reforms (the secret ballot, referendum and initiative, primary elections, the direct election of senators, the limitation of the office of president to one term) and economic reforms (a graduated income tax, "the free and unlimited coinage of silver at the present legal ratio of 16 to 1," the eight-hour day for industrial workers, and public ownership of the railroads). The platform also advocated limiting immigration so as to reduce competition for low-wage jobs.[12] For most Americans the

Populist Platform was a radical document, especially the planks calling for such socialist ideas as the nationalization of the railway and communication companies. However, several of their demands, such as the graduated income tax and the direct election of senators, were implemented early in the twentieth century.

The Populists, as third parties in the United States have discovered, faced formidable obstacles. In the South especially there was the daunting task of trying to unite poor and middle-class white farmers with black sharecroppers. Tom Watson, a Populist activist in Georgia, realized that it was necessary to convince people that the economic interests of the poor were a more significant unifying factor than race was a dividing factor. He addressed political gatherings in the South urging blacks and whites to join together in common cause. "You are kept apart," he warned, "that you may be separately fleeced of your earnings. You are made to hate each other because upon that hatred is rested the keystone of the arch of financial despotism which enslaves you both. You are deceived and blinded that you may not see how this race antagonism perpetuates a monetary system which beggars both."[13] But Watson and other Populists found that it was nearly impossible to achieve meaningful racial unity in the South. Most African Americans were reluctant to abandon the party of Lincoln and join the Populists, while Democratic politicians continued to play the race card, mercilessly fanning white fears that blacks would take away their jobs and destroy southern society unless they were put in their place.

Still, despite such obstacles, the Populists did make their voices heard in the election of 1892. More than a million Americans voted for Weaver, and he won four states (Nevada, Idaho, Colorado, and Kansas) with twenty electoral votes and one electoral vote each in Oregon and North Dakota. Populists also won the gubernatorial races in three states and fifteen congressional seats in the House of Representatives.

* * *

Unfortunately for the Farmers' Alliance the federal government was part of the problem. Ever since the end of Reconstruction Washington continued, unflinchingly, to favor big business. And the wealthiest business leaders in the country—the railroad tycoons, the steel magnates—along with the party bosses, were confident that they could control the man in the White House. The power of wealth created an environment that

encouraged corruption and a pervading attitude of rampant materialism and greed.

Furthermore, the presidents of the Gilded Age were a study in medi-
ocrity. What they had in common was a belief that the president should
do little to regulate the economy; in fact for the most part they acted as
though they were mere caretakers in the White House and their job was
simply to preside over a rapidly growing nation. They were incapable
of leading. Neither political party seemed interested in confronting the
significant problems facing the nation. The lack of political will characterized the era.

Despite the lack of leadership, the United States expanded rapidly
during the last quarter of the nineteenth century. As Americans pushed
into the West, the people who were already there felt the sting of losing
their property, their way of life, and their rights. But some fought back.
Some resisted encroachment by protesting. Some fought back by taking
their cases to court. Some literally fought by taking up arms. Throughout it all, by the end of the century the West had become a confluence
of cultures—Anglo-European, Chinese, Hispanic, African American,
and Native American—living uneasily together.

American expansion was both geographical and economic. Miners,
ranchers, land speculators, railroad companies, bankers, agribusinesses,
and others with the financial wherewithal extracted untold wealth from
the land and grew richer. Those who did not have the resources, who
were merely trying to improve their lives by staking a claim or a homestead, found that it was nearly impossible to eke out a living. By the late
1880s a protest movement had emerged in the Midwest that eventually
developed into a major political force challenging the powers that be. If
the federal government was not going to respond to their needs, they
were ready to force it to do so.

The abundant raw materials that were being extracted from the West
helped fuel industry back east. Along with the rise of a number of skillful entrepreneurs, new inventions, improved methods of production,
and an influx of countless immigrants to supply the labor force for a
rapidly developing factory system, the United States grew from a rural
agrarian society into an urban industrial power. By the last decade of
the century the United States was one of the major manufacturing
countries in the world. Within another decade the country was on the
cusp of becoming a force in international politics.

But not every American prospered, and many angrily opposed a system that they believed prevented them from reaping the rewards of their hard work and gave unfair advantage to the moneyed classes. Workers, like the farmers in the West and South, began to organize. Labor unrest led to strikes, to protest marches, and in a few significant instances to violence.

CHAPTER 12

Workers of the World Unite!

Workingmen, to Arms!!!! . . . You have for years endured the most abject humiliations; . . . you have worked yourself to death; . . . your Children you have sacrificed to the factory lord— . . . you have been miserable and obedient slaves all these years. Why? To satisfy the insatiable greed, to fill the coffers of your lazy thieving master? When you ask them now to lessen your burdens, he sends his bloodhounds out to shoot you, kill you! . . . To arms we call you, to arms!

—August Spies, summoning workers to a
rally at Haymarket Square, May 4, 1886

The Gilded Age was an era of unprecedented industrial and urban growth, a time of seemingly unlimited expansion of American business. The timber, iron ore, precious metals, and agricultural products from the West were a boon to the economy. Cornelius Vanderbilt, John D. Rockefeller, Andrew Carnegie, J. P. Morgan, and other entrepreneurs created huge monopolies and trusts and seemed to wield more power than the federal government itself. Inventions such as the electric light, the telephone, and the electrification of urban mass-transit systems, as well as innovations such as mass marketing, professional spectator sports, and department stores, transformed daily life.

But as the cities grew and the nation rapidly industrialized, so too did serious problems. Political corruption ran rampant in the cities. Unscrupulous employers and landlords took advantage of the poor and the new immigrants flooding in from Europe. Workers had little choice but to take jobs in unsafe factories and industrial plants where they barely earned enough to support themselves. Appalling working and living conditions led to mounting discontent. Discontent led to dissent. Dissent led to activism. Activist workers organized and showed a willingness to go on strike. They called for owners to recognize and negotiate with their unions, and they demanded a living wage and a safe working environment, while farmers, as we have seen, also organized cooperatives and a political party to push for their interests. By the 1890s it seemed that workers and farmers were on the brink of forming an extensive radical coalition that would force the government to address their concerns, recognize their contribution to American prosperity, alleviate their suffering, and protect their rights.

* * *

Business tycoons such as Carnegie, Vanderbilt, Rockefeller, and Morgan, encouraged and abetted by the laissez-faire attitude of the government, dominated the expansion of American industry. To some these men were "captains of industry" piloting the American economy to great wealth, while to others they were "robber barons" exploiting workers mercilessly in order to maximize profit. Whatever the designation, they combined great business acumen with political skill and a heavy dose of fearlessness and ruthlessness. They expanded their industries into great conglomerates and monopolies through shrewd, often ruthless and exploitive, methods. Not every entrepreneur who set out to build an industrial empire was successful, but those who were accrued incredible wealth, power, and influence.

These men were enamored with the writings of the English philosopher Herbert Spencer and Yale professor William Graham Sumner, who applied Darwin's theory of evolution to society. Coining the term "survival of the fittest," Spencer argued that those who arrive at the top of the social and economic ladder are more fit than their fellows. No matter what corrupt, exploitive, or predatory practices a man used to get to the pinnacle of success, he was justified because this was simply natural selection at work. If the workers were truly fit, then why were they living in poverty? Why were they working for the likes of Carnegie and Rockefeller? "Millionaires," Sumner wrote, "are a product of natural selection."[1] They are wealthy because they deserve to be wealthy. They are the fittest. It would be going against nature for the government to do anything to help the poor and the lower classes. It would be wrong to pass laws for a minimum wage or workers' compensation or unemployment insurance or welfare or aid for education. Such legislation would only enable more of the unfit to survive, thus weakening the whole human race. What is necessary is to support the *more* fit—if anything, the United States should aid the rich, not the poor. Taxing the rich, Sumner reasoned, "would be like killing off our generals in time of war."[2] The United States' core principles should not be "life, liberty, and equality." No. The United States is about life, *in*equality, and survival of the fittest!

Needless to say, Social Darwinism, as Spencer's and Sumner's philosophy came to be called, was music to the ears of business tycoons. Social Darwinism validated whatever practices they used to increase profit, destroy competition, and control the nation's wealth. It was a "scientifically proven" fact that the fit survive and the unfit perish.

By the 1880s Social Darwinism had entered the chambers of Congress, and politicians agreed with industrialists that capitalist exploitation was clearly a manifestation of natural law and that government should never act in any way as to disturb the natural order of things. Social Darwinism was also used to justify the Jim Crow laws—after all, African Americans were free, they were citizens, and males could vote; if they were fit, then obviously they would rise without any outside help, and if not, well, then so be it. Social Darwinism was used to justify the subjugation of the Indians. American culture and civilization was superior. That is why it was so easy to vanquish the Indians. If the Indians were the superior race, if they were meant to survive, they would have. The domination of whites was simply another example to Social Darwinists (and most Americans) of the survival of the fittest and proof of the superiority of American civilization. Additionally, Social Darwinism was used to justify imperialism. European nations had already taken over most of the "uncivilized" countries of the world in the name of the "white man's burden." Soon, too, the United States used similar reasoning to expand beyond its national borders. With these kinds of attitudes accepted as articles of faith by elected officials and the privileged classes, it is not surprising that the poor protested against a system that thwarted the hopes they had for improving their lives, a system that in fact blamed them for their own impoverishment.

With bankrupt farmers looking for jobs and European immigrants pouring into the country, factory owners had a huge supply of labor at their disposal, and this ensured that wages would never rise above subsistence. Most workers made $400 to $500 a year working twelve hours a day (sometimes longer) and six or seven days a week. Jobs in the steel industry, mining, and the railroads were so hazardous that every day workers were maimed or killed on the job. Moreover, with so many people needing employment, there was no motivation for owners to increase wages, offer job security, or provide decent, safe working conditions for their laborers. Jay Gould, realizing that competition among workers also acted as a brake on any attempt to unionize, once boasted that he could "hire one half of the working class to kill the other half."[3]

In addition to inadequate wages and unsafe working conditions, workers deeply resented the fact that they were treated as just another commodity by bosses who sought to extract the maximum amount of labor for the minimum amount of pay. Many workers had formerly been craftsmen who had taken great pride in their occupations. Now they were laboring in factories as part of the production process, making products to which they had no connection, goods that could be produced by anyone. As a result, there was no sense of job satisfaction, no sense of pride in their work.

One way workers dissented against the factory system was passively: by decreasing production. They knew that if they worked harder and produced more goods, it would lead to overproduction and thus result in layoffs. When new workers were hired, older hands ordered them to slow down and not work so fast. Workers who put in too much overtime or produced more than others were ostracized by their coworkers. Sometimes these "job wreckers," if they persisted, were "persuaded" by their comrades' fists. Other forms of resistance were shirking, shoddy work, and absenteeism. (Of course, if they were caught, they would lose their jobs.) Many also used their feet to protest when they could not bear it anymore by simply walking off the job without giving notice.

A key form of resistance was unionization. Before the Civil War skilled workers had organized craft unions—carpenters, printers, masons, and the like. In 1866 many of these craft unions joined together and formed the National Labor Union, but disagreement among the members caused it to fall apart within a few years. By the 1870s another union, the Knights of Labor, had formed and was on the way to becoming a viable and powerful national union representing the interests of unskilled industrial workers as well as artisans. The Knights of Labor even included women and African Americans among its membership. In 1879 the leader of the union was Terence V. Powderly. Powderly, who had served as the mayor of Scranton, Pennsylvania, believed that the best way for workers to gain their rights was through political power. He also proposed a cooperative system in order "to secure to the toilers a proper share of the wealth they create." To this end workers should be entitled to participate in owning the means of production. "There is no good reason," Powderly argued, "why labor cannot through co-operation, own and operate mines, factories and railroads." In addition to such basic socialist tenets, Powderly and the Knights of Labor called for an eight-hour day "so that the laborers may have more time for social enjoyment and intellectual improvement, and be enabled to reap the advantages conferred by the labor-saving machinery which their brains have created"; the prohibition of child labor; "equal pay for equal work" for women as well as men; and, demonstrating solidarity with western farmers, "the reserving of the public lands . . . for the actual settler; not another acre for railroads or speculators."[4]

The financial Panic of 1873 sent the nation into a recession, and business leaders' attempt to cope with the financial crisis as well as prevent workers from organizing exacerbated labor unrest. In the anthracite coal region of northeastern Pennsylvania most of the unskilled miners were Irish immigrants who worked for pathetic wages in brutally harsh conditions. In order to create a support network that would aid the families of the untold numbers of miners that had been severely injured or killed on the job, the miners organized the Ancient Order of Hibernians. A core group within the Order, known as the "Molly Maguires," often resorted to violence in retaliation against cruel bosses and foremen, as well as against policemen and mine owners. Through sabotage, physical assaults, and sometimes even murder, they sought to even the score. When the Mollies stepped up their activities after 1873, the mine operators hired Pinkerton detectives to infiltrate and destroy the organization. Twenty of the Molly Maguires, with the Pinkerton infiltrators giving testimony against them, were eventually arrested, tried, convicted, and hanged, while dozens of others were sent to prison. Protestors around the country, believing that the trial was unfair, demonstrated against the executions but to no avail. (Some historians argue that there is evidence that the Molly Maguires were indeed framed by the Pinkertons.)

Shortly after the Molly Maguire trials and executions a major railroad strike disrupted the entire nation. The Panic of 1873 had prompted several railroad companies to impose a series of wage cuts. When the Baltimore and Ohio Railroad Company announced its decision to reduce wages for the third time in three years by an additional 10 percent in

June 1877, workers exploded. The strike quickly spread to the Pennsylvania Railroad and other railway companies, and within weeks most rail traffic east of the Mississippi, as well as some in the West, ground to a halt. Strikers destroyed railroad property, tore up tracks, and torched freight cars, rail yards, and roundhouses. States called out their militias to restore order. Shots were exchanged. The violence escalated.

When the governor of Maryland mobilized the National Guard, thousands of townspeople, showing their solidarity with the railroad workers, surrounded the National Guard Armory in Baltimore. When the crowd began throwing rocks, the guardsmen opened fire, killing ten men and wounding scores of others. Thousands more now descended on the armory, and the federal government was forced to deploy the U.S. Army to put down the disturbance.

In Pittsburgh there was a confrontation between strikers and the Pennsylvania National Guard. Railroad officials worried that the Pittsburgh troops would be hesitant to fire on their townspeople, so they sent in Philadelphia troops instead. In the ensuing battle, shots were fired, and several strikers were killed. Hundreds of townsfolk now entered the fray on the side of the rail workers. They looted and torched buildings and surrounded the Philadelphia troops, who held out for a while in a roundhouse before escaping. When it was over, seventy-nine buildings had been destroyed and twenty-four people killed. The Pennsylvania National Guard was sent to other towns to crush the railroad strikers, but in some cases they refused to fire on their fellow citizens and even laid down their arms and fraternized with the strikers.

The disturbances spread. In New York thousands attended a rally in Tompkins Square calling for "a socialistic republic." In Chicago a mob of five thousand clashed with police and the National Guard. Twenty-one were killed. In St. Louis there were rallies in which over a thousand workers called for the nationalization of American industry. By the time the Great Railroad Strike of 1877 was quelled by federal troops in August, more than one hundred thousand Americans had taken part, more than a thousand had been arrested, and one hundred had been killed. The strike gained the workers nothing. Those who were not fired and who went back to work still faced the 10 percent wage cut. What the strike did do was convince wealthy and middle-class property owners that labor unrest had to be met with violent force and that the labor movement itself was a radical attempt to undermine the United States.

Between 1877 and 1886 there were hundreds of strikes, including sympathy strikes when workers in one plant struck to show solidarity with strikers in another plant. One of the more successful unions that emerged at this time was the American Federation of Labor (AFL), which was primarily a moderate organization bringing together an assortment of autonomous craft unions (for example, carpenters, cigar makers, iron workers, machinists) to lobby Congress to enact prolabor legislation. Fighting for such "bread-and-butter" issues as the eight-hour day and higher wages, the AFL by 1900 boasted a million members. Nevertheless, the union movement had a difficult time gaining the support of the public, especially after the Haymarket affair.

On May 1, 1886, 350,000 American workers, protesting the sixty-hour week and demanding an eight-hour workday, participated in a nationwide general strike. In Chicago on May 3, when striking workers at the McCormick Harvester Works were picketing in front of the plant, a skirmish broke out between strikers and scabs. The police arrived and fired into the crowd, killing three strikers. Outraged at the killings, August Spies and Albert Parsons, leaders of an anarchist organization, the International Working People's Association, called for a mass protest rally at Haymarket Square the following evening.

Nearly three thousand protestors attended the rally. For several hours they listened to union leaders and anarchists exhorting them to fight for their rights. Rain began falling, and much of the gathering began to disperse. At this point, with only a few hundred diehards remaining to listen to the last speaker, 180 policemen moved in to break up the rally. Suddenly someone threw a bomb into the advancing line of policemen. The police opened fire. When the smoke cleared, four protestors and seven police officers were mortally wounded, and more than two hundred people (fifty-nine of them policemen) were injured. Eight anarchists were arrested and charged with murder.

The nation was shocked. What happened at Haymarket convinced Americans that industrial workers were violent radicals. For the next several decades the public equated labor unions with anarchism. Unions were simply un-American. The union movement was dealt a devastating blow. The Knights of Labor, even though Powderly's organization had nothing to do with Haymarket, lost three-fourths of its membership within a year.

There was no evidence against any of the eight men arrested (only one of them was even at the square, and he was on the platform addressing the crowd at the time), but they were tried and convicted. Most observers maintained that the accused were put on trial because of their political beliefs, not for murder. Five of the eight were sentenced to death, and during the months before their execution there were major protest demonstrations in the United States, England, Holland, France, Spain, Italy, Russia, and elsewhere. In November 1887 Albert Parsons, August Spies, Adolph Fischer, and George Engel were hanged. The fifth condemned man, Louis Lingg, cheated the hangman the day before the execution by putting a stick of dynamite (which someone had smuggled into his cell) in his mouth and lighting the fuse. He was twenty-one years old.

Protests, however, continued. The day of the funerals twenty-five thousand people marched in Chicago and in other cities around the nation. For years afterward thousands of Americans attended memorial meetings for the Haymarket anarchists. When Illinois's next governor, John Peter Altgeld, took office, sixty thousand people signed a petition demanding that he investigate the case. He did so and pardoned the three anarchists who remained in jail. In the aftermath of the affair a conspiracy theory gained wide acceptance. According to this theory, the bomber was an undercover police agent, Rudolph Schnaubelt, and the bombing was part of a government plot to destroy the anarchist movement. But there is not sufficient evidence to substantiate this view. The identity of the bomb thrower was never discovered.

Although the Haymarket affair was a major setback for the union movement, workers continued to fight for their rights and protest the conditions under which they were forced to work. In the summer of 1892 a dramatic confrontation between workers and management took place at Carnegie's steel mill in Homestead, Pennsylvania. Andrew Carnegie, and his plant manager Henry Clay Frick, decided the time was ripe to topple the Amalgamated Association of Iron, Steel, and Tin Workers Union. While Carnegie went off for the summer to his castle in Scotland, Frick erected a fence around the Homestead plant and announced he was cutting wages. When workers refused to accept the pay cut, he ordered a "lockout" and brought in strikebreakers and the Pinkerton agency to protect the scabs. Three thousand workers took over the town and surrounded the plant in order to shut out the strike-breakers. When three hundred Pinkertons arrived on a barge on the Monongahela River (which bordered the plant), the steelworkers would not let them disembark. Shots rang out, and in the ensuing scuffle seven strikers were killed and the Pinkertons were forced to repair to the comparative safety of the barge. When the Pinkerton guards surrendered, the strikers beat them so severely that several died. The violence persisted for several days until the governor of Pennsylvania sent in the state militia to restore order. The militia kept the strikers at bay, while more strikebreakers were brought in by train and escorted under heavy guard by the Pinkertons into the steelworks.

In the midst of the violence Alexander Berkman, an anarchist who had been following Carnegie's and Frick's efforts to destroy the union, boarded a train in New York and headed for Pittsburgh. He could no longer sit idly by while Frick and the Pinkertons were brutalizing the Homestead steelworkers. Frick, Berkman decided (encouraged by his lover, Emma Goldman), must die. When Berkman arrived in Homestead, he went directly to Frick's office. Perhaps he was surprised that no one challenged him or perhaps he was too excited with the prospect of so easily accomplishing his mission, for when he pulled out his gun and squeezed the trigger, his aim was off. Frick was wounded but not seriously, and Berkman was apprehended. The assassination attempt destroyed whatever sympathy the public had for the strikers and shifted it to Frick. Soon the four-month strike that left fifteen people dead and dozens wounded was broken, and the Amalgamated Association of Iron, Steel, and Tin Workers Union was banned from the Carnegie works. It was another forty years before steelworkers were able to establish a permanent union. In the aftermath many of the organizers were charged with murder and other crimes, but no jury in the state would convict them. Berkman, however, was sentenced to fourteen years in prison.

Homestead, like Haymarket, was a radicalizing experience for American activists, and it had the effect of generating more dissent. Alexander Berkman and Emma Goldman (as we shall see) were two of many radicals committed to fighting against what they perceived as the abuses of capitalism. Anarchists and socialists were deeply concerned with the plight of workers, child laborers, women, blacks, and others in the United States whom they regarded as victims of capitalist exploitation.

And the outcome of Haymarket and Homestead convinced them that the struggle was only just beginning. Eugene V. Debs was one such radical thinker who moved further left because of Haymarket and Homestead and because of Washington's collusion with big business. To Debs the U.S. government itself was part of the problem that prevented workers and ordinary Americans from rising above poverty. The system gave them little opportunity to enjoy the liberty and equality that was supposedly the birthright of all Americans. "If the year 1892 taught the workingmen any lesson worthy of heed," Debs wrote, "it was that the capitalist class, like a devilfish, had grasped them with its tentacles and was dragging them down to fathomless depths of degradation."[5] Debs dedicated himself to doing all he could to promote the interests of the downtrodden, the poor, the destitute. Within a year he founded the American Railway Union.

In early 1893 a severe recession hit when the Reading Railroad declared bankruptcy. Before the end of the year nearly five hundred banks and fifteen thousand other business had collapsed, and by mid-1894 15 percent of Americans were unemployed. The Panic of 1893 (which lasted four years) was the worst the country had faced up to that time. Workers suffered most, and their discontent, unsurprisingly, was quick to surface. Thousands participated in demonstrations around the country demanding that lawmakers do something to alleviate the suffering of the poor. Some municipal governments responded to the demonstrations by setting up soup kitchens and creating programs to attend to the homeless. The federal government, however, did nothing.

Along with protest marches there were scores of strikes, the most militant of which was the 1894 strike in Chicago at the Pullman Company, which manufactured railroad cars. In order to deal with the economic downturn of the 1893 depression, Pullman laid off over 30 percent of its workforce. Most of these people lived in housing provided by the company, and despite the fact that they were now unemployed, Pullman refused to lower their rents. The workers called for a strike and appealed to the American Railway Union for support. The ARU offered to arbitrate the issue, but Pullman refused. ARU workers responded by refusing to run trains that included Pullman cars. Soon the dispute became a full-fledged nationwide railroad strike, paralyzing the nation's transportation network. President Grover Cleveland responded by sending federal troops to end the strike because it was interfering with the delivery of the U.S. mail. On July 7 the troops and the state militia fought with five thousand strikers and their supporters. For several days the railroad yard became a war zone. Rail cars and equipment were destroyed, thirty-four people were killed, and hundreds were wounded. In the end, the strike was crushed, and ARU leader Debs was arrested, tried, and sentenced to six months in prison. Ironically, during the trial, prosecutors kept trying to get him to admit that he was a socialist. He answered truthfully that he was not. But the constant harping on socialism aroused his curiosity so much that he read whatever socialist literature he could get his hands on while serving out his sentence. By the time Eugene V. Debs emerged from prison six months later, he had been converted to socialism.

So deep did discontent run in the United States in 1894 that close to a million workers went on strike that year. There was even a valiant, though unsuccessful, attempt at a march on Washington. A quarry owner in Massillon, Ohio, Jacob Coxey, put together a band of one hundred unemployed men to march from Massillon to Washington protesting the government's failure to enact legislation to combat the depression, to reduce unemployment, and to provide aid to people in distress. Coxey demanded that the government fund such public works projects as road construction in order to provide jobs for the unemployed. As "Coxey's Army" marched to Washington, hundreds of workers joined the protestors, and by the time they arrived in the nation's capital, they numbered more than five hundred. (Coxey was hoping for one hundred thousand.) Neither Congress nor President Cleveland paid any attention to the marchers' demands, although they sent in the police, who arrested Coxey and several of his supporters for walking on the grass near the Capitol. With Coxey in custody the soldiers moved in and easily dispersed the protestors. Although Coxey's Army accomplished nothing, it is an early example of a form of dissent that became increasingly effective in subsequent years—mobilizing like-minded individuals to march into the nation's capital to promote their cause. The government in this case did not respond to their demands. But there were other such marches on Washington (and elsewhere) in the future that achieved different results.

Although most labor militancy did little to improve workers' lives, the labor movement of the late nineteenth century was an important stepping-stone to gaining national recognition of the rights of work-ers. It is another example of dissenters keeping up the pressure in order to gain the rights that were denied them. Even when progress is only measured in fits and starts, in the end such persistence will lead to change. As the historian Howard Zinn has pointed out, even though workers' efforts to unionize were crushed by management and met with universal denunciation, the defeats did not destroy radicalism in the United States, nor did a constant string of setbacks end labor militancy. Though the labor movement was wounded, it lived on. And Haymarket, Homestead, and other attempts to destroy it actually served to inspire a later generation of radicals.

* * *

As the nineteenth century entered its last decade, the United States was swiftly leaving its rural past behind and developing into an urbanized multicultural civilization. Cities were flooded with tens of thousands of insolvent farmers and impoverished immigrants from southern, cen-tral, and eastern Europe. Urban centers brought together a wide variety of people with diverse political and religious views that provided the atmosphere for new ways of thinking, from narrow-minded bigotry to open-minded tolerance, from nativism to a more liberal set of values. The cities, in short, became a breeding ground for dissent.

Cities presented problems and challenges that were not known in rural areas. Immigrants were piled into overcrowded, unhealthy ten-ement houses. Open sewers, inadequate garbage removal, and con-taminated water were the norm. Public officials needed to find ways to develop a functional infrastructure that would alleviate the problems of housing, transportation, public works, sanitation, and crime. Political machines such as Tammany Hall, led by such indomitable figures as William Marcy Tweed and George Washington Plunkitt, were the driv-ing force building New York City's infrastructure. They took bribes from businessmen, skimmed off large percentages of money from the con-tracts they awarded, and used inside information for personal gain—a common practice was buying up real estate near a proposed station on a new subway line before the public announcement and then selling it for a huge profit afterward. (Though corrupt political bosses were more interested in personal gain than in the public good, historians point out that they did have a positive impact in professionalizing police, fire, and sanitation departments; expanding public transportation; constructing water and sewage pipelines; and building hospitals and schools.)

The influx of approximately twenty-five million immigrants who arrived between 1870 and 1914 has earned the United States the rather tired cliché of the "melting pot of nations." It is true that all these disparate groups did eventually identify themselves as "Americans" no matter what their ethnic background, but perhaps "fruit salad" is a more appropriate metaphor. Most ethnic groups in the United States have maintained and cherished their cultural heritage so deeply that it seems that each American is ingrained with something more than Americanness. One of the characteristics of being "American" is being multicultural. But the appreciation and acceptance of multiculturalism did not happen overnight. There was much protest and resistance to the new wave of immigration.

Americans of northern and western European ancestry were alarmed by the arrival of so many newcomers from southern and eastern Europe—Catholics and Jews who did not speak English, who seemed so foreign and out of sync with the Protestant Anglo-Saxon tradition. Native-born Americans protested, wrongly as it turned out, that these new immigrants would undermine "American" culture. And so a new wave of nativist protest, echoing the narrow-minded intolerance of the Know-Nothings of the 1850s, reared its head. Anti-Catholic bigotry was so intense that a group was founded in 1887—the American Protective Association—to defend the United States against the "Catholic menace." Other Americans (influenced by the Haymarket bombings) warned that the new arrivals were anarchists and extremists, communists and radicals that were seeking to destroy the United States, while elitist Social Darwinists argued that the new immigrants were the dregs of an inferior race. In the 1890s the Immigration Restriction League tried to convince Congress that immigrants should be required to pass a literacy test before being admitted to the United States.

Old-stock Americans wrote letters to congressmen and newspaper editors, drew offensive caricatures, invented insulting ethnic jokes, denounced immigrants in sermons and speeches, and verbally abused them in public. Name-calling frequently escalated into fights and physical assaults. Immigrants were severely beaten, their stores vandalized, their property stolen. The most common way prejudice was expressed in the workplace was through the barriers that prevented immigrants from being promoted to better jobs. Native-born foremen and managers saw to it that only relatives, friends, and other native-born Americans would be promoted to such positions.

Although nativists successfully persuaded Congress to pass the Chinese Exclusion Act, they could not convince lawmakers to restrict all immigration. Nativists did not have as much political clout as the industrialists and business leaders who lobbied Congress to keep the doors open so as to provide a limitless source of cheap labor. After World War I, however, when a new wave of xenophobia swept the country, nativists finally whipped up enough anti-immigrant feeling to force Congress to impose strict limits on immigration.

* * *

The bringing together of so many people of different ethnic backgrounds in rapidly growing urban centers and the concomitant tensions that surfaced, combined with the technological innovations of the era, brought about enormous social and cultural changes. An expanding middle class, the genesis of mass-market society, the proliferation of new forms of popular culture, and a genuine American high culture were all features of the era. The changes the United States went through expanded individuals' awareness of the diversity of the world at large, and this expanding awareness had an impact on fueling political debate and public protest.

A rapidly growing middle class, despite being less conspicuous than the opulent robber barons, underpaid workers, and anxious immigrants, was one of the most important facets of the Gilded Age. Expanding industries needed middle managers, technicians, engineers, bookkeepers, accountants, lawyers, and medical staff to conduct business. There was a growing need for bankers, stockbrokers, and insurance agents. In order to prepare people for such professions, it was necessary to expand education. Thus the nation needed more schools, more colleges, more teachers, and more educational administrators. The expanding middle class also meant there was a significant increase in the amount of discretionary income, and this in turn gave rise to a new mass-market economy. Mass production led to cheaper consumer goods, and department stores sprouted up in major cities. These vast, ornate emporiums selling all sorts of goods in "departments" under one roof, from men's clothing to women's clothing, stationery to perfumes, home furnishings to hardware, were veritable "cathedrals of capitalism."[6]

Spectator sports such as baseball, football, and basketball, theaters presenting Vaudeville shows and musicals, P. T. Barnum's circus, Buffalo Bill's Wild West Show, amusement parks, and the cinema all captivated Americans at the turn of the century. And the rise of these forms of popular culture was a significant coalescing force bringing together people from all walks of life, classes, and ethnicities. Americans also devoured the tabloid newspapers of the era, notably William Randolph Hearst's *New York Journal* and Joseph Pulitzer's *New York World*. These sensationalist newspapers were consumed so ravenously by the masses that they had an enormous impact on shaping (for good or for ill) public opinion. Magazines, too, took on a mass appeal. Vastly outselling such established highbrow periodicals as *Harper's* and the *Atlantic Monthly*, several new magazines came on the scene targeting the middle class: *Literary Digest, Forum, Frank Leslie's Illustrated Newspaper, McClure's Magazine, Ladies Home Journal*. They featured engravings and color illustrations and articles on a multitude of subjects from political controversies to gardening, from conservation to child care, and were read by so many millions of Americans that, like the tabloids, they helped shape popular attitudes and taste. The expansion of popular culture, especially the tabloids and periodicals, allowed people to share their views about politics and society. And eventually these forms gave people the opportunity not only to vent and left off steam but to question traditional morality and protest against the glaring injustices that permeated American society.

The harsh realities of industrialism and shifting philosophical points of view inspired by Darwin's theory of evolution and the scientific advances of the era motivated many writers to criticize a civilization that glorified wealth and devalued humans. Writers and philosophers scrutinized the United States through the prism of "realism." Their writings deplored the damaging effects of industrialism and greed on individuals and focused public awareness on many serious problems prevalent in the United States. Literature became a vehicle for encouraging social change. Samuel L. Clemens (Mark Twain) brilliantly used satire and humor to unmask the foibles and pretentiousness of human activity. In *The Gilded Age* and *Huckleberry Finn* he attacked unscrupulousness and hypocrisy, duplicity and vanity, and made fun of those who took themselves too seriously. Furthermore, Clemens was not afraid to confront the government itself when he penned blistering diatribes protesting the Spanish-American War and the occupation of the Philippine Islands. William Dean Howells's *The Rise of Silas Lapham* exposed the unethical nature of business in a society that only values money. Other writers, "naturalists," went even further than the realists by fully accepting the Darwinian view that humans are animals. Stephen Crane's *Maggie, Girl of the Streets* is an account of a young woman who is defeated by the excruciating struggle for existence in a Darwinian world. Kate Chopin, in *The Awakening*, tells the story of a middle-class married woman who through a "sexual awakening" rejects the societally imposed role of mother and wife. Contemporary critics condemned *The Awakening* as a dangerous challenge to middle-class morality, especially when Chopin committed suicide after an extramarital affair.

There were also writers who directly sought to remedy the ills of society through their books. Edward Bellamy wrote *Looking Backward* in 1887 about a future utopian/socialist society that he envisioned. The main character falls asleep in 1887 and awakens in the year 2000 to be enthralled by the marvels of a perfectly egalitarian civilization. Poverty, crime, inequality, and competition are all eliminated through the public ownership of industry. *Looking Backward* struck a responsive chord and was a best-seller for years. Bellamy hoped to bring about reform through fiction, while others offered their prescriptions for improving society through nonfiction. In *Progress and Poverty* Henry George grappled with the question of why so much poverty still existed amid so much wealth and progress.[7] The gap between the rich and the poor, he noted, was growing rapidly, but there was a way to turn this around. The wealthy got most of their wealth because the land and property they owned continued to increase in value without any effort of their own. The government should tax landowners by taking this unearned increment and redistributing it to the masses by funding schools and constructing hospitals, theaters, museums, and other such institutions for the public good. Enough revenue could be earned through this "single tax" that no other taxes would be needed. The government never seriously considered George's proposal, but his book was so popular that hundreds of thousands of Americans passionately discussed its pros and cons and joined single-tax clubs.

Artists used their talents to pass judgment on the social ills of the day and the appalling inequality that existed in a democratic country. The Ashcan School—John Sloan, Robert Henri, Edward Hopper, and others—specialized in unromantic, unsanitized, yet disquieting scenes of urban life: wash hanging on the clothesline behind tenement buildings, rats crawling out of garbage cans in filthy alleys, congested streets, poor people mingling in sidewalk markets—visual art that was intended to raise social conscience.

One of the most noteworthy events during the era was the advent of universal compulsory schooling for all Americans. Business leaders and industrialists realized that it was beneficial to have a literate workforce instructed in the basic values of republican government, ethics, and civility. Additionally, there was a conscientious effort to assimilate the millions of immigrants (especially those who did not speak English) who were pouring into the country. And certainly there was the unspoken fear harbored by many Americans that a vast, uneducated population of poor, immigrant, school-age children in urban ghettoes was a recipe for disaster. Universal compulsory education would keep them off the streets and make them productive citizens filling the ranks of the workforce and not the ranks of street gangs and the criminal element.

New pedagogical ideas influenced educators to pay more attention to nurturing children rather than treating them like little adults that should be rushed into the workforce. In 1873 the German educator Friedrich Fröbel's kindergarten (to teach young children with the tender care that gardeners nurtured their flowers) finally began to be implemented in a meaningful way in American public schools. At the same time, there was an increased emphasis on elementary education, which helped prepare more children for secondary school and also made life somewhat easier for working mothers. Furthermore, as Darwin's theory of evolution was gaining wider acceptance, many thinkers argued that education could be used to guide society in an ever-upward, ever-evolving direction. The University of Chicago professor John Dewey contended that education was "the fundamental method of social progress and reform." Education should center on the child, nurture the child's imagination, inspire the child to expand his or her mind, and saturate the child "with the spirit of service."[8] In this way children would become upright citizens, and all of society would benefit. Despite the fact that conservative business leaders supported public education for their own economic reasons, the transforming of American education at the turn of the century had a significant impact on expanding critical thinking and introducing Americans from all backgrounds to each other.

The expansion of universal education created a demand for teachers, which proved to be an unexpected boon for women. Society frowned on women who aspired to professions such as engineering or medicine or law, but teaching was a nurturing, service-oriented profession and therefore appropriately feminine. By 1900 dozens of colleges and universities throughout the nation were admitting women into courses of study to earn degrees in such fields as library science, nursing, social work, and above all, teaching. It was a liberating experience for women to identify themselves in connection with a career and not simply as some man's wife or daughter. These seemingly minor developments subtly altered gender stereotypes and strengthened the women's movement, which, as the new century dawned, turned into one of the most compelling dissent movements of the twentieth century.

* * *

The development of the United States into a major industrial power during the last three decades of the nineteenth century had as much of a revolutionary impact on the country as did the American Revolution itself. The prosperity that the nation experienced and the extraordinary wealth accumulated by a coterie of entrepreneurial tycoons had both positive and negative effects. Scientific and technological advances radically changed, and for the most part improved, the way people lived their daily lives. Opportunities for employment and the dream of participating in such riches made the United States a powerful magnet for the world's huddled masses, who flocked to the New World in unprecedented numbers. The influx of immigrants radically transformed the ethnic makeup of the United States. Cities expanded, along with the economy, at an exponential rate. Urbanization gave rise to new forms of popular culture and entertainment that brought people of different backgrounds together, people who would otherwise have never got to know each other. It widened people's horizons.

Industrialization and urbanization also produced significant problems. Monopolies and trusts, corruption and graft, swindlers and con artists were all part and parcel of the Gilded Age. The persistence of poverty, the exploitation of the poor, and the disasters that befell the victims of industrialization intensified dissent and conflict. Workers attempted to organize and fight for fairer pay and safe working conditions. They organized work stoppages and strikes. Some of the strikes turned violent. In 1877 striking workers destroyed millions of dollars of railroad property during the Great Railroad Strike, while hundreds were killed and wounded. The strike at the Carnegie Steel Works in Homestead, Pennsylvania, ended in death and catastrophe for steelworkers, while the Haymarket bombing and the subsequent execution of anarchists set the union movement back for decades. Still, discontent continued to seethe, and many workers, attracted to the radical message of socialists and anarchists, denounced the government just as vehemently as populist farmers protested their plight. During the 1890s many middle-class Americans, especially those living in cities where they came into close contact with a rapidly developing multicultural society, joined with the discontented and the downtrodden to form a new and influential reform movement that was to stamp its character on the first decades of the twentieth century. But just as reformers set out to create a better, more progressive society, the United States began looking beyond its own borders for new challenges and opportunities for expansion and prosperity. American expansionism led many to ponder, and ultimately to question, what the United States truly stands for.

CHAPTER 13

The New Manifest Destiny

We have pacified some thousands of the islanders and buried them; destroyed their fields; burned their villages, and
turned their widows and orphans out-of-doors; furnished
heartbreak by exile to some dozens of disagreeable patriots;
subjugated the remaining ten millions by Benevolent Assimilation, which is the pious new name of the musket; we have
acquired property in the three hundred concubines and other
slaves, . . . and hoisted our protecting flag over that swag.

And so, by these Providences of God—and the phrase is
the government's, not mine—we are a World Power.
—Samuel L. Clemens, 1902

As the nineteenth century drew to a close, industrialization and urbanization had radically transformed the nation from what it was in the first
half of the century. Not surprisingly this metamorphosis produced many
complex problems that clearly needed to be addressed. Dissident farmers, disgruntled workers, disappointed women, disillusioned minority
groups, anxious immigrants, and ardent moral crusaders were angry
that poverty, injustice, and inequality had become an impediment to
the fulfillment of America's promise. At the same time, it was clear that
the United States was on the cusp of a new phase in which, for better or
worse, it would become a player on the world stage. Since the creation
of the republic the United States had expanded westward, absorbing
more territory within its borders while remaining true to George Washington's injunction not to get involved in foreign (Washington meant
European) alliances and conflicts. But the realities of international commerce and national interest were converging at the dawn of the new
century to draw the United States out of its self-imposed isolation.
And so from 1896 to 1914 the United States entered a period of intense
debate about the direction the nation should take in the twentieth century. Expansionists sought to create a new, outward-looking United

States that would enter the global arena. Anti-imperialists, though, condemned those who they believed were setting the country on a path that was at odds with its most cherished principles.

* * *

The million votes cast for the Populist candidate James B. Weaver in 1892 and Populist gains in the 1894 midterm elections revealed the public's concern about federal monetary policy. And it revealed too how dissent can influence political discourse on the national stage. What started as a protest movement of angry farmers grew into a political party that forced Washington to take notice. The depression of 1893 further convinced Americans that something had to be done to stabilize the monetary system. As the 1896 presidential campaign got under way, Democrats and Republicans tackled the issue head-on. One of the central planks of the Populist Platform in 1892 had been the free and unlimited coinage of silver so that the dollar would be backed by both gold and silver, thus increasing the amount of money in circulation. This would reverse the deflationary spiral, increase the value of produce, and make it possible for farmers to pay off their debts and remain fiscally stable. By 1896 millions of Americans suffering from the depression (primarily western and southern farmers and debtors) believed that silver was the panacea for their money woes.

However, there were many defenders, especially in the Republican Party, of the gold standard—creditors, bankers, industrialists, and people living on fixed incomes—who argued that silver would cause severe inflation and thus undermine prosperity, economic growth, and their personal wealth. Implementing bimetallism and increasing the money supply, gold advocates claimed, would destroy the value of the dollar, strike at the foundations of the market system, and destabilize the economy. "We are unalterably opposed," the Republicans declared at their convention in June 1896 at St. Louis, "to every measure calculated to debase our currency or impair the credit of our country."[1] Vowing to keep the United States on the gold standard, they nominated Senator William McKinley of Ohio for president.

When the Democrats convened a month later in Chicago, they were especially captivated by the oratory of a young, thirty-six-year-old delegate from Nebraska, William Jennings Bryan. Bryan brought the convention to its feet when he spread his arms wide and directly addressed eastern bankers and stockbrokers. "You shall not," he challenged the moneyed elites, "press down upon the brow of labor this crown of thorns! You shall not crucify mankind upon a cross of gold!"[2]

The Democrats nominated Bryan for president and approved a platform calling for an income tax, the regulation of trusts and pools, limitations on immigration, and bimetallism. Gold, the Democrats believed, was the root of America's economic problems. "The appreciation of gold," the platform declared, "and a corresponding fall in the prices of commodities produced by the people [has led to] a heavy increase in the burdens of taxation and of all debts, public and private, the enrichment of the money-lending class at home and abroad, [and] the prostration of industry and impoverishment of the people." Therefore they were "unalterably opposed to the single gold standard, which . . . is not only un-American but anti-American": "We demand the free and unlimited coinage of both gold and silver at the present legal ration of 16 to 1. . . . We demand that the standard silver dollar shall be a full legal tender, equally with gold, for all debts, public and private."[3]

The Populists, hoping that a united front would defeat the Republicans, also nominated Bryan. But despite an energetic and hard-fought campaign, William McKinley won the election. The Republican victory was a clear triumph for business and financial interests over agrarian interests. The defeat was especially bitter for the Populist Party, for in the aftermath of the election it disintegrated. Nevertheless, many of the issues for which the Populists had fought so passionately—direct election of senators, a graduated income tax, women's suffrage, primary elections—all came to fruition within twenty-five years. Ideas that had been considered too radical in the 1890s became mainstream in less than a generation.

As fate would have it, shortly after the election new discoveries of gold in Alaska and Canada added significant reserves of bullion to the treasury, thus expanding the money supply and undermining the obsession with silver. At the same time, the economy got a boost when crop failures in Argentina, India, and Australia increased world demand for American agricultural products. It was clear to everyone that the economy was not just a domestic issue but was inextricably entwined with international economics. Business leaders were already aware that much of their wealth was dependent on international trade and that what happened in the rest of the world had repercussions in the

United States. They were also concerned that production had become so efficient that more goods were being manufactured than the domestic market could bear, so it was clear to them that opening Asian and Latin American markets to American products such as telephones and heavy machinery was a sensible (and lucrative) way to solve the problem. Clearly, if the United States wished to remain competitive in world markets and foster industrial growth, the wisest course of action was to look beyond the nation's borders. Perhaps it was time for the nation to abandon its distaste for international affairs.

* * *

Economic growth is contingent on continually expanding markets, abundant raw materials, and investments, but with the closing of the frontier it seemed inevitable that expansion would grind to a halt. Something had to be done to avoid economic retrenchment. Just as importantly, business leaders were alarmed by the specter of social unrest. The harsh conditions brought on by the Panic of 1893 had exacerbated farmer and worker discontent, strengthened the Populist Party, and widened the appeal of such radical political ideologies as socialism and anarchism. This combination of the profit motive with the fear of class conflict led industrialists and politicians to consider overseas expansion. This meant a fundamental rethinking of American isolationism and a willingness to engage in military intervention. Flexing military muscle, of course, could lead to war, but this would serve the purpose of defusing dissent by uniting Americans against a common foe.

Unfortunately for businessmen casting a covetous eye on the minerals, rubber, oil, tin, sugar, coffee, and other resources of the "undeveloped" world, Europeans had already seized much of it. By the end of the nineteenth century France had colonized Indochina; the Dutch the East Indies; the British Malaya, Hong Kong, Burma, and India; the Spanish the Philippines; the Japanese Korea and Taiwan; Russia had taken Manchuria; and all of these powers dominated trade with China by partitioning that country into economic spheres of interest. While the United States was expanding into the West, the nations of Europe had carved up the entire continent of Africa (only Ethiopia and Liberia remained independent). It was clear that the United States was going to have to jump on the imperial bandwagon immediately if it expected to expand its influence and become a significant player in international trade.

With these considerations in mind expansionists were captivated by Alfred Thayer Mahan's popular 1890 book *The Influence of Sea Power upon History, 1660–1783*, in which the navy captain argued that control of the seas was the essential ingredient for the rise of great civilizations. All great empires, he wrote, were great empires precisely because they dominated the seas. He called for the federal government to heed this historical lesson and begin the construction of a powerful, state-of-the-art navy. By expanding the navy the United States, with its extensive two-ocean coastline, could surpass other nations in naval power, even one day rivaling Great Britain's mighty fleet. Secondly, Mahan called for the acquisition of overseas bases, ports of call to be used as fueling stations for the American fleet. Finally, Mahan advocated the construction of a canal in Central America so that the fleet could move quickly between the Atlantic and Pacific.

Mahan's advice was enthusiastically received. (His argument also convinced Britain, Germany, and later Japan to expand their navies— decisions that had enormous consequences in the first half of the twentieth century.) Congress increased appropriations for enlarging and modernizing the navy, and throughout the 1890s the fleet was impressively expanded. At the same time, the United States established bases in Samoa in the South Pacific and the Midway Islands in the North Pacific as convenient way stations for American merchant ships on their crossing to China and Japan, and in 1898 the United States annexed the Hawaiian Islands.

While these events were transpiring, Americans were also keeping a close watch on the Spanish colony of Cuba. In 1895, after years of seething discontent, nationalist Cuban rebels launched a guerrilla war for independence from Spain. After a year of mounting violence the government in Madrid sent General Valeriano Weyler to Havana with orders to put down the revolt. Weyler rounded up thousands of peasants, confining them to unsanitary "reconcentration" camps, arrested scores of rebels, and quickly earned the reputation of a brutal and merciless tyrant. When reports of "Butcher" Weyler's activities surfaced in the United States, embellished and fanned by the sensationalist tabloid press, the American public (always well disposed to wars of independence) was nearly unanimous in its opinion that the United States should aid the Cuban rebels.

Although President McKinley was committed to not getting involved, the pressure of the tabloids and public opinion persuaded him to urge Spain to consider granting home rule to Cuba. Toward the end of 1897 the Spanish recalled General Weyler, but the situation did not improve. Street fighting broke out in Havana in January 1898, and in response McKinley sent the battleship *Maine* to the island to protect Americans and American businesses there. On February 15 the *Maine* exploded in Havana harbor. Over 250 sailors were killed, and expansionists in the United States, egged on by Hearst's and Pulitzer's sensationalist tabloids, went wild demanding retaliation for Spain's act of aggression. There was no evidence that the Spanish had deliberately targeted the ship (the evidence suggests that a boiler exploded), but most Americans blamed Spain for the sinking.

Still, the president refused to be stampeded into precipitate action. Although most Republicans pushed for intervention, McKinley was not interested in Cuban independence; he wanted Cuba to be stable so that American business interests could expand further into Cuba and dominate the island's economy. If Cuba gained its independence, it might not be so amenable to American business—a concern that most American businessmen shared with the president. Congressional Democrats, though, were eager to gain political capital at the Republicans' expense. They demanded that something be done to avenge the sinking of the *Maine*, and seeing McKinley as an easy target, they attacked the president for being spineless. Finally, in April, unable any longer to endure the pressures of the interventionists in both parties as well as the press and public opinion, McKinley asked Congress for a declaration of war. Congress complied on April 20, 1898, by authorizing the president to use force to expel the Spanish from the island.

The Spanish-American War, christened the "splendid little war" by Secretary of State John Hay, lasted barely four months, from April to August 1898. Ironically, despite the fact that the ostensible reason the United States entered the war was to back the Cuban revolutionaries, the first military campaign did not take place there but in a far more distant Spanish colony—the Philippines. During the crescendo of impassioned debate that led to the declaration of war, the assistant secretary of the navy, Theodore Roosevelt, had alerted Commodore George

Dewey, the commander of an American naval task force in Hong Kong, that war with Spain was imminent. Roosevelt cabled Dewey to prepare his fleet to engage the Spanish navy in the Philippines. Dewey promptly complied, even making secret arrangements to link up with a band of Filipino nationalist rebels led by Emilio Aguinaldo on the island of Luzon. Ten days after the declaration of war Dewey led his small squadron of six vessels into Manila Bay and engaged the antiquated Spanish fleet. Without losing a single man the Americans utterly destroyed the Spanish force. Dewey cabled Washington requesting U.S. Army troops to take and hold Manila. By August the troops had arrived, and in combination with Aguinaldo's guerrillas defeated the Spanish and seized Manila.

While events were unfolding in the Philippines, the main action took place in Cuba. In June an American invasion force landed on the eastern end of the island, pressed forward, and took the city of Santiago. By mid-August the Spanish conceded defeat. At the peace conference in Paris in December Spain granted Cuba its independence, ceded Puerto Rico and the island of Guam in the Pacific, and agreed to the sale of the Philippine Islands to the United States for $20 million. When Cubans drafted their constitution, they were required to ratify the Platt Amendment, which granted the United States the right to intervene militarily in Cuban domestic affairs whenever Washington deemed American interests were at stake. Thus the new government in Cuba would be, in effect, managed by the United States. Cuba also granted the U.S. a permanent base at Guantánamo Bay. And so the paradoxical outcome of the Spanish-American War—a war fought to liberate Cuba from imperial control—was that the United States itself became an imperial power.

The war was a jolt for the American military establishment. It was clear that the army was ill prepared for combat—especially in the tropics, where more men died of disease (over 4,000) than in battle (379). The standing army was pitifully small and outfitted with woolen uniforms that were wholly inappropriate in Cuba and the Philippines, food supplies were inadequate, and soldiers lived in unhygienic conditions. Now that the United States had acquired a small overseas empire, it was necessary to expand and modernize the military, as well as improve conditions for the troops. A federal commission investigating the woeful state of the nation's military preparedness concluded that the United

States should henceforth maintain a standing army of at least one hundred thousand troops ready for deployment. The commission also recommended the expansion of West Point and the establishment of a war college as well as additional military academies to train officers. And perhaps most importantly, it called for the creation of a General Staff—an organization of the heads of the various military services—that would coordinate the policies and activities of the armed forces (the General Staff evolved into the Joint Chiefs of Staff). With great determination, as the twentieth century dawned, the United States set in motion the modernizing of the military. Few people at the time foresaw how critical a role a powerful and well-coordinated military was to play in the twentieth century.

Another consequence of the war was that it embroiled the United States in combat in Southeast Asia. Emilio Aguinaldo had been waging a guerrilla war against the Spanish for years and was optimistic that the outcome of the Spanish-American War would lead to Filipino independence. But the terms of the Treaty of Paris infuriated him. The United States was the new occupier. The Filipinos had only exchanged one set of rulers for another. In January 1899 Aguinaldo, declaring that the Philippines was a free and independent republic, launched a violent uprising. Americans, basking in the glory of benevolently spreading American democracy to the Philippines, were shocked that the Filipinos were not grateful to Washington for having ousted the Spanish.

It took the United States three years to suppress what Washington called an insurgency (Filipinos called it a war for independence), during which time brutality and cruelty reached unimaginable levels. Filipino guerrillas harassed and ambushed American patrols and attacked American encampments in quick strikes before disappearing into the jungle. American troops, unable to distinguish between the insurgents and the civilian population, savagely torched Filipino villages, raped and pillaged, killed women and children, and in some localities confined civilians to specific zones (much like the "reconcentration" camps the Spanish had used in Cuba) in order to isolate the insurgents. They also systematically wiped out food supplies, which had the effect of starving both rebels and civilians. The guerrillas retaliated even more viciously by capturing unlucky soldiers and torturing them to death through mutilation and the hacking off of limbs and genitals. This intensified American fury. In the end, the "insurgency" was far more brutal and costly than the Spanish-American War. Of the 120,000 American troops who saw action in the Philippines, more than 4,200 were killed. There are no verifiable statistics for Filipino deaths, but estimates range from 100,000 to more than 200,000. Even after the insurgency was put down, outbreaks of violence continued for years. In 1916 the United States set a timetable for Filipino independence. Independence, however, did not come until a year after the end of World War II, on July 4, 1946.

The Spanish-American War also had a significant, though unanticipated, social impact on the United States. Twenty-five percent of the soldiers in the U.S. Army in 1898 were African Americans. As they traveled by train from their bases in the Midwest to Tampa, they were greeted by cheers in most of the towns along the way, but after they crossed into Kentucky and Tennessee, this all changed. Below the Mason-Dixon line they were no longer hailed as heroic soldiers going off to war but were refused service in railroad stations, denied admittance to restaurants, and forced to use segregated facilities. One African American soldier wrote, "it mattered not if we were soldiers of the United States, and going to fight for the honor of our country and the freedom of an oppressed and starving people, we were 'niggers' as they called us, and treated us with contempt."[4] On the night before embarking for Cuba, with tempers reaching a flashpoint, a race riot erupted in Tampa that left three whites and twenty-seven blacks wounded. Once the black soldiers arrived in Cuba, they were struck by the contrast between the way they were treated by white U.S. soldiers and by the Cuban revolutionaries. While the U.S. Army fought in segregated regiments, the Cuban rebels were a fully integrated army of whites and blacks that fully accepted the African American regiments. The Cubans, calling the Buffalo Soldiers "Smoked Yankees," treated them with the respect that was denied them by their white comrades in arms. To astonished African American soldiers fighting for the cause of Cuban freedom it seemed that black Cubans enjoyed more freedom than black Americans.

When four African American regiments were sent to the Philippines later to put down the insurrection, they were moved by the plight of the Filipinos, which they considered not much different from their own. Many African American troops deserted. Some of them even joined the rebels fighting the Americans. One black soldier recalled that a brown-skinned Filipino boy asked him why he was fighting against the Filipinos, who never did anything to him, and not against "those people in America who burn Negroes . . . [and] make a beast of you."[5] The African American experience in Cuba and the Philippines laid the groundwork for an expanding sense of racial consciousness and the stimulus, after the soldiers returned home, for grassroots civil rights activism.

* * *

In the United States the war brought about a surge of patriotic sentiment (just as business and political leaders had hoped). The victory over Spain and the acquisition of the Philippines, as well as Puerto Rico and Guam, seemed to verify the mission of the United States to spread democracy and American civilization to "less fortunate" people. The prospect of teaching "natives" in far-flung lands the virtues of republican government, sending missionaries to preach the gospel, and sending businessmen to expand markets and open the doors to trade in Latin America and Asia (especially China) filled American hearts with a patriotic glow and a sense of mission. However, despite the general enthusiasm, a wave of antiwar and anti-imperialist dissent swept over the country. Many Americans were profoundly troubled by what they saw as a betrayal of the basic principles on which the United States was founded.

At the outset socialists were universally opposed to the war. "It is a terrible thing," a socialist wrote in a San Francisco newspaper as the war broke out, "to think that the poor workers of this country should be sent to kill and wound the poor workers of Spain merely because a few leaders incite them to do so." In New York the Socialist Labor Party planned an antiwar march for May 1, 1898, but municipal authorities banned the parade. Mainstream workingmen who considered the socialists too radical nevertheless also opposed the war. Some pointed out, after the *Maine* incident, that although the loss of life was deplorable, the number of sailors killed was only a small percentage of the number of workers killed every month in on-the-job accidents and in violent confrontations with the police and mercenary strikebreakers. The unions demanded to know why there was never a comparable uproar in the press when American workingmen were killed in such large numbers. One trade union journal went so far as to warn that the war fever stirred up by the sinking of the *Maine* was a subterfuge to expand the military and "place the United States in the front rank as a naval and military power. . . . Capitalists will have the whole thing and, when any working-men dare to ask for the living wage . . . they will be shot down like dogs in the street."[6] But soon after war was declared, such dissent was stifled, and most labor leaders, perhaps fearing an antiradical backlash, urged workers to support the government.

Although most progressives were prowar, some well-known progressives, such as Charles Eliot Norton, spoke out against it. Norton was a celebrated professor of fine arts at Harvard, the editor of the *North American Review*, and a founder of the liberal journal the *Nation*. He was also an outspoken critic of the McKinley administration—especially the policies that led to the war. In June 1898, as American soldiers were about to embark for Cuba, Norton gave an emotional speech condemning the war and urging young men not to enlist in the army. Americans should always be willing to take up arms against lawlessness and injustice, he acknowledged, but "now of a sudden, without cool deliberation, without prudent preparation, the nation is hurried into war, and America . . . unsheathes her sword, compels a weak and unwilling nation to a fight, rejecting without due consideration her earnest and repeated offers to meet every legitimate demand of the United States. It is a bitter disappointment to the lover of his country; it is a turning-back from the path of civilization to that of barbarism." There are Americans, he said, who believe it is moral and just to go to war to topple the Spanish oppressors and win independence for Cuba. "But independence secured for Cuba by forcible overthrow of the Spanish rule means either practical anarchy or the substitution of the authority of the United States for that of Spain." There are people who argue that it is necessary for America to invade Cuba if only to relieve the suffering the Cubans are enduring at the hands of the Spanish. "As for the relief of suffering, surely it is a strange procedure to begin by inflicting worse suffering still. . . . The plea that the better government of Cuba and the relief of the reconcentrados could only be secured by war is the plea either of ignorance or of hypocrisy." Even though Congress declared war, Norton said, "a declaration of war does not change the moral law"; therefore it is every American's duty to protest the war and prevent men from enlisting. "The voice of protest, of warning, of appeal is never more needed than when the clamor of fife and drum, echoed by the press and too often by the pulpit, is bidding all men fall in and keep step and obey in silence the tyrannous word of command." It is precisely at such times, when war fever grips the land, that Americans *must* speak out. "Then, more than ever, it is the duty of the good citizen not to be silent, and insist on being heard, and with sober counsel to maintain the everlasting validity of the principles of the moral law."[7]

To Norton the Spanish-American War was unnecessary. The McKinley administration "have brought us into a war that might and should have been avoided, and which consequently is an unrighteous war." Because of this, he reiterated, "the duty of the good citizen is plain. He is to help . . . provide . . . every means that may serve to bring [the war] to the speediest end." Every day the war brings more death, more suffering, more grief. It is imperative to end the war as quickly as possible. "We mourn the deaths of our noble youth fallen in the cause of their country when she stands for the right; but we may mourn with a deeper sadness for those who have fallen in a cause which their generous hearts mistook for one worthy of the last sacrifice."[8]

When the brief war ended and the annexation of the Philippines was imminent, anti-imperialist dissent replaced antiwar dissent. Anti-imperialism, in fact, was more widespread than the antiwar protests. It was so extensive that it made for strange bedfellows. Mark Twain and William James, Carl Schurz and William Jennings Bryan, Andrew Carnegie and Samuel Gompers all took an adamant stance against American imperialism, and most of them participated in forming the Anti-Imperialists League in November 1898. Of course, as is so often the case with dissent, motives varied greatly. Many of those who protested against the acquisition of Puerto Rico and the Philippines did so for racist reasons. They feared that the United States' Anglo-Saxon heritage would be overwhelmed by "inferior" races. Moreover, they did not want large numbers of nonwhites to gain access to American society and jobs. The labor leader Samuel Gompers, for example, feared that "half-breeds and semi-barbaric people" would be imported as cheap labor, thus taking jobs away from white Americans. The Democrat Senator Benjamin Tillman of South Carolina bluntly protested against "incorporating any more colored men into the body politic." There were also partisan Democrats who opposed imperialism as a political tool, hoping to use their opposition to depose the Republicans in the upcoming presidential election. The steel magnate Andrew Carnegie believed colonies were essential for expanding the American economy, but he

was against the acquisition of colonies by force because military conquest and rule was a distraction from the primary undertaking—business investment and industrial development.[9]

But what most irked conscientious Americans across the political spectrum was that the occupation of Spain's former colonies went
against the core American principle of self-government—consent of
the governed. The United States, after all, was the result of a revolution against an imperial power. By annexing the Philippines, Guam,
and Puerto Rico the United States was undermining its own principles. The former Republican secretary of the interior Carl Schurz, for
example, categorically condemned the annexation of the Philippines. If
we become an imperial power, Schurz declared in an 1899 speech, "we
shall transform the government of the people, for the people, and by the
people . . . into a government of one part of the people, the strong, over
another part, the weak." Such a policy was just as hurtful to the United
States as it was to a subjugated population, for "such an abandonment
of a fundamental principle as a permanent policy . . . can hardly fail
in its ultimate effects to disturb the rule of the same principle in the
conduct of democratic government at home. And I warn the American
people that a democracy cannot so deny its faith as to the vital conditions of its being—it cannot long play the king over subject populations
without creating within itself ways of thinking and habits of action most
dangerous to its own vitality." There were expansionists who questioned
Schurz's patriotism, accusing him of disloyalty because of his refusal
to support the occupation of the Philippines. "The American flag, we
are told," he said, directly addressing those who supported the policy of
imperialism, "whenever once raised, must never be hauled down. Certainly, every patriotic citizen will always be ready, if need be, to fight
and to die under his flag wherever it may wave in justice and for the
best interests of the country." But this created a grave danger that could
undermine the United States. "But I say to you, woe to the republic if it
should ever be without citizens patriotic and brave enough to defy the
demagogues' cry and to haul down the flag wherever it may be raised
not in justice and not for the best interests of the country. Such a republic would not last long."[10]

Schurz was joined in the summer of 1900 by William Jennings
Bryan, who also denounced America's imperialist course. Bryan was
campaigning a second time against McKinley, and his anti-imperialist

Carl Schurz, Secretary of the Interior, 1877. In 1899 Schurz
became a leading anti-imperialist activist. Photograph
by Matthew B. Brady. (Public domain; courtesy Library
of Congress)

stance was part of the Democratic Party's attack on the president. But
beyond the political motive Bryan was also genuinely concerned about
what he called "the paralyzing influence of imperialism," which was
leading the United States to abandon its most fundamental principle.
"Those who would have this nation enter upon a career of empire must
consider not only the effect of imperialism on the Filipinos but they
must also calculate its effects upon our own nation. We cannot repudiate the principle of self-government in the Philippines without weakening that principle here." Americans have always been sympathetic

to and supported revolutions for civil liberty and self-government. If we become an imperial power, we would be giving up the moral high ground and become that which we oppose. Moreover, when the United States was founded, it had a deep distrust of a powerful military that could be used as a tool to enforce the will of a tyrant. Militarism, the founding fathers believed, led to despotism. Presciently, Bryan warned that if the United States became an imperialist power, it would create a dangerously powerful military. "If we have an imperial policy," he predicted, "we must have a great standing army as its natural and necessary complement. The spirit which will justify the forcible annexation of the Philippine Islands will justify the seizure of other islands and the domination of other people, and with wars of conquest we can expect a certain, if not rapid, growth of our military establishment." President McKinley had already authorized, Bryan reminded Americans, a significant increase in the size of the standing army. Such "a large standing army," Bryan argued, "is not only a pecuniary burden to the people, . . . but it is even a menace to a republican form of government."[11]

The writer Samuel L. Clemens was another active supporter of the Anti-Imperialist League and used his scathing wit in articles and speeches at antiwar rallies to denounce imperialism. "I am an anti-imperialist. I am opposed to having the eagle put its talons on any other land." While American troops were putting down the Filipino insurrection, Clemens irreverently proposed a flag design for this the newest American province: "just our usual flag," he suggested, "with the white stripes painted black and the stars replaced by the skull and crossbones." Clemens, the most quintessential of American writers, was so opposed to American policy in the Philippines and what he considered the hypocrisy of mindless patriotism that he penned a satirical "War Prayer" that was too controversial to be published during his lifetime.

O Lord our Father, our young patriots, idols of our hearts, go forth to battle—be Thou near them! . . . O Lord our God, help us to tear their soldiers to bloody shreds with our shells; help us to cover their smiling fields with the pale forms of their patriot dead; help us to drown the thunder of the guns with the shrieks of their wounded, writhing in pain; help us to lay waste their humble homes with a hurricane of fire; help us to wring the hearts of their unoffending widows with unavailing grief; help us to turn them out roofless with little children to wander unfriended the wastes of their desolated land in rags and hunger and thirst, . . . broken in spirit, worn with travail, imploring Thee for the refuge of the grave and denied it—for our sakes who adore Thee, Lord, blast their hopes, blight their lives, protract their bitter pilgrimage, make heavy their steps, water their way with their tears, stain the white snow with the blood of their wounded feet! We ask it, in the spirit of love, of Him Who is the Source of Love, and Who is the ever-faithful refuge and friend of all that are sore beset and seek His aid with humble and contrite hearts. Amen.[12]

In all his writings Clemens fervently denounced the "my country right or wrong" attitude that seemed to prevail in the United States. If that is our way of thinking, Clemens contended, then "we have thrown away the most valuable asset we had: the individual's right to oppose both flag and country when he . . . believed them to be in the wrong. We have thrown it away; and with it, all that was really respectable about that grotesque and laughable word, Patriotism."[13] For Clemens the right to dissent is the most fundamental element of what it means to be an American.

* * *

Throughout the pro-imperialist/anti-imperialist debate on the annexation of the Philippines, Theodore Roosevelt, like most progressives, came down steadfastly in favor of expansion. Roosevelt was convinced that the future of the nation lay in playing a major role in world affairs. His philosophy reflected much of the basic racial and ethnic assumptions of the day. Like the Social Darwinists, Roosevelt believed that the Anglo-Saxon and industrialized nations were more fit than the "backward" nations of Africa, Asia, and Latin America. In fact he felt that it was the *duty* of the United States to exploit and dominate inferior nations. He was keenly aware that the country in 1901 was emerging as one of the richest and most productive industrial nations in the world but that the United States did not yet have enough muscle to wield its developing authority. Once he was president, Roosevelt decisively pursued a vigorous foreign policy that set the United States on a path that had a seminal impact on the twentieth century and beyond. He encouraged a revolution in the Colombian province of Panama so that he could negotiate a treaty with an independent Panama for the rights to build a canal across the isthmus. He intervened in Venezuela and the Dominican Republic when those governments defaulted on their international debts. And he formulated the "Roosevelt Corollary" to the Monroe Doctrine that added the clause that it was the prerogative of the United States to intervene in any Latin American nation if U.S. interests were at stake. Although his actions were controversial and provoked protest, Roosevelt was, if nothing else, prophetic in seeing the future course of American foreign policy. The United States had no choice, Roosevelt believed, but to play a great role in the world.

A distinguishing feature of American imperialism as it evolved under Roosevelt and his successor, William Howard Taft, was that it was a more subtle form of imperialism than the brute form that had been perfected by the industrial powers of Europe. Although American military force was necessary in the Philippines, the United States relied more and more on commercial development and business investment—a policy called "dollar diplomacy"—to influence and control weaker countries. Taft, especially, encouraged American businesses to invest in world markets. As the historians Howard Zinn and William Appleman Williams have pointed out, American imperialism was more refined than the aggressive military intervention and colonization of undeveloped countries that was the modus operandi of European imperial ventures. American businesses were simply interested in expanding and dominating markets. As long as they had an "open door," it was not necessary to take over a country politically. From the nineteenth century to the present this has been the central feature of American imperialism that distinguishes it from European imperialism.

By joining the club of imperial nations (albeit with only a handful of colonies) the United States entered the twentieth century with a sense of self-righteous benevolence about its place in the world. Of course, many Americans knew that beneath the surface of the virtuous, high-minded claims justifying the war, the primary motive for American intervention in Cuba and the Philippines was economic. Acquiring and maintaining outposts in the Caribbean and the western Pacific was beneficial for American commerce and established the United States as a rising world power. "The Philippines are ours forever," the Republican Senator Albert Beveridge of Indiana declared, expressing a predominant American attitude of the time,

And just beyond the Philippines are China's illimitable markets. . . . We will not renounce our part in the mission of our race, trustee, under God, of the civilization of the world. . . .

The Pacific is our ocean. . . . China is our natural customer. . . . The Philippines give us a base at the door of all the East. . . .

It has been charged that our conduct of the war has been cruel. . . . [But we] must remember that we are not dealing with Americans or Europeans. We are dealing with Orientals.[14]

True, there were troubling similarities between the way the United States dealt with the Filipino insurrection and the tactics of the Spanish in Cuba that Hearst and Pulitzer had railed against. But most Americans were proud of the United States' engagement in the world, for they believed that America's motives were virtuous and that we had a duty to show the world the wonders and benefits of American society and democracy. *And* it was good for business too.

Although the profit motive was paramount in driving American expansionism, the discontent of the working class, the attempts to unionize, and the Populist movement in the 1890s also made expansionist impulses more attractive. Politicians and business leaders saw expansionism as a means to neutralize dissent and to diminish the prospect of class warfare by uniting Americans in a common cause. But the conflict with Spain and the subsequent brutal war in the Philippines did not create as much unity as anticipated. And it fueled dissent. Hundreds of thousands of Americans, including political, business, and cultural titans such as William Jennings Bryan, Andrew Carnegie, and Mark Twain, protested that the new imperial policy was at odds with American ideals. It was patently hypocritical for the United States to espouse self-determination and deny other people their freedom.

The American experience in the Spanish-American War and the Philippines is the first of many examples of international conflict breeding dissent. In this case those who protested American policy had little effect on changing it. Indeed, the arguments brought forth on both sides of the debate in some ways propelled that policy forward and helped mold the view that the United States should concentrate less on military/political control and more on economic intervention and investment. For the next century, whether it was World War I, World War II, or the Vietnam War, antiwar dissenters continued to speak out.

And in these cases, too, dissenters felt frustrated that their opposition did little to end the wars. But the debate *did* have an impact on policy and in some cases did curtail conflicts.

Overshadowing the discourse about America's international role as the new century dawned was the mounting concern for what was happening at home. Despite the incredible wealth produced by the expanding economy, it was all too clear that millions of Americans were mired in poverty with little opportunity to improve their lot. Distraught that there were too many victims of industrialization, thousands of middle-class Americans embarked on a crusade to create a more egalitarian society. As this "Progressive" movement grew, reformers and radicals tackled other endemic problems—rampant political corruption; business malpractice; and ethnic, racial, and gender discrimination—and fought hard to push a do-nothing government to enact progressive, humanitarian legislation that would ease the suffering of the poor and make the American Dream accessible to all.

CHAPTER 14

Progressives and Radicals

The chief purpose of the Christian Church in the past has
been the salvation of individuals. But the most pressing task
of the present is not individualistic. Our business is to make
over an antiquated and immoral economic system: to get rid
of laws, customs, maxims, and philosophies inherited from
an evil and despotic past; to create just and brotherly relations between great groups and classes of society; and thus
to lay a social foundation on which modern men individually
can live and work in a fashion that will not outrage all the
better elements in them.

—Walter Rauschenbusch,
Christianizing the Social Order, 1912

Despite the glittering wealth of the nation at the turn of the century
and the rise of a middle class, millions of Americans lived in abject poverty. (The wealthiest 10 percent of the population owned 72 percent
of the nation's wealth; the top 1 percent owned nearly a third.) While
rich industrialists and investors lived lives of opulent splendor, the
people who worked for them barely eked out a living. Whether they
were newly arrived immigrants or long-established citizens, unskilled
workers toiled intolerably long hours for intolerably low wages, they
were crammed into squalid urban slums, and there was little opportunity to improve their lot. The gospel of wealth had created a society
that encouraged a "get rich quick" mentality, which in turn encouraged
businessmen to think only of profits and very little about the exploitation of their workers. Industrialists resisted every attempt by workers to
organize, and they did whatever it took, including bribery, to make sure
lawmakers did nothing to regulate the consolidation of their businesses
into vast monopolies.

However, starting in the 1890s and continuing well into the twentieth
century, progressives, reformers, and radicals dedicated themselves to

righting these wrongs. They worked hard to alleviate the sufferings of the victims of industrialization, they led the fight for social justice for women and African Americans, they lobbied the federal government to regulate business and to bust monopolies and trusts, and they attacked graft and political corruption and pushed state legislatures and city councils to initiate a series of political reforms. Some were reformers whose goal was to improve the system. Some were radicals who were fed up with capitalism and sought to transform the system. Although not all the goals of the Progressive movement were achieved (and those that were realized fell far short of attaining an egalitarian society), the efforts of reformers during the first two decades of the twentieth century are a striking example of the impact dissenters have had in changing the status quo and in shaping (indeed, in many ways, redirecting) American society. Even the radicals had an impact. While they were unable to blow up the system and replace capitalism with socialism, their protests raised consciousness and influenced the debate.

The complexity of the political, economic, and social problems caused by rapid industrialization, urbanization, and mechanization spawned a range of responses. Middle-class reformers, appalled about unsafe working conditions, child labor, rampant political corruption, and the indifference of the public; leftist radicals determined to sweep away the negative features of capitalism; and even a number of wealthy philanthropists, fearing that excessive privation could lead to a violent uprising offered an assortment of remedies for the problems. And as historian Richard Hofstadter has pointed out, some middle-class Americans—educators, clergymen, lawyers, small shop owners—became reformers because they felt they were losing status in direct proportion to the rising power and dominance of the superrich.[1] Thus the impulse for their dissent was partly reactionary: they wanted to turn back the clock to the time when they enjoyed a prominent place in society.

The reform spirit was rising in the decades before the 1890s—civil service reformers, the Mugwumps, the Grangers and the Farmers' Alliance, and the Populists were precursors of the Progressive movement. Philosophically speaking, reformers were influenced by such progressive thinkers as Edward Bellamy, Henry George, and John Dewey, who offered recipes for enriching life and creating a better future. Darwin's theory of evolution also influenced many reformers. Just as Social Darwinists used evolutionary theory to justify inequality and the exploitive practices of big business as an example of natural selection at work, intellectuals such as Lester Frank Ward also adapted the theory but for more progressive purposes. The technological inventions of the nineteenth century seemed proof that the world was a constantly progressing, constantly evolving place. Just as humans harnessed science and technology to bring about progress, so too could human intelligence be used to create a more equitable, more just society. In "Mind as a Social Factor" Ward argued that it was intelligence and self-reflection that set *homo sapiens* apart from animals. Because of this, humans have the ability to guide the course of evolution. Ward's Reform Darwinism called for a system of planned government intervention in the economy and in social relations, replacing survival of the fittest with the fitting of as many as possible to survive. Through laws regulating industry, establishing a minimum wage, improving safety conditions, permitting workers to organize unions, and providing aid to education, the government can improve the lives of the poor and make them more fit for survival. The human species will evolve, Ward believed, more effectively through cooperation than through competition.[2] Ward's belief that humanity was moving ever upward, that society was ever progressing, and that human beings can expedite the process influenced and inspired many reformers, among them Jane Addams, Walter Rauschenbusch, Frances E. Willard, and John Muir.

* * *

One area that was of particular concern was unbridled political corruption. Alarmed that government was not responsive to the people and that politicians were increasingly in the pocket of corporations, reformers targeted corruption at the municipal, state, and federal levels and simultaneously sought to open up democracy so that more Americans could participate in the political process.

The complexity and anonymity of city life, along with the long-established reign of political bosses in urban centers, was a recipe for fraud and dishonesty. Politicians routinely accepted, indeed demanded, bribes from companies seeking construction contracts, tax breaks, or licenses of any kind. City councilmen and policemen took kickbacks from illegal gambling rings, houses of prostitution, and bars operating without liquor licenses. Dozens of investigative reporters wrote articles scrutinizing and exposing corruption in New York, Philadelphia,

Chicago, St. Louis, Minneapolis, and other cities, which riled up the public to demand that something be done to hold public officials to a basic standard of honesty. The articles roused reform-minded citizens to run for public office pledging to clean up city hall. Tom L. Johnson won election as a progressive mayor in Cleveland, Samuel M. "Golden Rule" Jones in Toledo, Hazen S. Pingree in Detroit, and Seth Low in New York. And all of them succeeded in rooting out much (but by no means all) of the corruption. Some progressive mayors curbed corruption by establishing nonpartisan commissions that independently monitored public officials, while others converted utility companies (electric, gas, water) into publicly run departments of the city government. Reform mindedness took hold so profoundly in Syracuse, Milwaukee, and Minneapolis that all three cities elected, to the shock of the business community, socialists as mayors. But Socialist Party success was the exception rather than the rule.

Reformers pushed state legislatures to pass laws establishing building codes for tenement housing (creating more space around and ventilation within the buildings, as well as requiring fire escapes and fireproofing); laws limiting working hours in the textile, railroad, and mining industries; and legislation banning child labor. Regardless of progressive attempts to improve working and living conditions, however, industries found numerous ways to circumvent the laws, and the courts frustrated reformers by frequently striking down many laws as unconstitutional— ruling that governments had no authority to regulate free enterprise.

In 1900 a progressive Republican, Robert M. La Follette, was elected governor of Wisconsin. As soon as he assumed office, he initiated a whole series of reforms aimed at ending political corruption in the state. He pushed bills that limited the lobbying of big business, curbed campaign financing, set standards for conservation, and appointed commissions regulating road construction and the railroad industry. La Follette also set up a direct primary system whereby the people, not professional political bosses in the proverbial "smoke-filled rooms," controlled the nomination process.

La Follette's efforts inspired other states to institute primaries, and several states also attempted to expand democracy by adopting initiative, referendum, and recall. Initiative was the process by which citizens could present a petition that would require the state legislature to deliberate and vote on legislation the public wanted. Referendum was the process whereby the public could review a bill that lawmakers had passed (or rejected) and vote to override the will of the legislators. And recall empowered voters to remove (essentially fire) incompetent and ineffective judges, legislators, or governors from office. (For officials who committed criminal or illegal acts, impeachment was the constitutional process already established to remove them.)

The most significant political reform of the era, though, was the culmination of the long struggle for women's suffrage. During the last quarter of the nineteenth century two groups, the American Woman Suffrage Association and the National Woman Suffrage Association led the campaign for women's rights. While the AWSA concentrated on the main goal, the more radical NWSA expanded the struggle beyond gaining the vote and promoted equal rights for women in the workplace, in politics, and in the eyes of the law. In 1890 the two groups combined as the National American Woman Suffrage Association (NAWSA), and they did achieve limited success in swaying several western state legislatures to grant women's suffrage; but by 1900 it became increasingly apparent that the state-by-state strategy was never going to achieve complete success.

During the first years of the twentieth century the torch of leadership in the women's movement was passed from Elizabeth Cady Stanton and Susan B. Anthony to a new generation of leaders, notably Carrie Chapman Catt (who succeeded Anthony as president of NAWSA), Harriot Stanton Blatch, Lucy Burns, and Alice Paul. All four women organized protest marches and applied increasing pressure on Congress to pass the women's suffrage amendment (first introduced to Congress in 1878 by Susan B. Anthony). From 1907 to 1910 Alice Paul studied in England, where she was influenced by Christabel Pankhurst and the more radical women suffragettes of Britain. (The "suffragettes" in England were more militant than their American counterparts, the "suffragists," frequently resorting to civil disobedience and even property damage during their protests. One English suffragette, Emily Davison, claiming that women's suffrage needed a martyr to compel Parliament to act, committed suicide in 1913 by stepping in front of the king's horse at Ascot—Britain's premier annual horse-racing event.) When Alice Paul returned to the States, she brought with her some of the more militant tactics—picketing, vigils, hunger strikes—that she had learned in England. On the day before Woodrow Wilson's inauguration in 1913 Paul

Suffragists parading in New York City, May 4, 1912. Photograph, titled "Youngest Parader in New York City Suffragist Parade," by the American Press Association. (Public domain; courtesy Library of Congress)

organized a parade in Washington, DC, demanding that Wilson support women's suffrage. She also formed the National Woman's Party in 1916 to campaign against politicians who did not support women's suffrage, and in January 1917 she coordinated a major civil disobedience campaign at the White House. For more than a year women held a silent vigil (the first of many such demonstrations that subsequent dissenters employed at the White House) condemning Wilson's lack of support for women's suffrage. After the United States declared war on Germany, the demonstrators' signs frequently, and irreverently, referred to the president's speeches in which he justified America's entry into the war as a noble effort to extend democracy to Europeans who had no say in their government. "Kaiser Wilson," one such sign cheekily proclaimed, "20,000,000 American Women Are Not Self-Governed. Take The Beam Out Of Your Own Eye." The protestors were daily derided, mocked, harassed, and even physically abused by passersby and policemen. Embarrassed by the picketing, Wilson ordered their arrest, but Paul continued her protest in her jail cell by going on a hunger strike. She was force-fed and eventually released but went right back to the

Alice Paul, c. 1915. Militant suffragist; National Chairman, Congressional Union for Woman Suffrage; Member, Ex-Officio, National Executive Committee, Woman's Party. Alice Paul was arrested several times while protesting at the White House. In jail she went on a hunger strike and was force-fed by correctional officers. In 1923 she introduced the Equal Rights Amendment to Congress. (Public domain; courtesy Library of Congress)

picket line. In the end, in 1918, an exasperated Wilson announced a change of position and urged Democrats in Congress to vote for the women's suffrage bill. The bill made it through both houses by June 1919, and in August 1920, when Tennessee became the thirty-sixth state to ratify the Nineteenth Amendment, it became the law of the land. And so, 48 years after Susan B. Anthony was arrested for casting a vote in Rochester, New York, 72 years after Elizabeth Cady Stanton and Lucretia Mott penned the Declaration of Sentiments, 144 years after Abigail Adams had exhorted her husband not to forget "the Ladies" in the "new Code of Laws," American women finally enjoyed the right to vote.

* * *

Reformers also sought to remedy social ills such as the rampant discrimination faced by immigrants and African Americans, while others sought to diminish poverty, domestic violence, and crime by waging war on alcohol. There were also reformers who went beyond secular humanism and drew on Christian morality to improve American society.

Between 1889 and 1893 the first settlement houses were established: Jane Addams's Hull House in Chicago, Robert A. Woods's South End House in Boston, and Lillian Wald's Henry Street Settlement in New York. Settlement houses were essentially community centers set up to alleviate the appalling conditions in urban slums, especially those overflowing with immigrants. Volunteer workers, mostly women, toiled to aid immigrants from rural areas of Europe who were having difficulty adjusting to urban life in the United States. They provided shelter and taught English, cooking, sewing, and hygiene, seeking to ease immigrants' path into American society. Soon the volunteers found that the work done in the settlement houses was simply not enough. Consequently they lobbied local governments to improve sanitation, to finance more schools, and to pass laws regulating child labor and tenement housing. They became expert at gathering statistical data that could be used to sway lawmakers to enact socially progressive legislation. Settlement-house workers also solicited private charities and benefactors to sponsor libraries, playgrounds, and day-care centers.

The basic philosophy underlying the movement, according to Jane Addams, was "the solidarity of the human race," and the goal was "to aid in the solution of the social and industrial problems which are engendered by the modern conditions of life in a great city . . . [and] attempt to relieve, at the same time, the overaccumulation at one end of society and the destitution at the other; but it assumes that this overaccumulation and destitution is most sorely felt in the things that pertain to social and educational privileges."[3]

Settlement houses also provided an outlet for the creative energies of many college-educated women, who were increasingly frustrated that there were not enough meaningful jobs open to them in a male-dominated society. By dedicating themselves to social progress and working in the settlement houses they experienced a sense of fulfillment while at the same time founding a new academic discipline—social work. Soon the University of Chicago established the Department of Social Research, which featured, as part of the curriculum, hands-on learning at Hull House. The underlying (and sometimes unconscious) goal of university-educated settlement workers, who were mostly culturally conservative middle-class Protestant women, was to enforce assimilation and social order.

Because settlement-house workers witnessed firsthand the debilitating effects of alcohol on the working class, many of them became staunch activists in the temperance crusade. The temperance movement had been going strong for decades, with people such as Frances Willard, Annie Wittenmeyr, and Carrie Nation and organizations such as the Woman's Christian Temperance Union, the Anti-Saloon League, and the Prohibition Party aggressively lobbying local governments to enact laws restricting alcohol. For women who experienced abuse from alcoholic husbands it was primarily a feminist issue, for conservative Protestants it was a moral issue, and for many rural folk it was linked to nativism. Most of the new immigrants flocking to the United States came from southern and eastern European countries where wine and beer was part of daily life. Some nativists supported temperance as a way to dissuade immigrants from Jewish, Roman Catholic, and Eastern Orthodox areas from coming to America. The temperance crusade is, in fact, a prime example of the overlapping motives that sometimes form the basis of dissent. Despite their diverse goals, radicals, reformers, and reactionaries all took part in the temperance movement.

The most legendary prohibitionist was Carrie Nation. In 1900, convinced she was doing God's will, Carrie Nation launched her "Hatchetation" campaign. She would regularly march into a saloon, carrying her Bible and singing hymns, and wielding a hatchet, proceed to destroy the place. She smashed liquor bottles, chopped up the bars, and lectured the owners and patrons on the evils of alcohol. "Men," she proclaimed, "I have come to save you from a drunkard's fate!"[4] She was arrested thirty times. In between incarcerations she toured the country lecturing in churches, vaudeville halls, and college campuses and earned enough money to pay her fines and legal costs. By the time of her death in 1911 she had literally destroyed dozens of bars and saloons.

While Carrie Nation was carrying on her entertaining campaign, thousands of women and men joined the crusade to eliminate alcohol. By the second decade of the twentieth century the temperance movement had gained considerable political clout. The argument continually put forth was that the elimination of alcohol would eliminate alcoholism, which in turn would reduce the number of people losing their jobs and sinking into lives of poverty and crime. What made Prohibition even more feasible was the ratification of the Sixteenth Amendment instituting the income tax, thus freeing the federal government from reliance on the excise tax on liquor as a primary source of revenue. By 1916 sixteen state legislatures had prohibited the sale of alcohol; and then in 1919 the Eighteenth Amendment was ratified, outlawing the sale of alcohol in the United States as of January 17, 1920.

By 1900 it was clear to many in the African American community that Booker T. Washington's injunction that blacks should not concern themselves with civil and political rights as long as they worked to lift themselves up economically was not a particularly effective strategy. In 1900 alone more than one hundred African Americans were lynched, many of whom *had* moved up the economic ladder. No one knows exactly how many blacks were murdered, for there are no reliable statistics, but historians estimate that between 1901 and 1914 more than a thousand lynchings took place. Racism was obviously too deeply entrenched in American society for whites to accept blacks as equals.

In 1905 W. E. B. Du Bois, William Monroe Trotter, John Hope, and more than thirty prominent black intellectuals met in Niagara Falls, Canada, to hammer out a strategy to secure African American civil rights. Denouncing Booker T. Washington's "accommodationism," they demanded the abolition of the Jim Crow laws, the reinstatement of the right to vote where that right had been contravened by literacy tests and poll taxes, equal educational and economic opportunity, and the right to protest for their civil rights. The following year they met again in

Harpers Ferry and further developed the strategy to secure civil rights, and in 1909 they became the National Association for the Advancement of Colored People (NAACP).

The NAACP was the first of the major civil rights organizations. Its chief focus was to use the judicial system to overturn the 1896 *Plessy v. Ferguson* decision and also to bring lawsuits challenging civil rights violations at the state and local level. Within a few years the NAACP had chapters in many states, with thousands of members. The organization also launched a monthly magazine, the *Crisis*, as a vehicle to publish stories bringing civil rights abuses (including lynchings) to public attention. It is arguable that the NAACP had very little impact during the first decades of its existence, but it did give hope to millions of African Americans who understood that, for the first time, there was an organization that was actively fighting for their rights.

Underlying many of the reforms of the early twentieth century was the Social Gospel movement, which brought a moral dimension to protest by applying Christian principles to reform. Traditionally clergymen counseled the poor that their suffering was God's will and that they would get their reward in heaven, but Walter Rauschenbusch, a Baptist pastor in New York's Lower East Side, rejected this approach. It is all well and good, he reasoned, to minister to people's souls, but it was just as essential to apply Christian principles to daily life and to do everything possible to make life better for the poor in the here and now. Rauschenbusch put his Social Gospel views into practice. In the Hell's Kitchen section of Manhattan he opened soup kitchens that gave aid and comfort to the poor and the homeless. In 1907 he published *Christianity and the Social Crisis* and in 1912 *Christianizing the Social Order*, in which he criticized capitalist exploitation of workers as being unchristian and argued for the Social Gospel and the establishment of a welfare state.

At the same time, Father John A. Ryan, responding to the papal encyclical *Rerum Novarum* (in which Pope Leo XIII declared that the state had an obligation to guarantee the rights of workers) implemented the Catholic social justice movement. Ryan argued that workers have the right to livable wages and reasonable working hours. He wrote, in *Distributive Justice: The Right and Wrong of Our Present Distribution of Wealth* (1916), that ethics and economics were inextricably entwined and that the government's duty was to ensure that workers were treated equitably. He called for a minimum wage and criticized the culture of consumption that was pervasive in the United States.

Charles Sheldon's popular novel *In His Steps* (1898) further popularized the Social Gospel. In it Sheldon argued that business leaders who were confronted with decisions about working conditions and wages or politicians debating a law for workers' compensation on an eight-hour day should first ask themselves one question before they made their decision: "What would Jesus do?" The message was clear. Would Jesus run a sweatshop? Would he try to extract the maximum labor from workers for minimum pay? Such sentiments had a profound impact on conservative Christians, who normally thought of reform as an expression of radical politics. To look at reform through a Christian prism led many such people to change their minds and get involved.

Later in the century the Social Gospel influenced other movements that espoused social justice, equality, and economic opportunity. From the beginning of Martin Luther King, Jr.'s engagement in the civil rights movement he frequently cited the works of Rauschenbusch, Reinhold Niebuhr, and other Social Gospel spokesmen, as well as the Bible and the teachings of Jesus, in arguing that civil rights was a moral issue.

* * *

Theodore Roosevelt was not a radical, as conservatives portrayed him. He was not against monopolies and trusts, for he believed that large corporations were efficient and helped spur economic growth. But he wished to rein in the rampant industrialization that was destroying the natural environment, and he was deeply concerned that capitalist exploitation was leading to dangerous discontent on the part of the working class and that unchecked corporate greed was sowing the seeds of class warfare. Reform, he believed, was far preferable to revolution.

In 1903 President Roosevelt spent several days camping in Yosemite National Park with John Muir. Muir, the founder of the Sierra Club, had been making it his life's mission to save the wilderness from developers and the mining and lumber companies. By the time he met Roosevelt, Muir's lobbying had already persuaded Congress to turn Yellowstone, Yosemite, and Sequoia into national parks. Roosevelt's rapport with Muir influenced the president to become even more proactive in his efforts to preserve the nation's natural resources. But Roosevelt was also influenced by the conservationist Gifford Pinchot, who represented another side of environmentalism. Whereas Muir was dedicated to the *preservation* of the wilderness from development, Pinchot advocated *conservation* through the managed use of natural resources. Roosevelt embraced both points of view. Believing that the wilderness experience was spiritually uplifting, he worked hard to preserve the pristine areas of the nation. He signed executive orders creating fifty-one bird sanctuaries, four national game preserves, and five national parks, as well as the Act for the Preservation of American Antiquities, in order to keep federal land out of the hands of developers. At the same time, Roosevelt appointed Pinchot to chair a National Conservation Commission to formulate a plan on how best to use the nation's natural resources. Acting on the commission's recommendations, Roosevelt created 150 national forests where lumber companies were given contracts to harvest the timber but were required by law to plant new trees for future harvesting. He also established the Public Lands Commission to analyze public land laws and the Inland Waterways Commission to recommend ways of improving flood control and hydroelectric power, and he signed the National Reclamation Act to fund irrigation projects that were especially advantageous to large agribusinesses. Thus TR combined Muir's and Pinchot's views so that millions of acres were preserved, while at the same time millions of acres were set aside for the prudent extraction of natural resources.

After Roosevelt took on J. P. Morgan, busted a few trusts, broke up several monopolies, pushed for laws to curb corporate abuse, and took labor's cause seriously by mediating a coal strike in 1902, progressives took heart. They were optimistic that with a sympathetic president in the White House there was hope for the progressive agenda. And so during Roosevelt's presidency the impetus for reform branched out. Writers and journalists throughout the country applied their analytical skills to an obsessive effort to root out and expose the ills of society. Some writers worked for the tabloid press, and part of their motivation was to produce sensational, scandalous stories that sold newspapers. But many of them were themselves progressives who were legitimately outraged at the corruption, abuse, and exploitation they uncovered, as well as the apathy of the public. Their intention was to awaken the nation's conscience and propel Americans into action. Roosevelt called them "muckrakers" because he thought they were too busy wallowing in the muck of scandal and ignored the positive side of American society, but at the same time they did influence him to act.

Lincoln Steffens wrote a series of investigative articles for *McClure's Magazine* (collected and published as *The Shame of the Cities* in 1904) about the relationship between corrupt politicians and unscrupulous business leaders. His book induced thousands of Americans to protest against graft and bribery and forced legislators and judges to investigate the corruption. Ida M. Tarbell wrote a scathing indictment of the Standard Oil Company, exposing John D. Rockefeller's ruthless business practices. Frank Norris's novel *The Octopus* (1901) compared the railroad companies of California, because of their extortionate shipping rates, with an octopus that was choking the life out of small farmers. The publisher S. S. McClure's editorials in his magazine hammered at the immorality of business leaders, landlords, politicians, judges, lawyers, and even workers and educators.

But the most influential of all the muckraking publications was Upton Sinclair's best-selling novel *The Jungle* (1906). Sinclair, a socialist, wrote the book as a paean to socialism. Sinclair described, in shocking detail, the unsanitary conditions rampant in the meat-packing industry and the appalling exploitation that destroyed an immigrant family. At the end of the book the protagonist, after losing everything, attends a socialist meeting, and for the first time he sees a ray of hope. Sinclair's message was clear: socialism was the cure for capitalism. But that was not the message readers took from the novel. The public was gripped by Sinclair's graphic descriptions of the butchering of the cattle, the sickening process for producing ground beef and stuffing sausages, the processing of contaminated meat from diseased cattle that had died on the way to the slaughterhouse, and the maiming of overworked men operating the meat grinders. As Sinclair later put it, "I aimed at the public's heart, and by accident I hit it in the stomach."[5] Roosevelt (carnivore that he was) was so sickened when he read the book that he stopped eating meat for several months until he got Congress to pass the Pure Food and Drug Act.

One of the worst abuses of the age was the exploitation of children in factories and mines. It was a common practice to hire child workers in order to cut production costs. In textile mills their small hands could reach into the power looms to extract defective threads, in mines boys as young as eight years old were employed sorting coal, and in all cases they were paid less than adults. Children frequently lost fingers and hands in factory accidents, developed fatal respiratory diseases in mines, worked ten hours and more a day for less than fifty cents, and forfeited any opportunity for education. Many were literally worked to death. One investigator wrote an article about a young girl, Roselie Randazzo, who died of a hemorrhage coughing up blood while working in the unsafe air of an artificial flower factory.

In the 1880s and 1890s Florence Kelley, who worked with Jane Addams at Hull House, brought cases to the Illinois courts seeking to get the state to outlaw child labor. In 1901 Kelley moved to New York, where she led the National Consumers League—its purpose was to encourage consumers to buy products only from companies that met minimum wage and safety standards. The league's slogan was "investigate, agitate, legislate." Kelley also organized consumer boycotts of sweatshops and other industries that exploited child labor; she pioneered the practice of assembling scientific and statistical data to influence courts and legislatures, and she came up with numerous creative ideas to eradicate child labor, for example, compulsory education and requiring labels on manufactured goods certifying that children were not used in its production.

Mary Harris Jones (the namesake of *Mother Jones* magazine—the distinguished present-day magazine of progressive news analysis) exemplifies two of the chief categories of dissent. At first Mother Jones was a liberal who sought to reform society, but later she grew increasingly radical and pushed hard to upend the entire capitalist system. In the nineteenth century she was an organizer for the Knights of Labor and the United Mine Workers of America, but by the turn of the century she became a socialist and was one of the founders of the Industrial Workers of the World. In 1903, at the age of seventy-three, she went to the Kensington neighborhood of Philadelphia to show her solidarity with seventy-five thousand textile workers who had walked off the job demanding shorter hours and increased wages. Ten thousand of the striking workers were children. "Every day," she wrote, "little children came into Union Headquarters, some with their hands off, some with the thumb missing, some with their fingers off at the knuckle. They were stooped things, round shouldered and skinny." Although state law prohibited employing children under the age of twelve, many of them were only ten years old. "I asked the newspaper men why they didn't

The mill children on Mother Jones's famous march from Philadelphia to Oyster Bay protesting child labor, 1903. (Public domain)

publish the facts about child labor in Pennsylvania. They said they couldn't because the mill owners had stock in the papers. 'Well, I've got stock in these little children,' said I, 'and I'll arrange a little publicity.'"[6]

And so Mother Jones organized the children for a protest march from Philadelphia to Oyster Bay, Long Island. "I decided to go with the children to see President Roosevelt to ask him to have Congress pass a law prohibiting the exploitation of childhood. I thought that President Roosevelt might see these mill children and compare them with his own little ones who were spending the summer on the seashore at Oyster Bay. I thought too, out of politeness, we might call on Morgan in Wall Street who owned the mines where many of these children's fathers worked." In Trenton, New Jersey, the police were ordered to stop the march, but instead "they just smiled and spoke kindly to the children, and said nothing at all about not going into the city." The children marched into the city, where Mother Jones spoke to the crowd, "and it was the wives of the police who took the little children and cared for them that night, sending them back in the morning with a nice lunch rolled up in paper napkins."[7]

The march's next stop was Princeton, where Jones told a gathering of professors and students that she would speak to them about higher education. "'Here's a text book on economics,' I said pointing to a little chap, James Ashworth, who was ten years old and who was stooped over like an old man from carrying bundles of yarn that weighed seventy-five pounds. 'He gets three dollars a week and his sister who is fourteen gets six dollars. They work in a carpet factory ten hours a day while the children of the rich are getting their higher education.'" In New York City they got donations from a crowd when she delivered a speech about the evils of child labor. "I showed them Eddie Dunphy, a little fellow of twelve, whose job it was to sit all day on a high stool, handing in the right thread to another worker. Eleven hours a day he sat on the high stool with dangerous machinery all about him. All day long, winter and summer, spring and fall, for three dollars a week." At Coney Island she told another crowd, "We want President Roosevelt to hear the wail of the children who never have a chance to go to school but work eleven and twelve hours a day in the textile mills of Pennsylvania; who weave the carpets that he and you walk upon and the lace curtains in your windows, and the clothes of the people. Fifty years ago there was a cry against slavery and men gave up their lives to stop the selling of black children on the block. Today the white child is sold for two dollars a week to the manufacturers. Fifty years ago the black babies were sold C.O.D. Today the white baby is sold on the installment plan."[8]

When the protestors finally got to Oyster Bay, President Roosevelt, despite his progressive credentials, refused to greet them. Still, the children's march raised public awareness and forced people to discuss the issue. (In most cases of dissent, whether protest marches to Oyster Bay or Washington or picketing the White House or acts of civil disobedience such as sit-ins, elevating the issue into public discourse was a primary goal.) "Our march," Mother Jones declared, "had done its work. We had drawn the attention of the nation to the crime of child labor. And while the strike of the textile workers in Kensington was lost and the children driven back to work, not long afterward the Pennsylvania legislature passed a child labor law that sent thousands of children home from the mills, and kept thousands of others from entering the factory until they were fourteen years of age."[9]

In 1904 anti-child-labor activists founded the National Child Labor Committee (NCLC) to lobby Congress to enact anti-child-labor legislation. In 1908 the NCLC commissioned the photographer Lewis B. Hine to travel the country documenting child labor. Hine was horrified at

Mother Jones, 1915. Photograph of the labor activist Mother Jones (1837–1930) attending the 1915 hearings of the federal Commission on Industrial Relations at New York City Hall. (Public domain; courtesy Library of Congress)

what he discovered, and his photographs remain a powerful and disturbing reminder of the terrible conditions under which children, some as young as five years old, worked. For years Hine exhibited his photos and urged audiences around the country to vote for politicians who took a stand against child labor. "Perhaps you are weary of child labor pictures," he said. "Well, so are the rest of us, but we propose to make you and the whole country so sick and tired of the whole business that when the time for action comes, child labor pictures will be records of the past."[10] Members of the NCLC also pressured the government to create a federal agency to look after children's welfare. In 1912 President Taft signed the bill creating the United States Children's Bureau and appointed Julia Lathrop as its chair to "investigate and report upon all matters pertaining to the welfare of children and child life among all classes of our people."[11]

Despite the efforts of Jones, Addams, Kelley, Hine, and so many other activists (both progressives and radicals), it was not until the New Deal in the 1930s that child labor was effectively regulated at the federal level, when another Roosevelt signed the Fair Labor Standards Act prohibiting child labor under the age of fourteen and setting strict limits on the hours and type of work for children between the ages of fourteen and eighteen.

Progressive reformers also targeted the working conditions of New York City's garment industry, which employed thousands of young women (mostly Italian and Jewish immigrants) in hundreds of sweatshops throughout lower Manhattan. These women worked long, fifty-six hour weeks, in unsafe, miserable conditions for one dollar a day making dresses and shirtwaists (blouses). The companies, seeking to maximize profits, forced the women to rent their sewing machines (sometimes even requiring that they pay for the electricity) and made them take their breaks at their stations. In 1909 nearly twenty thousand garment workers walked off their jobs, demanding better working conditions. Supported by the International Ladies' Garment Workers Union and dozens of the city's clergymen, the women won. But not all the shirtwaist manufacturers improved working conditions, and many of the sweatshops remained unsafe. The Triangle Shirtwaist Company, for example, still required employees to take their breaks at their sewing machines, and to ensure they did the managers routinely kept the doors to the workshop locked so the women could not even go out into the hallway.

On March 25, 1911, a fire broke out in the eighth-floor workshop. Most of the doors were locked; but even those that were unlocked swung inward, and the press of panicked women trying to escape prevented the doors from opening. The elevators did not work. There were no fire escapes. The fire department's ladders only reached to the seventh floor. The women were trapped. With flames and smoke engulfing them many women, in threes and fours, holding hands, leapt to their deaths. "They jumped with their clothing ablaze," one newspaper reported. "The hair of some of the girls streamed up aflame as they leaped. Thud after thud sounded on the pavements."[12] When it was all over, 146 women were dead. None of the managers died.

The public was outraged. The governor established a commission to investigate working conditions throughout the state. The commission's findings, after five years, eventually led to the enactment of legislation that set safety standards for the workplace, prohibited the employment of children under fourteen, and limited women's working hours to fifty-four per week. From 1911 on it became clear to politicians and the public that the government needed to establish regulations that would improve the safety of the workplace for all workers. In the long run, the Triangle Shirtwaist Company fire had a positive impact. It raised public awareness of work safety issues to the point that eventually, nearly sixty years later, the Occupational Safety and Health Administration (OSHA) was launched. As far as the victims were concerned, immediately after the disaster the factory owners were taken to court. After three years of litigation the final decision was that the company owners were obliged to pay seventy-five dollars for each life lost.

One of the most shocking incidents underscoring the need for labor reform was the Ludlow Massacre. The miners at the Colorado Fuel and Iron Company (owned by the Rockefeller family) lived in company towns, were paid in company scrip, and were forced to shop in company stores. In 1913 they went on strike, demanding the recognition of their union—the United Mine Workers of America (UMWA)—an eight-hour day, the right to choose where to live and shop, and finally to be paid for such "dead work" as shoring up the mines and laying track (miners were paid by the ton of coal they mined). As soon as they struck, the company evicted the strikers from the towns. Twelve hundred miners set up a tent city near the mines so they could prevent scab workers from being brought in. The company hired the Baldwin-Felts Detective Agency to break the strike. The detectives began routinely patrolling the encampment in an armored vehicle, arbitrarily shooting into the tents. In October the governor of Colorado sent in the National Guard. At first the mineworkers cheered, thinking they had come to protect them. But on April 20, 1914, the Guard moved in to disperse the strikers. During the ensuing melee seventeen people were killed, including two women and eleven children.

"The Ludlow camp is a mass of charred debris," the *New York Times* reported the following day, "and buried beneath it is a story of horror imparalleled [*sic*] in the history of industrial warfare. In the holes which had been dug for their protection against the rifles' fire the women and children died like trapped rats when the flames swept over them."[13] And an outraged Mother Jones could not restrain her righteous fury. "The women and children fled to the hills," she wrote. "All day long the firing continued. Men fell dead, their faces to the ground. Women dropped. The little Snyder boy was shot through the head, trying to save his kitten. A child carrying water to his dying mother was killed." The fighting continued for fourteen hours. "Night came. A raw wind blew down the canyons where men, women and children shivered and wept. Then a blaze lighted the sky. The soldiers, drunk with blood and with the liquor they had looted from the saloon, set fire to the tents of Ludlow with oil-soaked torches. The tents, all the poor furnishings, the clothes and bedding of the miners' families burned." Finally it ended. "The wretched people crept back to bury their dead. In a dugout under a burned tent, the charred bodies of eleven little children and two women were found—unrecognizable. Everything lay in ruins. . . . Oil and fire and guns had robbed men and women and children of their homes and slaughtered tiny babies and defenseless women."[14]

United Mine Worker officials urged mineworkers throughout Colorado to rise up in arms and defend themselves. For ten days guerrilla warfare broke out as nearly a thousand miners attacked and destroyed mine property and killed guards. Dozens more were killed during the uprising, and order was restored only after President Woodrow Wilson sent in the U.S. Army. Estimates of the number of dead ranged from sixty to two hundred. Hundreds of strikers were arrested. Twenty-two National Guardsmen were court-martialed after thousands of people demonstrated in front of the state capitol in Denver demanding that they be tried for murder. In the end, the strike was broken, the UMWA did not gain recognition, most of the striking workers were fired, and no National Guardsmen served time in prison.

The federal government set up the Commission on Industrial Relations to investigate the affair, interrogated the people involved, including

John D. Rockefeller, Jr., and concluded that many of the union's demands should be implemented, that child labor in the mines should be abolished, and that a national eight-hour day should be implemented. Rockefeller himself was so shaken by the event (and the negative publicity) that he hired labor-relations experts and instituted a whole series of reforms to improve working and living conditions, including building recreational facilities and paved roads in the towns, upgrading safety and health standards in the mines, and permitting miners to unionize.

* * *

Most of the progressives seeking to reform society were middle-class moderates. Many were liberals who wanted to see opportunity and equality extended to all Americans. But a lot of them were conservatives who wanted to reestablish a society that they believed was endangered by the changes wrought by the industrial revolution as well as by the extremist antidotes being recommended to address the problems. And then there was a smaller group of radical dissenters who desired deeper, more fundamental changes. In fact they sought a complete transformation of the way things were. They did not want to reform or fix the system; they wanted to destroy the system. The Socialist Party demanded the public ownership of factories, mines, and railroads; free education; fair wages; and humane working conditions. Declaring that "the capitalist system has outgrown its historical function, and has become utterly incapable of meeting the problems now confronting society," and denouncing "this outgrown system as incompetent and corrupt and the source of unspeakable misery and suffering to the whole working class," the Socialist Party Platform of 1912 called for a radical upheaval of the American system of government. "The Socialist party is the political expression of the economic interests of the workers. Its defeats have been their defeats and its victories their victories. It is a party founded on the science and laws of social development. It proposes that, since all social necessities to-day are socially produced, the means of their production and distribution shall be socially owned and democratically controlled." Thus the plutocracy that runs America must be thrown out, and a system of "collective ownership and democratic management of railroads, wire and wireless telegraphs and telephones, express service, steamboat lines, and all other social means of transportation and communication and of all large scale industries" including banking, mining, natural resources must immediately be inaugurated. This was only the beginning. Among the many other demands the Socialists put forward were the establishment of a minimum wage, a shorter workweek, safety inspection in mines and factories, women's suffrage, and the abolition of child labor.[15]

Eugene V. Debs, one of the founders of the American Socialist Party, was the party's candidate for president five times between 1900 and 1920. Business leaders, bankers, and politicians worried and fretted about Debs's increasing popularity and the surging growth of the Socialist Party. By the second decade of the century the party had well over one hundred thousand members actively engaged in politics, and Debs won nearly a million votes in both the 1912 and 1920 elections (despite the fact that he conducted his 1920 campaign from a prison cell). Debs was by far the most articulate and celebrated socialist leader, who in speeches all over the country consistently fought for the rights of labor, women, children, and the downtrodden. "While there is a lower class," Debs famously proclaimed, "I am in it; while there is a criminal element, I am of it; while there is a soul in prison, I am not free!" By 1916, as the United States moved ever closer to involvement in the Great War, he became a powerful antiwar activist. War, Debs believed, was a capitalist plot to preserve the political and economic status quo by pitting international workers against each other. "Years ago I declared that there was only one war in which I would enlist and that was the war of the workers of the world against the exploiters of the world. I declared moreover that the working class had no interest in the wars declared and waged by the ruling classes of the various countries upon one another for conquest and spoils."[16] In other words, workers of the world should be united and not allow themselves to be the pawns of the capitalists.

Although Debs never came close to challenging the Republican or Democratic candidates on the national level, socialist support was strong enough in certain immigrant, working-class, and Populist areas that local socialist candidates did score some success. Socialists elected mayors in Milwaukee, Wisconsin; Butte, Montana; Berkeley, California; and Reading, Pennsylvania. In 1914 socialists in Manhattan's Lower East Side elected Meyer London to the U.S. House of Representatives. And by a wide margin Wisconsin voters elected socialist Victor L. Berger to Congress in 1918.

In 1905 a band of radical union organizers, disgruntled about the lack of representation of unskilled workers in the American Federation of Labor and other unions, founded the Industrial Workers of the World (IWW). The purpose of the IWW was to ensure the representation of *all* workers regardless of ethnicity, race, gender, or skill, whether citizens or illegal migrant workers. The "Wobblies," as they were popularly called, proudly extended "a fraternal hand to every wage-worker, no matter what his religion, fatherland, or trade." Moreover, they advocated overthrowing the state and abolishing the wage system and demanded that workers seize the means of production. "The working class and the employing class," the preamble to the IWW constitution declares, "have nothing in common. There can be no peace so long as hunger and want are found among millions of the working people and the few, who make up the employing class, have all the good things of life." It is not merely an American problem but an international problem. "Between these two classes a struggle must go on until the workers of the world organize as a class, take possession of the means of production, abolish the wage system, and live in harmony with the Earth."[17]

When the IWW coordinated a strike, the leadership insisted on the complete solidarity of the striking workers. Previous strikes, such as those of the Knights of Labor and the American Railway Workers Union, failed because strikers did not maintain cohesion but became a powerless, disorganized mob. Within the IWW's first few years it organized dozens of strikes in Nevada, Ohio, Maine, Connecticut, and Pennsylvania, with mixed success. IWW restaurant and hotel workers in Nevada were successful in winning an eight-hour day, while sawmill workers in Pennsylvania secured a pay raise and a nine-hour day. But in Connecticut an IWW strike was broken when the AFL colluded with management and sent in scab workers, and another failed in Lancaster, Pennsylvania, when the silk mill was closed down. Occasionally the Wobblies turned violent when authorities deployed security forces to crush a walkout. During an eleven-week strike in McKees Rocks, Pennsylvania, in 1909 the company requested the Pennsylvania State Constabulary (referred to as the "American Cossacks" by the strikers) to break the strike. The confrontation led to a standoff in which several strikers and constables were killed and fifty wounded before it finally ended with a hard-fought victory for the strikers. The Wobblies were especially pleased with the outcome, for it was the first time, after multiple defeats, that the workers defeated the "Cossacks" and won their demands.

One of the founding members of the IWW was its leader, "Big Bill" Haywood. Haywood had been a member of the Western Federation of Miners before getting involved with the IWW. In 1907 he was arrested and tried for participating in the assassination of an antilabor former governor of Idaho. But Haywood's lawyer, the noted defense attorney Clarence Darrow, got one of the defendants (the confessed bomb thrower) to admit that he was paid off by the Mine Owners' Association. Haywood was acquitted. In 1912 more than twenty thousand textile workers in Lawrence, Massachusetts, walked off the job in opposition to the reduction of their wages (which were already an abysmal sixteen cents an hour). When the mill owners called in the police, violence broke out, and a number of strikers were killed. The workers asked for the IWW's assistance, and soon Big Bill Haywood arrived. Haywood suggested that the workers send their children to New York City for the duration of the strike in order to garner public sympathy and support. Socialist families in New York agreed to take them in, and when scores of hungry, destitute children marched from the train station through the middle of Manhattan, reporters were on hand to write heart-wrenching stories about their plight. "I have never found children who were so uniformly ill-nourished, ill-fed, and ill-clothed," one witness to the march exclaimed.[18] The resulting publicity led embarrassed Lawrence officials to forbid any other children from leaving the city. When a group of mothers and children tried to board a train in Lawrence, the police beat them back. When newspaper stories around the world expressed outrage at the heartless actions of the city officials and the company, the governor of Massachusetts was forced to step in on the workers' side and settle the strike.

Along with fighting for workers' rights the Wobblies had to put in just as much time fighting official efforts to prohibit their activities. A standard method that most state and local governments used to clamp down on strikes and protests was to issue injunctions forbidding public assembling, speeches, rallies, and picketing. Haywood and the IWW invariably challenged these injunctions. In Fresno, California, for example, when the city forbade street meetings during a strike of migrant agricultural workers, the IWW initiated a direct action campaign that led to the arrest of hundreds of its members and coordinated a "March on Fresno" of free-speech proponents from around the country. After four months the city gave up and rescinded the prohibition on free speech and public assemblies.

Perhaps the most famous Wobbly was the Swedish immigrant and songwriter Joel Haggland. When he arrived in the United States in 1902, Haggland was deeply disappointed that the hoped-for success promised to immigrants seemed beyond his grasp. For a number of years he tried to eke out a living however he could, including petty thievery. He changed his name to Joseph Hillstrom (to keep one step ahead of the law?), and then in 1910 he joined the IWW. Calling himself Joe Hill, he quickly became a leading recruiter and organizer for the union by effectively devoting his musical talent to the IWW cause.

His technique was to gather a crowd outside a factory at the end of a shift by singing a few songs. Then he and fellow organizers would hand out literature and make short speeches extolling the benefits of joining the Wobblies. Hill, in effect, was one of the country's first protest singers. His songs all had an anticapitalist, prounion message. Usually he took a popular tune or hymn to grab people's attention and added new lyrics to get them to think, as in "The Preacher and the Slave Girl." Sung to the tune of the hymn "Sweet Bye and Bye," the song began with an attack on Christianity's collusion with the robber barons:

> Long-haired preachers come out every night,
> Try to tell you what's wrong and what's right;
> But when asked how 'bout something to eat,
> They will answer with voices so sweet:
>
> You will eat,
> Bye and bye,
> In that glorious land above the sky;
> Work and pray, live on hay,
> You'll get pie in the sky when you die.

And it ended with the Wobblies' socialist message:

> Workingmen of all countries, unite,
> Side by side we for freedom will fight:
> When the world and its wealth we have gained
> To the grafters we'll sing this refrain:

You will eat, bye and bye,
When you've learned how to cook and to fry.
Chop some wood, 'twill do you good,
And you'll eat in the sweet bye and bye.[19]

   In 1913 Hill traveled to Utah, one of the most conservative and anti-union states in the country, in order to organize mine workers. Early in 1914 two men held up a grocery store; during the robbery two clerks were murdered. Hill was arrested for the crime. Consistently claiming his innocence in the courtroom, Hill was convicted on circumstantial evidence and sentenced to death. Immediately Big Bill Haywood organized mass demonstrations protesting the conviction. It was clear to all members of the IWW and even to huge numbers of the general public that the trial was a setup and that big business and the state of Utah was out to destroy Hill and discredit the IWW. For months the protests spread around the nation and around the world. There were demonstrations in New York and London and other major cities, Helen Keller and Elizabeth Gurley Flynn (both socialists and members of the IWW) protested the verdict, and even President Wilson urged the governor of Utah to commute Hill's sentence. Despite the public outcry, Hill was executed by firing squad in November 1915. Just before his execution he sent a telegram to Haywood urging the IWW and his supporters worldwide: "Don't waste any time in mourning. Organize."[20] Later in the twentieth century union organizers as well as musicians and protest singers from Woody Guthrie and Pete Seeger to Bob Dylan and Billy Bragg drew inspiration from Hill.
   Other radicals made waves demanding fundamental changes to the American way of life. Helen Keller, famously known for her extraordinary courage and ability to overcome blindness and deafness, campaigned for socialism and communism in speeches all over the world. From New York to Adelaide, Australia, she sang the praises of socialism, the Wobblies, and the Bolshevik Revolution. Elizabeth Gurley Flynn was a young radical activist who joined the Socialist Party and became an organizer for the IWW. A few years later she was one of the founders of the American Civil Liberties Union and went around the country lecturing and speaking out in support of radical causes.
   One of the most notorious radicals of the time was Emma Goldman. Goldman denounced nearly every aspect of capitalist society. A Russian

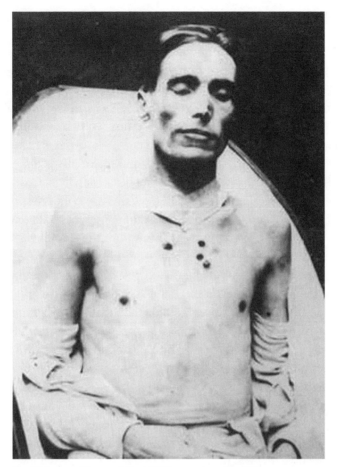

Joe Hill, 1915. The socialist IWW organizer Joe Hill was executed by firing squad in Utah on what most activists believed
were trumped-up charges of murder. Hundreds of thousands of
people around the world protested his conviction and execution.
(Public domain)

immigrant who was enamored with anarchism, socialism, and communism, Goldman was such an outspoken critic of America that she was
frequently and consistently harassed by law enforcement officials.[21] In a
1911 essay, "Marriage and Love," Goldman argued that women's fight for
suffrage, even if successful, was not going to accomplish any real change
unless the underlying evils of capitalism itself were addressed. In capitalist society, she contended, women (indeed, all people, all relationships)

were treated as commodities. Marriage was nothing more than an economic arrangement; in fact marriage was nothing more than legalized prostitution, an institution dedicated to keeping women subservient. "Marriage and love have nothing in common," she wrote; "they are as far apart as the poles; are, in fact, antagonistic to each other." Women cannot earn enough money to live independently, and so they must find a man to support them. Marriage condemns women to a life of servitude. "The moral lesson instilled in the girl is not whether the man has aroused her love, but rather . . . Can the man make a living? Can he support a wife? That is the only thing that justifies marriage. Gradually this saturates every thought of the girl; her dreams are not of moonlight and kisses, of laughter and tears; she dreams of shopping tours and bargain counters. This soul-poverty and sordidness are the elements inherent in the marriage institution. The State and the Church approve of no other ideal, simply because it is the one that necessitates the State and Church control of men and women."[22]

It is true, Goldman acknowledged, that things are changing, that more and more women are entering the workforce and that soon women may gain the right to vote. But in capitalist society, where workers are exploited, what sort of progress is this? If and when women gain all the benefits that men have, will there be real progress? She suspected that the only result would be that women would then have "the equal right with men to be exploited, to be robbed, to go on strike; aye, to starve even."[23] Still, she never wavered from her demand for "freedom for both sexes, freedom of action, freedom in love and freedom in motherhood."[24] Many thousands of Americans attended Goldman's speeches and read her essays, and many thousands were inspired by her message and imported her views into their daily lives. Greenwich Village, New York, where Goldman lived, was a vibrant enclave of cultural rebels—"Bohemians"—who rejected conventional morality. Avant-garde writers and painters, poets and dancers—Max Eastman, Isadora Duncan, and many others—published articles and poetry, exhibited paintings, produced experimental plays and dance, and yearned for the day when complete, uninhibited freedom would dawn in the United States. Such Bohemian views, however, horrified and frightened the majority of Americans, especially after the outbreak of World War I and the triumph of the Bolsheviks in Russia. Still, Goldman did not keep quiet or lower the tone of her rhetoric. Her defiant and ceaseless

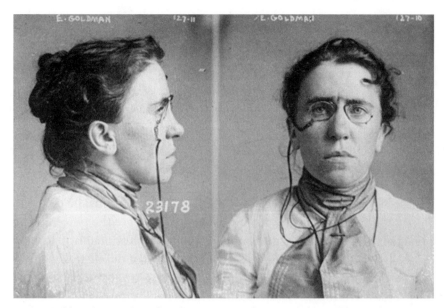

Emma Goldman's mug shot after she was arrested in 1901 to be interrogated concerning the assassination of President William McKinley. Anarchist, socialist, activist, and revolutionary, Goldman was involved in just about every radical cause of her time. (Public domain; courtesy Library of Congress)

dissent eventually led in 1919 to her deportation back to Russia, where she found, to her horror, that free speech was considered a bourgeois superstition. (She eventually did a lot of traveling and lecturing in Europe and Canada and was even briefly allowed back into the United States for a lecture tour in 1934.)

* * *

By 1912 the issues raised by progressives and radicals—the enormous power of monopolies, the plight of workers, political corruption, women's rights, and the role of government—were the focus of public discourse. Republican presidents Theodore Roosevelt and William Howard Taft had, to varying degrees, taken up the challenge of the times, but as the presidential election of 1912 loomed, all was not well within Republican circles.

Roosevelt's handpicked successor in 1908 had been Secretary of War William Howard Taft. Roosevelt believed that Taft would continue in the Roosevelt tradition, and to a large extent, Taft did. In fact he actually busted more trusts during his single term than TR did in two. However, by 1910 Roosevelt was disappointed that Taft had allied himself with the conservative wing of the Republican Party and was no longer aggressively carrying out Roosevelt's conservationist policies. In 1912 Roosevelt publicly broke with Taft and challenged him for the Republican nomination. When Taft was renominated, Roosevelt and his supporters walked out of the convention and formed a new party—the Progressive Party—that promptly nominated Roosevelt for president. In his acceptance speech he offered a progressive agenda on such items as tariff reform, minimum wage, workers' compensation, and child labor. But he also backed off from trust-busting. Large corporations, he claimed, were good for the country, but it was vital to increase the power of the president and the federal government (the "New Nationalism," Roosevelt called it) to regulate business as the "steward of public welfare."[25]

The Democrats for their part nominated the progressive governor of New Jersey, Woodrow Wilson. Calling his program the "New Freedom," Wilson advocated federal regulation of the economy, new legislation to improve working conditions, and strict measures to break up the trusts (unlike Roosevelt, who only wanted to regulate them). By eliminating the trusts, competition would be restored, and the free enterprise system would flourish to the benefit of all.

The most revealing statistic about the 1912 election was that the Americans who cast eleven million combined votes for Wilson, Roosevelt, and Debs chose candidates who advocated progressive and even (in Debs's case) radical ideas. The American people by 1912 were clearly sympathetic to the progressive vision.

As president, Wilson lowered the protective tariff, authorized a graduated income tax, established the Federal Trade Commission to prosecute companies accused of stifling competition, and enacted other progressive reforms. But despite his economic progressivism, socially he was a conservative. He dragged his feet on the crucial issue of women's suffrage (it took nearly both his terms as president before militant suffragists finally swayed him to support the vote for women), and he brought Jim Crow to Washington. In nearly all federal agencies and departments, lunchrooms, restrooms, and offices were officially segregated, and African American administrators were transferred or dismissed. Blacks who had been working side by side with whites in federal offices suddenly found themselves shunted aside. Wilson believed that the separation of races was ordained by God. Instituting segregation as official federal policy, he said, was not "a movement *against* Negroes": "I sincerely believe it to be in their interest."[26] Wilson ignored the protests of the NAACP and black leaders and even, to their dismay, praised the 1915 feature film *Birth of a Nation* (a shockingly racist hagiography of the Ku Klux Klan) as a masterpiece. "Have you a 'new freedom' for white Americans," the civil rights activist William Monroe Trotter acidly asked him, "and a new slavery for your African-American fellow citizens?"[27]

* * *

Both Roosevelt and Wilson, despite their antipathy for each other, were moderates who were tuned in to the voices of dissent and the progressive mood of the times. Both were opposed to socialism and radical organizations such as the Industrial Workers of the World, both supported free enterprise, both wanted capitalism to succeed. For the most part progressives, whether Republican or Democrat, were in agreement. Believing in the American credo of equality, they sought to end exploitation and protect the victims of industrialism through governmental intervention. During the Progressive era, dominated by the middle class, dissent became respectable. Most progressives were scientific in their approach to the problems created by industrial growth, and many also brought a moral, Christian element to their campaigns. Whether they based their philosophy on Reform Darwinism or the Social Gospel, progressives were on a mission to reform society. Muckrakers attempted, with some success, to jolt Americans out of their apathy and push the government to do something about political corruption, poverty, and the unchecked greed of the moneyed interests. Women fought for, and won, the vote. Temperance advocates successfully persuaded the federal government to prohibit the sale of alcohol. African Americans embarked on a campaign to reverse the *Plessy v. Ferguson* "separate but equal" decision and formed the first influential civil rights organization.

At the same time, radicals felt a far more drastic approach was needed to overcome the evils of capitalism. Socialists such as Eugene V. Debs and anarchists such as Emma Goldman believed that the system was too corrupt to be reformed and that capitalism itself had to be overthrown and a new egalitarian society created from its ashes. Although the radicals were unsuccessful in destroying the system, they did have the impact of pushing progressives like Wilson further than they had been willing to go. The radicals did not get the new world they hoped for, but they did push reformers' goals to be more inclusive; and this, in effect, influenced reformers to achieve more than they perhaps would have without radical prodding. Furthermore, although never more than a minority movement, the radicals of the Progressive era did lay the basis for American radicalism of the twentieth century, especially during the 1930s and 1960s, when radical thought again came to the forefront.

The Progressive movement faded during the 1920s but had a rebirth during the New Deal. Still, even to this day Americans continue to debate the question of how much the federal government, so distrusted by individualists, should intervene for the public good. As Americans attempted to solve this riddle, events in Europe signaled that the United States was at the threshold of a new and increasingly perilous age in which its isolation from the rest of the world would be severely challenged.

CHAPTER 15

Making the World Safe for Democracy

The flag is not a symbol of the country as a cultural group, following certain ideals of life, but solely a symbol of the political State, inseparable from its prestige and expansion. The flag is most intimately connected with military achievement, military memory. It represents the country not in its intensive life, but in its far-flung challenge to the world. The flag is primarily the banner of war; it is allied with patriotic anthem and holiday. It recalls old martial memories. A nation's patriotic history is solely the history of its wars, that is, of the State in its health and glorious functioning. So in responding to the appeal of the flag, we are responding to the appeal of the State, to the symbol of the herd organized as an offensive and defensive body, conscious of its prowess and its mystical herd strength.

—Randolph Bourne,
"War Is the Health of the State," 1918

When Europeans enthusiastically marched off to war in the summer of 1914 after the assassination of Archduke Franz Ferdinand, most Americans reacted with disbelief. It seemed preposterous that modern nations would go to war over outmoded notions of monarchy. However, even though the United States was not involved in the conflict, many Americans worried about the war's impact. Progressives worried that the war would weaken the reform impetus at home. Suffragists and settlement-house workers organized a massive peace parade in New York City. At the outset President Wilson announced that the United States would remain neutral, and he urged Americans to remain neutral even in their private thoughts. Americans, for the most part, had no wish to get involved, and certainly the knowledge that the Atlantic Ocean insulated the United States from the European conflict assured Americans that we would not get drawn in.

Although the official American policy was neutrality, most Americans (with the notable exception of those of German or Irish ancestry) tended to be more sympathetic to the Allies because Germany was perceived as the aggressor. The British also deluged the United States with propaganda reports about German atrocities in Belgium that inflamed anti-German sentiment. Still, the American people, though inwardly taking sides in the conflict, were in no mood to go to war. It was a European struggle. Let them fight each other. Americans should not get involved.

Neutrality was good for business. American merchants enjoyed a brisk trade supplying the belligerent nations with foodstuffs, raw materials, weapons, artillery shells, vehicles, and other equipment. The president supported the merchants, insisting that the United States, as a neutral power, had the right to trade with both sides in the conflict. Mostly, however, our trade was with the Allies because Britain, with its superior navy, established a blockade around the Central Powers and confiscated goods intended for the enemy.

But the all-out German effort to destroy the British blockade created a severe crisis that almost brought the United States into the war in May 1915 when a U-boat sank the British passenger liner the *Lusitania*. Among the 1,200 casualties were 128 Americans. Wilson issued a stern protest, and the crisis passed when the German government publicly apologized, announced it would rein in submarine warfare, and paid reparations to the victims' families.

As the 1916 election approached, Wilson worried that the Republicans might nominate the formidable Theodore Roosevelt. In order to solidify the progressive vote, he began a calculated push to enact many of the stalled bills that progressive activists had been advocating. For example, he got Congress to pass the Keatings-Owen Child Labor Bill, which outlawed interstate commerce in goods produced by children under the age of fourteen. He also got a Workmen's Compensation Bill passed as well as the Adamson Act, which established the eight-hour day for railway workers. These reforms had long been a part of the progressive agenda, but it was the looming election that finally induced politicians to support these measures. This illustrates one of the less dramatic, more modest ways that dissent brings about change. Dissenters are often a few steps ahead of their time and consequently are forced to wait for public opinion and political circumstances to catch up with them. Progressive activists such as Mother Jones, Florence Kelley, Jane Addams, Walter Rauschenbusch, and Eugene V. Debs had worked hard for years focusing public awareness on the need for such reforms, and now, within a few months and a few acts of Congress, change was rapidly coming to pass. Wilson's electoral strategy paid off. By promoting progressive legislation and campaigning to keep the country out of war, he won the votes of progressives, moderates, and anti-interventionists. The election was close, but Wilson eked out a victory.

In February 1917 the Germans announced that they were resuming unrestricted submarine warfare. Within days an American ship was torpedoed, and Wilson broke off diplomatic relations with Germany. And then on February 25 the British intercepted a telegram from the German government to Mexico that they passed on to Wilson. In it the German foreign secretary, Arthur Zimmermann, proposed an alliance with Mexico. If Mexico invaded the United States in the event of war between the U.S. and Germany, Mexico would regain the territories it had lost to the U.S. in 1848. Wilson was enraged. So too was the American public. Finally, on April 2 the president went to Congress and asked for a declaration of war. "It is a fearful thing," he said, "to lead this great, peaceful people . . . into the most terrible and disastrous of all wars." But to justify the sacrifice the war would entail, Wilson insisted that it would be a war to end all wars and that "the world must be made safe for democracy": "We have no selfish ends to serve. We desire no conquest, no dominion. . . . We are but one of the champions of the rights of mankind."[1] After four days of debate Congress voted in favor of the declaration.

It took nearly a year, however, before American troops began arriving in Europe in large enough numbers to make a difference. But by the spring of 1918, with hundreds of thousands of Americans finally deployed "over there," the tide finally turned. Although the Germans were bolstered by troops that had been fighting on the Eastern Front (after the Bolshevik Revolution in November 1917 Russia signed a separate peace treaty with Germany), the reinforcements were not enough to offset the arrival of the Americans. By the fall of 1918 an armistice was signed, and at the eleventh hour of the eleventh day of the eleventh month of 1918 the guns fell silent.

* * *

The war had an enormous impact on the home front, and that impact ushered in new attitudes about social relations, especially for women and African Americans, and it raised questions about the nature of American freedom and the meaning of democracy. All of this set in motion trends that fueled dissent and dominated political discourse for the rest of the century.

The large number of men entering the military created a labor shortage. This was a boon for workers, especially for minority groups that suffered discrimination. Millions of women landed better-paying jobs during the war as factory workers, agricultural workers, secretaries, nurses, and drivers. Some joined the army, mostly as nurses or secretaries. But although women experienced significant changes in their roles and enjoyed the salaries they earned, American involvement in the war was too brief for most of these changes to endure. As soon as the war was over, most jobs evaporated or were taken away from women and offered to returning veterans. Still, the war focused attention on women's rights and began to revolutionize the age-old assumptions about gender relationships and women's place in society.

African Americans too found that the war meant new opportunities. As the demand for workers increased in the all-important war-production industries, many companies sent agents into the Deep South to recruit black sharecroppers. By 1918 a "Great Migration" was well under way as hundreds of thousands of African Americans left their homes for jobs in the industrial plants of Chicago, Detroit, Cleveland, and other northern cities. As is usually the case in migrations of large populations there were both "push" and "pull" factors. The pull factor was the jobs and the wages beckoning from the North. The push factors, of course, were the Jim Crow laws, racial discrimination, and the constant fear of physical violence. This Great Migration to the "Promised Land" lasted far beyond the war. Indeed, the flow of African Americans northward swelled during the 1920s and 1930s and well beyond into the post–World War II era.

Many African Americans took W. E. B. Du Bois's advice to "forget about special grievances and close our ranks shoulder to shoulder with our own fellow white citizens . . . that are fighting for democracy"[2] and enlisted in the army. Their hope was, like African American soldiers who served in the Civil War, that they would be accepted more readily into American society if they proved themselves on the battle-field. Unfortunately such acceptance did not happen. The 367,000 who entered the military found themselves segregated and shunted mostly into quartermaster and labor regiments where they worked to supply white troops and performed the least desirable tasks; 42,000 did serve in combat battalions, but most did not.

Despite the patriotic efforts of African Americans during the war they continued to be faced with violent racism. There were forty-eight lynchings in 1917 and sixty-three in 1918, and these were *not* confined to the South. There were race riots in several northern cities. In 1917 in East St. Louis, Illinois, dozens of blacks were killed when employ-ers brought in African American workers in an effort to break a union. Thousands of blacks fervently protested against this outrage. They organized what they called a Silent Protest Parade, and on July 28, 1917, ten thousand African Americans marched down Fifth Avenue in New York City. "Mr. President," the signs they carried asked, "Why Not Make America Safe for Democracy?" White Americans were shocked at this bold display of militancy.

Shortly after the war in 1919 a major riot took place in Chicago. It was precipitated when whites drowned a black teenager who had inad-vertently crossed the invisible line segregating a Lake Michigan beach. The ensuing riot lasted for nearly a week and spread throughout the city. Five hundred people were injured and thirty-eight killed before the National Guard restored order. Lynchings and racial violence spread through other parts of the country well into the postwar period. In 1921 the worst of these disturbances took place when whites torched a black neighborhood in Tulsa, killing more than three hundred African Amer-icans. It was clear that the Great Migration was stirring up deep-seated fears and resistance to change on the part of many white Americans.

Still, despite persistent racism, for most African Americans the Great Migration offered hope and opportunity. Economically and psychologi-cally those who went north were certainly better off than those who stayed in the South. For many African Americans the opportunity to vote, to educate their children, and to be able to walk down a street without fear of being kidnapped or lynched was truly uplifting. By 1920 over half a million had moved north. Before the war 90 percent of America's black population lived below the Mason-Dixon line. After the war that percentage had fallen to 80 percent. And over the next three decades the percentage dropped even further as ever-larger numbers of African Americans abandoned the South.

* * *

The war, of course, had its protestors. In fact it was the most heavily protested war in American history up to that time, and it prompted many citizens to examine the nature of patriotism and what it means to be an American. Hundreds of thousands spoke out against the war, against the draft, and against Wilson's efforts to suppress dissent. Right from the beginning Wilson knew that it would not be easy to unite public opinion behind the war. He was also well aware that roughly 20 percent of Americans had German roots and were not keen on going to war against Germany, just as most Irish Americans (also about 20 percent of the population) were not keen on fighting on Britain's side. If anything, both groups favored Germany. And so the president established the Committee on Public Information, headed by George Creel, to shape public opinion, stifle antiwar opposition, and convince Americans that the war was necessary in order to preserve American principles. Creel hired advertising men and academics, journalists and artists, to depict Germans as the enemies of freedom and democracy. "Four Minute Men" were hired to give "spontaneous," four-minute, prowar speeches on street corners and in theaters. Posters were widely distributed depicting Germans as ruthless barbarians, apes, and monsters. One poster showed a caricature of a fiendish German soldier impaling a Belgian baby on his bayonet. Other posters portrayed attractive young women being ravished and brutalized by Germans. The kaiser was depicted as the "Beast of Berlin." Newspaper articles and short documentaries screened in movie theaters denounced Germans as a bloodthirsty race. By appealing to and manipulating the unconscious fears and angst that Sigmund Freud's psychological studies had uncovered, the Committee on Public Information elevated propaganda to an art.

The propaganda was successful. Anti-German sentiment became so intense that teaching the German language was banned, German books were removed from libraries (and in some cases burned), and German words and expressions were censured. Frankfurters became "hot dogs," hamburgers became "Salisbury steak" or "liberty sandwiches," sauerkraut became "liberty cabbage," and the German measles

became "liberty measles." The governor of Iowa announced that freedom of speech did not confer "the right to use a language other than the
language of the country."[3] Anti-German attitudes reached such intensity that German Americans were physically attacked, and some were
lynched. In one case a German American, Robert Prager, was hanged
from a street lamp in Illinois, his hands and feet tied with the remnants
of a shredded American flag.

So many Americans got into the patriotic spirit that it became a
sport to test other Americans whose patriotism was suspect to prove
their loyalty. Flag-waving mobs frequently forced alleged German sympathizers to march down the street repeatedly kissing the Stars and
Stripes. Congress also, in an attempt to promote patriotism and quash
mounting antiwar dissent, approved the Espionage and Sedition Acts in
1917 and 1918, respectively. Along with prohibiting spying and surveillance the Espionage Act also banned any attempt to interfere with the
draft (demonstrating at a draft office, encouraging men to dodge the
draft, or in any way aiding them in avoiding conscription or helping
them desert), as well as making disparaging "false statements" about
the military. Periodicals that were critical of the war or the government's policy in waging the war were banned from the mails. The Sedition Act prohibited any statements (printed or spoken) that could be
construed as critical of the administration, the military, or the war. It
condemned anyone who would "willfully utter, print, write, or publish
any disloyal, profane, scurrilous, or abusive language about the form
of government of the United States, or the Constitution of the United
States, or the military or naval forces of the United States, or the flag
of the United States . . . or shall willfully utter, print, write, or publish
any language intended to incite, provoke, or encourage resistance to
the United States, . . . or willfully advocate, teach, defend, or suggest the
doing of any of the acts or things in this section enumerated."[4] In 1918
alone more than two thousand American citizens were arrested under
the Sedition Act.

The Espionage and Sedition Acts reveal how deeply Washington saw
dissent as a threat. Many protestors found that denouncing the war got
them into a great deal of trouble. And they found that the civil liberties they believed were sacrosanct were not nearly as well protected as
they assumed. Ordinary Americans, Quakers, intellectuals, radicals,
many feminists, and some politicians spoke out adamantly against

the war and just as adamantly against official efforts to stifle dissent. Some of these people were public figures, most were unknown, many were arrested.

Before the war the Republican Robert M. La Follette had gained prominence as one of the most progressive and reform-minded politicians in the country. As governor of Wisconsin and later as U.S. senator, La Follette championed racial equality, women's suffrage, and the right of workers to organize unions. In 1912 he publicly supported the Democratic presidential candidate because of Wilson's commitment to social reform and the regulation of big business. However, he parted ways with the president in 1917 when Wilson called for war.

During the Senate debate on the declaration of war La Follette argued that there was something hypocritical about a war to promote democracy when our chief ally, Great Britain, was an imperialist monarchy—"with a hereditary ruler, with a hereditary House of Lords, with a hereditary landed system, with a limited and restricted suffrage for one class and a multiplied suffrage power for another, and with grinding industrial conditions for all the wageworkers"—that refused to give home rule to Ireland, India, and its other colonies. The war, he proclaimed, was being foisted on the American people. "The espionage bills, the conscription bills, and other forcible military measures . . . is the complete proof that those responsible for this war fear that it has no popular support."[5] La Follette, however, was only one of six senators who voted against the declaration. As he was leaving the Senate chamber, someone handed him a coil of rope, presumably so he could save the country the cost of a trial for treason by hanging himself. Still, he was not intimidated, and he kept up his criticism against the war and against the attempt to suppress antiwar dissent.

Six months later, in October 1917, La Follette delivered a blistering address in defense of free speech and dissent. "Since the declaration of war, the triumphant war press has pursued those Senators and Representatives who voted against war with malicious falsehood and recklessly libelous attacks, going to the extreme limit of charging them with treason against their country." There had been many attacks, he went on, against him personally and demands that he be expelled from the Senate. But such attacks were not just aimed at politicians but were also being directed at ordinary citizens in an attempt to coerce them into silence and acquiescence in an unjust war. "The mandate seems to have gone forth to the sovereign people of this country that they must be silent while those things are being done by their Government which most vitally concerns their well-being, their happiness, and their lives." This was deplorable. American citizens must not be "terrorized" in this way. He produced several affidavits of Americans being subjected to unlawful arrest merely for expressing opposition to the war. "Honest and law-abiding citizens of this country are being terrorized," he admonished, even though they have committed no crime. Throughout the nation "private residences are being invaded, loyal citizens of undoubted integrity and probity arrested, cross-examined, and the most sacred constitutional rights guaranteed to every American citizen are being violated." Of course, he conceded that citizens recognize that in time of war security measures are needed that might chip away at some civil liberties, but he emphasized, *the right to control their own Government according to constitutional forms is not one of the rights that the citizens of this country are called upon to surrender in time of war*" (La Follette's emphasis). When the country is at war, he went on, it is even more necessary to preserve this right than it is in time of peace. In wartime the American citizen

> must be most watchful of the encroachment of the military upon the civil power. He must beware of those precedents in support of arbitrary action by administration officials which, excused on the pleas of necessity in war time, become the fixed rule when the necessity has passed and normal conditions have been restored.
>
> More than all, the citizen and his representative in Congress in time of war must maintain his right of free speech. More than in times of peace it is necessary that the channels for free public discussion of governmental policies shall be open and unclogged.

The most important right the American people enjoy is the right "to discuss in an orderly way, frankly and publicly and without fear, from the platform and through the press, every important phase of this war; its causes, and manner in which it should be conducted, and the terms upon which peace should be made." And any attempt to stifle free speech, public discussion of the war, or even severe criticism of the administration's policies, is "a blow at the most vital part of our Government."[6]

Even former president Theodore Roosevelt was furious about Wilson's attempts to suppress dissent. When Wilson's supporters said it was wrong to criticize the president, especially in time of war, Roosevelt lashed out angrily. "To announce that there must be no criticism of the president," he said, "or that we are to stand by the president, right or wrong, is not only unpatriotic and servile, but is morally treasonable to the American public. Nothing but the truth should be spoken about him or anyone else. But it is even more important to tell the truth, pleasant or unpleasant, about him than about anyone else."[7]

But many of those who dared to "tell the truth, pleasant or unpleasant," found themselves in trouble with the law. In June 1918 Socialist Party leader Eugene V. Debs was arrested under the provisions of the Sedition Act for a scathing antiwar speech he gave in Canton, Ohio. "Wars throughout history," Debs reflected, "have been waged for conquest and plunder." When feudal lords in the Middle Ages sought to increase their domains, "they declared war upon one another. But they themselves did not go to war any more than the modern feudal lords, the barons of Wall Street go to war." It was the serfs, the peasants, who fought and died in the battles back then. "The poor, ignorant serfs had been taught . . . to believe that when their masters declared war upon one another, it was their patriotic duty to fall upon one another and to cut one another's throats for the profit and glory of the lords and barons who held them in contempt." This has not changed. Now, just as then, it is the master class that profits from war, the working class that dies in wars. "They have always taught and trained you to believe it to be your patriotic duty to go to war and to have yourselves slaughtered at their command. But in all the history of the world you, the people, have never had a voice in declaring war, and strange as it certainly appears, no war by any nation in any age has ever been declared by the people."[8]

The Great War, Debs insisted, is an imperialist war for the benefit of American businessmen and financiers—the Wall Street gentry—whom he likened to the Junkers, the autocratic Prussian ruling class that was the force behind German aggression. These "Wall Street Junkers" were lying about the war's goals when they say it is a war to make the world safe for American democracy. The war is really about profits, nothing

The Socialist Party leader Eugene V. Debs leaving the federal penitentiary in Atlanta, Georgia, on Christmas Day 1921. He had been imprisoned in 1918 under the Sedition Act for giving a speech against participation in the First World War. President Warren G. Harding commuted his sentence to time served in December 1921. "While there is a lower class," Debs declared, "I am in it; while there is a criminal element, I am of it; while there is a soul in prison, I am not free!" Photograph by Underwood & Underwood. (Pubic domain; courtesy Library of Congress)

else. They wrap themselves up in patriotism and intimidate the people by questioning the patriotism of anyone who does not wholeheartedly support the war. "These are the gentry who are today wrapped up in the American flag," Debs scoffed,

> who shout their claim from the housetops that they are the only patriots, and who have their magnifying glasses in hand, scanning the country for evidence of disloyalty, eager to apply the brand of treason to the men who dare to even whisper their opposition to Junker rule in the United Sates. No wonder Sam Johnson declared that "patriotism is the last refuge of the scoundrel." He must have had this Wall Street gentry in mind, or at least their prototypes, for in every age it has been the tyrant, the

oppressor and the exploiter who has wrapped himself in the cloak of patriotism, or religion, or both to deceive and overawe the people.

These deceivers are the real traitors, Debs insisted, not those who criticize the war, not those who stand up for liberty and justice. Those are the real patriots.[9]

Shortly after Debs delivered this speech, he was arrested, tried, and sentenced to ten years in prison. Along with his prison term he was stripped of his American citizenship. "I have been accused of obstructing the war," Debs said when he was permitted to speak to the jury before sentencing. "I admit it. Gentlemen, I abhor war. I would oppose war if I stood alone."[10] But then he also confessed that he believed in the Constitution. "Isn't it strange that we Socialists stand almost alone today in upholding and defending the Constitution of the United States? The revolutionary fathers who had been oppressed under king rule understood that free speech and the right of free assemblage by the people were fundamental principles in democratic government.... I believe in the right of free speech, in war as well as peace."[11]

At war's end Attorney General A. Mitchell Palmer suggested that Wilson commute Debs's sentence. Wilson refused to do so. Debs served nearly three years of his sentence, and despite losing his American citizenship, he was nominated as the Socialist Party's candidate for president in 1920 and conducted his entire campaign from behind bars. During the three years he was in prison, thousands of Americans (even those who abhorred Debs's socialist views) sent letters and petitions to the president and Congress calling for Debs (as well as others who had been jailed for antiwar dissent) to be pardoned. "A government that will deliberately take away the inalienable rights of natural born citizens," one woman wrote Wilson, "throttle free speech, institute espionage and intimidation systems, cannot be held in low enough contempt by its subjects."[12] Debs's views and imprisonment led to a vital and energetic national debate about the nature of free speech, the validity of the First Amendment, and how to balance national security needs with the fundamental rights guaranteed in the Bill of Rights—a debate that still rages in the United States. Wilson, however, was unimpressed and refused to pardon Debs. It was the new (Republican) president, Warren G. Harding, who released Debs from prison on Christmas morning 1921. Eventually, in 1976 (fifty years after Debs's death), Congress restored his citizenship.

Another prominent antiwar dissenter was Randolph Bourne. Bourne was a man of impressive intellect who suffered from severe physical deformity. Birth defects and spinal tuberculosis gave him the appearance of a hunchbacked dwarf. Yet he was an intellectual giant. By the time he graduated from Columbia, he was an influential spokesman for his generation, contributing articles to the *Atlantic*, the *New Republic*, the *Dial*, and *Seven Arts*, in which he encouraged the nation's youth to question conventional social roles, personal relationships, and American values. He also wrote essays criticizing corporate capitalism and condemning the Wilson administration's policy of suppressing dissent. His uncompromising opposition to America's entry into the Great War alienated so many of his contemporaries that he was fired from the *New Republic* and was put under surveillance by the Justice Department. Bourne could never accept President Wilson's conviction that the war would be the "war to end wars" or that it would "make the world safe for democracy," nor could he approve of the intellectuals who supported and condoned the war, especially those who wrote propaganda for Creel's Committee on Public Information. To Bourne, American participation in the war revealed that the United States, despite its deeply held belief in democracy, was no better than any nondemocratic nation.

Although Bourne's voice was silenced when he died at the age of thirty-two in the 1918 flu pandemic, his antiwar essays "War and the Intellectuals" and "War Is the Health of the State" remain two of the most articulate indictments of war—indictments that are as applicable to any war as they were to World War I. In these essays, especially the latter, Bourne analyzes the characteristics of the state, the psychology of a people at war, the nature of patriotism, and why it becomes necessary for the state to stifle dissent.

In "War and the Intellectuals" Bourne reproached the intellectuals and academics who supported the war or worked for the government or collaborated with the Creel committee in spreading prowar, anti-German propaganda. "The American intellectuals, in their preoccupation with reality," he wrote, "seem to have forgotten that the real enemy is War rather than imperial Germany." It is wrong to try to convince

Americans, as Wilson has tried to do, that the war is "a holy crusade. What shall we do with leaders who tell us that we go to war in moral spotlessness or who make 'democracy' synonymous with a republican form of government? There is work to be done in still shouting that all the revolutionary by-products will not justify the war or make war anything else than the most noxious complex of all the evils that afflict men."[13]

But it is in Bourne's posthumous essay "War Is the Health of the State" that he offers the most profound analysis of the historical role and the psychological basis of war. Bourne is writing about the Great War, but his conclusions can be applied to all wars. "Wartime brings the ideal of the State out into very clear relief," Bourne observed, "and reveals attitudes and tendencies that were hidden. In times of peace the sense of the State flags in a republic that is not militarized. For war is essentially the health of the State. The ideal of the State is that within its territory its power and influence should be universal. As the Church is the medium for the spiritual salvation of man, so the State is thought of as the medium for his political salvation." When a state goes to war, it gathers power and energy from the people's urgent need to feel protected, to feel one with the state. Bourne's definition of the state is that it "is the organization of the herd to act offensively or defensively against another herd similarly organized. The more terrifying the occasion for defense, the closer will become the organization and the more coercive the influence upon each member of the herd. War sends the current of purpose and activity flowing down to the lowest level of the herd."[14] During peacetime people go about their lives without a sense of their connection to the state, but war awakens them to this connection, arouses their sense of loyalty, and makes them feel empowered.

The people do not, however, have power. People in a democracy believe they have a voice in the operation of their government, but they have had no say whatsoever in the policies that have led to war. Those policies are exclusively in the domain of the executive branch of government. When it comes to foreign policy, "the Government, with no mandate from the people, without consultation of the people, conducts all the negotiations, the backing and filling, the menaces and explanations, which slowly bring it into collision with some other Government, and gently and irresistibly slides the country into war." The executive officer of a nation (whether president, prime minister, chancellor, or king) convincingly puts forward moral reasons for the necessity of war: that the enemy is evil or that going to war will create a better future. Such arguments win over the people and their representatives. "The result is that, even in those countries where the business of declaring war is theoretically in the hands of representatives of the people, no legislature has ever been known to decline the request of an Executive, which has conducted all foreign affairs in utter privacy and irresponsibility, that it order the nation into battle." It is clear to Bourne that "all foreign policy, the diplomatic negotiations which produce or forestall war, are equally the private property of the Executive part of the Government, and are equally exposed to no check whatever from popular bodies, or the people voting as a mass themselves." Even when people realize this, something magical happens when war is declared. Suddenly, in a wave of patriotic fervor, "the mass of the people," even the intellectual classes, "through some spiritual alchemy, become convinced that they have willed and executed the deed themselves. They then, with the exception of a few malcontents, proceed to allow themselves to be regimented, coerced, . . . and turned into a solid manufactory of destruction toward" the enemy.[15]

War is the health of the state because it "automatically sets in motion throughout society those irresistible forces for uniformity, for passionate cooperation with the Government in coercing into obedience the minority groups and individuals which lack the larger herd sense. The machinery of government sets and enforces the drastic penalties; the minorities are either intimidated into silence, or brought slowly around by a subtle process of persuasion which may seem to them really to be converting them." At this stage inevitably "minorities are rendered sullen, and some intellectual opinion bitter and satirical. But in general, the nation in wartime attains a uniformity of feeling, a hierarchy of values culminating at the undisputed apex of the State ideal, which could not possibly be produced through any other agency than war. . . . Loyalty— or mystic devotion to the State—becomes the major imagined human value."[16] Any critical thinking, any questioning of the meaning of loyalty, is considered treason.

Perspicaciously Bourne analyzes (evidently influenced by Freud) the "filial mysticism" that the citizenry invests in the state. When a people go to war, there is a deep-seated need for security. People want protection. And just as they looked to their fathers and mothers for protection when they were children, now in wartime they look to the state for protection. Thus the state is strengthened.

> It is not for nothing that one's State is still thought of as Father or Motherland, that one's relation towards it is conceived in terms of family affection. The war has shown that nowhere under the shock of danger have these primitive childlike attitudes failed to assert themselves again, as much in this country as anywhere. If we have not the intense Father-sense of the German who worships his Vaterland, at least in Uncle Sam we have a symbol of protecting, kindly authority, and in the many Mother-posters of the Red Cross, we see how easily in the more tender functions of war service, the ruling organization is conceived in family terms. A people at war have become in the most literal sense obedient, respectful, trustful children again, full of that naïve faith in the all-wisdom and all-power of the adult who takes care of them, imposes his mild but necessary rule upon them and in whom they lose their responsibility and anxieties. In this recrudescence of the child, there is great comfort, and a certain influx of power.[17]

And so the state is our protector, and any criticism, any dissent, is reviled and treated as treason. "In this great herd-machinery, dissent is like sand in the bearings." People seek unanimity of opinion. When everyone is pulling together, there is a deeper sense of security. Unity means security. "Any interference with that unity turns the whole vast impulse towards crushing it. Dissent is speedily outlawed, and the Government, backed by the significant classes and those who . . . identify themselves with them, proceeds against the outlaws. . . . The herd becomes divided into the hunters and the hunted, and war-enterprise becomes not only a technical game but a sport as well."[18]

Much of Bourne's writings speak directly to the Committee on Public Information's propaganda work and the laws restricting freedom of speech and press. Bourne himself, had he not died in December 1918, might very well have been imprisoned, as Debs was, under the Sedition Act. "War Is the Health of the State" is one of the most eloquent and intelligent analyses of the relationship between the citizen and the state. Along with Thoreau's "Resistance to Civil Government" and Martin Luther King, Jr.'s "Letter from Birmingham Jail" it is indispensable reading for dissenters or anyone interested in dissent.

La Follette, Debs, and Bourne were three well-known dissenters who denounced the war. There were also hundreds of thousands of ordinary Americans, workers, immigrants, political radicals, feminists, and middle-class citizens who protested in a variety of ways against U.S. involvement in the Great War and against the efforts on the part of the government to suppress dissent by restricting free speech. In Minnesota thousands of farmers attended public gatherings organized by socialists to protest the war and the draft. In Wisconsin thousands also participated in antiwar/antidraft demonstrations. There were antiwar parades in Boston in the summer of 1917. In local elections that year antiwar socialist candidates made a remarkably good showing—in New York State, for example, ten socialists were elected to the state assembly, and the socialist mayoral candidate in New York City received 22 percent of the vote.

Americans protested against the war even though they risked imprisonment under the provisions of the Espionage and Sedition Acts. One citizen was sent to jail when she proclaimed that "the government is for the profiteers," and another was arrested for calling President Wilson "a wooden-headed son of a bitch."[19] A socialist printer in Philadelphia, Charles Schenck, was sentenced to six months in prison for printing and distributing antiwar and antidraft leaflets. Sixty-five thousand Americans refused to serve in the armed forces on the grounds that they were conscientious objectors, while thousands more refused to register for the draft. In South Dakota Fred Fairchild was imprisoned for a year after publicly proclaiming that if drafted, he would not serve. "They could shoot me, but they could not make me fight," he said.[20] Underscoring Bourne's claim that in order to stifle dissent, "the herd becomes divided into the hunters and the hunted," more than one hundred thousand Americans joined the vigilante American Protective League (APL) to root out "slackers" and subversives and anyone who criticized the war or the president or refused to buy liberty bonds. They intercepted people's mail and tapped their telephones. APL vigilantes proudly claimed that they had uncovered three million disloyal Americans. Sometimes speaking out proved deadly. The IWW labor organizer Frank Little gave an antiwar speech urging American workers to resist the draft and to refuse to fight in the war. Shortly afterward six masked men dragged him from his home in Butte, Montana, and hanged him from a railroad trestle. They fastened a sign to his body proclaiming, "Agitator Called Our Troops 'Scabs in Uniform' and Denounced American Government."[21]

* * *

After the war Americans faced an uncertain future. Many believed that getting involved in the war was a disaster. The United States had not heeded George Washington's admonition to stay out of European affairs. The lesson was clear—the United States must remain neutral, must stay within the confines of the Western Hemisphere. The United States did not ratify the Versailles Treaty, nor did it join the League of Nations—dashing Wilson's naïve vision that the war would prove to be the war to end all wars. The Bolshevik Revolution raised the specter of revolution in the United States; the fear that communism might spread to these shores frightened millions of Americans, yet at the same time the Russian Revolution, with its vision of a working-class utopia, also inspired many American workers to join the struggle for better wages and working conditions. As a result, in 1919 a wave of labor unrest coupled with a frightening Red Scare swept over the country. Americans soon discovered that it was not going to be easy to return to the old prewar days.

Wilson's idealistic comments about fighting for political and economic freedom gave American workers the misleading impression that the president would actively support workers' rights, but he did not. In January 1919 shipyard workers walked off their jobs in Seattle. This precipitated a general strike of one hundred thousand workers. By February the city had ground to a halt. Committees of strikers kept some essential city services running, but most had stopped. The strike finally ended when the mayor called in federal troops. Strikes spread around the country in a variety of industries. There were strikes of textile workers, telephone operators, policemen, coal miners, and even actors. In some labor disputes the conservative American Federation of Labor, despite its fear of radicalism, combined with the socialist Industrial Workers of the World in an uneasy alliance.

Toward the end of the year the Boston Police Department went on strike for higher wages. When the officers walked off the job, violence and crime escalated, and public opinion turned against the striking policemen. Governor Calvin Coolidge, proclaiming that "there is no right to strike against the public safety, by anybody, anywhere, anytime,"²² fired the entire department and sent in the National Guard to take over police duties and restore order.

The most momentous of the strikes was the steel strike that started in Chicago in September and spread to Pittsburgh. Workers demanded an eight-hour day, increased wages, and union recognition. More than three hundred thousand steelworkers, many of them immigrants, participated in the strike. The owners countered by manipulating and inflaming native-born steelworkers' anti-immigrant prejudice, which helped management break the strike.

Approximately four million workers participated in a total of four thousand strikes in 1919. Labor unrest unsettled the public, and just as in the period after the Haymarket affair middle-class Americans equated unionism with radicalism, anarchism, socialism, and communism. To be sure, the radical IWW participated in the strikes, but most workers only demanded better wages and hours, not socialism. They simply wanted to reform the system, not overthrow it. Still, the strikes exacerbated the fear of communism.

And then came a wave of terrorist attacks. A few months after the mayor of Seattle had called for federal troops to crush the general strike, a package containing a bomb was sent to his residence. (It was discovered before it exploded.) Radicals targeted other politicians and public figures. An anarchist planted a bomb on the doorstep of Attorney General A. Mitchell Palmer in Washington, DC. (Unfortunately for the bomber the only person he killed was himself when the bomb exploded prematurely.) Anarchists also attempted to assassinate John D. Rockefeller and Supreme Court Justice Oliver Wendell Holmes, Jr.

The nation was jolted. Americans, unaware that there was little connection between anarchists and communists, believed that violent radicals were the vanguard of a worldwide communist conspiracy to topple the United States. Attorney General Palmer formed the General Intelligence Division within the Department of Justice and appointed the young J. Edgar Hoover as its director. Starting in November Palmer seized the opportunity to combat dissent and authorized hundreds of raids against suspected radicals. In multiple cities around the country Palmer's agents illegally broke into people's homes in the middle of the night and arrested them. Palmer targeted socialists, anarchists, communists, and immigrants from eastern Europe and Russia. One of the attorney general's goals was to destroy the Union of Russian Workers;

another was to destroy the IWW. Both goals were accomplished. Thousands of leftists, usually beaten up in the process, were arrested. On a single night in January 1920 more than four thousand suspected "reds" were arrested in coordinated raids in thirty-three American cites. Socialists who had been elected to state office were expelled from their seats. More than 250 radical aliens, including Emma Goldman, were deported. The Palmer Raids also fanned the flames of intolerance as many Americans eagerly joined in the "red hunt" with as much gusto as they had in the anti-German frenzy of the previous three years. Vigilante bands singled out "radical terrorists," harassed them, beat them, and in a few cases, lynched them. Patriotic organizations sprouted in the fertile soil of the anticommunist crusade (among them the United States Flag Organization and the American Legion), dedicated to promoting the "American way" and ferreting out subversives.

Of course not all Americans succumbed to the hysteria. Many liberals, intellectuals, and legal scholars, as well as ordinary citizens, protested against the abuses of civil liberties and the outrageous assault on the Bill of Rights. Alarmed at this attack on the Constitution, Crystal Eastman and Roger Baldwin founded the American Civil Liberties Union "to defend and preserve the individual rights and liberties guaranteed to every person in this country by the Constitution and laws of the United States."[23] By the spring of 1920 it was transparently clear to increasing numbers of people that the Palmer Raids were a serious abuse of civil liberties. Palmer's zeal (and the fact that he had one eye on the 1920 presidential nomination) led him to overstep so many bounds that the Red Scare finally imploded. Assistant Secretary of State Louis Post became critical of Palmer and insisted that legal rights must be provided for the detainees, and for the remainder of the year most of the six thousand who were arrested were gradually released. Attorney General Palmer also lost credibility when he announced that radical terrorists were planning a massive uprising on May 1, 1920. He put police forces around the nation on high alert, but nothing happened.

The Red Scare had peaked. Still, despite the fact that the sweeping arrests came to an end, the scare persisted, as two Italian immigrants, Nicola Sacco and Bartolomeo Vanzetti, were about to experience. In April 1920 a security guard and a paymaster were killed during a holdup at a South Braintree, Massachusetts, shoe factory. Soon thereafter

Sacco and Vanzetti were arrested for the crime. It was obvious to most observers that the men were accused of the crime because they were anarchists and because they were immigrants. Both men were associated with the followers of the Italian anarchist Luigi Galleani, who was suspected of being involved with the bombing of the attorney general's residence in June 1919, and both had avoided the draft during the war, facts that further doomed them in the eyes of the public.

The trial itself was a travesty of justice. No real evidence was offered as to their guilt, witnesses changed their testimony, while others verified the defendants' alibis. The biased judge referred to them as "those anarchist bastards" and instructed the jury that although Vanzetti "may not have actually committed the crime attributed to him, [he] is nevertheless culpable, because he is the enemy of our existing institutions."[24] Throughout the proceedings it was apparent that the two men were being railroaded because of their political beliefs and their nationality. They were convicted and sentenced to the electric chair. For the next seven years, as their lawyers appealed the case, a worldwide campaign for their release was waged. Liberals, intellectuals, lawyers, and writers in the United States and Europe, including Dorothy Parker, Edna St. Vincent Millay, John Dos Passos, H. G. Wells, and George Bernard Shaw, protested the verdict and called for a new trial. As the appeals process wound down, tens of thousands of protestors around the world took to the streets in massive demonstrations and vigils against the impending executions. The protests were so compelling that the governor of Massachusetts postponed the executions and appointed a special panel to review the case. However, when the panel upheld the verdict, the executions were finally carried out in August 1927. Even then the protests did not end. There were demonstrations and riots in London, Paris, and Germany, as well as in the United States. In the end, the Sacco and Vanzetti case established the model for future dissenters to organize vigils, protest marches, and demonstrations demanding the release of other condemned prisoners who were deemed wrongly convicted political prisoners. "I have had to suffer," Vanzetti said in April 1927, "for things that I am guilty of. I am suffering because I am a radical, and indeed I am a radical; I have suffered because I am an Italian, and indeed I am an Italian."[25]

* * *

When the United States emerged from the Great War, it was on the verge of becoming a global power. The U.S. was the world's largest creditor, American heavy industries were dominating world markets, and American diplomats had an important influence on shaping the peace. And yet the experience of the war turned Americans inward and fostered the desire to find security in isolation from the world. It was as though the United States was rejecting the invitation to become a major player on the world's stage. The American reaction to the Bolshevik Revolution further underscored the fear of engagement with the world. A Red Scare swept over the land as fearful Americans sought to flush out all those who would destroy the American way of life. The Palmer Raids and the Sacco and Vanzetti case heralded one of the most pervasive and pernicious trends of the next decade: intolerance.

Antiwar dissent, as well as the protests against the government's efforts to crush dissent and radicalism, was a significant legacy of the war. The tumultuous period saw changes in the way dissent was expressed and heard and responded to. Thousands of Americans found the courage to protest, and they found many ways to do so. Some refused to register for the draft. Some left the country. Some protested against the overzealous patriots who were undermining the Constitution by forming the American Civil Liberties Union to guard against infractions of the Bill of Rights. Some went to prison. Workers, pacifists, Quakers, and prominent public figures such as Republican Senator Robert M. La Follette, Socialist Party leader Eugene V. Debs, and intellectuals such as Randolph Bourne and Helen Keller spoke out eloquently against the war and against the curbing of civil liberties. When Sacco and Vanzetti were convicted of murder, hundreds of thousands of people took to the streets protesting an abuse of the judicial system.

The war had come to an end and the protests with it, but the legacy of the protests ensured that dissent was more deeply embedded than ever in the American consciousness. For the rest of the twentieth century American dissenters continued to draw inspiration from the protesters of 1917–1920.

CHAPTER 16

Traditionalism Collides with Modernism

No woman can call herself free who does not own and control her body. No woman can call herself free until she can choose consciously whether she will or will not be a mother.
—Margaret Sanger, 1920

Despite the booming economy of the 1920s, disillusion, insecurity, and uncertainty began to eat away at the nation's psyche. The war had been a terrible shock. How could God have let it happen? The experience of the war—the carnage, the devastation, the surfacing of such inhumane brutality—was a profound challenge to all traditional values. The belief in God, the belief in progress, even the belief in science all came under attack. Darwin's theory of evolution had laid bare the animal origins of humans, Nietzsche's famous dictum that "God is dead" struck at the heart of religious faith, Freud's analysis of the psyche and the tremendous hold the unconscious mind has on human behavior undermined the belief in human reason and rationality, and Einstein's theory of relativity and Heisenberg's uncertainty principle showed that even science was open to question. All this buttressed the existential philosophers' view that there is no meaning to life. In the 1920s it seemed that there was no certainty, no security, nothing to hold onto. Many Americans willingly embraced these modern ideas, but many others were aghast and steadfastly strove to return to a bygone, simpler era, when belief was not challenged. It is this conflict between a world of accelerating technological advances, automation, consumerism, changing social and gender relationships, and revolutionary philosophies challenging the existence of God on one side and the deeply entrenched conservatism that resisted the new trends on the other side that defined the decade. The Roaring Twenties, dubbed "The Jazz Age" by writer F. Scott Fitzgerald, was a vibrant, exciting decade characterized by this clash between traditionalism and modernism. It was an age of bifurcation. Dissent was everywhere. Liberal dissenters denounced the forces of reaction, while conservative dissenters denounced the forces that were taking the United States in a direction they did not want to go.

Warren G. Harding, the new president, promised to return the country to normalcy. But normalcy was irretrievably in the past. While Europe was struggling to rebuild, the United States was experiencing an astounding rate of economic growth. Business expanded, exports rose, unemployment declined, wages increased, and Americans had a voracious appetite for new consumer products. And the most important product that drove all sectors of the economy from steel to petroleum, road building to home construction in new suburbs, was Henry Ford's Model T. Aviation, advertising, radio broadcasting, and the cinema all boomed in the 1920s, while Americans filled jazz clubs to listen to African American music and dance halls to dance the trendy Charleston. And although the Eighteenth Amendment prohibited the sale of alcohol, rural bootleggers as well as urban crime bosses such as Al Capone provided booze illegally to anyone who wanted it. Americans flocked in huge numbers to speakeasies, where they consumed vast quantities of bootleg liquor. Nearly every American was a lawbreaker. The one good thing about Prohibition, as humorist Will Rogers reportedly quipped, was that it was better than no alcohol at all.

* * *

After more than a century of protest women found their horizons expanding. In most respects women's position in society and especially in the family did not change drastically, but employment opportunities were opening up, and the "new woman" was beginning to emerge.

Socially women's role *did* change. After gaining the right to vote many young women rejected the old Victorian ways of thinking and acting and dressing and adopted a new, confrontational style. They discarded the restricting clothing their mothers had worn—the Victorian dresses that covered all parts of the body—in favor of knee-length, close-fitting, seductively suggestive dresses. They wore shoes with buckles intentionally left unbuckled so that the flaps would strike the ground as they walked, thereby calling attention to themselves (thus the term *flapper*). Underscoring women's equality with men, they sought ways to present a more boyish figure, wore undergarments to flatten breasts, bobbed their hair short, and copied behaviors that were traditionally reserved for males. They smoked in public (a behavior that before the war would have horrified most people), went on their own or with other women to dance halls and speakeasies where they danced wildly, flirted openly, spoke candidly about sex, and acted in ways aimed at highlighting their liberation.

Despite all the looseness and apparent independence, women's freedom was somewhat illusory. Although large numbers of women, especially in cities such as New York, were employed, they were not earning enough to support themselves. Either they worked low-paying menial and service jobs—secretaries, sales clerks, telephone operators—or where they competed with men for teaching jobs or managerial work, they did not receive equal wages. In banks, business offices, department stores, law firms, and schools, women worked side by side with men but were paid at a much lower rate. When women protested, they were told that men received more because they had families to support. Some women urged unions to take up the cause, but union leaders turned their backs on their pleas. The basic assumption pervading society was that men needed to make more than women and that a woman's earnings were supplemental family income.

The upshot was that despite women's earnings, they were not self-sufficient. They were still dependent on men. Married women depended on their husband's income. Single women usually lived at home, where they did not have to pay rent. It was clear, as the English writer Virginia Woolf put it in *A Room of One's Own*, that women would never be completely emancipated until they were economically independent of men. Until they could afford to support themselves, until they could afford a room of their own, women would never be free. Women had been jubilant when the Nineteenth Amendment was ratified, but their experience in the 1920s revealed that the right to vote was not enough to ensure equality. Feminists, led by Alice Paul, resolved to do something about this. In 1923 Paul introduced the Equal Rights Amendment, which would guarantee full equality under the law, and began a campaign to force Congress to consider it. It was a straightforward statement—"Equality of rights under the law shall not be denied or abridged by the United States or by any state on account of sex"—but it was voted down.[1] Paul and the National Women's Party, as well as many other groups, continued to push for passage of the amendment for decades.

One of the leading activists of the era was Margaret Sanger. Earlier in the century Sanger had been involved with the Socialist Party and the IWW. She also regularly associated with Eugene V. Debs, Emma Goldman, Max Eastman, John Reed, and the Bohemian social critics of Greenwich Village. A committed feminist, Sanger was especially concerned with reproductive rights and the legal restrictions on birth control that posed a life-threatening danger, especially for poor immigrant women. In 1912, she began writing a column in the socialist *New York Call*, "What Every Girl Should Know," seeking to educate women on matters of sexual health. One of her columns on venereal disease got her in trouble with the censors, but she pressed on. She also worked in a women's health clinic on the Lower East Side, where she was exposed on a daily basis to poor women seeking medical aid for botched abortions. Most of the patients sought advice on how to avoid pregnancy, but federal law prohibited the dissemination of birth-control information. The Comstock Law (1873), for example, forbade sending birth-control information through the mail, while other laws stipulated that even members of the medical profession were not allowed to give verbal advice to patients about birth control. One day, Sanger later recalled, an immigrant woman named Sadie Sachs came into the clinic to receive treatment for a hemorrhage resulting from an illegal abortion. When she was about to be released, she begged the physician in charge to tell her how to avoid becoming pregnant. They were a poor family, she said, but as soon as she would return home, her husband would want to have sex, and they simply could not afford another mouth to feed. The doctor flippantly replied that Sachs should tell her husband "to sleep on the roof."[2] Sanger was taken aback but kept silent. Some time later Sadie Sachs returned to the clinic after another bungled back-alley abortion. This time, however, she died, and Margaret Sanger vowed that she would never again remain silent.

In 1914 Sanger launched a radical feminist magazine, the *Woman Rebel*, for the sole purpose of advancing women's rights, especially reproductive rights. The masthead of the periodical announced "No Gods, No Masters," and each issue provided explicit information on birth control and contained articles proclaiming women's right to control their own bodies. Within a few months Sanger was arrested for violating the Comstock Law, but during her trial she jumped bail and fled to England. When she returned to the United States, she went on a speaking tour to raise money and generate publicity for her cause. Charges against her were eventually dropped, and in 1916 she opened

The activist, socialist, and feminist Margaret Sanger, December 31, 1921. "No woman can call herself free who does not own and control her body. No woman can call herself free until she can choose consciously whether she will or will not be a mother." Photograph by Underwood & Underwood. (Public domain; courtesy Library of Congress)

a birth-control clinic in Brooklyn. She was arrested again and this time spent a month in jail. By the time Sanger founded the American Birth Control League in 1921, she and her supporters had enough influence that Congress passed a law that permitted *a physician* to offer birth-control advice if medical reasons warranted. This was only a partial victory, but Sanger was astute enough to capitalize on it and make it work even better for the cause. She saw it as an opportunity to increase the number of women physicians in the United States. In 1923 she opened a clinic staffed with female doctors and eventually set up clinics in other cities throughout the country where birth control became available to anyone who wanted it. Throughout the decade the demand for female doctors increased, and more women chose to enter medical school. In 1939 Sanger founded the Birth Control Federation of America, the forerunner of the Planned Parenthood Federation of America, and before her death in 1966 she was instrumental in the research and development of the birth-control pill. Although she embraced controversial views about eugenics that have been rightly criticized, Sanger was America's most successful proponent of reproductive rights.

For Sanger birth control was a vital feminist issue. The right to vote was not enough. Women would never be fully free until they had control over their own bodies. If they did not, their lives would continue to be dictated by men. When would a woman have time to pursue her own educational and creative goals if she was perpetually pregnant and forced into the role of caring for one child after another? If that was what a woman wanted, that was fine—as long as it was the path she chose. But if it was not what she wanted, then she *must*, according to Sanger, be free to choose the path she envisions. The only way to achieve this is to have complete reproductive control. Sanger was not in favor of abortion per se. She argued that if birth control was available to the public, then the abortion rate would fall drastically. Contraception was a way to avoid abortion. There have always been ways for educated and upper-class women to gain access to contraceptives, because of their privileged position in society. But it was the poor and immigrants who did not know how to acquire the information, and as a result "women of the impoverished strata of society" are forced to "violate those laws of their inner beings which tell them not to bring children into the world to live in want, disease and general misery. They break the first law of nature, which is that of self preservation. Bound by false morals, enchained by false conceptions of religion, hindered by false laws, they endure until the pressure becomes so great that morals, religion and laws alike fail to restrain them. Then they for a brief respite resort to the surgeon's instruments [abortion]."[3]

Women must protest. They must "assert themselves upon this fundamental right. . . . These laws were made by men and have been instruments of martyrdom and death for unnumbered thousands of women. Women now have the opportunity to sweep them into the trash heap." It is only by making birth control available that motherhood can become the fulfilling experience it should be. "When motherhood becomes the fruit of a deep yearning, not the result of ignorance or accident," Sanger wrote optimistically in 1920, "its children will become the foundation of a new race. There will be no killing of babies in the womb by abortion, nor through neglect in foundling homes, nor will there be infanticide. Neither will children die by inches in mills and factories. No man will dare to break a child's life upon the wheel of toil."[4]

Along with birth control women activists also continued to push the federal government for anti-child-labor legislation, safer workplaces, an eight-hour day, and other such reforms, but with the suffering wrought by the Great War still foremost in people's minds, thousands of American women joined pacifist organizations. The Woodrow Wilson Foundation, for example, sought to carry on the former president's idealistic goal of ending war by encouraging and giving grants of money to "the liberal forces of mankind throughout the world . . . who intend to promote peace by the means of justice."[5] And the Carnegie Endowment for International Peace also set up endowment funds to finance those who came up with plans "to hasten the abolition of war."[6] One of the leading organizations was the Women's International League for Peace and Freedom (WILPF). Under the leadership of Jane Addams and Carrie Chapman Catt the crux of its campaign was to lobby Congress to apply for U.S. membership in the League of Nations or, failing that, to create another such organization that would promote world peace. The WILPF was actively opposed to the National Defense Act of 1920, which provided for the maintenance of a standing army of 280,000 men. The way to prevent war, the WILPF maintained, was not through military preparedness but through being involved in global diplomacy, nipping disputes in the bud before they became international crises, and through complete disarmament. Because of its antiwar position the WILPF was accused by right-wing critics of being a communist-run front. Some conservatives even came up with a color-coded radicalism chart showing how "red" the individual members of the WILPF were. Even Henry Ford joined in the red-baiting by publishing in the *Dearborn Independent* in 1924 the "Spider Web Chart," which purportedly showed the web-like connections between the WILPF and various communist and socialist organizations. As a result of these attacks, the WILPF failed in its campaign to convince the United States to join the League of Nations, but its influence was considerable—considerable enough that Secretary of State Frank B. Kellogg signed (even though he regarded it as meaningless) the Kellogg-Briand Pact renouncing war as an instrument of international relations.

* * *

Women, of course, were not the only activists in the Roaring Twenties. Americans from all classes and political persuasions energetically spoke out for causes they deemed vital for the public good. Dissenters of the left—women and men, blacks and whites—protested racism, rampant consumerism, and the business-as-usual attitudes that permeated the nation in the aftermath of the Great War, while dissenters of the right protested the rapid societal changes that were too radical. Conservatives, for example, appalled at what they considered the libertine behavior of the "new woman," regularly harassed and ostracized women who adopted the flapper lifestyle.

One influential way that dissenting positions were promulgated was through literature. Many notable American writers and intellectuals were disheartened by the return to "normalcy." H. L. Mencken, Ernest Hemingway, F. Scott Fitzgerald, Gertrude Stein, Sinclair Lewis, John Dos Passos, and Eugene O'Neill were among those who criticized American materialism. From blistering satires and parodies to more subtle commentaries and poignant stories about what it means to be an American, scores of writers expressed their disillusionment with the United States. Some, such as Stein and Hemingway, were so disillusioned that they moved to Paris. Creative artists, these expatriates believed, were nurtured and valued in Europe, whereas the crass, stultifying materialism of the United States crushed the human spirit and poisoned creativity. Hemingway in *The Sun Also Rises* and *A Farewell to Arms* portrayed characters wrecked by the meaningless horrors of war and the vagaries of life; F. Scott Fitzgerald in *The Great Gatsby* described people caught up in soul-destroying materialism. The heroes of so many of the "Lost Generation's" novels had grown up, as Fitzgerald put it in *This Side of Paradise*, "to find all Gods dead, all wars fought, all faiths in man shaken."[7]

One of the most popular writers of the decade was Sinclair Lewis, who specialized in novels satirizing small-town middle-class America and chamber of commerce "boosterism." Two of his most successful novels, *Main Street* and *Babbitt*, were exposés of the smug provincialism that permeated the United States. Lewis's characters were utterly conventional and banal; they were self-righteous bigots who strove only for material goods, spoke in clichés and platitudes, and never came up with an original thought. Many Americans saw themselves in the pages of Lewis's novels but, to Lewis's dismay, did not realize they were being parodied.

Even more scathing in ridiculing middle-class American values was the newspaperman H. L. Mencken. Mencken was the ultimate curmudgeon. He took on nearly every aspect of the status quo and did so with scurrilous, outrageous humor (that bordered on libel) but equally remarkable perceptiveness. The only things Mencken valued were free speech and critical thinking because "the most dangerous man, to any government is the man who is able to think things out for himself, without regard to the prevailing superstitions and taboos. Almost inevitably he comes to the conclusion that the government he lives under is dishonest, insane and intolerable."[8] Everything about America—Democrats, Republicans, socialists, politicians, the common man, women, Victorian morality, democracy, religion, prohibition—were targets of his ridicule. However, as Mencken himself observed, "it is inaccurate to say that I hate everything. I am strongly in favor of common sense, common honesty, and common decency. This makes me forever ineligible for public office."[9]

In the magazine Mencken founded, the *American Mercury*, and thousands of newspaper articles he described Americans as unsophisticated, uncultured idiots. Americans never looked deeper than the surface. They were the most gullible people in the world, blindly believing everything politicians and advertisers told them. Labeling them the "booboisie," Mencken frequently declared that no one ever lost money betting on the stupidity of the American people.

As for democracy, which Mencken defined as the "pathetic belief in the collective wisdom of individual ignorance,"[10] he admitted that at least it is "the most charming form of government ever devised by man" and should not be dismissed out of hand. Still, it is important to keep in mind that democracy "is based upon propositions that are palpably not true and what is not true, as everyone knows, is always immensely more fascinating and satisfying to the vast majority of men than what is true." The average American believes in democracy, Mencken wrote, because he

> gets a feeling that he is really important to the world—that he is genuinely running things. Out of his maudlin herding after rogues and mountebanks there comes to him a sense of vast and mysterious power—which is what makes archbishops, police sergeants, the grand goblins of the Ku Klux and other such magnificoes happy. And out of it there comes, too, a conviction that he is somehow wise, that his views are taken seriously by his betters—which is what makes United States Senators, fortune tellers and Young Intellectuals happy. Finally, there comes out of it a glowing consciousness of a high duty triumphantly done which is what makes hangmen and husbands happy.

But Mencken gets more serious when he attacks what he considers a most dangerous tendency in a democracy—during times of a national crisis, when a democracy's natural instinct is to stifle dissent. Democracy is "a self-limiting disease," Mencken contends, but even worse it is "self-devouring":

> One cannot observe it objectively without being impressed by its curious distrust of itself—its apparently ineradicable tendency to abandon its whole philosophy at the first sign of strain. I need not point to what happens invariably in democratic states when the national safety is menaced. All the great tribunes of democracy, on such occasions, convert themselves, by a process as simple as taking a deep breath, into despots of an almost fabulous ferocity. Lincoln, [Theodore] Roosevelt and Wilson come instantly to mind. . . . Democracy always seems bent upon killing the thing it theoretically loves. I have rehearsed some of its operations against liberty, the very cornerstone of its political metaphysic. It not only wars upon the thing itself; it even wars upon mere academic advocacy of it. I offer the spectacle of Americans jailed for reading the Bill of Rights. . . . Try to imagine monarchy jailing subjects for maintaining the divine right of Kings! Or Christianity damning a believer for arguing that Jesus Christ was the Son of God![11]

Mencken is here echoing Randolph Bourne's criticism of the "herd mentality" in his essay "War Is the Health of the State"—by trying to root out dissent, democracy is violating its core principle, the principle of liberty that is vital to its very existence.

African American writers and intellectuals joined the chorus of voices that increasingly criticized American society and values. And, of course, they brought a racial perspective to the discourse. Marcus Garvey, a Jamaican émigré who came to the United States in 1916, had a vital impact on getting African Americans to rethink how to deal with the dilemma of being black in America. Garvey was the founder of the United Negro Improvement Association (UNIA), and from his head-quarters in Harlem he urged blacks, all over the world, to join the asso-ciation and form a powerful bloc to fight against oppression and racism. In rousing speeches Garvey claimed that the time had come for blacks to take charge of their own destiny. Whites would never willingly grant equality to blacks; therefore blacks *must* take charge of their own lives. America was a white man's country, Garvey declared, and would never fully accept blacks. He urged African Americans not to cooperate with whites and not to strive for integration but instead to demand power to regulate their own communities. Garvey coined the phrase "black power" and advocated a "back to Africa" movement. He also coined the phrase "black is beautiful," exhorting blacks to be proud of their innate beauty and the uniqueness of Africanness. They should forgo any effort to blend into white society; they should not adopt white clothing and hairstyles and mannerisms but should emphasize their African heri-tage. "No Negro," Garvey said, "let him be American, European, West Indian or African, shall be truly respected until his race as a whole has emancipated itself, through self-achievement and progress, from uni-versal prejudice." It was essential that blacks create their own culture and literature, their own society and government. Only then would whites take them seriously. "Until then, we are but wards of a superior race and civilization, and the outcasts of a standard social system."[12]

Garvey designed a red, green, and white flag to symbolize the Pan-Africa movement, composed a national anthem, and sold shares in a steamship company (the Black Star Line—a wordplay on Britain's White Star Line) that would build ships to take American blacks to Africa. African Americans, however, were not interested in moving to Africa, the Black Star Line did not build any ships, and Garvey's busi-ness venture failed. Although his ways of raising money were extremely controversial (notable African Americans such as W. E. B. Du Bois and

A. Philip Randolph accused him of trying to defraud poor blacks), and although he was convicted of mail fraud and deported back to Jamaica, Garvey had an important impact on racial politics in the United States. Most of his followers, and there were hundreds of thousands of them, were heartened by his message, and "Garveyism" helped deepen a sense of pride and solidarity in the black community and was an influence on the civil rights movement that emerged after World War II. "We were created equal," Garvey repeatedly told his audiences, "and were put into this world to possess equal rights and equal privileges, and the time has come for the black man to get his share."[13]

Amy Jacques Garvey, even before she married Marcus Garvey, was also a civil rights activist. She traveled thousands of miles around the United States delivering speeches that advanced the UNIA message and edited a page in the *Negro World* devoted to articles about the status of black women in America and worldwide. W. E. B. Du Bois continued working to end racial discrimination as a leader of the NAACP and as editor of the organization's magazine, the *Crisis*. A. Philip Randolph and Chandler Owen were African Americans who believed that socialism was the answer. It was the only political system that could overcome capitalist exploitation and had the potential to create an egalitarian society free of racism. The two men published a radical magazine, the *Messenger*, urging blacks to join unions and convert to socialism if they wanted to gain economic, social, and political equality. In 1925 Randolph founded the Brotherhood of Sleeping Car Porters to represent the interests of the thousands of porters—most of whom were black—who worked on the nation's passenger trains. Randolph successfully negotiated with the Pullman Company to gain recognition for the union and improvements in wages and job security for its members.

Just as important as the efforts of black activists seeking political and economic remedies for racism was the impact of the Harlem Renaissance. As hundreds of thousands of African Americans moved north during the Great Migration, many creative writers, musicians, and artists gravitated toward New York's Harlem. Writers such as Langston Hughes, Zora Neale Hurston, Jean Toomer, and Claude McKay wrote novels and poetry, short stories and plays, expressing what it means to be black in a racist society. Like the expatriate writers of the Lost Generation, the Harlem Renaissance writers articulated their discontent through critically acclaimed literature that not only offered a discerning commentary on American life but also persuaded white America that black America had something of profound significance to offer. As their books reached a wide audience, many of the stereotypes and assumptions that whites had about blacks were shattered. African Americans were not submitting to racism; they were proud, they were forceful, and they were not afraid to fight back. "If we must die," McKay wrote, "let it not be like hogs / Hunted and penned in an inglorious spot. . . . / Like men we'll face the murderous, cowardly pack, / Pressed to the wall, dying, but fighting back!"[14] It was clear to both African Americans and whites that black literature was the equal of anything white writers had to offer. The key to great writing, Hughes wrote in his essay "The Negro Artist and the Racial Mountain," was to be completely honest and to write fearlessly. "We younger Negro artists," he wrote, "now intend to express our individual dark-skinned selves without fear or shame. If white people are pleased we are glad. If they aren't, it doesn't matter. We know we are beautiful. And ugly too. . . . If colored people are pleased we are glad. If they are not, their displeasure doesn't matter either. . . . We . . . stand on the top of the mountain, free within ourselves."[15]

Music reached an even wider audience than literature and went a long way to opening America's mind (through its ears) to the vibrancy of black culture. Two forms of music that derived directly from the African American experience, jazz and the blues, became popular in the 1920s. Whites flocked to Harlem to listen to Duke Ellington, Louis Armstrong, and other jazz musicians. They purchased 78 rpm records of these artists as well as of such blues singers as Ma Rainey and Bessie Smith and guitarists Robert Johnson and Mississippi John Hurt. The uncommon rhythms and syncopations, harmonies and playing style, seemed exotic and alluring and, above all, liberating. Even Europeans who usually dismissed American art and literature as inconsequential were captivated by the sounds of jazz and the blues. Countless African American musicians went to London and Paris, where they enjoyed fame and notoriety and reveled in the less prejudiced atmosphere of those cities. Jazz was the perfect soundtrack for the 1920s, expressing musically the revolt against traditionalism and the exaltation of the modern. In many respects the allure of jazz, as well as the blues, created an atmosphere that fostered understanding and tolerance between the races.

* * *

Whereas liberal writers, intellectuals, and African Americans condemned racism, consumerism, and conservatism, conservatives condemned the rapid changes that were taking place as dangerous to American values—so dangerous that American identity was in jeopardy. The ending of the Red Scare did not eradicate fear and paranoia. Xenophobia entrenched itself ever more deeply in the United States as the decade wore on. Millions of rural and small-town whites were repulsed by anything and anybody they considered un-American, and many of them were so angry that they joined the Ku Klux Klan. Conservatives also feared that forces of modernization and the theories of Sigmund Freud threatened family values and that the teaching of Darwin's theory of evolution was undermining faith in God. The only way to resist a potential disaster, they reasoned, was to return to the fundamentals of Christianity and restore the "old-time religion." On the whole, significant numbers of Americans were so alarmed by the rapidly changing world that they dug in their heels and did all they could to resist change and return to the more familiar, more secure world of their fathers.

Urban Americans, for the most part and out of necessity, accepted the diversity of religions and ethnicities that exemplified city living. But those who lived outside the cities resisted such pluralism. America's white Anglo-Saxon heritage, they believed, was gravely endangered by the influx of so many Catholic and Jewish immigrants. A formidable nativist movement, which rivaled that of the Know-Nothings seventy years before, demanded that the government in Washington close America's doors to the hundreds of thousands of immigrants flocking to the United States. In 1921, responding to such demands, Congress set a quota system that strictly limited the number of immigrants from eastern and southern Europe. Only 357,000 immigrants would be allowed into the country each year, and a quota was set of 3 percent for each country, on the basis of the number of people from that country who lived in the United States in 1910. That meant that because there were far more people of English and northern European heritage in the United States in 1910 than the number of Italians or Poles or Russians, the quota for these southern and eastern European groups was significantly smaller than the quota for those from western or northern Europe. (The quota for Great Britain was approximately 65,000, whereas the quota for Italy was 6,000.) In 1924 the National Origins Act limited immigration to 150,000 per year, set the quota at 2 percent, and changed the base year to 1890. It also prohibited all immigration from Asia, with the exception of people from the American-held Philippine Islands. There were, however, no restrictions placed on immigration from the Western Hemisphere because California relied on Mexican agricultural workers to provide cheap labor. The act, however, established a border patrol to monitor the border.

The anti-immigration fervor was one manifestation of the rising racism, anti-Semitism, and bigotry that seemed to obsess the nation. The rebirth of the Ku Klux Klan was another. The second Klan was founded in 1915 by William J. Simmons, shortly after the release of D. W. Griffiths's film glorifying the Reconstruction-era Ku Klux Klan, *Birth of a Nation*. This time the Klan was not confined to the South, nor was its focus only on blacks. Along with its white supremacy views and commitment "to protect and defend the Constitution of the United States," the Klan was anti-Catholic, anti-Semitic, antiforeigner, antifeminist, anti-Bolshevik, and anti–Modernist Protestant. In fact it was against anything that it did not regard as "100 percent pure Americanism." The urban Northeast was a favorite target of KKK hostility. New York City, because of its large foreign population, was the "most un-American center on the American continent," the Klan's leader, Simmons, told a convention of the Kamelia—a women's Klan-like organization. "The foremost political and social economist of the world," Simmons said, "recently made a survey of New York City and after listening to its babel of tongues, after feeling its hot breath of anarchy, after touching its seething restlessness, he calmly turned away and said that Petrograd in its dust and desolation, was a picture of New York City of the future." And "New England," he continued, "is settled by French Roman Catholics, Canadians who continue to speak the French language, maintain parochial schools and multiply with amazing rapidity."[16]

By the mid-1920s the KKK had over three million members (some estimates go as high as six million) and had hundreds of chapters throughout the United States. Oregon, Pennsylvania, Rhode Island, Maine, Indiana, and many other northern states boasted numerous Klan chapters. More midwesterners joined the Klan than southerners, and at one time nearly every member of the Indiana state legislature, as well as Governor Edward Jackson, was a Klansman. The Klan was so

Formation of Ku Klux Klan parade in Washington, DC, August 8, 1925. The Klan held marches in the nation's capital several times in the 1920s, with the participation of tens of thousands of hooded Klansmen and women. They demanded "100% Pure Americanism" and denounced African Americans, Jews, Catholics, immigrants, liberals, flappers, modernist Protestants, and all those who did not fit their vision of a white-dominated America. Photograph by the National Photo Company. (Public domain; courtesy Library of Congress)

popular during the decade that tens of thousands of Klansmen marched in massive protest parades in the nation's capital in 1925 and 1928, campaigning against threats to "Americanism" (code for white supremacy). The Klan's power was such that it blocked the nomination for president of the Roman Catholic governor of New York, Alfred E. Smith, at the 1924 Democratic National Convention. Four years later, when Democrats did nominate Smith, the Klan campaigned so effectively against him that the Republicans were able to break the solid Democratic South for the first time since Reconstruction, taking five of the former Confederate states.

Klansmen intimidated blacks, Jews, and Catholics by boycotting businesses that hired them; burning crosses on their lawns, hoping to harry them out of town; beating them; and in some cases lynching them. Physical violence reached shocking levels. On several occasions African American World War I veterans were lynched in their uniforms. The Klan also viewed itself as the protector of family values and the purity of women by ferreting out "loose women" for punishment. In Alabama, for example, Klansmen frequently staked out the secluded spots where young couples met for a romantic rendezvous. They would catch the unlucky couple, strip them to the waist, tie them to a tree, and whip them as punishment for their "immoral behavior."

It was the Klan's own immoral behavior, though, that brought it down. A series of financial scandals in which it was disclosed that several Klan leaders had been swindling members discredited the organization. But the tipping point came when David Stephenson, the Grand Dragon of the Klan in Indiana, was convicted in a sensational trial for raping and murdering a young woman. Almost immediately thousands of Klansmen dropped out of the organization, and by 1930 membership had declined to less than ten thousand. Although the Klan died out, anti-Semitism, racism, and bigotry did not.[17]

Conservatives also protested the modern forces threatening traditional values by returning to the fundamental evangelical roots of Protestant Christianity. The moral depravity of the cities, rampant materialism, the changing role of women, the flagrant defiance of Prohibition, and the widespread acceptance of the theories of evolution and relativity and sexuality were all anathema to rural and small-town Americans. So too were the large numbers of Jews and Catholics residing in the nation's cities, as well as the influence of modernist Protestant theologians such as Harry Emerson Fosdick and Reinhold Niebuhr who sought to reconcile faith and science.

In response, millions of Americans were "born again" at the revival meetings of such flamboyant evangelical preachers as Billy Sunday and Aimee Semple McPherson. Millions more listened to the newly invented radio, as evangelists reached out to an ever-wider audience. In emotionally charged sermons Sunday and McPherson emphasized the fundamentals of the trinity, the virgin birth, the divinity of Christ, and the resurrection. The Bible was the word of God and was to be taken absolutely literally. To fundamentalists scientific theories, especially the theory of evolution, which contradicted the literal truth of the Bible, were simply wrong. Furthermore, "modernist" theologians' efforts to interpret scripture figuratively so as to accommodate the theory of evolution were just as dangerous to faith as the theory itself. In addition to evolution, fundamentalists denounced as sins promiscuity, alcohol, tobacco, profanity, nightclubs, burlesque, and all forms of liberal free-thinking. When Prohibition went into effect, fundamentalists rejoiced. The corruption and violence caused by bootlegging and organized crime, however, was proof that the fight against "demon rum" was far from over and convinced them they had to keep fighting against the evils of alcohol. The successful implementation of Prohibition (despite the difficulties in enforcing it) also encouraged them to take on the theory of evolution.

Conservative Christians launched a vigorous campaign to push local and state governments to enact laws banning the teaching of evolution in public schools. Before the end of the decade they successfully lobbied five states to do so. In Tennessee, for example, educators at all levels were forbidden "to teach any theory that denies the story of the divine creation of man as taught in the Bible and to teach instead that man has descended from a lower order of animals."[18] To be sure, many conservative Protestants *did* believe that there was some evidence for evolution, that the human race had evolved over time, and that God was instrumental in this evolutionary progress, but the implications of the theory of natural selection through the survival of the fittest posited a world devoid of compassion and love, a world in which God acted with cruel randomness. And this they could not accept.

In 1925 the evangelical crusade against "Darwinism" reached its high point in Dayton, Tennessee. Shortly after the passage of Tennessee's antievolution law the American Civil Liberties Union offered its services to any teacher who would challenge the law. John Scopes, a tenth-grade science teacher, agreed to be the guinea pig. On May 7, 1925, Scopes was arrested for teaching a lesson on evolution (ironically the lesson he taught was right out of the state-approved biology textbook). The ensuing "Monkey Trial" was the ultimate clash between opposing voices of dissent. Traditionalists and fundamentalists were determined to prevent the scientific community's attempt to impose ideas that threatened deeply held religious beliefs. Modernists and liberals were just as determined to prevent what they saw as a clumsy attempt to proscribe the free exchange of thought. Fundamentalists fought to protect religion and the "faith of our fathers," the ACLU to protect free speech and the separation of church and state.

Clarence Darrow, the most famous trial lawyer in the country, volunteered his services to the ACLU's team defending Scopes. Darrow first came to fame as a labor lawyer defending such radical union leaders as Eugene V. Debs during the Pullman strike trial and then became even more famous as a successful criminal lawyer. Darrow was an outspoken liberal, an ardent defender of free thinking who opposed capital punishment, traditional morality, and the narrow-minded intolerance of the "slave religion" of Christianity. The Christian view of sin and salvation, Darrow believed, was "dangerous," "wicked," and even "silly." "It is not the bad people I fear so much as the good people. When a person is sure that he is good, he is nearly hopeless; he gets cruel—he believes in punishment."[19]

The perennial Democratic presidential candidate William Jennings Bryan volunteered for the prosecution team. Bryan was a political progressive as well as a fundamentalist Christian. He sincerely believed that the Bible was the divinely inspired word of God and that it should be taken literally. But a major part of Bryan's motivation in taking on the theory of evolution was his political progressivism: if he could prove Darwin wrong, it would undermine the Social Darwinist argument against progressive legislation. The Darwinian view posited that man was an animal, that natural selection was cruel, that there was no teleological purpose to existence. The biblical view was that man was created in God's image, and though he was sinful, redemption was possible. For progressives such as Bryan it was essential to promote a worldview of decency and integrity and to disprove the gloomy cruelty of the Darwinian world. Bryan opposed the theory of evolution, he said, "because I fear we shall lose the consciousness of God's presence in our daily life, if we must accept the theory that through all the ages no spiritual force has touched the life of man and shaped the destiny of nations." But that was not his only objection. "The Darwinian theory," he contended, "represents man as reaching his present perfection by the operation of the law of hate—the merciless law by which the strong crowd out and kill off the weak."[20] For this reason the theory must be challenged.

From the outset the trial was a media circus. Two hundred reporters and correspondents from newspapers and magazines around the world descended on Dayton, Tennessee, in July 1925. The Chicago radio station WGN broadcast the proceedings live, and thousands of people (mostly eastern Tennesseans) flocked to Dayton to participate in the carnival-like festivities surrounding the trial. Tables were set up near the courthouse where antievolutionists and itinerant preachers denounced Darwin and handed out copies of the Bible, while evolutionists denounced narrow-mindedness and handed out offprints from *The Origin of the Species*. Enterprising individuals entertained the public by putting trained chimpanzees dressed in business suits through their tricks, took photographs of the public mugging for the camera through wooden cutouts of gorillas, and sold monkey dolls and all manner of simian souvenirs.

"Scopes is not on trial," Darrow told a packed courtroom as the trial began; "civilization is on trial. The prosecution is opening the doors for a reign of bigotry equal to anything in the Middle Ages. No man's belief will be safe if they win."[21] For several days the judge heard arguments from the defense requesting the testimony of evolutionary zoologists and biologists as expert witnesses. But the judge ruled that Scopes was simply being tried for violating the ban on teaching evolution, and thus there was no need for scientific witnesses to prove the validity of the theory. The highpoint of the trial came when Darrow and the other defense attorneys shifted tactics and surprised the entire courtroom when they called Bryan to the stand as a *defense* witness. Since they were denied experts on evolution, the defense reasoned, they would argue the case with the help of a biblical expert. First Darrow got Bryan to affirm under oath that every word of the Bible was the literal truth. Then he proceeded one by one, reading passages from the Bible, to expose the paradoxes of literalism. If there were only four people on Earth at the beginning (Adam, Eve, Cain, and Abel), where did Cain's wife come from? How could the sun have stood still when Joshua commanded it to, when even the most conservative fundamentalist knew that it was the Earth that revolved around the sun? Darrow's incessant badgering finally forced Bryan to acknowledge that there were passages open to interpretation and that he himself even believed that the twenty-four-hour days of creation were metaphorical days of indeterminate length.

The outcome of the trial was that Scopes was found guilty and Tennessee's antievolution law remained on the books until 1967. However, the literal interpretation of the Bible was discredited, and it opened the possibility for even conservative Christians to acknowledge that God created the heavens and the Earth *through* some sort of evolutionary process. Science and religion were not necessarily incompatible. Although fundamentalists still challenge the Darwinian view in the twenty-first century, and controversy continues to swirl around the subject, most recently in *Kitzmiller v. Dover Area School District* in Pennsylvania in 2005, scientific skepticism has dominated scholarship and science education ever since the "Monkey Trial."

* * *

When the 1920s began, the American people believed they were returning to "normalcy." But the decade was anything but normal. The economy boomed. The Model T transformed the face of the United States with a network of highways and expanding suburbs. Consumerism flourished, and the Republican Party dominated national politics. Women got the right to vote, fought for reproductive rights, and enjoyed a sense of liberation that they had never felt before. Nearly a million African Americans found better economic and social conditions in the North, and a literary and artistic renaissance blossomed in Harlem. A wide variety of dissenting voices spoke out against grievances real and imagined in every part of the nation. Margaret Sanger, Marcus Garvey, H. L. Mencken, Sinclair Lewis, and thousands of others protested against various aspects of American society and politics, while racial, religious, and ethnic intolerance rose to a fever pitch.

The underlying theme of the Roaring Twenties was the sharp division within American society between the forces of modernism and the forces of traditionalism. The expanding popularity of Darwin's, Einstein's, and Heisenberg's scientific theories, Freud's psychological hypotheses, and the invasion of European existentialism; the rapid technological developments and the expansion of a consumer culture; the Great Migration of African Americans into northern cities; the emergence of the "modern woman"—all of these changes underscored the philosophical divide that was rapidly growing and that made the 1920s a watershed decade separating modern America from its more naïve past. Many Americans embraced the modernist future wholeheartedly. But many others recoiled from it by putting up a powerful and sometimes effective resistance to the forces they believed would destroy traditional American values. Prohibitionists, nativists, the KKK, and fundamentalists fought mightily against speakeasies and bootlegging, immigrants and Catholics, Jews and blacks, Darwinists and modernist Protestants. In a sense the 1920s was an early chapter in conservatism's reaction to modernity, a cycle that repeats throughout the latter half of the twentieth century and still continues.

CHAPTER 17

A New Deal for America

These Punch and Judy Republicans, whose actions and words
were dominated by the ventriloquists of Wall Street, are so
blind that they do not recognize, even in this perilous hour,
that their gold basis and their private coinage of money have
bred more radicals than did Karl Marx or Lenin.
> —Father Charles Coughlin, 1936

The State, every government whatever its form, character
or color . . . is by its very nature conservative, static, intolerant of change and opposed to it. Whatever changes it
undergoes are always the result of pressure exerted upon it,
pressure strong enough to compel the ruling powers to submit peaceably or otherwise, generally "otherwise"—that is,
by revolution.
> —Emma Goldman,
> "The Individual, Society, and the State," 1936

For the American people the Great Depression was a catastrophe of
unprecedented proportions. Unemployment was a staggering 25 percent. And even those who were employed worked for reduced wages or
reduced hours. Farmers, workers, and minority groups were especially
hard hit, with virtually no prospects. Untold numbers took to the highways seeking jobs in other communities, only to find that there were
no jobs. "Okies"—impoverished farmers from the dust bowl of Kansas,
Oklahoma, and northern Texas—went west to California, where they
hoped to find jobs picking fruit, only to find disappointment and further
hardship. Migrants set up shantytowns of makeshift corrugated steel and
plywood shacks (irreverently called "Hoovervilles") in garbage dumps
on the outskirts of the unwelcoming cities and towns that refused them
admittance. Middle-class families defaulted on their mortgages, and
banks repossessed their houses. Americans believed that if they worked

hard and were virtuous, they would partake of the American Dream, but when they lost their jobs and homes, many were overwhelmed with a sense of shame that somehow it was *their* fault—not economic forces beyond their control—that *they*, individually, had failed. So it was not only the economy that was depressed; people were depressed—deeply depressed. Suicide rates increased. Birth rates dropped. Marriages broke up. Thousands of men left their families and rode the rails, going from one town to the next vainly seeking employment.

With more than five thousand banks failing between 1930 and 1932 millions of Americans began questioning capitalism itself, began questioning the ability of laissez-faire economics to extricate the nation from the depression. Many blamed the capitalist system for causing the depression. As the election of 1932 approached, dread and foreboding gripped the land. Something needed to be done. President Hoover seemed incapable of solving the problem. Would the Democratic candidate, Franklin Delano Roosevelt, be up to the task of reversing the downward slide? Americans certainly hoped so. They flocked to the polls and gave him the biggest margin of victory in presidential election history up to that point.

During the first hundred days of FDR's presidency the American people responded positively to the new president's assurance that "the only thing we have to fear is fear itself." And although the New Deal did not extricate the nation from the Great Depression, it did restore hope to a downhearted people. Even so, throughout the 1930s dissenters attacked the New Deal on a daily basis. Many denounced the president's policies as too radical and too socialistic, while others condemned the New Deal's attempt to save capitalism. For those on the right the New Deal was undermining the free enterprise system. For those on the left it did not go nearly far enough to punish Wall Street, redistribute income, and alleviate the suffering of the poor; ultimately leftist dissenters were incensed that FDR was working hand in hand with the moneyed classes to strengthen capitalism.

* * *

By 1932 hundreds of thousands of Americans were homeless. The possibility of starvation was all too real. Hoovervilles dotted the landscape, people were scavenging food from garbage cans, destitute farmers resorted to violence, unemployed whites assaulted minorities whom they viewed as competitors for jobs, and public officials lived in dread that protests and demonstrations could explode at any moment into riots and even rebellion.

While the depression affected most Americans, minority groups suffered disproportionately. African Americans, North and South, remained at the bottom of the economic ladder. When a job did become available, whites were hired before African Americans were even considered. In the South white-supremacist organizations saw to it that whites received preferential treatment over blacks in even the lowest-paying jobs. One group's slogan was "No Jobs for Niggers until Every White Man Has a Job!"[1] In California and the Southwest Latinos faced severe discrimination and harassment. Thousands of Mexican migrant workers who had been brought into the region as cheap labor during the 1920s were rounded up and deported, even those who were legally in the country.

One of the most startling protests in the nation's history took place in the summer of 1932 when World War I veterans marched on Washington demanding the immediate payment of their retirement bonuses. These were not due until 1945, but unemployed veterans had faith that Congress would do the right thing and pay the bonuses at a time when the veterans desperately needed financial assistance. Nearly twenty thousand veterans from all ethnic and racial backgrounds descended on Washington to push Congress to pass the bonus bill. For several weeks the Bonus Army demonstrated at the Capitol and the White House, but when the bill was defeated in mid-June, most of the protestors gave up and returned home. Several thousand, however, vowed to keep up the pressure and remain in the shantytown they had set up at Anacostia Flats near the Capitol building until Congress reversed its decision. The police tried to remove the demonstrators, shots were fired, two people were killed, and then President Hoover, embarrassed by the Bonus Army, ordered in the U.S. Army. What followed was a bizarre scene with General Douglas MacArthur, accompanied by his lieutenants Dwight D. Eisenhower and George S. Patton, leading tanks and troops up Pennsylvania Avenue to torch the encampment. In the ensuing chaos hundreds of panicked demonstrators were injured, and the shantytown was leveled.

People around the country, already critical of President Hoover's aloof attitude in dealing with the depression, were appalled. Photographs

The Bonus Army, July 1932. More than ten thousand World War I veterans from all over the country and from all ethnic and racial backgrounds took part in a protest march on Washington in June–July 1932. When Congress refused to pass the bonus bill, they occupied land near the Capitol building to pressure Congress to accede to their demands. President Hoover sent in the U.S. Army under the command of General Douglas MacArthur to evict the protestors. Photograph by Harris & Ewing. (Public domain; courtesy Library of Congress)

and newspaper accounts of veterans being violently removed from their encampment by heavily armored troops shocked Americans and destroyed whatever credibility Hoover still had. "What a pitiful spectacle," one newspaper reported. "The mightiest government in the world chasing unarmed men, women and children with Army tanks. If the Army must be called out to make war on unarmed citizens, this is no longer America."[2] The president's cavalier action convinced millions that he was out of touch with the suffering of the people and that the administration's parsimonious policies were actually exacerbating the economic crisis. It seemed almost certain that whomever the Democrats nominated to oppose Hoover in the general election would easily defeat the unpopular president.

President Hoover, of course, had not caused the depression, but he received the brunt of the people's displeasure. "Hard times," one sign proclaimed, "are Hoover-ing over us!" Hoover *did* make several attempts to use federal power to address the worst effects of the depression, but he was too wedded to his commitment to laissez faire, rugged individualism, and a balanced budget to put forward the bold initiatives necessary to tackle the complex economic problems. Most significantly, he was perceived as compassionless and arrogant and stubbornly unwilling to fully use the power of the federal government to turn the economy around.

To face Hoover in the upcoming election Democrats nominated the liberal governor of New York, Franklin D. Roosevelt. Roosevelt had impressed the party faithful with his aggressive hands-on approach in tackling the depression in New York State by implementing programs that provided relief for the poor and authorizing state funding for construction and power projects. There was a sense that a new feeling was in the air when Roosevelt broke all precedent by flying to the Democratic convention in Chicago to accept the nomination—the first presidential candidate ever to do so. "The appearance before a national convention of its nominee for President," Roosevelt told the cheering delegates, "is unprecedented, but these are unprecedented times." He announced that he would lead the party and the country in a new, liberal direction. "Ours must be a party of liberal thought, of planned action, of enlightened international outlook, and the greatest good to the greatest number of our citizens." He would use the full power of the federal government to rebuild the economy and put an end to the abuses, exploitation, and mismanagement that led to the depression. "I pledge you, I pledge myself," he concluded, "to a New Deal for the American people."[3]

Americans were desperate. They wanted change. They needed a new direction. The election was a landslide. Roosevelt defeated Hoover by seven million votes (22.8 million to 15.8 million). The electoral vote was even more lopsided: 472 to 59. The country had voted for a New Deal.

* * *

During the first hundred days of the new administration, FDR introduced (and Congress passed) more legislation than any of his predecessors had done. He signed into law an act establishing the Federal Deposit Insurance Corporation, which would guarantee all bank deposits up to $5,000. Congress passed the Federal Securities Act, which became the basis, a year later, for the Securities and Exchange Commission that would regulate and police the stock market. The Agricultural Adjustment Act (AAA) established controls limiting the production of milk, corn, wheat, rice, cotton, and hogs in order to raise prices and, it was hoped, to increase the income of impoverished farmers. But the act tended to benefit the owners of large farms and agribusinesses. Thousands of small family-run farms, as well as tenant farmers and sharecroppers, lost everything. In order to employ young men (and keep them off the streets where they might get in trouble) Roosevelt proposed the Civilian Conservation Corps. Men between the ages of eighteen and twenty-five were put to work on conservation projects in parks and forests around the country. They built hiking trails in national parks, planted trees in national forests, and lived in quasi-military-style camps where they were taught military drills, did calisthenics, and developed rapport with each other. They were given room and board as well as pocket money, and each month their families back home were sent sixty-five dollars. Other successful New Deal programs were the Tennessee Valley Authority (TVA), which brought hydroelectric power and jobs to the Tennessee River Valley and the Works Progress Administration (WPA), which provided jobs for millions of Americans building dams, roads, airports, bridges, libraries, and post offices, as well as commissioning creative individuals (artists, writers, musicians, sculptors, muralists, and playwrights) to produce their art.

Roosevelt's bold, controversial measures, however, were so unprecedented that soon there was a rising cacophony of dissenting voices. Most Americans were hopeful that FDR would restore the economy (and by the end of 1933 nearly two-thirds of Americans believed that the nation was on the road to recovery), but many millions of Americans looked on the New Deal with varying levels of horror, distaste, and anxiety. For conservatives the New Deal was a threat to American values and the free market system. Bankers, businessmen, industrialists, and right-wing newspaper publishers believed that Roosevelt's policies were nothing more than socialism in disguise. Roosevelt, they believed, was trying to transform the United States into a socialist state. By the summer of 1934 their antagonism to the New Deal turned into open defiance. A group of business leaders launched the Liberty League, ostensibly an "educational" association for the promotion of "American ideals" but primarily dedicated to the goal of electing anti–New Deal men to Congress. They were, however, unsuccessful in both 1934 and 1936. But as the decade wore on, the Liberty League began to chip away at FDR's support and remained adamantly determined to put an end to relief programs as well as to transfer government-planned initiatives, such as the TVA, to the private sector.

For the Liberty League, congressional Republicans, and other conservatives, every New Deal program was an attack on liberty and individualism. True, many businessmen at first embraced the National Industrial Recovery Act (NIRA) and the AAA (for they benefited from the acts), but they soon learned to hate the close relationship between government and business. Furthermore, the expansion of federal authority and government planning, they believed, would lead to regimentation, which would in turn lead to socialism and communism. These "economic royalists" (as FDR referred to them) were appalled that the president took the United States off the gold standard, and they demanded that FDR discontinue his deficit-spending spree. And perhaps most importantly, they despised the president for reversing the government's time-honored role of siding with business and instead supporting unions and workers' rights. The newspaper mogul William Randolph Hearst, for example, became an ardent antagonist of the New Deal when Roosevelt supported an inheritance tax. From 1935 on Hearst instructed his reporters to refer to the New Deal as the "Raw Deal" and the inheritance tax as the "soak-the-successful tax." Colonel

Robert Rutherford McCormack, owner of the influential *Chicago Tribune*, regularly demonized Roosevelt in his newspaper as the arch-enemy of capitalism and American democracy. The writer and activist Elizabeth Dilling attacked the New Deal as a socialist plot to take over the United States. The "Socialist administration" in Washington, Dilling wrote, has made sure that "economic serfdom has become a grim reality in the United States."[4] Dilling admired Adolf Hitler for rooting out communists in Germany, and like Hitler, she equated Marxism and "Jewry"—communism, she believed, was a Jewish conspiracy, and FDR, his cabinet, and even the First Lady, were in its grip.

What the Right did not fully understand was that FDR had to sound more left-wing than he indeed was, so that the more radical elements among his supporters were not attracted to the populist demagoguery of such adversaries as Huey Long or Father Coughlin or to the platforms of socialists such as Norman Thomas or communists such as William Z. Foster. The president for his part was deeply frustrated over "the failure of those who have property to realize that [he was] the best friend the profit system ever had."[5]

It is no surprise that in a country that was essentially conservative, peopled with individuals with a deep distrust of centralized authority, Roosevelt and his approach to tackling the depression would face powerful criticism from those whose chief article of faith was free enterprise and individual liberty. But many of Roosevelt's most vocal critics, ironically, were those who criticized him from the left: populists, socialists, communists, and other radicals who believed that the depression was a clear signal that capitalism had failed and that what the United States needed was a new economic structure. Indeed, in terminology that foreshadowed the Occupy movement of 2011–2012, leftists incessantly denounced Wall Street's influence on Washington. Concentrated wealth and power, they claimed, had ruined the country. The system was set up to benefit the wealthy at the expense of the middle and lower classes. It was time to change this.

One of FDR's most influential critics was Huey "Kingfish" Long. Long was elected governor of Louisiana in 1928, campaigning on the slogan "every man a king, but no one wears a crown." By 1932 he was nationally renowned for his internal improvement programs and educational reform initiatives in the state, as well as for his imperious rule and the graft, bribery, and corruption that surrounded him. Despite his notoriety, Long was elected to the U.S. Senate in 1930. He campaigned for Roosevelt in the 1932 election, but by 1934 the "Kingfish" was loudly protesting that the New Deal did not go nearly far enough in tackling the problems that lay at the core of the depression. Roosevelt, he declared, should throw the full weight of the presidency into redistributing wealth and breaking the stranglehold of power wielded by bankers and big business. In February 1934 he delivered a speech on the Senate floor in which he proposed his "Share Our Wealth" program to destroy the power of the moneyed interests and eliminate poverty. "There is nothing wrong with the United States," Long declared.

> We have more food than we can eat. We have more clothes and things out of which to make clothes than we can wear. We have more houses and lands than the whole 120 million can use if they all had good homes. So what is the trouble? Nothing except that a handful of men have everything and the balance of the people have nothing if their debts were paid. There should be every man a king in this land flowing with milk and honey instead of the lords of finance at the top and slaves and peasants at the bottom.[6]

Long proposed that no individual be permitted to earn more than $1 million a year. Any amount over that sum would be taxed at 100 percent. Each citizen would receive a guaranteed annual income of $2,500. He called for full employment of everyone, a thirty-hour week, thirty days of paid vacation, and free college education for every American who wanted to attend college.

Millions of Americans enthusiastically responded to Long's populist appeal. By early 1935 he was routinely calling the depression the "Roosevelt depression," and it was obvious that he was gearing up to challenge FDR for the Democratic nomination in 1936. Long boasted that there were close to eight million members of his Share Our Wealth societies and that he was ready to run on a third-party ticket if he did not get the Democratic nomination. But although Long's demagoguery gained him many followers, he had also trod on many toes during his career. In September 1935 the son-in-law of one of Long's political enemies in Louisiana confronted Long in the corridor of the state capitol in Baton Rouge and assassinated him. "God, don't let me die!" Long said, mortally wounded. "I have so much to do!"[7]

Father Charles Coughlin (the "Radio Priest") was another populist critic with a large following. In the late 1920s and early 1930s he hosted a popular radio show in which he offered spiritual guidance, but as the depression deepened, he grew more political by expressing hostility toward President Hoover and Wall Street bankers. In 1932 he supported Roosevelt and during the early days of the new administration opined, "the New Deal is Christ's Deal."[8] Coughlin was hoping to ingratiate himself with the Roosevelt administration as a sort of unofficial adviser, but when Coughlin soon realized that FDR was spurning his advances, he shifted his stance. By 1934 Coughlin was using his radio pulpit to denounce FDR's policies as inadequate for extricating the nation from the depression and punishing the moneyed interests. As many as forty-five million Americans listened to the Radio Priest's weekly condemnation of the New Deal, FDR, and capitalism. Coughlin founded the National Union for Social Justice as an organization to promote a new economic system that would find a middle way between the twin evils of capitalism and communism. Capitalism, he argued, was finished. And communism was a dead end that would destroy individualism and religion. "My friends, the outworn creed of capitalism is done for. The clarion call of communism has been sounded. I can support one as easily as the other. They are both rotten! But it is not necessary to suffer any longer the slings and arrows of modern capitalism any more than it is to surrender our rights to life, to liberty and to the cherished bonds of family to communism. . . . Away with both of them!"[9]

Coughlin called for the nationalization of banks, a currency based on both gold and silver, and the type of corporatist economics implemented by fascist Italy. His criticism of Roosevelt and the New Deal was laced with sarcasm. "No man in modern times," he said, "received such plaudits from the poor as did Franklin Roosevelt when he promised to drive the money-changers from the temple—the money-changers who had clipped the coins of wages, who had manufactured spurious money, and who had brought proud America to her knees." But Roosevelt betrayed the American people. He was still too cozy with the mandarins of finance. "Alas! The temple still remains the private property of the money-changers. The golden key has been handed over to them for safekeeping—the key which now is fashioned in the shape of a double cross!"[10]

During the 1936 election campaign Coughlin referred to the president as "Franklin Double-Crossing Roosevelt," called him "the great betrayer and liar," and endorsed the third-party candidate William Lemke. His vitriol increased as Election Day neared. He called Roosevelt an "anti-God" communist (while at the same time accusing Roosevelt of being in league with the money-changers), a "scab president," and an "upstart dictator," and he implied that it would not be a bad thing if Roosevelt were assassinated. This was too much for his superiors in the church, and Coughlin was ordered to issue a public apology.[11]

Still, Coughlin's attacks on Roosevelt intensified during FDR's second term. By this time, with much of the world taking notice of what was transpiring in Hitler's Germany, the Radio Priest's comments took on a progressively more anti-Semitic tone. The president, Coughlin asserted (sounding like the right-winger Elizabeth Dilling), was carrying out the policies of Jewish bankers and industrialists and the Jewish members of his cabinet. He began calling the New Deal the "Jew Deal." Coughlin's anti-Semitism proved to be his undoing. Shortly after Kristallnacht in Germany in 1938, when Jewish synagogues and businesses were destroyed during the "night of broken glass," Coughlin proclaimed that the Jews were only being paid back for their persecution of Christians. Even after Hitler invaded Poland, he continued his anti-Semitic diatribes while praising Hitler and Benito Mussolini. Finally, in 1940 the radio networks were so appalled at his pro-Nazi, anti-Semitic remarks that they took his show off the air.

A third populist critic of the New Deal was the retired physician Francis Townsend. Townsend protested that the president's relief and recovery programs, especially in regard to the elderly, were falling short. He proposed a plan that would distribute $200 a month to all citizens over the age of sixty, with the only stipulation being that they agree to retire and spend the money within a month of receiving it. The Townsend Plan was widely popular, especially among older Americans, and by the end of 1934 more than two million people had joined Townsend Clubs and were lobbying the administration to enact the doctor's plan.

All three of these populists, in their protests against what they regarded as Roosevelt's inadequate response to the Great Depression, offered radical solutions that would enlarge federal management of the economy. And all three had an impact on federal policy.

FDR understood that their message was attractive to many Americans (indeed, he feared the formidable challenge they would represent if they and their followers would ever unite to form a third party), and in order to diffuse their appeal, he co-opted some of their proposals. For example, Long's plan about taxing the rich was incorporated into the inheritance tax (although at a greatly reduced rate), Coughlin's anti-business, antibanker diatribes goaded the president into taking a more hard-line stance against business leaders, and Townsend's ideas about old-age pensions were absorbed into the Social Security Act that FDR signed into law in 1935 and that became one of the major legacies of the New Deal.

The populist critique of the New Deal clearly had a radical tinge to it, but other dissidents engaged in a far more radical condemnation of capitalism and FDR's attempt to save the free enterprise system. Many of those who were devastated by the depression were drawn to social-ism and communism. For these individuals it seemed that the sever-ity of the depression was proof that capitalism had failed and that the only way to escape from the boom/bust cycle was through a planned economy. The anarchist Emma Goldman continued writing blistering attacks on capitalism and called for a government that would truly rec-ognize the worth of the individual. Society does not exist to support the interests of the moneyed classes, as it does under a capitalist sys-tem, Goldman contended; it exists to elevate the individual. Anarchy, for Goldman, was the answer. "Of all social theories Anarchism alone steadfastly proclaims that society exists for man, not man for society. The sole legitimate purpose of society is to serve the needs and advance the aspiration of the individual."[12]

Socialists such as Upton Sinclair (the author of *The Jungle*) did not go quite so far. They believed that the nationalization of industry, rail-roads, and banks would be sufficient to create a more equitable society, to keep exploitation in check, and to restore prosperity. In the 1920s Sinclair ran (unsuccessfully) for Congress twice and once for the Sen-ate as a socialist candidate, but in 1934 he thought the time was ripe to "outflank" the enemies of socialism by running for governor of Cali-fornia "disguised" as a Democrat. He founded the organization End Poverty in California (EPIC), which put forth an essentially socialist program as the panacea for unemployment and poverty in the state. Conservatives, however, were not fooled, and they denounced him as a communist who was attempting to undermine democracy in the state. Still, he gained a huge following and won nearly one million votes. Reflecting on his incursion into politics, Sinclair later remarked that when he ran for office as a socialist, the most he ever got was 60,000 votes, but in 1934, he said, "running on the slogan to 'End Poverty in California' I got 879,000. I think we simply have to recognize the fact that our enemies have succeeded in spreading the Big Lie. There is no use attacking [capitalism] by a front attack, it is much better to outflank them."[13] Norman Thomas, the Socialist Party's regular presidential candidate, jumped from 200,000 votes in 1928 to nearly 900,000 in the 1932 election. Throughout the period socialists continued to draw large numbers of supporters but never were a serious challenge to the two major parties—and certainly did not make a dent in Roosevelt's electoral totals. Still, socialists did have an impact, and they were somewhat gratified to see Roosevelt incorporate many of their ideas into his New Deal programs. But Norman Thomas believed FDR was still not going far enough. Not known for his humor, Thomas wryly responded when a reporter asked him if Roosevelt was not actually carrying out his socialist program, "Yes, he is carrying it out in a coffin."[14]

In the Midwest hard-hit farmers, disenchanted with the Democrats for not proposing radical solutions, formed third parties to promote their interests. In Minnesota activists formed the Farmer-Labor Party and campaigned for Floyd Olson for governor. The party's platform proclaimed that "capitalism has failed" and demanded that "all the natural resources, machinery of production, transportation, and communication, shall be owned by the government."[15] Olson deprecated the liberal label. "I am a radical," he proudly proclaimed. "You bet your life I'm a radical. You might say I'm radical as hell!"[16] In Wisconsin thousands of farmers supported the equally radical Progressive Party and elected Philip La Follette as governor and Robert M. La Follette, Jr., as senator. "We are not liberals!" the new governor said. "Liberalism is nothing but a sort of milk-and-water tolerance. . . . I believe in a fundamental and basic change." Without explaining exactly what he meant, Philip La Follette called for a "cooperative society based on American traditions."[17]

More threatening, however, was the increasing popularity of the Communist Party. The Great Crash was proof to many radicals that American capitalism was through and a new political/economic structure modeled on that of Stalin's Russia was a necessity. The Soviet

Union was not as ravaged by the depression as were capitalist countries (mainly because the Soviet economy had never achieved a degree of prosperity), and this seemed proof that a communist economy was superior. In 1932 the presidential candidate of the Communist Party USA, William Z. Foster, won over one hundred thousand votes. By 1934 the party boasted a card-carrying membership of approximately thirty thousand and became increasingly vocal in condemning the New Deal. "Roosevelt's program," the party's general secretary, Earl Browder, contended, "is the same as that of finance capital the world over." The National Recovery Administration, communists insisted, was a "fascist slave program," and there must be no compromise with capitalism.[18] Pure and simply, the entire system needed to be overthrown.

Such condemnation had a powerful influence on unionism and industrial action, and consequently brought more radical tactics to the labor movement. From coast to coast communists organized strikes of agricultural workers, truck drivers, transportation workers, longshoremen, miners, and autoworkers. Some strikes escalated into riots. In May 1934 in Minneapolis communists helped lead a Teamster's strike of 20,000 people during which scores of strikers were shot and two died. A few months later a strike of San Francisco stevedores led to a citywide general strike that effectively closed down all business in the city for several days until the police, backed by 4,500 National Guardsmen, finally brought the strike to an end. Later that year 325,000 textile workers walked off their jobs in South Carolina, took control of the mills, immobilized the looms, and battled the police and guards. Seven were killed and twenty wounded before the strike ran its course. Newspapers reported that many of the protestors wore red armbands.

Even moderate, less radical labor militancy increased despite the fact that New Deal programs were ostensibly providing more jobs and better conditions for workers. Workers initiated new tactics that were effective in having their demands met and their unions recognized. Perhaps the most successful innovation was the "sit-down" strike. Instead of walking out of the plant (which invariably resulted in owners bringing in scabs to keep production going), striking workers occupied it. This meant that the workers themselves were in control of the factory, not management, not even union leaders. Such worker-controlled grassroots activism spread to other industries and forced management to recognize and bargain with unions. Workers of the fledgling United

Auto Workers union (UAW) were victorious at Goodyear and Firestone in Akron, Ohio, and at Fisher Body, General Motors, and Ford in Michigan. In 1937 alone nearly one million labor activists demanding union recognition participated in more than two thousand strikes. In response to these disputes President Roosevelt urged the automobile manufacturers to recognize and negotiate with the UAW, while Congress passed the Wagner Act establishing the National Labor Relations Board. The NLRB was empowered to oversee union activity, to determine the makeup of bargaining units, to prohibit "unfair business practices" (such as firing workers for joining the union), and to force employers to sit down at the bargaining table with union representatives.

Economic crises, because they affect nearly every segment of society, bring out more radical elements that have a tendency to become increasingly militant, rebellious, and if hopelessness and despair intensifies to the breaking point, revolutionary. Although the Great Depression saw a considerable upsurge of radicalism in the United States, that radicalism did not take root sufficiently to survive long after the depression. One reason for this, as the historian Alan Brinkley observes, is that there had never been a serious left-wing radical tradition in the United States. "The rhetoric of class conflict," Brinkley maintains, "echoed only weakly among men and women steeped in the dominant themes of their nation's history." The American Revolution and most protest movements throughout the nineteenth century were primarily motivated by a distrust of centralized authority. "Opposition to centralized authority and demands for the wide dispersion of power had formed the core of American social and political protest, the nation's constricted version of a radical tradition, for more than a century."[19] This distrust lay behind the reform movements of the 1830s and 1840s as well as the free-labor/free-soil ideology of the 1850s. By the time of the Great Depression the old dominant forces had been replaced by a new paradigm. Wall Street, big business, and the finance industry were the new centralized authority, and the protests against concentrated wealth and power were an echo of the American political tradition of opposition to the forces that prevented a wider dispersal of economic opportunity and therefore of power. This was the foundation of the protests of the 1930s, not the class struggle of Marxist ideology.

* * *

Along with direct political action, speeches, and demagoguery, dissent in the 1930s was also expressed very effectively through literature, music, and the arts. Even popular culture, while not outwardly protesting against business and government, reflected the profound level of discontent with the status quo that permeated the United States.

As the depression deepened, creative artists described the harsh realities that the hardest hit Americans faced in their daily lives. Writers, photographers, and artists focused public attention on the breadlines, the dust bowl, the dispossessed migrants, and the Hoovervilles that had become an indelible part of the American landscape. Raising consciousness through social realism, they hoped, would spur the government and the private sector to take more significant action in alleviating suffering and getting people back on their feet. Some of the most poignant images we have of the 1930s are the photographs of Walker Evans, Dorothea Lange, and Margaret Bourke-White depicting the despair of destitute Americans. Erskine Caldwell's novel *Tobacco Road* tells the story of white tenant farmers in Georgia, John Steinbeck's *The Grapes of Wrath* describes the countless misfortunes faced by the Joad family as they traveled from the dust bowl of Oklahoma to the promised land of California, lured by the false hope of finding decent-paying jobs as fruit pickers, Richard Wright's *Native Son* relates the story of an impoverished African American man living in Chicago's black ghetto who finds there is no escape from poverty and racism, and on a more political level, John Dos Passos's trilogy *U.S.A.* relentlessly blames the capitalist system for causing the depression. Murals and paintings by artists such as Thomas Hart Benton, John Steuart Curry, and Isaac Soyer were another form of social protest that portrayed the harsh realities of poverty as well as hopeful images of a more prosperous America that they hoped would soon come to pass.

In 1932 Myles Horton and Jim West founded the Highlander Folk School in Monteagle, Tennessee. The school was a grassroots educational institution that offered a variety of workshops that addressed social issues in the region and sought to get people involved in direct action campaigns for the purpose of creating a more humane society. Throughout much of its first decade the school concentrated on labor activism. The faculty taught miners and textile workers effective collective action strategies, such as picketing and the sit-down strike, and techniques for organizing successful recruitment drives. For a time

Highlander worked closely with the new Congress of Industrial Organizations (a more militant advocate for labor's unskilled rank-and-file
than the American Federation of Labor) organizing workers in Tennessee, the Carolinas, and other southern communities. One of the
features of Highlander was the emphasis on music. Harking back to
the tradition of Joe Hill and the Wobblies, Highlander taught workers
scores of inspirational prounion songs that would promote solidarity
and optimism on picket lines and protest marches. One of the songs it
introduced to activists was an African American hymn titled "I'll Overcome Someday." After World War II Highlander shifted its main focus
to civil rights activism, and the hymn was secularized when Pete Seeger,
Guy Carawan, and others quickened the tempo, wrote new verses, and
changed the title to "We Shall Overcome."

The volunteers at Highlander recognized the power of music in voicing dissent and promoting social change. The disorder and hard times
of the Great Depression produced a growing coterie of musicians and
songwriters who used their talent to fortify and propagate political
activism. Alfred Hayes and Earl Robinson paid homage to Joe Hill in
a song they hoped would inspire workers to stand up for their rights.
"I dreamed I saw Joe Hill last night," they wrote, "alive as you and me."
Florence Reese wrote "Which Side Are You On?"—a resounding union
song that was sung for decades at labor rallies and strikes and civil
rights marches. But it was Woody Guthrie who had the most significant
impact as a writer of protest songs during the Great Depression, and his
influence still resonates to this day.

During the depression, as Guthrie hitchhiked and rode the rails
around the country, he found himself very much engaged with the
unemployed, the migrant workers, and the Okies desperately seeking any kind of job that would bring in some money. Angered by the
discrimination and exploitation migrant workers faced in California,
Guthrie began writing and performing songs at Hoovervilles, union
meetings, migrant camps, protest rallies, and even on the radio. He
wrote what he called his "Dust Bowl Ballads," songs such as "Hard Trav-
elin'," "Blowin' Down This Old Dusty Road," "I Ain't Got No Home,"
"Tom Joad," and "Pastures of Plenty," detailing the stories of poor
migrant workers; union songs such as "Union Maid," "Ludlow Massacre," and "Union Burying Ground," extolling unionization; and political
protest songs such as "Pretty Boy Floyd," "Jesus Christ," and "Do Re Mi,"

Woody Guthrie, March 8, 1943, playing his guitar with a sticker that reads, "This Machine Kills Fascists." Guthrie wrote hundreds of protest songs and was a major force on the evolution of music as a means of expressing dissent. His influence was enormous and continues to this day—from Pete Seeger to Joan Baez, Bob Dylan, Phil Ochs, Bruce Springsteen, John Mellencamp, and countless other artists. (Public domain; courtesy Library of Congress)

attacking the hypocrisy and dishonesty of the establishment. In "Pretty Boy Floyd" Guthrie portrays the notorious bank robber as a modern-day Robin Hood who, unlike the bankers, gives money to the poor. He has seen so many different sorts of people as he has traveled around America, and as Guthrie sings in the song, "Some will rob you with a six-gun / And some with a fountain pen." In "Jesus Christ" Guthrie ponders how people would respond if Jesus Christ returned to preach his message around the United States today, and he concludes that the preachers and the bankers and the cops would crucify him all over again. In "Do Re Mi" Guthrie wryly observes that California was not exactly the "promised land" that existed in the minds of the thousands of Okies fleeing the dust bowl. The migrants arriving in California looking for jobs discovered all too soon the truth of Guthrie's lyrics that they were not going to make it unless they had the dough.

Guthrie's songs were always topical, often controversial and provocative, touching on the real-life misfortunes of the poor. Many of the songs were taken directly from his personal experience and the stories he read in newspapers. When a plane carrying illegal Mexican migrant workers who were being deported crashed over Los Gatos Canyon on the way to Mexico, Guthrie was appalled that the radio and newspapers reported that the victims "were just deportees." When he read this, Guthrie was inspired to write a song denouncing the exploitation of migrant workers.

He wrote his most famous song, "This Land Is Your Land," as a rejoinder to Irving Berlin's "God Bless America," which Guthrie considered the epitome of American sanctimoniousness. In the first version of the song the repetitive refrain he invoked was "God blessed America for me." Later he changed it to "this land was made for you and me." He also wrote several radical verses (later dropped from recordings of the song) that made it clear he believed America belonged to *all* the people, even the ones who wait in line outside relief offices, not just wealthy landlords and banks and corporations.

Many people accused Woody Guthrie of being a communist or at least a communist sympathizer. He often made fun of these accusations by denying he was a "red," even though he had always been "in the red" all his life. Although he was attracted to communism, the Soviet system, and Joseph Stalin, he did not join the Communist Party because he believed it was too authoritarian, especially its antireligious stance. Guthrie was too much of an individualist to adhere to strict party lines. When Stalin signed the Nazi-Soviet Nonaggression Pact with Hitler, Guthrie, like many leftists, grew disenchanted with communism. When World War II broke out, Guthrie aimed his militant songs at the Nazis. He was always opposed, as he wrote in his autobiography, to "Hitlerism and fascism homemade and imported."[20] He pasted a notice on his guitar's soundboard proclaiming, "This Machine Kills Fascists." Guthrie considered himself a true patriot, a man who sincerely believed in what the United States stood for. And when he felt American ideals were endangered, whether by Nazis and fascists or by business leaders and bankers, he spoke out strongly and eloquently in song. His songs were heard by millions of Americans, stirred people's consciousness, and were an enduring legacy that influenced Pete Seeger, Bob Dylan, Bruce Springsteen, Ani DiFranco, and hundreds of other artists who wrote songs of political protest and social activism later in the century.

Escapism, although not overtly political, was another form of dissent. The reality of the Great Depression was so harsh that millions of Americans escaped into a dream world of superheroes that promised salvation from the catastrophe and lavish musical comedies that, for the moment at least, permitted them to forget their troubles. Comic books, most notably *Superman*, whose title character fought for "truth, justice, and the American Way," were enormously popular. Americans were glued to their radios each night listening to serials such as *The Lone Ranger*, whose protagonist championed downtrodden common people. Hollywood comedies such as *It Happened One Night* and the Marx Brothers' films allowed people to laugh and feel good for a couple of hours. Musicals such as *42nd Street* were extravagant denials that a depression was gripping the land. And although most writers were penning realistic critiques of the harsh realities of life, the most popular book (and subsequently movie) of the decade was Margaret Mitchell's *Gone with the Wind*—a romantic and nostalgic tale of southern society during and after the Civil War. The story of Scarlet O'Hara surviving the cataclysm of Civil War and Reconstruction inspired Americans to believe they could survive the Great Depression. Ultimately 1930s popular culture reveals that Americans found the present to be so intolerable that they looked for escape and solace in diversions that transported them far from everyday reality.

* * *

By 1936 ominous events in the rest of the world were increasingly demanding America's attention. In East Asia, imperial Japan had occupied Manchuria and invaded China. In Africa the Italian dictator Benito Mussolini overran Ethiopia and turned it into an Italian colony. In Spain fascists led by Francisco Franco (with support from Mussolini and Hitler) launched a civil war against the democratically elected government. And in Germany Adolf Hitler violated the Versailles Treaty by rearming Germany and militarizing the Rhineland. Whereas Britain and France, unwilling to risk another war, tolerated Hitler's belligerent rhetoric and behavior, FDR regarded the German dictator as a major threat to world peace and was convinced that if Hitler was not reined in, war would be inevitable. Roosevelt believed that the only way to preserve world peace, the only way for the United States to have an influence on the course of world events and ensure the peace, was not by burying its head ostrich-like in the sand and hoping the problem would go away but by actively engaging in diplomacy, by pursuing a policy of internationalism. The problem was that the cornerstone of American foreign policy was isolationism, reaffirmed by America's disillusionment with getting involved in the Great War. Congress's response to the growing crisis in Europe was a series of Neutrality Acts between 1936 and 1939 that prohibited the United States from selling arms to belligerents, even those countries that needed to defend themselves against aggression.

And so, as the European peace deteriorated, Roosevelt embarked on the daunting task of educating the American public of the dangers of noninvolvement. Every move the president made to change America's course met with stiff opposition from isolationists in both parties. Progressives and liberals opposed any policy that would lead to American involvement because they feared it would undermine New Deal reforms. Business leaders and investors were isolationist because war would disrupt access to markets. But at the same time, many Republicans and conservative southern Democrats who seldom saw eye to eye with Roosevelt on domestic issues sided with him on foreign policy because they believed that the United States would never be more than a second-rate power in a world dominated by the Axis.

If anything, the advent of war in Europe in 1939 strengthened the isolationists' hand. Americans, above all, did not want to be dragged into another European conflict, and a potent antiwar/neutrality movement swung into high gear. Roosevelt's call for a special session of Congress at the end of September to reconsider neutrality legislation galvanized isolationist forces. Senator William Borah of Idaho warned that tampering with neutrality laws would surely drag the United States into the war. Other isolationist senators, along with Charles Coughlin and the aviation hero Charles Lindbergh (perhaps the most popular man in the country), gave radio speeches denouncing Roosevelt's efforts to get around the Neutrality Acts and aid the victims of Nazi aggression. "The destiny of this country," Lindbergh argued, "does not call for our

392 * A NEW DEAL FOR AMERICA

involvement in European wars. One need only glance at a map to see where our true frontiers lie. What more could we ask than the Atlantic Ocean on the east and the Pacific on the west . . . ?"[21] Millions of Americans sent letters and telegrams to Congress and the White House opposing any revision in the neutrality laws. Like Lindbergh, they believed that the Third Reich did not endanger "Fortress America."

Such opposition continued throughout 1940 and 1941 as Roosevelt sought ways to support Britain. In Chicago a group of anti-interventionist activists founded the America First Committee to coordinate the protests against FDR's course of action, which would inevitably drag the United States into the war. When Roosevelt introduced the Lend-Lease Bill in order to bypass the restrictions on selling military supplies to Britain, the America First Committee stepped up its attacks. Such a policy, they declared (rightly), would only lead the U.S. Navy to protect the convoys of goods going to England, and this in turn would lead to a shooting war with Nazi submarines. The anti-war "Mothers' Crusade" held a "pray-in" at the Capitol while Congress voted on the Lend-Lease Bill and then, when the bill was approved, picketed the White House demanding the president kill Lend-Lease, "not our sons." At the same time, America First organized additional rallies around the country. The antiwar activism delayed the passage of the Lend-Lease Bill, but Roosevelt eventually signed the bill into law in January 1941. Lindbergh and other America Firsters continued to give speeches all over the country. "In time of war," Lindbergh said at an April rally in New York, "truth is always replaced by propaganda. I do not believe we should be too quick to criticize the actions of a belligerent nation [Germany]. . . . But we in this country have a right to think of the welfare of America first. . . . When England asks us to enter this war, she is considering her own future, and that of her Empire. In making our reply, I believe we should consider the future of the United States and that of the Western Hemisphere." President Roosevelt and his interventionist cronies, Lindbergh claimed, are destroying American democracy. "It is they who are undermining the principles of Democracy when they demand that we take a course to which more than eighty percent of our citizens are opposed. . . . There is no better way to give comfort to an enemy than to divide the people of a nation over the issue of foreign war. There is no shorter road to defeat than by entering a war with inadequate preparation."[22]

CHAPTER 18

The Good War?

Before my first trip to Germany, I knew that the U.S. government and banks were supporting and arming Adolf Hitler. ... I also knew that a number of major U.S. corporations had set up plants in Nazi Germany. ... General Motors, ITT, and Ford come most readily to mind as having plants protected by Hitler.

—David Dellinger,
"Why I Refused to Register in the 1940 Draft"

In less than two hours on December 7, 1941, the Japanese were able to accomplish what FDR had been trying to accomplish for over two years—unite the American people behind the war. And yet, despite the fact that the vast majority of Americans in December 1941 believed it was necessary to declare war, and despite the fact that the attack on Pearl Harbor silenced the isolationist opposition, antiwar dissent continued unabated throughout the conflict.

The war ended the Great Depression. Unemployment was over. Anyone who wanted a job found one. Millions went to work in defense industries. The demand for workers and soldiers provided endless opportunities for everyone and accelerated social change, especially for women and minorities. Manufacturers and industrialists sent agents south of the border to recruit Mexican workers for their factories. Women's roles expanded as they were offered good-paying jobs in the defense industry that had previously only been open to men. And millions of Americans enlisted in the armed forces or were drafted. More than two hundred thousand women served in the army and navy. Thousands of Indians and Mexican Americans volunteered for the military, more than two million African Americans registered for the draft, and nearly a million of them served in segregated regiments, where they committed themselves to fighting for the "Double V Campaign"— victory abroad against fascism, victory at home against racism.

Five months before Pearl Harbor, A. Philip Randolph, the president of the Brotherhood of Sleeping Car Porters, gained an audience with the president and threatened that if African Americans were not hired on an equal-opportunity basis in the defense industries, he would lead a massive protest march on Washington. Worried that calling attention to racism in the United States at such a moment would be a propaganda victory for the Nazis, FDR acquiesced to Randolph's demand. Roosevelt issued Executive Order 8802 establishing the Fair Employment Practices Commission and prohibiting discrimination in the defense industry. In this way dissent, although merely the threat of a protest march, modified official federal racial policy. This was only the beginning. The experience of African American soldiers, pilots, and sailors in combat— some of them serving as officers, all of them confronting a much wider world—had a profound impact on their lives and proved to be one of the important factors in the rise of the postwar civil rights movement.

Despite the pride of African American soldiers in serving the nation they continued to protest against the racism, segregation, and unequal treatment they experienced on a daily basis in the military. In several states African American troops served as guards at the camps where German prisoners of war were incarcerated. Most prisoners were compelled to do forced labor, and it was common practice to take them to work in nearby fields. When the guards took the POWs back to the camps in the evening, they frequently stopped for food at a diner or restaurant along the way. While the German POWs would be served inside, their African American guards had to get their sandwiches handed to them out of the kitchen window. This happened not only in the South but in the North as well. "The people of Salina [Kansas]," one African American soldier recalled after the war, "would serve these enemy soldiers and turn away black American G.I.'s."[1] When FDR proclaimed that the United States was fighting "to make a world in which tyranny and aggression cannot exist; a world based upon freedom, equality, and justice; a world in which all persons regardless of race, color, and creed may live in peace, honor, and dignity,"[2] an African American soldier, Private First Class Charles Wilson, sent an angry letter of protest. "Dear President Roosevelt," he wrote, it is quite clear that the United States itself is undemocratic as long as "jim crow and segregation is practiced by our Armed Forces against its Negro members." Segregation means that "totally inadequate opportunities are given to the Negro members of our Armed Forces . . . to participate with 'equality' . . . 'regardless of race and color' in the fight for our war aims." He went on to describe the inferior conditions in the segregated barracks that African American soldiers had to endure. "How can we convince nearly one tenth of the Armed Forces, the Negro members," he reasoned, "that your pronouncement of the war aims of the United Nations means what it says, when their experience with . . . the United States of America, is just the opposite?"[3]

On the home front hundreds of thousands of African Americans, lured by good pay and job security, moved to industrial centers. This migration triggered a number of race riots. One riot in Detroit lasted several days, during which twenty-five blacks and nine whites were killed. Other riots took place in New York; Los Angeles; Beaumont, Texas; and Mobile, Alabama. In the face of such violence blacks became more militant. Hundreds of thousands joined the NAACP (membership jumped from 50,000 in 1940 to 405,000 by the end of the war), and in 1942 a new, more militant civil rights organization was founded: the Congress of Racial Equality (CORE). Unlike the NAACP, which confronted racism primarily through legal action, CORE organized and coordinated civil disobedience campaigns. Hundreds of CORE activists participated in the "Don't Shop Where You Can't Work" campaign urging the public to boycott stores, restaurants, and theaters in northern cities such as New York that did not hire African American workers. In 1944 fourteen black intellectuals published *What the Negro Wants*, a manifesto calling for voting rights in the South and full integration into the American way of life. World War II made it patently obvious that there was an inherent contradiction in fighting for freedom in a segregated military and a segregated nation. By the end of the war African Americans and white liberals envisioned an integrated society in which the U.S. recommitted itself to the nation's ideals of liberty and equality for all. Within a few years a full-fledged civil rights movement began to change America.

Mexican factory workers also were targets of racism and bigotry. In many locales they were considered "colored," and therefore they were segregated, forbidden access to public swimming pools and restaurants, and routinely harassed by local police forces. In Los Angeles in 1943 anti-Mexican sentiment boiled over in the so-called "Zoot Suit Riots" (many young Mexican and Mexican American men, in an act of defiance and dissent against prejudice and racial discrimination, wore wide-brimmed hats and baggy suits with peg-leg pants), during which soldiers, sailors, and local residents rampaged through the city beating up every zoot-suiter they came across. Hundreds were severely injured.

Despite prevailing gender attitudes and male resistance, millions of women took jobs in the defense plants, jobs that were normally seen as "men's work." Women worked long hours as welders, riveters, and tool operators. They built airplanes and jeeps, ships and tanks, guns and bombs. Posters published by the War Production Co-Ordinating Committee urged women to fill the abundant positions that were necessary for the war effort while the men were in combat in Europe and the Pacific. The apocryphal "Rosie the Riveter" became a dominant image in government posters. Women soon were so essential in the workforce that they compelled some industries to establish day-care centers for children while they were on the job. They even pressured unions, such as the United Auto Workers, to lobby employers for "equal pay for equal work." Even though women were indispensable for wartime manufacturing, and even though the federal government appealed to women's patriotism to go to work for the country, they were still confronted with gender stereotyping and male condescension. For example, in the aircraft industry women were usually trained in a gender-specific way—male managers would patronizingly explain a job such as riveting the wings of airplanes by likening the task to sewing a dress according to a pattern. And, of course, there was plenty of sexual harassment. Many women also joined the armed forces as WAVES (Women Accepted for Voluntary Emergency Service) and WACs (Women's Army Corps). Here they most frequently performed the usual service roles reserved for women, working predominantly in offices as clerks and typists or in hospitals at home and abroad as nurses. It was clear, though, that no matter what tasks women performed during the war, their horizons and expectations, like those of African Americans and Mexican Americans, were expanding.

* * *

Although most Americans regardless of race, ethnicity, or gender supported the "Good War," many thousands protested—against the war, against the draft, and against infringements on civil liberties and civil rights. Most isolationists and members of the America First Committee ceased protesting against Roosevelt's policies immediately after Pearl Harbor, but many of them simply shifted their protest to focus on Roosevelt's war strategy, arguing that the United States should throw the bulk of its might into the Pacific Theater fighting the "yellow peril" rather than the president's "Germany first" strategy. This expression of the deep-seated racism that persists in American society, coupled with the Japanese attack on Pearl Harbor, ignited an outbreak of anti-Japanese hysteria. This was especially problematic on the West Coast, where more than one hundred thousand Japanese Americans lived. Americans jumped to the conclusion that Japanese Americans could not be trusted, that their loyalty was not to the United States but to imperial Japan. Rumors spread that the Japanese living in California were spies, saboteurs, traitors; they were planning to guide Japanese warplanes to targets in California; they were hatching plots to blow up dams and hydroelectric power stations. Both the governor and attorney general of California called for their removal. Many whites saw it as a golden opportunity to acquire Japanese farms, orchards, businesses, and homes at bargain-basement prices. Anti-Japanese prejudice reached the boiling point. The respected *New York Times* columnist Walter Lippmann reported that "it is a fact that communication takes place between the enemy at sea and enemy agents on land."[4] The commander of the army's Western Command, General John DeWitt, urged Washington to remove the Japanese from the West Coast. "A Jap's a Jap," he declared; "it makes no difference whether he is an American citizen or not."[5] Public pressure was put on Roosevelt to do something, and in February 1942 FDR signed Executive Order 9066 authorizing the internment of Japanese Americans on the West Coast. (FBI director J. Edgar Hoover, surprisingly, was one of the few federal officials who opposed the internment. He counseled Roosevelt that the FBI had a complete list of Japanese spies in America and that there was no threat whatsoever from citizens of Japanese descent.) Without due process, without any charges being filed, without writs of habeas corpus, more than 110,000 Japanese Americans were forced out of their homes and sent to internment camps. More than half of them were *nisei*, born in the United States, American citizens. Civil liberties, civil rights were disregarded. The NAACP, the Communist Party, the Socialist Party, the American Jewish Committee—organizations that had traditionally fought for civil rights protections—were embarrassingly silent.

But there *was* dissent against this policy. Japanese Americans, as would be expected, fought against the removal order. Those who were removed to the camps resisted through strikes and disobedience, refusal to take loyalty oaths, even riots. Some refused to report for evacuation and were arrested. Some of those who were arrested took their cases to the Supreme Court. Gordon Hirabayashi, Minoru Yasui, and Fred Korematsu all challenged the constitutionality of the executive order. "The thing that struck me immediately," Minoru Yasui said about the evacuation order, "was that the military was ordering the civilian to do something. In my opinion, that's the way dictatorships are formed. And if I, as an American citizen stood still for this, I would be derogating the rights of all citizens. By God, I had to stand up and say, 'That's wrong.' I refused to report for evacuation."[6] As a result, he was arrested and served nine months in solitary confinement. Yasui, who had received a law degree from the University of Oregon in 1939, appealed his case to the Supreme Court. In November 1942, while in jail, he wrote his sister. "The insidious danger of creating a precedent of confining American citizens behind barbed wire fences and machine guns when they have committed no crime seemed reprehensible to me. . . . But surely as the attack on Pearl Harbor endangered our democracy, . . . [the] evacuation of American citizens on the basis of race is just as dangerous a threat to democracy!" Thus it was clear to Yasui that it was his *patriotic* duty, as a loyal American, to fight the internment policy. "Caucasian Americans are no better nor worse than I, for we are all human beings. It is only the principles of liberty, democracy and justice, and the adherence to these principles that made America great, and as a loyal American who can suffer his native land to do no wrong, I must hold true to those principles."[7] In 1943 in *Yasui v. United States* the Supreme Court upheld the evacuation order and denied Yasui's appeal. The Court also ruled against both Korematsu and Hirabayashi in their cases.

One of the ironies of the internment of Japanese Americans is that despite the fact that their civil liberties had been rescinded and they were incarcerated, they were also subject to the draft. Approximately two hundred refused to be drafted (and were sent to prison), but twenty thousand Japanese Americans served in the army and acquitted themselves heroically in the European theater. One *nisei* battalion, the 442nd Infantry Combat Team, received more combat decorations than any other battalion in the war.

When Japanese Americans received their internment orders, they had only a few days to sell their property. Thus they were forced to accept prices far below market value. When they were finally released from internment, they had no place to go. Those who returned to the communities where they had lived before the war discovered that anti-Japanese prejudice had not diminished, they faced harassment and persecution, and they were not welcome to return home. For decades after the war Japanese Americans continued to protest their treatment and demand restitution. Finally, in 1988 Congress issued a formal apology and approved a $20,000 payment to each surviving victim. Not a single American of Japanese descent was ever found guilty of sabotage or espionage.

* * *

Labor unions on the whole were eager to show they were fully behind the war effort by agreeing to the government's wage freeze and the no-strike pledges announced by the AFL and CIO. Even so, the wage freeze rankled workers, especially when it soon became clear that business profits were soaring at an unprecedented rate. Some workers protested the wage freeze by breaking the no-strike pledge. There were innumerable walkouts and "flash strikes," in which workers walked off the job for a day or two. Miners and steelworkers went on strike. There was a walkout at the Willow Run Liberator Bomber plant in Michigan that stopped production for more than twenty-four hours. In Chicago workers struck for three days at a plant that manufactured airplane engines. Dozens of times during the war President Roosevelt ordered the army to seize plants and mines and put them back into operation. Despite the no-strike pledge, it is estimated that there were over twelve thousand labor stoppages during the war involving more than six million workers. One effective way that companies dealt with these strikes and got workers back to work was to offer them health insurance and pension plans in lieu of wage increases.

Before the Japanese attack on Pearl Harbor the America First Committee, as we have seen, put enormous pressure on Roosevelt to stay out of the war. Along with America First there was also a communist organization—the American Peace Mobilization (APM)—that protested loudly at that time against American involvement in the war. The APM organized protest rallies and demonstrations and frequently picketed the White House. But after Hitler invaded the Soviet Union, American communists about-faced and became adamant anti-Nazi war hawks. Other Americans, though, took up the antiwar banner as doves. Quakers, as they have often done, led the way. Other religious groups also protested for moral reasons: Mennonites, Amish, Jehovah's Witnesses, Seventh Day Adventists, and Buddhists, as well as some Catholics. Particularly odious to many was the draft. The Selective Service Act of 1940 provided two classifications for those who were opposed to the war: 1-AO, for those who were willing to work in the medical corps, and 4-E, for those who were not willing to take any military assignment but would accept alternative civilian work. Between 1941 and 1945 thirty-seven thousand pacifists were given "conscientious objector" classifications, while seven thousand others refused to participate in any way in the war and wound up serving prison sentences. Those who did not enter the medical corps worked in Civil Public Service (CPS) work camps nine hours a day, six days a week. They were assigned to menial tasks and were expected to pay thirty-five dollars a month for their "room and board." They came from all walks of life. "We had PhDs," one inmate recalled later, "we had winners of Fulbright prizes, we had guys who had a third-grade education, we had stockbrokers, we had ballet dancers, we had atheists, we had fundamentalists . . . every possible kind of human being was there."[8] One conscientious objector was the Hollywood actor Lew Ayres, who played the starring role in the classic World War I antiwar film *All Quiet on the Western Front*. Ayres spent the war serving in the medical corps. Many of the conscientious objectors who went into the CPS camps performed valuable and necessary jobs. Some worked as assistants in mental institutions, where they had a positive impact in bringing about the humane treatment of mental patients (in fact their efforts induced *Life* magazine to run a widely read exposé that successfully reformed the way the mentally ill were treated); some worked as "fire jumpers" (combating forest fires); some worked as caregivers for juvenile delinquents; and some even volunteered for dangerous medical experiments to find cures for hepatitis, malaria, typhus, and other infectious diseases as well as for studies on the effects of starvation in order to improve the treatment of starvation victims. The government's main concern, however, was to isolate conscientious objectors from the public so that they would not have a demoralizing influence on the war effort. In reality it was a form of incarceration; some objectors were not released from the CPS camps until 1947.

Two of the draft resisters imprisoned during World War II, David Dellinger and Bayard Rustin, went on to become major players in the two principal dissent movements of the 1960s—Rustin in civil rights and Dellinger in the mobilization against the war in Vietnam. Dellinger was a young progressive activist who was inspired by the example of Mahatma Gandhi and the writings of the Social Gospel advocate Reinhold Niebuhr. Dellinger had visited Germany in 1936 and 1937 and was disgusted with American complicity in the rise of Adolf Hitler. American bankers and industrialists had supported Hitler throughout the 1930s. Sperry Gyroscope sold important aviation navigation technology to the Luftwaffe, DuPont was in cahoots with German explosive manufacturers, Pratt and Whitney had a brisk trade in selling aircraft engines to the Third Reich. "It was clear to me during this period," Dellinger wrote, "that England, France, and the United States were working with Hitler not only for the profits to be gained by U.S. banks and corporations, but also with the major aim of influencing the Nazis to expand militarily to the east, destroying, or at least crippling, the Communist enemy."[9] It was only after the Nazi-Soviet Nonaggression Pact that American financiers began to turn against Hitler. When the war broke out in Europe, Dellinger helped organize and take part in antiwar demonstrations, and then in 1941 he refused to register for the draft. He was arrested and sentenced to prison. He used his time in prison as a political activist by leading protests and staging hunger strikes against the practices of segregating white inmates from black, throwing uncooperative inmates into "The Hole" (where prisoners were subjected to sensory deprivation and solitary confinement), and censoring books and incoming mail.

Dellinger's first protest was a spontaneous act shortly after he began serving his sentence. Prisoners were allowed to view movies on Saturday nights. The first time he entered the prison theater, he accompanied an African American inmate. "The guard pointed to the white section for me and the black section for him, but I sat next to my friend in the black section. It was not a planned protest, just the instinctive, natural thing to do. Soon I was carried out and placed in a solitary cell in the maximum security 'troublemakers' cell block." Frequently during his

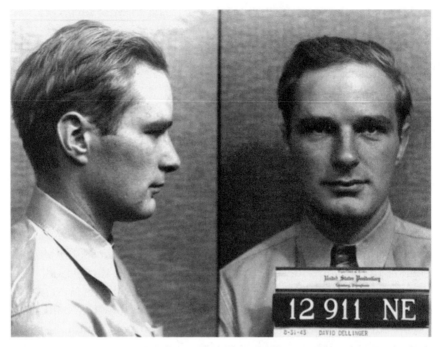

The antiwar protestor David Dellinger, August 31, 1943, in prison for resisting the draft during World War II. Dellinger went on to participate in many other protests after his release, including acting as one of the organizers of the anti–Vietnam War demonstrations at the Democratic Convention in Chicago, 1968. Photograph by the Federal Bureau of Prisons. (Public domain)

four years in prison guards abused him. Sometimes they would throw him into the overcrowded cells where the most violent criminals were held. The guards would tell the hardened inmates that Dellinger was "yellow" and urged them "to take care of this unpatriotic guy."[10]

The antiwar protestor Bayard Rustin was imprisoned for two years in the Lewisburg, Pennsylvania, federal penitentiary. At Lewisburg Rustin organized boycotts, strikes, and antisegregation protests. Such protests by Rustin, Dellinger, and other conscientious objectors eventually led to the integration of the federal prison system. Immediately after the war Rustin became an anticolonial/anti-imperialist activist demanding the end of colonial rule in Africa and Asia. In the 1950s Rustin was a leading force in the civil rights movement, joining Martin Luther King, Jr., in the Montgomery bus boycott and, most famously, organizing and coordinating the 1963 March on Washington.

Larry Gara, a lifelong pacifist, was devoted to his Quaker beliefs as well as the socialist theories of Eugene V. Debs. He refused to register for the draft and was arrested, convicted, and sentenced to three years in federal prison. It was in prison where he met Bayard Rustin. When Gara learned that Rustin's cell was in a segregated cell block, he organized a series of nonviolent demonstrations against segregation. "We planned to sit wherever we chose in the dining hall, and if we should be physically prevented from doing so we would go on work strike. Even the majority of Jehovah's Witnesses agreed to the plan." When the protestors struck, the prison put them all on "administrative segregation." This meant they were all "confined to [their] cells all day except for a brief period of exercise and for taking showers." After Gara was released from prison, he continued to protest the war as a history teacher—a stance that at one college led to his firing. Still he maintained his pacifist values and believed that he could make a difference. "I have questioned many of my beliefs and actions," he wrote several years after the war, "but have never once doubted that refusal to register for Selective Service was the correct path for me to follow. It was the strongest stand a male youth could take against war in 1942, and I instinctively knew it was what I had to do." Individuals must take a stand, Gara contended, even when it seems impossible to change things. And throughout American history individuals from William Lloyd Garrison to Martin Luther King did have the courage to take a stand. True, the Nazis committed horrible atrocities and *had* to be stopped. But killing untold thousands of German and Japanese civilians in the firebombing of Hamburg and Dresden and Tokyo or in the atomic bombs dropped on Hiroshima and Nagasaki was not the answer. "In truth," Gara admitted, "we had no answers, though we knew that much earlier there had been opportunities for governments to prevent the war." What the war resisters accomplished, though, "was to light a few candles in the darkness, to keep the ideal of nonviolence alive for use when the world came to its senses."[11]

What is perhaps most astonishing about the World War II antiwar movement is that there were so many conscientious objectors. The war had virtually zero organized opposition. The Socialist and Communist Parties as well as most anarchist groups that had previously taken antiwar positions were unanimous this time in their support for the war. To them it was a "people's war" against fascism. Of all the wars the United

States has ever fought, none had such unprecedented unanimity of support as World War II. Pacifists were viewed as cowards. And so it took extraordinary courage on their part to dissent. One conscientious objector, Desmond T. Doss, who served as a medic but refused to carry a gun and was therefore subjected to the ridicule and antagonism of his fellow soldiers, showed exceptional courage when he saved seventy-five men as a medic during a fierce battle in Okinawa. At the end of the war President Harry Truman awarded Doss the Congressional Medal of Honor.

The experience of conscientious objectors during World War II also shows how dissent can precipitate change in unexpected ways. Conscientious objectors opposed the war and were willing to pay the price of imprisonment or forced labor as well as the humiliation of becoming pariahs of society. They did not stop the war or hinder the war effort, yet they used their incarceration to publicize their antiwar position as well as to protest unequal conditions in prison and inhumane conditions in mental institutions. As a result, these activists left a lasting and positive impact on those institutions.

While conscientious objectors protested for religious or moral reasons, there were others who opposed the war from an intellectual stance. The controversial writer Henry Miller was one of many creative artists who protested the war, not because he endorsed Hitler or hated the United States but because he believed that war was ultimately irrational. Miller believed that life was to be lived to the fullest and that the forces that would repress joyousness and self-fulfillment were the same forces that led nations to believe that war could bring about peace. Miller was living in Europe when the Germans invaded Poland, and he returned (reluctantly) to the United States in December 1939 when American embassies ordered all Americans to evacuate from the war zones. In 1944 he published an antiwar pamphlet, *Murder the Murderer*, in which he presented an overview of American wars and the antiwar positions of American thinkers from Thoreau to Debs. Miller argued that World War II, despite the fact that the enemy was evil, was no better than the previous wars fought for economic reasons. "A period of darkness has set in," Miller wrote. "The world seems determined to resolve its problems by force. . . . Millions of men and women will sacrifice their lives; millions more will be maimed and mutilated." But it is our own fault, he argued. If we had been wise, we could have stopped Hitler long before war became inevitable. "To defeat Hitler and his gang is not a particularly brilliant goal to set oneself. Hitler and his gang could have been defeated without war had we possessed the intelligence, the will, and the purity to undertake the task." But the United States supported Hitler's rise to power and then sat by and allowed him to swallow up one nation after another. "When France fell we were full of bitterness. We cried 'Shame!' though we hadn't lifted a finger to help her. . . . Until the treacherous attack by Japan, which we should have anticipated, considering all the lessons we had been given, we were undecided what course to pursue. Now suddenly we are united and, as in the last war, we are pretending that we are fighting to free the world."[12]

Miller argued that Americans have a false sense that it is the United States' duty to spread democracy and liberty to the world. The press and the government, he maintained, emphasize America's special role every time we go to war, but this is to mask the real motives of expanding American business around the globe. He also condemned the efforts to stifle dissent, not only by the government but also by citizens incessantly monitoring each other's patriotism. In words reminiscent of Randolph Bourne's argument in "War Is the Health of the State," Miller contended that "nations make war upon one another on the assumption that the views of the people and those who govern them are one. The moment war is declared it is impossible to dissent. . . . The unanimity of a nation, in times of war, is brought about by coercion pure and simple."[13] Like conscientious objectors who endured ostracism and prison, Miller too, along with other antiwar intellectuals and writers, was vilified for his "unpatriotic" stance.

* * *

Before the war radical students and professors at the City College of New York (CCNY) organized a chapter of the Communist Party and sponsored a series of antifascist demonstrations denouncing America's indifference to the rise of Hitler, Mussolini, and Franco while publicly proclaiming their admiration for Soviet communism. In 1941 and 1942 the Board of Education and the college administration launched a campaign to destroy "communist subversion." They banned the Communist Party and other left-wing student organizations, expelled students, and fired faculty. Hundreds of protesters took to the streets blasting this inexcusable abrogation of freedom of speech, but to no avail.

On the heels of the CCNY protests and as the war wound down, the House Committee on Un-American Activities launched a systematic investigation of disloyal Americans. By the late 1940s more and more Americans were being subpoenaed to give testimony before the committee. And then in 1950 Senator Joseph McCarthy burst on the scene with allegations that the reason for the worldwide success of communism was that the United States was infiltrated with traitors. The State Department was riddled with communists. Spies were everywhere. Disloyal Americans must be rooted out. Anyone who dissented against American policy or subscribed to left-wing ideology or pacifist beliefs was suspect.

CHAPTER 19

Dissent in an Age of Conformity

Some of my ancestors were religious dissenters who came to America over 300 years ago. Others were abolitionists in New England of the 1840's and 50's.

For twenty years I have been singing folksongs of America and other lands to people everywhere. I am proud that I never refused to sing to any group of people because I might disagree with some of the ideas of some of the people listening to me. I have sung for rich and poor, for Americans of every possible political and religious opinion and persuasion, of every race, color, and creed.

The House committee wished to pillory me because it didn't like some few of the many thousands of places I have sung for. . . . A good song can only do good, and I am proud of the songs I have sung. I hope to be able to continue singing these songs for all who want to listen, Republicans, Democrats, and independents. Do I have the right to sing these songs?

—Pete Seeger, statement at his sentencing
for contempt of Congress, 1961

"From Stettin in the Baltic to Trieste on the Adriatic an iron curtain has descended on the Continent."[1] Thus Winston Churchill characterized the geopolitical reality of postwar Europe and coined the term that dominated the West's view of the Cold War. Soviet troops occupied an enslaved eastern Europe, while British and American forces were the occupiers in the free West. The tension between East and West, which intensified and spread around the globe at a dizzying pace, became the defining feature of international relations for the next forty-five years.

As the United States and the Soviet Union faced off against each other, rattling their swords and raising the rhetoric to a fearsome pitch, anxious Americans proudly rallied around the flag. By 1953 the division in Europe had hardened, the Soviet Union had successfully tested its own atomic bomb, China had gone communist, Congress was investigating communists and spies *within* the U.S. government, Julius and Ethel Rosenberg were tried, convicted, and executed as Soviet spies, a war had been fought in Korea, and a new, far more lethal, nuclear arms race was under way.[2] The prevailing attitude was that Armageddon was just around the corner and that an evil, totalitarian foe was aiming to enslave the United States. Americans, joining together in universal revulsion for communism and their belief in the American way, proudly proclaimed that everything about the United States was noble while everything about the Soviet Union was evil. Yet, despite this patriotic unity, a powerful groundswell of discontent simmered just below the seemingly placid surface of the 1950s.

Like the 1920s, the 1950s was a decade of contrasts. Whereas the 1920s featured a conflict between modernism and traditionalism, the 1950s was a schizophrenic age split between confidence and paranoia. On one hand the booming economy, suburban growth, and a plethora of new consumer goods produced an atmosphere of great optimism and faith in the future. Things were only going to get better. But on the other hand the arms race, Cold War anxiety, and the paranoid fear of communism produced a sense of foreboding that it all might end at any moment in a nuclear holocaust. The growth of the middle class, home ownership, and the consumer society also, conversely, underscored that there were serious discrepancies in the United States, that there were numerous marginalized groups within American society, that contrary to conventional wisdom the American Dream was not fully available to all.

* * *

One way that dissent reared its head during the early years of the Cold War was in the reaction to the Second Red Scare that swept over the nation. As the House Committee on Un-American Activities (HUAC) and then later the Senate, led by Senator Joseph McCarthy, held hearings in an attempt to root out communist infiltration in the United States, courageous Americans spoke out against what they regarded as a twentieth-century witch hunt.

Some of those who protested, not surprisingly, were the very people being investigated by Congress. John Howard Lawson, the president of

the Screen Writers' Guild, was a case in point. Because the film industry was a particularly powerful force in shaping public opinion, Congress targeted Hollywood. Lawson (who had joined the Communist
Party in the 1930s) was a screenwriter who, according to congressional investigators, was brainwashing Americans by slipping communist
propaganda into his screenplays. When he appeared before HUAC, he
denounced the committee itself for being "un-American" because of its
flagrant contempt for the Bill of Rights. During his testimony Lawson
attempted to read a statement criticizing the hearings, but the chairman refused to let him do so. A brief excerpt from the record conveys
the chaotic atmosphere in the room as the chairman did everything in
his power to prevent Lawson from reading his statement:

> THE CHAIRMAN. Mr. Lawson, you will have to stop or you will leave
> the witness stand. And you will leave the witness stand because you
> are in contempt. That is why you will leave the witness stand. And if
> you are just trying to force me to put you in contempt, you won't have
> to try much harder. You know what has happened to a lot of people
> that have been in contempt of this committee this year, don't you?
>
> MR. LAWSON. I am glad you have made it perfectly clear that you are
> going to threaten and intimidate the witnesses, Mr. Chairman.
>
> (*The chairman pounding gavel.*)
>
> MR. LAWSON. I am an American and I am not at all easy to intimidate,
> and don't think I am.
>
> (*The chairman pounding gavel.*) . . .
>
> THE CHAIRMAN (*pounding gavel*). Mr. Lawson, just quiet down again.
> Mr. Lawson, the most pertinent question that we can ask is whether
> or not you have ever been a member of the Communist Party. Now,
> do you care to answer that question?
>
> MR. LAWSON. You are using the old technique, which was used in
> Hitler Germany in order to create a scare here—
>
> THE CHAIRMAN (*pounding gavel*). Oh—
>
> MR. LAWSON. In order to create an entirely false atmosphere in which
> this hearing is conducted—. . .
>
> THE CHAIRMAN (*pounding gavel*). Stand away from the stand—
>
> MR. LAWSON. I have written Americanism for many years, and I shall
> continue to fight for the Bill of Rights, which you are trying to destroy.
>
> THE CHAIRMAN. Officers, take this man away from the stand—[3]

In the disallowed statement Lawson accused the committee of conducting "an illegal and indecent trial" that was a "gross violation of the Constitution of the United States, and especially of its First and Fifth Amendments." What HUAC was really trying to do, Lawson insisted, is "introduce fascism in this country. They know that the only way to trick the American people into abandoning their rights and liberties is to manufacture an imaginary danger, to frighten the people into accepting repressive laws which are supposedly for their protection." If the committee is not stopped, freedom of thought and conscience will be extinguished. "If I can be destroyed no American is safe. You can subpoena a farmer in a field, a lumberjack in the woods, a worker at a machine, a doctor in his office—you can deprive them of a livelihood, deprive them of their honor as Americans."[4] But Lawson's protestations were scornfully dismissed. He was convicted of contempt of Congress, sentenced to a year in prison, and blacklisted.

Pete Seeger, a member of the popular music group the Weavers, which had recorded a number of hit songs ("Goodnight Irene," "Kisses Sweeter than Wine," "Sixteen Tons"), also ran afoul of HUAC. In August 1955 he was subpoenaed by the committee to testify about his political affiliations. Seeger, who had been a member of the Communist Party, was responsible for introducing "We Shall Overcome" to civil rights activists and was the composer of such protest songs as "If I Had a Hammer" and "Where Have All the Flowers Gone?" Seeger's antiwar views and firm commitment to civil rights, as well as his former Communist Party membership, made him an obvious target for a HUAC investigation. Members of the committee interrogated Seeger about his attendance and performances at Communist rallies and meetings, but Seeger refused to answer the questions, not on the grounds of the Fifth Amendment, as so many defendants routinely pleaded, but on the grounds of the First Amendment—that Congress had no right to ask questions regarding personal political beliefs. "I am not going to answer any questions," Seeger told the committee, "as to my association, my philosophical or religious beliefs or my political beliefs, or how I voted in any election, or any of these private affairs. I think these are very improper questions for any American to be asked, especially under such compulsion as this. I would be very glad to tell you my life if you want to hear of it." When pressed repeatedly to admit that he sang his songs at Communist rallies, Seeger replied, "I have sung for Americans of every political persuasion, and I am proud that I never refuse to sing to an audience, no matter what religion or color of their skin, or situation in life. I have sung in hobo jungles, and I have sung for the Rockefellers, and I am proud that I have never refused to sing for anybody. That is the only answer I can give along that line." The committee kept insisting that Seeger answer the question.

MR. SEEGER: Except for the answer I have already given you, I have no answer. The answer I gave you you have, don't you? That is, that I am proud that I have sung for Americans of every political persuasion, and I have never refused to sing for anybody because I disagreed with their political opinion, and I am proud of the fact that my songs seem to cut across and find perhaps a unifying thing, basic humanity, and that is why I would love to be able to tell you about these songs, because I feel that you would agree with me more, sir. I know many beautiful songs from your home county, Carbon, and Monroe, and I hitchhiked through there and stayed in the homes of miners.

MR. TAVENNER: My question was whether or not you sang at these functions of the Communist Party. You have answered it inferentially, and if I understand your answer, you are saying you did.

MR. SEEGER: Except for that answer, I decline to answer further. . . .

MR. SCHERER: Do you understand it is the feeling of the Committee that you are in contempt as a result of the position you take?

MR. SEEGER: I can't say.

MR. SCHERER: I am telling you that that is the position of the Committee. . . .

MR. SEEGER: I decline to discuss, under compulsion, where I have sung, and who has sung my songs, and who else has sung with me, and the people I have known. I love my country very dearly, and I greatly resent this implication that some of the places that I have sung and some of the people that I have known, and some of my opinions, whether they are religious or philosophical, or I might be a vegetarian, make me any less of an American. I will tell you about my songs, but I am not interested in telling you who wrote them, and I will tell you about my songs, and I am not interested in who listened to them.[5]

Seeger, like Lawson, was convicted of contempt of Congress and sentenced to a year in prison. Seeger appealed, and the sentence was overturned seven years later. But he was blacklisted and banned from radio and television until 1967.

Another target of HUAC was the African American actor-singer Paul Robeson. Starting in the 1930s, Robeson, who had achieved great fame for his acclaimed performances in *Othello*, *The Emperor Jones*, and *Show Boat*, traveled extensively abroad, where he assertively expressed his political views. He condemned segregation in the United States, denounced the fascist dictators in Europe, and expressed support for the Loyalists in Spain and his admiration of Soviet communism. Robeson was especially impressed with his treatment in the Soviet Union, where he found that he could walk the streets, eat in restaurants, and take public transportation without being subjected to racial discrimination. Communism, Robeson declared, was more egalitarian than American democracy was. After World War II he continued to speak favorably of communism, protested against the Jim Crow laws, and urged African Americans not to participate in an "imperialist war" if the United States went to war against the Soviet Union. In 1949 anticommunism was so extreme that when Robeson was booked to perform a concert in Peekskill, New York, all hell broke loose. Militant anticommunist protesters, wielding baseball bats, attacked concertgoers and forced the postponement of the concert. The following week more than twenty thousand people were in attendance at the open-air event when Robeson and other performers finally took the stage. But when people were leaving at the end of the concert, they were violently attacked. Hundreds of protesters screamed epithets at the performers and concertgoers, condemning them as unpatriotic, anti-American communists. With the police looking on, rock-throwing vigilantes attacked the cars and buses leaving the area. Dozens of people were severely injured. In the aftermath producers canceled Robeson's bookings, and there were public burnings of his records.

In 1950 the State Department revoked Paul Robeson's passport. With Robeson unable to travel abroad and not being booked in American concert halls, his career came to a crashing halt. With the FBI keeping him under surveillance, Robeson sued the government to reinstate his passport. Finally, in 1956 he was summoned to testify before the House Committee on Un-American Activities. Despite the constant browbeating by members of the committee and despite his continued invocation of the Fifth Amendment, Robeson managed to lecture them on the meaning of "Americanism" and insisted that it was the committee, not he, that was unpatriotic. "Whether I am or not a Communist is irrelevant," he declared. "The question is whether American citizens, regardless of their political beliefs or sympathies, may enjoy their constitutional rights." Furthermore, he asked at another point, "what do you mean by the Communist Party? As far as I know it is a legal party like the Republican Party and the Democratic Party. Do you mean a party of people who have sacrificed for my people, and for all Americans and workers, that they can live in dignity? Do you mean that party?" Robeson admitted that he admired the Soviet Union. "In Russia," he said, "I felt for the first time like a full human being. No color prejudice like in Mississippi, no color prejudice like in Washington. It was the first time I felt like a human being. Where I did not feel the pressure of color as I feel [it] in this Committee today." One of the interlocutors then asked him why he did not stay in Russia, to which Robeson replied, "Because my father was a slave, and my people died to build this country, and I am going to stay here, and have a part of it just like you. And no Fascist-minded people will drive me from it. Is that clear? I am for peace with the Soviet Union, and I am for peace with China, and I am not for peace or friendship with the Fascist Franco, and I am not for peace with Fascist Nazi Germans. I am for peace with decent people." He was a true patriot, Robeson insisted, unlike the members of the committee, the very existence of which goes against the most fundamental principles of the United States. "You gentlemen belong with the Alien and Sedition Acts, and you are the nonpatriots, and you are the un-Americans, and you ought to be ashamed of yourselves."[6] This was too much for the congressmen, and they abruptly adjourned the hearing.

Many Americans were appalled by the proceedings of HUAC as well as of the McCarthy hearings in the Senate, and hundreds protested against the attempt to root out Americans with left-wing political beliefs, to destroy their careers, and to tarnish them as unpatriotic. The playwright Arthur Miller responded to the hearings with his play *The Crucible*, in which he drew on the 1692 Salem witchcraft trials as a thinly veiled allegory for the anticommunist witch hunt. Actors and actresses spoke out against HUAC. "As an American," Katharine Hepburn declared, "I shall always resist any attempt at the abridgement of freedom."[7] And Humphrey Bogart and Lauren Bacall led a score of actors in a march in Washington, DC, protesting HUAC's hounding of the Hollywood Ten. Even a Republican senator, Margaret Chase Smith of Maine, protested the McCarthy hearings. According to Smith, her fellow senator's crusade was endangering one of the most cherished American principles—freedom of conscience. In 1950 she issued a "Declaration of Conscience" in which she denounced Senator McCarthy and appealed to all Americans to stand up for the principles of democracy. "I think that it is high time for the United States Senate and its members to do some soul searching—for us to weigh our consciences—on the manner in which we are performing our duty to the people of America—on the manner in which we are using or abusing our individual powers and privileges." The Constitution, she pointed out, is about freedom of speech and the right to a jury trial. It is *not* about "trial by accusation" or character assassination. "Those of us who shout the loudest about Americanism in making character assassinations," she said,

> are all too frequently those who, by our own words and acts, ignore some of the basic principles of Americanism—
> The right to criticize;
> The right to hold unpopular beliefs;
> The right to protest;
> The right of independent thought.
> The exercise of these rights should not cost one single American citizen his reputation or his right to a livelihood nor should he be in danger of losing his reputation or livelihood merely because he happens to know some one who holds unpopular beliefs. . . .
> The American people are sick and tired of being afraid to speak their minds lest they be politically smeared as "Communists" or "Fascists" by their opponents. Freedom of speech is not what it used to be in America. It has been so abused by some that it is not exercised by others.

The tactics employed by Senator McCarthy and others, Smith concluded, are worse than the evils they are trying to expose. They are "totalitarian techniques" that threaten the very existence of the United States and "that, if continued here unchecked, will surely end what we have come to cherish as the American way of life."[8]

Even so, despite such pleas for sanity and rational discourse, hundreds of creative artists were blacklisted, and careers were destroyed. In addition to Pete Seeger and Paul Robeson, Charlie Chaplin, Leonard Bernstein, John Garfield, Orson Welles, Arthur Miller, Dashiell Hammett, Lillian Hellman, Lee Grant, and Aaron Copeland were among those blacklisted.

* * *

Most Americans accepted the administration's portrayal of the Cold War as Us versus Them, Good versus Evil. And the prosecution of the Korean War was part of that scenario. If we do not fight the spread of communism in Korea, the party line went, then we will have to fight it in Kansas. Still, there were some Americans who protested against the Korean War, not so much from a moralistic or pacifist standpoint but from the more conservative stance that the war did not seem worth fighting. These dissenters did not accept the "official narrative" that the war was necessary to contain communism. If it was necessary, then why was it a limited war? Why not prosecute it to the fullest extent of American power? Why not use the atomic bomb? President Truman and the Joint Chiefs believed that if the war was not limited to the Korean peninsula, there was too much risk that it would widen into World War III. And in the aftermath of Hiroshima and the Soviets' successful test of an atomic bomb, there was no doubt in anyone's mind that a Third World War would be a nuclear war. Some dissenters on the right argued that Truman was not tough enough; they wanted him to expand the war and destroy communism. Antiwar dissenters on the left were simply not concerned that communism would spread from North Korea to South Korea. And for many of the troops on the ground the limited prosecution of the war was an outrage, and while they did not actively protest against the war, they bitterly complained, publicly declaring that they were not fighting for democracy but simply fighting to stay alive. But antiwar sentiment never became a full-fledged movement because the vast majority of the public believed the official line that the communists were determined to take over the free world. Anyone who dissented was considered a "communist dupe" or a "pinko" or "soft on communism" or a "fellow traveler," disloyal to the United States.

* * *

At the same time that American soldiers were fighting Communism in Korea and anticommunist hysteria was gripping the nation at home, the United States was experiencing unprecedented prosperity. This created an eerie, nearly schizophrenic, fixation within the American psyche. Pride in the "American way of life" was at odds with the obsessive fear that the nuclear powers could unleash Armageddon on the world, which would in an instant destroy civilization. Patriotic Americans believed that the Soviet Union was a malevolent, godless, totalitarian society while the United States represented all that was good and virtuous in the world. Such an attitude generated enormous pressure for conformity. The message was clear. Everyone should aspire to live the American Dream in a nice suburban house with a large picture window, have a stable job in a prosperous company, purchase consumer goods every week, faithfully watch television every night, value the American way, and be constantly vigilant against communism at home as well as abroad. But as the social critic John Keats pointed out, there was a "crack in the picture window" of suburbia.[9] Not everyone found happiness living the American Dream. Many found that material possessions did not bring contentment, while large numbers of Americans were too poor even to participate in the American Dream. The sociologists William Whyte and David Riesman condemned the conformity that had engulfed the United States. In *The Organization Man* Whyte argued that Americans were more concerned with fitting in than with standing out, that they had lost their ability to generate innovative ideas. And Riesman postulated in *The Lonely Crowd* that Americans were no longer "inner directed" individuals acting according to their deep-seated principles and morality but were "other directed," without original thoughts of their own, lacking inner values, and more concerned with pleasing others and "keeping up with the Joneses." Such insights were only the tip of the iceberg. Many Americans, in the midst of the conformist 1950s, resisted the impulse to conform.

Signs of dissent were apparent, if implicit, in art and music. Abstract expressionists such as Mark Rothko, Robert Motherwell, and Jackson Pollack painted canvases that ignored all the traditional conventions of visual art. Viewers did not know what to think of their paintings. Charlie Parker, Dizzy Gillespie, Thelonious Monk, and scores of other musicians took jazz to a new level of improvisation and individual inventiveness that puzzled listeners. Perhaps the musicians and artists themselves were not fully conscious that they were expressing in their own creative way a form of protest (or at least a nagging dissatisfaction) against the suffocating conformity of the era.

In literature too there were abundant signs of discontent with mainstream America. In addition to Arthur Miller's spot-on criticism in *The Crucible* of Congress's obsession with unearthing communists, novelist J. D. Salinger attacked the shallowness and phoniness of American society in *The Catcher in the Rye*. But it was in the Beat movement that a literature of dissent made a frontal assault on the political, social, and cultural orthodoxy of the times.

William Burroughs, Allen Ginsberg, and Jack Kerouac formed the core of a phalanx of rebellious writers in New York City during the late 1940s. By the early 1950s in their writings (mostly unpublished at that time) and lifestyle they were a living reproof to the conformist, strait-laced mentality of the affluent society. Condemning the split-level American Dream, they denounced middle-class values, anticommunist hysteria, Cold War propaganda, and the unbridled materialism that dominated the era. To the Beats mainstream America was in denial about the millions of marginalized individuals who were ignored by television and the media—blacks, Hispanics, homosexuals, drug addicts, ex-cons, Indians, creative artists, dropouts. And so in their poetry and novels they extolled the outcasts. Ginsberg was especially outspoken and unapologetic about his homosexuality and never missed an opportunity to celebrate it. In October 1955 he electrified the underground scene when he performed his poem "Howl" at the Six Gallery in San Francisco. "I greet you at the beginning of a great career," fellow poet and publisher Lawrence Ferlinghetti cabled Ginsberg after the performance.[10] When Ferlinghetti's City Lights Books published *Howl and Other Poems*, the San Francisco Police confiscated the books, arrested the clerk at City Lights Bookstore for selling an "obscene" book, and charged Ferlinghetti with obscenity. The publicity generated by the resulting trial was a marketing boon for the book. Everyone wanted to read it, even after the judge ruled that "Howl" was not obscenity but literature. "I saw the best minds of my generation destroyed by / madness, starving hysterical naked, / dragging themselves through the negro streets at / dawn looking for an angry fix," Ginsberg begins, and then he continues with a mesmerizing litany of American outcasts struggling to survive any way they can in the consumer society. He speaks of "angelheaded hipsters," "saintly motorcyclists," "visionary Indian angels," and the Old Testament deity Moloch, who demands the sacrifice of children.[11]

In another poem in the collection, "America," Ginsberg uses humor and history to effectively challenge Americans to reexamine their assumptions, their values, and the way they live their lives. Like Socrates, he implies that the unexamined life is not worth living. He extols the Wobblies, the Scottsboro Boys, Communists, radicals, and marijuana while condemning tired Cold War clichés and *Time* magazine. "Are you going to let your emotional life be run by Time Magazine?" "America," Ginsberg says, "go fuck yourself with your atom bomb."[12]

In interviews, Ginsberg recalled that when he and Kerouac were young men, they were constantly lectured to about morality and ethics. Parents and teachers and politicians and clergymen were always telling them what was right and what was wrong, that marriage was good but premarital or homosexual sex was bad, that conformity and middle-class values were good but holding radical views and doing drugs was bad. And it occurred to them that the generation that was responsible for the Holocaust and Hiroshima had no right to lecture on morality. "In the forties the Bomb dropped, the entire planet was threatened biologically. . . . [We] suddenly [had] the realization, why are we being intimidated by a bunch of jerks who don't even know about life? Who are they to tell us what we feel and how we're supposed to behave and why take all that bullshit?"[13]

Jack Kerouac's *On the Road*, published in 1957, was an instant success, especially with the nation's youth. Young people (including Bob Dylan and Jim Morrison) responded to Kerouac's message of going against the grain, being in the here and now, and living life to the fullest. The journey, the road itself, not the destination, was the purpose of life. To Kerouac it was the downtrodden, the outsiders, who were the most exciting people. "The only people for me," Kerouac wrote, "are the mad ones, the ones who are mad to live, mad to talk, mad to be saved, desirous of everything at the same time, the ones who never yawn or say a commonplace thing, but burn, burn, burn."[14]

The fact that so many baby boomers read *On the Road* as well as "Howl" and other Beat works was a symptom of an undercurrent of rebellion that lay below the surface of the complacent 1950s. The writings of William Burroughs, Gregory Corso, Gary Snyder, and other Beat writers, with the emphasis on hipness, jazz, unconventional thinking, individuality, sexual freedom, drugs, and Zen Buddhism, had a significant influence on the generation that shaped the counterculture of the 1960s.

* * *

There was another sign that young Americans were chafing at the oppressive conformity of middle-class American life. In the early 1950s "race music" (as it was first called) was gaining in popularity. Record stores and radio stations were increasingly promoting African American rhythm and blues, but then interest in the music exploded in 1951 when a Cleveland radio station began airing disc jockey Alan Freed's *Moondog's Rock 'n' Roll Party*. Within a few years hundreds of radio stations throughout the country featured rock-and-roll shows. By the mid-1950s American teenagers were hungrily consuming the music of black artists such as Fats Domino, Little Richard, and Chuck Berry as well as whites such as Bill Haley, Jerry Lee Lewis, and above all, Elvis Presley. Presley was a phenomenon whose huge popularity hinted at cultural, racial, and sexual unrest. Adolescent girls were obsessed with Presley's music and overt (and somewhat ambiguous) sexuality, which flew in the face of conventional morality. They screamed so loudly at his concerts that it was impossible to hear him sing. Adults were horrified. They viewed Presley as a threat to morals and decency; they feared he would corrupt the nation's youth. But when Elvis performed on Ed Sullivan's popular television show in 1956, it was clear that, no matter how emphatically adults objected, rock and roll was here to stay.

Right-wingers loudly (and ludicrously) denounced rock and roll as part of the "international communist conspiracy to corrupt America's youth." But in a sense rock and roll was indeed "revolutionary" music— not in the sense that its goal was to overthrow the United States (and certainly not in the sense that the teeny-bopper lyrics emphasizing puppy love and teenage lust were at all political) but because the music itself, the visceral, uninhibited, sensual beat and the culture and lifestyle it represented, was inherently a powerful criticism of middle-class values and the repressive political culture of anticommunism. (A decade later, of course, rock-and-roll lyrics *did* become overtly political.) The rock-and-roll phenomenon in the 1950s, which inspired young people to religiously listen every day to the Top Forty hits on the radio and to watch *American Bandstand* on television, to purchase the latest hit singles and to line up to buy tickets to rock-and-roll concerts, was a clear indication that American teenagers had an indefinable longing for something that the material comforts of the affluent society were not providing.

* * *

America's restlessness and discontent, especially among young people, was one sign that all was not well in the affluent society. But the most important indicator that the American Dream was not quite living up to its billing was the emergence of the civil rights movement. After a century of waiting for equal rights African Americans refused to wait any longer. By the end of the decade the modern civil rights movement challenged the fundamental assumptions about the meaning of democracy and forced Americans to reevaluate their most basic and cherished principles.

There were signs, long before World War II, that the winds of change were impacting race relations in the United States. The founding of the NAACP, Marcus Garvey's United Negro Improvement Association, the Harlem Renaissance, and the Communist Party's staunch defense of the Scottsboro Boys were just a few of the important early steps in the long civil rights movement. During the New Deal, First Lady Eleanor Roosevelt had pushed her husband hard to do more for African Americans in the programs he submitted to Congress. In 1939, when a concert at Washington's Constitution Hall featuring the famed African American opera singer Marian Anderson was canceled because the venue was a segregated facility, Eleanor Roosevelt made headlines when she arranged for Anderson to perform on the steps of the Lincoln Memorial on Easter Sunday. Seventy-five thousand people attended the widely publicized event, and it was not lost on the public that the First Lady was clearly a champion of civil rights. Many applauded her stance. Many hated her for it.

During World War II more than seven hundred thousand blacks served in the military. Even though they fought in segregated regiments from the Pacific to the European theater, the experience was a transformative one. Many had become officers and commanded platoons and companies. They saw a wider world and were welcomed as heroes in Europe as the Allied armies liberated Italy, France, Belgium, and the Netherlands. And when American troops crossed into Germany, African Americans were among those who entered the extermination camps, witnessing firsthand the consequences of Hitler's racist policies. But when black GIs returned home, especially those returning to the South, they were not treated as conquering heroes. And the "Colored Only" and "Whites Only" signs were a galling reminder that though they had just played a part in the liberation of Europe and the destruction of fascism, not much had really changed at home. Tens of thousands of African Americans vowed that they were not going to take it anymore.

Other factors helped ignite the modern civil rights movement. Many African American veterans were able to use the low-interest loans provided by the GI Bill to pay for college tuition or to start up a business. This meant that more African Americans graduated from college and entered a wide variety of professions. By the 1950s there was a rapidly growing black middle class of physicians, lawyers, teachers, scientists, businessmen, and clergymen. African American role models became increasingly visible. Ralph Bunche was appointed the United States' first ambassador to the United Nations. Jackie Robinson broke the color line in major-league baseball and in doing so electrified the African American community (as well as millions of white Americans) and opened the way for Roy Campanella, Don Newcombe, Willie Mays, Ernie Banks, and eventually hundreds of others. Writers such as Ralph Ellison, Richard Wright, and James Baldwin were putting their mark on American literature. Musicians and performers such as Paul Robeson, Dizzy Gillespie, Charlie Parker, and Louis Armstrong became household names. All this elevated African Americans to a more prominent place in the American consciousness.

When President Truman learned that a black soldier, Isaac Woodard, was severely beaten by South Carolina police and heard about the lynching of other African American veterans returning home at war's end, he was galvanized into action. He appointed a Committee on Civil Rights to make recommendations about what should be done. In early 1948, armed with the committee's report (*To Secure These Rights*), Truman went to Congress and called for legislation that would establish "a permanent Commission on Civil Rights, a Joint Congressional Committee on Civil Rights, and a Civil Rights Division in the Department of Justice."[15] He also asked Congress to establish a Fair Employment

Practice Commission and enact federal antilynching laws. And then five months later Truman issued Executive Order 9980 desegregating the civil service and Executive Order 9981 desegregating the armed forces. The impact of Truman's executive orders was far-reaching and, despite significant resistance, went a long way toward establishing a level of equality in federal jobs and the military. Truman's commitment to civil rights, however, nearly cost him the 1948 election when southern Democrats bolted the convention, formed the States' Rights Party (dubbed by the press the "Dixiecrats"), and nominated the segregationist governor of South Carolina, Strom Thurmond, for president.

It was clear by the early 1950s that change was in the air regarding the issue of race and that that change, when it came, would not be easy. The invention of television also had a profound impact on the emergence of the civil rights movement. It meant that Americans, no matter where they lived in the United States, were exposed to escalating news coverage about racial matters—from Supreme Court decisions to lynchings and protests and boycotts in the South. Not only did television coverage of these events force Americans to form their own opinions about race, but also it embarrassingly revealed to the world at the height of the Cold War that American democracy was imperfect. This was especially discomforting to the American government because U.S. foreign policy focused on proving to the world, specifically the new independent nations of Africa, that the "American way" was superior to the Soviet system. In this way the emerging civil rights movement had an impact on the propaganda war being waged between the United States and the Soviet Union for the hearts and minds of the Third World. And that ideological war had an impact on civil rights. If the United States was committed to containing communism and preventing the Soviet Union from extending its influence in the Third World, it was absolutely necessary that the federal government, no matter how reluctantly, respond to the demands of civil rights activists. The harsh realities of the Cold War struggle between democracy and totalitarianism turned civil rights into an issue of national security.

For decades NAACP lawyers had fought diligently to overturn the 1896 *Plessy v. Ferguson* "separate but equal" decision, which validated the Jim Crow laws, by taking case after case to the Supreme Court. Many of the cases were attempts to force poor southern school districts to abide by the *Plessy* decision, that is, to compel them to build separate schools for black children in districts where the community could not afford to do so. This moderate form of protest by the NAACP actually did have some success in getting poor school districts to quietly open their existing schools to blacks rather than to incur the expense of constructing another building. But the organization understood that it would take centuries to desegregate southern schools with this approach. By the 1940s the NAACP shifted its focus from enforcing the letter of the law to attacking head-on the doctrine of segregation itself. In two 1950 decisions the Court ruled that colleges in Oklahoma and Texas could not segregate students on the basis of race, and then the Court took on five separate cases dealing with segregation in public schools in Virginia, Kansas, Delaware, South Carolina, and Washington, DC. On May 17, 1954, the Supreme Court unanimously overturned the 1896 *Plessy v Ferguson* decision. After listening to testimony from legal authorities, psychologists, anthropologists, and educators the Court ruled in *Brown v. Board of Education* that separating black children "from others of similar age and qualifications solely because of their race generates a feeling of inferiority as to their status in the community that may affect their hearts and minds in a way unlikely ever to be undone." Even if black children are placed in a superior school, the fact that they are set apart creates a feeling of inferiority and deeply affects their motivation to learn. "We conclude that, in the field of public education, the doctrine of 'separate but equal' has no place. Separate educational facilities are inherently unequal."[16]

Throughout the nation African Americans rejoiced. But the Supreme Court did little to enforce compliance with the decision other than urging that desegregation be carried out with "all deliberate speed." And when President Dwight D. Eisenhower commented that he did not think it wise to try to alter southern traditions overnight that had been in effect for generations, southern whites were emboldened to resist. What the president's reticence meant for African Americans was that more than a decade of activism, protest, and resistance lay ahead before the decision was fully implemented.

CHAPTER 20

Civil Rights: An American Revolution

> The only weapon that we have in our hands this evening is the weapon of protest. . . . And certainly, certainly, this is the glory of America, with all of its faults. This is the glory of our democracy. If we were incarcerated behind the iron curtains of a Communistic nation, we couldn't do this. . . . But the great glory of American democracy is the right to protest for right.
>
> —Martin Luther King, Jr., address in
> Montgomery, Alabama, December 5, 1955

In August 1955 fourteen-year-old Emmett Till of Chicago, visiting relatives in Mississippi, was abducted by J. W. Mylam and Roy Bryant, beaten, shot, and dumped in the Tallahatchie River. His offense? He had "talked fresh" to a white woman. When photographs of Till's brutalized, decomposed body were published in the African American press, the nation was shocked. How could a fourteen-year-old be so savagely murdered for such a minor infraction? The publicity surrounding the case generated immense interest in the trial, and when it commenced at the end of September, hundreds of reporters descended on the courthouse in Sumner, Mississippi. Although Moses Wright (Till's great-uncle) testified that he had witnessed Milam and Bryant taking his nephew away and though it was clear that the two men were guilty of the crime, the all-white jury deliberated for less than an hour before acquitting the defendants. Around the world newspapers denounced the obvious miscarriage of justice. In Germany a newspaper proclaimed that a black person's life in the United States was worth nothing. In Belgium a paper called it "a judicial scandal." And France's *Le Monde* prophetically reported that perhaps the Till murder would serve to awaken America's consciousness.[1]

Two months later Rosa Parks refused to give up her seat on a Montgomery, Alabama, bus to a white man. Parks was not a "tired seamstress," as she is conventionally portrayed; she was a longtime community organizer and labor and civil rights activist. She had disobeyed segregation laws in the past and had been fined for doing so, she was an active member of the Montgomery NAACP, and she had attended civil disobedience workshops at the Highlander Folk School in Tennessee. But her deliberate act of dissent on December 1, 1955, and the decision not to pay the fine ignited the spark that pushed the United States another step in the direction of fulfilling its promise. The century-long civil rights movement, stretching from the Thirteenth Amendment to the Niagara Movement, from Marcus Garvey to the *Brown* decision, was reaching critical mass.

After Rosa Parks was arrested, black lawyers, ministers, and NAACP officials held a meeting during which they called on the African American community to boycott Montgomery's buses. The one-day boycott was so successful that they formed the Montgomery Improvement Association (MIA) and held another meeting, with nearly seven thousand attendees, at the Holt Street Baptist Church in order to coordinate a longer boycott. At this meeting a new minister in town, the twenty-six-year-old Martin Luther King, Jr., electrified the crowd with his stirring oratory. "We are not wrong in what we are doing," King proclaimed. "If we are wrong, the Supreme Court of this nation is wrong. If we are wrong, the Constitution of the United States is wrong. If we are wrong, God Almighty is wrong."[2]

The people mobilized quickly. King was elected to head the MIA (mainly because none of Montgomery's established African American leaders wanted the job), and with the hard work of JoAnn Robinson, the association printed and distributed thousands of leaflets and fliers and organized car pools for workers who lived long distances from their jobs. At first the MIA only asked for amelioration of the harshest indignities of segregation. They asked for the end of "floating" sections on the buses (which meant that when the white section filled up, blacks would have to give up the first row of the black section and so on), not for the eradication of the segregated sections. And they demanded that the bus company hire some black drivers. City authorities, however, would not budge an inch, and so the MIA eventually upped its demands to push for complete desegregation. The boycott continued month after month without any movement on the part of the city but with a great deal of harassment of the drivers running the car pools and the bombing of several civil rights leaders' homes. Still the boycott held.

And still the protestors heeded King's call for nonviolence. Not only did King bring his eloquence to the civil rights movement; he also brought the message of nonviolent civil disobedience. Drawing on the ideas of Henry David Thoreau and Mahatma Gandhi, as well as the teachings of Jesus and the Social Gospel, King preached the philosophy of using the "weapon of love" as a tactic to defeat racism and segregation. The oppressed should not hate the oppressor, even when being beaten. Hate the system that turned a person into a racist, not the person. Violence, King believed, only begat more violence. Violence hardened attitudes on both sides of a dispute. Through nonviolence one could shame the system into seeing the injustice of racial discrimination; through nonviolence one could transform one's enemy into a friend.

The boycott continued. The black citizens of Montgomery walked and walked and walked. Finally, in June 1956 the U.S. Supreme Court ruled that bus segregation was unconstitutional. After appeals the ruling went into effect a year after the boycott began. On December 20, 1956, blacks ended the campaign and resumed riding the buses—this time sitting in the front.

Early in 1957 King and a number of civil rights leaders founded the Southern Christian Leadership Conference (SCLC), which drew its membership from the South's African American churches. It conducted educational programs and civil disobedience workshops throughout the region, coordinated protests and demonstrations, organized voter registration drives, and emphasized the moral element of the campaign against racism. By the 1960s SCLC was one of the most important organizations fighting Jim Crow and putting pressure on the federal government to address racial injustice.

In 1957 a federal court ordered the Little Rock, Arkansas, school district to comply with the *Brown* decision and desegregate Little Rock Central High School. During the first days of September whites gathered at the school protesting the desegregation order. On September 4, 1957, citing the fear of possible violence, Governor Orval Faubus defied the court order by ordering the Arkansas National Guard to prevent the admission of nine black students. The standoff continued for two weeks until a federal court ordered the governor to remove the National Guard. On September 23 the students gained admittance to the school, but a white mob outside began breaking windows and beating up black reporters who had come to Little Rock to cover the story. The police then stepped in and, in order to defuse the situation, removed the students from the school.

Though President Eisenhower had originally been critical of the *Brown* decision, it was his duty as president to uphold federal law. Fed up with Faubus's defiance, Eisenhower deployed the 101st Airborne Division to protect the students and restore order. And so, on September 24, the Little Rock Nine finally began taking classes at the high school. Throughout the country Americans could watch the daily scenes on television news of soldiers escorting the nine students up the steps and into the school. Despite the presence of the 101st Airborne surrounding the school, each of the students endured hostility (punching, shoving, cursing, spitting) from the white students. After a few days of this each of the nine was assigned his or her own personal bodyguard—one of the soldiers—in order to minimize the harassment. It was perhaps appropriate that Eisenhower chose the 101st Airborne, for it was the 101st that parachuted into Normandy in the predawn hours of June 6, 1944, to liberate France. And now, thirteen years later, the division was sent to Little Rock to secure access to equal education for African Americans.

After several months the 101st Airborne was withdrawn, and the federalized Arkansas National Guard took over for the rest of the school year. But during the summer of 1958, in order to make a last defiant statement against integration, the Little Rock school board, the state legislature, and Governor Faubus canceled the entire 1958–1959 school year. With Central High closed, students attended private schools or traveled to other districts for their education. But before the year was out federal courts ordered Little Rock to reopen for the 1959–1960 school year. From that point on school integration became a reality.

Like the Emmett Till case and the Montgomery bus boycott, the events in Little Rock focused the nation's attention on civil rights. What exactly *are* our rights? What is it exactly that the Constitution guarantees for American citizens? It was clear that America believed deeply in its most cherished principle, that "all men are created equal." But what exactly did that mean? Why were African Americans in the South demonstrating to end state-mandated segregation, job discrimination, and voter suppression? Why were African Americans in the North demanding an end to housing segregation, non-legally-mandated segregation of schools and facilities, and endemic job discrimination? Why were

African Americans fighting for empowerment and the opportunity to determine their own lives, culture, and communities? Newspaper accounts and televised broadcasts of the African American struggle to secure these rights underscored for most Americans that not all people were considered equal in the United States, that America was not living up to its own ideals. All of this served to broaden consciousness and to accelerate the dialogue. Americans who knew nothing about the African American experience were increasingly confronted with the evils of racism and segregation (de jure and de facto). And as time wore on, those who had no opinion about civil rights found that they were forced to develop an opinion, forced to choose sides.

Dissent against segregation reached a new level on February 1, 1960, when four black college students walked into the local Woolworths in Greensboro, North Carolina, and sat down at the lunch counter. Even though African Americans were permitted to shop at the store, they were forbidden service at the lunch counter. As the four young men expected, they were not served. Over the ensuing days they returned, accompanied by ever-increasing numbers of their fellow students. Within a week the sit-ins spread to Nashville, Atlanta, Charlotte, and dozens of other cities throughout the South. As the sit-ins proliferated, whites began a campaign of harassing the demonstrators—calling them names, punching them, pouring ketchup and mustard on their heads, extinguishing cigarettes on the backs of their necks—until finally store management called in the police. Instead of arresting the white thugs for assault, the police arrested the protestors for disorderly conduct. Many of the stores simply closed their lunch counters. Since most of the five-and-dime stores targeted were part of national chains, civil rights activists launched a nationwide campaign to boycott all the stores, even though the northern branches did not discriminate against blacks. Thus, around the nation, outside of Woolworths and Kresges and other stores demonstrators formed picket lines and carried signs urging shoppers not to do business with chain stores that practiced segregation in the South.

By summer, after thousands of arrests in dozens of cities throughout the South, the sit-ins bore fruit. Although some stores continued to refuse service to African Americans for a number of years, most did desegregate their lunch counters. Feeling the economic pinch, corporate headquarters of national chains ordered their southern stores to serve blacks. In Nashville hundreds of protestors marched to city hall, where, with the media recording the confrontation, they held a dialogue with the mayor on the building's steps. When student activist Diane Nash asked Mayor Ben West if he thought it was wrong to discriminate against someone on the basis of race, he answered honestly that he *did* think it was wrong. Nash followed up by asking him if he thought Nashville stores should serve blacks. West said "yes." Within a month Nashville desegregated its lunch counters. It took six months in Greensboro, but by July most stores began serving blacks. Other cities, such as Atlanta, took more than a year, but in the end desegregation came there too.

* * *

Even though most of the nation's youth were more interested in watching *American Bandstand* on television than civil rights demonstrations, they were aware of the news reports coming out of the South. And many of them, as they entered college in the last years of the decade and the first years of the 1960s, perceived the African American struggle for civil rights as a just cause. Baby boomers had been taught that the United States was the greatest nation on earth, that the United States was superior to totalitarian Russia and China because the United States was the world's champion of human rights. The United States was superior because in America everyone was free and equal. But the events in Montgomery and then Little Rock contradicted that notion. The reality was that not everyone was free and equal. Unconsciously, and in many cases consciously, it occurred to young Americans that if they pointed out that there was some discrepancy between what is and what should be, then there was a chance that they could put things right so that the reality in America would more closely resemble the ideal. "We can change the world" became a rallying cry just at the moment that the 1960 presidential race went into gear.

Both candidates, Richard M. Nixon and John F. Kennedy, considered the Cold War the most critical issue facing the nation. And each claimed that *he* would be the best man to deal with the Soviet threat. Both were moderates on civil rights, but the issue rarely surfaced during the campaign. But civil rights did effect the election. In October Martin Luther King was arrested at a sit-in in Atlanta and sentenced to four months hard labor in Reidsville State Prison. Civil rights activists worried that "something might happen" to King isolated in a cell far from the public eye. Senator Kennedy was also worried and telephoned Coretta Scott King voicing his concern over her husband's incarceration. Later that afternoon Kennedy's brother Robert called the judge who sentenced King, and the next day the judge released King on bond. The civil rights movement rejoiced, and on the Sunday before Election Day black ministers throughout the land urged their congregations to vote for Kennedy because he got King out of jail. Kennedy won the election with a plurality of less than one-half of one percent of the popular vote. Clearly the hundreds of thousands of African American votes helped swing the election for him.

When John F. Kennedy was sworn in as president on January 20, 1961, he tapped into the idealism of the nation's youth. The repercussions lasted for more than a decade, but at the beginning his challenge to "ask not what your country can do for you, ask what you can do for your country" reinforced the belief that with enough energy and dedication young people could indeed change the world. The idealism that JFK symbolized and promoted, along with the example of African American student activists, motivated white college students to participate in the struggle for civil rights.

And in May 1961 the next phase of the civil rights movement commenced with the participation of larger numbers of whites than previously. The Congress of Racial Equality (CORE) sponsored a "Freedom Ride" in an effort to force the federal government to enforce the Supreme Court's 1960 *Boynton v. Virginia* decision, which outlawed segregation in interstate travel facilities: bus terminals, waiting rooms, restrooms. Although the ruling was already in effect, buses and bus terminals in the South remained segregated. The plan was for small groups of black and white activists to travel on interstate buses from Washington, DC, to New Orleans. As the buses entered the South, white Freedom Riders would sit in the back of the bus and black Freedom Riders in the front. At each rest stop along the way the whites would use the black restrooms and lunch counters, and the blacks would use the white facilities. They reasoned that somewhere along the line they would meet with resistance and that an incident would trigger a federal response. On May 4, 1961, two buses left Washington, DC. In South Carolina two riders were beaten, another arrested. But the major confrontation took place shortly after the buses crossed from Georgia into Alabama. One of the buses was stopped and firebombed by Klansmen near Anniston, Alabama. The bus was destroyed, and the Freedom Riders suffered burns and smoke inhalation and were beaten—it was a miracle that no one was killed. The second bus made it all the way to Birmingham, where it was met by another mob of Klansmen. Again no one was killed, but several riders were beaten so severely that they were hospitalized. James Farmer, the national director of CORE, canceled the rest of the ride, and the riders abandoned the attempt.

The Student Nonviolent Coordinating Committee (SNCC) now stepped into the fray. "We can't let them stop us with violence," proclaimed Diane Nash, one of the leaders of the Nashville sit-ins of the previous year. "If we do, the movement is dead."[3] She and other members of SNCC organized a second Freedom Ride, this time from Nashville to Birmingham. Before the bus arrived in Birmingham, however, state police stopped it and arrested the ten Freedom Riders. By this time the Kennedy administration, albeit reluctantly, was finally beginning to respond (President Kennedy in the midst of escalating tensions with the Soviet Union had asked his civil rights adviser, Harris Wofford, to tell the protestors to call off the Freedom Rides while the country was facing a showdown over Berlin). Attorney General Robert Kennedy worked out an agreement with the governor of Alabama that the state police would escort the bus from Birmingham to Montgomery. But when the bus arrived at Montgomery's city limits, the state police withdrew, leaving the riders unprotected. At the bus terminal the SNCC people were attacked by hundreds of stick- and pipe-wielding Klansmen and beaten so brutally (one rider was set on fire) that several suffered permanent brain damage. Even Justice Department official John Seigenthaler was beaten unconscious. When the Montgomery police stepped in, they issued an injunction prohibiting the continuation of the Freedom Ride.

At this point Martin Luther King flew to Montgomery and held a mass meeting in support of the Freedom Riders at the First Baptist Church. "The federal government," King proclaimed, "must not stand idly by while bloodthirsty mobs beat nonviolent students with impunity."[4] But even as King addressed the rally, a violent mob surrounded the church shouting epithets and threats, overturned and set vehicles on fire, and threw bricks and tear-gas canisters through the church's windows. Federal marshals were barely holding the line against the enraged mob. With the congregation choking on smoke and teargas and King describing the situation over the telephone to Robert Kennedy, the Alabama National Guard finally arrived on the scene. Even so, it took the rest of the night for the guardsmen and the marshals to disperse the mob and get the congregation safely home.

At the end of May, President Kennedy ordered the Interstate Commerce Commission (ICC) to establish a procedure to enforce the desegregation ruling, but nothing changed. And the Freedom Riders kept coming. Every week dozens of activists boarded buses in northern cites and rode into the Deep South. They never got farther than Alabama or Mississippi before they were arrested and thrown into prison. Mississippi's infamous Parchman Prison was overflowing with Freedom Riders. But the activists did not lose heart. Confined to their cells, they sang freedom songs—"We Shall Overcome," "If I Had a Hammer," "Oh Freedom," "We Shall Not Be Moved," "Ain't Gonna Let Nobody Turn Me Around"—even after guards removed their mattresses in an effort to silence them. Still, they kept singing. Finally, in September the ICC enforced the ban on segregated facilities and buses. Like the sit-in campaign of the previous year, direct action once again achieved a small victory.

The objective of the direct action campaigns was to force the federal government to acknowledge that African Americans were deprived of their basic citizenship rights and then to force Washington to intervene in the South to secure those rights. With a liberal Democrat in the White House civil rights protestors had high hopes that Washington would respond to their demands, but Kennedy's reluctance to commit the administration (because he feared negative political fallout) frustrated and angered civil rights protesters. Kennedy continued to put pressure on the leaders of the movement to tone down the rhetoric and be less confrontational. But Martin Luther King, James Farmer, Diane Nash, John Lewis, and thousands of other dedicated protestors vowed to keep the pressure on until African Americans achieved the full rights of first-class citizenship.

* * *

The sit-ins and Freedom Rides inspired millions and spawned a host of demonstrations. In scores of cities and rural communities throughout the South activists marched, demonstrated, protested, and demanded the end of Jim Crow. Black students took the lead, but ordinary members of African American churches, elderly people, children, and even many whites also participated. And in every region of the country Americans of all ethnicities and socioeconomic backgrounds were forced to think about civil rights and answer the question "which side are you on?"

When James Meredith was refused admittance to the University of Mississippi, he appealed to the Supreme Court that he had been rejected solely on the basis of his race. In September 1962 the Court ruled in Meredith's favor and ordered the all-white university to admit him. But when Meredith attempted to enroll, the governor of Mississippi, Ross Barnett, personally barred him from entering the registrar's office. Barnett's grandstanding was a calculated political ploy on his part to enhance his popularity as a defender of states' rights against the "despotic" federal government. He knew that if he blocked Meredith but was forced by the federal government to yield, he would be a hero in Mississippi. A few days later federal marshals escorted Meredith as he enrolled at the university. A mob of two thousand angry students rioted and attacked the marshals, trying to get at Meredith. For more than twelve hours federal marshals fought a desperate battle through the night with the mob. By daybreak more than a hundred marshals had been wounded (twenty-eight with gunshot wounds), and two people were killed. In order to restore peace, President Kennedy finally sent in more federal marshals. The riot was quelled, and the University of Mississippi was at last integrated. But every day Meredith, whether in his dormitory room, walking across campus, or attending classes, faced constant harassment, threats, and intimidation.

As these events were transpiring in Mississippi, the civil rights movement was engaged in a major campaign in Albany, Georgia. For most of 1962 civil rights activists initiated a bus boycott, conducted citizenship classes, participated in protest marches and rallies, and got arrested trying to integrate lunch counters and railroad cars. Hundreds were arrested, including Martin Luther King and Ralph Abernathy. However, because the Albany police showed restraint in arresting the demonstrators, the protests just did not gain any traction. Nonviolent civil disobedience is most effective in garnering public approval and potential recruits when authorities react with heavy-handed tactics to crush the action. By refraining from violence and treating the protestors civilly the Albany police successfully defused the protests. By early 1963, after more than two years of strenuous campaigning, the civil rights movement seemed to be hitting a wall in Albany, Georgia, with little movement toward desegregation despite the collective efforts of so many. As Easter approached in 1963, SCLC shifted its attention from Albany to Birmingham, Alabama.

At the urging of the Reverend Fred Shuttlesworth, Martin Luther King and SCLC launched a series of sit-ins in Birmingham. On April 6, as protestors began a march from the Sixteenth Street Baptist Church to city hall, the Birmingham police moved in and arrested dozens of demonstrators. At the next day's march more arrests were made. This time police chief Bull Connor, not heeding the example set by the Albany police, sent in the fire department and a K-9 unit to confront the protestors. Around the country Americans were shocked at the photographs showing police dogs attacking peaceful demonstrators and firefighters using high-pressure fire hoses to knock people down. On Good Friday Martin Luther King was arrested. While King sat in solitary confinement, eight Alabama clergymen published an open letter in the *New York Times* in which they blamed King and the "outsiders" who had come to Birmingham for the violence provoked by the demonstrations. "We recognize the natural impatience of people," they wrote, "who feel that their hopes are slow in being realized. But we are convinced that these demonstrations are unwise and untimely."[5]

It was a critical moment for the civil rights movement. After the failure at Albany the movement could not afford to lose further ground in Birmingham. King was acutely aware of this as he sat in his cell. Writing in the margins of the newspaper, King responded to the clergymen in one of the most seminal statements of dissent in American history. For dissenters King's letter, like Thoreau's "Resistance to Civil Government" and Bourne's "War Is the Health of the State," is holy writ. Dissenters, whatever their cause, frequently and inevitably refer to these documents for tactics and inspiration.

"I have yet to engage in a direct action campaign that was 'well timed,'" King writes, "in the view of those who have not suffered unduly from the disease of segregation. For years now I have heard the word 'Wait!' It rings in the ear of every Negro with a piercing familiarity. This 'Wait' has almost always meant 'Never.'" He understands the difficulty, he acknowledges, for whites to empathize with African Americans' impatience. After all, blacks have waited for centuries for their rights. "The nations of Asia and Africa are moving with jetlike speed toward the goal of political independence, but we still creep at horse-and-buggy pace toward the gaining of a cup of coffee at a lunch counter." And then King writes one of the most extraordinary sentences in American letters:

> But when you have seen vicious mobs lynch your mothers and fathers at will and drown your sisters and brothers at whim; when you have seen hate-filled policemen curse, kick, brutalize and even kill your black brothers and sisters with impunity; when you see the vast majority of your twenty million Negro brothers smothering in an airtight cage of poverty in the midst of an affluent society; when you suddenly find your tongue twisted and your speech stammering as you seek to explain to your six-year-old daughter why she can't go to the public amusement park that has just been advertised on television, and see tears welling up in her eyes when she is told that Funtown is closed to colored children, and see the depressing clouds of inferiority begin to form in her little mental sky, and see her begin to distort her little personality by unconsciously developing a bitterness toward white people; when you have to concoct an answer for a five-year-old son asking in agonizing pathos: "Daddy, why do white people treat colored people so mean?"; when you take a cross-country drive and find it necessary to sleep night after night in the uncomfortable corners of your automobile because no motel will accept you; when you are humiliated day in and day out by nagging signs reading "white" and "colored"; when your first name becomes "nigger," your middle name becomes "boy" (however old you are) and your last name becomes "John," and your wife and mother are never given the respected title "Mrs."; when you are harried by day and haunted by night by the fact that you are a Negro, living constantly at tip-toe stance never quite knowing what to expect next, and plagued with inner fears and outer resentments; when you are forever fighting a degenerating sense of "nobodiness"; then you will understand why we find it difficult to wait.[6]

Throughout the letter King expounds the philosophy of nonviolence, defines civil disobedience, and lays out the aims of a direct action campaign. In response to the criticism that he has no respect for the law, King argues that he only breaks "unjust laws." Echoing Thoreau, King elaborates on the difference between "just laws" (laws that coincide with natural law or God's law and apply equally to everyone, such as laws against murder), which he honors, and "unjust laws" (those that do not coincide with natural law or God's law and that do not apply equally to all people, such as the Jim Crow laws).

To the charge that he is an "outsider," King replies, "I am in Birmingham because injustice is here. . . . I cannot sit idly by in Atlanta and not be concerned about what happens in Birmingham. Injustice anywhere is a threat to justice everywhere." And to the criticism that he is an "extremist," King simply responds, "was not Jesus an extremist for love?" and then he goes on to categorize other historical figures, from St. Paul to Abraham Lincoln, as extremists too. In this context King positions himself as a reformer who stands "in the middle of two opposing forces in the Negro community": the conservative accommodationist and the radical revolutionary. He is not one of the complacent ones who "have been so completely drained of self-respect and a sense of 'somebodiness' that they have adjusted to segregation." Nor is he a radical who is so filled with "bitterness and hatred" that he advocates violence. If whites do not embrace his nonviolent approach "millions of Negroes," he predicts, "out of frustration and despair, will seek solace and security in black-nationalist ideologies, a development that will lead inevitably to a frightening racial nightmare."[7] King in essence is warning white America, not so subtly, that he is the only reasonable alternative to black militants.

Shortly after King's release James Bevel and other organizers set in motion the most controversial tactic of the campaign: relying on children between the ages of eight and eighteen to be the bulk of the marchers. The reasoning was that if a child is arrested at a demonstration, it does not put the economic pressure on a family that would result if the parents were arrested. Controversial though it was (and many in the black community were very much against using children as demonstrators), the result was that within a few days all local jails were filled. Finally, Birmingham's business community, concerned about the loss of revenue, agreed to remove the segregation signs, integrate the stores, and hire more black clerks. Once again protest resulted in change—perhaps not a lot of change but some progress for the African American community.

The day after King left Birmingham, the motel where he had been staying was bombed. When blacks gathered around as firefighters and police arrived on the scene, tensions mounted, tempers flared, and a riot erupted. In the ensuing days frustration and impatience in black communities across the country boiled over into civil disturbances. In response to the violence President Kennedy finally took a bold stand on civil rights. He did this in the face of much opposition from his closest advisers. All of them, with the exception of his brother Robert, the attorney general, counseled him *not* to address the nation and *not* to propose a civil rights bill. Southern Democrats and conservative Republicans, the president's advisers argued, would destroy the bill. It would not pass, and consequently he would lose support for the rest of his legislative program. It was clear that Kennedy would lose so much political capital that it would jeopardize his reelection prospects for 1964. But Kennedy felt he had vacillated enough for the past two years. He had been sympathetic to the civil rights movement, but he had distanced himself from it as far as possible because he did not want to alienate southern white support. But now he believed it was the right thing to do. He had to take a stand.

Calling civil rights a "moral issue," Kennedy addressed the nation on June 11. "One hundred years of delay have passed since President Lincoln freed the slaves," Kennedy said,

> yet their heirs, their grandsons, are not fully free. They are not yet freed from the bonds of injustice. They are not yet freed from social and economic oppression. And this Nation, for all its hopes and all its boasts, will not be fully free until all its citizens are free. We preach freedom around the world, and we mean it, and we cherish our freedom here at home, but are we to say to the world, and much more importantly, to each other that this is a land of the free except for the Negroes; that we have no second-class citizens except Negroes; that we have no class or caste system, no ghettoes, no master race except with respect to Negroes?

He announced that he was sending a civil rights bill to Congress that would abolish the Jim Crow laws and prohibit segregation in public housing, public accommodation, and workplaces. The time has come, he said, for every American to acknowledge that "race has no place in American life or law."[8]

Kennedy's advisers were right. Southern senators balked and began using every means at their disposal to prevent the bill from even coming up for a vote. It seemed the bill was doomed. In order to put pressure on Congress to pass the bill, civil rights and union leaders coordinated a March on Washington for Jobs and Freedom to take place at the end of the summer. The Kennedy administration was apprehensive that the march would turn violent or that it would be construed as critical of the president. But the event, on August 28, was peaceful as well as inspirational. As we have seen, A. Philip Randolph, the head of the Brotherhood of Sleeping Car Porters, had planned such a march on Washington in 1941 but agreed to call it off after President Roosevelt signed an executive order prohibiting racial discrimination in the defense industry. Now, in 1963, Randolph was one of the proud organizers for the march. Two hundred and fifty thousand people took part in the symbolic march from the Washington Monument to the Lincoln

A twelve-year-old girl at the March on Washington for Jobs and Freedom, August 28, 1963. The original caption reads, "Photograph of a Young Woman at the Civil Rights March on Washington, D.C., with a Banner, 08/28/1963," photographed by Rowland Scherman of the U.S. Information Agency. For decades Edith Lee-Payne did not know her photograph was one of the iconic images of the March on Washington, until one day in 2008 when a friend spotted it in a black history calendar. National Public Radio did a story on Lee-Payne on the occasion of the fiftieth anniversary of the march in August 2013. (Courtesy National Archives)

Bob Dylan and Joan Baez at the March on Washington, August 28, 1963. Photographer unknown. (Public domain; courtesy National Archives)

Memorial. There they listened to protest singers Peter, Paul, and Mary, Joan Baez, and Bob Dylan and speeches by Randolph, James Farmer, Floyd McKissick, John Lewis, and others. (Lewis's speech was inflammatory, and his fellow organizers prevailed on him to tone down the angry, threatening rhetoric before delivering it.) The highlight of the day was Martin Luther King's speech. "I still have a dream. It is a dream deeply rooted in the American dream that one day this nation will rise up and live out the true meaning of its creed—'We hold these truths to be self-evident, that all men are created equal'"—King proclaimed. "I have a dream that my four little children will one day live in a nation where they will not be judged by the color of their skin but by the content of their character. I have a *dream* today!"[9] At the end of the speech he repeatedly intoned "let freedom ring" and went into a litany of the mountaintops from which it should ring, including Stone Mountain, Georgia, and Lookout Mountain, Tennessee—locations associated with the Ku Klux Klan.

Much of white America, at least outside the South, was impressed with the nonviolent crowd and the moving eloquence of Martin Luther

King's oratory. The march won new converts to civil rights, and it elevated King to the status of undisputed leader of the movement. However, not all African Americans were in lockstep with King's message of nonviolence and hope, passive resistance and civil disobedience. Many felt that the government was responding far too slowly to the movement's demands and that the black revolution needed to be more militant and not keep turning the other cheek. Malcolm X was one of the outspoken critics of King's nonviolent approach. The March on Washington, Malcolm X proclaimed later, "was a sellout." The Kennedy administration co-opted it and controlled it from beginning to end. "It lost its militancy. It ceased to be angry, it ceased to be hot, it ceased to be uncompromising."[10]

For several years Malcolm X had been the leading spokesman of the Nation of Islam, whose philosophy went against the grain of King's Christian Social Gospel message. Malcolm denounced whites as "blue-eyed devils" that would never treat blacks equally. He called for African Americans to fight against white dominance and take charge of their own communities. He scorned integration for it implied that black society was inferior to white society. Black society, he repeated over and over again, black values, black culture were *superior*. He called for "black nationalism" which meant that blacks must have "complete control over the politics and the politicians of [their] own community": "We should also gain economic control over the economy of our own community, the businesses and the other things which create employment so that we can provide jobs for our own people instead of having to picket and boycott and beg someone else for a job."[11] He argued for self-defense. If a white man hits you, Malcolm X repeatedly advised, do not turn the other cheek. Hit him back harder. And he will not hit you again. In some ways it can be argued that many white Americans began to embrace Martin Luther King and support the civil rights struggle precisely because they were afraid of Malcolm X.

But even among King's most loyal followers there was a sense that his tactics were too slow, that the movement was not accomplishing enough. After all, the struggle had been going on for some time. Why does Congress not immediately pass the needed legislation? Why does the Justice Department not provide adequate protection for civil rights activists? Why does the federal government drag its heels? As if to underscore the frustrations of those who sought a quicker end to racial injustice, less than three weeks after the March on Washington a bomb exploded at the Sixteenth Street Baptist Church, in Birmingham. Fourteen children attending Sunday school were injured. Four girls were killed. The euphoria and elevated hopes that the March on Washington had brought to the movement vanished in the explosion. How could whites be filled with so much hatred that they could kill four children in Sunday school? It was a sobering moment as civil rights activists realized that there was a long way to go.

The assassination of President Kennedy two months later was another important turning point. On one hand the movement had lost an ally who, although he had been slow to support civil rights, had finally thrown the weight of the Oval Office behind the movement. But on the other hand Kennedy's assassination was a boost for civil rights. It prompted the new president, Lyndon B. Johnson, to take up the cause more passionately than Kennedy had. "Let us continue," Johnson declared as he vowed his commitment to carrying on JFK's legacy in a speech to Congress and the nation on November 27. Johnson used the occasion to boost the civil rights bill that was languishing in Congress. "No memorial oration or eulogy could more eloquently honor President Kennedy's memory than the earliest possible passage of the civil rights bill for which he fought so long."[12] Johnson used all of his power and persuasion over the next several months to cajole, convince, and coerce conservative Republicans and southern Democrats into supporting the bill. Had JFK lived, the bill would have died. But LBJ got it done. In July he signed into law the Civil Rights Act of 1964. The comprehensive bill did away with the Jim Crow laws and empowered the attorney general to enforce school desegregation. "All persons shall be entitled to the full and equal enjoyment of the goods, services, facilities, and privileges, advantages, and accommodations of any place of public accommodation . . . without discrimination or segregation on the ground of race, color, religion, or national origin." The act prohibited federal funding to segregated schools or businesses that discriminated on the basis of race, and significantly, it outlawed discrimination in the workplace. "It shall be an unlawful employment practice for an employer . . . to fail or refuse to hire or to discharge any individual, or otherwise to discriminate against any individual with respect to his compensation, terms, conditions, or privileges of employment, because of such individual's race, color, religion, sex, or national origin."[13]

Kennedy's assassination strengthened the civil rights movement in another way. Countless numbers of baby boomers had been inspired by Kennedy's appeal to their idealism, and many of them began to find ways to carry on his legacy. Kennedy might be gone, they reasoned, but we can take up the causes he fought for. Many volunteered for the Peace Corps, some enlisted in the military, others decided to get involved in politics, and untold thousands threw themselves into the civil rights movement. In the spring of 1964 SNCC and CORE began organizing for "Freedom Summer." It was one thing, they reasoned, to gain access to a lunch counter to buy a cup of coffee or to be allowed to sit in the front of the bus. But none of these advances for blacks did anything to enhance political power. Only through the ballot box could African Americans hope to gain some leverage in the American political system. And so Freedom Summer was conceived as a campaign to go into Mississippi in the summer of 1964, to set up "freedom schools" that would teach political awareness and encourage African Americans to take part in the political process, and to fan out through the state getting African Americans to register to vote. Blacks constituted about 50 percent of the population of Mississippi, but only 6.7 percent of them were registered. If African Americans voted, not only would they have a say in state politics and be able to elect members of their own community to political office, but even white politicians would have to address black concerns if they hoped to win elections.

During the planning stages CORE and SNCC debated whether to invite whites to participate in the project. Those who wanted to do so felt that white participation would increase press coverage of the campaign. Those who were against the idea were actually against it for the same reason—they felt that whites would get the bulk of the media's attention, thus diverting attention from all the hard work of the African American volunteers who, after all, had been fighting and dying for civil rights for years. Finally, they voted by a slim margin to invite whites to participate. In June volunteers trained at a small college in Oxford, Ohio, where they were taught what to expect when they entered Mississippi, how to avoid encounters with hostile whites, and the basics of nonviolent resistance and self-protection.

No sooner had the first cohort of CORE volunteers arrived in Mississippi than three of them disappeared. On June 21, 1964, James Chaney, Andrew Goodman, and Michael Schwerner drove to the site of a burned-down black church near Philadelphia, Mississippi. They were arrested for a traffic violation by the sheriff and held for some hours in the town jail. When they were released, members of the Klan picked them up, beat them, and shot them. Chaney was black, Goodman and Schwerner white. For six weeks the FBI conducted a massive statewide manhunt for the three civil rights workers, but only after receiving a tip from a local resident did they find the bodies buried in an earthen dam. Instead of curtailing the number of civil rights workers descending on Mississippi during that summer, the disappearance and murder of the three men dominated headlines around the country, intensified interest in the struggle, and prompted more individuals to volunteer. The violence that southern whites perpetrated on civil rights activists was one of the most powerful forces galvanizing support for civil rights in the North. From Little Rock to Birmingham, from Freedom Summer to Selma, the beatings and killings of nonviolent civil rights activists invariably strengthened the movement.

One of the accomplishments of Freedom Summer was the creation of the Mississippi Freedom Democratic Party (MFDP). At the end of August the MFDP sent delegates to the Democratic National Convention in Atlantic City who they claimed were more representative of the state population than the all-white delegation of the regular Mississippi Democratic Party. But the reality of power politics in the United States proved to be a bitter disappointment for the MFDP. President Johnson, wanting to avoid a controversy that threatened to divide the Democratic Party, insisted that the regular delegation be seated. When the credentials committee held a hearing about the conflicting demands of the two delegations, as one of the MFDP delegates, Fannie Lou Hamer, launched into her compelling and emotional testimony, a fuming Johnson held a spur-of-the-moment (meaningless) press conference that preempted televised coverage of the hearing.

But Hamer's testimony was replayed again and again on newscasts. When she attempted to register to vote, she told the committee, she was arrested and thrown into a jail cell.

> I was carried out of that cell into another cell where they had two Negro prisoners. The State Highway Patrolmen ordered the first Negro to take the blackjack. The first Negro prisoner ordered me, by orders from the State Highway Patrolman for me, to lay down on a bunk bed on my

face, and I laid on my face. . . . The first Negro began to beat, and I was beat by the first Negro until he was exhausted, and I was holding my hands behind me at that time on my left side because I suffered from polio when I was six years old. After the first Negro had beat until he was exhausted the State Highway Patrolman ordered the second Negro to take the blackjack. . . .

All of this is on account of us wanting to register, to become first-class citizens, and if the Freedom Democratic Party is not seated now, I question America. Is this America, the land of the free and the home of the brave where we have to sleep with our telephones off of the hooks because our lives be threatened daily because we want to live as decent human beings, in America?[14]

Despite Hamer's powerful testimony, the credentials committee, pressured by the vice presidential nominee Hubert Humphrey as well as President Johnson, refused to seat the MFDP delegation. The delegates protested, sang freedom songs, and vowed that they would be heard, but to no avail. Disheartened African Americans, closely watching the drama unfold at the convention, grew bitterly skeptical about America's commitment to equality. Many felt that the normative political process was not responsive to their demands and that more militant ways were going to be necessary in order to gain equal rights.

* * *

In September, Freedom Summer volunteers, overflowing with quasi-missionary fervor about their experiences in Mississippi, returned to college campuses around the nation. The first thing they told their friends and professors at the beginning of the fall semester was about the work they did at the freedom schools and registering voters. Scores of volunteers had been beaten by southern racists, hundreds had been arrested and harassed by the police, all of them felt they were risking their lives for the cause. And now as they told their stories, they urged others to make donations or to join one of the civil rights organizations or to volunteer for a voter registration drive in Alabama planned for 1965. At the University of California at Berkeley school authorities told students that they could not set up their tables, hand out leaflets, solicit donations, or otherwise proselytize for a political cause on campus property. The students responded with shock and outrage. The university was telling them they could not discuss the most significant issue facing the nation! This was too much. Spontaneous protests erupted. Students from all political persuasions, from left to right, protested the university's heavy-handed trampling on free speech. Thus was born a new dissent movement—the Berkeley Free Speech Movement—a direct offspring of the activists on the cutting edge of the civil rights movement. And the FSM, as it was called, instantly spread to other campuses, thus giving birth to the student movement. At first the primary issues that student protestors focused on was First Amendment rights, civil rights, and the policy of in loco parentis—the set of guidelines followed by most universities at the time that the institution acts in place of the parents as the moral and social guardian of its students. In loco parentis, students demanded, must be abolished. "We have an autocracy which runs this university," proclaimed Mario Savio in an impassioned speech to a crowd of thousands of protestors at Berkeley, which treats students as though they were mere "raw materials" and not human beings. "There is a time when the operation of the machine becomes so odious, makes you so sick at heart, that you can't take part; you can't even passively take part, and you've got to put your bodies upon the gears and upon the wheels, upon the levers, upon all the apparatus, and you've got to make it stop. And you've got to indicate to the people who run it, to the people who own it, that unless you're free, the machine will be prevented from working at all!"[15]

As the student movement was getting off the ground in the fall of 1964 and winter of 1965, Bernard Lafayette, John Lewis, C. T. Vivian, Martin Luther King, and others launched a voter registration campaign in Selma, Alabama. During the early weeks of 1965 protestors conducted a series of demonstrations at the Selma courthouse, where they had been vainly attempting to register. In February, as club-wielding police were breaking up one of the demonstrations, Jimmie Lee Jackson stepped in front of his mother in order to protect her. A state trooper opened fire, mortally wounding the young man. Jackson lingered in the hospital for eight days before dying.

African Americans and civil rights demonstrations were hitting the front pages of newspapers and were the top stories on radio and television every day in February and March 1965. Whether it was the mainstream media or the African American press or publications such as the *Nation, I. F. Stone's Weekly,* or *National Review,* civil rights was reported on, analyzed, criticized, lauded. It was not only news about the protests in Selma, but it was also during this time (February 21) that Malcolm X was assassinated in New York City. Was the civil rights movement going to be able to continue working for change through nonviolence? It was a question that went through many Americans' minds.

On Sunday, March 7, five hundred protestors set out from Selma for a planned march to Montgomery to demand that Governor George Wallace protect civil rights demonstrators. They only got to the far side of the Edmund Pettis Bridge when state troopers and the Selma police confronted them. Policemen attacked the marchers with billy clubs and tear gas. Mounted police trampled some of the demonstrators. Reporters and photographers captured it all, and that evening Americans watched newsreel footage of the brutal assault on the evening news. In many cities supporters took to the streets in demonstrations of solidarity with the Selma marchers. Martin Luther King issued a call for Americans to come to Selma to take part in a second march on March 9. More than two thousand people responded to the call.

But a federal judge issued a restraining order prohibiting the march. King was in a quandary. As he had emphasized in "Letter from Birmingham Jail," he made a distinction between just laws and unjust laws. Invariably the unjust laws that he transgressed, the laws upholding segregation, were state laws. King's strategy was to use the federal government to step in and force noncompliant state leaders to abide by federal law. King was reluctant to violate the federal restraining order. The standard SCLC course of action in cases like this was to get the injunction overturned in court. So, as the marchers set out from the Brown Chapel on March 9, this time more than twenty-five hundred strong, King settled on the idea of a "symbolic" march. He led the marchers across the bridge, where they were confronted by the police. King knelt and led the protestors in prayer, then turned everyone around and headed back to the chapel. Most of the marchers were confused. What was King doing? SNCC activists, especially, were angry that King turned the march around and did not continue toward Montgomery. (SNCC people were already irritated that as soon as King arrived in Selma, the media focused on him and not on those who had been beaten on "Bloody Sunday.") Back at the chapel King promised the throng that SCLC lawyers would get the injunction overturned and that the march would take place later in the week. He urged as many of the demonstrators as possible to remain in Selma and to be on hand for the march.

That evening three white ministers who had come to Selma from Boston were assaulted by baseball-bat-wielding Klansmen as they were walking back to their motel. One of the ministers, James Reeb, was so severely beaten that he died two days later. The clergyman's death was reported on the front pages of just about every newspaper in the country and garnered a tremendous outpouring of public opinion in favor of civil rights. President Johnson commented that the murder was "an American tragedy,"[16] and he called for Congress to begin work on a voting rights bill. But many African Americans, although they too mourned Reeb, were angry that the death of a white man engendered so much outrage, whereas Jimmie Jackson's death had hardly been noticed by white America.

On March 15 President Johnson went to Congress to introduce the voting rights bill. In perhaps the most eloquent speech of his career Johnson made it clear that he had listened to the demands of civil rights protestors and that he was committing himself and the nation to their cause. Calling racism an "American problem," LBJ spoke about what was happening in Selma. "There is no cause for pride in what has happened in Selma," Johnson said. "There is no cause for self-satisfaction in the long denial of equal rights of millions of Americans. But there is cause for hope and for faith in our Democracy in what is happening here tonight. For the cries of pain and the hymns and protests of oppressed people have summoned into convocation all the majesty of this great government." He went on to discuss the complexity of the issues surrounding civil rights. He spoke of the voting rights bill that he was submitting to Congress, and he urged the lawmakers to pass it swiftly. But it was not just a matter of law, he acknowledged; it was a matter of attitude, a matter of conscience, a matter of consciousness. "But even if we pass this bill the battle will not be over. What happened in Selma is part of a far larger movement which reaches into every section and state of America. It is the effort of American Negroes to secure for themselves the full blessings of American life. Their cause must be our cause too. Because it's not just Negroes, but really it's all of us, who must overcome the crippling legacy of bigotry and injustice." At this point the president paused, and then, looking directly into the camera, on national television, he said, "And we *shall* overcome."[17]

The speech electrified civil rights activists. They saw, for the first time clearly and unambiguously, that the man in the Oval Office was paying attention, that the purpose of the demonstrations—to persuade the people in power to exercise that power to guarantee fundamental rights to *all* Americans—was bearing fruit. Dissent was working.

Within a few days the federal judge in Selma rescinded the injunction, and on March 21 more than three thousand people from all walks of life, black and white, young and old, ordinary citizens and celebrities, set out for the fifty-four-mile trek to Montgomery. This time when they crossed the Edmund Pettus Bridge, the heavily armed Alabama state troopers and Selma police officers allowed them to pass. Marchers linked arms and sang "We Shall Overcome" as they crossed over. Averaging about eleven miles a day, it took the marchers five days to arrive in the state capital. By the time they got to Montgomery, the number of protestors had swelled from three thousand to approximately twenty-five thousand. They went to the statehouse with a petition. "We have come not only five days and 50 miles," the petition read, "but we have come from three centuries of suffering and hardship. We have come to you, the Governor of Alabama, to declare that we must have our freedom NOW. We must have the right to vote; we must have equal protection of the law, and an end to police brutality."[18] Governor George Wallace was conveniently not there, but Martin Luther King addressed the crowd. "We must come to see that the end we seek is a society at peace with itself, a society that can live with its conscience. That will be a day not of the white man, not of the black man. That will be the day of man as man." King acknowledged that the frustration of waiting for equal rights weighed heavily on those who had suffered and fought so long. "I know you are asking today, 'How long will it take?' I come to say to you this afternoon however difficult the moment, however frustrating the hour, it will not be long, because truth pressed to earth will rise again. How long? Not long, because no lie can live forever. How long? Not long, because you still reap what you sow. How long? Not long. Because the arc of the moral universe is long but it bends toward justice."[19]

Weary yet hopeful, the marchers began dispersing in carpools. One of the volunteers was Viola Liuzzo, a civil rights activist from Detroit, Michigan, who had come to Selma to assist with shuttling demonstrators to airports and bus stations after the march. As she was driving between Montgomery and Selma, a car pulled up alongside her vehicle, and three passengers started shooting. Liuzzo, a white mother of five children, was killed instantly. Once again television, radio, and newspaper headlines around the nation trumpeted the story of the murder of another civil rights worker.

* * *

Selma was the climax of the southern struggle against segregation. In the aftermath of Selma, President Johnson signed into law the Voting Rights Act, which did away with the most egregious discriminatory abuses such as the literacy tests that prevented blacks from voting. By the end of the year 250,000 new black voters had registered, and they became a powerful new voting bloc in the South. African Americans in the South were gaining, slowly but surely, political power. But Selma also signified a major turning point in the civil rights movement for another reason—the movement was falling apart. Discontent, especially on the part of SNCC, with Martin Luther King's dominance of the movement and frustration that his tactics were not going fast enough and far enough, created a fissure in the movement. When Stokely Carmichael assumed the leadership of SNCC, he took up the black separatism mantle of Malcolm X and other radical black thinkers. "Black Power" became Carmichael's signature phrase as he went on a speaking tour of the nation's universities. Black Power meant that blacks must seize equality for themselves, because whites will never grant it. Carmichael urged African Americans to unite "to recognize their heritage, to build a sense of community, . . . to define their own goals, to lead their own organizations." Furthermore, blacks must do this for themselves, not with white help. "We cannot have white people working in the black community—on psychological grounds. The fact is that all black people question whether or not they are equal to whites, since every time they start to do something, white people are around showing them how to do it. If we are going to eliminate that for the generation that comes after us, then black people must be in positions of power, doing and articulating for themselves." Blacks, in short, must be self-reliant. Carmichael acknowledged that the phrase "Black Power" was intimidating for whites. "White people associate Black Power with violence because of their own inability to deal with blackness. If we had said 'Negro power' nobody would get scared. Everybody would support it."[20]

After Selma, with the split within the movement widening, civil rights moved north. And when it did, civil disobedience and demonstrations became less effective because the problems for African Americans in the North were more complex than those that could be solved by passing new laws. In northern inner cities the problems were economic. There were no Jim Crow laws, but black neighborhoods in the North were just as rigidly segregated from white neighborhoods as they were in the South. And there seemed to be no easy solution for black demands for economic justice. Martin Luther King observed that it had cost the federal government nothing to pass laws ensuring that African Americans had the right to have a cup of coffee at a lunch counter or to ride at the front of a bus, but it would cost millions of dollars for the government to do something about economic injustice and the crushing poverty of the ghetto.

Just days after President Johnson signed the Voting Rights Act, in August 1965 a routine traffic stop in the African American Watts neighborhood of south central Los Angeles escalated into an altercation between black residents and the police officer. The situation got out of hand, more police were called in, a bystander was clubbed, and scores of African Americans gathered around, taunting and threatening the cops. Years of anger at police brutality and resentment about exploitive white landlords exploded. For five days Watts went up in flames. Hundreds of buildings and white-owned businesses were damaged or destroyed, thousands were arrested, hundreds were injured, twenty-five blacks and nine whites were killed. The riot was only quelled after 16,000 National Guardsmen were deployed. But Watts was just the first of these inner-city rebellions. In 1966 there were riots in Cleveland and Chicago. In 1967 there were eight major uprisings. Those in Newark and Detroit eclipsed Watts. In Detroit five days of carnage left millions of dollars of property damage, 1,200 injured, and 43 dead. In Newark, there were 725 injured and 23 dead and also millions of dollars of destruction. President Johnson had to send in army and National Guard troops to restore order.

Johnson, like most white Americans, was shaken by the uprisings and appointed a commission to investigate the causes and to propose a remedy. "White racism is essentially responsible," the Kerner Commission reported in 1968, "for the explosive mixture which has been accumulating in our cities since the end of World War II." Blacks living in the inner cities have been excluded from economic progress in the United States. There is no opportunity for young people to escape. "What white Americans have never fully understood—but what the Negro can never forget—is that white society is deeply implicated in the ghetto. White institutions created it, white institutions maintain it, and white society condones it." The commission proposed numerous programs for federal, state, and local governments to initiate that would "expand opportunities for ghetto residents to participate in the formulation of public policy and the implementation of programs affecting them through improved political representation, creation of institutional channels for community action, expansion of legal services, and legislative hearings on ghetto problems."[21] Although Congress increased funding for welfare, the commission's recommendations were never implemented, and before the year was out, the white backlash against civil rights demonstrations and what was perceived as a government that was too accommodating to black America gave Richard Nixon the victory in the presidential election.

Finding Martin Luther King's message of nonviolent resistance ineffective in dealing with the reality of the ghetto and fed up with the poverty, racial discrimination, and police brutality that African Americans faced every day, Huey Newton and Bobby Seale founded the Black Panther Party in Oakland, California. Adopting a more radical approach to dissent, they combined the philosophy of black nationalism with Marxism. The Black Panthers believed that racism was essentially part of the global class struggle. And they believed in self-defense. African Americans have the right to protect themselves against racists. Armed Black Panthers wearing black leather jackets and black berets patrolled the streets of Oakland as a sort of town watch, looking to defuse volatile situations before they got out of hand. For example, if a black man was stopped for a traffic infraction, Panthers would arrive on the scene and stand with rifles slung over their shoulders observing the interaction between the police officer and the detained person just to make sure that the officer did not use excessive force. White Americans were intimidated by the Panthers, but in reality the Panthers rarely engaged in any violence. They primarily concerned themselves with community action programs: they distributed food to schools and families in need, they fought for better employment and decent housing opportunities, they demanded equal opportunity for high-quality education, and they demanded an immediate end to police brutality. The Black Panther Party is a prime example of dissent taking a different form on the basis of a different set of convictions around the same issue. Whereas Martin Luther King's vision was to work within the system to reform race relations, Black Panthers moved in the direction of radically altering the system. Even so, the Black Panthers' reputation as extremists and revolutionaries has been wildly exaggerated by an antagonistic media and paranoid political officials. Their impact was more moderate. They raised new questions and offered new solutions to age-old problems and created a stronger sense of solidarity within the black community. The FBI, however, treated the Panthers like a terrorist organization and, under Director J. Edgar Hoover, launched a relentless counteroffensive against the Panthers that eventually, by the early 1970s, destroyed the organization and killed most of its leaders. The most infamous episode of the FBI Counter Intelligence Program (COINTELPRO) targeting Black Panthers was the raid on the Chicago Panther leader Fred Hampton's house in December 1969. Hampton and another Panther, Mark Clark, were killed in their beds at four a.m., although the FBI and the Chicago police insisted that they were shot resisting arrest. It was the beginning of the end for the Black Panther Party.

CHAPTER 21

Make Love, Not War

We're going to march in singing "We Shall Overcome."
Slowly, there are a lot of us.
—Mario Savio, 1964

LSD offers vast possibilities of accelerated learning and
scientific-scholarly research, but for initial sessions, intellectual reactions can become traps. "Turn your mind off" is
the best advice for novitiates. After you have learned how to
move your consciousness around—into ego loss and back,
at will—then intellectual exercises can be incorporated into
the psychedelic experience. The objective is to free you from
your verbal mind for as long as possible.
—Timothy Leary, 1964

The young are in the forefront of those who live and fight for
Eros against Death, and against a civilization which strives to
shorten the "detour to death" while controlling the means for
lengthening the detour. . . . Today the fight for life, the fight
for Eros, is the *political* fight.
—Herbert Marcuse, 1966

Dissent exploded in the "long" 1960s. Starting with civil rights protests in the last years of the 1950s and not culminating until the end of
the Vietnam War in the mid-1970s the United States experienced an
explosion of dissent, demonstrations, disturbances, riots, and rebellion.
Everything was fair game. Everything was questioned—from race to
gender, from war to the environment, from consumerism to middle-
class values, indeed the American way of life itself. All was subject to
debate, dissection, analysis, criticism, reevaluation. Dissenters of all
varieties—reformers, reactionaries, revolutionaries—expressed their
grievances through civil disobedience, speeches, demonstrations,

petitions, music, art, street theater, comedy, and even violence. By 1975 the United States was transformed, and the fallout from that period is still felt today.

* * *

JFK's appeal to youthful idealism when he challenged Americans to "ask not what your country can do for you, ask what you can do for your country" and the bitter reality that sank in after his assassination was one of the factors that gave rise to the counterculture of the 1960s. The suffocating conformity of suburbs and shopping malls and McCarthyism, coupled with the iconoclastic attitude of the Beats and 1950s rock and roll, also had a profound effect on making the 1960s what they were. Most importantly it was the inspiring example of courageous African American college students confronting Jim Crow with sit-ins and Freedom Rides and demonstrations that propelled a generation of white college students to rebel, to dissent, to question authority.

As the war in Vietnam began to escalate in middecade, dissent intensified at an exponential rate, not only in opposition to the war but also in questioning *everything* about American society. As more and more young radicals criticized the wisdom and motivation of U.S. involvement in Vietnam, their protests soon embraced all aspects of American policy and values. They recognized the demonization of communism and communists from Fidel Castro to Patrice Lumumba as pure propaganda, and they condemned Washington's inadequate and sluggish response to African Americans' century-long struggle for equal rights. If American government and society was suspect in these things, many young people reasoned, then American values themselves needed to be reevaluated.

In August 1964 Congress passed the Gulf of Tonkin Resolution (at LBJ's request), giving the president carte blanche in protecting American interests in Vietnam. During the election campaign that fall, while the Republican candidate Barry Goldwater demanded that the United States unleash the full power of its military in Vietnam, the Democrats portrayed Goldwater as a warmonger and urged Americans to vote for Johnson, who would maintain peace. But with the election safely won, Johnson stepped up America's presence in Vietnam. As events in Selma dominated the nation's headlines, Johnson authorized Operation Rolling Thunder. This was a series of daily bombing sorties, originally designed as an eight-week campaign, in an all-out effort to crush the communists of Vietnam. Soon after the launching of the operation Johnson deployed ground troops to Vietnam. From this point on the die was cast, and hostilities escalated at an inexorable and accelerating pace.

At first many young men, answering JFK's call to pay any price and bear any burden in the struggle against communism, enlisted in the armed forces. But as the war escalated and the number of American troops in Vietnam swelled, so too did dissent against the war. In fact in March 1965, as B-52s were dropping thousands of tons of bombs on Vietnam and civil rights activists were protesting in Selma, the first "teach-in" took place at the University of Michigan. This was an all-night event in which students and faculty participated in lectures and discussions examining the historical roots of the conflict and U.S. Cold War policy. For eleven hours they debated the arguments both for and against the war. During the night three bomb threats were called in by opponents of the teach-in who believed that the mere act of investigating U.S. policy was an act of treason. But the student participants saw the teach-in as an expression of heartfelt patriotism. From time to time they had to move outside while the police searched the rooms for bombs, but the speakers continued speaking in the freezing weather until they could return inside. A number of anti-teach-in protestors attending the event repeatedly challenged the speakers and in some cases heckled and disrupted them. But this only enhanced and deepened the intellectual analysis. All night long the presenters continued espousing the argument that the Vietnamese had been struggling for independence for centuries against the Chinese, the French, and the Japanese and that the United States was merely the latest nation seeking to control Vietnam. The war, they contended, was not about democracy versus communism; the war was about Vietnamese nationalism. When the teach-in ended, most (but by no means all) of the students agreed that the United States should pull out of Vietnam, and they endorsed a strong antiwar position. Over the next few weeks the teach-in phenomenon swept over scores of campuses from Berkeley to Columbia, from the University of Chicago to the University of Pennsylvania, as students and scholars discussed what was happening in Vietnam. And then in May thousands, including some members of Congress, attended a National Teach-In in Washington, DC. The antiwar movement was born.

Events moved quickly. More than twenty thousand protestors took part in an antiwar demonstration on the steps of the Capitol building in Washington, DC, in April, and then in June thousands protested at the Pentagon. On November 2 Quaker pacifist Norman Morrison, calling for an immediate withdrawal of American troops, committed self-immolation below the window of Secretary of Defense Robert McNamara's Pentagon office. And later that same month more than forty thousand demonstrated at the White House and the Washington Monument. Still, at year's end most Americans (64 percent according to the Gallup Poll) supported Johnson's policy in Vietnam (only 20 percent were against it).

One of the organizations backing the 1965 antiwar demonstrations was the left-wing Students for a Democratic Society. Formed in 1960 at the University of Michigan, SDS was mostly involved in labor and civil rights activism during its first five years. Calling for "participatory democracy," hundreds of SDS members strove to radicalize local auto-workers in southeastern Michigan and also journeyed south to participate in the sit-ins, Freedom Rides, Freedom Summer, and civil rights protest marches. Influenced by such left-wing political thinkers as Herbert Marcuse, C. Wright Mills, and Frantz Fanon, SDS was deeply critical of American capitalism. It denounced Cold War stereotypes and U.S. efforts to contain communism, which meant supporting right-wing dictators who were guilty of flagrant human rights violations. According to SDS, America's demonization of communism was a smokescreen to mask U.S. imperialism, and the escalating war in Vietnam was a perfect example of this. Washington was not interested in democracy in Vietnam; it was simply interested in maintaining American economic dominance in Southeast Asia.

In November 1965 the Committee for a Sane Nuclear Policy, with significant support from SDS, Women Strike for Peace, and the National Coordinating Committee to End the War in Vietnam, organized the largest antiwar demonstration to that date. Thirty-five thousand antiwar protestors marched from the White House to the Washington Monument, where they listened to Carl Oglesby, the president of SDS, give a compelling speech in which he denounced both conservatives and liberals and posited a radical analysis of American foreign policy. The men who created the policy that led the United States into

Vietnam, Oglesby argued, were not monsters or right-wing ideologues but liberals, and their goal in Vietnam was not to stop the spread of communism but to preserve and expand the American corporate system. The National Liberation Front was fighting a revolution not unlike America's own revolution against Britain, he said, but Americans were turning a blind eye to this fact. We were so caught up in opposing the Soviet Union and Communist China that we could only see Red, and this was blinding us to the fact "that our proper human struggle is not with Communism or revolutionaries, but with the social desperation that drives good men to violence."[1]

Oglesby went on to summarize American foreign policy of the Cold War years to prove his point that business interests were dictating that policy—oil in Iran, fruit in Guatemala, sugar in the Dominican Republic, and so on. The people behind the policy, Oglesby contended, were "good men." But they were caught in the system and thus lost their compassion. "People become instruments. Generals do not hear the screams of the bombed; sugar executives do not see the misery of the cane cutters: for to do so is to be that much less the general, that much less the executive." We do not admit that our presence in Third World countries is based on such selfish grounds; we insist that we are pursuing loftier principles of liberty and freedom. Though we might exploit a nation, we are bestowing the blessings of democracy and Western civilization. This attitude allows us to depict "our presence in other lands not as a coercion, but a protection. It allows us even to say that the napalm in Vietnam is only another aspect of our humanitarian love— like those exorcisms in the Middle Ages that so often killed the patient. So we say to the Vietnamese peasant, the Cuban intellectual, the Peruvian worker: 'You are better dead than Red. If it hurts or if you don't understand why—sorry about that.'"[2]

Most of us, Oglesby contended, are unaware of our personal responsibility for the war. It is not just the politicians and businessmen who are responsible but *all* of us. "All of us are born to the colossus of history, our American corporate system—in many ways an awesome organism. There is one fact that describes it: With about five per cent of the world's people, we consume about half the world's goods. We take a richness that is in good part not our own, and we put it in our pockets, our garages, our split-levels, our bellies, and our futures." So in the end,

Vietnam War protestors in Washington, DC, October 21, 1967.
(Public domain; courtesy Lyndon B. Johnson Library)

we have to accept our responsibility, and if we truly believe in America's human rights ideals, then we must do everything we can to change the status quo and bring about a "humanist reformation."[3]

Media coverage of the demonstrations was, for the most part, negative. From *Time, Newsweek,* the *Washington Post,* and the *New York Times* to ABC, CBS, and NBC, the mainstream media portrayed antiwar protestors as an unwashed, unruly mob of disloyal, procommunist radicals. Even the term "peacenik" that was applied to antiwar activists—an attempt to Russify them by evoking the image of disgruntled ne'er-do-wells who were really Soviet agents or at best sympathizers and dupes—indicted their loyalty. The truth is, however, that antiwar protestors came from a wide variety of backgrounds. Most of them were, like Oglesby, thoughtful, intellectual critics of American policy. And certainly the scholarly expertise of many antiwar dissenters from the academic community did bestow a level of respectability on the movement. Any American who took his or her patriotism seriously was aware that complex historical and political issues were at the crux of the Vietnam conflict. If one wished to develop an informed opinion one way or the other about the war, it was imperative to study history and examine these issues. And many did just that. In addition to academics and students, there were literally thousands of groups working locally and coming together several times a year for massive protests. As the war intensified, so too did the protests, and cogent antiwar arguments gained traction with millions and even tens of millions of Americans. Demonstrators were not, as the media liked to portray them, just hippies. Nuns, clergymen, politicians, housewives, Quakers, and groups such as Another Mother for Peace, Businessmen Against the War, and American Writers Against the Vietnam War were among those that took to the streets in thousands of antiwar demonstrations.

Intellectual opposition to the war was only part of the picture. Many opposed the war because of the draft. For some it was purely a matter of self-preservation—they did not want to *be* killed. For others it was less self-interested than that—they did not want *to* kill. They questioned the morality of the war. As young men (many of whom had begun to question the validity of the war) received their draft notices, more and more of them began to actively oppose the war. Some joined demonstrations and protest marches, some refused to report for their physical examination, some were arrested, some fled to Canada. At demonstrations as early as 1965 antiwar protestors of draft age began publicly burning their draft cards—an act that could get them arrested. And hundreds were arrested. Antiwar protestors regularly held sit-ins at induction centers and Selective Service offices, attempting to block inductees and recruits from entering. Others engaged in more militant tactics. The Catholic priests Daniel and Philip Berrigan, leaders in the Catholic peace movement,[4] were arrested for breaking into draft offices in Baltimore and pouring blood on Selective Service files and in Catonsville, Maryland, where they destroyed draft documents with homemade napalm. Over the next few years there were break-ins in dozens of Selective Service offices around the country, during which an estimated five hundred antiwar activists stole or destroyed files. Before the war ended, more than one hundred thousand men refused induction into the U.S. Army, while more than half a million evaded the draft. More than twenty thousand men were put on trial, nine thousand were convicted, and four thousand served prison terms of up to five years. There is no accurate way of knowing how many men fled the country, but estimates are that between thirty thousand and fifty thousand draft-age American men left. Many of them never returned.

Each year the antiwar movement grew. By 1969 there were thousands of demonstrations annually, not only in large metropolitan areas but also in smaller cities and towns all over the nation. The demonstrations spread around the world as people took to the streets in London, Rome, Berlin, Tokyo, Paris, and nearly every major metropolis in every country. Still, despite the growing antiwar movement, most Americans were hawks who supported the president's policies and who believed in the legitimacy of preventing a communist takeover of Vietnam. They accepted the common wisdom of the domino theory (first espoused by President Eisenhower) that postulated that if one country fell to communism, then, like a row of dominoes, neighboring countries would also fall. Eventually the falling dominoes would reach the United States. Johnson more than once stated that it was better to fight the communists in the jungles of Vietnam than it would be to fight them on the beaches of California. The hawks vilified the doves as being un-American. To support the war, to support the troops, was patriotic. To question the war was to be on the side of the enemy. Prowar Americans frequented antiwar demonstrations, where they heckled the demonstrators, calling them cowards and traitors and holding counter-demonstrations of their own.

* * *

Concurrent with the antiwar movement, many thousands of Americans, especially young people, began questioning the prevalent assumptions of the social order. From the American way of life to *all* bourgeois values, from the nature of patriotism to the sanctity of religious doctrine, from obeying authority to the legitimacy of society's time-honored rules and regulations, everything was examined, questioned, and challenged. And from this cauldron of reevaluation the counterculture was born.

Hundreds of thousands of college students, inspired by JFK and the civil rights movement, still believed in the idealistic, somewhat naïve, mantra that "we can change the world!" But it seemed increasingly clear to them that the government was intentionally obfuscating, if not lying about, the necessity for American military intervention in Vietnam. If the authorities were not being entirely up-front with the American people about Vietnam, many students believed, then perhaps the "Establishment" was not to be trusted about anything. Slowly at first but accelerating rapidly, large numbers of America's youth began questioning all authority, all rules, all values, all morality. Dissent permeated the atmosphere.

Baby boomers had been brought up steeped in middle-class morality. They were taught that the ideal life consisted of the nuclear churchgoing family living in a comfortable house in suburbia far from the crime and grime (code for racial issues) of the city. Patriotism, religious faith, consumer products, and prosperity were the highest ideals. Those who did not exhibit such values were suspect, shady, un-American. Baby boomers had also been taught that sexual feelings and urges were basically sinful. Premarital sex was immoral. Sexual desire should be satisfied *only* in marriage, and homosexuality was unspeakably abnormal and particularly wicked. They were brought up in an environment of sharply delineated gender roles. Men were the breadwinners whose authority was not to be questioned, while women did the housework and cared for the children. Drugs too, especially marijuana, were classified as immoral. Only criminals and people living in the ghettoes of the nation's cities used drugs. But by the end of the 1960s millions of baby boomers, through politics, lifestyle, and relationships, challenged *all* of these assumptions.

Dissent in the 1960s was expressed in a multitude of ways—music, art, comedy, theater, fashion, lifestyle, drugs, sex—and because of technological advances in television, radio, and recordings, the message that activists wished to disseminate reached a far wider audience in the 1960s and 1970s than in previous decades. Perhaps the most effective way of getting out the dissenting message was through song. By the end of the 1950s the civil rights movement and the popularity of the blacklisted folk group the Weavers brought about the folk music revival. Folk songs told stories. And many of the stories recounted the difficulties of the poor. Miners owing their souls to the company store in "Sixteen Tons," workers dreaming of a better life in "I Dreamed I Saw Joe Hill Last Night," and above all, African Americans fighting for equal rights in "If You Miss Me at the Back of the Bus" and "We Shall Not Be Moved." Starting in 1958, the recordings of such popular performers as the Kingston Trio, the Brothers Four, Peter, Paul, and Mary, and Joan Baez increasingly invaded the pop charts and the consciousness of teenagers as they graduated from high school. Although the songs were easy enough for amateurs to play and the words and melodies were simple, many of the songs raised serious issues that stimulated critical thinking. Thousands of young people entering college were drawn to the reflective lyricism of the genre, and soon folk music (in an age before Facebook and Twitter and other forms of social media) linked Americans all over the country in a burgeoning culture of protest.

When Bob Dylan burst on the folk scene, protest music really took off. He recorded mostly traditional folk songs on his first album but then began recording his own songs, in which he dealt with personal as well as civil rights and antiwar themes. "The Lonesome Death of Hattie Carroll," "Blowin' in the Wind," and "Only a Pawn in Their Game" drew attention to the African American struggle for civil rights. In "The Lonesome Death of Hattie Carroll" Dylan sings of the murder of a black maid by a wealthy, white Baltimore socialite who gets off with a mere six-month sentence—a realistic depiction of the racial inequality in America. "Only a Pawn in Their Game" is a powerful and nuanced examination of the 1963 murder of Medgar Evers in which Dylan depicts the assassin as an ignorant white man who is "only a pawn" in southern racist politicians' "game." And in "Blowin' in the Wind" Dylan raises a litany of questions about the struggle for freedom that only the wind can answer. Such songs impelled listeners, even those who had never thought about civil rights or the plight of African Americans, to examine where they stood on the issue, to find the answers to the questions, and to form their own judgments. Dylan, obviously, was moved enough by the struggle for civil rights that it inspired him to write such songs. And these songs, in turn, wound up influencing Americans who had been apathetic about civil rights to reflect on these things and, in the end, to decide which side they were on. Many Americans joined the movement and as early as the 1963 March on Washington helped turn civil rights into an unstoppable force. Perhaps the lines in "Blowin' in the Wind" that resonated most with listeners were the ones in which Dylan wonders "how many ears must one man have / before he can hear people cry?" and "how many times must a man turn his head / pretending he just doesn't see?"[5] In essence Dylan is saying that you personally *must* get involved. The time for indifference is over. If you are not part of the solution, you are part of the problem. Soon civil rights protestors were singing "Blowin' in the Wind" along with "We Shall Overcome" in marches and demonstrations.

Dylan also tackled the issues of war, American militarism, and the potential consequences of the Cold War. In "With God on Our Side" Dylan ridicules the cliché that God is always on America's side in its military conflicts, and in "Masters of War" he excoriates the arms manufacturers who create the weapons for war and hide in their mansions "as young people's blood / flows out of their bodies / and is buried in the mud."[6] At the height of the Cold War, during the Cuban missile crisis, Dylan tapped into the powerful foreboding that held Americans in its grip in his apocalyptic vision of a postnuclear future, in "A Hard Rain's A-Gonna Fall."

Even after Dylan went electric at the Newport Folk Festival in 1965, abandoning his openly political lyrics for a more surrealistic commentary, moving from political dissent to countercultural dissent, his songs remained critical of the fake morals and superficiality of modern life. "Like a Rolling Stone," a song that many people consider to be the "anthem of the sixties," is a surrealistic critique of American culture, including underground culture. What is so significant about so many of Dylan's songs is that they imaginatively reflected the stresses and anxieties of contemporary life while at the same time pushed individuals to think for themselves and live a more thoughtful and, consequently, more meaningful life. The songs encouraged active participation and being a part of one's own time. And Dylan was not alone. Hundreds of other musicians wrote politically and socially charged songs: Phil Ochs, Tom Paxton, Buffy Sainte-Marie, Paul Simon. Soon it seemed that the majority of the songs aired on the radio had some sort of sociopolitical message. And by middecade the example of Bob Dylan and other singer-songwriters wound up having a transformative influence on rock and roll. The Beatles led the way. With songs like "Eleanor Rigby" and

"Nowhere Man" the Beatles opened up pop music to broader social issues than the hackneyed teenage lust that had dominated rock and roll since its inception. They instinctively understood that young people like themselves were not only interested in love and jealousy, holding hands and sexuality; they were also caught up in finding their own place in the world and living a meaningful life. When the band sang about a "Nowhere Man" who "doesn't have a point of view," it resonated with thousands of young people who were trying to find their way in life. By 1967 political rock and roll permeated the airwaves. Whether it was the Doors beseeching "come on, baby, light my fire" or the Mothers of Invention disparaging "plastic people! / oh, baby, now you're such a drag" or Jefferson Airplane observing that the pills "that mother gives you / don't do anything at all" or the Motown artist Edwin Starr shouting, "war, what's it good for?";[7] whether it was the Grateful Dead, the MC5, Janis Joplin, Jimi Hendrix, or the Beatles and the Rolling Stones invading from England, rock and roll had become a critical commentary on modern-day life.[8]

One of the first things people think about when they think about the sixties is drugs. But drug use was not simply about self-indulgence or escaping from reality. Drugs, especially LSD and marijuana, were part of the 1960s search for authenticity. After psychology professor Timothy Leary was fired from Harvard for experimenting with lysergic acid diethylamide (LSD) with his students, he began touring college campuses around the country preaching the gospel of psychedelic drugs. Repeating his mantra of "Tune In, Turn On, and Drop Out," Leary urged listeners to tune in to their spiritual nature, turn on with LSD, and drop out of the bourgeois consumerist rat race. LSD, Leary proclaimed, was a mind-expanding drug that enabled the user to see into the true nature of things, to recognize the interconnectedness of all being, and as a result live a deeper, more fulfilling life. LSD led to *satori*, the enlightenment that Buddhist monks achieved after years of meditation. Leary struck a responsive chord with tens of thousands of young people who were already protesting against racism and the war in Vietnam, reevaluating middle-class values, and distrusting authority, especially when he advised them, "never trust anyone over thirty" (Leary was in his forties). By the late sixties untold numbers of young people had experimented with LSD and other psychedelic drugs, while the other popular drug, marijuana, was almost de rigueur for any person claiming to be hip and wishing to show his or her countercultural credentials. Although Leary encouraged widespread drug *use*, he warned against drug *abuse*. What many people missed was his injunction that drugs were not for everyone. Unless you were seriously interested in expanding your mind and deepening your awareness, you should abstain. "Acid is not for every brain," Leary wrote; "only the healthy, happy, wholesome, handsome, hopeful, humorous, high-velocity should seek these experiences."[9]

Left-wing political philosopher Herbert Marcuse also tapped into the naturally rebellious impulses of the counterculture. In his *Eros and Civilization* Marcuse combined Freud's ideas about sexual repression with Marx's critique of capitalism. Unlike totalitarian societies that control people through physical oppression, capitalism maintains control by restricting sexuality. In the United States, Marcuse argues, political, legal, and religious authorities have established a system in which there is excessive sexual repression—people are made to feel guilty for their sexual urges, premarital sex is taboo, homosexuality is forbidden. This "surplus repression" is manipulated by advertisers and manufacturers to fuel consumer capitalism. Individuals try to fill the inner void and find happiness through consumption—buying consumer goods, smoking, consuming alcoholic beverages, overeating, frequenting movies and sporting events, watching television (where they are exposed to even more consumer goods). If we become aware that we are sexually repressed, Marcuse contends, and if we develop a healthy, honest attitude about sex, then we will not only find erotic satisfaction, but we will be performing an act of revolution against consumer capitalism. Such ideas, coupled with the invention of the birth-control pill, became the basis for the sexual revolution of the 1960s. Young people everywhere rejected outmoded sexual morals and sought to establish a new model of sexual behavior. Like drugs, sex was perceived as a path to self-discovery and self-fulfillment—all part of the quest for authenticity. For many young Americans unrepressed sexuality was political. It was both an act of personal liberation and radical politics—the slogan "Make Love, Not War" became one of the catchphrases of the era.

Humor, too, was another form of dissent. From Mark Twain to H. L. Mencken, heirs to the court-jester tradition of medieval Europe, societal critics employed humor as a way to express dissenting opinions. Lenny Bruce, a champion of the free expression guaranteed in the First Amendment, used every four-letter word in the book in his offensive, wry observations about American values. On Steve Allen's prime-time television show he admitted there were some words that offended even him: "Governor Faubus, segregation offend me; . . . the shows that exploit homosexuality, narcotics, and prostitution under the guise of helping these societal problems; . . . motion pictures that exploit race relations."[10] Other stand-up comedians, from Dick Gregory to Richard Pryor, Mort Sahl to the Smothers Brothers and George Carlin, used their acerbic wit to challenge Americans to question the bourgeois, racist, classist, sexist ethos of the time.

Even the fashions of the 1960s were a manifestation of dissent. Because it was more important to be concerned with the serious issues of war and racism, to resist the forces of conformity, and to live an authentic life, young people everywhere rejected the accepted bourgeois notions of grooming and wearing such proper attire as suits and ties, modest skirts and blouses. Conservative clothing made everyone look alike. There was little space for self-expression. And so young people playfully chose to wear bell-bottom jeans, old military-surplus shirts, tie-dye T-shirts, Indian shirts, miniskirts, and colorful earth-mother dresses. Men grew beards and let their hair grow long. Women stopped shaving their legs and armpits. And though many people belittled hippies as being just as conformist as the culture they were rejecting, the cultural rebels were *consciously* conforming to a new style, a new set of rules, a new set of values. Anyone encountering a hippie knew instantly where that person stood on civil rights, the war in Vietnam, drugs, and sexuality just by looking at him or her. And while not overtly political, the "hippie look" was a political statement. Sex, drugs, rock and roll, long hair—all of it was an individual expression of dissent and a refusal to go along with business as usual. By 1970 there was little to distinguish cultural and social dissent from political dissent. It was all part and parcel of the heartfelt determination to reject conventional values and political orthodoxy in favor of living an examined life honestly and fully.

* * *

The radical values of the 1960s were also expressed in paintings, posters, literature, and the performing arts. Art is always on the cutting edge of change. To be an artist is to question accepted norms. Perhaps no artist more exemplifies the sixties revolt against conventional standards than Andy Warhol. His celebrated paintings of Campbell's tomato soup cans, in which he challenges the viewer to look at the everyday images of modern society with new eyes, simply baffled most people. Warhol's "pop art" commented on the assembly-line nature of contemporary American life, in which all consumer products (including art) and the mundane experience of daily living were all repeated endlessly. Whether it was a Campbell's soup can, a Brillo box, or Marilyn Monroe, Mick Jagger, or Jacqueline Kennedy Onassis, Warhol's iconic images forced people to ponder, and presumably to question, the routine dreariness of their own lives. In a consumer society everything, even individuals, is mass-produced.

Other visual artists were more explicit in their protests against the political status quo. This was especially true in the realm of poster art. As the war in Vietnam heated up and public debates about the antiwar protests and the counterculture grew more contentious, hundreds of artists, both well-known and anonymous, produced thousands of images that attacked everything from the war to laws against drugs. One of the most famous posters was painted by Lorraine Schneider, a member of the antiwar group Another Mother for Peace. It was a simple drawing of a sunflower with the phrase "War is not healthy for children and other living things." Sister Mary Corita Kent, a nun in the Order of the Immaculate Heart, used her artistic talent to create antiwar silkscreen posters. Conservatives accused her of being subversive, but her art was primarily a conservative depiction of the golden rule. She advocated peace, love, and nonviolence. "I am not brave enough," she once said, "to not pay my income tax and risk going to jail. But I can say rather freely what I want to say with my art."[11]

Graphic artists designed thousands of antiwar and antidraft posters. One of the most widely distributed was a politically incorrect photo of three "hippie chicks" sitting on a couch, with the caption "GIRLS SAY YES to boys who say NO," that is, say no to the draft. And another was simply a photo of a young man burning his draft card, with the caption "FUCK THE DRAFT." Posters proliferated on walls, on telephone poles, on fences all over the country urging solidarity with the Chicago 8 during their trial, promoting the Black Panther Party, and demanding the legalization of marijuana, while others were psychedelic paintings proclaiming the virtues of getting high and taking acid trips or enjoining everyone to "Make Love, Not War." One of the most famous antimainstream posters of all featured Frank Zappa, the long-haired iconoclastic leader of the rock group Mothers of Invention, sitting on a toilet with his pants rolled down to his ankles and glaring at the camera.

Performance artists also employed their talents to protest the Vietnam War and to advocate alternative lifestyle choices. The experimental theater troupe the Living Theatre, founded by Judith Malina and Julian Beck, produced plays in which the theater itself became the medium to promote social and political change. In plays such as *Paradise Now*, *Mysteries and Smaller Pieces*, and *Frankenstein* they challenged audiences to reassess their ways of thinking and behaving. Often the challenge was uncomfortably confrontational, as when actors descended from the stage, forcing members of the audience to participate in the action, turning them into (sometimes reluctant) actors in the play. The antiwar activist Barbara Garson's *MacBird* was a droll retelling of Shakespeare's *Macbeth* satirizing President Johnson's rise to power. The surprise off-Broadway hit was a devastating and controversial critique of power that went so far as to accuse LBJ of murdering his predecessor. The activist Bread and Puppet Theatre performed regularly at antiwar marches and demonstrations. Using massive puppets ten to twenty feet tall, the performers translated political activism into street theater. The puppets, papier-mâché caricatures of Johnson, Nixon, Kissinger, Uncle Sam, and other political figures, invariably added a festive, humorous quality to the demonstrations. When the mischievous and subversive musical *Hair* moved to Broadway in 1967, the counterculture went mainstream. Although many theatergoers disapproved of *Hair*'s radical message—the joyous espousal of free love, marijuana, and the hippie lifestyle—they were nevertheless fascinated (and titillated) by the full-frontal nudity of the actors in the play's finale.

Dozens of films during the decade promoted a dissenting point of view. Andy Warhol's experimental films, such as *Chelsea Girls* and *Blow Job*, were unapologetic critiques of middle-class morality. The independent film *Prologue* was a fictional semidocumentary analyzing the schism between cultural rebels and political rebels during the 1968 Chicago demonstrations, and *Medium Cool*, also set in Chicago in 1968, was Hollywood's take on the Marshall McLuhan thesis about the interplay between the media and cultural events—"the medium is the message." A number of provocative plays were also translated into cinema. *A Thousand Clowns* was a paean to nonconformity, and the film version of the Royal Shakespeare Company's *Marat/Sade* (a play by the East German communist Peter Weiss) was a riveting and profound view of 1960s activism as seen through the prism of the French Revolution's Reign of Terror. Hollywood, too, got on the bandwagon with such enormously popular films as *The Graduate*, a humorous and poignant reflection on trying to be an individual in a conformist world; *Alice's Restaurant*, a film version of Arlo Guthrie's antidraft song; and *Easy Rider*, the story of two young men's disastrous motorcycle odyssey to free themselves from the constraints of conventional society. Millions of young Americans saw versions of themselves in these films.

* * *

By 1967 it seemed that dissent was becoming a way of life. Most of America's youth were turning into critics of business as usual. They favored civil rights. They opposed the war and the draft. They called for the legalization of marijuana. They renounced inhibition. And they insisted on their God-given right to "do their own thing." On top of this civil rights and the antiwar movement were coalescing in the person of Martin Luther King. King's sermon at New York's Riverside Church in April was a seminal event in 1967. Against the advice of his SCLC advisers King came out against the war in Vietnam. Civil rights activists feared that a public antiwar stance on King's part would lead to massive defections from the civil rights movement, especially by those who viewed protesting the war as unpatriotic. But King believed that he had to speak out because it was a question of morality, a question of morality no less significant than the cause of civil rights. It is time, King said, "to break the silence." He spoke about his role as a civil rights leader and his commitment to the methods of nonviolence. But it is hard to convince people that the way to solve problems is through nonviolence when the United States is "using massive doses of violence to solve its problems, to bring about the changes it wanted": "the greatest purveyor of violence in the world today [is] my own government." After killing more than a million Vietnamese, we must take stock of ourselves and "admit that we have been wrong from the beginning of our adventure in Vietnam, that we have been detrimental to the life of the Vietnamese people."[12]

King's speech was a thunderclap. Around the nation millions of Americans denounced him as anti-American. President Johnson, who was King's most important ally and who was responsible for pushing the Civil Rights and Voting Rights Acts through Congress, was furious.

Even many of King's supporters felt he had gone too far, that he should not have taken up a cause that was viewed as outside his domain. But many others paused to reflect on his words and to reflect on whether they could continue to support America's actions in Vietnam.

Senator Robert Kennedy also broke publicly with President Johnson over the war. He did not blame the war entirely on Johnson. He acknowledged that he had participated in decisions during his brother's presidency that led to deepening America's involvement in Vietnam. And so if there was blame to go around, he was to blame too. He did not try to duck responsibility. But the time had come to acknowledge that mistakes were made, that we were wrong. We must come to understand, Kennedy told Americans in his speeches, that it is not Johnson's war, it is not McNamara's war; it is *our* war. And what we are doing in Vietnam is immoral. "It is we who live in abundance and send our young men out to die. It is our chemicals that scorch the children and our bombs that level the villages. We are all participants." It was time to end the war and to negotiate a peace settlement. Later Kennedy reiterated the immorality of the war. "We're killing children, we're killing women, we're killing innocent people . . . because [the Viet Cong are] 12,000 miles away and they might get to be 11,000 miles away. Do we have the right here in the United States to say we're going to kill tens of thousands, make millions of people, as we have . . . refugees, kill women and children?"[13]

With public figures such as Robert Kennedy and Martin Luther King speaking out against the war, many more Americans began to question U.S. policy in Vietnam. At the end of October seventy thousand protestors marched on the Pentagon in one of the biggest antiwar demonstrations in American history. Dr. Benjamin Spock, Noam Chomsky, Norman Mailer, and Abbie Hoffman were among the celebrated "peaceniks" participating in the march. Hoffman, vowing to exorcise the Pentagon, led a contingent of hippies in chanting "Om" in order to levitate the building and end the war in Vietnam. Meanwhile thousands of other demonstrators approached the main entrance of the building, where they were confronted by twenty-five hundred troops. Those who tried to break through the barrier were arrested. A famous photograph from the standoff depicts a young protestor inserting a carnation into the barrel of a soldier's gun: flower power. A month later, on November 30, Senator Eugene McCarthy of Minnesota declared his candidacy for the Democratic presidential nomination in 1968 with the pledge that if elected president, he would end the war immediately. "I am hopeful that this challenge," McCarthy said, "may alleviate at least in some degree this sense of political helplessness and restore to many people a belief in the processes of American politics and of American government."[14] The Johnson administration was beginning to feel the heat.

* * *

The year 1968 was a watershed. At the beginning of the year more than 50 percent of Americans supported the Vietnam War; by December more than 50 percent opposed the war. The year began with the Tet Offensive, in which the Viet Cong launched a series of attacks throughout the length and breadth of Vietnam. There was no delineated front. They attacked American bases in every corner of the country. They even occupied the American embassy in Saigon for a few days. Up to this point most Americans believed the administration's reports that we were winning the war. After all, we were killing far more of the Viet Cong than they were killing us. But as early as February 1968 disturbing images coming out of Vietnam on the nightly news seemed to contradict the official reports and expose a serious "credibility gap" between what the administration said about the progress of the war and what people saw on the evening news. U.S. Marines had to fight their way back into the American embassy, children were running down roads with napalm burns on their bodies, and the most searing image of all that appeared on the front pages of newspapers throughout the country was the photograph of the South Vietnamese police chief Nguyễn Ngọc Loan summarily executing a Viet Cong guerrilla on a Saigon street. Despite the fact that after several weeks of intensive fighting American troops beat back the Viet Cong, it certainly did not seem like the United States was winning the hearts and minds of the Vietnamese. It was clear that the light at the end of the tunnel that General William Westmoreland claimed he saw was more likely (as waggish antiwar critics put it) the headlight of an onrushing locomotive.[15]

In March, while the Tet Offensive was still commanding headlines, Eugene McCarthy won 42 percent of the votes in the New Hampshire primary. The fact that an antiwar candidate had such an impressive showing against an incumbent president in a conservative state was a shock to the Democratic Party. Four days later Robert Kennedy entered the race. Many in the antiwar movement saw Kennedy's decision as opportunistic; they had, after all, been trying for months to convince the senator to take on Johnson, and they viewed his decision, after McCarthy had tested the waters, to be somewhat less than courageous. Nevertheless, Kennedy (who wore the mystical mantle of his brother's legacy) had a vast following, not only antiwar radicals but also minority groups and civil rights activists, as well as the working class. It seemed that Kennedy had a legitimate chance to wrest the nomination away from Johnson. And if he did, there was every reason to believe that with the magic of the Kennedy name he would win the general election in November.

On March 31 Johnson stunned the nation with his televised announcement that he would not seek the nomination for another term as president. The antiwar movement was elated. For four days a sense of euphoria swept through the ranks of antiwar activists. After all, it was clear that their demonstrations and protests had succeeded. They had forced the abdication of Lyndon Baines Johnson. But on April 4, 1968, the euphoria vanished when Martin Luther King was assassinated. Most Americans were fed up with dissenters, and perhaps the majority was indifferent to King's assassination. But his death was deeply mourned by liberals and civil rights activists, student protestors and antiwar militants. And in the days following his funeral a sense of doom overwhelmed the Left.

In April students at Columbia University, angered at the university's exploitive dealings with the African American residents of neighboring Harlem and furious with the university's connections with a weapons research think tank that worked with the Pentagon, initiated a series of protests that led to their occupying the university's administrative offices. After several days the New York police were called in and cleared the protestors out of the buildings. Most surrendered without resistance, but in some cases the police used violent means to remove them. Hundreds were arrested, 148 protestors and bystanders were injured.

The protests at Columbia continued in May and helped inspire students at the Sorbonne in Paris to carry out their own protests against the university's martinet rules and regulations. Soon the Paris uprising turned violent. Property destruction was widespread as student demonstrators set up barricades in the streets, and when the working class joined the students (an alliance that did not take place in any of the protests in the United States), President Charles de Gaulle was forced to call for a new election. For the next several months protests spread to Berlin, London, Tokyo, Mexico City, Prague, and many other cities as the spirit of dissent swept around the world. It seemed that forces had been unleashed that no one could control or even fully understand. Rebellion was contagious.

On June 5, just moments after winning the Democratic primary in California, Robert Kennedy was gunned down by an assassin. The hopes of activists for a quick end to the war in Vietnam died with Kennedy. For the next two months some clung to the flimsy chance that against-all-odds McCarthy would get the Democratic nomination or that antiwar delegates would at least be able to insert a peace plank into the platform. But this was not to be. Party professionals were able to secure the nomination for Vice President Hubert Humphrey at the convention in Chicago and fend off the peace-plank effort. With thousands of militants protesting the war on the streets and with the Chicago police beating, tear-gassing, and arresting the demonstrators, a bizarre scene played out on the convention floor. Antiwar Democrats from New York, California, Wisconsin, and other states joined in with the spirit of dissent when they began singing "We Shall Overcome." On national television, before the eyes of millions of viewers, the Democratic Party was disintegrating in a wave of frustration and anger.

In November, Richard Nixon was elected president of the United States.

* * *

Despite the assassinations and the violence and the crushed hopes of those who so desperately desired change, the protests continued. In fact they mushroomed. And Nixon's unwillingness to end the war or even to listen to the nonviolent demonstrators radicalized the movement. Some of the largest demonstrations against the war took place in 1969, 1970, and 1971. When the Democratic Party nominated the fierce, uncompromising antiwar Senator George McGovern as its candidate for president in 1972, it underscored the power of dissent to shape history. The politics of dissent that seemed on the fringe in 1964 had become insider politics by 1972—changing forever the direction of the Democratic

Party and ending the hawkish warmongering both major parties had embraced since the onset of the Cold War.

As more and more people joined the antiwar protests, dissent extended into other spheres. Many dissented against American values by dropping out. Some went off to live in the country, where they established utopianesque communes and collectives. Others experimented with communal living in urban areas. They took up meditation, yoga, and macrobiotic diets. They read books about Zen Buddhism and holistic medicine and used *The Whole Earth Catalog* as a resource for innovative, alternative living. In San Francisco the Diggers experimented with a community free of money by preparing and distributing free food and organizing free parties, free concerts, and free theatrical performances. Since so many of the old values had been challenged and so many of them found wanting, everything was open to experimentation and trying out. The main thing was to live life fully and authentically.

Other activists took a different route. Some felt that since they could not change society either through the political process or nonviolent protest, it was time to embrace violence. The most notorious faction that took up revolutionary violence was the Weathermen. Claiming that the only way to change the system was through destruction, a splinter group of SDS formed the Weathermen (later the Weather Underground). They viewed, as did most leftists, the war in Vietnam as an imperialist war that had nothing to do with supporting democracy and containing communism but everything to do with extending American business interests. Unlike other radical groups, however, the Weather Underground eschewed nonviolent protest in favor of taking down the whole imperialist system through violence. Their slogan was "bringing the war home," which meant overthrowing the American power structure that was waging the war. Pulling the troops out was not enough. Bringing down imperialism was the goal.

In October 1969 Weathermen launched their "Days of Rage" campaign in Chicago. It started when Bill Ayers and Terry Robbins blew up the statue in Haymarket Square memorializing the policemen who had died there in the infamous 1886 confrontation with labor organizers, and it continued with several hundred Weathermen parading through the streets of Chicago's Gold Coast smashing car and store windows. For a total of three days they clashed with police and National Guardsmen (who outnumbered the Weathermen approximately three thousand to six hundred) in a series of separate incidents. Nearly three hundred Weathermen were arrested, scores injured, and several shot. Americans were outraged at the Days of Rage, and the Weather Underground's action did not win any new converts to the antiwar cause; nor was it supported by even the most radical members of SDS. Most antiwar dissenters viewed the Days of Rage as senseless. The reaction of a socialist newspaper in New York was typical of leftist opinion: "the most significant aspect of the surrealistic contretemps created by the Weatherman microfaction of SDS last week was that the rest of the movement had the revolutionary sense to stay away."[16]

By 1970 the Weather Underground had truly gone underground. The group commenced a bombing campaign that started off disastrously when three members hiding out in a Greenwich Village townhouse and assembling a bomb that was intended to be used at the U.S. Army base in Fort Dix, New Jersey, were killed when the bomb prematurely exploded. This incident prompted some to quit the organization, while others spent a long time reevaluating their tactics. Nevertheless, over the next few years the group placed bombs at several government buildings, including the Pentagon and the Capitol, but only set them off outside business hours when the building was empty or after they had called in a warning. "We were very careful," Bill Ayers later reflected, "from the moment of the townhouse on to be sure we weren't going to hurt anybody, and we never did hurt anybody. Whenever we put a bomb in a public space, we had figured out all kinds of ways to put checks and balances on the thing and also to get people away from it, and we were remarkably successful."[17] By the mid-1970s the steam had gone out of the group. Many turned themselves in. Their campaign, in the end, proved counterproductive.

* * *

In October 1969 the Vietnam Moratorium Committee organized a "Moratorium" against the war—a day of coordinated protest marches in Washington, DC, New York City, San Francisco, and most major cities in the country. More than two million people took part in the demonstrations. A month later a coalition of antiwar groups formed the New Mobilization Committee to End the War in Vietnam and organized a "March Against Death" that would, like the October Moratorium, be a day of coordinated protests around the country. Before the demonstrations took place, President Nixon informed the press that he had no intention of watching them on television but was instead going to spend the afternoon watching college football. (The Nixon White House later admitted that the president did indeed pay attention to what was going on in the streets of the nation. Perhaps it only fed his determination to order FBI spies and informants to infiltrate and undermine all radical movements.) The March Against Death was a massive event. Millions of people, not only in the United States but at American embassies in London,[18] West Berlin, and Paris, participated in the demonstrations. For hours solemn demonstrators marched past the White House in Washington and the American embassies reading out the names of American soldiers killed in Vietnam and placing a card with each individual soldier's name in a coffin. It took two days to read all the names.

The Moratorium and the March Against Death were sandwiched between two significant countercultural events that revealed both a buoyant festive side of the counterculture and a destructive side. Woodstock and Altamont gave thousands of young people the opportunity to do their own thing and flaunt conservative, traditional values. In August hippies, college students, and high school kids descended on Bethel, New York, to participate in a huge rock festival. Jimi Hendrix, Janis Joplin, the Grateful Dead, Jefferson Airplane, Santana, and dozens of other performers celebrated the birth of a new lifestyle, of a new America, of "Woodstock Nation." Pot and LSD and sex and jubilation filled the air, and inhibition fell by the wayside as festivalgoers greeted what they thought was the dawn of a new age. Everyone could be free. But in December at Altamont, California, all inhibitions collapsed, and a dark side appeared. Too many people got wasted. Too many people equated freedom with license. Too many people lost control. And the festival turned truly ugly when a contingent of Hell's Angels assaulted a young man and killed him in front of horrified onlookers. The incident seemed to confirm middle-class Americans' worst fears— that the counterculture would destroy all values, all sense of decency. Newspapers, pundits, commentators, and politicians had a field day pronouncing, with a noticeable trace of schadenfreude, the demise of the counterculture.

* * *

Despite the predictions of opponents and the disillusionment of adherents, the counterculture and the antiwar movement became even more radical and more intense in the first years of the 1970s. Three of the most momentous events were the massive protests greeting the public disclosure that the United States had been secretly bombing Cambodia for more than a year, the burglary of an FBI office that made public J. Edgar Hoover's extraordinary, and illegal, efforts to suppress dissent, and the emotional antiwar rally led by Vietnam veterans in Washington, DC.

On April 30, 1970, President Nixon acknowledged the bombing of Cambodia and revealed that he had authorized U.S. forces to invade that country. Nixon called it an "incursion" and stressed that we were *not* "invading" Cambodia. Nevertheless, hundreds of thousands of protestors took to the streets denouncing the widening of the war. At Kent State University in Ohio student protestors set fire to the ROTC building on May 2, and the governor sent in the National Guard to quell the disturbance. Two days later guardsmen fired into a crowd of two thousand protestors. Nine were wounded, four were killed. The reaction around the country was overwhelming. On nearly every campus students held protests and vigils. Polls showed that close to 90 percent of students had serious misgivings about the government and believed that the administration was lying to the American people. But other Americans, especially working-class Americans and those whom President Nixon called the "silent majority," just as loudly and passionately proclaimed that the student protestors got exactly what they deserved. In New York City a group of protestors spontaneously marched to city hall and lowered the flag to half-staff. Shortly thereafter a group of hard-hat construction workers assaulted the demonstrators and raised the flag back up to full staff. In the end, the Kent State shootings revealed the depth of how far the nation had become polarized.

In early 1971 eight activists, frustrated at the inability of the antiwar movement to end the war and consumed by the nagging conviction that antiwar groups were being spied on, infiltrated, disrupted, and undermined by the FBI, worked out a plan to uncover evidence that the FBI was illegally repressing dissent. On the night of March 8, 1971, they broke into the FBI office in Media, Pennsylvania, and not even knowing what they were looking for or even if proof of FBI subversion was located in the office, they stole *all* the files. Two weeks later, calling themselves the Citizens' Commission to Investigate the FBI, they began anonymously distributing secret documents to the *Washington Post* and the *New York Times* showing that the FBI was conducting a shadow campaign to destroy not only the antiwar movement but all dissent movements in the U.S. It was these documents that revealed the FBI's Counter Intelligence Program (COINTELPRO) and led eventually to a full-scale congressional investigation of the FBI and its attempt to crush dissent. Despite one of the most massive manhunts in FBI history, the eight burglars were never caught.[19]

A month after the burglary, in April 1971, hundreds of Vietnam veterans marched on Washington to protest the war. For several days they demonstrated at Arlington National Cemetery, the Pentagon, the Capitol building, and the steps of the Supreme Court. At the Supreme Court the veterans demanded to know why the Court had not ruled on the constitutionality of the war. At the Pentagon fifty vets attempted to turn themselves in to the bewildered guard as war criminals. And at the Capitol building nearly one thousand veterans denounced the war, voiced their sense of guilt at having taken part in it, and in a gesture of disgust threw their medals and ribbons onto the Capitol steps.

During the week that Vietnam Veterans Against the War (VVAW) protested in the nation's capital, one of them, John Kerry, the future senator, presidential candidate, and secretary of state, gave two hours of emotional testimony to the Senate Foreign Relations Committee. Kerry said that he was not just speaking for himself but for the hundreds of "winter soldiers" (as they called themselves) who had come to Washington to protest the war. "We could come back to this country," he said, "we could be quiet, we could hold our silence, we could not tell what went on in Vietnam, but we feel because of what threatens this country, not the reds, but the crimes which we are committing that threaten it, that we have to speak out." The United States should never have involved itself militarily in Vietnam, Kerry argued. What was happening in Vietnam was a civil war and posed no threat whatsoever to the United States. The Vietnamese only sought independence. Most of them

> didn't even know the difference between communism and democracy. They only wanted to work in rice paddies without helicopters strafing them and bombs with napalm burning their villages and tearing their country apart. They wanted everything to do with the war, particularly

with this foreign presence of the United States of America, to leave them alone in peace, and they practiced the art of survival by siding with whichever military force was present at a particular time, be it Viet Cong, North Vietnamese or American.

What the United States had done, Kerry continued, was the height of hypocrisy and immorality. "We rationalized destroying villages in order to save them. We saw America lose her sense of morality as she accepted very coolly a My Lai and refused to give up the image of American soldiers who hand out chocolate bars and chewing gum." We must look into our hearts and question our motivations, and we must immediately pull our soldiers out of Vietnam. "We are asking Americans to think about that because how do you ask a man to be the last man to die in Vietnam? How do you ask a man to be the last man to die for a mistake?"[20]

The impact of Kerry's testimony, and even more so the sight of veterans throwing their Purple Hearts, Silver Stars, Bronze Stars, and Service Crosses onto the Capitol's steps, unnerved many Americans who had enthusiastically supported the war. World War II and Korean War veterans who cherished their own medals and ribbons were especially troubled by the Vietnam vets' demonstration. It hit them in a flash that anyone who willingly threw away his medals must be overwhelmed by anguish and despair and guilt. World War II vets were proud of the medals they earned. But they believed in their war. Clearly, Vietnam veterans had experienced something far different, far more disturbing. Thus, for the first time, many of these older vets began seriously questioning American involvement in Vietnam. In one week the VVAW protests convinced more mainstream Americans to question the war than six years of student protests had done.

* * *

It was another four years before the war finally came to an end. Many protestors despaired that their demonstrations, their petitions, their speeches, and their rallies had virtually no impact on changing policy. But there is little doubt that the massed power of the antiwar movement put significant pressure on the government and that it did hasten the end of the war (although not fast enough for antiwar activists). Dissent mobilized tens of millions against the war and eventually persuaded

A group of antiwar activists celebrates the end of the Vietnam War in New York's Central Park, May 1975. (Image © Leif Skoogfors; courtesy Leif Skoogfors, Corbis)

enough members of Congress to pull the plug on financing the war. One victory of dissent was the eventual elimination of the draft, and to this day it does not seem feasible that any politician would suggest reinstating it, especially for a limited conflict somewhere in the world that does not obviously and immediately threaten national security. The impact of the antiwar movement also influenced American foreign policy for the rest of the twentieth century. "No more Vietnams!" became the mantra for policy makers when considering intervention in Latin America or the Middle East.

The counterculture's criticism of middle-class values changed America. Social and cultural critics forced Americans to reevaluate their basic assumptions about race, gender, relationships, and indeed, even dissent. In the decades following the 1960s Americans developed more open relationships (marriage was no longer considered the only option for people who wanted to live together); fashion and style became less constricting and more eclectic and expressive; life became more open; and increasing numbers of Americans, some for purely selfish purposes, others for more spiritual reasons, engaged in self-help and self-improvement programs. And because dissent had toppled the Jim Crow laws, expanded rights for black Americans, and helped end the Vietnam War, Americans clearly saw dissent as an effective instrument for change. Witnessing the impact of dissent on the big issues of civil rights and the war in Vietnam, Americans abandoned whatever reticence they may have harbored about dissent and became willing participants in dissent movements for the causes they believed in: feminism, Chicano rights, Native American rights, gay rights, environmentalism. The 1960s spawned a mobilization of minorities of every imaginable stripe as dissent took center stage. If civil rights activists could end segregation and antiwar activists could hasten the end of the war, then surely women and gays and Chicanos and Indians and all the others could make their voices heard too.

CHAPTER 22

Mobilization and Backlash

Feminism is the radical notion that women are people.
— Marie Shear, 1986

When did you ever see a fag fight back? . . . Now, times are
a-changin'. Tuesday night was the last night for bullshit. . . .
Predominantly, the theme [w]as, "this shit has got to stop!"
— anonymous participant in the Stonewall riot, 1969

In the name of all Indians, therefore, we reclaim this island
for our Indian nations, for all these reasons. We feel this
claim is just and proper, and that this land should rightfully
be granted to us for as long as the rivers run and the sun shall
shine. We hold the rock!
— "A Proclamation: To the Great White Father and All
His People on the Takeover of Alcatraz Island," 1969

The 1960s produced irreversible change in the United States. The civil
rights movement sent currents of inspiration so deeply throughout
the land that there was no going back to the days when any American would settle for less than full constitutional rights. But still, during
the 1970s and 1980s, even as American society continued to evolve, as
more and more people from every conceivable ethnic and racial background demanded their rights, there was a powerful backlash against
what many conservatives viewed as the excesses of the immoral, licen-
tious sixties. Dissenting values of the 1960s set off another chapter in
the culture wars.

The most significant movement to come out of this period was
second-wave feminism. Winning the right to vote in 1920 was a political victory for women, but women's status did not really change much.
As early as 1923 the feminist leader Alice Paul initiated the fight for
economic equality by introducing the Equal Rights Amendment to

Congress. It was ignored. Forty years later women were still experiencing second-class status and what Betty Friedan called "the problem that has no name." Friedan was interviewing her classmates from Smith College fifteen years after graduation when it became apparent to her that even though most of the women were living successful lives, married to successful men, raising successful children, they themselves felt inexplicably unfulfilled. They were victims of the "feminine mystique," the belief that women's source of satisfaction came from being homemakers. It is foolish, Friedan insisted, to expect that women achieve orgiastic bliss from waxing the kitchen floor. Women needed an outlet for their creative energies, a way of experiencing their full potential. And the only way for that was to overthrow the outmoded male-dominated ways of thinking. Friedan called for a reevaluation of gender assumptions and demanded equal educational and career opportunities for women as well as equal pay for equal work. The publication of her book *The Feminine Mystique* in 1963 inaugurated a new era in the struggle for women's rights. "The problem lay buried," Friedan wrote, "unspoken, for many years in the minds of American women. . . . As she made the beds, shopped for groceries, matched slipcover material, ate peanut butter sandwiches with her children, chauffeured Cub Scouts and Brownies, lay beside her husband at night—she was afraid to ask even of herself the silent question—'Is this all?'"[1]

The book resonated for untold thousands of American women, and they began openly questioning the expectations that society exacted on them. A Presidential Commission on the Status of Women issued a report on the extent of discrimination against women in education and salaries. President Kennedy signed the Equal Pay Act and an executive order prohibiting discrimination in the civil service.

In 1966 Friedan, along with Congresswoman Shirley Chisholm, the Reverend Pauli Murray, and twenty-five other women and men, founded the National Organization for Women (NOW) in order "to take action to bring women into full participation in the mainstream of American society now, exercising all the privileges and responsibilities thereof in truly equal partnership with men." NOW issued a "Statement of Purpose" delineating its goals: "We believe the time has come . . . to confront, with concrete action, the conditions that now prevent women from enjoying the equality of opportunity and freedom of choice which is their right, as individual Americans, and as human beings." Women, the statement read, were "first and foremost" human beings and thus deserved exactly the same opportunities available for men.[2]

NOW pushed for enforcement of equal pay for equal work and demanded that the Equal Opportunity Employment Commission enforce Title VII of the 1964 Civil Rights Act, which prohibited discrimination in the workplace on account of sex. It pressured colleges and universities to open up professional programs to women and to include women's studies courses in their curriculum. It pushed the government and private business to provide day-care centers for children. And perhaps most importantly, certainly most controversially, NOW lobbied vigorously for women's reproductive rights and to decriminalize abortion.

The women reading *The Feminine Mystique* and joining NOW were one of three factions propelling second-wave feminism. Many members of NOW were professional women with connections, looking for equality and self-determination. Another group, influenced by the general milieu of 1960s dissent, were housewives who were frustrated by the constraints of the 1950s and looking to gain greater opportunity and possibilities in a world that was not structured by rigid gender lines and subordination to men/husbands. The third faction consisted of radical women looking to rethink the meaning and practice of gender and gender relations. Involvement in the civil rights movement, antiwar protests, and the counterculture had deepened these women's political consciousness, made them keenly aware of the limitations placed on them in the social structure, and radicalized them. They studied the works of radical political philosophers from Marx and Lenin to Marcuse and Fanon and consequently began examining their own lives through the prism of leftist analysis. More and more they argued for the restructuring of gender relationships in postcapitalist society. But paradoxically their radicalization came about only partly because of their engagement in New Left ideology; it was also brought about because they discovered that even within left-wing organizations like SDS sexism ran rampant. At the national SDS convention in 1965 women staged a walkout to protest the expectation that after an evening of intellectual discourse they were expected to make coffee and sandwiches, to clean up, and to be available for sex. Radical men, it seems, were just as chauvinistic as the rest of American men. The gender attitudes of New Left males, as much as dialectical materialism, radicalized the women's movement.

The most important phase of the radicalization process took place in the women's caucuses that developed in response to sexism. These were consciousness-raising sessions in which women sat in a circle, opening up and discussing what had always been taboo: their thoughts and feelings about sexuality, lesbianism, masturbation, menopause, unwanted pregnancy, and the illegal abortions that many of them had experienced. They encouraged each other to see through and cast aside the artificial existence and role-playing imposed on them by a male-dominated society. The sense of solidarity, of sisterhood, that these sessions generated strengthened the women's movement and gave women the daring to become more militant.

Feminist groups promoted these consciousness-raising workshops and urged their members to participate. One of them was the left-wing organization Redstockings, which was founded in New York City by Shulamith Firestone and Ellen Willis in early 1969. "Women are an oppressed class," the Redstockings Manifesto declared. "Our oppression is total, affecting every facet of our lives. We are exploited as sex objects, breeders, domestic servants, and cheap labor. We are considered inferior beings, whose only purpose is to enhance men's lives. Our humanity is denied." Arguing that relationships between men and women are class relationships, Redstockings identifies "the agents of [women's] oppression as men. Male supremacy is the oldest, most basic form of domination. All other forms of exploitation and oppression (racism, capitalism, imperialism, etc.) are extensions of male supremacy; men dominate women, a few men dominate the rest." Relationships between "men and women are political conflicts that can only be solved collectively." The sooner women recognize this, the sooner they will be liberated.[3]

By the end of the 1960s radical feminist groups were proliferating throughout the nation, and their members were eager to experiment with all sorts of in-your-face tactics. Taking a cue, perhaps, from the type of street theater practiced by activists such as Abbie Hoffman, hundreds of women on September 7, 1968, shortly after the Chicago demonstrations and riots, protested the Miss America Pageant in Atlantic City. They dressed a sheep in a bikini and "Miss America" sash and paraded her up and down the boardwalk, announcing that she was a prime piece of American meat. Demonstrators carried signs that read, "Let's Judge Ourselves as People" and "Welcome to the Miss America

Cattle Auction," while inside the convention hall activists unfurled a huge banner from the balcony proclaiming, "Women's Liberation." With dozens of male hecklers surrounding them, they threw their bras, girdles, curlers, high-heel shoes, makeup, and other symbols of male oppression into a "Freedom Trash Can." They had planned to set the contents of the trash can on fire, but they were unable to obtain a fire permit from city officials. Even so, the episode was inaccurately characterized in newspapers as a "bra-burning," a clever association of the feminists with the antiwar activists who were publicly burning their draft cards.

A month later, on Halloween night, another widely covered piece of radical feminist street theater took place: a Witches' Dance in front of the New York Stock Exchange. Women from W.I.T.C.H. (Women's International Terrorist Conspiracy from Hell) dressed up as witches, danced on Wall Street, and put a hex on the stock market. Later in the year they protested the House Committee on Un-American Activities, and in 1969, wearing black veils, they held another guerrilla-style protest at a Bridal Fair at Madison Square Garden. As the women's liberation movement grew and became more threatening to conservatives, such radical actions, although they were obviously humorous, tongue-in-cheek attempts to raise consciousness, only served to provoke a powerful antifeminist backlash. Antifeminists portrayed feminists as male-bashing, antisexual, humorless shrews. The word *feminist* became, in their lexicon, a pejorative term, a joke even, and for many Americans this association has endured despite numerous gains that feminists have won for women.

Still, the essential arguments put forth by feminists resonated—with men as well as women—and set in motion a growing impulse to reconsider age-old labels and stereotypes. What does it mean to be a man or a woman in a society that imposes strict roles on individuals on the basis of gender? Women's liberation sought to free women from oppressive stereotyping that denied their individuality and hindered them from pursuing their full creative potential. What many men began to realize was that women's liberation also freed men from the roles and expectations that constricted their own individuality. "'Women's liberation,'" as the feminist activist Gloria Steinem wrote in a *Washington Post* op-ed piece in 1970, "aims to free men, too." The movement is not really a "feminist" movement; it is a "humanist" movement. "The first problem

Feminist protest during the bicentennial in Philadelphia, Pennsylvania, July 4, 1976. (Image © Leif Skoogfors; courtesy Leif
Skoogfors, Corbis)

for all of us, men and women, is not to learn, but to unlearn." We must
examine and question the antiquated assumptions that dominate our
thinking. "Patriotism means obedience, age means wisdom, woman
means submission, black means inferior: these are preconceptions
imbedded so deeply in our thinking that we honestly may not know
that they are there." If we can recognize these erroneous assumptions
and get beyond them, we will all be free to experience *who* we are in
our unique individuality. Men will not have to prove their masculinity,

women will not have to prove their submissiveness, men will be permitted to give their feminine side free rein, and women, their masculine side, for in truth we are all yin and yang, black and white, masculine and feminine. Denying one side of ourselves limits us. There are enough limitations in life; why impose artificial limitations on ourselves? Women's liberation frees everyone. "No more alimony. Fewer boring wives. Fewer childlike wives. No more so-called 'Jewish mothers,' who are simply normally ambitious human beings with all their ambitiousness confined to the house. No more wives who fall apart with the first wrinkle because they've been taught that their total identity depends on their outsides. No more responsibility for another adult human being who has never been told she is responsible for her own life." What both women and men need is a revolution in consciousness.[4]

Despite alarmists' warnings that feminism would destroy marriage and family life, the primary focus of second-wave feminism was simply to bring about a revolution in attitudes and consciousness. Even to this day individuals are transforming their lives each time they question basic gender assumptions about their relationships with other individuals.

The most controversial accomplishment of the movement was the successful campaign to legalize abortion. After years of debate and lobbying, organizations such as NOW and the National Association for the Repeal of Abortion Laws stepped up the pressure by coordinating demonstrations and rallies demanding the decriminalization of abortion. Redstockings organized a series of "abortion speakouts" in New York and other cities, giving women a public platform to openly discuss the illegal and risky abortions that so many of them had undergone as a means of raising consciousness about the issue. Finally, a case on abortion rights that had slowly moved its way through the court system made it to the Supreme Court, and on January 22, 1973, the justices, in a 7–2 decision, decriminalized abortion. Writing the majority opinion in *Roe v. Wade*, Associate Justice Harry Blackmun (a Nixon appointee) declared that the "right of privacy, whether it be founded in the Fourteenth Amendment's concept of personal liberty and restrictions upon state action, as we feel it is, or, as the district court determined, in the Ninth Amendment's reservation of rights to the people, is broad enough to encompass a woman's decision whether or not to terminate her pregnancy."[5] The broader question of "women's rights" was not an issue in the case; the Court was more concerned with physicians' rights to perform abortions legally and with women's privacy rights. Regardless of the rationale behind the decision, women rejoiced that they were freed from governmental interference in a difficult and emotional personal decision. Women's reproductive rights were recognized and affirmed by the federal government.

Activists for women's reproductive rights had company—the movement for gay and lesbian rights. On June 28, 1969, the police raided the Stonewall Inn, a well-known gay bar in New York's Greenwich Village. This was not an unusual occurrence. Gay bars were habitually raided, with patrons apprehended and then released. It was an attempt to intimidate and humiliate homosexuals, who for the most part lived secret lives, fearful for their jobs, parental disapproval, and societal condemnation. Some bars, such as the Stonewall Inn, were operated by the Mafia; the owners paid off the police and served watered-down, overpriced drinks to people seeking a welcoming place where they could meet, dance, hook up, and be openly themselves. There were organizations in the 1950s, such as the Mattachine Society and the Daughters of Bilitis, that created a supportive community for gays and lesbians. And over the years there were protests and demonstrations and even a riot (in 1966) when police tried to arrest several drag queens and transvestites at a cafeteria in San Francisco, but for the most part the gay and lesbian world stayed below the radar. By 1969 the social and political unrest of the times, the example of civil rights and antiwar protestors, and the do-your-own-thing values of the counterculture emboldened homosexuals. On that June night in 1969 when the police raided the Stonewall Inn, the clientele fought back. Some refused to leave, and they forced six officers back into the bar as hundreds of gay men in the neighborhood gathered on Christopher Street outside the bar. For several days protestors and police clashed in the streets, while activists distributed flyers urging others to join the demonstrations and take to the streets of Greenwich Village. "Get the mafia and the cops out of gay bars," demanded one of the flyers. "The nights of Friday, June 27, 1969 and Saturday, June 28, 1969," it went on to explain to the public, "will go down in history as the first time that thousands of Homosexual men and women went out into the streets to protest the intolerable situation which has existed in New York City for many years—namely, the Mafia (or syndicate) control of this city's Gay bars in collusion with certain elements in the Police Dept. of the City of New York." Calling themselves HYMN (the Homophile Youth Movement) and taking a page from the philosophy of the Black Power movement, the writers of the flyer made clear that "the only way this monopoly can be broken is through the action of Homosexual men and women themselves." They demanded the boycotting of Mafia-owned establishments and that "Gay businessmen step forward and open Gay bars that will be run legally with competitive pricing and a healthy social atmosphere." And they also appealed to Mayor John Lindsay to open "a thorough investigation and effective action to correct this intolerable situation."[6]

The Stonewall Riots lasted for only six days, but the movement was gaining momentum. In July gay activists called for strategy meetings and more demonstrations. "Do you think homosexuals are revolting?" one widely distributed placard asked. "You bet your sweet ass we are. We're going to make a place for ourselves in the revolutionary movement. We challenge the myths that are screwing up this society." And they announced a planning meeting for July 24, 1969. Another handout from the summer of '69 that was pasted on walls, nailed to trees, and slipped under parked cars' windshield wipers read,

> Homosexuals Are Coming Together at Last
> To examine how we are oppressed and how we oppress ourselves. To fight for gay control of gay businesses. To publish our own newspaper. To these and other radical ends.[7]

In the ensuing months several gay rights organizations were founded, among them the Gay Liberation Front (equating itself with the Vietnamese National Liberation Front) and the Gay Activists Alliance. And this was only the start. From these beginnings scores of organizations were formed throughout the 1970s and 1980s (and indeed in the 1990s and the first decade of the twenty-first century) that increasingly demanded equal rights for gays, lesbians, bisexuals, and transgender persons.

As the gay rights movement grew, people's attitudes and public policy slowly began to evolve. In cities with large gay populations, such as New York, Philadelphia, and San Francisco, politicians gradually began endorsing proposals and passing statutes that modestly improved the standing of gays. For example, in California, State Assemblyman

George Moscone openly supported gay rights and was instrumental in pushing the legislature to repeal the state's sodomy law. Later, when he was mayor of San Francisco, he continued his support for gay rights and backed candidate Harvey Milk for election to the San Francisco Board of Supervisors. Milk, a vocal leader of San Francisco's gay community, had run for political office several times in the past, but his election as a supervisor in 1977 was his first victory. It was the first time that an openly gay man was elected to political office in the United States. Milk was hoping to make a difference through the conventional political process, and his major achievement was a civil rights bill that banned discrimination against anyone for sexual orientation. However, after only eleven months in office Milk (along with Mayor Moscone) was assassinated. His assassination and the enormous outpouring of grief by the citizens (gay and straight) of San Francisco focused attention on the gay rights movement at a critical moment and went a long way toward expanding Americans' consciousness in the same way that violence against Freedom Riders did for the civil rights movement.

During the 1980s and 1990s gays were even more in the public eye. By the mid-1980s Gay Pride festivals and parades celebrating the anniversary of Stonewall were held around the country, and scores of cities boasted gay softball leagues, with the North American Gay Amateur Athletic Alliance (NAGAA) sponsoring tournaments and an annual "Gay World Series." And more and more politicians saw the political wisdom of embracing these events. For example, in Philadelphia, Mayor (and later Governor) Ed Rendell regularly threw out the ceremonial first ball of the season for the City of Brotherly Love Softball League. (Consequently the gay community always threw its full support behind him at election time.)

Civil rights demonstrations and antiwar activism inspired others to organize and to demand their rights. In California Mexican American (Chicano) migrant workers banded together and, using civil rights tactics, protested against the fruit and vegetable growers that routinely exploited them by paying far less than minimum wage for long hours of backbreaking work. One of these workers, César Chávez, organized the National Farm Workers Association (NFWA) to stand up to the growers. From 1965 to 1970 the NFWA (changing its name in 1966 to the United Farm Workers, or UFW) coordinated a grape strike that focused national attention on the plight of California migrant workers. Throughout the strike (*La Huelga*) Chávez adopted the nonviolent tactics of Martin Luther King and even took a page out of Gandhi's book by carrying out a twenty-five-day hunger strike in 1968 that garnered much-needed publicity for the workers' cause. By 1970 the nationwide grape boycott pressured growers to recognize and negotiate with the union. The UFW's success inspired other Latinos around the country to fight against discrimination. In 1969 activists formed La Raza Unida to engage in political battles on a local level with the goal of organizing Latinos as a bloc to elect state and national representatives committed to passing legislation to end discrimination. La Raza Unida and Chávez's UFW formed the basis of what evolved into a growing and significant movement to apply pressure on federal, state, and local governments to guarantee equal rights for Spanish-speaking Americans.

After enduring centuries of injustice, prejudice, brutality, and outright murder, American Indians too were propelled to action by the radical currents of the times. By 1968 thousands of Native Americans adopted 1960s-style militancy and protest as the means to fight for equality and the basic civil rights they had been denied. African Americans' demand for "Black Power" especially resonated with Native Americans. Using the phrase "Red Power" as their rallying cry, Indian activists formed the American Indian Movement (AIM) in 1968 and organized protests and acts of civil disobedience to force the federal government to redress their grievances. Over the next few years Dennis Banks, Russell Means, and Leonard Peltier emerged as three of AIM's most prominent militants, and they became national figures in the struggle for Native American rights. In November 1969 AIM and about six hundred Indians from fifty tribes occupied Alcatraz Island in San Francisco Bay. For more than a year they stayed put, fending off federal authorities and demanding that they be allowed to keep the island (since the federal government had closed Alcatraz Prison), where they hoped to set up an Indian university, museum, and cultural center. "We are a proud people!" they proclaimed. "We have observed and rejected much of what so-called civilization offers. We are Indians! We will preserve our traditions and ways of life by educating our own children. We are Indians! We will join hands in a unity never before put into practice. We are Indians! Our Earth Mother awaits our voices. . . .

WE HOLD THE ROCK!"[8] Though the occupation created publicity for the deplorable conditions Indians were subjected to, it ended in June 1971 without their demands being met when President Nixon ordered federal marshals and the FBI to retake the island and evict the protestors. Undaunted, AIM and members of other Indian organizations next organized a march on Washington. Calling it the "Trail of Broken Treaties," hundreds of activists drove in a caravan to the nation's capital, arriving in DC just before the 1972 presidential election. When members of Congress refused to meet with them, they occupied the Bureau of Indian Affairs and issued a proclamation of twenty demands. Among their demands was the insistence that the United States honor all the treaties it has broken, that those that have not been ratified be submitted to the Senate, that Congress "relinquish their control over Indian Affairs," that 110 million acres be restored to the Indians, that Indians' civil rights be restored, and that all crimes against Native Americans be treated as federal crimes.[9] In essence they demanded Indian Power, Red Power.

In 1973 some members of AIM seized the Wounded Knee battlefield site (where more than 140 Miniconjou Sioux had been massacred by the U.S. Army in 1890) and demanded that the United States honor the Fort Laramie Treaty of 1868 guaranteeing the Black Hills to the Lakota in perpetuity. The Wounded Knee siege was the most notorious of the American Indian Movement's encounters with the federal government; it led to a seventy-one-day confrontation between AIM and federal marshals, during which a federal officer and two Lakota were killed. In the end, however, as with the Alcatraz standoff, the protestors were removed, and their demands went unmet.

Even groups with the least power of all, prison inmates, were motivated by the radical activism of the time to launch their own rebellions. Prisoners in New Jersey, California, Massachusetts, and most notoriously Attica Prison in New York mutinied against the inhumane conditions to which they were subjected. Employing the rhetoric of Marx, the Black Panthers, and other revolutionary groups, they issued a series of political demands. But inmates' rebellions were invariably crushed. Indeed, although the uprisings called attention to their legitimate grievances and although there was some governmental response at least to evaluate and study their grievances, the inmates achieved only limited success. Still, public consciousness was expanding. Americans were realizing that there were problems that needed to be addressed.

One of the long-term movements that emerged from the 1960s was the environmental movement. As early as the nineteenth century environmentalists such as John Muir and John Burroughs toiled to raise awareness of the fragility of the environment. By the 1960s, after the publication of Rachel Carson's influential book *Silent Spring*, thousands of Americans, concerned about water and air pollution and the rapid destruction of natural resources, began organizing in a serious way to "save the planet." Implementing the slogan "think globally, act locally," environmentalists argued that doing something in their own neighborhoods, their own cities, to reverse the negative human impact on the environment was the best way to find a solution for a global problem. The longtime dissenter and folk singer Pete Seeger, who had been involved in the struggle for workers' rights as well as the civil rights and antiwar movements, began a campaign in 1968 to clean up the Hudson River. He raised money to build a replica of a nineteenth-century sloop, and then he and his crew sailed the sloop *Clearwater* up and down the river, performing concerts at towns along the way, raising political awareness about the devastating effects of the PCBs and other pollutants dumped into the river by such companies as General Electric. By 1978 the concerts had evolved into an annual two-day folk festival that has been going on for more than forty years and has been a major factor in cleaning up the Hudson River. In fact the efforts to decontaminate the river were successful enough that sturgeon reappeared in the Hudson after an absence of a century. Beginning in 1970, environmentalists also inaugurated "Earth Day," which has become an annual environmental awareness rally in cities around the nation. Also founded in the early 1970s was the militant organization Greenpeace, which continues to confront companies and countries that endanger the Earth's ecology. Greenpeace has interfered with Japanese and Norwegian whaling ships, American military tests, and French vessels carrying nuclear waste. But nonviolent efforts, civil disobedience, or even disruptive tactics to purify the atmosphere, rivers, and oceans; to protect endangered species; and to fight against the proliferation of nuclear power is a very slow process. It might take years, if not decades, before the hard work pays off.

Many of these movements are still unfolding, still evolving. Women, gays, Hispanics, and undocumented immigrants continue to press for their rights. And environmentalists, in an age of increasingly devastating climate change and dwindling resources, still fight on. Such movements will continue to expand, and so too will the discourse as dissenters push to broaden and deepen the dialogue.

* * *

By the end of the 1970s a full-fledged backlash exploded against the radical 1960s. Frightened by the radicalism of, and angry at the attention paid to, African Americans, women, Hispanics and gays, many whites, especially those of modest income, felt victimized. They resented a government that ignored their struggles while giving preferential treatment to minorities; they felt Congress was giving handouts to people who did not deserve it; they felt cheated. And they hated the challenges posed to traditional American mores, religion, and ethical values. And they began to revolt. This conservative backlash to 1960s radicalism fostered new dissent movements that sought to overturn the gains made by African Americans, women, gays, and radicals.

One of the most conspicuous manifestations of this backlash was the "prolife" movement. As soon as *Roe v. Wade* established a new norm expanding women's rights, a new dissent movement—the antiabortion movement—was born. Hundreds of thousands of Americans formed organizations and political action groups with the specific goal of overturning *Roe*. One of the leading organizations spearheading the backlash was the National Right to Life Committee, which argued on moral grounds that a fetus's right to life trumps a woman's right to choose. Antiabortion activists lobbied politicians and held demonstrations on a regular basis, they picketed Planned Parenthood clinics and the offices of physicians who perform abortions, they organized demonstrations on college campuses, and every year on the anniversary of the *Roe* decision, they held a protest rally at the Supreme Court. The movement quickly gained the backing of fundamentalists, the Roman Catholic Church, and after the 1980s, the Republican Party. In fact, since the 1980s, prolife has become so central to Republican ideology that it is regarded as a litmus test for would-be Republican political candidates. What feminists regarded as a personal issue is now a public political issue. As prolife rallies and demonstrations mounted in the 1980s and 1990s, NOW and other feminist groups fought against the backlash by organizing prochoice rallies supporting *Roe* and abortion rights.

By the 1990s protests at Planned Parenthood clinics and other abortion facilities escalated to the point that several abortion-provider physicians and clinical workers were murdered by zealots who justified such acts as necessary to save the lives of the innocent, the unborn. The majority of prolife advocates deplored such murderous deeds, but such actions underscored the raw emotions that were unleashed on both sides of the issue. The issue, of course, is far more complicated than the reductive terms of "prolife" and "prochoice," which give the false impression that there are two, mutually exclusive points of view.

Conservative activists targeted other progressive accomplishments of the 1960s. After the Supreme Court upheld busing as a tool to integrate de facto segregated school districts (busing African American students to school districts where most of the students were white, and vice versa), a number of cities experimented with the policy. The hope was that mixing students from diverse ethnic and racial backgrounds would reduce prejudice and racial strife and produce more equal education opportunities. But white lower- and lower-middle-class Americans who could not afford to send their children to private schools were enraged and took to the streets in dozens of protests. Boston was not the only city that witnessed such protests, but it became the most notorious with the publication of a Pulitzer Prize–winning photograph of a white protestor attempting to impale an African American lawyer on the pole of the American flag he was wielding. This image of unrestrained rage being expressed in the streets of the city that launched the American Revolution left an unforgettable and paradoxical impression on Americans' minds. Clearly, overcoming centuries of racism was not going to be an easy task.

Supreme Court decisions strengthening separation of church and state by banning prayer in public schools also angered many conservatives, particularly evangelical Christians. The ban, they believed, endangered religious freedom and was an existential threat that would destroy the United States. And so they protested. If they could get the ban overturned, if they could soften the impenetrable barrier separating church and state that had existed from the nation's founding, they believed it would help prevent, or at least slow down, the country's slide into immorality. Emerging from such religiously motivated protests, a new movement was born. Conservative Christians, led by preachers such as Pat Robertson and Jerry Falwell, launched a political movement with the goal of electing born-again Christians to office. The idea was to work in political campaigns at a local level and then from an empowered local base expand nationally. Jerry Falwell founded the Moral Majority in 1979 as a proevangelical Christian lobby group that would back only candidates who were profamily, prolife, pro-prayer, pro-Israel, and staunchly anticommunist. The Moral Majority threw its support behind Reagan in the 1980 presidential campaign (this, despite the fact that Reagan was not, as his opponent Jimmy Carter professed to be, a "born-again" Christian). Reagan supported the Moral Majority's socially conservative agenda, while the Democrat Carter, in Falwell's eyes, was too liberal, too soft on communism, and a traitor to family and Christian values. A second powerful Christian lobbying group was the Christian Coalition, headed by another evangelical minister, Pat Robertson. Robertson also founded the Christian Broadcasting Network, which became a means to disseminate his sermons and political diatribes. Planned Parenthood, he warned, "is teaching kids to fornicate, teaching people to have adultery, every kind of bestiality, homosexuality, lesbianism—everything the Bible condemns."[10] This sentence succinctly enunciates the Christian Coalition's position and its goal of electing politicians who would put an end to such offenses. Along with this moral stance the Christian Right is a dyed-in-the-wool supporter of Israel. Part of the fundamentalist belief is that the book of Revelations prophesizes the return of Christ and that the onset of the Millennium will occur after the Jews have returned to Jerusalem. This "Christian Zionism" is a central feature of the Christian Right's foreign policy. The United States, in this view, should do everything in its power to fully restore the Holy Land to the Jews, thus hastening Christ's return. Although not all politicians, even some conservative politicians, fully accepted the Christian Right's position on Israel (they did not exactly reject it either), such radical views do impact elections and U.S. policy regarding the Israeli-Palestinian conflict.

At the height of dissent in the 1960s and 1970s the United States also embarked on a War on Crime that was in no small part a backlash to the civil rights dissent/unrest of that same period. Equating antiwar and civil rights protests with disorder and crime allowed first President

Johnson and then President Nixon to police African American, Latino, and poor neighborhoods much more aggressively. With President Reagan's War on Drugs in the 1980s more aggressive policing was augmented by new laws as well as much harsher sentencing policies, which in turn led to a major incarceration crisis in this country. By the close of the twentieth century the United States had more people incarcerated than any other country in the world, and those people were overwhelmingly and disproportionately African American, Latino, and poor.

With Reagan in the White House the conservative backlash against 1960s–1970s dissent swelled dramatically. The Christian Right acquired considerable power and prestige, right-wing talk-show hosts gained enormous followings on radio and television, and Democrats—not just moderate Democrats—for the most part went along with the backpedaling on social programs and the stepping up of defense spending. Reagan eschewed détente, denounced any easing of tensions with "the evil empire" (as Reagan called the Soviet Union), and heated up Cold War rhetoric. Academics, pundits, and media personalities, such as Paul Weyrich, Edward Feulner, Phyllis Schlafly, Irving Kristol, David Horowitz, and Rush Limbaugh, won considerable followings by vilifying liberalism and the extremists of the 1960s and 1970s. They promoted family values, prolife militancy, antifeminism, homophobia, religion in the public sphere, the sanctity of marriage, and other conservative values, while smearing 1960s radicals, such as Timothy Leary, Abbie Hoffman, Jane Fonda, and H. Rap Brown, as disloyal, as un-American, as traitors.

* * *

In 1968 it had appeared that an increasingly radicalized United States was on the verge of revolution, and when Richard M. Nixon won the presidency, political commentators believed it was because the Left was fatally split. However, in retrospect we see unmistakably that the 1968 election was an early sign of the rising conservative backlash. Nixon won not because the Left was split (although that did help the Republicans) but mostly because the white middle class, the "silent majority," was fed up with radicalism, disorder, and the defiance of American values. The election was a sign of the potency of a white backlash against the civil rights movement. It was a sign of middle-class abhorrence (and fear) of the radical challenge to the affluent consumerist society, to Christian values, to the American way of life. Indeed, when one adds the votes cast for the racist third-party candidate George Wallace to Nixon's totals, the conservative vote was a landslide against liberalism. The backlash was immediately evident with the National Guard shooting of unarmed demonstrators at Kent State and with the brutal no-holds-barred suppression of the Attica Prison rebellion. It was visible in the forceful retaking of Alcatraz and Wounded Knee from Indian protestors and in the massive nationwide campaign to prevent the ratification of the Equal Rights Amendment. By the 1980s the long-term white backlash set in: the gutting of welfare programs, the defunding of the Justice Department's Civil Rights Division, the beginnings of mass incarceration. In some ways this was comparable to the backlash against the abolition of slavery during Reconstruction. In the immediate aftermath of the Civil War the Ku Klux Klan and other organizations used violence and terrorism to maintain white supremacy; then, with the end of Reconstruction, long-term backlash against the abolition of slavery set in through legal and political means, with the Republican Party's abandonment of its focus on the freedmen and southern state legislatures' instituting Jim Crow laws, literacy tests, and poll taxes and redefining crime and incarceration in such a way that increased the African American prison population. Some historians have labeled the backlash against the 1960s a "Second Reconstruction."[11]

By the time Reagan became president in 1981, it was clear that the majority of Americans *had* turned their backs on the radical sixties. Still, dissent continued. There were demonstrations and protests in the 1980s, although not on the scale of those of the 1960s and 1970s, against the Reagan administration's pouring money into the Star Wars missile-shield system and the Reagan Doctrine of backing and aiding brutal regimes, most notably in El Salvador, where death squads roamed at will exterminating peasants and leftists who opposed the CIA-supported right-wing dictatorship. When the United States armed and trained the Contras in Nicaragua, thousands of Americans protested. And left-wing activists initiated a series of annual demonstrations at Fort Benning, Georgia, where the Department of Defense's School of the Americas trained (still trains) Latin American dictators and their security forces in the finer points of suppression and torture to eliminate political dissidents.

When the Cold War ended with the fall of the Soviet Union in 1991, the United States was the last superpower standing. Americans, cheering that "we won the Cold War," were filled with optimism that a new era of peace was about to dawn. But such hopes were chimerical, and it soon became clear that American policy was partly to blame for the evaporation of prospects of a peaceful new world order. As the United States transitioned from the last decade of the twentieth century into the new millennium, Americans continued to raise a dissenting voice.

CHAPTER 23

A New Age of Dissent

It is my belief that the writer, the free-lance author, should be
and must be a critic of the society in which he lives. . . . The
moral duty of the free writer is to begin his work at home:
to be a critic of his own community, his own country, his
own culture. If the writer is unwilling to fill this part, then
the writer should abandon pretense and find another line of
work: become a shoe repairman, a brain surgeon, a janitor, a
cowboy, a nuclear physicist, a bus driver.
—Edward Abbey, 1988

When President George H. W. Bush launched Operation Desert Storm
with the backing of the UN Security Council to oust Saddam Hussein
from Kuwait in 1991, another (albeit small) antiwar movement was born.
Even before the war began, some students and Vietnam veterans organized marches in Boston, Boulder, Missoula, Minneapolis, Ann Arbor,
and San Francisco protesting the stationing of American troops in the
Persian Gulf. They carried signs that read, "No Blood for Oil" and "No
More Vietnams." Behind the scenes, in the military, antiwar sentiment
was expressed by a surprising number of troops. When Marine Corporal Jeff Paterson's unit was ordered to deploy to Saudi Arabia, Paterson
sat down on the tarmac and refused to board the plane. He could have
remained quiet and gone with the flow, he said, but he believed it was
his duty to resist. "I will not," he said, "be a pawn in America's power
plays for profit and oil in the Middle East." Paterson was not the only
service member to protest the war. West Point graduate David Wiggins,
Marine Glen Motil, Army physician Harlow Ballard, and Army Reserve
Medical Corps Captain Yolanda Huet-Vaughn all spoke out against the
war, while more than a thousand Army reservists applied for conscientious objector status.

This Gulf War, however, was too brief for a full-fledged antiwar
movement to emerge. If it had gone on longer, there is little doubt that

more Americans, still unnerved by the bitter experience of the Vietnam War, would have protested the war. Because of its brevity the war was more of a television spectacle for Americans as they watched the daily images of the bombing of Iraq and the chaotic finishing off of Iraqi land forces on the evening news. Twelve years later, as we shall see, when the United States invaded Iraq a second time and stayed for nearly a decade, antiwar and antioccupation sentiment became a significant force that helped determine the outcome of the 2008 presidential election.

For most of the 1990s domestic issues dominated dissenting discussions. Ecological concerns, because the effects of environmental degradation are seen only gradually, usually do not get people as worked up as a war, with its more immediate impact. Nevertheless, environmentalists became increasingly more militant during the 1990s and the first decade of the twenty-first century. Julia Butterfly Hill, for example, garnered a lot of media attention when she climbed into a thousand-year-old giant redwood that the Pacific Lumber Company was about to cut down and vowed not to return to earth until the company agreed to spare the tree. She wound up living in the branches of the redwood, 180 feet from the ground, for 738 days. Television and radio crews gathered around. Reporters were lifted up into the tree on cherry pickers to interview her. Supporters brought food and supplies, which she hauled up in a bucket. Finally, after more than two years of negative publicity, the Pacific Lumber Company acquiesced in Hill's demands and pledged not to cut down the tree.

For years the literary genius and incorrigible gadfly Edward Abbey wrote essays, journals, and novels calling for the preservation of the wilderness and denouncing politicians and developers that were destroying these pristine areas. People must experience national parks on foot, not sitting on their fat butts inside air-conditioned Winnebagos and SUVs. If people must visit the national parks, Abbey insisted, let them walk.

Let the people walk. Or ride horses, bicycles, mules, wild pigs—anything—but keep the automobiles and the motorcycles and all their motorized relatives out. We have agreed not to drive our automobiles into cathedrals, concert halls, art museums, legislative assemblies, private bedrooms and the other sanctums of our culture; we should treat our national parks with the same deference, for they, too, are holy places. . . . The forests and mountains and desert canyons are holier than our churches. Therefore let us behave accordingly.[1]

Abbey's most popular book was the best-selling novel *The Monkey Wrench Gang*, which developed a sizeable cult following among environmental radicals. It is the humorous account of an anarchistic gang of ecoterrorists who travel around the American Southwest blowing up billboards, dams, bridges, and other symbols of civilization that are destroying all that is good about America.

One of Abbey's readers was Theodore Kaczynski, aka the Unabomber, who evidently took the tongue-in-cheek message of ecoterrorism a bit more seriously than Abbey might have liked. A sort of twentieth-century Luddite, Kaczynski was opposed to technological progress. "I read Edward Abbey," he said in an interview after he was sentenced to prison; "that was one of the things that gave me the idea that, 'yeah, there are other people out there that have the same attitudes that I do.' I read *The Monkey Wrench Gang*, I think it was. But what first motivated me wasn't anything I read. I just got mad seeing the machines ripping up the woods and so forth."[2] Kaczynski lived in a remote cabin in Montana and for eighteen years mailed to academics and scientists at research and development laboratories letter bombs that killed three people and maimed more than twenty others. He was finally caught after the *New York Times* published his "Manifesto," and his brother, recognizing his writing style and philosophy, tipped off the FBI. Kaczynski's goal was to start a revolution against technology, which he believed was destroying human life. "The Industrial Revolution and its consequences," he proclaimed in the Manifesto, "have been a disaster for the human race." They have "destabilized society, have made life unfulfilling, have subjected human beings to indignities, have led to widespread psychological suffering (in the Third World to physical suffering as well) and have inflicted severe damage on the natural world. The continued development of technology will worsen the situation." Therefore, he argued, there must be "a revolution against the industrial system . . . to overthrow . . . the economic and technological basis of the present society."[3] Though Kaczynski's vision was misguided and unrealistic, it did draw attention to important problems that would otherwise be ignored.

The Unabomber was a solo act, but there were organizations that resorted to violence (although against property, not persons) to protest the degradation of the environment. The Earth Liberation Front (ELF) and Earth First! were two of the more notorious groups that grabbed headlines. Both organizations, like Greenpeace, used civil disobedience, but they went beyond protests and disruptive direct action campaigns such as tree sitting and road blockages. They also engaged in sabotage (which they call "ecotage"). Destroying ski lodges, pouring sugar into the gas tanks of Hummers parked in automobile-dealership lots, pouring chemicals on golf-course greens. The Earth Liberation Front, the more radical of the two organizations, has been designated a domestic terrorist organization by the FBI. ELF does not shrink from the term *ecoterrorism*, but it does not seek to harm individuals. It has taken credit for torching a ski lodge in Vail, Colorado (because the lodge was expanding into a forest that endangered the habitat of the Canada lynx), and attempting to burn down the U.S. Forestry Service facility in Irvine, Pennsylvania. One of the spokespersons for ELF, Craig Rosebraugh, was subpoenaed in 2002, when the United States was embarking on the "War on Terror," to testify at a congressional hearing investigating both foreign and domestic terrorism. The history of the United States, Rosebraugh said in his statement, shows that social change only comes about through civil disobedience. Working conditions were only improved when workers went on strike or participated in protests and riots, women only got the vote when they picketed the White House, civil rights only became successful after the civil disobedience campaigns against segregation and the denial of voting rights, the Vietnam War only ended after massive demonstrations in the streets. "Perhaps the most obvious . . . historical example," he said, "of this notion supporting the importance of illegal activity as a tool for positive, lasting change, came just prior to our war for independence. Our educational systems in the United States glorify the Boston Tea Party while simultaneously failing to recognize and admit that the dumping of tea was perhaps one of the most famous early examples of politically motivated property destruction." We do not label our founding fathers as terrorists, but this is what the similar actions of the Earth Liberation Front are labeled by the federal government: ecoterrorism. "Yet, in the history of the Earth Liberation Front, . . . no one has ever been injured by the group's many actions. . . . Simply put and most fundamentally, the goal of the Earth Liberation Front is to save life. The group takes actions directly against the property of those who are engaged in massive planetary destruction in order for all of us to survive. This noble pursuit does not constitute terrorism, but rather seeks to abolish it." ELF has to take action because the government is not passing the laws and regulations needed to prevent the destruction of the forests. Those who take action "to stop the destruction of the natural world . . . are the heroes, risking their freedom and lives so that we as a species as well as all life forms can continue to exist on the planet. In a country so fixated on monetary wealth and power, these brave environmental advocates are engaging in some of the most selfless activities possible."[4]

Along with the radicalization of environmentalism a burgeoning antigovernment movement got a lot of press coverage in the 1990s, especially in the aftermath of events in Ruby Ridge, Waco, and Oklahoma City. Believing that individual liberty and the Constitution must be protected from an intrusive federal government, right-wing paramilitary militias in Michigan and Montana attracted many discontented supporters. They were antitax, antigovernment, and pro–Second Amendment. They armed themselves in order to prepare for the day when governmental restrictions on liberty would become intolerable. Just as the minutemen at Lexington and Concord stood up to unjust taxes and a despotic Parliament, so too must Americans stand up to the tyranny in Washington. The government must not interfere in their lives. They yearned for the supposedly good old days of the nineteenth-century pioneers who built this country through their rugged individualism. However, these modern-day minutemen overlooked the fact that it was the federal government that subsidized the railroads and irrigation projects that made it possible for settlers and homesteaders to move into the West and farm the land. Still, oftentimes what people *believe* about the past is more influential than what *actually* happened. When the FBI had shoot-outs with the Freemen of Montana at Ruby Ridge, Idaho, in 1992, killing two people, and with the Branch Davidians (a religious cult) at their compound in Waco, Texas, in 1993, which resulted in the deaths of seventy-six men, women, and children, membership in right-wing militias soared. These heavy-handed attacks were proof to many people of a vast government conspiracy to stamp out personal liberty and to establish a dictatorship. In 1995 the Michigan Militia posted a "Statement of Purpose and Mission" on its website:

"It shall be the sworn duty of this Militia to protect, defend, support, uphold and obey the Constitutions of the State of Michigan and the United States of America. Notice is hereby given that violations of either the State or National Constitution, by any alliance, nation, power, state, organization, agency, office, or individual shall be met with a fierce and determined resistance."[5]

On the second anniversary of the Waco shoot-out Timothy McVeigh (who was associated with, but not a member of, the Michigan Militia) staged a horrifying protest against the U.S. government by blowing up the Alfred P. Murrah Federal Building in Oklahoma City: 168 people, including children in a day-care center, were killed, hundreds wounded. This act of violent dissent sickened Americans. For days the nation was in shock. McVeigh and his accomplices were quickly apprehended, tried, and convicted. (McVeigh was executed in June 2001; his accomplices received prison sentences.) Though McVeigh was not actually a member of any of the right-wing militias, the bombing and the trials discredited much of the antigovernment militia ideology. Still, these militias continue to gain members as they prepare to defend themselves against all enemies, foreign or domestic.

* * *

Throughout the 1970s and 1980s gay rights activists kept increasing pressure on local governments to end antigay discrimination. When the federal government essentially ignored the AIDS crisis that exploded in the 1980s, gays founded the AIDS Coalition to Unleash Power (ACT UP) and took to the streets in a series of protests demanding that the federal government authorize funds for AIDS research and that the Food and Drug Administration approve and release new experimental AIDS drugs. By the mid-1990s gay activism was gaining considerable visibility, and with increased visibility came increased success. In 1994 dozens of gay men and women testified before a congressional hearing about antigay discrimination. Phill Wilson, a gay African American man, testified that "when you deny someone a job because they are gay or you deny someone a job because they are a woman or you deny someone a job because they are black, when you deny someone a home because they are gay or lesbian, or you deny someone a home because they are black or you deny someone a home because they are a woman, in the end, you have people who are jobless, you have people who are homeless." And lesbian Letitia Gomez urged the committee, "Seriously consider the merit of legislation that will protect the rights of gay men, lesbians and bisexual people and our friends to work regardless of their sexual orientation. And please do not be led into the discussion that we, lesbians, gay men and bisexual people, want special rights. This is about the equal right to work in the U.S. As we are all painfully aware in this day and time, we need to be about keeping people employed and providing safe workplace environments so that they can carry out their jobs."[6] Wilson and Gomez were two of many gay rights activists who testified before the House committee supporting the passage of antidiscrimination measures.

During Bill Clinton's presidency the issue that provoked the most dissent was globalization. With bipartisan support Clinton signed the North American Free Trade Agreement (NAFTA), creating a free-trade zone linking the United States with Canada and Mexico, and the General Agreement on Tariffs and Trade (GATT), establishing the World Trade Organization. "Antiglobalists" denounced these measures as corporate power rolling over workers, merely a dressed-up version of imperialism. When the World Trade Organization met in Seattle in November 1999, more than forty thousand protestors, representing dozens of disparate groups that normally do not see eye to eye with each other, descended on the city. Environmentalists concerned that environmental standards were nonexistent in the Third World countries where the WTO was sponsoring free trade, thus exacerbating climate change, labor unions worried about the loss of American jobs, and human rights activists denouncing sweatshops that exploited children and the poor got together for several days of massive demonstrations. The media, of course, focused most of its attention on a small group of masked anarchists that began breaking shop windows and destroying property, which had the effect of damaging the movement in the public's eye. No matter how much the government, industry, and media played down the demonstrations, the fact remains that Seattle marked the beginning of a recurring series of protests against globalization that intensified over the next dozen years.

The most famous proponent of antiglobalization was the consumer advocate Ralph Nader, who was nominated as the Green Party candidate for president in 1996 and 2000. The Green Party warned Americans that *both* the Democrats and the Republicans were owned by corporate interests, and they were not at all responsive to the needs of the people. Democracy was endangered because NAFTA and GATT concentrated too much power and wealth in the hands of multinational corporations. Americans, Nader pointed out, have a moral objection to those who need a handout from the federal government. They believe there is something morally lacking in welfare recipients and that is why they are poor. They are lazy. They deserve nothing. But the small amount of money that welfare recipients receive, Nader insisted, is nothing compared to the welfare the government doles out to corporations in the form of subsidies, tax breaks, and sweetheart deals. "By any yardstick," Nader said, there is "far more welfare disbursement . . . in the corporate world than in the impoverished street arena." Americans need to wake up. "We're supposed to have a government of, by and for the people. Instead we have a government of the Exxons, by the General Motors and for the DuPonts. We have a government that recognizes the rights and liabilities and privileges of corporations, which are artificial entities created by state charters, against the rights and privileges of ordinary people."[7]

* * *

Millions of Americans believed that the world changed on September 11, 2001. But the world did not change. What did change was that Americans suddenly had to come to grips with the fact that the world viewed us differently than we viewed ourselves. For several weeks, as Americans rallied around the president and proudly flew flags from their cars and houses, they tried to understand why "they hate us." Was it because the Arab world hated our freedom? Our way of life? Was it because our policies had the effect of denying those rights to the people of the Middle East while enriching the autocratic regimes that ruled them?

While Americans pondered these imponderables, Washington retaliated. With a 90 percent approval rating President George W. Bush sent American forces into Afghanistan to hunt down Osama Bin Laden and to destroy Al-Qaeda and the Taliban. But as the War on Terror escalated, as more and more troops were sent to Afghanistan, as Bin Laden proved too elusive, and as the United States geared up for a war with Iraq, dissent intensified. Some argued that the United States should not be going to war but should be reevaluating the policies that provoked the attacks. Some felt that the attacks were a product of what the CIA calls "blowback"—unanticipated consequences of CIA activity. Some protested against the PATRIOT Act. Within weeks of the attacks Congress had passed the act, which expanded the definition of terrorism and eased restrictions on the government's ability to wiretap telephones, monitor financial transactions and Internet use, engage in secret background checks and surveillance of citizens and noncitizens suspected of terrorist sympathies, increase border security, and hold aliens for questioning. Although most Americans were sufficiently concerned about security to support these measures, many, both on the right and on the left, were infuriated at this misguided move to restrict individual liberty. They feared that in our quest for security we were fatally eroding the constitutional principles that made this country great.

In the weeks immediately following the attacks there was an extraordinary show of unity in the United States. Pundits, regardless of political leanings, were calling for the destruction of Afghanistan. "Bomb them back to the Stone Age" was one of the sentiments expressed. But there were also those who questioned the wisdom of retaliatory attacks that would likely kill far more innocent civilians than Al-Qaeda terrorists or their Taliban allies. Some argued that what the United States needed to do was to revise its foreign policy. In October 2001 the singer-songwriter Ani DiFranco penned "self evident," a poem about "the day that america / fell to its knees / after strutting around for a century / without saying thank you / or please" that struck a chord with those who were critical of U.S. foreign policy. In the poem she catalogs decades of American imperialism in Latin America and the Middle East that she believes prompted the terrorist attacks.[8] Of course, many Americans were deeply offended by DiFranco's leftist critique, calling her unpatriotic, a traitor, even a terrorist. But anyone who dissented against the government's response to 9/11 in those first weeks after the attacks found themselves labeled un-American or traitors—or worse. Every point of view, every thought, every action seemed black or white; there were no shades of gray in people's thinking.

But there were hundreds of thousands of dissenters even in the midst of this almost jingoist, knee-jerk reaction on the part of so many Americans. Those who did not go along with the herd mentality questioned the bombing of Afghanistan and U.S. Middle East policy in general, but they were also severely critical of the PATRIOT Act and the blanket arrests of noncitizens. Amnesty International was one of the organizations leading the way. It released a report in March 2002 that exposed the extent of the sweeps. More than twelve hundred aliens, mostly of South Asian or Arab ethnicity, were incarcerated during the first two months after the attacks, and hundreds, without having formal charges levied against them, were still in custody six months later. "A significant number of detainees," the report stated, "continue to be deprived of certain basic rights guaranteed under international law. These include the right to humane treatment, as well as rights which are essential to protection from arbitrary detention, such as the right of anyone deprived of their liberty to be informed of the reasons for the detention; to be able to challenge the lawfulness of the detention; to have prompt access to and assistance from a lawyer; and to the presumption of innocence." While granting that Washington needs to protect national security, Amnesty International is nevertheless "concerned that the government has used its expanded powers to detain non-nationals in the wake of September 11 without the necessary safeguards under international law. AI [Amnesty International] is concerned that the detentions in some cases may amount to arbitrary deprivation of liberty in violation of Article 9(1) of the ICCPR [International Covenant on Civil and Political Rights]. The secrecy surrounding the detention process has, further, created a serious lack of public accountability." The organization then spells out the ways the government could protect basic civil liberties.[9] Still, more than a decade after the attacks and with a new administration in Washington, the debate continues to rage in the United States about the abuse of civil liberties.

The American Civil Liberties Union, as would be expected, condemned the attempts to stifle dissent. The ACLU published *Freedom under Fire: Dissent in Post-9/11 America* in 2003. "In the tense time following the Sept. 11, 2001, terrorist attacks," the report announced, "Attorney General John Ashcroft mocked government critics and assailed their patriotism, calling their concerns 'phantoms of lost liberty.'" But Americans, the ACLU insisted, have the right to be *both* "safe and free." The report claimed that the administration was making a determined effort to question the patriotism of its critics. And it was not just the administration but also the media and other members of the power structure that were engaged in the policy of intimidation. "White House spokesman Ari Fleischer," the report declared, "also warned Americans to 'watch what they say.' Conservative commentators like

Bill O'Reilly suggested prosecuting war protesters as 'enemies of the state.' Since 2001, hundreds have been arrested for exercising their constitutionally protected freedoms, and some have lost their jobs or been suspended from school." Clearly, Americans "need to stop and consider the direction in which we are going, for we are in danger of allowing ourselves to be governed by our fears rather than our values. We are not the first generation to face this challenge."[10] The rest of the document recapitulated the history of past attempts to stifle dissent, from John Adams and the Alien and Sedition Acts to Lincoln's suspension of the writ of habeas corpus to the Sedition Act of World War I to the incarceration of Japanese Americans during World War II. Although the administration continued its campaign of labeling critics unpatriotic, the ACLU and other organizations championing free speech kept the issue in people's consciousness.

All through 2002 the Bush administration made a strong (if knowingly inflated) case for invading Iraq. Saddam Hussein, key officials insisted, had weapons of mass destruction (WMD). They claimed the CIA had irrefutable evidence that Iraq had a stockpile of chemical and biological weapons and was nearing completion of an atomic bomb. They claimed that we must invade Iraq and topple Saddam Hussein before it is too late. "The problem here," National Security Adviser Condoleezza Rice said, in a metaphor that was to be repeated countless times by other members of the administration, "is that there will always be some uncertainty about how quickly he can acquire nuclear weapons. But we don't want the smoking gun to be a mushroom cloud."[11] Such scare tactics worked. In October 2002 Congress passed a resolution granting the president the necessary powers to go to war with Iraq without a formal declaration of war (much like the Gulf of Tonkin Resolution gave Lyndon Johnson carte blanche in Vietnam).

But as the inexorable buildup for war escalated, so too did antiwar dissent—not only in the United States but also worldwide. On February 15, 2003, coordinated protests took place in hundreds of cities around the globe. Millions demonstrated in Rome, London, Dublin, Paris, Berlin, Athens, New York, Philadelphia, Chicago, San Francisco, Los Angeles, Seattle, and other cities, demanding that the United States not embark on this war, not invade Iraq. Protestors insisted that there was literally no proof that Iraq had weapons of mass destruction, nor was there any evidence whatsoever that Iraq was involved with or supported the terrorists who were responsible for 9/11. The outpouring of public sentiment at these demonstrations was extraordinary. It seemed that more Americans opposed the war with Iraq *before* it started then opposed the Vietnam War even four years into that ill-advised conflict.

But the demonstrations and marches had no influence on the administration. Bush dismissed the protestors as a "focus group" and went ahead with the invasion on March 19. Still, antiwar activists, though disheartened, continued to organize protests, demonstrations, vigils, acts of civil disobedience, and teach-ins. On April 9–10, 2003, the American Historical Association's "Historians Against the War" coordinated a nationwide teach-in that took place on scores of college campuses around the country. From UCLA to NYU, from Stanford to Rutgers, from the University of Montana to the University of South Carolina, hundreds of students and faculty attended teach-ins. At Temple University in Philadelphia more than a hundred students attended a seven-hour teach-in analyzing the policy behind the war—a war that at that time was less than a month old. And on many campuses teach-ins continued on a regular basis.

An antiwar organization calling itself Not in Our Name issued a statement, signed by more than sixty-five thousand people, condemning the Bush administration's wars.

> In our name, the Bush administration, with near unanimity from Congress, not only attacked Afghanistan but abrogated to itself and its allies the right to rain down military force anywhere and anytime. The brutal repercussions have been felt from the Philippines to Palestine, where Israeli tanks and bulldozers have left a terrible trail of death and destruction. The government has waged an all-out war on and occupied Iraq—a country which has no connection to the horror of September 11. What kind of world will this become if the U.S. government has a blank check to drop commandos, assassins, and bombs wherever it wants?

For several paragraphs the statement expanded on the policies that the administration was pursuing "in our name" but that the signers utterly reject. "We refuse to allow you to speak for all the American people. We will not give up our right to question. We will not hand over our consciences in return for a hollow promise of safety. We say NOT IN OUR NAME. We refuse to be party to these wars and we repudiate any inference that they are being waged in our name or for our welfare." Among the thousands of signatories were celebrities and leftist intellectuals: Robert Altman, Kevin Bacon, Spike Lee, Yoko Ono, Bonnie Raitt, Pete Seeger, Martin Sheen, Noam Chomsky, Angela Davis, Barbara Ehrenreich, Gloria Steinem, and Howard Zinn.[12]

Vietnam Veterans Against War as well as veterans of the Gulf War also leapt into the fray. They issued a "Call to Conscience from Veterans to Active Duty Troops and Reservists," in which they urged troops to resist the war. "We are veterans of the United States armed forces," they began. "We stand with the majority of humanity, including millions in our own country, in opposition to the United States' all-out war on Iraq. We span many wars and eras, have many political views and we all agree that this war is wrong."[13] David Wiggins, a West Point graduate, posted an online statement to the troops about to be deployed in which he urged them to look deeply into the ethical ramifications of what they were about to do and, ultimately, to follow their conscience. "With all due respect, I want you to know that if you participate in this conflict, you are not serving me, and I don't support you." If you participate in the war, you "will be damaging my reputation as an American, and further endangering me and my children by creating hatred that will someday be returned to us—perhaps someday soon. Your actions will not lead to a safer world, but a more dangerous world of pre-emption and unilateral decisions to commit mayhem. I don't support that."[14]

With each passing month, with each passing year, as American troops got bogged down in a poorly conceived occupation and casualties kept mounting, antiwar dissent grew. MoveOn.org, a liberal political action committee, urged Americans to get active in the antiwar movement. It produced a documentary film, *Uncovered: The Whole Truth about the Iraq War*, which persuasively argued that the Bush administration "cherry picked" intelligence reports about the so-called weapons of mass destruction that Saddam Hussein was stockpiling, and thus the rationale for going to war was a lie. The filmmaker Michael Moore produced a scathing (if somewhat overstated) documentary blasting the hubris of the Bush administration and the lies used to justify the war. People flocked to see *Fahrenheit 9/11* in movie theaters the world over. After Cindy Sheehan's son, Army Specialist Casey Sheehan, was killed in April 2004, Sheehan attended a meeting with the president. She was so outraged at the president's indifference to the suffering of the families of soldiers who had been killed in action and his apparent inability to grasp the implications of the war that she dedicated herself to the antiwar movement. She helped found Gold Star Families for Peace and held a vigil at President Bush's Crawford, Texas, ranch in 2005, demanding that the president meet with her and explain why her son was killed. She also told the press she wanted the president to explain why troops were still stationed in Iraq even after it was acknowledged that weapons of mass destruction did not exist. The president refused to meet with her. She continued her protests, getting arrested a number of times at demonstrations in Washington and other cities. Michael Berg was another parent who became a leading antiwar figure. In May 2004 his son Nick, a contractor in Iraq, was kidnapped and beheaded by an Al-Qaeda-linked terrorist group. Millions of people were horrified at his grisly execution, which the terrorists posted on the Internet. For the next four years Michael Berg went around the country participating in demonstrations and giving speeches blaming President Bush, not the terrorists, for his son's murder. He even ran for Congress in Delaware in 2006 as the Green Party's candidate.

Recording artists, inspired by the antiwar songs from times past, protested against the Iraq War with their music. (Some musicians even recorded new versions of earlier antiwar songs, such as Pearl Jam's take on Dylan's "Masters of War," which the band performed on the *Late Night with David Letterman* television show.) One of the most powerful indictments of American foreign policy, the war in Iraq, and the cheerleading role of the media was the hip-hop artist Immortal Technique's 2003 song "The 4th Branch." It is a compelling and relentlessly in-your-face denunciation of American foreign policy. "You really think this country, never sponsored terrorism? / Human rights violations, we continue the saga / El Salvador and the contras in Nicaragua / And on top of that, you still wanna take me to prison / Just cause I won't trade humanity for patriotism." In the end, he orders listeners to "turn off the news and read . . . ! Read . . . read . . . read."[15] Countless artists recorded songs protesting against the war, against President Bush, and against American policy. Here is just a sampling: Eminem's "Mosh," OutKast's "War," Pearl Jam's "World Wide Suicide," and Neil Young's "Let's Impeach the President." In the tradition of Woody Guthrie and Pete Seeger, Billy Bragg recorded "The Price of Oil," and Steve Earle "Rich Man's War." The latter song is a particularly poignant reflection on the impact of war on ordinary individuals caught up in fighting, not for their own dreams or interests but for the benefit of global corporations and politicians. For those facing the guns, whether a working-class U.S. soldier or a desperate Palestinian suicide bomber, there are no winners. Earle gives a twenty-first-century take on a sentiment expressed by antidraft rioters in New York City in 1863: "Just another poor boy off to fight a rich man's war."[16] Although protest music and the recording industry has changed since its heyday in the 1960s and 1970s, music still has the power to raise important questions and shape the conversation about controversial issues. It can still transform apathy into commitment.

* * *

Despite the historic election of Barack Obama, the ending of the Iraq War, and the elimination of Osama Bin Laden, dissent is still commonplace in the second decade of the twenty-first century. Pundits, talking heads, and comedians still denounce and mock the people in power. Right-wing political commentators such as Glenn Beck and Sean Hannity, as well as left-wing commentators such as Rachel Maddow and Chris Matthews, have many devoted fans, although it is doubtful that their critiques change any minds since they are preaching to their respective choirs. More effective are comedians like Stephen Colbert and Jon Stewart, who are truly subversive in their use of humor to ridicule the power structure. Like H. L. Mencken before them, they induce people to look with new eyes at the underlying absurdity of the things corporate executives and political leaders say and do.

Ever since the New Deal, conservative Americans opposed what they saw as an out-of-control Big Brother–style government. They wanted less government, less regulation, less taxes, less intrusion into their lives. It was not just the Democratic Party that was anathema to them; the Republican Party under George W. Bush too was just as guilty of expanding a vast, bloated, inefficient federal bureaucracy. Conservative organizations such as Americans for Prosperity and FreedomWorks, founded by the ultraconservative billionaires David and Charles Koch, promote political action to resist big government and support ultra-conservative politicians. The passage of the Troubled Asset Relief Program, the election of the nation's first African American president, the implementation of the Homeowners Affordability and Stability Plan,

Tea Party protestors in Washington, DC, September 12, 2009, venting their anger at what they perceive as an over-the-top intrusive federal government. This march was sponsored in part by an organization named 9.12dc.org, which was founded by Fox Television's Glenn Beck. Photograph by David King. (Courtesy dbking on Flickr, shared under a Creative Commons license at https://creativecommons.org/licenses/by/2.0/legalcode)

and in 2010 the passage of health-care reform inflamed conservatives. During 2009 and 2010 a new organization, the Tea Party, held hundreds of demonstrations and rallies around the country. Many activists dressed in eighteenth-century costumes, wigs, and tricornered hats. They carried signs and shouted slogans paraphrasing the rallying cries of 1776. They compared Obama, variously, to George III, Adolf Hitler, and Joseph Stalin. They portrayed the government in Washington as the archenemy of liberty and Christian values. Many on the left ridiculed the Tea Party, but they stopped laughing when the 2010 midterm election resulted in a thorough repudiation of Obama and the Democratic Party. Republicans gained in just about every state legislative and gubernatorial election in the country, they gained seats in the Senate, and they won an overwhelming majority in the House of Representatives. The new legislators were passionately devoted to principle; they vowed to overturn "Obamacare" and the other measures that had been passed to deal with the economy, and they vowed to lower taxes. The Tea Party had tapped into a deep vein of populist anger and developed a massive following.

Within a year of the Tea Party's successes protestors from the left, outraged at the economic inequality that is growing out of control in the United States, also took to the streets. The protests started on September 17, 2011, when protestors converged on the statue of the Wall Street bull in New York City. Within a few days hundreds had descended on lower Manhattan and began camping out in Zuccotti Park, renamed Liberty Park. "We are the 99 percent!" they proclaimed, referring to the fact that 42 percent of the nation's wealth is possessed by the elite 1 percent, while 99 percent share the rest. Within weeks Occupy Wall Street spread to other cities: Philadelphia, Boston, Los Angeles, Oakland, Seattle, Denver, Atlanta. Even small towns had versions of the Occupy movement. Soon it spread to London, Rome, Athens, Frankfurt, and other international cities. Something was happening around the world: a deep, unfathomable discontent with the harsh economic realities that most people face on a daily basis. In the United States so many Americans, most of them middle class, were feeling that the American Dream was slipping through their fingers, that no matter how hard they tried, they would only take baby steps in getting ahead, whereas the 1 percent kept accumulating more and more wealth at the expense of the 99 percent. Indeed the government bailout of the banks and industries that were "too big to fail" mostly profited the 1 percent. The Occupy protestors had a plethora of grievances—unemployment, mortgage defaults, loss of savings and pensions, overwhelming student debt—but they were united in demanding that the government in Washington, the president, the Senate, and the House of Representatives, listen to them.

Shortly after the occupation began, the protestors issued a declaration. "As one people, united, we acknowledge the reality: that the future of the human race requires the cooperation of its members; that our system must protect our rights, and upon corruption of that system, it

Occupy Wall Street, November 15, 2011. Photograph by David Shankbone. (Freely licensed; courtesy of David Shankbone on Wikimedia Commons, shared under a Creative Commons license at http://creativecommons.org/licenses/by/3.0/deed.en)

is up to the individuals to protect their own rights, and those of their neighbors; that a democratic government derives its just power from the people, but corporations do not seek consent to extract wealth from the people and the Earth; and that no true democracy is attainable when the process is determined by economic power." They went on to denounce the corporations that "place profit over people, self-interest over justice, and oppression over equality, [that] run our governments." Emulating the Declaration of Independence, they listed numerous specific grievances that they demanded must be addressed.[17]

It is probable that many of the Occupy protestors voted for Obama and were deeply disappointed that he had not done enough to alleviate their distress. Perhaps they formed the Occupy movement because they realized that the problems were so complex, so entrenched, that no one person, not even the president of the United States, could fix them. It was only through solidarity, through working together, that there was a chance to solve the economic crisis.

Occupy Wall Street was not particularly radical in that most of the demonstrators called for the reform, not the destruction, of capitalism.

In some ways they were more akin to the Progressive movement of the early twentieth century than to the IWW or the radical socialists and anarchists who sought to smash capitalism. But by year's end most of the occupations around the country were dislodged by law enforcement officials, and the movement lost its momentum. The problem that Occupy Wall Street faced was that linking a protest with a specific space is an existential problem. It is one thing to stage a civil disobedience action for a day or two, occupying a space or blocking traffic, but it is quite another to attempt an indefinite occupation without an end date. If the protest and the space are separated, if the protestors are removed, it ends the demonstration. The Bonus Army experienced this in 1932. Columbia student radicals experienced it in 1968. Occupy Wall Street experienced it in 2011. Still, in all those cases the ending of a specific dramatic action did not silence the protesting voices. The fight continued.

Superficially there are some similarities between the Tea Party and Occupy Wall Street. Both movements hate the vast amounts of taxpayer money that bailed out the financial industry. But after that their views diverge. Whereas Occupy Wall Street sees government as part of the solution, the Tea Party sees it as *the* problem. Furthermore, the Occupy movement is more of a "grassroots" movement than is the Tea Party, which because of the financial backing of the Koch brothers and favorable promotion by the conservative media could be more accurately labeled an "Astroturf" movement. The Tea Party obviously had more success in the voting booth, but one thing Occupy Wall Street accomplished was to change the focus of the political discussion. Before Occupy everyone was talking about the deficit. By the time Occupy was evicted, economic inequality was the focal point. Everyone, even the Republican leadership, who of course had vastly different ideas than Occupy about how to address the problem, was talking about the 99 percent.

Conclusion

The Arc of Dissent

The more of the 99 percent that begin to see themselves as sharing needs, the more the guards and the prisoners see their common interest, the more the Establishment becomes isolated, ineffectual.

—Howard Zinn

From the streets of Cairo and the Arab Spring, to Occupy Wall Street, . . . social media was not only sharing the news but driving it.

—Dan Rather

Since the election of Barack Obama it seems that political discourse has taken on a nastier (although not necessarily new) tone of bitterness and partisanship. The rise of the Tea Party movement and its irreconcilable stance against big government and taxation, angry protests against health-care reform, vilification of "illegal aliens," and relentless questioning of the religion and even the nationality of the nation's first black president reflect a deep-seated fear reminiscent of the 1920s clash between modernism and traditionalism that the United States is moving too rapidly into an unknown, frightening future. A variation of this fear was a motivating force for the Occupy Wall Street movement—the fear that the United States has abandoned the principles of the founding fathers and that democracy of the people, by the people, and for the people has truly perished under the onslaught of corporate power.

The Tea Party and Occupy Wall Street are the largest and most recognizable dissent movements of recent years, but dissent continues to be expressed by many groups, for many causes. Thousands of protestors rally on a regular basis demanding immigration reform to fix the broken immigration laws and provide a way for undocumented

migrants to become American citizens. Gays and lesbians are seeing a remarkable level of success in a relatively short period of time
in their fight for marriage equality. Thousands of Americans protest
against the Supreme Court's *Citizens United* decision, against the Keystone XL Pipeline, against fracking, against mountaintop-removal coal
mining, against gun violence, against attempts to restrict voting rights
with voter ID laws, against the exploitation of migrant workers, against
racially motivated police and town watch shootings of young unarmed
black men, and in the light of whistle-blower Edward Snowden's revelations, against the National Security Agency's violation of the Fourth
Amendment. The list goes on.

In the twenty-first century new elements have entered the dissent
narrative. Viral videos on YouTube have the impact of reaching massive audiences and raising public awareness of an injustice. Postings on
Twitter and Facebook spread the word to protestors of the time and
place of the next rally or demonstration or civil disobedience action or
spontaneous "flash protest." Individuals backing a specific cause use the
Internet to obtain millions of signatures on petitions that are then sent
to government officials or corporations, demanding they change a law
or policy. The possibilities are endless for dissenters to utilize these new
tools to spread the word, educate people, and increase participation
in their movement. And clearly, both the Tea Party and Occupy Wall
Street, as well as the recent Occupy movements in Europe and the Arab
Spring in the Middle East, successfully used social media and the Internet to expand their message and mobilize supporters. There has been,
however, a downside to electronic media. It can misrepresent a cause,
distort a message, or paint a false picture of what actually happened at
a protest march. So, viewers, beware. Furthermore, unlike the antiwar
and civil rights protests of the 1960s, which called for a real commitment on the part of activists to go to a public space and participate in a
demonstration, the use of electronic media has produced the phenomenon of what is called "slacktivism" or "clicktivism." By clicking "like" on
a group's Facebook page or signing an online petition, individuals have
the tendency to feel that they have done their part, that they have participated, that they have fought the good fight, without actually doing
so, without actually making a physical commitment. Still, while passive
advocacy is no replacement for activism, it is clear that social media is
one of the most powerful tools to fan the fires of dissent.

I have written elsewhere that dissent is the fuel for the engine of progress. But "progress," like "dissent" itself, is a disputed concept. For some, progress is creating a more just society in which all Americans enjoy the rights set forth in the Declaration of Independence and the Constitution. For some, the progress that dissenters seek is an unmitigated disaster, a drastic deviation from the ideals of the founders that will bring the country to ruin. Throughout the country's tumultuous history the long tradition of skepticism and questioning authority has moved the United States, somewhat erratically in fits and starts, generally in the direction of "all men are created equal." Whether it is progress or not, whether it is evolution or devolution, is in the eye of the beholder.

And in the eyes of this beholder dissenters need to push people to a broader consciousness, to open their minds to see beyond their own narrow self-interests, to realize that what is good for everyone is good for them and ultimately coincides with their own self-interest. And we need to understand too that, in the end, the arc of dissent, to paraphrase Martin Luther King, Jr., in a different context, bends toward justice.

At a time when more and more Americans claim they get a more accurate, more nuanced perspective of the events happening in the world from Comedy Central shows hosted by Jon Stewart and Stephen Colbert than they do from "real" network evening news or political punditry, it is clear that it is our duty, if we value American democracy, to be informed citizens. And we need to demand more responsible journalism, we need to demand politicians who are beholden to the people and not to those who bankroll them, we need to question authority, we need to speak out, we need to make sure that "We the People" really means something. We need to dissent.

NOTES

INTRODUCTION: DISSENT AND AMERICA

1. Eric Foner, *The Story of American Freedom* (New York: Norton, 1998), xiv.
2. Martin Luther King, Jr., "Letter from Birmingham Jail," in *Why We Can't Wait* (New York: Mentor, 1964), 77.
3. David Wiggins, "Message to the Troops: Resist!," October 11, 2002, Strike the Root, posted March 10, 2003, http://www.strike-the-root.com/3/wiggins/wiggins3.html.

1. THE "FREE AIRE OF A NEW WORLD"

1. Robert Baillie, *A Dissuasive from the Errours of the Time* (London, 1645), 55. Baillie, a Presbyterian critic of New England Congregationalism, was using the term pejoratively.
2. H. L. Mencken, *A Mencken Chrestomathy: His Own Selection of His Choicest Writing* (New York: Random House, 1949), 624.
3. Roger Williams, *The Bloudy Tenent of Persecution* (London, 1644), ed. Samuel L. Caldwell (Providence, RI: Narragansett Club, 1867), 138–139, 248–249.
4. Thomas Hutchinson, *The History of the Province of Massachusetts-Bay*, vol. 2 (London, 1758), 508.
5. Lawrence H. Leder, ed., "Records of the Trials of Jacob Leisler and His Associates," *New-York Historical Society Quarterly* 36 (1952): 454.

2. DISSENT IN AN AGE OF REASON

1. See Jon Butler, *Awash in a Sea of Faith: Christianizing the American People* (Cambridge: Harvard University Press, 1990).
2. For an excellent analysis of the rebellion see Jill Lepore, *New York Burning: Liberty, Slavery, and Conspiracy in Eighteenth-Century Manhattan* (New York: Random House, 2005).
3. Garret Hendericks et al., "The Germantown Protest," February 18, 1688, available online at http://www.yale.edu/glc/aces/germantown.htm (accessed September 14, 2014).
4. Ralph Sandiford, *A Brief Examination of the Practice of the Times* (Philadelphia: Franklin and Meredith, 1729), 6.
5. Wendy M. Zirngibl, "Lay, Benjamin," in *Encyclopedia of American History: Colonization and Settlement, 1608 to 1760*, rev. ed., ed. Billy G. Smith and Gary B. Nash, vol. 2 (New York: Facts On File, 2010).
6. Elihu Coleman, *A Testimony against the Antichristian Practice of Making Slaves of Men* (New Bedford, MA, 1733), 22.

7. John Woolman, *Considerations on Keeping Negroes, Part Second,* in *The Journals and Essays of John Woolman,* ed. Amelia Mott Gummere (New York: Macmillan, 1922), 381.

8. Ibid., 378.

9. Anthony Benezet, *A Short Account of That Part of Africa Inhabited by Negroes, with General Observations on the Slave Trade and Slavery* (1762), in *The Complete Antislavery Writings of Anthony Benezet, 1754–1783,* ed. David L. Crosby (Baton Rouge: Louisiana State University Press, 2014), 29.

10. Ottobah Cugoano, *Thoughts and Sentiments on the Evil and Wicked Traffic of the Slavery and Commerce of the Human Species* (London, 1787), 143.

11. Equiano's autobiography has recently been challenged as a fiction. According to historian Vincent Carretta in *Equiano, the African: Biography of a Self-Made Man* (Athens: University of Georgia Press, 2005), there is some evidence that he was born in South Carolina; thus his description of the Middle Passage is not drawn from personal experience. This, of course, does not impinge on the *Narrative*'s power as an antislavery document.

12. Olaudah Equiano, *The Interesting Narrative of Olaudah Equiano, or Gustavus Vassa the African* (London, 1789), n.p. (end of chap. 5).

13. Loron Sauguaarum, "Letter from a Penobscot Chief Explanatory of the Treaty of Peace Concluded at Caskebay, between the English and Indians," August 1727, in *Documents Relative to the Colonial History of the State of New York,* ed. E. B. O'Callaghan, vol. 9 (Albany, NY: Weed, Parsons, 1855), 966–967.

14. "Letter to Mr. Jeremiah Langhorne & all Magistrates of Pennsilvania, 1740" (from unnamed Delaware chiefs), in *Pennsylvania Indian Treaties, 1737–1756,* ed. Donald H. Kent (Frederick, MD: University Publications of America, 1984), 45.

15. Atiwaneto, "Propositions of the Abenakis of St. Francis to Captain Phineas Stevens, Delegate from the Governor of Boston, in Presence of the Baron De Longueuil, Governor of Montreal, Commandant of Canada and of the Iroquois of the Sault Saint Louis and of the Lake of the Two Mountains," July 5, 1752, in *Documents Relative to the Colonial History of the State of New York,* ed. E. B. O'Callaghan, vol. 10 (Albany, NY: Weed, Parsons, 1887), 252–253.

16. "Mashpee Petition to the Massachusetts General Court," June 11, 1752, in *Native Writings in Massachusetts,* by Ives Goddard and Kathleen J. Bragdon (Philadelphia: American Philosophical Society, 1988), 373.

17. John Killbuck, "Speech to the Governors of Pennsylvania, Maryland, and Virginia," December 4, 1771, in *Documents of the American Revolution,* ed. K. G. Davies, vol. 3 (Shannon: Irish University Press, 1981), 255.

18. Elizabeth Dunlap, advertisement in the *Pennsylvania Gazette,* June 17, 1742, in *Runaway Women: Elopements and Other Miscreant Deeds as Advertised in the "Pennsylvania Gazette," 1728–1789 (Together with a Few Abused Wives and Unfortunate Children),* ed. Judith Ann Highley Meier (Apollo, PA: Closson, 1993), 6; Mary Fenby, advertisement in the *Pennsylvania Gazette,* August 7, 1746, in ibid., 11.

19. Hannah Griffiths, "The Female Patriots. Address'd to the Daughters of Liberty in America. By the Same," 1768, in *Milcah Martha Moore's Book: A Commonplace Book from Revolutionary America*, ed. Catherine La Courreye Blecki and Karin A. Wulf (University Park: Pennsylvania State University Press, 1997), 172.

20. Report from the New Jersey government to the Lords of Trade in London, quoted in Howard Zinn, *A People's History of the United States: 1492–Present* (New York: HarperCollins, 2001), 52.

21. John Peter Zenger, editorial, *New York Weekly Journal*, November 19, 1733.

22. Quoted in Livingston Rutherfurd, *John Peter Zenger, His Press, His Trial, and a Bibliography of Zenger Imprints* (New York: Dodd, Mead, 1904), 116.

3. REVOLUTION

1. James Wolfe, quoted in Guy Chet, *Conquering the American Wilderness: The Triumph of European Warfare in the Colonial Northeast* (Amherst: University of Massachusetts Press, 2003), 127.

2. 10 March 1764, House of Commons *Journals*, vol. 29, 934–935, quoted in Merrill Jensen, *The Founding of a Nation: A History of the American Revolution, 1763–1776* (Indianapolis: Hackett, 2004), 48.

3. Samuel Adams, "The Rights of the Colonists as Men, as Christians, and as Subjects," November 20, 1772, in *The Writings of Samuel Adams*, vol. 2, *1770–1773*, ed. Harry Alonso Cushing (New York: Putnam, 1906), 350.

4. Ibid., 350, 357.

5. Quoted in "A History of Edenton, North Carolina," Carolana, http://www.carolana .com/NC/Towns/Edenton_NC.html (accessed September 16, 2014).

6. Abigail Adams to John Adams, September 20, 1776, in *Adams Family Correspondence*, vol. 2, *June 1776–March 1778*, ed. L. H. Butterfield (Cambridge: Harvard University Press, 1963), 129.

7. "A Declaration by the Representatives of the United Colonies of North-America, Now Met in Congress at Philadelphia, Setting Forth the Causes and Necessity of Their Taking Up Arms," available online at http://avalon.law.yale.edu/18th_century/arms.asp#1 (accessed September 16, 2014).

8. George III, "A Proclamation, by The King, for Suppressing Rebellion and Sedition," August 23, 1775, available online at http://www.digitalhistory.uh.edu/disp_textbook.cfm?smtID=3&psid=4105 (accessed September 16, 2014).

9. Thomas Paine, *Common Sense, Addressed to the Inhabitants of America* (Philadelphia, 1776), 38, 45, 34, 60.

10. Thomas Hutchinson, *Strictures upon the Declaration of the Congress at Philadelphia, in a Letter to a Noble Lord, &c.* (London, 1776), 4.

11. Ibid., 32.

12. Ibid., 8, 9–10.

13. "Slave Petition for Gradual Emancipation: To the Honorable Legislature of the State of Massachusetts Bay, January 13, 1777," *Massachusetts Historical Society Collections*, 5th ser., vol. 3 (Boston, 1877), 437.

14. David Waldstreicher, *Runaway America: Benjamin Franklin, Slavery, and the American Revolution* (New York: Hill and Wang, 2004), 210.

15. Quoted in Mary Beth Norton, *Liberty's Daughters: The Revolutionary Experience of American Women, 1750–1800* (Ithaca: Cornell University Press, 1996), 171–172, 179.

16. Abigail Adams to John Adams, March 31, 1776, in *Adams Family Correspondence*, vol. 1, *December 1761–May 1776*, ed. L. H. Butterfield (Cambridge: Harvard University Press, 1963), 370.

17. George Washington, "General Orders, October 25 [1781]," in *The Writings of George Washington from the Original Manuscript Sources 1745–1799*, vol. 23, *August 16, 1781–February 15, 1782*, ed. John C. Fitzpatrick (Washington, DC: Government Printing Office, 1937), 264–265.

4. DISCORD IN THE NEW REPUBLIC

1. Articles of Confederation, art. 3.

2. Articles of Confederation, art. 2.

3. Jefferson to James Madison, January 30, 1787, in *The Writings of Thomas Jefferson*, ed. Paul Leicester Ford, vol. 4 (New York: Putnam, 1894), 362–363.

4. Quoted in John Marshall, *The Life of George Washington: Commander in Chief of the American Forces*, 2nd ed., vol. 2 (Philadelphia: James Crissy & Thomas Cowperthwait, 1845), 137.

5. Quoted in Kathleen DuVal, "Independence for Whom? Expansion and Conflict in the South and Southwest," in *The World of the Revolutionary Republic: Land, Labor, and the Conflict for a Continent*, ed. Andrew Shankman (New York: Routledge, 2014), 102.

6. Shawnee, Miami, Ottawa, and Seneca, "Proposal to Maintain Indian Lands," 1793, in *The Correspondence of Lieut. Governor John Graves Simcoe*, ed. E. A. Cruikshank, vol. 2 (Toronto: Ontario Historical Society, 1923–1931), 20.

7. Judith Sargent Murray, "On the Equality of the Sexes," in *Selected Writings of Judith Sargent Murray*, ed. Sharon M. Harris (New York: Oxford University Press, 1995), 7–8.

8. Hannah Webster Foster's *The Coquette; or, The History of Eliza Wharton, a Novel: Founded on Fact* was first published anonymously in 1797. It was a daring novel about the daughter of a minister who dies giving birth to an illegitimate child. Susanna Rowson was an actress who wrote poetry, an opera, and novels, the most popular of which, *Charlotte Temple* (1791), outsold all other novels in the United States until Harriet Beecher Stowe's *Uncle Tom's Cabin* appeared. Both *The Coquette* and *Charlotte Temple* dealt with the taboo subjects of seduction and betrayal.

9. 1 Stat. 570.

10. 1 Stat. 596.

11. Quoted in "Alien and Sedition Acts," *The Founder's Blog*, June 22, 2012, http://williamdbailey.wordpress.com/tag/5th-united-states-congress/.

12. *Annals of Congress*, 12th Cong., 1st sess. (1812), vol. 2, cols. 2219–2221.

13. Tecumseh, "Sleep Not Longer, O Choctaws and Chicawaws," 1811, in *Indian Oratory: Famous Speeches by Noted Indian Chieftains*, comp. W. C. Vanderwerth (Norman: Oklahoma University Press, 1971), 63–64.

14. Tecumseh, "Speech at Vincennes," in *The Library of Oratory*, ed. Chauncey M. Depew, vol. 4 (New York: Current Literature, 1902), 363.

15. "Free Blacks of Philadelphia Protest against Colonization Policy," 1817, in *A Documentary History of the Negro People in the United States*, vol. 1, *From Colonial Times through the Civil War*, ed. Herbert Aptheker (Secaucus, NJ: Citadel, 1973), 71–72.

16. Jefferson to John Holmes, April 22, 1820, in *The Writings of Thomas Jefferson*, ed. Paul Leicester Ford, vol. 10 (New York: Putnam, 1899), 157.

17. Quoted in Caleb William Loring, *Nullification, Secession, Webster's Argument and the Kentucky and Virginia Resolutions Considered in Reference to the Constitution and Historically* (New York: Putnam, 1893), 24.

18. *Register of Debates in Congress*, 21st Cong., 1st sess. (April 9, 1830), vol. 6, part 1, 311, 312, 318.

19. *The Cherokee Nation v. The State of Georgia*, 30 U.S. 1, 17 (1831); *Worcester v. Georgia*, 31 U.S. 515, 559 (1832); Jackson's famous comment is quoted in Edwin A. Miles, "After John Marshall's Decision: *Worcester v. Georgia* and the Nullification Crisis," *Journal of Southern History* 39, no. 4 (1973): 519.

20. John Ross, *Letter from John Ross, Principal Chief of the Cherokee Nation of Indians, in Answer to Inquires from a Friend Regarding the Cherokee Affairs with the United States* (Washington, DC, 1836), 23.

21. William Apess, "An Indian's Looking-Glass for the White Man," in *On Our Own Ground: The Complete Writings of William Apess, a Pequot*, ed. Barry O'Connell (Amherst: University of Massachusetts Press, 1992), 156, 157.

22. Laborers of Boston, "Ten-Hour Circular," 1835, in *The Faith of Our Fathers: An Anthology of Americana, 1790–1860*, ed. Irving Mark and E. E. Schwaab (New York: Knopf, 1952), 342–343.

23. For an insightful discussion of worker resistance to industrial discipline throughout the nineteenth century see Herbert Gutman, *Work, Culture, and Society in Industrializing America: Essays in American Working-Class and Social History* (New York: Knopf, 1976).

5. SLAVERY AND ITS DISCONTENTS

1. C. W. Larison, *Silvia Dubois: A Biografy of the Slav Who Whipt Her Mistres and Gand Her Fredom*, ed. Jared C. Lobdell (New York: Oxford University Press, 1988), 64, 65–66.

2. Nat Turner, *The Confessions of Nat Turner, the Leader of the Late Insurrection in Southampton, VA* (Baltimore: Thomas R. Gray, 1831), 9–10.

3. Ibid., 11, 12–13.

4. David Walker, *Walker's Appeal in Four Articles; Together with a Preamble, to the Colored Citizens of the World, with a Brief Sketch of his Life by Henry Highland Garnet* (New York: J. H. Tobitt, 1848), 76, 31, 37, 17.

5. Ibid., 24.

6. Ibid., 27–28.

7. William Lloyd Garrison, "To the Public," *Liberator* (Boston), January 1, 1831, 1.

8. William Lloyd Garrison, "Triumph of Mobocracy in Boston," in *Selections from the Writings and Speeches of William Lloyd Garrison* (Boston: R. F. Wallcut, 1852), 387.

9. Quoted in Eric H. Walther, *The Fire-Eaters* (Baton Rouge: Louisiana State University Press, 1992), 297.

10. Angelina E. Grimké, *Appeal to the Christian Women of the South* (New York: New York Anti-Slavery Society, 1836), 24, 35.

11. Ralph Waldo Emerson, "'Address to the Citizens of Concord' on the Fugitive Slave Law," in *Emerson's Antislavery Writings*, ed. by Len Gougeon and Joel Myerson (New Haven: Yale University Press, 1995), 57.

12. Frederick Douglass, "What to the Slave Is the Fourth of July?," in *The Frederick Douglass Papers: Series One: Speeches, Debates, and Interviews, 1847–1854*, ed. John W. Blassingame, vol. 2 (New Haven: Yale University Press, 1982), 386–387.

13. Martin R. Delany, "Political Destiny of the Colored Race, on the American Continent," in *Martin R. Delany: A Documentary Reader*, ed. Robert S. Levine (Chapel Hill: University of North Carolina Press, 2003), 251, 247, 320.

6. REFORMERS AND DISSIDENTS

1. "*La propriété, c'est le vol!*" from Proudhon's 1840 book, the English title of which is *What Is Property? or, An Inquiry into the Principle of Right and of Government*, in *Property Is Theft! A Pierre-Joseph Proudhon Anthology*, ed. Iain McKay (Oakland, CA: AK Press, 2011), 88.

2. William Wordsworth, "The Tables Turned," in *Lyrical Ballads, with a Few Other Poems* (London: J. & A. Arch, 1798), 188.

3. Ralph Waldo Emerson, *The Essay on Self-Reliance* (East Aurora, NY: Roycroft, 1908), 9, 11, 14.

4. Ibid., 18–19.

5. Ibid., 19–20, 23.

6. Henry David Thoreau, *Walden* (New York: Thomas Y. Crowell, 1910), 8, 427, 430.

7. Margaret Fuller, *Woman in the Nineteenth Century* (New York: Greeley and McElrath, 1845), 103, 107.

8. "The Drunkard's Progress from the First Glass to the Grave," 1846, poster by Nathaniel Currier.

9. Quoted in Thomas Dublin, *Women at Work* (New York: Columbia University Press, 1979), 93.

10. Harriet Hanson Robinson, "The Lowell Mill Girls Go on Strike, 1836," 1898, available online at http://historymatters.gmu.edu/d/5714 (accessed September 13, 2014).

11. Sarah Begley to Angelique Martin, Springfield, March 13, 1847[?], quoted in Teresa Murphy, "Sarah Bagley: Laboring for Life," in *The Human Tradition in American Labor History*, ed. Eric Arnesen (Wilmington, DE: Scholarly Resources, 2004), 41.

12. Quoted in Gary B. Nash et al., *The American People: Brief Edition*, vol. 1 (New York: Pearson/Longman, 2006), 358.

13. Quoted in David L. Gollaher, *Voices for the Mad: The Life of Dorothea Dix* (New York: Free Press, 1995), 143.

14. Horace Mann, "Twelfth Annual Report to the Secretary of the Massachusetts Board of Education," 1848, available online at http://www.tncrimlaw.com/civil_bible/horace_mann.htm (accessed September 16, 2014).

15. *Seneca County Courier*, 1848, quoted in Elisabeth Griffith, *In Her Own Right: The Life of Elizabeth Cady Stanton* (New York: Oxford University Press, 1984), 52.

16. Elizabeth Cady Stanton, "Address Delivered at Seneca Falls," July 19, 1848, available online at http://womenshistory.about.com/library/etext/bl_1848_stanton1.htm (accessed September 16, 2014).

17. "Declaration of Sentiments," in *History of Woman Suffrage*, vol. 1, *1848–1861*, ed. Elizabeth Cady Stanton, Susan B. Anthony, and Matilda Joslyn Gage (1881; repr., New York: Arno / *New York Times*, 1969), 70–71.

18. Frederick Douglass, "The Women's Association of Philadelphia, *The North Star*, June 15, 1849," in *Frederick Douglass on Women's Rights*, ed. Philip S. Foner (New York: Da Capo, 1992), 51.

19. Isaac Dayton, ed., *The Office of Surrogate, Surrogates, and Surrogates Courts, and Executors, Administrators, and Guardians, in the State of New York: A Compilation of the Statutes, and a Summary of the Judicial Decisions of the State of New York Relating to the Office of Surrogate . . . and the Powers, Duties, and Liabilities of Executors, Administrators, and Guardians, Arranged in the Form of a Treatise* (New York: Banks & Brothers, 1861), 237.

7. EXPANSION AND CONFLICT

1. John L. O'Sullivan, "Annexation," *United States Democratic Review* 17, no. 85 (1845): 5.

2. Ethan Allen Hitchcock, *Fifty Years in Camp and Field: Diary of Major-General Ethan Allen Hitchcock, U.S.A.*, ed. W. A. Croffut (New York: Putnam / Knickerbocker, 1909), 212–213.

3. Taylor to Polk, April 26, 1846, in *Messages of the President of the United States: With the Correspondence Therewith Communicated, between the Secretary of War and Other Officers of the Government, on the Subject of the Mexican War* (Washington, DC, 1848), 288.

4. "Message from the President of the United States Relative to an Invasion and Commencement of Hostilities by Mexico," May 11, 1846, in ibid, 8.

5. Quoted in Zinn, *People's History*, 155.

6. Quoted in ibid.,159, 168.

7. Quoted in ibid., 159, 160–161.

8. Henry David Thoreau, *"Walden" and "Resistance to Civil Government,"* 3rd ed., ed. William Rossi (New York: Norton, 2008), 230.

9. Ibid., 234.

10. Ibid., 236.

11. Ibid., 238–239.

12. Quoted in Nash et al., *American People*, 451.

13. Quoted in Tom Rea, *Devil's Gate: Owning the Land, Owning the Story* (Norman: University of Oklahoma Press, 2012), 32.

14. Quoted in Frederick Law Olmstead, *A Journey through Texas; or, A Saddle-Trip on the Southwestern Frontier* (New York: Dix, Edwards, 1857), 502.

15. "Juan Nepomuceno Cortina," in *The Mythical West: An Encyclopedia of Legend, Lore, and Popular Culture*, ed. Richard W. Slatta (Santa Barbara, CA: ABC-CLIO, 2001), 108–109.

16. Quoted in James M. McPherson, *Battle Cry of Freedom: The Civil War Era* (New York: Oxford University Press, 1988), 62.

17. Quoted in Ronald Seavoy, *An Economic History of the United States: From 1607 to the Present* (New York Routledge, 2013), 173.

18. Quoted in Perry Miller, *Errand into the Wilderness* (Cambridge: Harvard University Press, 1956), 10.

8. DISSENT IMPERILS THE UNION

1. Quoted in Allen C. Guelzo, *Fateful Lightning: A New History of the Civil War and Reconstruction* (New York: Oxford University Press, 2012), 74.

2. Quoted in ibid., 85.

3. Frederick Douglass, "The End of All Compromises with Slavery—Now and Forever," 1854, in *The Life and Writings of Frederick Douglass*, vol. 2, *Pre–Civil War Decade*, ed. Philip S. Foner (New York: International, 1950), 282.

4. Lincoln, quoted in Michael Burlingame, *Abraham Lincoln: A Life* (Baltimore: Johns Hopkins University Press, 2013), 363.

5. Quoted in Eric Foner, *The Fiery Trial: Abraham Lincoln and American Slavery* (New York: Norton, 2010), 66.

6. Quoted in McPherson, *Battle Cry of Freedom*, 89, 90.

7. Hinton Rowan Helper, *The Impending Crisis of the South: How to Meet It* (New York: A. B. Burdick, 1857), 153.

8. George Fitzhugh, *Cannibals All! or, Slaves without Masters* (Richmond, VA: A. Morris, 1857), 49, 206.

9. Quoted in Ethan Greenberg, *Dred Scott and the Dangers of a Political Court* (Lanham, MD: Lexington Books, 2009), 53.

10. Charles Sumner, *The Crime against Kansas: The Apologies for the Crime; The True Remedy* (Boston: John P. Jewett, 1856), 9, 31.

11. Quoted in Greenberg, *Dred Scott*, 113, 114.

12. Frederick Douglass, "The Dred Scott Decision: Speech Delivered before American Anti-Slavery Society, New York, May 14, 1857," in *Selected Speeches and Writings*, ed. Philip Foner (Chicago: Lawrence Hill Books, 1999), 355, 348.

13. Quoted in William Cooper Nell, *William Cooper Nell, Nineteenth-Century African American Abolitionist, Historian, Integrationist: Selected Writings from 1832–1874*, ed. Constance Porter Uzelac (Baltimore: Black Classic, 2002), 512.

14. Abraham Lincoln, "Speech at Springfield, Illinois," June 26, 1857, in *The Collected Works of Abraham Lincoln*, ed. Roy P. Basler, 9 vols. (New Brunswick: Rutgers University Press, 1953), 2:405–406.

15. Abraham Lincoln, "Speech at New Haven, Connecticut," March 6, 1860, in ibid., 4:24.

16. Abraham Lincoln to Albert G. Hodges, April 4, 1864, in ibid., 7:281.

17. Abraham Lincoln to Joshua Speed, August 24, 1855, in ibid., 2:323.

18. Abraham Lincoln, "Speech at Peoria, Illinois," October 16, 1854, in ibid., 2:265, 266.

19. Abraham Lincoln, first debate with Stephen A. Douglas, Ottawa, Illinois, August 21, 1858, in ibid., 3:6, 9, 16.

20. Frederick Douglass, "Lincoln and the Colored Troops," in *Reminiscences of Abraham Lincoln by Distinguished Men of His Time*, ed. Allen Thorndike Rice (New York: Harper, 1909), 323.

21. John Brown, statement to the court, in *A John Brown Reader*, ed. Louis Ruchames (London: Abelard-Schuman, 1959), 126–127.

22. John Brown, note of December 2, 1859, in *The Life and Letters of John Brown*, ed. F. B. Sanbourn (Concord, MA: F. B. Sanbourn, 1910), 517.

23. Doris Kearns Goodwin, *Team of Rivals: The Political Genius of Abraham Lincoln* (New York: Simon and Schuster, 2005), 228; Herman Melville, "The Portent," 1866, available online at http://www.melville.org/hmbattle.htm (accessed September 18, 2014); David W. Blight, "'He Knew How to Die': John Brown on the Gallows, December 2, 1859," History News Network, http://historynewsnetwork.org/article/120730 (accessed September 18, 2014).

24. *Charleston (South Carolina) Mercury*, November 8, 1860.

25. Alexander H. Stephens, "Cornerstone Speech," Savannah, Georgia, March 21, 1861, available online at http://www.civilwar.org/education/history/primarysources/alexander-h-cornerstone.html (accessed September 13, 2014).

9. A NATION DIVIDES

1. Abraham Lincoln, First Inaugural Address, March 4, 1861, in *Collected Works of Abraham Lincoln*, 4:271.

2. Quoted in James M. McPherson, *For Cause and Comrades: Why Men Fought in the Civil War* (New York: Oxford University Press, 1997), 106.

3. Abraham Lincoln to Winfield Scott, April 27, 1861, in *Collected Works of Abraham Lincoln*, 4:347.

4. Abraham Lincoln, message to Congress in special session, July 4, 1861, in ibid., 4:420.

5. Clement L. Vallandigham, *The Record of the Hon. C. L. Vallandigham on Abolition, the Union, and the Civil War* (Cincinnati, OH: J. Walter, 1863), 105.

6. For a full discussion of the Arkansas Peace Society see Ted R. Worley, "The Arkansas Peace Society of 1861: A Study in Mountain Unionism," *Journal of Southern History* 24, no. 4 (1958): 445–456; and Ted R. Worley, "Documents Relating to the Arkansas Peace Society of 1861," *Arkansas Historical Quarterly* 17, no. 1 (1958): 82–111.

7. Brown to Stephens, September 1, 1862, in *The Correspondence of Robert Toombs, Alexander H. Stephens, and Howell Cobb,* ed. Ulrich Bonnell Phillips (Washington, DC, 1913), 605.

8. Joseph E. Brown, *Message of His Excellency Joseph E. Brown, to the Extra Session of the Legislature, Convened March 10th, 1864* (Milledgeville, GA: Boughton, Nisbet, Barnes & Moore, 1864), 12, 20.

9. Lincoln to Greeley, August 22, 1862, in *Collected Works of Abraham Lincoln,* 5:388.

10. Abraham Lincoln, "Preliminary Emancipation Proclamation," September 22, 1862, in ibid., 5:434.

11. Quoted in Frederic May Holland, *Frederick Douglass: The Colored Orator* (New York: Funk and Wagnalls, 1891), 301.

12. Quoted in Scott Reynolds Nelson and Carol Sheriff, *A People at War: Civilians and Soldiers in America's Civil War* (New York: Oxford University Press, 2007), 199.

13. Quoted in Thomas Lynch, *Booking Passage: We Irish and Americans* (New York: Norton, 2006), 199.

14. Quoted in John A. Garraty and Mark C. Carnes, *The American Nation: A History of the United States,* 10th ed. (New York: Pearson Education, 1999), 417.

15. Cyrus Pringle, *The Record of a Quaker Conscience: Cyrus Pringle's Diary* (New York: Macmillan, 1918), 26, 77.

16. Ibid., 92.

17. H.I.W., letter to the editor, *Christian Recorder* (Philadelphia), July 23, 1864; J. H. Hall, letter to the editor, *Christian Recorder* (Philadelphia), August 27, 1864.

18. Quoted in Elna C. Green, *This Business of Relief: Confronting Poverty in a Southern City, 1740–1940* (Athens: University of Georgia Press, 2003), 78.

10. LIBERATION AND SUPPRESSION

1. Robert Brown Elliott, "The Civil Rights Bill," in *Masterpieces of Negro Eloquence 1818–1913,* ed. Alice Moore Dunbar (1914; repr., Mineola, NY: Dover, 2000), 43, 54.

2. Frederick Douglass, "What the Black Man Wants," 1865, in *The Life and Writings of Frederick Douglass,* vol. 4, *Reconstruction and After,* ed. Philip S. Foner (New York: International, 1950), 164.

3. Quoted in Eric Foner, *Reconstruction: America's Unfinished Revolution, 1863–1877* (New York: Harper and Row, 1988), 444.

4. "Memorial of the American Equal Rights Association to the Congress of the United States," May 1867, in *History of Woman Suffrage,* vol. 2, *1861–1876,* ed. Elizabeth Cady Stanton, Susan B. Anthony, and Matilda Joslyn Gage (New York: Fowler and Wells, 1882), 226–227n.

5. Elizabeth Cady Stanton, "Address to the National Woman Suffrage Convention," Washington, D.C., January 19, 1869, in *The Concise History of Woman Suffrage: Selections from "History of Woman Suffrage,"* ed. Paul Buhle and Mary Jo Buhle (Urbana: University of Illinois Press, 2005), 254. Also see Elizabeth K. Helsinger, *The Woman Question: Social Issues, 1837–1883* (Manchester: Manchester University Press, 1983), 102.

6. Victoria Claflin Woodhull, *A Speech on The Principles of Social Freedom* (New York: Woodhull, Claflin, 1872), 4, 23.

7. Susan B. Anthony, "Remarks by SBA in the Circuit Court of the United States for the Northern District of New York," June 19, 1873, in *The Selected Papers of Elizabeth Cady Stanton and Susan B. Anthony*, vol. 2, *Against an Aristocracy of Sex, 1866–1873*, ed. Ann D. Gordon (New Brunswick: Rutgers University Press, 2000), 613.

8. Susan B. Anthony, "Is It a Crime for a U.S. Citizen to Vote?," January 16, 1873, in ibid., 556.

9. Jim Crow was a fictional character created in the 1830s by Thomas Rice—a white entertainer who performed songs and skits in blackface in the antebellum minstrel shows that were popular throughout the country. By the time of the Civil War the term *Jim Crow* was a commonly used derogatory term reinforcing the stereotype of blacks as inferior, simpleminded people.

10. See Douglas A. Blackmon, *Slavery by Another Name: The Re-enslavement of Black Americans from the Civil War to World War II* (New York: Random House, 2008), for a detailed account of the intricate procedure through which southern states reenslaved African Americans. African Americans would be arrested for vagrancy, and because they could not pay the fine, they were handed over to a business or corporation to work off the fine. "Under a standing arrangement between the county and a vast subsidiary of the . . . U.S. Steel Corporation—the sheriff turned the young man over to the company for the duration of the sentence. In return the subsidiary . . . paid the county $12 a month" until the fine was paid off. Prisoners were often ensnared in such an arrangement for years (ibid., 1–2).

11. Ida B. Wells-Barnett, *Lynch Law in Georgia: A Six-Weeks' Record in the Center of Southern Civilization, as Faithfully Chronicled by the "Atlanta Journal" and the "Atlanta Constitution"* (Chicago: Chicago Colored Citizens, 1899), 7, 10.

12. Ida B. Wells-Barnett, "Lynch Law in America," 1900, available online at http://www.digitalhistory.uh.edu/disp_textbook.cfm?smtID=3&psid=1113 (accessed September 20, 2014).

13. Booker T. Washington, "Speech to the Atlanta Cotton States and International Exposition," Atlanta, Georgia, October 18, 1895, in *Up from Slavery: An Autobiography* (New York: Doubleday, Page, 1907), 223, 221–222.

14. W. E. B. Du Bois, *The Souls of Black Folk* (1903), ed. Henry Louis Gates, Jr. (New York: Oxford University Press, 2007), 26, 27.

II. PROTEST AND CONFLICT IN THE WEST

1. Chief Joseph, "An Indian's View of Indian Affairs," *North American Review* 128 (April 1879): 431–432.

2. Quoted in James McLaughlin, *My Friend the Indian* (Boston: Houghton Mifflin, 1910), 185.

3. James Mooney, *The Ghost-Dance Religion and the Sioux Outbreak of 1890*, fourteenth annual report of the Bureau of American Ethnology, part 2 (Washington, DC: Government Printing Office, 1896), 885–886.

4. For a full and moving account of the Wounded Knee Massacre see Dee Brown, *Bury My Heart at Wounded Knee* (New York: Bantam, 1970).

5. Quoted in Ronald Takaki, *A Different Mirror: A History of Multicultural America* (Boston: Little, Brown, 1993), 196.

6. Rutherford B. Hayes, diary entry, February 20, 1879, in *The Diary and Letters of Rutherford Birchard Hayes: Nineteenth President of the United States*, ed. Charles Richard Williams, vol. 3 (Columbus: Ohio State Archaeological and Historical Society, 1922), 52.

7. Saum Song Bo, letter, 1885, available online at http://caamedia.org/separatelives brokendreams/statue.html (accessed September 20, 2014).

8. Emmeline Wells, "Is It Ignorance?," *Woman's Exponent*, July 1, 1883.

9. For a penetrating and revealing examination of relations between blacks and poor whites in this period see Glenn Feldman's groundbreaking work, *The Disfranchisement Myth: Poor Whites and Suffrage Restriction in Alabama* (Athens: University of Georgia Press, 2004). Feldman overturns C. Vann Woodward, V. O. Key, and J. Morgan Kousser's long-accepted thesis that poor, hill-country white farmers favored black enfranchisement because they recognized that they had common economic problems and needed to band together to confront the power structure that was keeping them down. Feldman provides abundant evidence that poor southern whites were just as opposed to the enfranchisement of African Americans as were the ruling elites. Even though there were moments when it seemed that the two groups could unite within the Populist movement, that unity never materialized.

10. Mary Elizabeth Lease, "Speech to the Woman's Christian Temperance Union," quoted in Joan M. Jensen, *With These Hands: Women Working on the Land* (Old Westbury, NY: Feminist Press / McGraw-Hill, 1981), 158, 160.

11. "People's Party Platform," *Omaha Morning World-Herald*. July 5, 1892.

12. Ibid.

13. Quoted in Donald Lee Grant, *The Way It Was in the South: The Black Experience in Georgia* (Athens: University of Georgia Press, 1993), 176.

12. WORKERS OF THE WORLD UNITE!

1. William Graham Sumner, "The Concentration of Wealth: Its Economic Justification," *Independent* 54 (April–June 1902).

2. William Graham Sumner, *What Social Classes Owe to Each Other* (1883; repr., New York: Cosimo Classics, 2007), 48.

3. Quoted in Nell Irvin Painter, *Standing at Armageddon: The United States, 1877–1919* (New York: Norton, 1987), 33.

4. Terence V. Powderly, *Thirty Years of Labor, 1859–1889* (Philadelphia, 1890), 236, 136, 129–130.

5. Quoted in Zinn, *People's History*, 278.

6. John Wanamaker's Department Store in Philadelphia even installed one of the grandest pipe organs in the United States, thus (perhaps unconsciously) going along with the "cathedral" motif.

7. Henry George, *Progress and Poverty* (New York, 1879).
8. John Dewey, *My Pedagogic Creed* (New York: Kellogg, 1897), 16; John Dewey, *The School and Society* (Chicago: University of Chicago Press, 1907), 44.

13. THE NEW MANIFEST DESTINY

1. Charles M. Harvey, ed., *History of the Republican Party Together with the Proceedings of the Republican National Convention at St. Louis June 16th–June 18th, 1896* (St. Louis: I. Haas, 1896), 159.
2. Quoted in Paul F. Boller, Jr., *Presidential Campaigns: From George Washington to George W. Bush* (New York: Oxford University Press, 2004), 168.
3. Democratic National Committee, *Campaign Text-Book of the National Democratic Party, 1896* (Chicago, 1896), 11.
4. Quoted in Edward A. Johnson, *History of Negro Soldiers in the Spanish-American War* (Raleigh, NC: Capital, 1899), 37.
5. Quoted in Zinn, *People's History*, 319.
6. Quoted in ibid., 308, 307.
7. Charles Eliot Norton, "True Patriotism," speech delivered at the Men's Club of the Prospect Street Congregational Church in Cambridge, Massachusetts, June 7, 1898.
8. Ibid.
9. Gompers and Carnegie quoted in Mary Beth Norton et al., *A People and a Nation: A History of the United States*, vol. 2, *Since 1865*, 7th ed. (Boston: Houghton Mifflin, 2006), 609, 610; Benjamin R. Tillman, "Causes of Southern Opposition to Imperialism," *North American Review* 171 (1900): 445.
10. Carl Schurz, "The Issue of Imperialism," January 4, 1899, in *Speeches, Correspondence, and Political Papers of Carl Schurz*, vol. 6, *January 1, 1899–April 8, 1906*, ed. Frederic Bancroft (New York: Putnam, 1913), 11, 28, 29.
11. William Jennings Bryan, "Notification Speech," August 8, 1900, in *Life and Speeches of Hon. Wm. Jennings Bryan* (Baltimore: R. H. Woodward, 1900), 394–396.
12. Mark Twain, *The War Prayer* (1923; repr., New York: Harper Colophon, 2001), 5–6. Twain withheld *The War Prayer* from publication fearing the public would find it too sacrilegious. It was originally published posthumously in 1923.
13. Mark Twain, *Mark Twain's Notebook*, comp. Albert Bigelow Paine (New York: Harper, 1935), 395, available online at https://archive.org/stream/MarkTwains Notebook/TXT/00000401.txt (accessed May 10, 2014).
14. *Congressional Record*, 56th Cong., 1st sess., vol. 33, 704–712, available online at http://teachingamericanhistory.org/library/document/in-support-of-an-american -empire/ (accessed October 2, 2014).

14. PROGRESSIVES AND RADICALS

1. Richard Hofstadter, *The Age of Reform: From Bryan to FDR* (New York: Knopf, 1955).
2. Lester Frank Ward, "Mind as a Social Factor," *Mind* 9, no. 36 (1884): 563–573.

3. Jane Addams, *Twenty Years at Hull House* (New York: Macmillan, 1910), 100.

4. Quoted in Herbert Asbury, *Carry Nation* (New York: Knopf, 1929), 87.

5. Sinclair's comment was originally published in *Cosmopolitan* (October 1906), quoted in John Milton Cooper, *Pivotal Decades: The United States, 1900–1920* (New York: Norton, 1990), 86.

6. Mary Harris Jones, "The March of the Mill Children," chap. 10 in *The Autobiography of Mother Jones*, ed. Mary Field Parton (Chicago: Charles H. Kerr, 1925), 71–72.

7. Ibid., 74, 75.

8. Ibid., 76–77, 79, 80.

9. Ibid., 83.

10. Quoted in Neil A. Hamilton, *American Social Leaders and Activists* (New York: Infobase, 2002), 197.

11. Quoted in Chaim M. Rosenberg, *Child Labor in America: A History* (Jefferson, NC: McFarland, 2013), 175.

12. *New York World*, quoted in Zinn, *People's History*, 326.

13. *New York Times*, April 21, 1914, quoted in "Primary Resources: The Ludlow Massacre," American Experience, PBS.org, http://www.pbs.org/wgbh/american experience/features/primary-resources/rockefellers-ludlow/ (accessed August 12, 2014).

14. Jones, *Autobiography of Mother Jones*, 192, 193.

15. "The Socialist Party's Platform," 1912, available online at http://www.laborhistory links.org/PDF%20Files/Socialist%20Party%20Platform%201912.pdf (accessed June 9, 2014).

16. Eugene V. Debs, "Statement to the Court upon Being Convicted of Violating the Sedition Act," September 18, 1918, available online at https://www.marxists.org/archive/debs/works/1918/court.htm (accessed September 21, 2014); Debs, quoted in "Pacifism," Eugene V. Debs Foundation, http://debsfoundation.org/pacifism.html (accessed September 21, 2014).

17. Ralph Darlington, *Syndicalism and the Transition to Communism: An International Comparative Analysis* (Aldershot, UK: Ashgate, 2008), 114; Industrial Workers of the World, "Preamble to the IWW Constitution," http://www.iww.org/culture/official/preamble.shtml (accessed September 21, 2014).

18. Quoted in Michael Miller Topp, *Those without a Country: The Political Culture of Italian American Syndicalists* (Minneapolis: University of Minnesota Press, 2001), 102. The witness was Margaret Sanger.

19. Industrial Workers of the World, *Little Red Songbook*, 19th ed. (Chicago: IWW, 1923), 22–23.

20. Quoted in William M. Adler, *The Man Who Never Died: The Life, Times, and Legacy of Joe Hill, American Labor Icon* (New York: Bloomsbury, 2011), 13.

21. Goldman was suspected of being involved in plotting, with her lover, Alexander Berkman, the assassination of Henry Clay Frick during the Homestead Strike in 1892, and she was arrested and questioned intensively in connection with the assassination of William McKinley by an anarchist in 1901.

22. Emma Goldman, *Anarchism and Other Essays*, 2nd ed. (New York: Mother Earth, 1911), 233, 238.

23. Ibid., 238.

24. Emma Goldman, "Essay in the *Firebrand*, New York, 18 July 1897," in *Emma Goldman: A Documentary History of the American Years*, vol. 1 *Made for America, 1890–1901*, ed. Candace Falk (Berkeley: University of California Press, 2003), 273.

25. Quoted in Cooper, *Pivotal Decades*, 159.

26. Quoted in Bruce Bartlett, *Wrong on Race: The Democratic Party's Buried Past* (New York: Macmillan, 2008), 102.

27. Quoted in Nina Mjagkij, *Loyalty in Time of Trial: The African American Experience during World War I* (Lanham, MD: Rowman and Littlefield, 2011), 21.

15. MAKING THE WORLD SAFE FOR DEMOCRACY

1. Woodrow Wilson, "Address to Congress Advising That Germany's Course Be Declared War against the United States," April 2, 1917, in *The Messages and Papers of Woodrow Wilson*, vol. 1 (New York: Review of Reviews Corporation, 1924), 382, 381.

2. W. E. B. Du Bois, "Close Ranks," *Crisis* 16, no. 3 (1918): 111.

3. Quoted in Foner, *Story of American Freedom*, 178.

4. Sedition Act of 1918, Pub. L. No. 65-150, 40 Stat. 553 (1918).

5. Robert M. La Follette, "The People Do Not Want This War," April 4, 1917, in *We Who Dared to Say No to War: American Antiwar Writing from 1812 to Now*, ed. Murray Polner and Thomas E. Woods, Jr. (New York: Basic Books, 2008), 127, 128–129.

6. Robert M. La Follette, speech to the Senate, *Congressional Record*, 65th Cong., 1st sess., vol. 55, 7878–7888 (October 6, 1917).

7. Theodore Roosevelt, editorial in the *Kansas City Star*, May 7, 1918.

8. Eugene V. Debs, "The Canton, Ohio Speech, Anti-War Speech," June 16, 1918, available online at http://www.marxists.org/archive/debs/works/1918/canton.htm (accessed October 4, 2014).

9. Ibid.

10. Quoted in Ernest Freeberg, *Democracy's Prisoner: Eugene V. Debs, the Great War, and the Right to Dissent* (Cambridge: Harvard University Press, 2008), 99.

11. The full speech is in Scott Nearing, *The Debs Decision*, 2nd ed. (New York: Rand School of Social Science, 1919), 18, 24, 25. Also see Debs, "Address to the Jury (1918)," in *Protest Nation: Words That Inspired a Century of American Radicalism*, ed. Timothy Patrick McCarthy and John Campbell McMillian (New York: New Press, 2010), 30; and Freeberg, *Democracy's Prisoner*, 100.

12. Quoted in Freeberg, *Democracy's Prisoner*, 181.

13. Randolph Bourne, "War and the Intellectuals," *Seven Arts* 2 (June 1917): 136.

14. Randolph Bourne, "The State," in *The Radical Will: Selected Writings, 1911–1918*, ed. Olaf Hansen (New York: Urizen Books, 1977), 359. (The original manuscript is in the Randolph Silliman Bourne Papers, Rare Book & Manuscript Library,

Columbia University Libraries, New York.) The full (unfinished) essay can also be found online at http://struggle.ws/hist_texts/warhealthstate1918.html (accessed September 22, 2014).

15. Ibid., 356.
16. Ibid., 360–361.
17. Ibid., 364.
18. Ibid., 372.
19. Quoted in Ronald Schaffer, *America in the Great War* (New York: Oxford University Press, 1991), 16.
20. Quoted in Bill Kauffman, *Ain't My America: The Long, Noble History of Antiwar Conservatism and Middle-American Anti-Imperialism* (New York: Macmillan, 2008), 74.
21. Richard Halworth Rovere and Gene Brown, *Loyalty and Security in a Democratic State* (New York: Arno, 1979), 21.
22. Quoted in William J. Chambliss, ed., *Police and Law Enforcement* (Los Angeles: Sage, 2011), 161.
23. The American Civil Liberties Union's "Statement of Purpose" is available on the ACLU website: https://www.aclu.org/about-aclu-0 (accessed September 23, 2014).
24. Quoted in Jay Feldman, *Manufacturing Hysteria: A History of Scapegoating, Surveillance, and Secrecy in Modern America* (New York: Anchor Books, 2012), 135.
25. Quoted in Susan Tejada, *In Search of Sacco and Vanzetti: Doubles Lives, Troubled Times, and the Massachusetts Case That Shook the World* (Lebanon, NH: University Press of New England, 2012), 228.

16. TRADITIONALISM COLLIDES WITH MODERNISM

1. Available online at http://www.equalrightsamendment.org/ (accessed September 23, 2014). Congress eventually passed the amendment in 1972, but it was never ratified.
2. Quoted in Vicki Cox, *Margaret Sanger* (New York: Infobase, 2009), 26.
3. Margaret Sanger, *Woman and the New Race* (New York: Brentano's, 1920), 192–193.
4. Ibid., 197, 232.
5. Quoted in Frank Freidel, *Franklin D. Roosevelt: The Ordeal* (Boston: Little, Brown, 1973), 124.
6. Quoted in Matthew C. Price, *The Wilsonian Persuasion in American Foreign Policy* (Youngstown, NY: Cambria, 2007), 252.
7. F. Scott Fitzgerald, *This Side of Paradise* (New York: Scribner, 1920), 304.
8. Mencken, *Mencken Chrestomathy*, 145.
9. Roger Butterfield, "Mr. Mencken Sounds Off," *Life*, August 5, 1946, 52.
10. Quoted in Kirby Goidel, *America's Failing Experiment: How We the People Have Become the Problem* (Lanham, MD: Rowman and Littlefield, 2013), 4.
11. H. L. Mencken, "Last Words," 1926, available online at http://www.etsu.edu/cas/history/documents/menckenlast.htm (accessed September 23, 2014).

12. Marcus Garvey, *The Philosophy and Opinions of Marcus Garvey; or, Africa for the Africans*, comp. Amy Jacques Garvey, vol. 1 (New York: Universal, 1923), 24.

13. Marcus Garvey, "Address to the UNIA Supporters in Philadelphia, October 21, 1919," in *African American Political Thought, 1890–1930: Washington, Du Bois, Garvey, and Randolph*, ed. Cary D. Wintz (Armonk, NY: M. E. Sharpe, 1996), 203.

14. Claude McKay, "If We Must Die," in *Harlem Shadows: The Poems of Claude McKay* (New York: Harcourt, Brace, 1922), available online at http://history matters.gmu.edu/d/5130 (accessed September 23, 2014). Howard Zinn notes that Senator Henry Cabot Lodge was so alarmed at the sentiment expressed in McKay's poem that he had it printed in the *Congressional Record* (*People's History*, 444).

15. Langston Hughes, "The Negro Artist and the Racial Mountain," *Nation*, June 23, 1926.

16. *El Paso Herald*, April 20, 1923, 5.

17. One of the best analyses of the Ku Klux Klan is Glenn Feldman, *Politics, Society, and the Klan in Alabama, 1915–1949* (Tuscaloosa: University of Alabama Press, 1999). Feldman links the Reconstruction-era KKK with the 1920s KKK and beyond to the 1950s Klan in its xenophobia to anything considered "foreign"—racially, ethnically, religiously, *and morally.*

18. Tennessee law of 1925, quoted in William E. Leuchtenburg, *The Perils of Prosperity, 1914–1932* (Chicago: University of Chicago Press, 1958), 220.

19. Quoted in Edward J. Larson, *Summer for the Gods: The Scopes Trial and America's Continuing Debate over Science and Religion* (New York: Basic Books, 2006), 71.

20. Quoted in ibid., 39, 27.

21. Quoted in Diana Klebanow and Franklin L. Jonas, *People's Lawyers: Crusaders for Justice in American History* (Armonk, NY: M. E. Sharpe, 2003), 129.

17. A NEW DEAL FOR AMERICA

1. Quoted in Terry H. Anderson, *The Pursuit of Fairness: A History of Affirmative Action* (New York: Oxford University Press, 2004), 10.

2. Quoted in Jean Edward Smith, *FDR* (New York: Random House, 2007), 284.

3. Quoted in ibid., 276, 277.

4. Elizabeth Kirkpatrick Dilling, *The Red Network: A "Who's Who" and Handbook of Radicalism for Patriots* (Chicago: Elizabeth Dilling, 1934), 74, 75.

5. Franklin D. Roosevelt to Felix Frankfurter, February 9, 1937, in *Roosevelt and Frankfurter: Their Correspondence, 1928–1945*, ed. Max Freedman (Boston: Little, Brown, 1968), 382.

6. *Congressional Record*, 73rd Cong., 2nd sess., February 5, 1934.

7. Quoted in David M. Kennedy, *Freedom from Fear: The American People in Depression and War, 1929–1945* (New York: Oxford University Press, 1999), 278.

8. Quoted in Alan Brinkley, *Voices of Protest: Huey Long, Father Coughlin, and the Great Depression* (New York: Knopf, 1982), 108.

9. Charles E. Coughlin, "Address on the National Union for Social Justice," November 11, 1934, in *A Series of Lectures on Social Justice* (Royal Oak, MI: Radio League of

the Little Flower, 1935), available online at http://web.mit.edu/21h.102/www/
Primary%20source%20collections/The%20New%20Deal/Coughlin,%20Address%
20on%20the%20Ntl%20Union%20for%20Social%20Justice.htm (accessed September 23, 2014).

10. Charles E. Coughlin, "National Radio Address," June 19, 1936, in ibid., available online at http://www.austincc.edu/lpatrick/his2341/rooseveltandruin.htm (accessed September 23, 2014).

11. Quoted in Conrad Black, *Franklin Delano Roosevelt: Champion of Freedom* (New York: PublicAffairs, 2005), 386.

12. Emma Goldman, "The Individual, Society, and the State," in *Red Emma Speaks: Selected Writings and Speeches*, ed. Alix Kates Shulman (New York: Random House, 1972), 100.

13. Quoted in Leon A. Harris, *Upton Sinclair, American Rebel* (New York: Crowell, 1975), 351.

14. Quoted in Black, *Franklin Delano Roosevelt*, 331.

15. Quoted in ibid., 329.

16. Quoted in Kennedy, *Freedom from Fear*, 220.

17. Quoted in ibid.

18. Quoted in ibid., 222.

19. Brinkley, *Voices of Protest*, 160–161.

20. Woody Guthrie, *Pastures of Plenty: A Self Portrait*, ed. Dave Marsh and Harold Leventhal (New York: HarperCollins, 1990), 10. Also see Ronald D. Cohen, *Woody Guthrie: Writing America's Songs* (New York: Routledge, 2012), 25.

21. Quoted in Kennedy, *Freedom from Fear*, 433.

22. Charles A. Lindbergh, *Address by Charles Lindbergh: Delivered at an America First Committee Meeting in New York City on April 23, 1941* (New York: America First Committee, 1941), available online at http://www.pbs.org/wgbh/amex/lindbergh/filmmore/reference/primary/firstcommittee.html (accessed October 4, 2014).

18. THE GOOD WAR?

1. Lloyd Brown, quoted in Leon F. Litwack, *How Free Is Free? The Long Death of Jim Crow* (Cambridge: Harvard University Press, 2009), 75.

2. Quoted in Ethan Fishman, "The Prudential FDR," in *FDR and the Modern Presidency: Leadership and Legacy*, ed. Mark J. Rozell and William D. Pederson (New York: Greenwood, 1997), 157.

3. Charles F. Wilson to President Franklin Delano Roosevelt, May 9, 1944, in *Taps for a Jim Crow Army: Letters from Black Soldiers in World War II*, ed. Phillip McGuire (Santa Barbara, CA: ABC-CLIO, 1983), 134, 135, 137.

4. Quoted in H. W. Brands, *Traitor to His Class: The Privileged Life and Radical Presidency of Franklin Delano Roosevelt* (New York: Doubleday, 2008), 657.

5. Quoted in Shirley Castelnuovo, *Soldiers of Conscience: Japanese American Military Resisters in World War II* (Westport, CT: Greenwood, 2008), 13.

6. Minoru Yasui, response to Executive Order 9066, available online at http://www.hrcr.org/ccr/yasui.html (accessed September 24, 2014).

7. Minoru Yasui to Yuka Yasui, November 30, 1942, in Yuka Yasui Fujikura's private collection; used by permission.

8. Steve Cary, World War II conscientious objector, quoted in "In the Camps," *The Good War and Those Who Refused to Fight It*, PBS.org, http://www.pbs.org/itvs/thegoodwar/camps.html (accessed September 24, 2014).

9. David Dellinger, "Why I Refused to Register in the October 1940 Draft and a Little of What It Led To," in *A Few Small Candles: War Resisters of World War II Tell Their Stories*, ed. Larry Gara and Lenna Mae Gara (Kent, OH: Kent State University Press, 1999), 27.

10. Ibid., 32, 34.

11. Larry Gara, "My War on War," in ibid., 87, 95, 97.

12. Henry Miller, *Murder the Murderer* (1944), in *Remember to Remember* (New York: New Directions, 1947), 164–165, 168, 167.

13. Ibid., 133, 134.

19. DISSENT IN AN AGE OF CONFORMITY

1. Winston Churchill, speech at Westminster College, Fulton, Missouri, March 5, 1946, available online at http://www.fordham.edu/halsall/mod/churchill-iron.asp (accessed September 25, 2014).

2. The high-profile Rosenberg espionage case, combined with the House Committee on Un-American Activities and McCarthy hearings, created a tremendous outpouring of paranoia in the country. And as paranoia increased, it had a hampering effect on dissent because liberals and other left-of-center commentators were afraid to express legitimate criticism of American foreign policy for fear of being labeled unpatriotic "pinkoes" or denounced as communists. The fear of being ostracized and blacklisted inhibited healthy, robust political debate and dissenting opinions. Well into the next decade everyone was, or at least proclaimed they were, vehemently anticommunist.

3. U.S. Congress, House, Committee on Un-American Activities, *Hearings Regarding the Communist Infiltration of the Motion Picture Industry*, 80th Cong., 1st sess., October 29, 1947.

4. John Howard Lawson, "A Statement by John Howard Lawson," in *Thirty Years of Treason: Excerpts from Hearings before the House Committee on Un-American Activities, 1938–1968*, ed. Eric Bentley (New York: Viking, 1971), 161–165.

5. U.S. Congress, House, Committee on Un-American Activities, *Investigation of Communist Activities, New York Area (Entertainment): Hearings*, 84th Cong., 1st sess., August 18, 1955.

6. U.S. Congress, House, Committee on Un-American Activities, *Investigation of the Unauthorized Use of U.S. Passports*, 84th Cong., 2nd sess., June 12, 1956.

7. Quoted in Anne Edwards, *Katharine Hepburn: A Remarkable Woman* (New York: Macmillan, 2000), 345.

8. Margaret Chase Smith, "Declaration of Conscience" and "Statement of Seven Senators," *Congressional Record*, 82nd Cong., 1st sess., June 1, 1950.

9. John Keats, *The Crack in the Picture Window* (Boston: Houghton Mifflin, 1957).

10. Quoted in Bill Morgan, *I Celebrate Myself: The Somewhat Private Life of Allen Ginsberg* (New York: Viking, 2006), 209.

11. Allen Ginsberg, *Howl and Other Poems* (San Francisco: City Lights Books, 1956), 9, 12, 17.

12. Ibid., 32, 31.

13. Allen Ginsberg, interviewed in the documentary film *The Source: The Story of the Beats and the Beat Generation*, dir. Chuck Workman (Beat/Calliope, 1999).

14. Jack Kerouac, *On the Road* (New York: Viking, 1957), 5–6.

15. Harry S. Truman, "Special Message to the Congress on Civil Rights," February 2, 1948, in *Public Papers of the Presidents of the United States, Harry S. Truman, 1948*, vol. 4 (Washington, DC: U.S. Government Printing Office, 1963), 122.

16. Brown v. Board of Education, 347 U.S. 483, 494, 495 (May 17, 1954).

20. CIVIL RIGHTS: AN AMERICAN REVOLUTION

1. "*Le Peuple*, the daily Belgian Socialist newspaper, calls the acquittal 'a judicial scandal in the United States.' *Le Drapeau Rouge* (the Red Flag) publishes: 'Killing a black person isn't a crime in the home of the Yankees: The white killers of young Emmett Till are acquitted!' In France, *L'Aurore* newspaper publishes: 'The Scandalous Acquittal in Sumner' and the daily newspaper *Le Figaro* adds: 'The Shame of the Sumner Jury.' . . . The French daily newspaper *Le Monde* runs an article: 'The Sumner Trial Marks, Perhaps, an Opening of Consciousness.' . . . In Germany, the newspaper *Freies Volk* publishes: 'The Life of a Negro Isn't Worth a Whistle.'" American Experience documentary *The Murder of Emmett Till*, PBS, available online at http://www.pbs.org/wgbh/amex/till/timeline/timeline2.html (accessed September 25, 2014).

2. Martin Luther King, Jr., "MIA Mass Meeting at Holt Street Baptist Church," speech in Montgomery, Alabama, December 5, 1955, in *The Papers of Martin Luther King, Jr.: Birth of a New Age, December 1955–December 1956*, ed. Clayborne Carson (Berkeley: University of California Press, 1997), 73.

3. Quoted in Lynne Olson, *Freedom's Daughters: The Unsung Heroines of the Civil Rights Movement from 1830 to 1970* (New York: Simon and Schuster, 2001), 184.

4. Martin Luther King, Jr., "Acceptance Address for the Nobel Peace Prize," in *A Call to Conscience: The Landmark Speeches of Dr. Martin Luther King, Jr.*, ed. Clayborne Carson (New York: Grand Central, 2001), 105.

5. "White Ministers' Good Friday Statement, April 12, 1963," in *Blessed Are the Peacemakers: Martin Luther King, Jr., Eight White Religious Leaders, and the "Letter from Birmingham Jail,"* by S. Jonathan Bass (Baton Rouge: Louisiana State University Press, 2001), 235.

6. King, "Letter from Birmingham Jail," 80–82, 86–87.

7. Ibid., 82, 77, 88, 86, 87.

8. John F. Kennedy, "Address on Civil Rights," June 11, 1963, available online at http://millercenter.org/president/speeches/detail/3375 (accessed May 14, 2014).

9. Martin Luther King, Jr., "I Have a Dream," in *A Testament of Hope: The Essential Writings and Speeches of Martin Luther King, Jr.*, ed. James M. Washington (San Francisco: HarperCollins, 1991), 219.

10. Malcolm X, "Message to the Grass Roots," November 10, 1963, in *Malcolm X Speaks: Selected Speeches and Statements*, ed. George Breitman (New York: Grove, 1965), 16.

11. Malcolm X, "Speech on 'Black Revolution,'" April 8, 1964, in *Two Speeches by Malcolm X* (New York: Merit, 1965), 5, 14.

12. Quoted in Robert A. Caro, *The Passage of Power: The Years of Lyndon Johnson* (New York: Knopf, 2012), 430.

13. Pub. L. 88-352, 78 Stat. 241, enacted July 2, 1964.

14. Fannie Lou Hamer, "Testimony before the Credentials Committee at the Democratic National Convention, Atlantic City, New Jersey, August 22, 1964," in *The Speeches of Fannie Lou Hamer: To Tell It Like It Is*, ed. Maegan Parker Brooks and Davis W. Houck (Jackson: University Press of Mississippi, 2011), 45.

15. Quoted in Robert Cohen, *Freedom's Orator: Mario Savio and the Radical Legacy of the 1960s* (New York: Oxford University Press, 2009), 327.

16. Quoted in Barbara Harris Combs, *From Selma to Montgomery and Freedom: The Long March to Freedom* (New York: Routledge, 2014), 43.

17. Lyndon B. Johnson, "Special Message to the Congress: The American Promise," March 15, 1965, in *Public Papers of the Presidents of the United States, Lyndon B. Johnson, 1965*, no. 1 (Washington, DC: U.S. Government Printing Office, 1965), 281–287; also available online at the LBJ Presidential Library, http://www.lbjlib .utexas.edu/johnson/archives.hom/speeches.hom/650315.asp (accessed September 25, 2014).

18. Petition to Alabama Governor George C. Wallace by Selma-to-Montgomery Marchers, March 25, 1965, available online at http://www.fofweb.com/History/ MainPrintPage.asp?iPin=afdCR11&DataType=AFHC&WinType=Free (accessed September 25, 2014).

19. Martin Luther King, Jr., "Address at the Conclusion of the Selma to Montgomery March," March 25, 1965, text and audio available online at http://mlk-kpp01 .stanford.edu/index.php/encyclopedia/documentsentry/doc_address_at_the_ conclusion_of_selma_march/ (accessed September 25, 2014).

20. Stokely Carmichael, "Berkeley Speech," in *Contemporary American Voices: Significant Speeches in American History, 1945–Present*, ed. James R. Andrews and David Zarefsky (White Plains, NY: Longman, 1992), 106.

21. The Kerner Report, available online at http://www.archive.org/stream/kernerre-portreviooasse/kernerreportreviooasse_djvu.txt (accessed October 4, 2014).

21. MAKE LOVE, NOT WAR

1. Carl Oglesby, "Let Us Shape the Future," November 27, 1965, available online at the Students for a Democratic Society Document Library, http://www.antiauthoritarian .net/sds_wuo/sds_documents/oglesby_future.html (accessed May 15, 2014).

2. Ibid.

3. Ibid.

4. The Catholic peace movement was a bloc of dedicated Catholic pacifists influenced by Pope John XXIII's encyclical *Pacem in Terris*, in which he urged Catholics to work for world peace, as well as by the teachings of the pacifist social activists Dorothy Day (founder of the Catholic Worker Movement) and Trappist monk Thomas Merton.

5. Bob Dylan, "Blowin' in the Wind," *The Freewheelin' Bob Dylan*, Columbia Records, 1963.

6. Bob Dylan, "Masters of War," ibid.

7. The Beatles, "Nowhere Man," *Rubber Soul*, Parlophone, 1965; The Doors, "Light My Fire," *The Doors*, Elektra, 1967; The Mothers of Invention, "Plastic People," *Absolutely Free*, Verve, 1967; Jefferson Airplane, "White Rabbit," *Surrealistic Pillow*, RCA Victor, 1967; Edwin Starr, "War," single, Gordy, 1970.

8. The impact of these artists' antiwar, antimainstream message cannot be overstated. Who can forget Jimi Hendrix's mesmerizing and ferocious version of the national anthem at Woodstock? Or the Rolling Stones singing about "Street Fighting Man" or "Sympathy for the Devil"? Or the MC5 screaming "kick out the jams motherfuckers!"? Or Janis Joplin's version of Kris Kristofferson's cautionary observation that "freedom's just another word for nothing left to lose"?

9. Quoted in Peter Stafford, *Psychedelics* (Oakland, CA: Ronin, 2003), 63.

10. Lenny Bruce on *The Steve Allen Show*, April 9, 1959; the full performance is available online at http://www.youtube.com/watch?v=0CplnUgaohU (accessed September 26, 2014).

11. Quoted in "Sister Corita Kent Biography," Corita Art Center, https://www.corita .org/component/content/article/5-sister-corita-kent-biography.html (accessed September 26, 2014).

12. Martin Luther King, Jr., "Beyond Vietnam: A Time to Break the Silence," speech at Riverside Church, New York, April 4, 1967, available online at http://www.digital history.uh.edu/disp_textbook.cfm?smtid=3&psid=3621 (accessed May 15, 2014).

13. Quoted in Arthur M. Schlesinger, Jr., *Robert Kennedy and His Times* (Boston: Houghton Mifflin, 1978), 773, 824.

14. Quoted in G. Calvin Mackenzie and Robert Weisbrot, *The Liberal Hour: Washington and the Politic of Change in the 1960s* (New York: Penguin, 2008), 343–344.

15. Robert Buzzanco, *Masters of War: Military Dissent and Politics in the Vietnam Era* (Cambridge: Cambridge University Press, 1996), 311. Westmoreland may have not actually used the exact words "light at the end of the tunnel," but antiwar critics frequently quoted him as saying it and then appended some version of the onrushing train or locomotive metaphor.

16. *Guardian*, October 18, 1969, quoted in Jeremy Varon, *Bringing the War Home: The Weather Underground, the Red Army Faction, and Revolutionary Violence in the Sixties and Seventies* (Berkeley: University of California Press, 2004), 84.

17. Bill Ayers, interview in the film *The Weather Underground*, dir. Sam Green and Bill Siegel (Free History Project, 2002), quoted in Beth Massey, "Bill Ayers and the

Weather Underground," PSLweb.org, October 31, 2008, http://www2.pslweb.org/site/News2?page=NewsArticle&id=10290.

18. I took part in the London demonstration. It was a very moving vigil. Thousands of us marched around Grosvenor Square, and as each person passed in front of the U.S. embassy, we were handed a card with the name of a U.S. soldier killed in Vietnam. We stepped up to a microphone, read the soldier's name, and then placed the card in a coffin on the embassy steps. I was there for more than eight hours, and it was still going on when I left.

19. The burglars came forward more than forty years later. See Betty Medsger, *The Burglary: The Discovery of J. Edgar Hoover's Secret FBI* (New York: Knopf, 2014).

20. U.S. Congress, Senate, Committee on Foreign Relations, "Legislative Proposals Relating to the War in Southeast Asia," *Hearings before the Committee on Foreign Relations*, 92nd Cong., 1st sess., April–May 1971 (Washington, DC: Government Printing Office, 1971), 180, 181, 182.

22. MOBILIZATION AND BACKLASH

1. Betty Friedan, *The Feminine Mystique* (1963; repr., New York: Dell, 1970), 11.

2. National Organization for Women, "Statement of Purpose," 1966, http://www.now.org/about/history/statement-of-purpose/ (accessed October 5, 2014).

3. Redstockings, "Manifesto," 1969, in *Dear Sisters: Dispatches from the Women's Liberation Movement*, ed. Rosalyn Baxandall and Linda Gordon (New York: Basic Books, 2000), 90.

4. Gloria Steinem, "'Women's Liberation' Aims to Free Men, Too," *Washington Post*, June 7, 1970.

5. Roe v. Wade, 410 U.S. 113, 153 (January 22, 1973).

6. Quoted in Don Teal, *The Gay Militants* (New York: St. Martin's, 1971), 24, 25.

7. Quoted in ibid., 36, 37.

8. Indians Of All Tribes, "We Hold the Rock!," in *Alcatraz: Indian Land Forever*, ed. Troy R. Johnson (Los Angeles: UCLA American Indian Studies Center, 1995), 11.

9. The complete list of their twenty demands is available online at https://faculty.utep.edu/LinkClick.aspx?link=20+Points.pdf&tabid=31574&mid=166322 (accessed September 27, 2014).

10. Quoted in "Pat Robertson Thinks the GOP Base Is Too Extreme? Hehehehe," *Daily Kos* (blog), October 24, 2011, http://www.dailykos.com/story/2011/10/24/1029543/-Pat-Robertson-Thinks-The-GOP-Base-Is-Too-Extreme-Hehehehe.

11. Among them are Manning Marable, *Race, Reform, and Rebellion: The Second Reconstruction in Black America* (Jackson: University Press of Mississippi, 1991); Mary Louise Frampton, Ian F. Haney López, and Jonathan Simon, eds., *After the War on Crime: Race, Democracy, and a New Reconstruction* (New York: NYU Press, 2008); David Garland, *The Culture of Control: Crime and Social Order in Contemporary Society* (Chicago: University of Chicago Press, 2002); Bruce Western, *Punishment and Inequality in America* (New York: Russell Sage Foundation, 2007); Todd Clear, *Imprisoning Communities: How Mass Incarceration Makes Disadvantaged Neighborhoods Worse* (New York: Oxford University Press, 2009);

and Heather Ann Thompson, "Why Mass Incarceration Matters: Rethinking Crisis, Decline, and Transformation in Postwar American History," *Journal of American History* 97, no. 3 (December 2010): 703–734.

23. A NEW AGE OF DISSENT

1. Edward Abbey, *Desert Solitaire: A Season in the Wilderness* (New York: McGraw-Hill, 1968), 52.

2. Ted Kaczynski, "Interview with Ted Kaczynski" (interview with the *Earth First! Journal*, Administrative Maximum Facility Prison, Florence, Colorado, USA, June 1999), available online at http://www.primitivism.com/kaczynski.htm (accessed May 15, 2014).

3. Ted Kaczynski, "Industrial Society and Its Future," available online at "The Unabomber Trial: The Manifesto," *Washington Post*, September 22, 1995, http://www.washingtonpost.com/wp-srv/national/longterm/unabomber/manifesto.text.htm (accessed May 15, 2014).

4. Carl Rosebraugh, "Written Testimony Submitted on February 7, 2002 to the U.S. House Subcommittee on Forests and Forest Health for the February 12, 2002, Hearing on 'Ecoterrorism,'" in *The Earth Liberation Front, 1997–2002*, by Leslie James Pickering (Oakland, CA: PM, 2007), 134, 135, 142.

5. Michigan Militia, "Statement of Purpose," http://www.michiganmilitia.com/literature/in_defense_of_liberty.htm (accessed May 15, 2014).

6. U.S. Congress, House, Committee on Education and Labor, *Employment Discrimination against Gay Men and Lesbians*, 103rd Cong., 2nd sess., June 20, 1994 (Washington, DC: U.S. Government Printing Office, 1994).

7. Ralph Nader, "It's Time to End Corporate Welfare as We Know It," 1996, in *The Ralph Nader Reader* (New York: Seven Stories, 2000), 154, 158.

8. Ani Di Franco, "self evident," 2001, available on her website, http://www.righteousbabe.com/pages/so-much-shouting-so-much-laughter (accessed October 7, 2014).

9. Amnesty International, "Amnesty International's Concerns Regarding Post September 11 Detentions in the USA," March 14, 2002, http://www.amnesty.org/en/library/asset/AMR51/044/2002/en/154256a9-d882-11dd-ad8c-f3d4445c118e/amr510442002en.pdf.

10. ACLU, "Freedom under Fire: Dissent in Post-9/11 America," May 8, 2013, https://www.aclu.org/national-security/freedom-under-fire-dissent-post-911-america.

11. The original CNN interview with Wolf Blitzer on September 8, 2002, is available online at http://transcripts.cnn.com/TRANSCRIPTS/0209/08/le.00.html (accessed September 28, 2014).

12. Not in Our Name, "Statement of Conscience," 2003, in *Dissent in America: The Voices That Shaped a Nation*, ed. Ralph Young (New York: Pearson Longman, 2006), 753, 754. (The website where the statement was posted during the lead-up to and duration of the Iraq War has been taken down.)

13. "Call to Conscience from Veterans to Active Duty Troops and Reservists," December 6, 2002, available online at http://www.vvawai.org/CtC/vcc-poster-tall.pdf (accessed September 28, 2014).

14. Wiggins, "Message to the Troops: Resist!"
15. Immortal Technique, "The 4th Branch," *Revolutionary, Vol. 2* (Viper Records, 2003).
16. Steve Earle, "Rich Man's War," *The Revolution Starts Now* (Artemis Records, 2004).
17. "Declaration of the Occupation of New York City," September 29, 2011, available at the NYC General Assembly website, http://www.nycga.net/resources/documents/declaration/ (accessed May 17, 2014).

BIBLIOGRAPHY

Abbey, Edward. *Desert Solitaire: A Season in the Wilderness*. New York: McGraw-Hill, 1968.

———. *The Monkey Wrench Gang*. Philadelphia: Lippincott, 1975.

Adams, John, and Abigail Adams. *Adams Family Correspondence*. Edited by L. H. Butterfield. 9 vols. Cambridge: Harvard University Press, 1963.

Adams, Samuel. "The Rights of the Colonists as Men, as Christians, and as Subjects." November 20, 1772. In *The Writings of Samuel Adams*, vol. 2, *1770–1773*, edited by Harry Alonzo Cushing, 350–359. New York: Putnam, 1906.

Addams, Jane. *Twenty Years at Hull-House*. New York: Macmillan, 1910.

Adler, William M. *The Man Who Never Died: The Life, Times, and Legacy of Joe Hill, American Labor Icon*. New York: Bloomsbury, 2011.

"Alien and Sedition Acts." *The Founder's Blog*, June 22, 2012. http://williamdbailey
.wordpress.com/tag/5th-united-states-congress/.

Almaguer, Tomás. *Racial Fault Lines: The Historical Origins of White Supremacy in California*. Berkeley: University of California Press, 1994.

Alperowitz, Gar. *Atomic Diplomacy: Hiroshima and Potsdam*. New York: Vintage, 1967.

American Civil Liberties Union. "Freedom under Fire: Dissent in Post-9/11 America." May 8, 2013. https://www.aclu.org/national-security/freedom-under-fire-dissent
-post-911-america.

———. "Statement of Purpose." https://www.aclu.org/about-aclu-0 (accessed September 23, 2014).

Amnesty International. "Amnesty International's Concerns Regarding Post September 11 Detentions in the USA." March 14, 2002. http://www.amnesty.org/en/
library/asset/AMR51/044/2002/en/154256a9-d882-11dd-ad8c-f3d4445c118e/
amr510442002en.pdf.

Anderson, Bonnie S. *Joyous Greetings: The First International Women's Movement, 1830–1860*. New York: Oxford University Press, 2000.

Anderson, Robert, ed. *Voices from Wounded Knee, 1973*. Mohawk Nation, Rooseveltown, NY: Akwesasne Notes, 1974.

Anderson, Terry H. *The Movement and the Sixties*. New York: Oxford University Press, 1995.

———. *The Pursuit of Fairness: A History of Affirmative Action*. New York: Oxford University Press, 2004.

———. *The Sixties*. New York: Longman, 1999.

Anthony, Susan B. *An Account of the Proceedings on the Trial of Susan B. Anthony, on the Charge of Illegal Voting*. Rochester, NY: Daily Democrat and Chronicle, 1874.

Anthony, Susan B. "Is It a Crime for a U.S. Citizen to Vote?," January 16, 1873. In *The Selected Papers of Elizabeth Cady Stanton and Susan B. Anthony*, vol. 2, *Against an Aristocracy of Sex, 1866–1873*, edited by Ann D. Gordon, 554–583. New Brunswick: Rutgers University Press, 2000.

———. "Remarks by SBA in the Circuit Court of the United States for the Northern District of New York." June 19, 1873. In *The Selected Papers of Elizabeth Cady Stanton and Susan B. Anthony*, vol. 2, *Against an Aristocracy of Sex, 1866–1873*, edited by Ann D. Gordon, 612–615. New Brunswick: Rutgers University Press, 2000.

Apess, William. "An Indian's Looking-Glass for the White Man." In *On Our Own Ground: The Complete Writings of William Apess, a Pequot*, edited by Barry O'Connell, 155–161. Amherst: University of Massachusetts Press, 1992.

Aptheker, Herbert. *American Negro Slave Revolts*. New York: International, 1969.

———, ed. *A Documentary History of the Negro People in the United States*. Vol. 1, *From Colonial Times through the Civil War*. Secaucus, NJ: Citadel, 1973.

Arnold, James R. *The Moro War: How America Battled a Muslim Insurgency in the Philippine Jungle, 1902–1913*. New York: Bloomsbury, 2011.

Arsenault, Raymond. *Freedom Riders: 1961 and the Struggle for Racial Justice*. New York: Oxford University Press, 2006.

Asbury, Herbert. *Carry Nation*. New York: Knopf, 1929.

Ash, Stephen V., ed. *Secessionists and Other Scoundrels: Selections from Parson Brownlow's Book*. Baton Rouge: Louisiana State University Press, 1999.

Atiwaneto. "Propositions of the Abenakis of St. Francis to Captain Phineas Stevens, Delegate from the Governor of Boston, in Presence of the Baron De Longueuil, Governor of Montreal, Commandant of Canada and of the Iroquois of the Sault Saint Louis and of the Lake of the Two Mountains." July 5, 1752. In *Documents Relative to the Colonial History of the State of New York*, edited by E. B. O'Callaghan, vol. 10, 252–254. Albany, NY: Weed, Parsons, 1887.

Avrich, Paul. *The Haymarket Tragedy*. Princeton: Princeton University Press, 1984.

Axtell, James. *The Invasion Within: The Contest of Cultures in North America*. New York: Oxford University Press, 1985.

Bailey, Beth. *Sex in the Heartland*. Cambridge: Harvard University Press, 2002.

Baillie, Robert. *A Dissuasive from the Errours of the Time*. London, 1645.

Bailyn, Bernard. *Ideological Origins of the American Revolution*. Cambridge: Belknap Press of Harvard University Press, 1965.

———. *The Ordeal of Thomas Hutchinson*. Cambridge: Belknap Press of Harvard University Press, 1974.

Barber, Benjamin R. *Jihad vs. McWorld: How the Planet Is Both Falling Apart and Coming Together and What This Means for Democracy*. New York: Ballantine Books, 2001.

Barry, John M. *Roger Williams and the Creation of the American Soul: Church, State, and the Birth of Liberty*. New York: Viking, 2012.

Bartlett, Bruce. *Wrong on Race: The Democratic Party's Buried Past*. New York: Macmillan, 2008.

Barton, Josef. *Peasants and Strangers: Italians, Rumanians, and Slovaks in an American City, 1890–1950*. Cambridge: Harvard University Press, 1975.

Bass, S. Jonathan. *Blessed Are the Peacemakers: Martin Luther King, Jr., Eight White Religious Leaders, and the "Letter from Birmingham Jail."* Baton Rouge: Louisiana State University Press, 2001.

Beale, Howard K. *Theodore Roosevelt and the Rise of America to World Power*. New York: Macmillan, 1962.

Beard, Charles A. *An Economic Interpretation of the Constitution of the United States*. New York: Macmillan, 1941.

Beatles, The. *Rubber Soul*. Parlophone, 1965.

Bederman, Gail. *Manliness and Civilization: A Cultural History of Gender and Race in the United States, 1880–1917*. Chicago: University of Chicago Press, 1995.

Beeman, Richard. *Plain, Honest Men*. New York: Random House, 2009.

Bellamy, Edward. *Looking Backward: 2000–1887*. Boston: Ticknor, 1888.

Benezet, Anthony. *A Short Account of That Part of Africa Inhabited by Negroes, with General Observations on the Slave Trade and Slavery*. 1762. In *The Complete Antislavery Writings of Anthony Benezet, 1754–1783*, edited by David L. Crosby, 25–83. Baton Rouge: Louisiana State University Press, 2014.

———. *Some Historical Account of Guinea*. 1771. In *The Complete Antislavery Writings of Anthony Benezet, 1754–1783*, edited by David L. Crosby, 112–196. Baton Rouge: Louisiana State University Press, 2014.

Berkin, Carol. *A Brilliant Solution: Inventing the American Constitution*. New York: Harcourt, 2002.

Berman, William C. *America's Right Turn: From Nixon to Bush*. Baltimore: Johns Hopkins University Press, 1994.

Bernstein, Iver. *The New York City Draft Riots: Their Significance in American Society and Politics in the Age of the Civil War*. New York: Oxford University Press, 1990.

Black, Conrad. *Franklin Delano Roosevelt: Champion of Freedom*. New York: Public Affairs, 2005.

Blackmon, Douglas A. *Slavery by Another Name: The Re-enslavement of Black Americans from the Civil War to World War II*. New York: Random House, 2008.

Blassingame, John W. *The Slave Community: Plantation Life in the Antebellum South*. New York: Oxford University Press, 1979.

———, ed. *Slave Testimony: Two Centuries of Letters, Speeches, Interviews, and Autobiographies*. Baton Rouge: Louisiana State University Press, 1977.

Blewett, Mary H. *Men, Women, and Work: Class, Gender, and Protest in the New England Shoe Industry, 1780–1910*. Urbana: University of Illinois Press, 1988.

Blight, David W. "'He Knew How to Die': John Brown on the Gallows, December 2, 1859." History News Network. http://historynewsnetwork.org/article/120730 (accessed September 18, 2014).

Blum, John Morton. *Woodrow Wilson and the Politics of Morality*. Boston: Little, Brown, 1956.

Bodnar, John. *The Transplanted: A History of Immigrants in Urban America*. Bloomington: Indiana University Press, 1985.

Boller, Paul F., Jr. *Presidential Campaigns: From George Washington to George W. Bush.* New York: Oxford University Press, 2004.

Borstelmann, Thomas. *The Cold War and the Color Line: American Race Relations in the Global Arena.* Cambridge: Cambridge University Press, 2001.

Bourne, Randolph. "The State." In *The Radical Will: Selected Writings, 1911–1918,* edited by Olaf Hansen, 355–395. New York: Urizen Books, 1977.

———. "War and the Intellectuals." *Seven Arts* 2 (June 1917): 133–146.

Bouvier, Virginia Marie. *Women and the Conquest of California, 1542–1840: Codes of Silence.* Tucson: University of Arizona Press, 2001.

Bowie, Robert R., and Richard H. Immerman, *Waging Peace: How Eisenhower Shaped an Enduring Cold War Strategy.* New York: Oxford University Press, 1998.

Boyle, Kevin. *Arc of Justice: A Saga of Race, Civil Rights, and Murder in the Jazz Age.* New York: Holt, 2004.

Branch, Taylor. *At Canaan's Edge: America in the King Years, 1965–68.* New York: Simon and Schuster, 2006.

———. *Parting the Waters: America in the King Years, 1954–63.* New York: Simon and Schuster, 1988.

———. *Pillar of Fire: America in the King Years, 1963–65.* New York: Simon and Schuster, 1998.

Brands, H. W. *The First American: Life and Times of Benjamin Franklin.* New York: Random House, 2000.

———. *Traitor to His Class: The Privileged Life and Radical Presidency of Franklin Delano Roosevelt.* New York: Doubleday, 2008.

Breen, T. H. *The Character of the Good Ruler: Puritan Political Ideas in New England, 1630–1730.* New York: Norton, 1974.

Bremer, Francis J. *Congregational Communion: Clerical Friendship in the Anglo-American Puritan Community, 1610–1692.* Boston: Northeastern University Press, 1994.

———. *The Puritan Experiment: New England Society from Bradford to Edwards.* Hanover, NH: University Press of New England, 1995.

Brewer, Susan A. *Why America Fights: Patriotism and War Propaganda from the Philippines to Iraq.* New York: Oxford University Press, 2009.

Brinkley, Alan. *The End of Reform: New Deal Liberalism in Recession and War.* New York: Knopf, 1995.

———. *Voices of Protest: Huey Long, Father Coughlin, and the Great Depression.* New York: Knopf, 1982.

Brown, Dee. *Bury My Heart at Wounded Knee.* New York: Bantam, 1970.

Brown, John. *A John Brown Reader.* Edited by Louis Ruchames. London: Abelard-Schuman, 1959.

———. *The Life and Letters of John Brown.* Edited by F. B. Sanbourn. Concord, MA: F. B. Sanbourn, 1910.

Brown, Joseph E. *Message of His Excellency Joseph E. Brown, to the Extra Session of the Legislature, Convened March 10th, 1864.* Milledgeville, GA: Boughton, Nisbet, Barnes & Moore, 1864.

Brownmiller, Susan. *Against Our Will: Men, Women and Rape*. New York: Simon and Schuster, 1975.

Bruce, Lenny. Performance on *The Steve Allen Show*. April 9, 1959. Available online at http://www.youtube.com/watch?v=oCplnUgaohU (accessed September 26, 2014).

Bruchey, Stuart W. *Enterprise: The Dynamic Economy of a Free People*. Cambridge: Harvard University Press, 1990.

Bryan, William Jennings. "Notification Speech." August 8, 1900. In *Life and Speeches of Hon. Wm. Jennings Bryan*, 390–411. Baltimore: R. H. Woodward, 1900.

———. *Speeches of William Jennings Bryan, Revised and Arranged by Himself*. New York: Funk and Wagnalls, 1909.

Burlingame, Michael. *Abraham Lincoln: A Life*. Baltimore: Johns Hopkins University Press, 2013.

Butler, Jon. *Awash in a Sea of Faith: Christianizing the American People*. Cambridge: Harvard University Press, 1990.

Butterfield, Roger. "Mr. Mencken Sounds Off." *Life*, August 5, 1946, 52.

Buzzanco, Robert. *Masters of War: Military Dissent and Politics in the Vietnam Era*. Cambridge: Cambridge University Press, 1996.

Bynum, Victoria E. *The Long Shadow of the Civil War: Southern Dissent and Its Legacies*. Chapel Hill: University of North Carolina Press, 2010.

Caldwell, Erskine. *Tobacco Road*. New York: Scribner, 1932.

"Call to Conscience from Veterans to Active Duty Troops and Reservists." December 6, 2002. Available online at http://www.vvawai.org/CtC/vcc-poster-tall.pdf (accessed September 28, 2014).

Capper, Charles. *Margaret Fuller: An American Romantic Life*. 2 vols. New York: Oxford University Press, 1992–2007.

Carmichael, Stokely. "Berkeley Speech." In *Contemporary American Voices: Significant Speeches in American History, 1945–Present*, edited by James R. Andrews and David Zarefsky, 100–107. White Plains, NY: Longman, 1992.

Caro, Robert. *Master of the Senate: The Years of Lyndon Johnson*. New York: Knopf, 2002.

———. *The Passage of Power: The Years of Lyndon Johnson*. New York: Knopf, 2012.

Carretta, Vincent. *Equiano, the African: Biography of a Self-Made Man*. Athens: University of Georgia Press, 2005.

Carson, Rachel. *Silent Spring*. Boston: Houghton Mifflin, 1963.

Castelnuovo, Shirley. *Soldiers of Conscience: Japanese American Military Resisters in World War II*. Westport, CT: Greenwood, 2008.

Chalberg, John. *Emma Goldman: American Individualist*. New York: Pearson Longman, 2008.

Chambliss, William J., ed. *Police and Law Enforcement*. Los Angeles: Sage, 2011.

Charters, Ann, ed. *The Portable Sixties Reader*. New York: Penguin, 2003.

Chernow, Ron. *Alexander Hamilton*. New York: Penguin, 2004.

Chet, Guy. *Conquering the American Wilderness: The Triumph of European Warfare in the Colonial Northeast*. Amherst: University of Massachusetts Press, 2003.

Chief Joseph. "An Indian's View of Indian Affairs." *North American Review* 128 (April 1879): 431–432.

Chomsky, Noam. *9-11*. New York: Seven Stories, 2002.

———. *Power and Terror: Post-9/11 Talks and Interviews*. New York: Seven Stories, 2003.

Chopin, Kate. *The Awakening*. Chicago: Herbert S. Stone, 1899.

Churchill, Ward, and Jim Vanderwall. *The COINTELPRO Papers: Documents from the FBI's Secret Wars against Domestic Dissent*. Boston: South End, 1990.

Churchill, Winston. Speech at Westminster College Fulton, Missouri, March 5, 1946. Available online at http://www.fordham.edu/halsall/mod/churchill-iron.asp (accessed September 25, 2014).

Clear, Todd. *Imprisoning Communities: How Mass Incarceration Makes Disadvantaged Neighborhoods Worse*. New York: Oxford University Press, 2009.

Cochran, Thomas. *The Age of Enterprise: A Social History or Industrial America*. New York: Macmillan, 1942.

———. *The Inner Revolution: Essays on the Social Sciences in History*. New York: Harper and Row, 1964.

Cohen, Lizbeth. *Making a New Deal: Industrial Workers in Chicago, 1919–1939*. Cambridge: Cambridge University Press, 1990.

Cohen, Robert. *Freedom's Orator: Mario Savio and the Radical Legacy of the 1960s*. New York: Oxford University Press, 2009.

Cohen, Ronald D. *Woody Guthrie: Writing America's Songs*. New York: Routledge, 2012.

Cole, Phyllis. *Mary Moody Emerson and the Origins of Transcendentalism: A Family History*. New York: Oxford University Press, 1998.

Coleman, Elihu. *A Testimony against the Antichristian Practice of Making Slaves of Men*. New Bedford, MA, 1733.

Collier-Thomas, Bettye. *Jesus, Jobs, and Justice: African American Women and Religion*. New York: Knopf, 2010.

Combs, Barbara Harris. *From Selma to Montgomery and Freedom: The Long March to Freedom*. New York: Routledge, 2014.

Cook, Adrian. *The Armies of the Streets: The New York City Draft Riots of 1863*. Lexington: University Press of Kentucky, 1982.

Cook, Blanche Wiesen. *Eleanor Roosevelt: 1884–1932*. New York: Viking, 1992.

———. *Eleanor Roosevelt: The Defining Years, 1933–1938*. New York: Viking. 1999.

Cooper, John Milton, Jr. *Pivotal Decades: The United States, 1900–1920*. New York: Norton, 1990.

———. *The Warrior and the Priest: Woodrow Wilson and Theodore Roosevelt*. Cambridge: Harvard University Press, 1983.

Cooper, Thomas V., and Hector T. Fenton. *American Politics from the Beginning to Date*. Chicago: Charles R. Brodix, 1882.

Cooper, W. D. *The History of North America*. London: E. Newberry, 1789.

Cornell, Saul. *The Other Founders: Anti-Federalism and the Dissenting Tradition in America, 1788–1828*. Chapel Hill: University of North Carolina Press, 1999.

Cott, Nancy F. *The Grounding of Modern Feminism*. New Haven: Yale University Press, 1987.

Coughlin, Charles E. "Address on the National Union for Social Justice." November 11, 1934. In *A Series of Lectures on Social Justice*. Royal Oak, MI: Radio League of the Little Flower, 1935.

———. "National Radio Address." June 19, 1936. In *A Series of Lectures on Social Justice*. Royal Oak, MI: Radio League of the Little Flower, 1935.

Cox, Vicki. *Margaret Sanger*. New York: Infobase, 2009.

Crane, Stephen. *Maggie, a Girl of the Streets: A Tale of New York*. New York, 1892.

Cugoano, Ottobah. *Thoughts and Sentiments on the Evil and Wicked Traffic of the Slavery and Commerce of the Human Species*. London, 1787.

Dallek, Robert. *An Unfinished Life: John F. Kennedy, 1917–1963*. Boston: Little, Brown, 2003.

Dangerfield, George. *The Awakening of American Nationalism, 1815–1828*. New York: Harper and Row, 1965.

Dannenbaum, Jed. *Drink and Disorder: Temperance Reform in Cincinnati from the Washington Revival to the Woman's Christian Temperance Union*. Urbana: University of Illinois Press, 1983.

Darlington, Ralph. *Syndicalism and the Transition to Communism: An International Comparative Analysis*. Aldershot, UK: Ashgate, 2008.

Dass, Ram. *Remember, Be Here Now*. San Cristobel, NM: Lama Foundation, 1971.

Dayton, Isaac, ed. *The Office of Surrogate, Surrogates, and Surrogates Courts, and Executors, Administrators, and Guardians, in the State of New York: A Compilation of the Statutes, and a Summary of the Judicial Decisions of the State of New York Relating to the Office of Surrogate . . . and the Powers, Duties, and Liabilities of Executors, Administrators, and Guardians, Arranged in the Form of a Treatise*. New York: Banks & Brothers, 1861.

Debs, Eugene V. "Address to the Jury (1918)." In *Protest Nation: Words That Inspired a Century of American Radicalism*, edited by Timothy Patrick McCarthy and John Campbell McMillian, 27–31. New York: New Press, 2010.

———. "The Canton, Ohio Speech, Anti-War Speech." June 16, 1918. Available online at http://www.marxists.org/archive/debs/works/1918/canton.htm (accessed October 4, 2014).

———. "Statement to the Court upon Being Convicted of Violating the Sedition Act." September 18, 1918. Available online at https://www.marxists.org/archive/debs/works/1918/court.htm (accessed October 7, 2014).

"Declaration by the Representatives of the United Colonies of North-America, A, Now Met in Congress at Philadelphia, Setting Forth the Causes and Necessity of Their Taking Up Arms." Available online at http://avalon.law.yale.edu/18th_century/arms.asp#1 (accessed September 16, 2014).

"Declaration of the Occupation of New York City." September 29, 2011. Available at the NYC General Assembly website, http://www.nycga.net/resources/documents/declaration/ (accessed May 17, 2014).

Delany, Martin R. "Political Destiny of the Colored Race, on the American Continent." In *Martin R. Delany: A Documentary Reader*, edited by Robert S. Levine, 245–279. Chapel Hill: University of North Carolina Press, 2003.

De León, Arnoldo. *The Tejano Community, 1836–1900*. Dallas: Southern Methodist University Press, 1982.

Dellinger, David. "Why I Refused to Register in the October 1940 Draft and a Little of What It Led To." In *A Few Small Candles: War Resisters of World War II Tell Their Stories*, edited by Larry Gara and Lenna Mae Gara, 20–37. Kent, OH: Kent State University Press, 1999.

D'Emilio, John, and Estelle Freedman. *Intimate Matters: A History of Sexuality in America*. New York: Harper and Row, 1988.

Democratic National Committee. *Campaign Text-Book of the National Democratic Party, 1896*. Chicago, 1896.

De Voto, Bernard. *Across the Wide Missouri*. Boston: Houghton Mifflin, 1964.

Dewey, John. *My Pedagogic Creed*. New York: Kellogg, 1897.

———. *The School and Society*. Chicago: University of Chicago Press, 1907.

Di Franco, Ani. "self evident." 2001. Available on her website, http://www.righteous babe.com/pages/so-much-shouting-so-much-laughter (accessed October 7, 2014).

Dilling, Elizabeth Kirkpatrick. *The Red Network: A "Who's Who" and Handbook of Radicalism for Patriots*. Chicago: Elizabeth Dilling, 1934.

Dodds, Gordon B., ed. *Varieties of Hope: An Anthology of Oregon Prose*. Corvallis: Oregon State University Press, 1993.

Donald, David Herbert. *Lincoln*. New York: Simon and Schuster, 1996.

Doors, The. *The Doors*. Elektra, 1967.

Dos Passos, John. *U.S.A.* New York: Library of America, 1996.

Douglass, Frederick. "The Dred Scott Decision: Speech Delivered before American Anti-Slavery Society, New York, May 14, 1857." In *Selected Speeches and Writings*, edited by Philip S. Foner, 344–357. Chicago: Lawrence Hill Books, 1999.

———. "The End of All Compromises with Slavery—Now and Forever." 1854. In *The Life and Writings of Frederick Douglass*, vol. 2, *Pre–Civil War Decade*, edited by Philip S. Foner, 282–283. New York: International, 1950.

———. "Lincoln and the Colored Troops." In *Reminiscences of Abraham Lincoln by Distinguished Men of his Time*, edited by Allen Thorndike Rice, 315–325. New York: Harper, 1909.

———. *Narrative of the Life of Frederick Douglass, an American Slave, Written by Himself*. Edited by Benjamin Quarles. Cambridge: Belknap Press of Harvard University Press, 1960.

———. "What the Black Man Wants." 1865. In *The Life and Writings of Frederick Douglass*, vol. 4, *Reconstruction and After*, edited by Philip S. Foner, 157–165. New York: International, 1950.

———. "What to the Slave Is the Fourth of July?" In *The Frederick Douglass Papers: Series One: Speeches, Debates, and Interviews, 1847–1854*, edited by John W. Blassingame, 359–388. New Haven: Yale University Press, 1982.

———. "The Women's Association of Philadelphia, *The North Star*, June 15, 1849." In *Frederick Douglass on Women's Rights*, edited by Philip S. Foner, 51–52. New York: Da Capo, 1992.

Dowd, Gregory E. *A Spirited Resistance: The North American Indian Struggle for Unity, 1745–1815*. Baltimore: Johns Hopkins University Press, 1992.

Drinnon, Richard. *Violence in the American Experience: Winning the West*. New York: New American Library, 1979.

Dublin, Thomas. *Women at Work*. New York: Columbia University Press, 1979.

Dubois, Ellen Carol. *Feminism and Suffrage: The Emergence of an Independent Women's Movement in America, 1848–1869*. Ithaca: Cornell University Press, 1978.

Du Bois, W. E. B. "Close Ranks." *Crisis* 16, no. 3 (1918): 111.

———. *The Souls of Black Folk*. 1903. Edited by Henry Louis Gates, Jr. New York: Oxford University Press, 2007.

Dunbar, Anthony P. *Against the Grain: Southern Radicals and Prophets, 1929–1959*. Charlottesville: University of Virginia Press, 1981.

DuVal, Kathleen. "Independence for Whom? Expansion and Conflict in the South and Southwest." In *The World of the Revolutionary Republic: Land, Labor, and the Conflict for a Continent*, edited by Andrew Shankman, 97–115. New York: Routledge, 2014.

Dylan, Bob. *Another Side of Bob Dylan*. Columbia Records, 1964.

———. *Blonde on Blonde*. Columbia Records, 1966.

———. *Bringing It All Back Home*. Columbia Records, 1965.

———. *Chronicles, Volume One*. New York: Simon and Schuster, 2004.

———. *The Freewheelin' Bob Dylan*. Columbia Records, 1963.

———. *Highway 61 Revisited*. Columbia Records, 1965.

———. *The Times They Are A-Changin'*. Columbia Records, 1964.

Earle, Steve. *The Revolution Starts Now*. Artemis Records, 2004.

Echols, Alice. *Daring to Be Bad: Radical Feminism in America, 1967–1975*. Minneapolis: University of Minnesota Press, 1989.

Edwards, Anne. *Katharine Hepburn: A Remarkable Woman*. New York: Macmillan, 2000.

Ehle, John. *Trail of Tears: The Rise and Fall of the Cherokee Nation*. New York: Doubleday, 1988.

Ehrenreich, Barbara. *The Worst Years of Our Lives: Irreverent Notes from a Decade of Greed*. New York: Pantheon Books, 1990.

Elkins, Stanley. *Slavery: A Problem in American Institutional and Intellectual Life*. New York: Grosset and Dunlap, 1963.

Elliott, Robert Brown. "The Civil Rights Bill." In *Masterpieces of Negro Eloquence 1818–1913*, edited by Alice Moore Dunbar, 40–54. 1914. Reprint, Mineola, NY: Dover, 2000.

Ellis, Joseph. *Founding Brothers: The Revolutionary Generation*. New York: Knopf, 2001.

———. *His Excellency George Washington*. New York: Knopf, 2004.

Elshtain, Jean Bethke. *Jane Addams and the Dream of American Democracy*. New York: Basic Books, 2001.

Eltis, David. *The Rise of African Slavery in the Americas*. Cambridge: Cambridge University Press, 2000.

Emerson, Ralph Waldo. "'Address to the Citizens of Concord' on the Fugitive Slave Law." In *Emerson's Antislavery Writings*, edited by Len Gougeon and Joel Myerson, 53–72. New Haven: Yale University Press, 1995.

———. *The Essay on Self-Reliance*. East Aurora, NY: Roycroft, 1908.

Epstein, Barbara. *The Politics of Domesticity: Women, Evangelism, and Temperance in Nineteenth-Century America*. Middletown, CT: Wesleyan University Press, 1980.

Equiano, Olaudah. *The Interesting Narrative of Olaudah Equiano, or Gustavus Vassa the African*. London, 1789.

Etulain, Richard W. *Does the Frontier Make America Exceptional?* New York: Bedford / St. Martin's, 1999.

Ewen, Alexander, ed. *Voices of Indigenous Peoples*. Santa Fe, NM: Clear Light, 1994.

Fahrenheit 9/11. Directed by Michael Moore. Dog Eat Dog Films, 2004.

Farber, David R. *The Age of Great Dreams: America in the 1960s*. New York: Hill and Wang, 1994.

———. *Chicago '68*. Chicago: University of Chicago Press, 1988.

Feldman, Glenn, ed. *Before "Brown": Civil Rights and White Backlash in the Modern South*. Tuscaloosa: University of Alabama Press, 2004.

———. *The Disfranchisement Myth: Poor Whites and Suffrage Restriction in Alabama*. Athens: University of Georgia Press, 2004.

———. *Politics, Society, and the Klan in Alabama, 1915–1949*. Tuscaloosa: University of Alabama Press, 1999.

Feldman, Jay. *Manufacturing Hysteria: A History of Scapegoating, Surveillance, and Secrecy in Modern America*. New York: Anchor Books, 2012.

Fellman, Michael D. *The Unbounded Frame: Freedom and Community in Nineteenth-Century American Utopianism*. Westport, CT: Greenwood, 1969.

Firestone, Shulamith. *The Dialectics of Sex*. New York: Bantam, 1970.

Fischer, David Hackett. *Washington's Crossing*. Oxford: Oxford University Press, 2004.

Fischer, Kirsten. *Suspect Relations: Sex, Race, and Resistance in Colonial North Carolina* Ithaca: Cornell University Press, 2002.

Fishman, Ethan. "The Prudential FDR." In *FDR and the Modern Presidency: Leadership and Legacy*, edited by Mark J. Rozell and William D. Pederson, 147–166. Westport, CT: Greenwood, 1997.

Fitzgerald, F. Scott. *The Great Gatsby*. New York: Scribner, 1925.

———. *Tales of the Jazz Age*. New York: Scribner, 1922.

———. *This Side of Paradise*. New York: Scribner, 1920.

Fitzhugh, George. *Cannibals All! or, Slaves without Masters*. Richmond, VA: A. Morris, 1857.

Flexner, Eleanor. *Century of Struggle: The Woman's Rights Movement in the United States*. Cambridge: Belknap Press of Harvard University Press, 1975.

Foner, Eric. *The Fiery Trial: Abraham Lincoln and American Slavery.* New York: Norton, 2010.

———. *Free Soil, Free Labor, Free Men: The Ideology of the Republican Party before the Civil War.* 1970. Reprint, New York: Oxford University Press, 1995.

———. *Reconstruction: America's Unfinished Revolution, 1863–1877.* New York: Harper and Row, 1988.

———. *A Short History of Reconstruction: 1865–1877.* New York: Harper and Row, 1990.

———. *The Story of American Freedom.* New York: Norton, 1998.

———. *Tom Paine and Revolutionary America.* New York: Oxford University Press, 1976.

Foner, Philip S. *The Great Labor Uprising of 1877.* New York: Monad, 1977.

———. *A History of the Labor Movement in the United States.* 4 vols. New York: International, 1947–1964.

Foreman, Grant. *Indian Removal.* Norman: University of Oklahoma Press, 1972.

Foster, Hannah Webster. *The Coquette; or, The History of Eliza Wharton, a Novel: Founded on Fact.* Boston, 1797.

Foster, Stephen. *The Long Argument: English Puritanism and the Shaping of New England Culture, 1570–1700.* Chapel Hill: University of North Carolina Press, 1991.

Frampton, Mary Louise, Ian F. Haney López, and Jonathan Simon, eds. *After the War on Crime: Race, Democracy, and a New Reconstruction.* New York: NYU Press, 2008.

Franklin, John Hope. *From Slavery to Freedom: A History of African Americans.* New York: Knopf, 2000.

Freeberg, Ernest. *Democracy's Prisoner: Eugene V. Debs, the Great War, and the Right to Dissent.* Cambridge: Harvard University Press, 2008.

Freehling, William W. *Prelude to Civil War: The Nullification Controversy in South Carolina, 1816–1836.* New York: Harper and Row, 1966.

Freidel, Frank. *Franklin D. Roosevelt: The Ordeal.* Boston: Little, Brown, 1973.

Friedan, Betty. *The Feminine Mystique.* 1963. Reprint, New York: Dell, 1970.

Fuller, Margaret. *Woman in the Nineteenth Century.* New York: Greeley and McElrath, 1845.

Gabaccia, Donna. *From the Other Side: Women, Gender, and Immigrant Life in the U.S., 1820–1990.* Bloomington: Indiana University Press, 1994.

Gaddis, John Lewis. *The Cold War: A New History.* New York: Penguin, 2005.

———. *The Long Peace: Inquiries into the History of the Cold War.* New York: Oxford University Press, 1987.

Gara, Larry. "My War on War." In *A Few Small Candles: War Resisters of World War II Tell Their Stories,* edited by Larry Gara and Lenna Mae Gara, 78–97. Kent, OH: Kent State University Press, 1999.

———. *War Resistance in Historical Perspective.* Wallingford, PA: Pendle Hill, 1970.

Garland, David. *The Culture of Control: Crime and Social Order in Contemporary Society.* Chicago: University of Chicago Press, 2002.

Garraty, John A., and Mark C. Carnes. *The American Nation: A History of the United States.* 10th ed. New York: Pearson Education, 1999.

Garrison, William Lloyd. "Triumph of Mobocracy in Boston." In *Selections from the Writings and Speeches of William Lloyd Garrison*, 373–389. Boston: R. F. Wallcut, 1852.

Garvey, Marcus. "Address to the UNIA Supporters in Philadelphia, October 21, 1919." In *African American Political Thought, 1890–1930: Washington, Du Bois, Garvey, and Randolph*, edited by Cary D. Wintz, 199–207. Armonk, NY: M. E. Sharpe, 1996.

———. *The Philosophy and Opinions of Marcus Garvey; or, Africa for the Africans.* Compiled by Amy Jacques Garvey. Vol. 1. New York: Universal, 1923.

Genovese, Eugene D. *Roll Jordan Roll: The World the Slaves Made*. New York: Pantheon Books, 1974.

George III. "A Proclamation, by The King, for Suppressing Rebellion and Sedition." August 23, 1775. Available online at http://www.digitalhistory.uh.edu/disp_textbook .cfm?smtID=3&psid=4105 (accessed September 16, 2014).

George, Henry. *Progress and Poverty*. New York, 1879.

Gienapp, William E. *The Origins of the Republican Party, 1852–1856*. New York: Oxford University Press, 1987.

Ginger, Ray. *Age of Excess: The United States from 1877 to 1914*. New York: Macmillan, 1965.

———. *The Bending Cross: A Biography of Eugene Victor Debs*. New Brunswick: Rutgers University Press, 1969.

———. *Six Days or Forever? Tennessee v. John Thomas Scopes*. New York: Oxford University Press, 1958.

Ginsberg, Allen. *Howl and Other Poems*. San Francisco: City Lights Books, 1956.

———. *Journals: Early Fifties, Early Sixties*. Edited by Gordon Ball. New York: Grove, 1977.

Gitlin, Todd. *The Sixties: Years of Hope, Days of Rage*. New York: Bantam, 1987.

———. *The Twilight of Common Dreams: Why America Is Wracked by Culture Wars*. New York: Holt, 1995.

Glazer, Nathan, and Irving Kristol. *The American Commonwealth 1976*. New York: Basic Books, 1976.

Goddard, Ives, and Kathleen J. Bragdon. *Native Writings in Massachusetts*. Philadelphia: American Philosophical Society, 1988.

Goidel, Kirby. *America's Failing Experiment: How We the People Have Become the Problem*. Lanham, MD: Rowman and Littlefield, 2013.

Goldman, Emma. *Anarchism and Other Essays*. 2nd ed. New York: Mother Earth, 1911.

———. "Essay in the *Firebrand*, New York, 18 July 1897." In *Emma Goldman: A Documentary History of the American Years*, vol. 1, *Made for America, 1890–1901*, edited by Candace Falk, 269–273. Berkeley: University of California Press, 2003.

———. "The Individual, Society, and the State." In *Red Emma Speaks: Selected Writings and Speeches*, edited by Alix Kates Shulman, 86–100. New York: Random House, 1972.

Gollaher, David L. *Voices for the Mad: The Life of Dorothea Dix*. New York: Free Press, 1995.

Good War and Those Who Refused to Fight It, The. Directed by Judith Ehrlich and Rick Tejada-Flores. Bull Frog Films / PBS / ITVS / Paradigm Productions, 2000. http://www.pbs.org/itvs/thegoodwar/camps.html (accessed September 24, 2014).

Goodwin, Doris Kearns. *The Bully Pulpit: Theodore Roosevelt, William Howard Taft, and the Golden Age of Journalism*. New York: Simon and Schuster, 2013.

———. *No Ordinary Time: Franklin and Eleanor Roosevelt: The Home Front in World War II*. New York: Simon and Schuster, 1994.

———. *Team of Rivals: The Political Genius of Abraham Lincoln*. New York: Simon and Schuster, 2005.

Goodwyn, Lawrence. *The Populist Moment: A Short History of the Agrarian Revolt in America*. New York: Oxford University Press, 1978.

Graham, Hugh Davis. *The Civil Rights Era: Origins and Development of National Policy, 1960–1972*. New York: Oxford University Press, 1990.

Grant, Donald Lee. *The Way It Was in the South: The Black Experience in Georgia*. Athens: University of Georgia Press, 1993.

Green, Elna C. *This Business of Relief: Confronting Poverty in a Southern City, 1740–1940*. Athens: University of Georgia Press, 2003.

Green, Michael D. *The Politics of Indian Removal: Creek Government and Society in Crisis*. Lincoln: University of Nebraska Press, 1982.

Greenberg, Ethan. *Dred Scott and the Dangers of a Political Court*. Lanham, MD: Lexington Books, 2009.

Griffith, Elizabeth. *In Her Own Right: The Life of Elizabeth Cady Stanton*. New York: Oxford University Press, 1984.

Griffiths, Hannah. "The Female Patriots. Address'd to the Daughters of Liberty in America. By the Same." 1768. In *Milcah Martha Moore's Book: A Commonplace Book from Revolutionary America*, edited by Catherine La Courreye Blecki and Karin A. Wulf, 172. University Park: Pennsylvania State University Press, 1997.

Grimké, Angelina E. *Appeal to the Christian Women of the South*. New York: New York Anti-Slavery Society, 1836.

Grimké, Sarah, and Angelina E. Grimké. *The Public Years of Sarah and Angelina Grimké: Selected Writings 1835–1839*. Edited by Larry Ceplair. New York: Columbia University Press, 1989.

Guelzo, Allen C. *Fateful Lightning: A New History of the Civil War and Reconstruction*. New York: Oxford University Press, 2012.

Gura, Philip F. *A Glimpse of Sion's Glory: Puritan Radicalism in New England, 1620–1660*. Middletown, CT: Wesleyan University Press, 1984.

Guthrie, Woody. *Bound for Glory*. New York: E. P. Dutton, 1943.

———. *Pastures of Plenty: A Self Portrait*. Edited by Dave Marsh and Harold Leventhal. New York: HarperCollins, 1990.

———. *The Woody Guthrie Songbook*. Edited by Harold Leventhal and Marjorie Guthrie. New York: Grosset and Dunlap, 1976.

Gutman, Herbert. *Work, Culture, and Society in Industrializing America: Essays in American Working-Class and Social History*. New York: Knopf, 1976.

Hajdu, David. *Positively Fourth Street: The Life and Times of Joan Baez, Bob Dylan, Mimi Baez Fariña, and Richard Fariña*. New York: Farrar, Straus, and Giroux, 2001.

Halberstam, David. *The Fifties*. New York: Ballantine Books, 1994.

Hall, David D. *The Faithful Shepherd: A History of the New England Ministry in the Seventeenth Century*. Chapel Hill: University of North Carolina Press, 1972.

———. *Worlds of Wonder, Days of Judgment: Popular Religious Belief in Early New England*. Cambridge: Harvard University Press, 1990.

Hamby, Alonzo. *Beyond the New Deal: Harry S. Truman and American Liberalism*. New York: Columbia University Press, 1973.

Hamer, Fannie Lou. "Testimony before the Credentials Committee at the Democratic National Convention, Atlantic City, New Jersey, August 22, 1964." In *The Speeches of Fannie Lou Hamer: To Tell It Like It Is*, edited by Maegan Parker Brooks and Davis W. Houck, 42–45. Jackson: University Press of Mississippi, 2011.

Hamilton, Neil A. *American Social Leaders and Activists*. New York: Infobase, 2002.

Harris, Leon A. *Upton Sinclair, American Rebel*. New York: Crowell, 1975.

Hartmann, Susan. *The Home Front and Beyond: American Women in the 1940s*. Boston: Twayne, 1982.

Harvey, Charles M., ed. *History of the Republican Party Together with the Proceedings of the Republican National Convention at St. Louis June 16th–June 18th, 1896*. St. Louis: I. Haas, 1896.

Hawley, Ellis. *The New Deal and the Problem of Monopoly: A Study in Economic Ambivalence*. Princeton: Princeton University Press, 1995.

Hay, Harry. *Radically Gay: Gay Liberation in the Words of Its Founder*. Edited by Will Roscoe. Boston: Beacon, 1997.

Hayden, Tom. *Rebel: A Personal History of the 1960s*. Los Angeles: Red Hen, 2003.

———. *Reunion: A Memoir*. New York: Random House, 1988.

Helper, Hinton Rowan. *The Impending Crisis of the South: How to Meet It*. New York: A. B. Burdick, 1857.

Helsinger, Elizabeth K. *The Woman Question: Social Issues, 1837–1883*. Manchester: Manchester University Press, 1983.

Hemingway, Ernest. *A Farewell to Arms*. New York: Scribner, 1929.

———. *The Sun Also Rises*. New York: Scribner, 1926.

Hersh, Seymour. *My Lai 4: A Report on the Massacre and Its Aftermath*. New York: Random House, 1970.

Higham, John. *Strangers in the Land: Patterns of American Nativism, 1860–1925*. New Brunswick: Rutgers University Press, 1955.

Hill, Christopher, *Society and Puritanism in Pre-Revolutionary England*. London: Secker and Warburg, 1964.

Hill, Julia Butterfly. *The Legacy of Luna: The Story of a Tree, a Woman, and the Struggle to Save the Redwoods*. New York: Harper, 2000.

Hilty, James W. *Robert Kennedy: Brother Protector*. Philadelphia: Temple University Press, 1997.

Hiltzik, Michael. *The New Deal: A Modern History*. New York: Free Press, 2011.

Hine, Lewis. *America and Lewis Hine: Photographs 1904–1940*. New York: Aperture, 1977.

Hinks, Peter P. *To Awaken My Afflicted Brethren: David Walker and the Problem of Antebellum Slave Resistance*. University Park: Pennsylvania State University Press, 1997.

Hitchcock, Ethan Allen. *Fifty Years in Camp and Field: Diary of Major-General Ethan Allen Hitchcock, U.S.A.* Edited by W. A. Croffut. New York: Putnam / Knickerbocker, 1909.

Hoffman, Abbie. *Steal This Book*. New York: Pirate Editions, 1971.

———. *Woodstock Nation*. New York: Vintage Books, 1969.

Hofstadter, Richard. *The Age of Reform: From Bryan to FDR*. New York: Knopf, 1955.

———. *The American Political Tradition*. New York: Random House, 1954.

———. *Social Darwinism in American Thought*. Boston: Beacon, 1955.

Holland, Frederic May. *Frederick Douglass: The Colored Orator*. New York: Funk and Wagnalls, 1891.

Howe, Daniel Walker. *What Hath God Wrought: The Transformation of America, 1815–1848*. New York: Oxford University Press, 2007.

Howells, William Dean. *The Rise of Silas Lapham*. Edinburgh, UK: David Douglas, 1884.

Hoxie, Frederick E. *A Final Promise: The Campaign to Assimilate the Indians, 1880–1920*. Lincoln: University of Nebraska Press, 1984.

Huggins, Nathan Irvin. *The Harlem Renaissance*. New York: Oxford University Press, 1971.

Hughes, Langston. "The Negro Artist and the Racial Mountain." *Nation*, June 23, 1926.

———. *Selected Poems of Langston Hughes*. New York: Knopf, 1959.

Hurmence, Belinda, ed. *Before Freedom: 48 Oral Histories of Former North and South Carolina Slaves*. New York: Mentor, 1990.

Hurtado, Albert L. *Intimate Frontiers: Sex, Culture, and Gender in California*. Albuquerque: University of New Mexico Press, 1999.

Hutchinson, Thomas. *The History of the Province of Massachusetts-Bay*. Vol. 2. London, 1758.

———. *Strictures upon the Declaration of the Congress at Philadelphia; In a Letter to a Noble Lord*. London, 1776.

Hyman, Michael R. *The Anti-Redeemers: Hill-Country Political Dissenters in the Lower South from Redemption to Populism*. Baton Rouge: Louisiana State University Press, 1990.

Immortal Technique. *Revolutionary, Vol. 2*. Viper Records, 2003.

Indians Of All Tribes. "We Hold the Rock!" In *Alcatraz, Indian Land Forever*, edited by Troy R. Johnson. Los Angeles: UCLA American Indian Studies Center, 1995.

Industrial Workers of the World. *Little Red Songbook*. 19th ed. Chicago: IWW, 1923.

———. "Preamble to the IWW Constitution." http://www.iww.org/culture/official/preamble.shtml (accessed September 21, 2014).

Jacobs, Harold. *Weatherman*. Berkeley, CA: Ramparts, 1970.

Jefferson, Thomas. *The Writings of Thomas Jefferson*. Edited by Paul Leicester Ford. 10 vols. New York: Putnam, 1892–1899.

Jefferson Airplane. *Surrealistic Pillow*. RCA Victor, 1967.

Jensen, Joan M. *With These Hands: Women Working on the Land*. Old Westbury, NY: Feminist Press / McGraw-Hill, 1981.

Jensen, Merrill. *The Founding of a Nation: A History of the American Revolution, 1763–1776*. Indianapolis: Hackett, 2004.

Johnson, Chalmers. *Blowback: The Costs and Consequences of American Empire*. New York: Metropolitan Books, 2000.

———. *Nemesis: The Last Days of the American Republic*. New York: Metropolitan Books, 2006.

———. *The Sorrows of Empire: Militarism, Secrecy, and the End of the Republic*. New York: Metropolitan Books, 2004.

Johnson, Edward A. *History of Negro Soldiers in the Spanish-American War*. Raleigh, NC: Capital, 1899.

Johnson, Lyndon B. "Special Message to the Congress: The American Promise." March 15, 1965. In *Public Papers of the Presidents of the United States, Lyndon B. Johnson, 1965*, no. 1. Washington, DC: U.S. Government Printing Office, 1965.

Jones, Mary. *The Autobiography of Mother Jones*. Edited by Mary Field Parton. Chicago: Charles H. Kerr, 1925.

Jones, William P. *The March on Washington: Jobs Freedom, and the Forgotten History of Civil Rights*. New York: Norton, 2013.

Joplin, Janis. *Pearl*. Columbia Records, 1971.

Jordan, Winthrop. *White over Black: American Attitudes toward the Negro, 1550–1812*. Chapel Hill: University of North Carolina Press, 1968.

Josephson, Matthew. *The Robber Barons: The Great American Capitalists, 1861–1901*. New York: Harcourt, Brace, and World, 1962.

Josephy, Alvin M., Jr. *Red Power: The American Indians' Fight for Freedom*. New York: American Heritage, 1971.

Juster, Susan. *Disorderly Women: Sexual Politics and Evangelicalism in Revolutionary New England*. Ithaca: Cornell University Press, 1994.

Kaczynski, Ted. "Industrial Society and Its Future." Available online at "The Unabomber Trial: The Manifesto," *Washington Post*, September 22, 1995, http://www.washingtonpost.com/wp-srv/national/longterm/unabomber/manifesto.text.htm (accessed May 15, 2014).

———. "Interview with Ted Kaczynski." Interview with the *Earth First! Journal*, Administrative Maximum Facility Prison, Florence, Colorado, USA, June 1999. Available online at http://www.primitivism.com/kaczynski.htm (accessed May 15, 2014).

Kaplan, Sidney, and Emma Nogrady Kaplan. *The Black Presence in the Era of the American Revolution*. Amherst: University of Massachusetts Press, 1989.

Karl, Barry. *The Uneasy State: The United States from 1915 to 1945*. Chicago: University of Chicago Press, 1983.

Karlsen, Carol. *The Devil in the Shape of a Woman: Witchcraft in Colonial New England*. New York: Norton, 1998

Karnow, Stanley. *Vietnam: A History*. New York: Viking, 1991.

Katznelson, Ira. *Fear Itself: The New Deal and the Origins of Our Time*. New York: Liveright, 2013.

Kauffman, Bill. *Ain't My America: The Long, Noble History of Antiwar Conservatism and Middle-American Anti-Imperialism*. New York: Macmillan, 2008.

Kaufman, Stuart B. *Samuel Gompers and the Origins of the American Federation of Labor, 1848–1896*. Westport, CT: Greenwood, 1973.

Keats, John. *The Crack in the Picture Window*. Boston: Houghton Mifflin, 1957.

Kelley, Robin D. G. *Hammer and Hoe: Alabama Communists during the Great Depression*. Chapel Hill: University of North Carolina Press, 1990.

Kennedy, David M. *Birth Control in America: The Career of Margaret Sanger*. New Haven: Yale University Press, 1970.

———. *Freedom from Fear: The American People in Depression and War, 1929–1945*. New York: Oxford University Press, 1999.

Kennedy, John F. "Address on Civil Rights." June 11, 1963. Available online at http://millercenter.org/president/speeches/detail/3375 (accessed May 14, 2014).

Kent, Donald, ed. *Pennsylvania Indian Treaties, 1737–1756*. Frederick, MD: University Publications of America, 1984.

Kerouac, Jack. *On the Road*. New York: Viking, 1957.

Kessler-Harris, Alice. *Out to Work: A History of Wage-Earning Women in the United States*. New York: Oxford University Press, 1982.

Killbuck, John. "Speech to the Governors of Pennsylvania, Maryland, and Virginia." December 4, 1771. In *Documents of the American Revolution*, edited by K. G. Davies, vol. 3. Shannon: Irish University Press, 1977–1981.

King, Martin Luther, Jr. "Acceptance Address for the Nobel Peace Prize." In *A Call to Conscience: The Landmark Speeches of Dr. Martin Luther King, Jr.*, edited by Clayborne Carson, 101–110. New York: Grand Central, 2001.

———. "Address at the Conclusion of the Selma to Montgomery March," March 25, 1965. Text and audio available online at http://mlk-kpp01.stanford.edu/index.php/encyclopedia/documentsentry/doc_address_at_the_conclusion_of_selma_march/ (accessed September 25, 2014).

———. "Beyond Vietnam: A Time to Break the Silence." Speech at Riverside Church, New York, April 4, 1967. Available online at http://www.digitalhistory.uh.edu/disp_textbook.cfm?smtid=3&psid=3621 (accessed May 15, 2014).

———. "I Have a Dream." In *A Testament of Hope: The Essential Writings and Speeches of Martin Luther King Jr.*, edited by James M. Washington, 217–220. San Francisco: HarperCollins, 1991.

———. "MIA Mass Meeting at Holt Street Baptist Church." Speech in Montgomery, Alabama, December 5, 1955. In *The Papers of Martin Luther King, Jr.: Birth of a New Age, December 1955–December 1956*, edited by Clayborne Carson, 71–79. Berkeley: University of California Press, 1997.

———. *Why We Can't Wait*. New York: Mentor, 1964.

Klebanow, Diana, and Franklin L. Jonas. *People's Lawyers: Crusaders for Justice in American History.* Armonk, NY: M. E. Sharpe, 2003.

Knaut, Andrew L. *The Pueblo Revolt of 1680: Conquest and Resistance in Seventeenth-Century New Mexico.* Norman: University of Oklahoma Press, 1995.

Knight, Louise W. *Citizen: Jane Addams and the Struggle for Democracy.* Chicago: University of Chicago Press, 2005.

Kolko, Gabriel. *Triumph of Conservatism: A Reinterpretation of American History.* New York: Free Press, 1977.

Kovic, Ron. *Born on the Fourth of July.* New York: McGraw-Hill, 1976.

Kusmer, Kenneth L. *Down and Out, on the Road: The Homeless in American History.* New York: Oxford University Press, 2002.

LaFeber, Walter. *America, Russia, and the Cold War, 1945–1996.* New York: McGraw-Hill, 1997.

La Follette, Robert M. "The People Do Not Want This War." April 4, 1917. In *We Who Dared to Say No to War: American Antiwar Writing from 1812 to Now,* edited by Murray Polner and Thomas E. Woods, Jr., 123–132 New York: Basic Books, 2008.

———. *The Political Philosophy of Robert M. La Follette as Revealed in His Speeches and Writings.* Madison, WI: Robert M. La Follette, 1920.

Larison, C. W. *Silvia Dubois: A Biografy of the Slav Who Whipt Her Mistres and Gand Her Fredom.* Edited by Jared C. Lobdell. New York: Oxford University Press, 1988.

Larson, Edward J. *Summer for the Gods: The Scopes Trial and America's Continuing Debate over Science and Religion.* New York: Basic Books, 2006.

Lawson, John Howard. "A Statement by John Howard Lawson." In *Thirty Years of Treason: Excerpts from Hearings before the House Committee on Un-American Activities, 1938–1968,* edited by Eric Bentley, 153–165. New York: Viking, 1971.

Lay, Benjamin. *All Slave-Keepers That Keep the Innocent in Bondage, Apostates.* Philadelphia, 1737.

Leary, Timothy. *Flashbacks: An Autobiography.* 1983. Reprint, New York: Putnam 1990.

———. *The Psychedelic Experience: A Manual Based on the Tibetan Book of the Dead.* New York: Citadel, 1964.

Leder, Lawrence H., ed. "Records of the Trials of Jacob Leisler and His Associates." *New-York Historical Society Quarterly* 36 (1952): 431–457.

Leffler, Melvyn P. *A Preponderance of Power: National Security, the Truman Administration, and the Cold War.* Stanford: Stanford University Press, 1992.

Lepore, Jill. *The Name of War: King Philip's War and the Origins of American Identity.* New York: Vintage, 1998.

———. *New York Burning: Liberty, Slavery, and Conspiracy in Eighteenth-Century Manhattan.* New York: Random House, 2005.

———. *The Whites of Their Eyes: The Tea Party's Revolution and the Battle over American History.* Princeton: Princeton University Press, 2010.

Leuchtenburg, William E. *Franklin D. Roosevelt and the New Deal, 1932–1940.* New York: Harper and Row, 1963.

———. *The Perils of Prosperity, 1914–1932.* Chicago: University of Chicago Press, 1958.

Levy, Peter B., ed. *Documentary History of the Modern Civil Rights Movement*. New York: Greenwood, 1992.

Lewis, Sinclair. *Babbitt*. New York: Harcourt, Brace, 1922.

———. *Main Street*. New York: Harcourt, Brace, and Howe, 1920.

Limerick, Patricia. *The Legacy of Conquest: The Unbroken Past of the American West*. New York: Norton, 1987.

———. *Something in the Soil: Legacies and Reckonings in the New West*. New York: Norton, 2000.

Lincoln, Abraham. *The Collected Works of Abraham Lincoln*. Edited by Roy P. Basler. 9 vols. New Brunswick: Rutgers University Press, 1953,

Lindbergh, Charles A. *Address by Charles Lindbergh: Delivered at an America First Committee Meeting in New York City on April 23, 1941*. New York: America First Committee, 1941.

Link, Arthur S. *Woodrow Wilson and the Progressive Era, 1910–1917*. New York: Harper and Row, 1954.

Litwack, Leon F. *How Free Is Free? The Long Death of Jim Crow*. Cambridge: Harvard University Press, 2009.

Livesay, Harold C. *American Made: Men Who Shaped the American Economy*. Boston: Little, Brown, 1979.

Lobo, Susan, and Steve Talbot, eds. *Native American Voices: A Reader*. New York: Longman, 1998.

Logan, Rayford W., ed. *What the Negro Wants*. Chapel Hill: University of North Carolina Press, 1944.

Loring, Caleb William. *Nullification, Secession, Webster's Argument and the Kentucky and Virginia Resolutions Considered in Reference to the Constitution and Historically*. New York: Putnam, 1893.

Lynch, Thomas. *Booking Passage: We Irish and Americans*. New York: Norton, 2006.

Lynd, Staughton. *Intellectual Origins of American Radicalism*. 2nd ed. Cambridge: Cambridge University Press, 2009.

Mackenzie, G. Calvin, and Robert Weisbrot. *The Liberal Hour: Washington and the Politic of Change in the 1960s*. New York: Penguin, 2008.

MacLean, Nancy. *Behind the Mask of Chivalry: The Making of the Second Ku Klux Klan*. New York: Oxford University Press, 1994.

Mahan, Alfred Thayer. *The Influence of Sea Power upon History, 1660–1783*. Boston: Little, Brown, 1890.

Maier, Pauline. *From Resistance to Revolution: Colonial Radicals and the Development of American Opposition to Britain, 1765–1776*. New York: Knopf, 1972.

Mailer, Norman. *The Armies of the Night: History as a Novel, the Novel as History*. New York: New American Library, 1968.

———. *Miami and the Siege of Chicago: An Informal History of the Republican and Democratic Conventions of 1968*. New York: World, 1968.

Mann, Horace. "Twelfth Annual Report to the Secretary of the Massachusetts Board of Education." 1848. Available online at http://www.tncrimlaw.com/civil_bible/horace_mann.htm (accessed September 16, 2014).

Marable, Manning. *Malcolm X: A Life of Reinvention*. New York: Viking, 2011.

———. *Race, Reform, and Rebellion: The Second Reconstruction in Black America*. Jackson: University Press of Mississippi, 1991.

Marcuse, Herbert. *Eros and Civilization: A Philosophical Inquiry into Freud*. Boston: Beacon, 1955.

———. *One-Dimensional Man: Studies in the Ideology of Advanced Industrial Society*. Boston: Beacon, 1964.

Laborers of Boston. "Ten-Hour Circular." 1835. In *The Faith of Our Fathers: An Anthology of Americana, 1790–1860*, edited by Irving Mark and E. E. Schwaab, 342–343. New York: Knopf, 1952.

Marshall, John. *The Life of George Washington: Commander in Chief of the American Forces*. 2nd ed. Vol. 2. Philadelphia: James Crissy & Thomas Cowperthwait, 1845.

Massey, Beth. "Bill Ayers and the Weather Underground." PSLweb.org, October 31, 2008. http://www2.pslweb.org/site/News2?page=NewsArticle&id=10290.

May, Elaine Tyler. *Homeward Bound: American Families in the Cold War Era*. New York: Basic Books, 1988.

Mayer, Henry. *All on Fire: William Lloyd Garrison and the Abolition of Slavery*. New York: St. Martin's, 1998.

McCarthy, Timothy Patrick, and John Campbell McMillian, eds. *Protest Nation: Words That Inspired a Century of American Radicalism*. New York: New Press, 2010.

McCartin, Joseph A. *Labor's Great War: The Struggle for Industrial Democracy and the Origins of Modern American Labor Relations, 1912–1921*. Chapel Hill: University of North Carolina Press, 1997.

McCormick, Richard L. *From Realignment to Reform: Political Change in New York State, 1893–1910*. Ithaca: Cornell University Press, 1981.

McCullough, David. *John Adams*. New York: Simon and Schuster, 2001.

———. *The Path between the Seas*. New York: Simon and Schuster, 1977

———. *Truman*. New York: Simon and Schuster, 1992

McGerr, Michael. *A Fierce Discontent: The Rise and Fall of the Progressive Movement in America, 1870–1920*. New York: Free Press, 2003.

McGuire, Phillip, ed. *Taps for a Jim Crow Army: Letters from Black Soldiers in World War II*. Santa Barbara, CA: ABC-CLIO, 1983.

McKay, Claude. "If We Must Die." In *Harlem Shadows: The Poems of Claude McKay*, 53. New York: Harcourt, Brace, 1922.

McLaughlin, James. *My Friend the Indian*. Boston: Houghton Mifflin, 1910.

McNamara, Robert S. *In Retrospect: The Tragedy and Lessons of Vietnam*. New York: Times Books, 1996.

McNeill, J. R. *Something New under the Sun: An Environmental History of the Twentieth-Century World*. New York: Norton, 2000.

McPherson, James M. *Battle Cry of Freedom: The Civil War Era*. New York: Oxford University Press, 1988.

———. *For Cause and Comrades: Why Men Fought in the Civil War*. New York: Oxford University Press, 1997.

Meacham, Jon. *American Lion: Andrew Jackson in the White House*. New York: Random House, 2008.

———. *Franklin and Winston: An Intimate Portrait of an Epic Friendship*. New York: Random House, 2004.

Medsger, Betty. *The Burglary: The Discovery of J. Edgar Hoover's Secret FBI*. New York: Knopf, 2014.

Meier, Judith Ann Highley, ed. *Runaway Women: Elopements and Other Miscreant Deeds as Advertised in the "Pennsylvania Gazette," 1728–1789 (Together with a Few Abused Wives and Unfortunate Children)*. Apollo, PA: Closson, 1993.

Melville, Herman. "The Portent." 1859. Available online at http://www.melville.org/hmbattle.htm (accessed September 18, 2014).

Mencken, H. L. "Last Words." 1926. Available online at http://www.etsu.edu/cas/history/documents/menckenlast.htm (accessed September 23, 2014).

———. *A Mencken Chrestomathy: His Own Selection of His Choicest Writing*. New York: Random House, 1949.

———. *Prejudices: A Selection*. Edited by James T. Farrell. Baltimore: Johns Hopkins University Press, 1996.

Merry, Robert W. *A Country of Vast Designs: James K. Polk, the Mexican War, and the Conquest of the American Continent*. New York: Simon and Schuster, 2009.

Messages of the President of the United States: With the Correspondence Therewith Communicated, between the Secretary of War and Other Officers of the Government, on the Subject of the Mexican War. Washington, DC, 1848.

Michigan Militia. "Statement of Purpose." http://www.michiganmilitia.com/literature/in_defense_of_liberty.htm (accessed May 15, 2014).

Middlekauf, Robert. *The Glorious Cause: The American Revolution, 1763–1789*. New York: Oxford University Press, 2005.

———. *The Mathers: Three Generations of Puritan Intellectuals, 1596–1728*. New York: Oxford University Press, 1971.

Miles, Edwin A. "After John Marshall's Decision: *Worcester v. Georgia* and the Nullification Crisis." *Journal of Southern History* 39, no. 4 (1973): 519–544.

Millard, Candice. *Destiny of the Republic: A Tale of Madness, Medicine, and the Murder of a President*. New York: Doubleday, 2011.

Miller, Arthur. *The Crucible*. New York: Viking, 1953.

Miller, Douglas T. *The Birth of Modern America, 1820–1850*. New York: Pegasus, 1970.

———. *Jacksonian Aristocracy: Class and Democracy in New York, 1830–1860*. New York: Oxford University Press, 1967.

Miller, Henry. *Murder the Murderer*. 1944. In *Remember to Remember*. New York: New Directions, 1947.

Miller, James. *Democracy Is in the Streets: From Port Huron to the Siege of Chicago*. Cambridge: Harvard University Press, 1987.

Miller, John C. *The Federalist Era, 1789–1801*. New York: Harper and Row, 1960.

Miller, Perry. *Errand into the Wilderness*. Cambridge: Harvard University Press, 1956.

———. *Jonathan Edwards*. New York: W. Sloane, 1949.

———. *The New England Mind: The Seventeenth Century*. New York: Macmillan, 1939.

Miller, Perry. *Orthodoxy in Massachusetts, 1630–1650*. Cambridge: Harvard University Press, 1933.

Mintz, Steven. *Moralists and Modernizers: America's Pre–Civil War Reformers*. Baltimore: Johns Hopkins University Press, 1995.

Mitchell, Margaret. *Gone with the Wind*. New York: Macmillan, 1936.

Mjagkij, Nina. *Loyalty in Time of Trial: The African American Experience during World War I*. Lanham, MD: Rowman and Littlefield, 2011.

Montgomery, David. *The Fall of the House of Labor: The Workplace, the State, and American Labor Activism, 1865–1925*. Cambridge: Cambridge University Press, 1987.

Mooney, James. *The Ghost-Dance Religion and the Sioux Outbreak of 1890*. Fourteenth annual report of the Bureau of American Ethnology. Part 2. Washington, DC: Government Printing Office, 1896.

Morgan, Bill. *I Celebrate Myself: The Somewhat Private Life of Allen Ginsberg*. New York: Viking, 2006.

Morgan, Edmund S. *American Slavery, American Freedom: The Ordeal of Colonial Virginia*. New York: Norton, 1975.

———. *Benjamin Franklin*. New Haven: Yale University Press, 2002.

———. *The Puritan Dilemma: The Story of John Winthrop*. Boston: Little, Brown, 1958.

———. *The Puritan Family: Religion and Domestic Relations in Seventeenth-Century New England*. 1944. Reprint, New York: Harper and Row, 1966.

———. *Visible Saints: The History of a Puritan Idea*. Ithaca: Cornell University Press, 1963.

Morgan, H. Wayne. *The Gilded Age*. Syracuse: Syracuse University Press, 1963.

Morgan, Philip. *Slave Counterpoint: Black Culture in the Eighteenth-Century Chesapeake and Lowcountry*. Chapel Hill: University of North Carolina Press, 1998.

Morison, Samuel Eliot. *The Founding of Harvard College*. Cambridge: Harvard University Press, 1935.

———. *The Intellectual Life of Colonial New England*. Ithaca: Cornell University Press, 1956.

Morris, Edmund. *Colonel Roosevelt*. New York: Random House, 2010.

———. *The Rise of Theodore Roosevelt*. New York: Coward, McCann, and Geoghegan, 1979.

———. *Theodore Rex*. New York: Random House, 2001.

Mothers of Invention, The. *Absolutely Free*. Verve, 1967.

MoveOn.org. *50 Ways to Love Your Country: How to Find Your Political Voice and Become a Catalyst for Change*. Makawao, HI: Inner Ocean, 2004.

Mowry, George. *Theodore Roosevelt and the Progressive Movement*. New York: Hill and Wang, 1946.

Muncy, Robyn. *Creating a Female Dominion in American Reform, 1890–1935*. New York: Oxford University Press, 1994.

Murder of Emmett Till, The. Directed by Stanley Nelson. American Experience, PBS. 2003. Available online at http://www.pbs.org/wgbh/amex/till/timeline/timeline2 .html (accessed September 25, 2014).

Murphy, Paul L. *World War I and the Origin of Civil Liberties in the United States.* New York: Norton, 1979.

Murphy, Teresa. "Sarah Bagley: Laboring for Life." In *The Human Tradition in American Labor History*, edited by Eric Arnesen, 31–45. Wilmington, DE: Scholarly Resources, 2004.

Murray, Judith Sargent. "On the Equality of the Sexes." In *Selected Writings of Judith Sargent Murray*, edited by Sharon M. Harris, 3–14. New York: Oxford University Press, 1995.

Nader, Ralph. *Crashing the Party.* New York: St. Martin's, 2001.

———. "It's Time to End Corporate Welfare as We Know It." 1996. In *The Ralph Nader Reader*, 154–158. New York: Seven Stories, 2000.

Nash, Gary B. *Quakers and Politics: Pennsylvania, 1681–1726.* Princeton: Princeton University Press, 1968.

———. *The Urban Crucible: Social Change, Political Consciousness, and the Origins of the American Revolution.* Cambridge: Harvard University Press, 1979.

Nash, Gary B., Julie Roy Jeffrey, John R. Howe, Peter J. Frederick, and Allen F. Davis. *The American People: Brief Edition.* Vol. 1. New York: Pearson/Longman, 2006.

National Organization for Women. "Statement of Purpose." 1966. http://www.now.org/about/history/statement-of-purpose/ (accessed October 5, 2014).

Nearing, Scott. *The Debs Decision.* 2nd ed. New York: Rand School of Social Science, 1919.

Neely, Mark E., Jr. *The Fate of Liberty: Abraham Lincoln and Civil Liberties.* New York: Oxford University Press, 1992.

Nell, William Cooper. *William Cooper Nell, Nineteenth-Century African American Abolitionist, Historian, Integrationist: Selected Writings from 1832–1874.* Edited by Constance Porter Uzelac. Baltimore: Black Classic, 2002.

Nelson, Bruce. *Beyond the Martyrs: A Social History of Chicago's Anarchists, 1870–1900.* New Brunswick: Rutgers University Press, 1988.

Nelson, Scott Reynolds, and Carol Sheriff. *A People at War: Civilians and Soldiers in America's Civil War.* New York: Oxford University Press, 2007.

Newman, Louise Michelle. *White Women's Rights: The Racial Origins of Feminism in the United States.* New York: Oxford University Press, 1999.

Norris, Frank. *The Octopus: A Story of California.* New York: Doubleday, Page, 1901.

Norton, Charles Eliot. "True Patriotism." Speech delivered at the Men's Club of the Prospect Street Congregational Church in Cambridge, Massachusetts, June 7, 1898.

Norton, Mary Beth. *Founding Mothers and Fathers: Gendered Power and the Forming of American Society.* New York: Knopf, 1996.

———. *Liberty's Daughters: The Revolutionary Experience of American Women, 1750–1800.* Ithaca: Cornell University Press, 1996.

Norton, Mary Beth, David M. Katzman, David W. Blight, Howard P. Chudacoff, Fredrik Logevall, Beth Bailey, Thomas G. Paterson, and William M. Tuttle, Jr. *A People and a Nation: A History of the United States.* Vol. 2, *Since 1865.* 7th ed. Boston: Houghton Mifflin, 2006.

Not in Our Name. "Statement of Conscience." 2003. In *Dissent in America: The Voices That Shaped a Nation*, edited by Ralph Young, 752–755. New York: Pearson Longman, 2006.

Nugent, Walter. *Crossings: The Great Transatlantic Migrations, 1870–1914*. Bloomington: Indiana University Press, 1981.

Nuttall, Geoffrey F. *Visible Saints: The Congregational Way, 1640–1660*. Oxford, UK: Blackwell, 1957.

Nye, Russel Blaine. *The Cultural Life of the New Nation, 1776–1830*. New York: Harper and Row, 1960.

Oates, Stephen B. *Let the Trumpet Sound: A Life of Martin Luther King, Jr.* New York: Harper and Row, 1982.

Oberholzer, Emil. *Delinquent Saints: Disciplinary Action in the Early Congregational Churches of Massachusetts*. New York: Columbia University Press, 1956.

Ochs, Phil. *I Ain't Marching Anymore*. Elektra, 1965.

Oglesby, Carl. "Let Us Shape the Future." November 27, 1965. Available online at the Students for a Democratic Society Document Library, http://www.antiauthoritarian .net/sds_wuo/sds_documents/oglesby_future.html (accessed May 15, 2014).

Okrent, Daniel. *Last Call: The Rise and Fall of Prohibition*. New York: Scribner, 2010.

Olmstead, Frederick Law. *A Journey through Texas; or, A Saddle-Trip on the Southwestern Frontier*. New York: Dix, Edwards, 1857.

Olson, Lynne. *Freedom's Daughters: The Unsung Heroines of the Civil Rights Movement from 1830 to 1970*. New York: Simon and Schuster, 2001.

———. *Those Angry Days: Roosevelt, Lindbergh, and America's Fight over World War II, 1939–1941*. New York: Random House, 2013.

O'Neill, William. *American High: The Years of Confidence, 1945–1960*. New York: Free Press, 1986.

O'Sullivan, John L. "Annexation." *United States Democratic Review* 17, no. 85 (1845): 5–10.

Packard, Jerrold M. *American Nightmare: The History of Jim Crow*. New York: St. Martin's, 2002.

Paine, Thomas. *Common Sense, Addressed to the Inhabitants of America*. Philadelphia, 1776.

Painter, Nell Irvin. *Exodusters: Black Migration to Kansas after Reconstruction*. New York: Knopf, 1977.

———. *Standing at Armageddon: The United States, 1877–1919*. New York: Norton, 1987.

Pardun, Robert. *Prairie Radical: A Journey through the Sixties*. Los Gatos, CA: Shire, 2001.

"Pat Robertson Thinks the GOP Base Is Too Extreme? Hehehehe." *Daily Kos* (blog), October 24, 2011. http://www.dailykos.com/story/2011/10/24/1029543/-Pat -Robertson-Thinks-The-GOP-Base-Is-Too-Extreme-Hehehehe.

Patterson, James T. *Grand Expectations: The United States, 1945–1974*. New York: Oxford University Press, 1996.

"People's Party Platform." *Omaha Morning World-Herald*, July 5, 1892.

Pete Seeger: The Power of Song. Directed by Jim Brown. Weinstein Company and Live Nation Artists, 2008.

Petition to Alabama Governor George C. Wallace by Selma-to-Montgomery Marchers. March 25, 1965. Available online at http://www.fofweb.com/History/MainPrintPage.asp?iPin=afdCR11&DataType=AFHC&WinType=Free (accessed September 25, 2014).

Philbrick, Nathaniel. *Mayflower: A Story of Courage, Community, and War*. New York: Penguin, 2007.

Pickering, Leslie James. *The Earth Liberation Front, 1997–2002*. Oakland, CA: PM, 2007.

Pollack, Norman. *The Populist Response to Industrial America*. New York: Norton, 1966.

Powderly, Terence V. *Thirty Years of Labor, 1859–1889*. Philadelphia, 1890.

President's Committee on Civil Rights. *To Secure These Rights: The Report of the President's Committee on Civil Rights*. New York: Simon and Schuster, 1947.

Price, Matthew C. *The Wilsonian Persuasion in American Foreign Policy*. Youngstown, NY: Cambria, 2007.

Pringle, Cyrus. *The Record of a Quaker Conscience: Cyrus Pringle's Diary*. New York: Macmillan, 1918.

Proudhon, Pierre-Joseph. *What Is Property? or, An Inquiry into the Principle of Right and of Government*. In *Property Is Theft! A Pierre-Joseph Proudhon Anthology*, edited by Iain McKay, 87–138. Oakland, CA: AK, 2011.

Rauschenbusch, Walter. *Christianity and the Social Crisis*. New York: Macmillan, 1907.

———. *Christianizing the Social Order*. New York: Macmillan, 1912.

Rea, Tom. *Devil's Gate: Owning the Land, Owning the Story*. Norman: University of Oklahoma Press, 2012.

Reagan, Leslie. *When Abortion Was a Crime: Women, Medicine, and the Law in the United States, 1867–1973*. Berkeley: University of California Press, 1997.

Redding, J. Saunders. "A Negro Looks at This War." *American Mercury* 55 (November 1942).

Redkey, Edwin S., ed. *A Grand Army of Black Men: Letters from African-American Soldiers in the Union Army, 1861–1865*. Cambridge: Cambridge University Press, 1992.

Redstockings. "Manifesto." 1969. In *Dear Sisters: Dispatches from the Women's Liberation Movement*, edited by Rosalyn Baxandall and Linda Gordon, 90–91. New York: Basic Books, 2000.

Reid, Ronald F., ed. *American Rhetorical Discourse*. 2nd ed. Prospect Heights, IL: Waveland, 1994.

Reynolds, David S. *John Brown, Abolitionist*. New York: Random House, 2005.

Richter, Daniel K. *Facing East from Indian Country: A Native History of Early America*. Cambridge: Harvard University Press, 2001.

Riesman, David. *The Lonely Crowd*. New York: Doubleday, 1953.

Riis, Jacob. *How the Other Half Lives: Studies among the Tenements of New York*. New York: Dover, 1971.

Robinson, Harriet Hanson. "The Lowell Mill Girls Go on Strike, 1836." 1898. Available online at http://historymatters.gmu.edu/d/5714 (accessed September 13, 2014).

Roeder, George H., Jr. *The Censored War: American Visual Experience during World War Two*. New Haven: Yale University Press, 1993.

Roosevelt, Franklin Delano, and Felix Frankfurter. *Roosevelt and Frankfurter: Their Correspondence, 1928–1945*. Edited by Max Freedman. Boston: Little, Brown, 1968.

Roosevelt, Theodore. Editorial. *Kansas City Star*, May 7, 1918.

Rosen, Ruth. *The World Split Open: How the Modern Women's Movement Changed America*. New York: Viking, 2000.

Rosenberg, Chaim M. *Child Labor in America: A History*. Jefferson, NC: McFarland, 2013.

Ross, John. *Letter from John Ross, Principal Chief of the Cherokee Nation of Indians, in Answer to Inquires from a Friend Regarding the Cherokee Affairs with the United States*. Washington, DC, 1836.

Rothman, Hal K. *Saving the Planet: The American Response to the Environment in the Twentieth Century*. Chicago: Ivan R. Dee, 2000.

Rotolo, Suze. *A Freewheelin' Time: A Memoir of Greenwich Village in the Sixties*. New York: Broadway Books, 2008.

Rovere, Richard Halworth, and Gene Brown. *Loyalty and Security in a Democratic State*. New York: Arno, 1979.

Rowson, Susanna. *Charlotte Temple*. London, 1791.

Rubin, Jerry. *We Are Everywhere*. New York: Harper and Row, 1971.

Rutherfurd, Livingston. *John Peter Zenger, His Press, His Trial, and a Bibliography of Zenger Imprints*. New York: Dodd, Mead, 1904.

Ryan, Fr. John A. *Distributive Justice: The Right and Wrong of Our Present Distribution of Wealth*. New York: Macmillan, 1916.

Sainte-Marie, Buffy. *It's My Way!* Vanguard Records, 1964.

Sale, Kirkpatrick. *SDS*. New York: Random House, 1973.

Salinger, J. D. *The Catcher in the Rye*. Boston: Little, Brown. 1951.

Salvatore, Nick. *Eugene V. Debs: Citizen and Socialist*. Urbana: University of Illinois Press, 1982.

Sandiford, Ralph. *A Brief Examination of the Practice of the Times*. Philadelphia: Franklin and Meredith, 1729.

Sanger, Margaret. *Woman and the New Race*. New York: Brentano's, 1920.

Sauguaarum, Loron. "Letter from a Penobscot Chief Explanatory of the Treaty of Peace Concluded at Caskebay, between the English and Indians." August 1727. In *Documents Relative to the Colonial History of the State of New York*, edited by E. B. O'Callaghan, vol. 9, 966–967. Albany, NY: Weed, Parsons, 1855.

Schaffer, Ronald. *America in the Great War*. New York: Oxford University Press, 1991.

Scheiber, Harry N. *The Wilson Administration and Civil Liberties, 1917–1921*. Ithaca: Cornell University Press, 1960.

Schirmer, Daniel Boone. *Republic or Empire: American Resistance to the Philippine War*. Cambridge, MA: Schenkman, 1972.

Schlesinger, Arthur M., Jr. *Robert Kennedy and His Times*. Boston: Houghton Mifflin, 1978.

Schlesinger, Arthur M., Jr., and Roger Burns, eds. *Congress Investigates: A Documented History, 1792–1974*. New York: Chelsea House, 1975.

Schneir, Miriam, ed. *Feminism in Our Time: The Essential Writings, World War II to the Present*. New York: Vintage Books, 1994.

Schrecker, Ellen. *Many Are the Crimes: McCarthyism in America*. Boston: Little, Brown, 1998.

Schurz, Carl. "The Issue of Imperialism." January 4, 1899. In *Speeches, Correspondence, and Political Papers of Carl Schurz*, vol. 6, *January 1, 1899–April 8, 1906*, edited by Frederic Bancroft, 1–35. New York: Putnam, 1913.

Seavoy, Ronald. *An Economic History of the United States: From 1607 to the Present*. New York Routledge, 2013.

Seeger, Pete. *We Shall Overcome: The Complete Carnegie Hall Concert*. Columbia Records, 1963; rereleased 1989.

Shawnee, Miami, Ottawa, and Seneca. "Proposal to Maintain Indian Lands." 1793. In *The Correspondence of Lieut. Governor John Graves Simcoe*, edited by E. A. Cruikshank, vol. 2, 17–20. Toronto: Ontario Historical Society, 1923–1931.

Sheldon, Charles. *In His Steps: "What Would Jesus Do?"* Chicago: Advance, 1898.

Shesol, Jeff. *Supreme Power: Franklin Roosevelt vs. the Supreme Court*. New York: Norton, 2010.

Shilts, Randy. *And the Band Played On: Politics, People, and the AIDS Epidemic*. New York: St. Martin's, 1987.

Silbey, David J. *A War of Frontier and Empire: The Philippine-American War, 1899–1902*. New York: Hill and Wang, 2008.

Sinclair, Andrew. *Prohibition: The Era of Excess*. Boston: Little, Brown, 1962.

Sinclair, Upton. *The Jungle*. 1906. Reprint, New York: Bantam, 1981.

Slatta, Richard W., ed. *The Mythical West: An Encyclopedia of Legend, Lore, and Popular Culture*. Santa Barbara, CA: ABC-CLIO, 2001.

"Slave Petition for Gradual Emancipation: To the Honorable Legislature of the State of Massachusetts Bay, January 13, 1777." *Massachusetts Historical Society Collections*, 5th ser., vol. 3. Boston, 1877.

Small, Melvin. *The Presidency of Richard Nixon*. Lawrence: University Press of Kansas, 1999.

Smith, George Winston, and Charles Judah, eds. *Chronicles of the Gringos: The U.S. Army in the Mexican War, 1846–1848*. Albuquerque: University of New Mexico Press, 1966.

Smith, Henry Nash. *Virgin Land: The American West as Symbol and Myth*. 1950. Reprint, Cambridge: Harvard University Press, 1970.

Smith, James Morton. *Freedom's Fetters: The Alien and Sedition Laws and American Civil Liberties*. Ithaca: Cornell University Press, 1956.

Smith, Jean Edward. *Eisenhower in War and Peace*. New York: Random House, 2012.

———. *FDR*. New York: Random House, 2007.

Smith-Rosenberg, Carol. *Disorderly Conduct: Visions of Gender in Victorian America.* New York: Knopf, 1985.

Solanas, Valerie. *S.C.U.M. Manifesto.* Oakland, CA: AK, 1968.

Sounes, Howard. *Down the Highway: The Life of Bob Dylan.* New York: Grove, 2001.

Source, The: The Story of the Beats and the Beat Generation. Directed by Chuck Workman. Beat/Calliope, 1999.

Spurr, John. *English Puritanism, 1603–1689.* New York: St. Martin's, 1998.

Stafford, Peter. *Psychedelics.* Oakland, CA: Ronin, 2003.

Stampp, Kenneth M. *The Peculiar Institution: Slavery in the Ante-Bellum South.* New York: Random House, 1956.

Stanton, Elizabeth Cady. "Address Delivered at Seneca Falls." July 19, 1848. Available online at http://womenshistory.about.com/library/etext/bl_1848_stanton1.htm (accessed September 16, 2014).

———. "Address to the National Woman Suffrage Convention." Washington, D.C., January 19, 1869. In *The Concise History of Woman Suffrage: Selections from "History of Woman Suffrage,"* edited by Paul Buhle and Mary Jo Buhle, 249–256. Urbana: University of Illinois Press, 2005.

Stanton, Elizabeth Cady, and Susan B. Anthony. *The Elizabeth Cady Stanton–Susan B. Anthony Reader: Correspondence, Writings, Speeches.* Edited by Ellen Carol Dubois. Boston: Northeastern University Press, 1992.

Stanton, Elizabeth Cady, Susan B. Anthony, and Matilda Joslyn Gage, eds. *History of Woman Suffrage.* Vol. 1, *1848–1861.* 1881. Reprint, New York: Arno / *New York Times,* 1969.

———, eds. *History of Woman Suffrage.* Vol. 2, *1861–1876.* New York: Fowler and Wells, 1882.

Starkey, Marion. *The Devil in Massachusetts: A Modern Enquiry into the Salem Witch Trials.* New York: Knopf, 1949.

Starr, Edwin. "War." Single. Gordy Records, 1970.

Steffens, Lincoln. *The Shame of the Cities.* New York: McClure, Phillips, 1904.

Stein, Judith. *The World of Marcus Garvey: Race and Class in Modern Society.* Baton Rouge: Louisiana State University Press, 1986.

Steinbeck, John. *The Grapes of Wrath.* New York: Viking. 1939.

Steinem, Gloria. *Outrageous Acts and Everyday Rebellions.* New York: Holt, Rinehart, and Winston, 1983.

———. "'Women's Liberation' Aims to Free Men, Too." *Washington Post,* June 7, 1970.

Stephens, Alexander H. "Cornerstone Speech." Savannah, Georgia, March 21, 1861. Available online at http://www.civilwar.org/education/history/primarysources/alexander-h-cornerstone.html (accessed September 13, 2014).

Stevens, Jay. *Storming Heaven: LSD and the American Dream.* New York: Grove, 1987.

Stowe, Harriet Beecher, *Uncle Tom's Cabin; or, Life among the Lowly.* Boston: John P. Jewett, 1852.

Sugden, John. *Tecumseh: A Life.* New York: Holt, 1998.

Sugrue, Thomas J. *Sweet Land of Liberty: The Forgotten Struggle for Civil Rights in the North.* New York: Random House, 2008.

Sullivan, Patricia. *Days of Hope: Race and Democracy in the New Deal Era.* Chapel Hill: University of North Carolina Press, 1996.

Sumner, Charles. *The Crime against Kansas: The Apologies for the Crime; The True Remedy.* Boston: John P. Jewett, 1856.

Sumner, William Graham. "The Concentration of Wealth: Its Economic Justification." *Independent* 54 (April–June 1902).

———. *What Social Classes Owe to Each Other.* 1883. Reprint, New York: Cosimo Classics, 2007.

Takaki, Ronald. *A Different Mirror: A History of Multicultural America.* Boston: Little, Brown, 1993.

———. *Double Victory: A Multicultural History of America in World War II.* Boston: Little, Brown, 2000.

———. *Strangers from a Different Shore: A History of Asian Americans.* Boston: Little, Brown, 1989.

Tarbell, Ida M. *The History of the Standard Oil Company.* New York: McClure, Phillips, 1905.

Tateishi, John, ed. *And Justice for All: An Oral History of the Japanese American Detention Camps.* New York: Random House, 1984.

Taylor, Alan. *American Colonies: The Settling of North America.* New York: Penguin, 2002.

Teal, Donn. *The Gay Militants.* New York: St. Martin's, 1971.

Tecumseh. "Sleep Not Longer, O Choctaws and Chicawaws." 1811. In *Indian Oratory: Famous Speeches by Noted Indian Chieftains,* compiled by W. C. Vanderwerth, 62–66. Norman: University of Oklahoma Press, 1971.

———. "Speech at Vincennes." In *The Library of Oratory,* edited by Chauncey M. Depew, vol. 4, 363–364. New York: Current Literature, 1902.

Tejada, Susan. *In Search of Sacco and Vanzetti: Doubles Lives, Troubled Times, and the Massachusetts Case That Shook the World.* Lebanon, NH: University Press of New England, 2012.

Thelen, David P. *Robert M. La Follette and the Insurgent Spirit.* Boston: Little, Brown, 1976.

Thernstrom, Stephan. *Poverty and Progress: Social Mobility in a Nineteenth Century City.* Cambridge: Harvard University Press, 1964.

Thomas, Keith, *Religion and the Decline of Magic.* New York: Scribner, 1971.

Thompson, Heather Ann. "Why Mass Incarceration Matters: Rethinking Crisis, Decline, and Transformation in Postwar American History." *Journal of American History* 97, no. 3 (December 2010): 703–734.

Thoreau, Henry David. *Walden.* New York: Thomas Y. Crowell, 1910.

———. *"Walden" and "Resistance to Civil Government."* 3rd ed. Edited by William Rossi. New York: Norton, 2008.

Tillman, Benjamin R. "Causes of Southern Opposition to Imperialism." *North American Review* 171 (1900): 439–446.

Tolles, Frederick B. *Meeting House and Counting House: The Quaker Merchants of Colonial Philadelphia 1682–1763.* New York: Norton, 1963.

Toombs, Robert, Alexander H. Stephens, and Howell Cobb. *The Correspondence of Robert Toombs, Alexander H. Stephens, and Howell Cobb*. Edited by Ulrich Bonnell Phillips. Washington, DC, 1913.

Topp, Michael Miller. *Those without a Country: The Political Culture of Italian American Syndicalists*. Minneapolis: University of Minnesota Press, 2001.

Trachtenberg, Alan. *The Incorporation of America: Society and Culture in the Gilded Age*. New York: Hill and Wang, 1982.

Truman, Harry S. "Special Message to the Congress on Civil Rights." February 2, 1948. In *Public Papers of the Presidents of the United States, Harry S. Truman, 1948*, vol. 4, 121–126. Washington, DC: U.S. Government Printing Office, 1963.

Turner, Frederick Jackson. *The Frontier in American History*. New York: Holt, 1920.

Turner, Jeffrey A. *Sitting In and Speaking Out: Student Movements in the American South, 1960–1970*. Athens: University of Georgia Press, 2010.

Turner, Nat. *The Confessions of Nat Turner, the Leader of the Late Insurrection in Southampton, VA*. Baltimore: Thomas R. Gray, 1831.

Twain, Mark. *Adventures of Huckleberry Finn*. New York: Webster, 1885.

———. *Mark Twain's Notebook*. Compiled by Albert Bigelow Paine. New York: Harper, 1935.

———. *Mark Twain's Weapons of Satire: Anti-imperialist Writings on the Philippine-American War*. Edited by Jim Zwick. Syracuse: Syracuse University Press, 1992.

———. *The War Prayer*. 1923. Reprint, New York: Harper Colophon, 2001.

Twain, Mark, and Charles Dudley Warner. *The Gilded Age: A Tale of To-Day*. Hartford, CT: American, 1873.

Tyack, David B. *The One Best System: A History of American Urban Education*. Cambridge: Harvard University Press, 1974.

Uncovered: The Whole Truth about the Iraq War. Directed by Robert Greenwald. Disinformation Company, 2004.

U.S. Congress, House, Committee on Education and Labor. *Employment Discrimination against Gay Men and Lesbians*. 103rd Cong., 2nd sess., June 20, 1994. Washington, DC: U.S. Government Printing Office, 1994.

U.S. Congress, Senate, Committee on Foreign Relations. "Legislative Proposals Relating to the War in Southeast Asia." *Hearings before the Committee on Foreign Relations*. 92nd Cong., 1st sess., April–May 1971. Washington, DC: Government Printing Office, 1971.

Utley, Robert M. *The Indian Frontier of the American West, 1846–1890*. Albuquerque: University of New Mexico Press, 1984.

Vallandigham, Clement L. *The Record of Hon. C. L. Vallandigham on Abolition, the Union, and the Civil War*. Cincinnati, OH: J. Walter, 1863.

Van Ronk, Dave, with Elijah Wald. *The Mayor of MacDougal Street*. New York: Da Capo, 2005.

Varon, Elizabeth R. *Disunion: The Coming of the American Civil War, 1789–1859*. Chapel Hill: University of North Carolina Press, 2008.

Varon, Jeremy. *Bringing the War Home: The Weather Underground, the Red Army*

Faction, and Revolutionary Violence in the Sixties and Seventies. Berkeley: University of California Press, 2004.

Vaughan, Leslie J. *Randolph Bourne and the Politics of Cultural Radicalism*. Lawrence: University Press of Kansas, 1997.

Waldstreicher, David. *In the Midst of Perpetual Fetes: The Making of American Nationalism*. Chapel Hill: University of North Carolina Press, 1997.

———. *Runaway America: Benjamin Franklin, Slavery, and the American Revolution*. New York: Hill and Wang, 2004.

———. *Slavery's Constitution: From Revolution to Ratification*. New York: Hill and Wang, 2009.

Walker, David. *Walker's Appeal in Four Articles; Together with a Preamble, to the Colored Citizens of the World, with a Brief Sketch of His Life by Henry Highland Garnet*. New York: J. H. Tobitt, 1848.

Wall, Robert Emmet, Jr. *Massachusetts Bay: The Crucial Decade, 1640–1650*. New Haven: Yale University Press, 1972.

Walther, Eric H. *The Fire-Eaters*. Baton Rouge: Louisiana State University Press, 1992.

Ward, John William. *Andrew Jackson: Symbol for an Age*. New York: Oxford University Press, 1962.

Ward, Lester Frank. "Mind as a Social Factor." *Mind* 9, no. 36 (1884): 563–573.

Washburn, Wilcomb E. *The Governor and the Rebel: A History of Bacon's Rebellion in Virginia*. New York: Norton, 1972.

Washington, Booker T. *The Booker T. Washington Papers*. Edited by Louis R. Harlan. Urbana: University of Illinois Press, 1974.

———. "Speech to the Atlanta Cotton States and International Exposition." Atlanta, Georgia, October 18, 1895. In *Up from Slavery: An Autobiography*, 217–237. New York: Doubleday, Page, 1907.

Washington, George. "General Orders, October 25 [1781]." In *The Writings of George Washington from the Original Manuscript Sources 1745–1799*, vol. 23, *August 16, 1781–February 15, 1782*, edited by John C. Fitzpatrick, 264–265. Washington, DC: Government Printing Office, 1937.

Weather Underground, The. Directed by Sam Green and Bill Siegel. Free History Project, 2002.

Weinstein, James. *The Corporate Ideal in the Liberal State, 1900–1918*. Boston: Beacon, 1968.

Wells, Emmeline. "Is It Ignorance?" *Woman's Exponent*, July 1, 1883.

Wells-Barnett, Ida B. "Lynch Law in America." 1900. Available online at http://www .digitalhistory.uh.edu/disp_textbook.cfm?smtID=3&psid=1113 (accessed October 7, 2014).

———. *Lynch Law in Georgia: A Six-Weeks' Record in the Center of Southern Civilization, as Faithfully Chronicled by the "Atlanta Journal" and the "Atlanta Constitution."* Chicago: Chicago Colored Citizens, 1899.

Western, Bruce. *Punishment and Inequality in America*. New York: Russell Sage Foundation, 2007.

Weyrich, Paul, and Connaught Marshner, eds. *Future 21: Directions for America in the 21st Century*. Old Greenwich, CT: Devin-Adair, 1984.

Whites, Lee Ann. *The Civil War as a Crisis in Gender: Augusta, Georgia, 1860–1890*. Athens: University of Georgia Press, 1995.

Whyte, William H. *The Organization Man*. New York: Simon and Schuster, 1956.

Wiebe, Robert H. *The Search for Order, 1877–1920*. New York: Hill and Wang, 1967.

Wiggins, David. "Message to the Troops: Resist!" October 11, 2002. Strike the Root, posted March 10, 2003, http://www.strike-the-root.com/3/wiggins/wiggins3.html.

Wilentz, Sean. *Bob Dylan in America*. New York: Doubleday, 2010.

Wilkerson, Isabel. *The Warmth of Other Suns: The Epic Story of America's Great Migration*. New York: Random House, 2010.

Wilkins, Roger. *Jefferson's Pillow: The Founding Fathers and the Dilemma of Black Patriotism*. Boston: Beacon, 2002.

Williams, Roger. *The Bloudy Tenent of Persecution*. 1644. Edited by Samuel L. Caldwell. Providence, RI: Narragansett Club, 1867.

Williams, William A. *The Contours of American History*. Cleveland, OH: World, 1961.

———. *The Tragedy of American Diplomacy*. New York: Dell, 1962.

Wills, Gary. *Explaining America: The Federalist*. Garden City, NY: Doubleday, 1981.

———. *Negro President: Jefferson and the Slave Power*. Boston: Houghton Mifflin, 2003.

Wilson, Woodrow. "Address to Congress Advising That Germany's Course Be Declared War against the United States." April 2, 1917. In *The Messages and Papers of Woodrow Wilson*, vol. 1. New York: Review of Reviews Corporation, 1924.

Winkler, Allan M. *"To Everything There Is a Season": Pete Seeger and the Power of Song*. New York: Oxford University Press, 2009.

Wintz, Cary D. *African American Political Thought, 1890–1930: Washington, Du Bois, Garvey, and Randolph*. Armonk, NY: M. E. Sharpe, 1996.

Wofford, Harris. *Of Kennedys and Kings: Making Sense of the Sixties*. Pittsburgh: University of Pittsburgh Press, 1980.

Wollstonecraft, Mary. *A Vindication of the Rights of Woman; With Strictures on Political and Moral Subjects*. London, 1792.

Wood, Gordon S. *The Americanization of Benjamin Franklin*. New York: Penguin, 2004.

———. *Empire of Liberty: A History of the Early Republic, 1789–1815*. Oxford: Oxford University Press, 2009.

———. *The Radicalism of the American Revolution*. New York: Knopf, 1992.

Woodhull, Victoria Claflin. *A Speech on the Principles of Social Freedom*. New York: Woodhull, Claflin, 1872.

Woodward, C. Vann. *The Strange Career of Jim Crow*. New York: Oxford University Press, 1974.

Woolf, Virginia. *A Room of One's Own*. New York: Harcourt, Brace, 1929.

Woolman, John. *The Journal and Major Essays of John Woolman*. Edited by Phillips P. Moulton. New York: Oxford University Press, 1971.

———. *The Journals and Essays of John Woolman*. Edited by Amelia Mott Gummere. New York: Macmillan, 1922.

Wordsworth, William. "The Tables Turned." In *Lyrical Ballads, with a Few Other Poems*. London: J. & A. Arch, 1798.

Worley, Ted R. "The Arkansas Peace Society of 1861: A Study in Mountain Unionism." *Journal of Southern History* 24, no. 4 (1958): 445–456.

———. "Documents Relating to the Arkansas Peace Society of 1861." *Arkansas Historical Quarterly* 17, no. 1 (1958): 82–111.

Wright, Lawrence. *The Looming Tower: Al Qaeda and the Road to 9/11*. New York: Knopf, 2006.

Wright, Richard. *Native Son*. New York: Harper, 1940.

Wrobel, David, and Michael Steiner, eds. *Many Wests: Place, Culture, and Regional Identity*. Lawrence: University Press of Kansas, 1997.

X, Malcolm. "Message to the Grass Roots." November 10, 1963. In *Malcolm X Speaks: Selected Speeches and Statements*, edited by George Breitman, 3–17. New York: Grove, 1965.

———. "Speech on 'Black Revolution.'" April 8, 1964. In *Two Speeches by Malcolm X*, 7–21. New York: Merit, 1965.

Yee, Shirley J. *Black Women Abolitionists: A Study in Activism, 1828–1860*. Knoxville: University of Tennessee Press, 1992.

Young, Ralph. "Breathing the 'Free Aire of the New World': The Influence of the New England Way on the Gathering of Congregational Churches in Old England, 1640–1660." *New England Quarterly* 83, no. 1 (March 2010): 5–46.

———. *Dissent in America: The Voices That Shaped a Nation*. New York: Pearson Longman, 2006.

Zagarri, Rosemarie. *Revolutionary Backlash: Women and Rights in the Early American Republic*. Philadelphia: University of Pennsylvania Press, 2007.

Zinn, Howard. *A People's History of the United States: 1492–Present*. New York: HarperCollins, 2001.

———. *Terrorism and War*. New York: Seven Stories, 2002.

Zirngibl, Wendy M. "Lay, Benjamin." In *Encyclopedia of American History: Colonization and Settlement, 1608 to 1760*, rev. ed., edited by Billy G. Smith and Gary B. Nash, vol. 2. New York: Facts On File, 2010.

INDEX

ABOUT THE AUTHOR

Ralph Young is Professor of History at Temple University. He has won several teaching awards and is the author of *Dissent in America: The Voices That Shaped a Nation*, a collection of four hundred years of dissenting speeches, petitions, letters, songs, poems, and essays that called for change, reform, or even revolution. He is also the founder of weekly campus-wide teach-ins at Temple in which students and faculty examine the historical context of controversial contemporary issues.